College Accounting

A Practical Approach

CHAPTERS 1–12

Eleventh Edition

Jeffrey Slater

North Shore Community College
Danvers, Massachusetts

Prentice Hall

Boston Columbus Indianapolis New York San Francisco Upper Saddle River
Amsterdam Cape Town Dubai London Madrid Milan Munich Paris
Montreal Toronto Delhi Mexico City Sao Paulo Sydney Hong Kong Seoul
Singapore Taipei Tokyo

To Nanny Shelley
With Love,
Papa Jeff

Library of Congress Cataloging-in-Publication Data information is available.

VP/Editorial Director: Natalie Anderson
AVP/Executive Editor: Jodi McPherson
Development Editor: Karen Misler
Assistant Editor: Melissa Arlio
Editorial Assistant: Christina Rumbaugh
AVP/Director of Marketing: Kate Valentine
Senior Marketing Manager: Maggie Moylan Leen
Marketing Assistant: Justin Jacob
Senior Managing Editor: Cynthia Zonneveld
Project Manager: Rhonda Aversa
Senior Operations Specialist: Nick Sklitsis
Senior Art Director: Jonathan Boylan
Text and Cover Designer: Kathy Mrozek
Manager, Visual Research: Beth Brenzel
Photo Researcher: Rachel Lucas
Manager, Rights and Permissions: Zina Arabia
Image Permission Coordinator: Joanne Dippel
Manager, Cover Visual Research & Permissions: Karen Sanatar
Cover Art: © Shutterstock ®
AVP/Director of Product Development: Lisa Strite
Media Editors: Ashley Lulling/Allison Longley
Media Project Manager, Production: John Cassar
Full-Service Project Management: GEX Publishing Services
Composition: GEX Publishing Services
Printer/Binder: Courier/Kendallville
Cover Printer: Lehigh-Phoenix Color/Hagerstown
Text Font: Times Roman 10/12

Credits and acknowledgments borrowed from other sources and reproduced, with permission, in this textbook appear on appropriate page within text and on photo credits page.

Pearson Education LTD.
Pearson Education Singapore, Pte. Ltd
Pearson Education, Canada, Ltd
Pearson Education–Japan
Pearson Education Australia PTY, Limited
Pearson Education North Asia Ltd
Pearson Educación de Mexico, S.A. de C.V.
Pearson Education Malaysia, Pte. Ltd

Prentice Hall
is an imprint of

www.pearsonhighered.com

10 9 8 7 6
ISBN 10: 0-13-606566-X
ISBN 13: 978-0-13-606566-1

Brief Contents

Contents

A Memo from the Desk of Jeff Slater . . .

I asked: "What do *college accounting* students really need to know?"

You told me: "Less is more . . . . They just need to *get it*."

I said: "Agreed, but tell me more about *it*."

"It" is

- Basic accounting concepts and processes
- Plenty of ways to practice
- Basic overview of accounting in technologically driven 2009 and beyond

I really listened to you and, in this edition of *College Accounting, A Practical Approach 11e,* I give your students three ways to really "get" accounting like they need to. I thought about "less is more" and took out any material that didn't absolutely focus students on learning accounting. Just by quickly flipping through this edition of my book, you'll see crystal-clear graphics, lots of white space, and new, relevant content.

I also thought about you, the instructor, and "less is more." So no more will you need to fill a cart with your instructor resources. Now you'll have an instructor's edition of the text with teaching notes, tips, and solutions . . . all in an easy-to-use, online format. But I'm getting ahead of myself. All the information you really need can be found on the next few pages.

Get "IT" from IN-CHAPTER LEARNING TOOLS

- **Accounting Cycle Tutorial:** Online practice and review of the accounting cycle. Margin logos direct students to the appropriate ACT section and material. The tutorial provides review, application, and practice. Available in Chapters 1–5.
- **Learning Unit Reviews:** Each chapter is organized into small, bite-sized units. Students are introduced to a new concept in the learning unit, and then they can immediately test their understanding in the learning unit review.
- **Need Help?:** This new feature has been added to each self-review quiz at the end of each learning unit for the first five chapters. This feature is like a private tutoring session with the author, as he anticipates students' questions and walks them through the provided solution, step by step. These Need Help? sections are provided for the first five chapters of the book, as they are the key to retention.
- **Chapter Opening Did You Know?:** Each chapter opens with some new and interesting information about a recognizable company. Each opener is accompanied by a matching photo.
- **Margin Notes:** Short, sweet, and to the point. They're not found on every page; instead they're provided only when a study hint is really needed.
- **In-Text Practice Set:** The in-text Sullivan Realty Practice Set (Chapter 5) enables students to complete two cycles of transactions (in your choice of manual or Peachtree/Quickbooks format).

Get "IT" from END-OF-CHAPTER PRACTICE MATERIAL

- **Student Demonstration Problem/Accounting Cycle Review:** Students need practice in order to master the accounting cycle. This problem is designed around the *Steps in the Accounting Cycle* and can be found at the ends of Chapters 1–5.
- **Blueprint:** A visual summary of the chapter. Students can use it as a roadmap to review what they have learned. It stresses when to perform specific activities.
- **Classroom Demonstration Exercises:** Short exercises (A and B sets) that can be assigned or used in class for difficult topics.
- **Learning Objectives:** A learning objective number and the average time to complete each exercise is now included for all end-of-chapter material.
- **Exercises:** Short exercises that can be assigned or used in class to focus on building skills.
- **Group A and Group B Problems:** Approximately 20% of the problems have been updated for this edition.
- **On the Job Applications:** Real-world scenarios that challenge students to think and act like managers.
- **Financial Report Problem:** Students use the annual financial report of Kellogg's Company (found in Appendix A) to apply theory and applications completed in the chapter.
- **Internet Project:** A new feature that directs students to the Web site of the chapter opening company to find more information.
- **Discussion Questions:** Include ethical questions and critical thinking questions.
- **Computerized Accounting:** Selected end-of-chapter problems can be completed with Peachtree or Quickbooks.
- **Continuing Problem (Sanchez Computer Center):** Students follow the activities of a single company and then are asked to apply concepts to solve specific accounting problems for the company. Problems can be found in Chapters 1–12 and can be solved manually or by using Peachtree or Quickbooks.
- **Computer Workshops:** Seven computer workshops (for Peachtree and QuickBooks) have been added with detailed step-by-step instructions on how to take a manual problem from the end of the chapter and computerize it in both types of software.

  Students need to do accounting manually before they can use the computer. These workshops allow the student to see how fast accounting theory and procedures can be done on the computer. They will need these computer skills when applying for jobs in the field.

  These workshops assume no computer knowledge and provide adjunct and full time faculty a step-by-step teaching package. Each step tells the student (or instructor) exactly what to press on the computer along with detailed explanations of what should print out. Initial instructions appear in the textbook itself and then students are led to the computer to do the actual work online.
- **MyAccountingLab:** Give your students the power of practice! *College Accounting* is now available with MyAccountingLab, an online homework and assessment software for accounting that not only gives students more "I Get It" moments, but also gives instructors the flexibility to make technology an integral part of their course, or a supplementary resource for students. MyAccountingLab content is available for Chapters 1–5 of the student textbook, where students need the most practice. All end-of-chapter Demonstration Exercises, Exercises, Problems, and Continuing Problems in Chapters 1–5 are included.

Special Section for Current Users

Thank you for your continued use of Slater's *College Accounting*. To ease your transition, here are highlights of chapter changes for the 11th edition.

Chapter 1 Accounting Concepts and Procedures

- New chapter opener on Best Buy, with Did You Know? information
- New Need Help? sections to explain the solutions to the learning unit quizzes
- New Internet project

Chapter 2 Debits and Credits: Analyzing and Recording Business Transactions

- New chapter opener on Staples, with Did You Know? information
- New Need Help? sections
- New Internet project

Chapter 3 Beginning the Accounting Cycle

- New chapter opener on Continental Airlines, with Did You Know? information
- New Need Help? sections
- New Internet project
- New Computer Workshop after Chapter 3

Chapter 4 The Accounting Cycle Continued

- New chapter opener on Black & Decker, with Did You Know? information
- New Need Help? sections
- New Internet project
- New Computer Workshop after Chapter 4

Chapter 5 The Accounting Cycle Completed

- New chapter opener on Amazon, with Did You Know? information
- New Need Help? sections
- New Internet project
- Updated 2008 numbers for the Sullivan Realty Mini-Practice set
- New Computer Workshop after Chapter 5

Chapter 6 Banking Procedure and Control of Cash

- New chapter opener on Bankrate, Inc., with Did You Know? information
- Updated information on trends in banking
- New Internet project

Chapter 7 Calculating Pay and Payroll Taxes: The Beginning of the Payroll Process

- New chapter opener on Johnson & Johnson, with Did You Know? information
- Updated figures and tables throughout to include 2008 rates
- Continued focus on integrating role of employee and employer
- New Internet project

Chapter 8 Paying, Recording, and Reporting Payroll and Payroll Taxes: The Conclusion of the Payroll Process

- New chapter opener on Coca-Cola, with Did You Know? information
- Updated figures and tables throughout to include 2008 rates
- New tax forms updated along with streamlined discussion of payroll deposits
- New Internet project
- New Computer Workshop after Chapter 8

Chapter 9 Sales and Cash Receipts

- New chapter opener on Big Lots, with Did You Know? information
- Special journals moved to an appendix at the end of Chapter 10
- New Internet project

Chapter 10 Purchases and Cash Payments

- New chapter opener on Del Monte, with Did You Know? information
- Clarification of periodic versus perpetual methods of inventory
- New Internet project
- Special journal appendix now appears at the end of Chapter 10
- New Computer Workshop after Chapter 10

Chapter 11 Preparing a Worksheet for a Merchandise Company

- New chapter opener on Build-a-Bear, with Did You Know? information
- More detailed explanation of merchandise inventory adjustment
- New Internet project

Chapter 12 Completion of the Accounting Cycle for a Merchandise Company

- New chapter opener on Chiquita, with Did You Know? information
- New Internet project
- New Computer Workshop after Chapter 12

For Instructors

Instructor's Resource Center (IRC): Register. Redeem. Login.

www.pearsonhighered.com/slater is where instructors can access a variety of print, media, and presentation resources available with this text in downloadable, digital format. For most texts, resources are also available for course management platforms such as Blackboard, WebCT, and Course Compass.

It gets better. Once you register, you will not have additional forms to fill out or multiple usernames and passwords to remember to access new titles and/or editions. As a registered faculty member, you can log in directly to download resource files and receive immediate access and instructions for installing course management content to your campus server.

Need help? Our dedicated technical support team is ready to assist instructors with questions about the media supplements that accompany this text. Visit http://247pearsoned.custhelp.com for answers to frequently asked questions and toll-free user support phone numbers.

The following supplements for this text and for College Accounting, 11e (Chapters 1–25) are available to adopting instructors. For detailed descriptions, please visit: www.pearsonhighered.com/slater.

Instructor's Resource Center (IRC) online: Login at www.pearsonhighered.com/slater.
Instructor's Resource CD-ROM: ISBN: 0-13-6065694
Study Guide and Working Papers (Chapters 1–12): 0-13-606572-4
Study Guide and Working Papers (Chapters 13–25): 0-13-606571-6
Instructor's Edition with Solutions: Visit the IRC for this supplement.

TestGen Test Generating Software: Visit the IRC for this supplement.
Test Item File: Visit the IRC for this supplement.
Working Papers in Excel format: Visit the IRC for this supplement.
PowerPoint Presentation Slides: Visit the IRC for this supplement.

MyAccountingLab is a Web-based tutorial and assessment software for accounting that not only gives students more "I Get It" moments, but also gives instructors the flexibility to make technology an integral part of their course, or a supplementary resource for students.

MyAccountingLab provides instructors with a rich and flexible set of course materials, along with course-management tools that make it easy to deliver all or a portion of the course online.

- Powerful homework and test manager
- Comprehensive gradebook tracking
- Department-wide solutions

For Students

Textbook Volumes

Textbook Chapters 1–25: ISBN 0-13-606380-2 *Includes payroll and additional blank worksheets

Textbook Chapters 1–12: ISBN 0-13-606566-X *Includes study guide and working papers for Chapters 1–12

Print Study Aids

Study Guide and Working Papers Chapters 1–12: ISBN 0-13-606572-4
Study Guide and Working Papers Chapters 13–25: ISBN 0-13-606571-6

MyAccountingLab provides students with a personalized interactive learning environment where they can learn at their own pace and measure their progress.

Key Student Features:

- Accounting cycle video tutorial
- Interactive tutorial exercises
- Multimedia learning aids including author and topic videos
- Study plan for self-paced learning
- Full e-text and e-study guide
- RSS feeds for ABC News in accounting and finance

Online Resources

www.pearsonhighered.com/slater contains valuable resources for both students and professors. Don't forget to preview the Accounting Cycle Tutorial and additional NEW videos on the Companion Web site.

Who I Listened To

Reviewers

Terry Aime, Delgado Community College
Cornelia Alsheimer, Santa Barbara City College
Julia Angel, North Arkansas College
Julie Armstrong, St. Clair County Community College
Marjorie Ashton, Truckee Meadows Community College
John Babich, Kankakee Community College
Cecil Battiste, Valencia Community College
Donald Benoit, Mitchell College
Peggy A. Berrier, Ivy Technical State College
Michelle Berube, Everest University
Anne Bikofsky, College of Westchester
Michael Bitting, John A. Logan College
David Bland, Cape Fear Community College
Suzanne Bradford, Angelina College
Beverly Bugay, Tyler Junior College
Gary Bumgarner, Mountain Empire Community College
Betsy Crane, Victoria College
Noel Craven, El Camino College
Don Curfman, McHenry County College
John Daugherty, Pitt Community College
Susan Davis, Green River Community College
Michael Discello, Pittsburgh Technical Institute
Sylvia Dorsey, Florence-Darlington Technical College
Sid Downey, Cochise College
Donna Eakman, Great Falls College of Technology
Steven Ernest, Baton Rouge Community College
John Evanson, Williston State College
Marilyn Ewing, Seward County Community College
Nancy Fallon, Albertus Magnus College
Nicole Fife, Bucks County Community College
Brian Fink, Danville Area Community College
Paul Fisher, Rogue Community College
Carolyn Fitzmorris, Hutchinson Community College
Trish Glennon, Central Florida Community College
Nancy Goehring, Monterey Peninsula College
Jane Goforth, North Seattle Community College
Lori Grady, Bucks County Community College
Gretchen Graham, Community College of Allegheny County
Marina Grau, Houston Community College
Mary Jane Green, Des Moines Area Community College
Joyce Griffin, Kansas City Kansas Community College
Becky Hancock, El Paso Community College
Toni Hartley, Laurel Business Institute
Raymond Hartman, Triton Community College
Scott Hays, Central Oregon Community College
Kathy Hebert, Louisiana Technical College
Sueanne Hely, West Kentucky Community & Technical College
Maggie Hilgart, Mid-State Technical College
Michele Hill, Schoolcraft College
Michelle Hoeflich, Elgin Community College
Mary Hollars, Vincennes University
Donna Jacobs, University of New Mexico-Gallup
Judy Jager, Pikes Peak Community College
Jane Jones, Mountain Empire Community College
Jenny Jones, Central Kentucky Technical College
Patrick Jozefowicz, Southwest Wisconsin Technical College
Nancy Kelly, Middlesex Community College
Karen Kettelson, Western Wisconsin Technical College
Elizabeth King, Sacramento City College
Ken Koerber, Bucks County Community College
David Krug, Johnson County Community College
Christy Land, Catawba Valley Community College
Ronald Larner, John Wood Community College
Lee Leksell, Lake Superior College
Lolita Lockett, Florida Community College at Jacksonville
Sue Mardock, Colby Community College
John Masserwick, Five Towns College
Pam Mattson, Tulsa Community College
Bonnie Mayer, Lakeshore Technical College
Sally McMillin, Katharine Gibbs School
John Miller, Metropolitan Community College
Cora Newcomb, Technical College of Lowcountry
Jon Nitschke, Great Falls Technical College
Lorinda Oliver, Vermont Technical College
Barbara Pauer, Gateway Technical College
Nicholas Peppes, St. Louis Community College
Richard Pettit, Mountain View College
Lisa Phillips, City College
Margaret Pollard, American River College
Shirley Powell, Arkansas State University
Claudia Quinn, San Joaquin Delta College
Jerry Rhodes, Daymar College
Ed Richter, Southeast Technical Institute
Alberta Robinson, Indiana Business College
Beth Sanders, Hawaii Community College
Bob Sanner, Central Community College
Debra Schmidt, Cerritos College
Karen Scott, Bates Technical College

Carolyn Seefer, Diablo Valley College
Jeri Spinner, Idaho State University
Alice Steljes, Illinois Valley Community College
Jack Stone, Linn-Benton Community College
Rick Street, Spokane Community College
Domenico Tavella, Pittsburgh Technical Institute
Bill Taylor, Cossatot Community College
Mary J. Tobaben, Collin County Community College
Elaine Tuttle, Bellevue Community College
Ski Vanderlaan, Delta College
Andy Williams, Edmonds Community College
Jack Williams, Tulsa Community College

Supplement Authors and Invaluable Assistance

Instructor's Edition: Marianne Rexer, Wilkes University

Test Item File: Allan Sheets, International Business College, Indianapolis; Michele Hill, Schoolcraft College

PowerPoint Presentations: Tim Samolis, Pittsburgh Technical Institute

Computerized Workshops: Terri Brunsdon

End-of-chapter Peachtree/QuickBooks problems: Toni Hartley, Laurel Business Institute

Who Dun It? Practice Set: Toni Hartley, Laurel Business Institute

Update of Chapters 7, 8, and Corner Dress Shop Practice Set: Rick Street, Spokane Community College

Text Accuracy Checkers: Richard Pettit, Mountain View College; Susan Davis, Green River Community College

Supplement Quality Assurance: Karen Sneary, Northwestern Oklahoma State University; Marina Grau, Houston Community College; Donald Benoit, Mitchell College; Michelle Berube, Everett University; Toni Hartley, Laurel Business Institute; Jonea Shade, Clarence Perkins, Bronx Community College; Richard Pettit, Mountain View College; Michele Hill, Schoolcraft College; Allan Sheets, International Business College; Wanda Edwards, Troy University; Susan Davis, Green River Community College

I Want to Hear from You

How to "get to me": Please e-mail me at jeffslater@aol.com, and I promise to get back to you within 24 hours or less. You are my customer, and I want to provide you with the best service possible.

1

Accounting Concepts and Procedures

DID YOU KNOW? By 2007 Best Buy employed 10,000 geek squad agents, 3,000 home theatre installers, and 3,000 vehicle installers. Revenues and net income are greatest for Best Buy in quarter 4 (the holiday seasons for the United States and Canada). Visit *www.BestBuy.com* to find more information about Best Buy.

LEARNING OBJECTIVES

1. Defining and listing the functions of accounting.
2. Recording transactions in the basic accounting equation.
3. Seeing how revenue, expenses, and withdrawals expand the basic accounting equation.
4. Preparing an income statement, a statement of owner's equity, and a balance sheet.

Companies like Best Buy have to comply with many federal statutes. In 2002 a federal statute called the Sarbanes-Oxley Act was passed to prevent fraud at public companies. This act requires a closer look at the internal controls and the accuracy of the financial results of a company.

Accounting is the language of business; it provides information to managers, owners, investors, government agencies, and others inside and outside the organization. Accounting provides answers and insights to questions like these:

- Should I invest in Best Buy or Wal-Mart stock?
- How will increasing fuel costs affect American Airlines?
- Can United Airlines pay its debt obligations?
- What percentage of Ford's marketing budget is allocated to e-business? How does that percentage compare with the competition? What is the overall financial condition of Ford?

Smaller businesses also need answers to their financial questions:

- At a local Walgreens, did business increase enough over the last year to warrant hiring a new assistant?
- Should Local Auto Detailing Co. spend more money to design, produce, and send out new brochures in an effort to create more business?
- What role should the Internet play in the future of business spending?

Accounting is as important to individuals as it is to businesses; it answers questions like these:

- Should I take out a loan to buy a new Toyota FJ Cruiser or wait until I can afford to pay cash for it?
- Would my money work better in a money market or in the stock market?

The accounting process analyzes, records, classifies, summarizes, reports, and interprets financial information for decision makers—whether individuals, small businesses, large corporations, or governmental agencies—in a timely fashion. It is important that students understand the "whys" of this accounting process. Just knowing the mechanics is not enough.

The three main categories of business organization are (1) sole proprietorships, (2) partnerships, and (3) corporations. Let's define each of them and look at their advantages and disadvantages. This information also appears in Table 1.1.

Sole Proprietorship A **sole proprietorship,** such as Lee's Nail Care, is a business that has one owner. That person is both the owner and the manager of the business. An advantage of a sole proprietorship is that the owner makes all the decisions for the business. A disadvantage is that if the business cannot pay its obligations, the business owner must pay them, which means that the owner could lose some of his or her personal assets (e.g., house or savings).

Sole proprietorships are easy to form. They end if the business closes or when the owner dies.

Partnership A **partnership,** such as Miller and Kaminsky, is a form of business ownership that has at least two owners (partners). Each partner acts as an owner of the company, which is an advantage because the partners can share the decision making and the risks of the business. A disadvantage is that, as in a sole proprietorship, the partners' personal assets could be lost if the partnership cannot meet its obligations.

Partnerships are easy to form. They end when a partner dies or leaves the partnership, or when the partners decide to close the business.

Corporation A **corporation,** such as Best Buy, is a business owned by stockholders. The corporation may have only a few stockholders, or it may have many stockholders. The

TABLE 1.1 Types of Business Organizations

	Sole Proprietorship (Lee's Nail Care)	Partnership (Miller and Kaminsky)	Corporation (Best Buy)
Ownership	Business owned by one person.	Business owned by more than one person.	Business owned by stockholders.
Formation	Easy to form.	Easy to form.	More difficult to form.
Liability	Owner could lose personal assets to meet obligations of business.	Partners could lose personal assets to meet obligations of partnership.	Limited personal risk. Stockholders' loss is limited to their investment in the company.
Closing	Ends with death of owner or closing of business.	Ends with death of partner or closing of business.	Can continue indefinitely.

stockholders are not personally liable for the corporation's debts, and they usually do not have input into the business decisions.

Corporations are more difficult to form than sole proprietorships or partnerships. Corporations can exist indefinitely.

Many corporate executives feel that Sarbanes-Oxley is too strict and results in too high of a cost to implement.

Classifying Business Organizations

Whether we are looking at a sole proprietorship, a partnership, or a corporation, the business can be classified by what the business does to earn money. Companies are categorized as service, merchandise, or manufacturing businesses.

A limo service is a good example of a **service company** because it provides a service. The first part of this book focuses on service businesses.

Gap and JCPenney sell products. They are called merchandise companies. **Merchandise companies** can either make their own products or sell products that are made by another supplier. Companies such as Intel and Ford Motor Company that make their own products are called **manufacturers.** (See Table 1.2.)

Definition of Accounting

LO1

Accounting (also called the accounting process) is a system that measures the activities of a business in financial terms. It provides various reports and financial statements that show how the various transactions the business undertook (e.g., buying and selling goods) affected the business. This accounting process performs the following functions:

- **Analyzing:** Looking at what happened and how the business was affected.
- **Recording:** Putting the information into the accounting system.
- **Classifying:** Grouping all the same activities (e.g., all purchases) together.
- **Summarizing:** Totaling the results.
- **Reporting:** Issuing the statements that tell the results of the previous functions.

TABLE 1.2 Examples of Service, Merchandise, and Manufacturing Businesses

Service Businesses	Merchandise Businesses	Manufacturing Businesses
Lee's Nail Care	Macy's	Anheuser-Busch
eBay	JCPenney	Ford
Dr. Wheeler, M.D.	Amazon.com	Toro
Accountemps	Home Depot	Levi's
Langley Landscaping	Gap	Intel

- **Interpreting:** Examining the statements to determine how the various pieces of information they contain relate to each other.
- **Communication:** Providing the reports and financial statements to people who are interested in the information, such as the business's decision makers, investors, creditors, and government agencies (e.g., the Internal Revenue Service).

Appendix A will look at the annual report of Kellogg Company.

As you can see, a lot of people use these reports. A set of procedures and guidelines were developed to make sure that everyone prepares and interprets them the same way. These guidelines are known as **generally accepted accounting principles (GAAP).**

Now let's look at the difference between bookkeeping and accounting. Keep in mind that we use the terms *accounting* and the *accounting process* interchangeably.

Difference between Bookkeeping and Accounting

Confusion often arises concerning the difference between bookkeeping and accounting. **Bookkeeping** is the recording (record keeping) function of the accounting process; a bookkeeper enters accounting information in the company's books. An accountant takes that information and prepares the financial statements that are used to analyze the company's financial position. Accounting involves many complex activities. Often, it includes the preparation of tax and financial reports, budgeting, and analyses of financial information.

Today, computers are used for routine bookkeeping operations that used to take weeks or months to complete. The text explains how the advantages of the computer can be applied to a manual accounting system by using hands-on knowledge of how accounting works. Basic accounting knowledge is needed even though computers can do routine tasks. QuickBooks, Excel, and Peachtree are popular software packages in use today.

Learning Unit 1-1 The Accounting Equation

Assets, Liabilities, and Equities

Let's begin our study of accounting concepts and procedures by looking at a small business: Mia Wong's law practice. Mia decided to open her practice at the end of August. She consulted her accountant before she made her decision. The accountant told her some important things before she made this decision. First, he told her the new business would be considered a separate business entity whose finances had to be kept separate and distinct from Mia's personal finances. The accountant went on to say that all transactions can be analyzed using the basic accounting equation: Assets = Liabilities + Owner's Equity.

Mia had never heard of the basic accounting equation. She listened carefully as the accountant explained the terms used in the equation and how the equation works.

Assets Cash, land, supplies, office equipment, buildings, and other properties of value *owned* by a firm are called **assets.**

Equities The rights of financial claim to the assets are called **equities.** Equities belong to those who supply the assets. If you are the only person to supply assets to the firm, you have the sole rights or financial claims to them. For example, if you supply the law firm with $6,000 in cash and $8,000 in office equipment, your equity in the firm is $14,000.

Relationship between Assets and Equities The relationship between assets and equities is

Assets = Equities
(Total value of items *owned* by business) (Total claims against the assets)

The total dollar value of the assets of your law firm will be equal to the total dollar value of the financial claims to those assets, that is, equal to the total dollar value of the equities.

The total dollar value is broken down on the left-hand side of the equation to show the specific items of value owned by the business and on the right-hand side to show the types of claims against the assets owned.

Liabilities A firm may have to borrow money to buy more assets; when it does, it means the firm *buys assets on account* (buy now, pay later). Suppose the law firm purchases a new computer for $3,000 on account from Dell, and the company is willing to wait 10 days for payment. The law firm has created a **liability:** an obligation to pay that comes due in the future. Dell is called the **creditor.** This liability—the amount owed to Dell—gives the store the right, or the financial claim, to $3,000 of the law firm's assets. When Dell is paid, the store's rights to the assets of the law firm will end because the obligation has been paid off.

Basic Accounting Equation To best understand the various claims to a business's assets, accountants divide equities into two parts. The claims of creditors—outside persons or businesses—are labeled *liabilities.* The claim of the business's owner is labeled **owner's equity.** Let's see how the accounting equation looks now.

Assets − Liabilities = Owner's Equity

Assets = Equities

1. Liabilities: rights of creditors
2. Owner's equity: rights of owner

Assets = Liabilities + Owner's Equity

The total value of all the assets of a firm equals the combined total value of the financial claims of the creditors (liabilities) and the claims of the owners (owner's equity). This calculation is known as the **basic accounting equation.** The basic accounting equation provides a basis for understanding the conventional accounting system of a business. The equation records business transactions in a logical and orderly way that shows their impact on the company's assets, liabilities, and owner's equity. *LO2*

Importance of Creditors Another way of presenting the basic accounting equation is

Assets – Liabilities = Owner's Equity

This form of the equation stresses the importance of creditors. The owner's rights to the business's assets are determined after the rights of the creditors are subtracted. In other words, creditors have first claim to assets. If a firm has no liabilities—therefore no creditors—the owner has the total rights to assets. Another term for the owner's current investment, or equity, in the business's assets is **capital.**

As Mia Wong's law firm engages in business transactions (paying bills, serving customers, and so on), changes will take place in the assets, liabilities, and owner's equity (capital). Let's analyze some of these transactions.

In accounting, capital does not mean cash. Capital is the owner's current investment, or equity, in the assets of the business.

Transaction A Aug. 28: Mia invests $6,000 in cash and $200 of office equipment into the business.

On August 28, Mia withdraws $6,000 from her personal bank account and deposits the money in the law firm's newly opened bank account. She also invests $200 of office equipment in the business. She plans to be open for business on September 1. With the help of her accountant, Mia begins to prepare the accounting records for the business. We put this information into the basic accounting equation as follows:

Assets			= Liabilities + Owner's Equity	
Cash	+	Office Equipment	=	Mia Wong, Capital
$6,000	+	**$200**	=	**$6,200**

$6,200 = $6,200

Note that the total value of the assets, cash, and office equipment—$6,200—is equal to the combined total value of liabilities (none, so far) and owner's equity ($6,200). Remember, Mia has supplied all the cash and office equipment, so she has the sole financial claim to the assets. Note how the heading "Mia Wong, Capital" is written under the owner's equity heading. The $6,200 is Mia's investment, or equity, in the firm's assets.

Transaction B Aug. 29: Law practice buys office equipment for cash, $500.

From the initial investment of $6,000 cash, the law firm buys $500 worth of office equipment (such as a computer desk), which lasts a long time, whereas **supplies** (such as pens) tend to be used up relatively quickly.

	Assets			= Liabilities +	Owner's Equity
	Cash	+	Office Equipment	=	Mia Wong, Capital
BEGINNING BALANCE	$6,000	+	$200	=	$6,200
TRANSACTION	**−500**		**+500**		
ENDING BALANCE	$5,500	+	$700	=	$6,200

$6,200 = $6,200

Shift in Assets As a result of the last transaction, the law office has less cash but has increased its amount of office equipment. This **shift in assets** indicates that the makeup of the assets has changed, but the total of the assets remains the same.

Suppose you go food shopping at Wal-Mart with $100 and spend $60. Now you have two assets, food and money. The composition of the assets has *shifted*—you have more food and less money than you did—but the *total* of the assets has not increased or decreased. The total value of the food, $60, plus the cash, $40, is still $100. When you borrow money from the bank, on the other hand, you increase cash (an asset) and increase liabilities at the same time. This action results in an increase in assets, not just a shift.

An accounting equation can remain in balance even if only one side is updated. The key point to remember is that the left-hand-side total of assets must always equal the right-hand-side total of liabilities and owner's equity.

Transaction C Aug. 30: Buys additional office equipment on account, $300.

The law firm purchases an additional $300 worth of chairs and desks from Wilmington Company. Instead of demanding cash right away, Wilmington agrees to deliver the equipment and to allow up to 60 days for the law practice to pay the invoice (bill).

This liability, or obligation to pay in the future, has some interesting effects on the basic accounting equation. Wilmington Company accepts as payment a partial claim against the assets of the law practice. This claim exists until the law firm pays off the bill. This unwritten promise to pay the creditor is a liability called **accounts payable.**

	Assets			=	Liabilities	+	Owner's Equity
	Cash	+	Office Equipment	=	Accounts Payable	+	Mia Wong, Capital
BEGINNING BALANCE	$5,500	+	$700	=			$6,200
TRANSACTION			**+300**		**+$300**		
ENDING BALANCE	$5,500	+	$1,000	=	$300	+	$6,200

$6,500 = $6,500

When this information is analyzed, we can see that the law practice increased what it owes (accounts payable) as well as what it owns (office equipment) by $300. The law practice gains $300 in an asset but also takes on an obligation to pay Wilmington Company at a future date.

The owner's equity remains unchanged. This transaction results in an increase of total assets from $6,200 to $6,500.

Finally, note that after each transaction the basic accounting equation remains in balance.

LEARNING UNIT 1-1 REVIEW

AT THIS POINT you should be able to

- Define and explain the purpose of the Sarbanes-Oxley Act.
- Define and explain the differences between sole proprietorships, partnerships, and corporations.
- List the functions of accounting.
- Compare and contrast bookkeeping and accounting.
- Explain the role of the computer as an accounting tool.
- State the purpose of the accounting equation.
- Explain the difference between liabilities and owner's equity.
- Define capital.
- Explain the difference between a shift in assets and an increase in assets.

For additional help go to www.pearsonhighered.com/slater

To test your understanding of this material, complete Self-Review Quiz 1-1. The blank forms you need for all Self-Review quizzes and end-of-chapter material throughout the textbook can be found in the *Study Guide and Working Papers*. The solution to the quiz immediately follows here in the text. If you have difficulty doing the problems, review Learning Unit 1-1 and the solution to the quiz along with a detailed explanation from Jeff Slater, your author. Be sure to check the Slater Web site for student study aids.

Keep in mind that learning accounting is like learning to type: The more you practice, the better you become. You will not be an expert in one day. Be patient. It will all come together.

Self-Review Quiz 1-1

Record the following transactions in the basic accounting equation:

1. Gracie Ryan invests $17,000 to begin a real estate office.
2. The real estate office buys $600 of computer equipment from Wal-Mart for cash.
3. The real estate company buys $800 of additional computer equipment on account from Circuit City.

Solution to Self-Review Quiz 1-1

Assets			=	Liabilities	+	Owner's Equity	
Cash	+	Computer Equipment	=	Accounts Payable	+	Gracie Ryan, Capital	
+$17,000						**+$17,000**	
17,000			=			17,000	**1. BALANCE**
−600		**+$600**					
16,400	+	600	=			17,000	**2. BALANCE**
		+800		**+$800**			
$16,400	+	$1,400	=	$800	+	$17,000	**3. ENDING BALANCE**

$17,800 = $17,800

NEED HELP?

Let's review first: The left side of the accounting equation shows what is owned by the business and the right side of the equation shows you who supplied those assets to a business. Now let's look at the transactions in the solution:

Transaction 1: In your head you must say to yourself, "What did the business get and how did it get it?" The business is getting or increasing its cash by $17,000 and that cash is being supplied by Gracie Ryan. Think of Gracie as increasing her rights in the business since she is supplying cash. Keep in mind that capital does not mean cash. Instead it is what the owner supplies to the business. (Gracie may in the future supply other items to the business.)

So the end result is to put $17,000 on the left side of the equation under cash and put $17,000 under Gracie Ryan, Capital on the right side. The sum of the left side must equal the sum on the right side.

Transaction 2: Here we are NOT looking at the personal finances of Gracie. You must focus on the business. What did the business get and who supplied it to the business?

In this transaction the business is getting $600 of computer equipment by using some of its cash. IT IS SHIFTING ITS ASSETS: MORE EQUIPMENT FOR LESS CASH. Note that capital is not affected since Gracie has not supplied anything new to the business. Note that the right side of the equation is not touched, but the equation still remains in the balance. We are just rearranging the composition of the assets.

Transaction 3: Now the business is getting more equipment but is not paying cash. The equipment is being supplied by a creditor called Accounts Payable. Hopefully in the future the business will be able to pay the creditor back the $800 that it owes. The end result is that the business now has $1,400 in equipment. Note that capital is not affected since no new investments were made by Gracie into the business.

Summary: At the end of these three transactions this company is made up of two assets, Cash $16,400 and Computer Equipment $1,400. The total of the assets was supplied by creditors $800 and the owner Gracie Ryan, Capital $17,000. The sum of the left side must equal the sum of the right side.

Learning Unit 1-2 The Balance Sheet

The balance sheet shows the company's financial position as of a particular date. (In our example, that date is at the end of August.)

In the first learning unit, the transactions for Mia Wong's law firm were recorded in the accounting equation. The transactions we recorded occurred before the law firm opened for business. A statement called a **balance sheet** or **statement of financial position** can show the history of a company before it opened. The balance sheet is a formal statement that presents the information from the ending balances of both sides of the accounting equation. Think of the balance sheet as a snapshot of the business's financial position as of a particular date.

Let's look at the balance sheet of Mia Wong's law practice for August 31, 200X, shown in Figure 1.1. The figures in the balance sheet come from the ending balances of the accounting equation for the law practice as shown in Learning Unit 1-1.

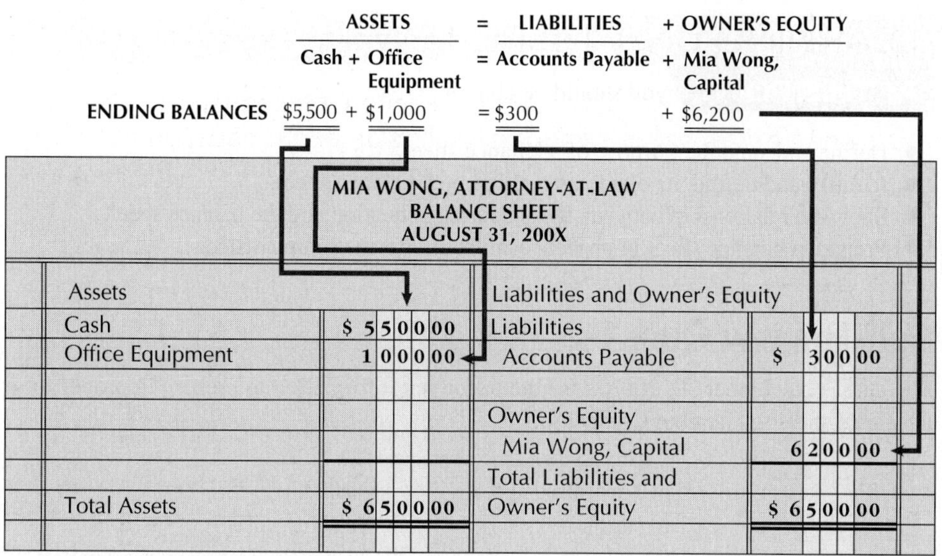

	ASSETS	=	LIABILITIES	+ OWNER'S EQUITY
	Cash + Office Equipment	=	Accounts Payable	+ Mia Wong, Capital
ENDING BALANCES	$5,500 + $1,000	=	$300	+ $6,200

MIA WONG, ATTORNEY-AT-LAW
BALANCE SHEET
AUGUST 31, 200X

Assets		Liabilities and Owner's Equity	
Cash	$ 5 5 0 0 00	Liabilities	
Office Equipment	1 0 0 0 00	Accounts Payable	$ 3 0 0 00
		Owner's Equity	
		Mia Wong, Capital	6 2 0 0 00
		Total Liabilities and	
Total Assets	$ 6 5 0 0 00	Owner's Equity	$ 6 5 0 0 00

FIGURE 1.1 The Balance Sheet

Note in Figure 1.1 that the assets owned by the law practice appear on the left-hand side and that the liabilities and owner's equity appear on the right-hand side. Both sides equal $6,500. This *balance* between left and right gives the balance sheet its name. In later chapters we look at other ways to set up a balance sheet.

Points to Remember in Preparing a Balance Sheet

The Heading The heading of the balance sheet provides the following information:

- The company name: Mia Wong, Attorney-at-Law
- The name of the statement: Balance Sheet
- The date for which the report is prepared: August 31, 200X

Use of the Dollar Sign Note that the dollar sign is not repeated each time a figure appears. As shown in Figure 1.2, the balance sheet for Mia Wong's law practice, it usually is placed to the left of each column's top figure and to the left of the column's total.

The three elements that make up a balance sheet are assets, liabilities, and owner's equity.

Distinguishing the Total When adding numbers down a column, use a single line before the total and a double line beneath it. A single line means that the numbers above it have been added or subtracted. A double line indicates a total. It is important to align the numbers in the column; many errors occur because these figures are not lined up. These rules are the same for all accounting reports.

The balance sheet gives Mia the information she needs to see the law firm's financial position before it opens for business. This information does not tell her, however, whether the firm will make a profit.

FIGURE 1.2 Partial Balance Sheet

MIA WONG, ATTORNEY-AT-LAW
BALANCE SHEET
AUGUST 31, 200X

Assets	
Cash	$ 5 5 0 0 00
Office Equipment	1 0 0 0 00
Total Assets	$ 6 5 0 0 00

A single line means the numbers above it have been added or subtracted.

A double line indicates a total.

LEARNING UNIT 1-2 REVIEW

AT THIS POINT you should be able to

- Define and state the purpose of a balance sheet.
- Identify and define the elements making up a balance sheet.
- Show the relationship between the accounting equation and the balance sheet.
- Prepare a balance sheet in proper form from information provided.

Self-Review Quiz 1-2

The date is November 30, 200X. Use the following information to prepare in proper form a balance sheet for Janning Company:

Accounts Payable	$40,000
Cash	18,000
A. Janning, Capital	9,000
Office Equipment	31,000

For additional help go to www.pearsonhighered.com/slater

Solution to Self-Review Quiz 1-2

FIGURE 1.3 Balance Sheet

JANNING COMPANY
BALANCE SHEET
NOVEMBER 30, 200X

Assets		Liabilities and Owner's Equity	
Cash	$18 000 00	Liabilities	
Office Equipment	31 000 00	Accounts Payable	$ 40 000 00
		Owner's Equity	
		A. Janning, Capital	9 000 00
		Total Liabilities and	
Total Assets	$49 000 00	Owner's Equity	$ 49 000 00

act Accounting Cycle Tutorial

Capital does not mean cash. The capital amount is the owner's current investment of assets in the business.

NEED HELP?

Let's review first: A photo of your family as of a particular date is like a balance sheet. It gives you a history of your family as of a particular date. The balance sheet is a formal report that lists assets, liabilities, and owner's equity for a business as of a particular date.

Before making the report, identify whether each title is an asset, liability, or owner's equity. Accounts payable is a liability. Hopefully the business will be able to pay. Cash is an asset, or something of value owned by the business. A. Janning, Capital is owner's equity, or what the owner is supplying to the business.

The heading of a balance sheet answers three questions:

Who? Janning Company

What report? Balance Sheet

When? November 30, 200X

The left side of the balance sheet lists out the assets, cash, and office equipment.

The right side lists out who supplies the assets to the business: creditors (accounts payable) or the owner, A. Janning, Capital. Use single rules to add and double rules for totals. The sum of the left side must equal the sum of the right side.

Learning Unit 1-3 The Accounting Equation Expanded: Revenue, Expenses, and Withdrawals

LO3

As soon as Mia Wong's office opened, she began performing legal services for her clients and earning revenue for the business. At the same time, as a part of doing business, she incurred various expenses such as rent.

When Mia asked her accountant how these transactions fit into the accounting equation, she began by defining some terms.

Remember: Accounts receivable results from earning revenue even when cash is not yet received.

Record an expense when it is incurred, whether it is paid immediately or is to be paid later.

Revenue A service company earns **revenue** when it provides services to its clients. Mia's law firm earned revenue when she provided legal services to her clients for legal fees. When revenue is earned, owner's equity is increased. In effect, revenue is a subdivision of owner's equity.

Assets are increased. The increase is in the form of cash if the client pays right away. If the client promises to pay in the future, the increase is called **accounts receivable.** When revenue is earned, the transaction is recorded as an increase in revenue and an increase in assets (either as cash or as accounts receivable, depending on whether it was paid right away or will be paid in the future).

Expenses A business's **expenses** are the costs the company incurs in carrying on operations in its effort to create revenue. Expenses are also a subdivision of owner's equity; when expenses are incurred, they *decrease* owner's equity. Expenses can be paid for in cash or they can be charged.

Net Income/Net Loss When revenue totals more than expenses, **net income** is the result; when expenses total more than revenue, **net loss** is the result.

Withdrawals At some point Mia Wong may need to withdraw cash or other assets from the business to pay living or other personal expenses that do not relate to the business. We will record these transactions in an account called **withdrawals.** Sometimes this account is called the *owner's drawing account.* Withdrawals is a subdivision of owner's equity that records personal expenses not related to the business. Withdrawals decrease owner's equity (see Fig. 1.4 on the following page).

It is important to remember the difference between expenses and withdrawals. Expenses relate to business operations; withdrawals are the result of personal needs outside the normal operations of the business.

Now let's analyze the September transactions for Mia Wong's law firm using an **expanded accounting equation** that includes withdrawals, revenues, and expenses.

Expanded Accounting Equation

Transaction D Sept. 1–30: Provided legal services for cash, $2,000.

FIGURE 1.4 Owner's Equity

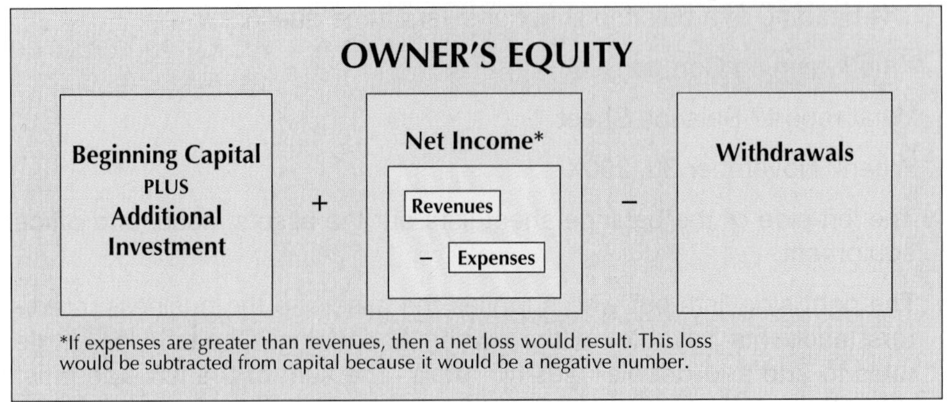

Transactions A, B, and C were discussed earlier, when the law office was being formed in August. See Learning Unit 1.1.

	Assets			= Liabilities +		Owner's Equity		
	Cash	+ Accts. Rec.	+ Office Equip.	= Accts. Pay.	+ M. Wong, Capital	− M. Wong, Withdr.	+ Revenue	− Expenses
BALANCE FORWARD	$5,500		+ $1,000	= $ 300	+ $6,200			
	+2,000						**+ $2,000**	
ENDING BALANCE	$7,500		+ $1,000	= $ 300	+ $6,200		+ $2,000	

$8,500 = $8,500

In the law firm's first month of operation, a total of $2,000 in cash was received for legal services performed. In the accounting equation, the asset Cash is increased by $2,000. Revenue is also increased by $2,000, resulting in an increase in owner's equity.

A revenue column was added to the basic accounting equation. Amounts are recorded in the revenue column when they are earned. They are also recorded in the assets column under Cash and/or Accounts Receivable. Do not think of revenue as an asset. It is part of owner's equity. It is the revenue that creates an inward flow of cash and accounts receivable.

Transaction E Sept. 1–30: Provided legal services on account, $3,000.

	Assets			= Liabilities +		Owner's Equity		
	Cash	+ Accts. Rec.	+ Office Equip.	= Accts. Pay.	+ M. Wong, Capital	− M. Wong, Withdr.	+ Revenue	− Expenses
BAL. FOR. TRANS.	$7,500		+ $ 1,000	= $ 300	+ $6,200		+ $2,000	
		+3,000					**+ $3,000**	
END. BAL.	$7,500	+ $3,000	+ $ 1,000	= $ 300	+ $6,200		+ $5,000	

$11,500 = $11,500

Mia's law practice performed legal work on account for $3,000. The firm did not receive the cash for these earned legal fees; it accepted an unwritten promise from these clients that payment would be received in the future.

Transaction F Sept. 1–30: Received $900 cash as partial payment from previous services performed on account.

During September some of Mia's clients who had received services and promised to pay in the future decided to reduce what they owed the practice by making payment of $900. This decision is shown as follows on the expanded accounting equation:

Assets			= Liabilities +	Owner's Equity				
Cash	+ Accts. Rec.	+ Office Equip.	= Accts. Pay.	+ M. Wong, Capital	− M. Wong, Withdr.	+ Revenue	− Expenses	
$7,500	+ $3,000	+ $ 1,000	= $ 300	+ $6,200		+ $5,000		**BAL. FOR. TRANS.**
+900	**−900**							
$8,400	+ $2,100	+ $ 1,000	= $ 300	+ $6,200		+ $5,000		**END. BAL.**

$11,500 = $11,500

The law firm increased the asset Cash by $900 and reduced another asset, Accounts Receivable, by $900. The *total* of assets does not change. The right-hand side of the expanded accounting equation has not been touched because the total on the left-hand side of the equation has not changed. The revenue was recorded when it was earned, and the *same revenue cannot be recorded twice.* This transaction analyzes the situation *after* the revenue has been previously earned and recorded. Transaction F shows a shift in assets resulting in more cash and less accounts receivable.

Transaction G Sept. 1–30: Paid salaries expense, $700.

Assets			= Liabilities +	Owner's Equity				
Cash	+ Accts. Rec.	+ Office Equip.	= Accts. Pay.	+ M. Wong, Capital	− M. Wong, Withdr.	+ Revenue	− Expenses	
$8,400	+ $2,100	+ $ 1,000	= $ 300	+ $6,200		+ $5,000		**BAL. FOR. TRANS.**
−700							**+$700**	
$7,700	+ $2,100	+ $ 1,000	= $ 300	+ $6,200		+ $5,000	− $700	**END. BAL.**

$10,800 = $10,800

As expenses increase, they decrease owner's equity. This incurred expense of $700 reduces the cash by $700. Although the expense was paid, the total of our expenses to date has *increased* by $700. Keep in mind that owner's equity decreases as expenses increase, so the accounting equation remains in balance.

Transaction H Sept. 1–30: Paid rent expense, $400.

Assets			= Liabilities +	Owner's Equity				
Cash	+ Accts. Rec.	+ Office Equip.	= Accts. Pay.	+ M. Wong, Capital	− M. Wong, Withdr.	+ Revenue	− Expenses	
$7,700	+ $2,100	+ $ 1,000	= $ 300	+ $6,200		+ $5,000	− $ 700	**BAL. FOR. TRANS.**
−400							**+400**	
$7,300	+ $2,100	+ $ 1,000	= $ 300	+ $6,200		+ $5,000	− $1,100	**END. BAL.**

$10,400 = $10,400

During September the practice incurred rent expenses of $400. This rent was not paid in advance; it was paid when it came due. The payment of rent reduces the asset Cash by $400 as well as increases the expenses of the firm, resulting in a decrease in owner's equity. The firm's expenses are now $1,100.

Transaction I Sept. 1–30: Incurred advertising expenses of $200, to be paid next month.

	Assets			= Liabilities +	Owner's Equity			
	Cash	+ Accts. Rec.	+ Office Equip.	= Accts. Pay.	+ M. Wong, Capital	− M. Wong, Withdr.	+ Revenue	− Expenses
BAL. FOR. TRANS.	$7,300	+ $2,100	+ $ 1,000	= $ 300	+ $6,200		+ $5,000	− $1,100
				+200				**+200**
END. BAL.	$7,300	+ $2,100	+ $ 1,000	= $ 500	+ $6,200		+ $5,000	− $1,300

$10,400 = $10,400

Mia ran an ad in the local newspaper and incurred an expense of $200. This increase in expenses caused a corresponding decrease in owner's equity. Because Mia has not paid the newspaper for the advertising yet, she owes $200. Thus her liabilities (Accounts Payable) increase by $200. Eventually, when the bill comes in and is paid, both Cash and Accounts Payable will be decreased.

Transaction J Sept. 1–30: Mia withdrew $100 for personal use.

	Assets			= Liabilities +	Owner's Equity			
	Cash	+ Accts. Rec.	+ Office Equip.	= Accts. Pay.	+ M. Wong, Capital	− M. Wong, Withdr.	+ Revenue	− Expenses
BAL. FOR. TRANS.	$7,300	+ $2,100	+ $ 1,000	= $ 500	+ $6,200		+ $5,000	− $1,300
	−100					**+$100**		
END. BAL.	$7,200	+ $2,100	+ $ 1,000	= $ 500	+ $6,200	− $100	+ $5,000	− $1,300

$10,300 = $10,300

By taking $100 for personal use, Mia *increased* her withdrawals from the business by $100 and decreased the asset Cash by $100. Note that as withdrawals increase, the owner's equity *decreases.* Keep in mind that a withdrawal is *not* a business expense. It is a subdivision of owner's equity that records money or other assets an owner withdraws from the business for *personal* use.

Subdivision of Owner's Equity Take a moment to review the subdivisions of owner's equity:

- As capital increases, owner's equity increases (see transaction A).
- As withdrawals increase, owner's equity decreases (see transaction J).
- As revenue increases, owner's equity increases (see transaction D).
- As expenses increase, owner's equity decreases (see transaction G).

Mia Wong's Expanded Accounting Equation The following is a summary of the expanded accounting equation for Mia Wong's law firm.

Mia Wong
Attorney-at-Law
Expanded Accounting Equation: A Summary

Assets						= Liabilities +				Owner's Equity					
Cash	+	Accts. Rec.	+	Office Equip.	=	Accts. Pay.	+	M. Wong, Capital	−	M. Wong, Withdr.	+	Revenue	−	Expenses	
$6,000				+$200	=			+$6,200							**A.**
6,000			+	200	=			6,200							**BALANCE**
–500				+500											**B.**
5,500			+	700	=			6,200							**BALANCE**
				+300		+$300									**C.**
5,500	+			1,000	=	300	+	6,200							**BALANCE**
+2,000												+$2,000			**D.**
7,500			+	1,000	=	300	+	6,200			+	2,000			**BALANCE**
		+$3,000										+3,000			**E.**
7,500	+	3,000	+	1,000	=	300	+	6,200			+	5,000			**BALANCE**
+900		–900													**F.**
8,400	+	2,100	+	1,000	=	300	+	6,200			+	5,000			**BALANCE**
–700														+$700	**G.**
7,700	+	2,100	+	1,000	=	300	+	6,200			+	5,000	−	700	**BALANCE**
–400														+400	**H.**
7,300	+	2,100	+	1,000	=	300	+	6,200			+	5,000	−	1,100	**BALANCE**
						+200								+200	**I.**
7,300	+	2,100	+	1,000	=	500	+	6,200			+	5,000	−	1,300	**BALANCE**
–100										+$100					**J.**
$7,200	+	$2,100	+	$1,000	=	$500	+	$6,200	−	$100	+	$5,000	−	$1,300	**END BALANCE**

$10,300 = $10,300

LEARNING UNIT 1-3 REVIEW

AT THIS POINT you should be able to

- Define and explain the difference between revenue and expenses.
- Define and explain the difference between net income and net loss.
- Explain the subdivisions of owner's equity.
- Explain the effects of withdrawals, revenue, and expenses on owner's equity.
- Record transactions in an expanded accounting equation and balance the basic accounting equation as a means of checking the accuracy of your calculations.

For additional help go to www.pearsonhighered.com/slater

Self-Review Quiz 1-3

Record the following transactions into the expanded accounting equation for the Bing Company. Note that all titles have a beginning balance.

1. Received cash revenue, $4,000.
2. Billed customers for services rendered, $6,000.
3. Received a bill for telephone expenses (to be paid next month), $125.

4. Bob Bing withdrew cash for personal use, $500.
5. Received $1,000 from customers in partial payment for services performed in transaction 2.

Solution to Self-Review Quiz 1-3

	Assets			= Liabilities +	Owner's Equity			
	Cash +	Accts. Rec. +	Cleaning Equip. =	Accts. Pay. +	B. Bing, Capital −	B. Bing, Withdr. +	Revenue −	Expenses
BEG. BALANCE	$10,000 +	$ 2,500 +	$ 6,500 =	$1,000 +	$11,800 −	$ 800 +	$ 9,000 −	$2,000
1.	**+4,000**						**+4,000**	
BALANCE	14,000 +	2,500 +	6,500 =	1,000 +	11,800 −	800 +	13,000 −	2,000
2.		+6,000					+6,000	
BALANCE	14,000 +	8,500 +	6,500 =	1,000 +	11,800 −	800 +	19,000 −	2,000
3.				+125				+125
BALANCE	14,000 +	8,500 +	6,500 =	1,125 +	11,800 −	800 +	19,000 −	2,125
4.	**–500**					**+500**		
BALANCE	13,500 +	8,500 +	6,500 =	1,125 +	11,800 −	1,300 +	19,000 −	2,125
5.	**+1,000**	**–1,000**						
END. BALANCE	$14,500 +	$ 7,500 +	$ 6,500 =	$1,125 +	$11,800 −	$1,300 +	$19,000 −	$2,125

$28,500 = $28,500

NEED HELP?

Let's review first: You only record revenue when it is earned. What can the business get? Cash and/or promises from customers called Accounts Receivable. Revenue is not an asset but does provide an inward flow of assets into the business. Revenue is part of owner's equity. Think of expenses as always increasing in a business. The end result will be a decrease in owner's equity. Expenses are recorded when they happen and can be paid for by cash or charged as Accounts Payable.

Withdrawals work just like expenses, but they represent personal withdrawals by the owner. Expenses and withdrawals are not recorded together. Each has a separate title.

Transaction 1: The company has done the work. It now records revenue of $4,000 in the revenue column (we only put numbers in this column when we do the work). This time the inward flow from the revenue is all in the form of cash of $4,000.

Transaction 2: This time the company does the work but is not getting the cash. It is receiving promises that it will be paid in the future. You record the $6,000 in the revenue column because you did the work. The inward flow from this revenue is not cash but promises called Accounts Receivable. Thus, the Accounts Receivable column is increased by $6,000.

Transaction 3: An expense has happened and should be recorded whether money is paid or not. The expenses for telephone have

INCREASED by $125, resulting in the total expenses rising to $2,125. As expenses in a business rise, the end result is a reduction in owner's equity.

Since the expense was charged, the $125 is recorded under Accounts Payable because hopefully the expense will be paid in the future. At this point this telephone expense has created a liability. Remember that an expense is not a liability.

Transaction 4: This transaction relates to a personal transaction and does not affect any expenses in the business. Bob Bing takes $500 cash from the business. Think of Bob as gaining the $500, but in reality his owner's rights will be reduced. This is shown by a $500 gain under withdrawals, which now results in a total of $1,300 (a reduction to owner's equity) and a decrease to cash. Note that expenses are not affected since this is a personal transaction.

Transaction 5: No new work is earned, so we do not record any new revenue. Here customers are paying part of what they owe. The result is that company cash increased by $1,000 and Accounts Receivable is reduced by $1,000. This is a shift in assets: more cash, less accounts receivable.

Summary: Note the four subdivisions of owner's equity: Capital, Withdrawals, Revenues, and Expenses. As capital and revenue increases, owner's equity will increase. As expenses and withdrawals increase, owner's equity will decrease. Revenue is not an asset. Rather, it provides assets in the form of cash and/or accounts receivable. Only record revenue when work is done. Only record expenses when they happen, regardless whether cash is received.

Learning Unit 1-4 Preparing Financial Statements

LO4

Mia Wong would like to be able to find out whether her firm is making a profit, so she asks her accountant whether he can measure the firm's financial performance on a monthly basis. Her accountant replies that a number of financial statements that he can prepare, such as the income statement, will show Mia how well the law firm has performed over a specific period of time. The accountant can use the information in the income statement to prepare other reports.

The Income Statement

An **income statement** is an accounting statement that shows business results in terms of revenue and expenses. If revenues are greater than expenses, the report shows net income. If expenses are greater than revenues, the report shows net loss. An income statement can cover 1, 3, 6, or 12 months. It cannot cover more than one year. The statement shows the result of all revenues and expenses throughout the entire period and not just as of a specific date. The income statement for Mia Wong's law firm is shown in Figure 1.5 on the following page.

Points to Remember in Preparing an Income Statement

The income statement is prepared from data found in the revenue and expense columns of the expanded accounting equation. The inside column of numbers ($700, $400, $200) is used to subtotal all expenses ($1,300) before subtracting from revenue.

Heading The heading of an income statement tells the same three things as all other accounting statements: the company's name, the name of the statement, and the period of time the statement covers.

The Setup As you can see on the income statement, the inside column of numbers ($700, $400, and $200) is used to subtotal all expenses ($1,300) before subtracting them from revenue ($5,000 − $1,300 = $3,700).

FIGURE 1.5 The Income Statement

Software programs may call this statement a profit and loss statement or an earnings statement.

MIA WONG, ATTORNEY-AT-LAW INCOME STATEMENT FOR MONTH ENDED SEPTEMBER 30, 200X		
Revenue:		
Legal Fees		$ 5 0 0 0 00
Operating Expenses:		
Salaries Expense	$ 7 0 0 00	
Rent Expense	4 0 0 00	
Advertising Expense	2 0 0 00	
Total Operating Expenses		1 3 0 0 00
Net Income		$ 3 7 0 0 00

Operating expenses may be listed in alphabetical order, in order of largest amounts to smallest, or in a set order established by the accountant.

The Statement of Owner's Equity

As we said, the income statement is a business statement that shows business results in terms of revenue and expenses, but how does net income or net loss affect owner's equity? To find out, we have to look at a second type of statement, the **statement of owner's equity.**

If this statement of owner's equity is omitted, the information will be included in the owner's equity section of the balance sheet.

The statement of owner's equity shows for a certain period of time what changes occurred in Mia Wong, Capital. The statement of owner's equity is shown in Figure 1.6.

The capital of Mia Wong can be

Increased by: Owner Investment
Net Income (Revenue − Expenses) and Revenue Greater Than Expenses
Decreased by: Owner Withdrawals
Net Loss (Revenue − Expenses) and Expenses Greater Than Revenue

Remember, a withdrawal is *not* a business expense and thus is not involved in the calculation of net income or net loss on the income statement. It appears on the statement of owner's equity. The statement of owner's equity summarizes the effects of all the subdivisions of owner's equity (revenue, expenses, withdrawals) on beginning capital. The ending capital figure ($9,800) will be the beginning figure in the next statement of owner's equity.

Suppose Mia's law firm had operated at a loss in the month of September. Suppose instead of net income, a $400 net loss occurred and an additional investment of $700 was made on September 15. Figure 1.7 shows how the statement would look with this net loss and additional investment.

FIGURE 1.6 Statement of Owner's Equity—Net Income

This statement, called a statement of retained earnings in Peachtree, is not available as a report in QuickBooks.

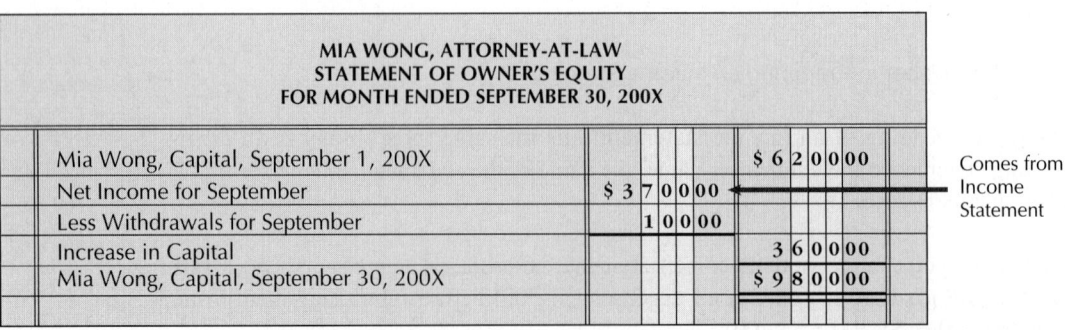

MIA WONG, ATTORNEY-AT-LAW STATEMENT OF OWNER'S EQUITY FOR MONTH ENDED SEPTEMBER 30, 200X		
Mia Wong, Capital, September 1, 200X		$ 6 2 0 0 00
Net Income for September	$ 3 7 0 0 00	
Less Withdrawals for September	1 0 0 00	
Increase in Capital		3 6 0 0 00
Mia Wong, Capital, September 30, 200X		$ 9 8 0 0 00

Comes from Income Statement

MIA WONG, ATTORNEY-AT-LAW
STATEMENT OF OWNER'S EQUITY
FOR MONTH ENDED SEPTEMBER 30, 200X

Mia Wong, Capital, September 1, 200X		$ 6 2 0 0 00
Additional Investment, September 15, 200X		7 0 0 00
Total Investment for September*		$ 6 9 0 0 00
Less: Net Loss for September	$ 4 0 0 00	
Withdrawals for September	1 0 0 00	
Decrease in Capital		5 0 0 00
Mia Wong, Capital, September 30, 200X		$ 6 4 0 0 00

*Beginning capital and additional investments.

FIGURE 1.7 Statement of Owner's Equity—Net Loss

The Balance Sheet

Now let's look at how to prepare a balance sheet from the expanded accounting equation (see Fig. 1.8). As you can see, the asset accounts (cash, accounts receivable, and office equipment) appear on the left side of the balance sheet.

Accounts payable and Mia Wong, Capital appear on the right side. Notice that the $9,800 of capital can be calculated within the accounting equation or can be read from the statement of owner's equity.

FIGURE 1.8 The Accounting Equation and the Balance Sheet

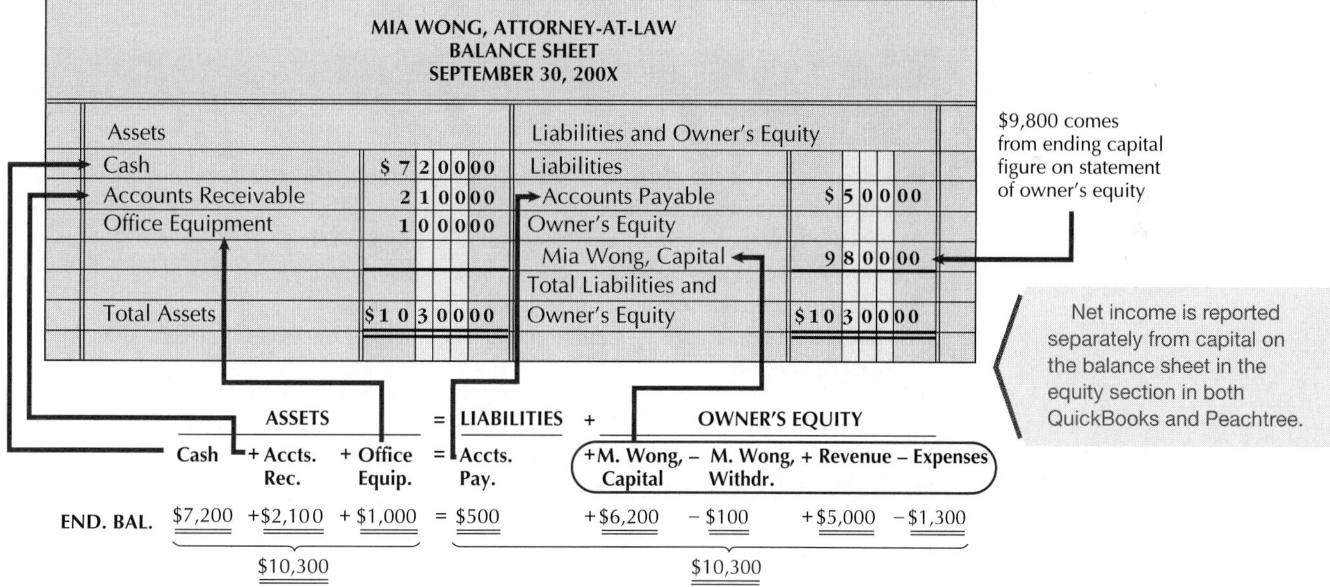

MIA WONG, ATTORNEY-AT-LAW
BALANCE SHEET
SEPTEMBER 30, 200X

Assets		Liabilities and Owner's Equity	
Cash	$ 7 2 0 0 00	Liabilities	
Accounts Receivable	2 1 0 0 00	Accounts Payable	$ 5 0 0 00
Office Equipment	1 0 0 0 00	Owner's Equity	
		Mia Wong, Capital	9 8 0 0 00
		Total Liabilities and	
Total Assets	$1 0 3 0 0 00	Owner's Equity	$1 0 3 0 0 00

Net income is reported separately from capital on the balance sheet in the equity section in both QuickBooks and Peachtree.

Main Elements of the Income Statement, the Statement of Owner's Equity, and the Balance Sheet

In this chapter we have discussed three financial statements: the income statement, the statement of owner's equity, and the balance sheet. A fourth statement, called the statement of cash flows, will not be covered at this time. Let us review what elements of the expanded accounting equation go into each statement and the usual order in which the statements are prepared. Figure 1.8 presents a diagram of the accounting equation and the balance sheet. Table 1.3 on the following page summarizes the following points:

- The income statement is prepared first; it includes revenues and expenses and shows net income or net loss. This net income or net loss is used to update the next statement, the statement of owner's equity.

TABLE 1.3 What Goes on Each Financial Statement

	Income Statement	Statement of Owner's Equity	Balance Sheet
Assets			X
Liabilities			X
Capital* (beg.)		X	
Capital (end)		X	X
Withdrawals		X	
Revenues	X		
Expenses	X		

**Note:* Additional Investments go on the statement of owner's equity.

- The statement of owner's equity is prepared second; it includes beginning capital and any additional investments, the net income or net loss shown on the income statement, withdrawals, and the total, which is the **ending capital.** The balance in Capital comes from the statement of owner's equity.
- The balance sheet is prepared last; it includes the final balances of each of the elements listed in the accounting equation under Assets and Liabilities. The balance in Capital comes from the statement of owner's equity.

LEARNING UNIT 1-4 REVIEW

AT THIS POINT you should be able to

- Define and state the purpose of the income statement, the statement of owner's equity, and the balance sheet.
- Discuss why the income statement should be prepared first.
- Show what happens on a statement of owner's equity when a net loss occurs.
- Compare and contrast these three financial statements.
- Calculate a new figure for capital on the statement of owner's equity and the balance sheet.

For additional help go to www.pearsonhighered.com/slater

Self-Review Quiz 1-4

From the balances listed next for Rusty Realty prepare the following:

1. Income statement for the month ended November 30, 200X.
2. Statement of owner's equity for the month ended November 30, 200X.
3. Balances as of November 30, 200X.

Cash	$4,000	R. Rusty, Capital	
Accounts Receivable	1,370	November 1, 200X	$5,000
Store Furniture	1,490	R. Rusty, Withdrawals	100
Accounts Payable	900	Commissions Earned	1,500
		Rent Expense	200
		Advertising Expense	150
		Salaries Expense	90

Solution to Self-Review Quiz 1-4

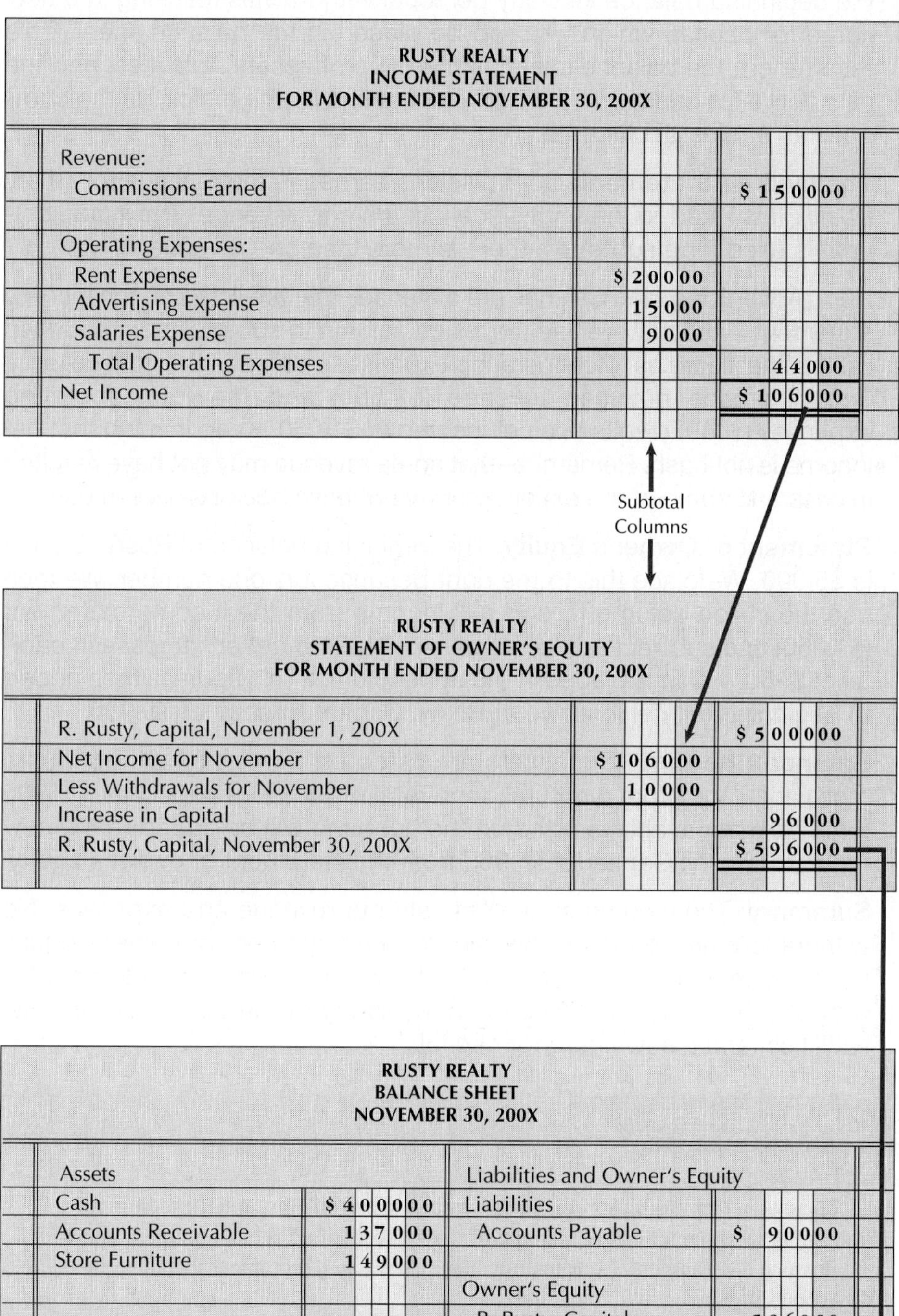

RUSTY REALTY
INCOME STATEMENT
FOR MONTH ENDED NOVEMBER 30, 200X

Revenue:		
Commissions Earned		$ 1500 00
Operating Expenses:		
Rent Expense	$ 200 00	
Advertising Expense	150 00	
Salaries Expense	90 00	
Total Operating Expenses		440 00
Net Income		$ 1060 00

RUSTY REALTY
STATEMENT OF OWNER'S EQUITY
FOR MONTH ENDED NOVEMBER 30, 200X

R. Rusty, Capital, November 1, 200X		$ 5000 00
Net Income for November	$ 1060 00	
Less Withdrawals for November	100 00	
Increase in Capital		960 00
R. Rusty, Capital, November 30, 200X		$ 5960 00

RUSTY REALTY
BALANCE SHEET
NOVEMBER 30, 200X

Assets		Liabilities and Owner's Equity	
Cash	$ 4000 00	Liabilities	
Accounts Receivable	1370 00	Accounts Payable	$ 900 00
Store Furniture	1490 00		
		Owner's Equity	
		R. Rusty, Capital	5960 00
		Total Liabilities and	
Total Assets	$ 6860 00	Owner's Equity	$ 6860 00

FIGURE 1.9 Financial Reports

NEED HELP?

Let's review first: The first formal report is the income statement, which is made up of only revenues and expenses. This report shows how a company is performing for a specific period of time. The second report is the statement of the owner's equity. This report shows how capital has changed from its beginning balance. The net income is added to the beginning balance less any personal withdrawals resulting in a new figure for capital, which will also be placed in the balance sheet. This third report, the balance sheet, is made up of assets, liabilities, and the new figure for capital. The balance sheet shows the history of the company as of a particular date.

The Income Statement: Commissions earned is the revenue for Rusty Realty. It is listed to the right since it is the only revenue. The inside column is used for a subtotal if there is more than one revenue.

Rent, Advertising, and Salaries are expenses that are listed on the income statement. Note that we use the inside column to subtotal them and then list the final figure as total operating expenses of $440 in the right column. The difference between revenue ($1,500) and the total operating expenses ($440) results in a net income of $1,060. Keep in mind that net income is not cash. Remember that some revenue may not have resulted in cash and some of the expenses may not have been paid for in cash.

Statement of Owner's Equity: The beginning balance of Rusty, Capital is $5,000. We place this to the right because it is one number. We then use the inside column to add net income from the income statement ($1,060) and subtract any withdrawals ($100) to get an increase in capital of $960, which is placed in the right column. This figure is then added to beginning capital to arrive at Rusty, Capital (ending) of $5,960.

Balance Sheet: All the assets are listed on the left (cash, accounts receivable, and store furniture), for a total of $6,860. The liability of $900 for accounts payable is listed on the right and will be added to the new figure for Rusty, Capital of $5,960 from the statement of owner's equity.

Summary: The income statement lists out revenue and expenses. No withdrawals are found on this report. The statement of owner's equity will show how capital changes by net income, net loss, and/or withdrawals. The balance shows the new history of the company's assets, liabilities, and a new figure for capital.

CHAPTER ASSIGNMENTS

All Classroom Demonstration Exercises, Exercises, Problems, and the Continuing Problem in this chapter can be found within MyAccountingLab, an online homework and practice environment. Your instructor may ask you to complete this material using MyAccountingLab.

DEMONSTRATION PROBLEM

Michael Brown opened his law office on June 1, 200X. During the first month of operations, Michael conducted the following transactions:

1. Invested $6,000 in cash into the law practice.
2. Paid $600 for office equipment.
3. Purchased additional office equipment on account, $1,000.
4. Received cash for performing legal services for clients, $2,000.
5. Paid salaries, $800.
6. Performed legal services for clients on account, $1,000.

7. Paid rent, $1,200.
8. Withdrew $500 from his law practice for personal use.
9. Received $500 from customers in partial payment for legal services performed, transaction 6.

ASSIGNMENT

Record these transactions in the expanded accounting equation.
Prepare the financial statements at June 30 for Michael Brown, Attorney-at-Law.

Solution to Demonstration Problem

	Assets			= Liabilities +	Owner's Equity			
A.	Cash	+ Accts. Rec.	+ Office Equip.	= Accounts Payable	+ M. Brown, Capital	− M. Brown, Withdr.	+ Legal Fees	− Expenses
1.	**+$6,000**				**+$6,000**			
BAL.	6,000		=		6,000			
2.	**–600**		**+$600**					
BAL.	5,400		+ 600 =		6,000			
3.			**+1,000**	**+$1,000**				
BAL.	5,400		+ 1,600 =	1,000	+ 6,000			
4.	**+2,000**						**+$2,000**	
BAL.	7,400		+ 1,600 =	1,000	+ 6,000		+ 2,000	
5.	**–800**							**+$800**
BAL.	6,600		+ 1,600 =	1,000	+ 6,000		+ 2,000 −	800
6.		**+$1,000**					**+1,000**	
BAL.	6,600 +	1,000 +	1,600 =	1,000	+ 6,000		+ 3,000 −	800
7.	**–1,200**							**+1,200**
BAL.	5,400 +	1,000 +	1,600 =	1,000	+ 6,000		+ 3,000 −	2,000
8.	**–500**					**+$500**		
BAL.	4,900 +	1,000 +	1,600 =	1,000	+ 6,000 −	500	+ 3,000 −	2,000
9.	**+500**	**–500**						
END. BAL.	$5,400 +	$ 500 +	$1,600 =	$1,000	+ $6,000 −	$500	+ $3,000 −	$2,000

$7,500 = $7,500

Solution Tips to Expanded Accounting Equation

- **Transaction 1:** The business increased its Cash by $6,000. Owner's Equity (capital) increased when Michael supplied the cash to the business.
- **Transaction 2:** A shift in assets occurred when the equipment was purchased. The business lowered its Cash by $600, and a new column—Office Equipment—was increased for the $600 of equipment that was bought. The amount of capital is not touched because the owner did not supply any new funds.
- **Transaction 3:** When creditors supply $1,000 of additional equipment, the business Accounts Payable shows the debt. The business had increased what it *owes* the creditors.
- **Transaction 4:** Legal Fees, a subdivision of Owner's Equity, is increased when the law firm provides a service even if no money is received. The service provides an inward flow of $2,000 to Cash, an asset. Remember that Legal Fees are *not* an asset. As Legal Fees increase, Owner's Equity increases.
- **Transaction 5:** The salary paid by Michael shows an $800 increase in Expenses and a corresponding decrease in Owner's Equity as well as a decrease in Cash.

- **Transaction 6:** Michael did the work and earned the $1,000. That $1,000 is recorded as revenue. This time the Legal Fees create an inward flow of assets called Accounts Receivable for $1,000. Remember that Legal Fees are *not* an asset. They are a subdivision of Owner's Equity.
- **Transaction 7:** The $1,200 rent expense reduces Owner's Equity as well as Cash.
- **Transaction 8:** Withdrawals are for personal use. Here the business decreases Cash by $500 while Michael's withdrawals increase $500. Withdrawals decrease the Owner's Equity.
- **Transaction 9:** This transaction does not reflect new revenue in the form of Legal Fees. It is only a shift in assets: more Cash and less Accounts Receivable.

Solution Tips to Financial Statements

B-1. The income statement lists only revenues and expenses for a period of time. The inside column is for subtotaling. Withdrawals are not listed here.

B-2. The statement of owner's equity takes the net income figure of $1,000 and adds it to beginning capital less any withdrawals. This new capital figure of $6,500 will go on the balance sheet. This statement shows changes in capital for a period of time.

B-3. The $5,400, $500, $1,600, and $1,000 came from the totals of the expanded accounting equation. The capital figure of $6,500 came from the statement of owner's equity. This balance sheet reports assets, liabilities, and a new figure for capital at a specific date.

B-1.

MICHAEL BROWN, ATTORNEY-AT-LAW
INCOME STATEMENT
FOR MONTH ENDED JUNE 30, 200X

Revenue:		
Legal Fees		$3,000
Operating Expenses:		
Salaries Expense	$ 800	
Rent Expense	1,200	
Total Operating Expenses		2,000
Net Income		$1,000

B-2.

MICHAEL BROWN, ATTORNEY-AT-LAW
STATEMENT OF OWNER'S EQUITY
FOR MONTH ENDED JUNE 30, 200X

Michael Brown, Capital, June 1, 200X		$6,000
Net income for June	$1,000	
Less withdrawls for June	500	
Increase in Capital		500
Michael Brown, Capital, June 30, 200X		$6,500

B-3.

MICHAEL BROWN, ATTORNEY-AT-LAW
BALANCE SHEET
JUNE 30, 200X

Assets		**Liabilities and Owner's Equity**	
Cash	$5,400	Liabilities	
Accounts Receivable	500	Accounts Payable	$1,000
Office Equipment	1,600	Owner's Equity	
		M. Brown, Capital	$6,500
Total Assets	$7,500	Total Liabilities and Owner's Equity	$7,500

SUMMARY OF KEY POINTS

LEARNING UNIT 1-1

1. The Sarbanes-Oxley rule helps prevent fraud at trading companies.
2. The functions of accounting involve analyzing, recording, classifying, summarizing, reporting, and interpreting financial information.
3. A sole proprietorship is a business owned by one person. A partnership is a business owned by two or more persons. A corporation is a business owned by stockholders. All forms of business organizations are found in Internet businesses.
4. Bookkeeping is the recording part of accounting.
5. The computer is a tool to use in the accounting process.
6. Assets = Liabilities + Owner's Equity is the basic accounting equation that aids in analyzing business transactions.
7. Liabilities represent amounts owed to creditors, whereas capital represents what is invested by the owner.
8. Capital does not mean cash. Capital is the owner's current investment. The owner could have invested equipment that was purchased before the new business was started.
9. In a shift of assets the composition of assets changes but the total of assets does not change. For example, if a bill is paid by a customer, the firm increases Cash (an asset) but decreases Accounts Receivable (an asset), so no overall increase in assets occurs; total assets remain the same. When you borrow money from a bank, you have an increase in cash (an asset) and an increase in liabilities; overall, assets increase rather than simply shift.

LEARNING UNIT 1-2

1. The balance sheet is a statement written as of a particular date. It lists the assets, liabilities, and owner's equity of a business. The heading of the balance sheet answers the questions *who, what,* and *when* (as of a specific date).
2. The balance sheet is a formal statement of a financial position.

LEARNING UNIT 1-3

1. Revenue generates an inward flow of assets. Expenses generate an outward flow of assets or a potential outward flow. Revenue and expenses are subdivisions of owner's equity. Revenue is not an asset.
2. When revenue totals more than expenses net income is the result; when expenses total more than revenue net loss is the result.
3. Owner's equity can be subdivided into four elements: capital, withdrawals, revenue, and expenses.
4. Withdrawals decrease owner's equity, revenue increases owner's equity, and expenses decrease owner's equity. A withdrawal is not a business expense; it is for personal use.

LEARNING UNIT 1-4

1. The income statement is a statement written for a specific period of time that lists earned revenue and expenses incurred to produce the earned revenue. The net income or net loss will be used in the statement of owner's equity.
2. The statement of owner's equity reveals the causes of a change in capital. This statement lists any investments, net income (or net loss), and withdrawals. The ending figure for capital will be used on the balance sheet.
3. The balance sheet uses the ending balances of assets and liabilities from the accounting equation and the capital from the statement of owner's equity.
4. The income statement should be prepared first because the information on it about net income or net loss is used to prepare the statement of owner's equity, which in turn provides information about capital for the balance sheet. In this way one statement builds upon the next, beginning with the income statement.

KEY TERMS

Accounting A system that measures the business's activities in financial terms, provides written reports and financial statements about those activities, and communicates these reports to decision makers and others.

Accounts payable Amounts owed to creditors that result from the purchase of goods or services on account—a liability.

Accounts receivable An asset that indicates amounts owed by customers.

Assets Properties (resources) of value owned by a business (cash, supplies, equipment, land).

Balance sheet A statement, as of a particular date, that shows the amount of assets owned by a business as well as the amount of claims (liabilities and owner's equity) against these assets.

Basic accounting equation Assets = Liabilities + Owner's Equity.

Bookkeeping The recording function of the accounting process.

Capital The owner's investment of equity in the company.

Corporation A type of business organization that is owned by stockholders. Stockholders usually are not personally liable for the corporation's debts.

Creditor Someone who has a claim to assets.

Ending capital Beginning Capital + Additional Investments + Net Income − Withdrawals = Ending Capital. Or: Beginning Capital + Additional Investments − Net Loss − Withdrawals = Ending Capital.

Equities The interest or financial claim of creditors (liabilities) and owners (owner's equity) who supply the assets to a firm.

Expanded accounting equation Assets = Liabilities + Capital − Withdrawals + Revenue − Expenses.

Expense A cost incurred in running a business by consuming goods or services in producing revenue; a subdivision of owner's equity. When expenses increase, there is a decrease in owner's equity.

Generally accepted accounting principles (GAAP) The procedures and guidelines that must be followed during the accounting process.

Income statement An accounting statement that details the performance of a firm (revenue minus expenses) for a specific period of time.

Liabilities Obligations that come due in the future. Liabilities result in increasing the financial rights or claims of creditors to assets.

Manufacturer Business that makes a product and sells it to its customers.

Merchandise company Business that buys a product from a manufacturing company to sell to its customers.

Net income When revenue totals more than expenses, the result is net income.

Net loss When expenses total more than revenue, the result is net loss.

Owner's equity Rights or financial claims to the assets of a business (in the accounting equation, assets minus liabilities).

Partnership A form of business organization that has at least two owners. The partners usually are personally liable for the partnership's debts.

Revenue An amount earned by performing services for customers or selling goods to customers; it can be in the form of cash or accounts receivable. A subdivision of owner's equity: As revenue increases, owner's equity increases.

Service company Business that provides a service.

Shift in assets A shift that occurs when the composition of the assets has changed but the total of the assets remains the same.

Sole proprietorship A type of business ownership that has one owner. The owner is personally liable for paying the business's debts.

Statement of financial position Another name for a balance sheet.

Statement of owner's equity A financial statement that reveals the change in capital. The ending figure for capital is then placed on the balance sheet.

Supplies One type of asset acquired by a firm; it has a much shorter life than equipment.

Withdrawals A subdivision of owner's equity that records money or other assets an owner withdraws from a business for personal use.

BLUEPRINT: FINANCIAL STATEMENTS

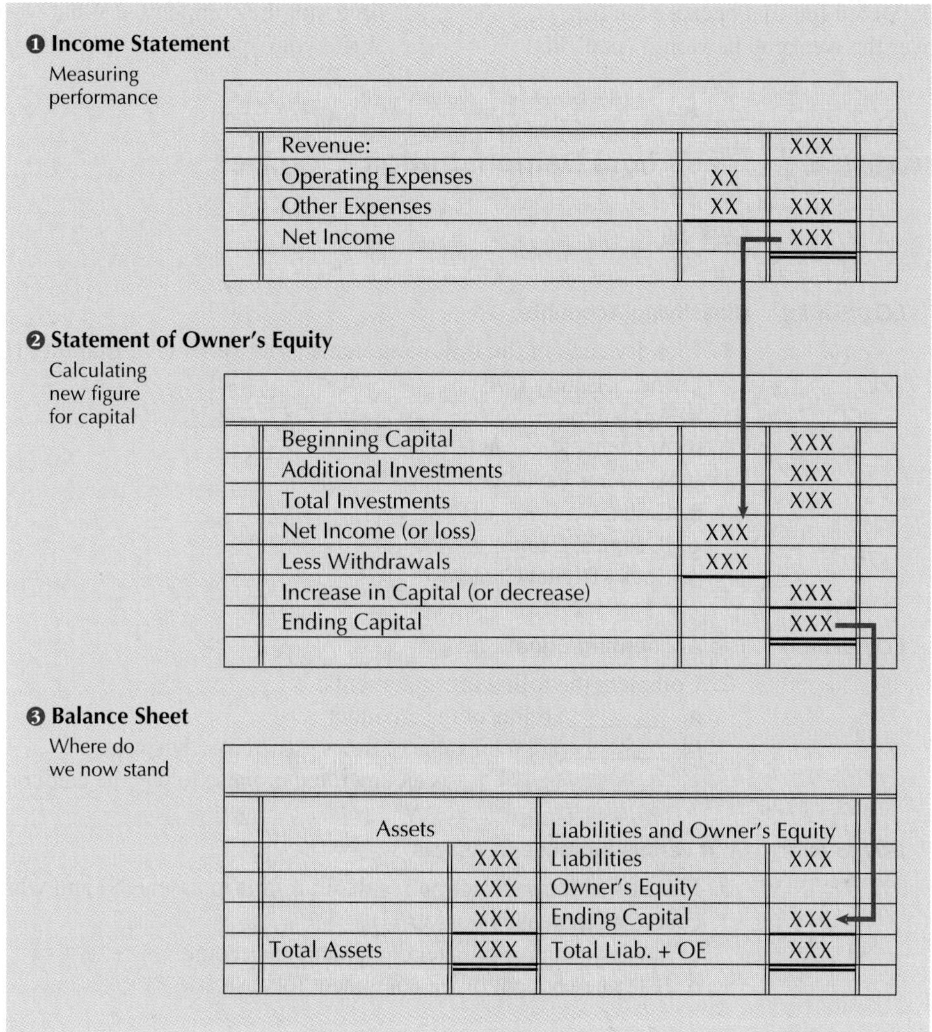

1 Income Statement
Measuring performance
Revenue:
XXX
Operating Expenses
XX
Other Expenses
XX
XXX
Net Income
XXX
2 Statement of Owner's Equity
Calculating new figure for capital
Beginning Capital
XXX
Additional Investments
XXX
Total Investments
XXX
Net Income (or loss)
XXX
Less Withdrawals
XXX
Increase in Capital (or decrease)
XXX
Ending Capital
XXX
3 Balance Sheet
Where do we now stand
Assets
Liabilities and Owner's Equity
XXX
Liabilities
XXX
XXX
Owner's Equity
XXX
Ending Capital
XXX
Total Assets
XXX
Total Liab. + OE
XXX

QUESTIONS, CLASSROOM DEMONSTRATION EXERCISES, EXERCISES, AND PROBLEMS

Discussion and Critical Thinking Questions/Ethical Case

1. What are the functions of accounting?
2. Define, compare, and contrast sole proprietorships, partnerships, and corporations.
3. How are businesses classified?
4. What is the relationship of bookkeeping to accounting?
5. List the three elements of the basic accounting equation.
6. Define capital.
7. The total of the left-hand side of the accounting equation must equal the total of the right-hand side. True or false? Please explain.
8. A balance sheet tells a company where it is going and how well it performs. True or false? Please explain.
9. Revenue is an asset. True or false? Please explain.
10. Owner's equity is subdivided into what categories?
11. A withdrawal is a business expense. True or false? Please explain.
12. As expenses increase they cause owner's equity to increase. Defend or reject.
13. What does an income statement show?
14. The statement of owner's equity only calculates ending withdrawals. True or false? Please explain.

15. Paul Kloss, accountant for Lowe & Co., traveled to New York on company business. His total expenses came to $350. Paul felt that because the trip extended over the weekend he would "pad" his expense account with an additional $100 of expenses. After all, weekends represent his own time, not the company's. What would you do? Write your specific recommendations to Paul.

MyAccountingLab Classroom Demonstration Exercises

SET A

LO1 (5 min)

Classifying Accounts

1. Classify each of the following items as an Asset (A), Liability (L), or part of Owner's Equity (OE).

a. Apple iPod ________
b. Accounts Receivable ________
c. Accounts Payable ________
d. Cash ________
e. B. James, Capital ________
f. Kodak Digital Camera ________

LO1 (5 min)

The Accounting Equation

2. Complete the following statements.

a. ________: rights of the creditors
b. ________ are total value of items owned by a business.
c. ________ ________ is an unwritten promise to pay the creditor.

LO1 (5 min)

Shift versus Increase in Assets

3. Identify which transaction results in a shift in assets (S) and which transaction causes an increase in assets (I).

a. Staples bought computer equipment on account.
b. JCPenney bought office equipment for cash.

LO2, 4 (5 min)

The Balance Sheet

4. From the following, calculate what would be the total of assets on the balance sheet.

B. Fleese, Capital	$18,000
Computer Equipment	4,000
Accounts Payable	6,000
Cash	12,000

LO3 (5 min)

The Accounting Equation Expanded

5. From the following, which are subdivisions of owner's equity?

a. Trees ________
b. J. Penny, Capital ________
c. Accounts Payable ________
d. J. Penny, Withdrawals ________
e. Accounts Receivable ________
f. Advertising Expense ________
g. Taxi Fees Earned ________
h. Computer Equipment ________

Identifying Assets

LO2 (5 min)

6. Identify which of the following are *not* assets.

a. DVD Player ________
b. Accounts Receivable ________
c. Accounts Payable ________
d. Grooming Fees Earned ________

The Accounting Equation Expanded

LO3 (5 min)

7. Which of the following statements are false?

a. ________ Revenue provides only outward flows of cash.
b. ________ Revenue is a subdivision of Assets.
c. ________ Revenue provides an inward flow of cash or accounts receivable.
d. ________ Expenses are part of Total Assets.

Preparing Financial Statements

LO4 (5 min)

8. Indicate whether the following items would appear on the income statement (IS), statement of owner's equity (OE), or balance sheet (BS).

a. ________ Tutoring Fees Earned
b. ________ Office Equipment
c. ________ Accounts Receivable
d. ________ Office Supplies
e. ________ Legal Fees Earned
f. ________ Advertising Expenses
g. ________ J. Earl, Capital (Beg.)
h. ________ Accounts Payable

Preparing Financial Statements

LO4 (5 min)

9. Indicate next to each statement whether it refers to the income statement (IS), statement of owner's equity (OE), or balance sheet (BS).

a. ________ Withdrawals found on it
b. ________ List total of all assets
c. ________ Statement that is prepared last
d. ________ Statement listing net income

SET B

Classifying Accounts

LO1 (5 min)

1. Classify each of the following items as an Asset (A), Liability (L), or part of Owner's Equity (OE).

a. Salaries Payable ________
b. Accounts Payable ________
c. J. Free, Capital ________
d. Office Supplies ________
e. Cash ________
f. Sony Digital Camera ________

The Accounting Equation

LO1 (5 min)

2. Complete the following statements.

a. A ________ ________ ________ results when the total of the assets remains the same but the makeup of the assets has changed.
b. Assets − ________ = Owner's Equity.
c. Capital does not mean ________.

LO1 (5 min) **Shift versus Increase in Assets**

3. Identify which transaction results in a shift in assets (S) and which transaction causes an increase in assets (I).

a. Office Max bought computer equipment for cash.
b. The Gap bought office equipment on account.

LO2, 4 (5 min) **The Balance Sheet**

4. From the following, calculate what would be the total of assets on the balance sheet.

B. Bryan, Capital	$15,000
Word Processing Equipment	2,000
Accounts Payable	8,000
Cash	14,000

LO3 (5 min) **The Accounting Equation Expanded**

5. From the following, which are subdivisions of owner's equity?

a. Land ________
b. M. Kaminsky, Capital ________
c. Accounts Receivable ________
d. M. Kaminsky, Withdrawals ________
e. Accounts Payable ________
f. Rent Expense ________
g. Office Equipment ________
h. Hair Salon Fees Earned ________

LO2 (5 min) **Identifying Assets**

6. Identify which of the following are *not* assets.

a. Fax Machines
b. Accounts Payable
c. Legal Fees Earned
d. Accounts Receivable

LO3 (5 min) **The Accounting Equation Expanded**

7. Which of the following statements are false?

a. ________ Revenue is an asset.
b. ________ Revenue is a subdivision of Owner's Equity.
c. ________ Revenue provides an inward flow of cash or accounts receivable.
d. ________ Withdrawals are part of Total Assets.

LO4 (5 min) **Preparing Financial Statements**

8. Indicate whether the following items would appear on the income statement (IS), statement of owner's equity (OE), or balance sheet (BS).

a. ________ B. Clo, Withdrawals
b. ________ Office Supplies
c. ________ Accounts Payable
d. ________ Computer Equipment
e. ________ Commission Fees Earned
f. ________ Salaries Expense
g. ________ B. Clo, Capital (Beg.)
h. ________ Accounts Receivable

Preparing Financial Statements *LO4 (5 min)*

9. Indicate next to each statement whether it refers to the income statement (IS), statement of owner's equity (OE), or balance sheet (BS).

a. ________ Calculate new figure for capital
b. ________ Prepared as of a particular date
c. ________ Statement that is prepared first
d. ________ Statement listing revenues and expenses

Exercises

MyAccountingLab

1-1. Complete the following table: *LO2 (5 min)*

	Assets	=	Liabilities	+	Owner's Equity
a.	$19,000	=	?	+	$4,000
b.	?	=	$6,000	+	$9,000
c.	$10,000	=	$4,000	+	?

1-2. Record the following transactions in the basic accounting equation. Treat each one separately. *LO2 (5 min)*

Assets = Liabilities + Owner's Equity

a. Matty invests $120,000 in company.
b. Bought equipment for cash, $600.
c. Bought equipment on account, $900.

1-3. From the following, prepare a balance sheet for Range Co. Cleaners at the end of November 200X: Cash, $50,000; Equipment, $7,000; Accounts Payable, $14,000; B. Range, Capital. *LO2, 4 (10 min)*

1-4. Record the following transactions into the expanded accounting equation. The running balance may be omitted for simplicity. *LO3 (15 min)*

Assets			= Liabilities +	Owner's Equity			
Cash	+ Accounts Receivable	+ Computer Equipment	= Accounts Payable	+ B. Bell, Capital	− B. Bell, Withdrawals	+ Revenues	− Expenses

a. Bell invested $60,000 in a computer company.
b. Bought computer equipment on account, $7,000.
c. Bell paid personal telephone bill from company checkbook, $200.
d. Received cash for services rendered, $14,000.
e. Billed customers for services rendered for month, $30,000.
f. Paid current rent expense, $4,000.
g. Paid supplies expense, $1,500.

1-5. From the following account balances, prepare in proper form for June (a) an income statement, (b) a statement of owner's equity, and (c) a balance sheet for French Realty. *LO4 (20 min)*

Cash	$3,310	S. French, Withdrawals	$ 40
Accounts Receivable	1,490	Professional Fees	2,900
Office Equipment	6,700	Salaries Expense	500
Accounts Payable	2,000	Utilities Expense	360
S. French, Capital, June 1, 200X	8,000	Rent Expense	500

Group A Problems

MyAccountingLab

1A-1. Mia Anabelle decided to open Mia's Nail Spa. Mia completed the following transactions: *LO2 (15 min)*

a. Invested $20,000 cash from her personal bank account into the business.
b. Bought store equipment for cash, $4,000.

Check Figure:
Cash $15,000

c. Bought additional store equipment on account, $6,000.
d. Paid $1,000 cash to partially reduce what was owed from transaction C.

Based on this information, record these transactions into the basic accounting equation.

LO2, 4 (15 min)

1A-2. Bill See is the accountant for See's Internet Service. From the following information, his task is to construct a balance sheet as of September 30, 200X, in proper form. Could you help him?

Check Figure:
Total Assets $52,000

Building	$20,000	Cash	$18,000
Accounts Payable	15,000	Equipment	14,000
See, Capital	37,000		

LO3 (20 min)

1A-3. At the end of November, Rick Fox decided to open his own typing service. Analyze the following transactions he completed by recording their effects into the expanded accounting equation.
a. Invested $10,000 in his typing service.
b. Bought new office equipment on account, $4,000.
c. Received cash for typing services rendered, $500.
d. Performed typing services on account, $2,100.
e. Paid secretary's salary, $350.
f. Paid office supplies expense for the month, $210.
g. Rent expenses for office due but unpaid, $900.
h. Withdrew cash for personal use, $400.

Check Figure:
Total Assets $15,640

LO4 (30 min)

1A-4. Jane West, owner of West Stenciling Service, has requested that you prepare from the following balances (a) an income statement for June 200X, (b) a statement of owner's equity for June, and (c) a balance sheet as of June 30, 200X.

Check Figure:
Total Assets $3,385

Cash	$2,300	Stenciling Fees	$3,000
Accounts Receivable	400	Advertising Expense	110
Equipment	685	Repair Expense	25
Accounts Payable	310	Travel Expense	250
J. West, Capital, June 1, 200X	1,200	Supplies Expense	190
J. West, Withdrawals	300	Rent Expense	250

LO2, 3, 4 (45 min)

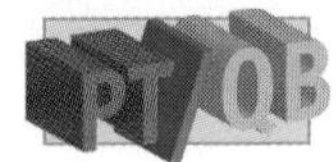

1A-5. John Tobey, a retired army officer, opened Tobey's Catering Service. As his accountant, analyze the transactions listed next and present them in proper form.
a. The analysis of the transactions by using the expanded accounting equation.
b. A balance sheet showing the position of the firm before opening for business on October 31, 200X.
c. An income statement for the month of November.
d. A statement of owner's equity for November.
e. A balance sheet as of November 30, 200X.

200X

Oct. 25	John Tobey invested $20,000 in the catering business from his personal savings account.
27	Bought equipment for cash from Munroe Co., $700.
28	Bought additional equipment on account from Ryan Co., $1,000.
29	Paid $600 to Ryan Co. as partial payment of the October 28 transaction.

Check Figure:
Total Assets,
Nov. 30 $24,060

(You should now prepare your balance sheet as of October 31, 200X.)

Nov. 1	Catered a graduation and immediately collected cash, $2,400.
5	Paid salaries of employees, $690.
8	Prepared desserts for customers on account, $300.

10 Received $100 cash as partial payment of November 8 transaction.
15 Paid telephone bill, $60.
17 Paid his home electric bill from the company's checkbook, $90.
20 Catered a wedding and received cash, $1,800.
25 Bought additional equipment on account, $400.
28 Rent expense due but unpaid, $600.
30 Paid supplies expense, $400.

Group B Problems

1B-1. Mia Annabelle began a new business called Mia's Nail Spa. The following transactions resulted:

LO2 (15 min)

a. Mia invested $16,000 cash from her personal bank account into the Nail Spa.
b. Bought store equipment on account, $1,500.
c. Paid $800 cash to partially reduce what was owed from transaction B.
d. Purchased additional store equipment for cash, $3,000.

Record these transactions into the basic accounting equation.

Check Figure:
Cash $12,200

1B-2. Bill See, accountant, has asked you to prepare a balance sheet as of September 30, 200X, for See's. Could you assist Bill?

LO2, 4 (15 min)

Blues, Capital	$24,000
Accounts Payable	60,000
Equipment	40,000
Building	28,000
Cash	16,000

Check Figure:
Total Assets $84,000

1B-3. Rick Fox decided to open his own typing service company at the end of November. Analyze the following transactions by recording their effects on the expanded accounting equation:

LO3 (20 min)

a. Rick invested $9,000 in the typing service.
b. Purchased new office equipment on account, $3,000.
c. Received cash for typing services rendered, $1,290.
d. Paid secretary's salary, $310.
e. Billed customers for typing services rendered, $2,690.
f. Paid rent expense for the month, $500.
g. Rick withdrew cash for personal use, $350.
h. Advertising expense due but unpaid, $100.

Check Figure:
Total Assets $14,820

1B-4. Jane West, owner of West Stenciling Service, has requested that you prepare from the following balances (a) an income statement for June 200X, (b) a statement of owner's equity for June, and (c) a balance sheet as of June 30, 200X.

LO3 (30 min)

Check Figure:
Total Assets $3,723

Cash	$2,043	Stenciling Fees	$1,098
Accounts Receivable	1,140	Advertising Expense	135
Equipment	540	Repair Expense	45
Accounts Payable	45	Travel Expense	90
J. West, Capital, June 1, 200X	3,720	Supplies Expense	270
J. West, Withdrawals	360	Rent Expense	240

LO2, 3, 4 (45 min)

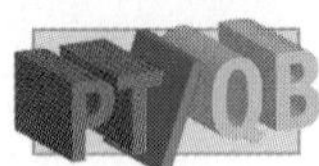

1B-5. John Tobey, a retired army officer, opened Tobey's Catering Service. As his accountant, analyze the transactions and present the following information in proper form:

a. The analysis of the transactions by using the expanded accounting equation.
b. A balance sheet showing the financial position of the firm before opening on November 1, 200X.
c. An income statement for the month of November.
d. A statement of owner's equity for November.
e. A balance sheet as of November 30, 200X.

200X		
Oct.	25	John Tobey invested $17,500 in the catering business.
	27	Bought equipment on account from Munroe Co., $900.
	28	Bought equipment for cash from Ryan Co., $1,500.
	29	Paid $300 to Munroe Co. as partial payment of the October 27 transaction.
Nov.	1	Catered a business luncheon and immediately collected cash, $2,000.
	5	Paid salaries of employees, $350.
	8	Provided catering services to Northwest Community College on account, $4,500.
	10	Received from Northwest Community College $1,000 cash as partial payment of November 8 transaction.
	15	Paid telephone bill, $95.
	17	John paid his home mortgage from the company's checkbook, $650.
	20	Provided catering services and received cash, $1,800.
	25	Bought additional equipment on account, $300.
	28	Rent expense due but unpaid, $750.
	30	Paid supplies expense, $600.

Check Figure:
Total Assets,
Nov. 30 $25,005

ON-THE-JOB TRAINING

LO3, 4 (20 min)

T-1. You have just been hired to prepare, if possible, an income statement for the year ended December 31, 200X, for Roger's Window Washing Company. The problem is that Roger Smith kept only the following records (on the back of a piece of cardboard):

FIGURE 1.10 Financial Records

Dollars in:

My investment	*$ 1,200*
Window cleaning	*11,376*
Loan from brother-in-law	*4,000*

Dollars out:

Salaries	*$5,080*
Withdrawals	*6,200*
Supplies expense	*1,400*

What I owe or they owe me
A. People who work for me but I still owe salaries to $1,800
B. Owe bank interest of $300
C. Work done but clients still owe me $2,900
D. Advertising bill due but not paid $95

Assume that Roger's Window Washing Company records all revenues when earned and all expenses when incurred.

You feel that it is part of your job to tell Roger how to organize his records better. What would you tell him?

T-2. While Jon Lune was on a business trip, he asked Abby Slowe, the bookkeeper for Lune Co., to try to complete a balance sheet for the year ended December 31, 200X. Abby, who had been on the job only two months, submitted the following: *LO2, 4 (30 min)*

FIGURE 1.11 Balance Sheet

LUNE CO. FOR THE YEAR ENDED DECEMBER 31, 200X			
Building	$44600 00	Accounts Payable	$127604 00
Land	72935 00	Accounts Receivable	104337 00
Notes Payable	75328 00	Auto	14268 00
Cash	10016 00	Desks	6825 00
J. Lune, Capital	?	Total Equity	$250034 00

1. Could you help Abby fix as well as complete the balance sheet?
2. What written recommendations would you make about the bookkeeper? Should she be retained?
3. Suppose that (a) Jon Lune invested an additional $20,000 in cash as well as additional desks with a value of $8,000, and (b) Lune Co. bought an auto for $6,000 that was originally marked $8,000, paying $2,000 down and issuing a note for the balance. Could you prepare an updated balance sheet?

FINANCIAL REPORT PROBLEM

Reading the Kellogg Annual Report

LO2, 4 (5 min)

Go to the annual report for Kellogg Company in Appendix A. Find the balance sheet and calculate the following: How much did cash increase in 2006 from 2005?

INTERNET PROJECT

Best Buy

Go to the Web and search: Annual Report Best Buy 2008.
Click on Investors Relations.
List out the latest news Best Buy is providing to its investors.
Order a free annual report.

CONTINUING PROBLEM

MyAccountingLab

Sanchez Computer Center

LO3, 4 (45 min)

The following problem continues from one chapter to the next, carrying the balances of each month forward. Each chapter focuses on the learning experience of the chapter and adds information as the business grows.

Assignment

1. Set up an expanded accounting equation spreadsheet using the following accounts:

Assets	Liabilities	Owner's Equity
Cash	Accounts Payable	Freedman, Capital
Supplies		Freedman, Withdrawal
Computer Shop		Service Revenue
Equipment		Expenses (notate type)
Office Equipment		

2. Analyze and record each transaction in the expanded accounting equation.

3. Prepare the financial statements ending July 31 for Sanchez Computer Center.

On July 1, 200X, Tony Freedman decided to begin his own computer service business. He named the business the Sanchez Computer Center. During the first month Tony conducted the following business transactions:

a. Invested $4,500 of his savings into the business.
b. Paid $1,200 (check # 8095) for the computer from Multi Systems, Inc.
c. Paid $600 (check # 8096) for office equipment from Office Furniture, Inc.
d. Set up a new account with Office Depot and purchased $250 in office supplies on credit.
e. Paid July rent, $400 (check # 8097).
f. Repaired a system for a customer and collected $250.
g. Collected $200 for system upgrade labor charge from a customer.
h. Electric bill due but unpaid, $85.
i. Collected $1,200 for services performed on Taylor Golf computers.
j. Withdrew $100 (check # 8098) to take his wife, Carol, out in celebration of opening the new business.

SUBWAY Case

A FRESH START

LO4 (20 min)

"Hey, Stan the man!" a loud voice boomed. "I never thought I'd see you making sandwiches!" Stan Hernandez stopped layering lettuce in a foot-long submarine sandwich and grinned at his old college buddy, Ron.

"Neither did I. But then again," said Stan, "I never thought I'd own a profitable business either."

That night, catching up on their lives over dinner, Stan told Ron how he became the proud owner of a Subway sandwich restaurant.

"After working like crazy at Xellent Media for five years and *finally* making it to marketing manager, then wham . . . I got laid off," said Stan. "That very day I was having my lunch at the local Subway as usual, when. . . . "

"Hmmm, wait a minute! I did notice you've lost quite a bit of weight," Ron interrupted and began to hum the bars of Subway's latest ad featuring Clay Henry, yet another hefty male who lost weight on a diet of Subway sandwiches.

"Right!" Stan quipped, "Not only was I laid off, but I was 'downsizing'! *Anyway,* I was eating a Dijon horseradish melt when I opened up an *Entrepreneur* magazine someone had left on the table—right to the headline 'Subway Named #1 Franchise in All Categories for 11th Time in 15 Years.'"

Well, to make a foot-long submarine sandwich story short, Stan realized his long-time dream of being his own boss by owning a business with a proven product and highly successful business model. When you look at Stan's restaurant, you are really seeing two businesses. Even though Stan is the sole proprietor of his business, he operates under an agreement with Subway of Milford, Connecticut. Subway supplies the business know-how and support (like training at Subway University, national advertising, and gourmet bread recipes). Stan supplies capital (his $12,500 investment) and his food preparation, management, and elbow grease. Subway and Stan operate interdependent businesses, and both rely on accounting information for their success.

Subway, in business since 1965, has grown dramatically over the years and now has more than 18,000 locations in 73 countries. It has even surpassed McDonald's in the number of locations in the United States and Canada. To manage this enormous service business requires careful control of each of its stores. At a Subway regional office, Mariah Washington, a field consultant for Stan's territory, monitors Stan's restaurant closely. In addition to making monthly visits to check whether Stan is complying with Subway's model in everything from décor to uniforms to food quality and safety, she also looks closely at Stan's weekly sales and inventory reports. When Stan's sales go up, Subway's do too, because each Subway franchisee, like Stan, pays Subway, the franchiser, a percentage of sales in the form of royalties.

Why does headquarters require accounting reports? Accounting reports give the information both Stan and the company need to make business decisions in a number of vital areas. For example:

- Before Stan could buy his Subway restaurant, the company needed to know how much cash Stan had and his assets and liabilities (such as credit card debt). Stan prepared a personal balance sheet to give them this information.
- Stan must have the right amount of supplies on hand. If he has too few, he can't make the sandwiches. If he has too many for the amount he expects to sell, items such as sandwich meats and bread dough may spoil. The inventory report tells Mariah what supplies are on hand. In combination with the sales report, it also alerts Mariah to potential red flags: If Stan is reporting that he is using far too much bread dough for the amount of sandwiches he is selling, a problem would be indicated.
- Although Subway does not require its restaurant owners to report operating costs and profit information, Subway gives them the option and most franchisees take it. Information on profitability helps Mariah and Stan make decisions such as whether and when to remodel or buy new equipment.

So that its restaurant owners can make business decisions in a timely manner, Subway requires them to submit the weekly sales and inventory report to headquarters electronically every Thursday by 2:00 P.M. Stan has his latest report in mind as he makes a move to pay the bill for his dinner with Ron. "We had a great week. Let me get this," he says. "Thanks, Stan the Man. I'm going to keep in touch because I may just be ready for a business opportunity of my own!"

Discussion Questions

1. What makes Stan a sole proprietor?
2. Why are Stan and Subway interdependent businesses?
3. Why did Stan have to share his personal balance sheet with Subway? Do you think most interdependent businesses operate this way?
4. What does Subway learn from Stan's weekly sales and inventory reports?

2

Debits and Credits: Analyzing and Recording Business Transactions

DID YOU KNOW? In 2006 20% of sales came from Staples brands. The company plans to increase that number to 30%. Staples has recycled more than 17 million ink and toner cartridges. Visit *www.staples.com* to find more information about Staples.

LEARNING OBJECTIVES

1. Setting up and organizing a chart of accounts.
2. Recording transactions in T accounts according to the rules of debit and credit.
3. Preparing a trial balance.
4. Preparing financial statements from a trial balance.

In Chapter 1 we used the expanded accounting equation to document the financial transactions performed by Mia Wong's law firm. Remember how long it was: The cash column had a long list of pluses and minuses, with no quick system of recording and summarizing the increases and decreases of cash or other items. Can you imagine the problem Staples would have if it used the expanded accounting equation to track the thousands of business transactions it makes each day?

Learning Unit 2-1 The T Account

Let's look at the problem a little more closely. Each business transaction is recorded in the accounting equation under a specific **account.** Different accounts are used for each of the subdivisions of the accounting equation: asset accounts, liabilities accounts, expense accounts, revenue accounts, and so on. What is needed is a way to record the increases and decreases in specific account *categories* and yet keep them together in one place. The answer is the **standard account** form (see Figure 2.1). A standard account is a formal account that includes columns for date, item, posting reference, debit, and credit. Each account has a separate form, and all transactions affecting that account are recorded on the form. All the business's account forms (which often are referred to as *ledger accounts*) are then placed in a **ledger.** Each page of the ledger contains one account. The ledger may be in the form of a bound or a loose-leaf book. If computers are used, the ledger may be part of a computer file. For simplicity's sake, we use the **T account** form. This form got its name because it looks like the letter T. Generally, T accounts are used for demonstration purposes. Each T account contains three basic parts:

1 Title of Account	
2 **Left side**	**Right side** 3

All T accounts have this structure.

In accounting, the left side of any T account is called the **debit** side.

***DEBIT* DEFINED:**
1. The *left* side of any T account.
2. A number entered on the left side of any account is said to be *debited* to an account.

Left side **Dr. (debit)**	

Just as the word *left* has many meanings, the word *debit* for now in accounting means a position, the left side of an account. Do not think of it as good (+) or bad (−).

Amounts entered on the left side of any account are said to be *debited* to an account. The abbreviation for debit, Dr., is from the Latin *debere.*

The right side of any T account is called the **credit** side.

***CREDIT* DEFINED:**
1. The *right* side of any T account.
2. A number entered on the right side of any account is said to be *credited* to an account.

	Right side **Cr. (credit)**

Amounts entered on the right side of an account are said to be *credited* to an account. The abbreviation for credit, Cr., is from the Latin *credere.*

At this point do not associate the definition of debit and credit with the words *increase* or *decrease.* Think of debit or credit as only indicating a *position* (left or right side) of a T account.

Account Title							Account No.
Date	Item	PR	Debit	Date	Item	PR	Credit

FIGURE 2.1 The Standard Account Form Is the Source of the T Account's Shape

Balancing an Account

No matter which individual account is being balanced, the procedure used to balance it is the same.

	Dr.	Cr.
Entries →	5,000	400
	600	500
Footings →	5,600	900
Balance	4,700	

In the "real" world, the T account would also include the date of the transaction. The date would appear to the left of the entry:

	Dr.		Cr.
4/2	5,000	4/3	400
4/20	600	4/25	500
	5,600		900
Bal 4,700			

Note that on the debit (left) side the numbers add up to $5,600. On the credit (right) side the numbers add up to $900. The $5,600 and the $900 written in small type are called **footings.** Footings help in calculating the new (or ending) balance. The **ending balance** ($4,700) is placed on the debit or left side, because the balance of the debit side is greater than that of the credit side.

If the balance is greater on the credit side, that is the side the ending balance would be on.

Remember that the ending balance does not tell us anything about increase or decrease. It only tells us that we have an ending balance of $4,700 on the debit side.

LEARNING UNIT 2-1 REVIEW

AT THIS POINT you should be able to

- Define ledger.
- State the purpose of a T account.
- Identify the three parts of a T account.
- Define debit.
- Define credit.
- Explain footings and calculate the balance of an account.

Self-Review Quiz 2-1

Respond True or False to the following:

1.

Dr.	Cr.
3,000	200
200	600

The balance of the account is $2,400 Cr.

2. A credit always means increase.
3. A debit is the left side of any account.
4. A ledger can be prepared manually or by computer.
5. Footings replace the need for debits and credits.

For additional help go to www.pearsonhighered.com/slater

Solutions to Self-Review Quiz 2-1

1. False
2. False
3. True
4. True
5. False

NEED HELP?

Let's review first: Debit does not mean good or bad. Instead, it represents a position, the left side of any account. Credit does not mean good or bad either. It represents a position, the right side of any account.

1. It is false because if you add the two debits of 3,000 and 200 you get 3,200 on the debit, or left side. A dr. + dr. = Debit balance. Now if you add the credit side of 200 and 600 you get a balance of 800 on the credit side. A cr. + cr. = Credit balance. To find the ending balance we take 3,200 less the 800 to arrive at a balance that is still larger on the DEBIT side by 2,400.
2. A credit is a position. It is the right side of any account.
3. Yes, the debit is always the left-hand side of any account. It does not mean good or bad.
4. Years ago the ledger, a group of accounts, was prepared manually; however, today most ledgers are updated by computer software.
5. Footings are used to add debits and credits to arrive at a new balance. Think of footings as the totals of a column.

Learning Unit 2-2 Recording Business Transactions: Debits and Credits

Can you get a queen in checkers? In a baseball game, does a runner rounding first base skip second base and run over the pitcher's mound to get to third? No; most of us don't do such things because we follow the rules of the game. Usually we learn the rules first and reflect on the reasons for them afterward. The same is true in accounting.

Instead of first trying to understand all the rules of debit and credit and how they were developed in accounting, it is easier to learn the rules by "playing the game."

T Account Entries for Accounting in the Accounting Equation

Have patience. Learning the rules of debit and credit is like learning to play any game: The more you play, the easier it becomes. Table 2.1 shows the rules for the side on which you enter an increase or a decrease for each of the separate accounts in the accounting equation. For example, an increase is entered on the debit side in the asset account but on the credit side for a liability account.

LO2

TABLE 2.1 Rules of Debit and Credit

Account Category	Increase (Normal Balance)	Decrease
Assets	Debit	Credit
Liabilities	Credit	Debit
Owner's Equity		
Capital	Credit	Debit
Withdrawals	Debit	Credit
Revenue	Credit	Debit
Expenses	Debit	Credit

It might be easier to visualize these rules of debit and credit if we look at them in the T account form, using + to show increase and − to show decrease.

Assets = Liabilities + Owner's Equity

Assets		Liabilities		Capital		Withdrawals		Revenue		Expenses	
Dr.	Cr.	Dr.	Cr.	Dr.	Cr.	Dr.	Cr.	Dr.	Cr.	Dr.	Cr.
+	−	−	+	−	+	+	−	−	+	+	−

(Owner's Equity: + Capital − Withdrawals + Revenue − Expenses)

Rules for Assets Work in the Opposite Direction to Those for Liabilities When you look at the equation you can see that the rules for assets work in the opposite direction to those for liabilities. That is, for assets the increases appear on the debit side and the decreases are shown on the credit side; the opposite is true for liabilities. As for the owner's equity, the rules for withdrawals and expenses, which *decrease* owner's equity, work in the opposite direction to the rules for capital and revenue, which *increase* owner's equity.

Assets + Withdrawals + Expenses = Liabilities + Capital + Revenue

Assets		Withdrawals		Expenses		Liabilities		Capital		Revenue	
Dr.	Cr.	Dr.	Cr.	Dr.	Cr.	Dr.	Cr.	Dr.	Cr.	Dr.	Cr.
+	−	+	−	+	−	−	+	−	+	−	+

This setup may help you visualize how the rules for withdrawals and expenses are just the opposite of those for capital and revenue.

A **normal balance of an account** is the side that increases by the rules of debit and credit. For example, the balance of cash is a debit balance, because an asset is increased by a debit. We discuss normal balances further in Chapter 3.

Balancing the Equation It is important to remember that any amount(s) entered on the debit side of a T account or accounts also must be on the credit side of another T account or accounts. This approach ensures that the total amount added to the debit side will equal the total amount added to the credit side, thereby keeping the accounting equation in balance.

Normal Balance	
Dr.	Cr.
Assets	Liabilities
Withdrawals	Capital
Expenses	Revenue

LO1

Chart of Accounts Our job is to analyze Mia Wong's business transactions—the transactions we looked at in Chapter 1—using a system of accounts guided by the rules of debit and credit that will summarize increases and decreases of individual accounts in the ledger. The goal is to prepare an income statement, statement of owner's equity, and balance sheet

TABLE 2.2 Chart of Accounts for Mia Wong, Attorney-at-Law

Balance Sheet Accounts	
Assets	**Liabilities**
111 Cash	211 Accounts Payable
112 Accounts Receivable	**Owner's Equity**
121 Office Equipment	311 Mia Wong, Capital
	312 Mia Wong, Withdrawals
Income Statement Accounts	
Revenue	**Expenses**
411 Legal Fees	511 Salaries Expense
	512 Rent Expense
	513 Advertising Expense

The chart of accounts aids in locating and identifying accounts quickly.

for Mia Wong. Sound familiar? If this system works, the rules of debit and credit and the use of accounts will give us the same answers as in Chapter 1, but with greater ease.

Mia's accountant developed what is called a **chart of accounts.** The chart of accounts is a numbered list of all of the business's accounts. It allows accounts to be located quickly. In Mia's business, for example, 100s are assets, 200s are liabilities, and so on. As you see in Table 2.2, each separate asset and liability account has its own number. Note that the chart may be expanded as the business grows.

The Transaction Analysis: Five Steps

We will analyze the transactions in Mia Wong's law firm using a teaching device called a *transaction analysis chart* to record these five steps. (Keep in mind that the transaction analysis chart is not a part of any formal accounting system.) The five steps to analyzing each business transaction include the following:

Step 1 Determine which accounts are affected. Example: Cash, Accounts Payable, Rent Expense. A transaction always affects at least two accounts.

Step 2 Determine which categories the accounts belong to: assets, liabilities, capital, withdrawals, revenue, or expenses. Example: Cash is an asset.

Step 3 Determine whether the accounts increase or decrease. Example: If you receive cash, that account increases.

Step 4 What do the rules of debit and credit say (Table 2.1)?

Step 5 What does the T account look like? Place amounts into accounts either on the left or right side depending on the rules in Table 2.1.

Remember that the rules of debit and credit only tell us on which side to place information. Whether the debit or credit represents increases or decreases depends on the account category: assets, liabilities, capital, and so on. Think of a business transaction as an exchange: You get something and you give or part with something.

The following chart shows the five-step analysis from another perspective.

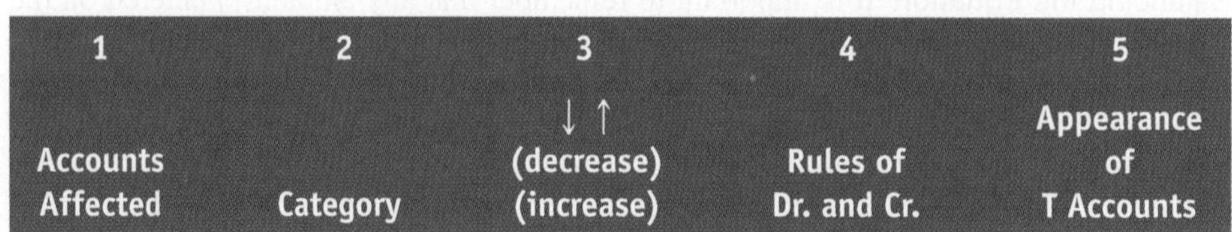

1	2	3	4	5
Accounts Affected	Category	↓ ↑ (decrease) (increase)	Rules of Dr. and Cr.	Appearance of T Accounts

Let us emphasize a major point: *Do not try to debit or credit an account until you go through the first three steps of the transaction analysis.*

Applying the Transaction Analysis to Mia Wong's Law Practice

Transaction A August 28: Mia Wong invests $6,000 cash and $200 of office equipment in the business.

1 Accounts Affected	2 Category	3 ↓ ↑	4 Rules of Dr. and Cr.	5 Appearance of T Accounts
Cash	Asset	↑	Dr.	Cash 111 (A) 6,000 |
Office Equipment	Asset	↑	Dr.	Office Equipment 121 (A) 200 |
Mia Wong, Capital	Capital	↑	Cr.	Mia Wong, Capital 311 | 6,200 (A)

Note in column 3 of the chart that it doesn't matter if both arrows go up, as long as the sum of the debits equals the sum of the credits in the T accounts in column 5.

Note again that every transaction affects at least two T accounts and that the total amount added to the debit side(s) must equal the total amount added to the credit side(s) of the T accounts of each transaction.

Analysis of Transaction A

Step 1 Which accounts are affected? The law firm receives its cash and office equipment, so three accounts are involved: Cash, Office Equipment, and Mia Wong, Capital. These account titles come from the chart of accounts.

Step 2 Which categories do these accounts belong to? Cash and Office Equipment are assets. Mia Wong, Capital, is capital.

Step 3 Are the accounts increasing or decreasing? The Cash and Office Equipment, both assets, are increasing in the business. The rights or claims of Mia Wong, Capital, are also increasing, because she invested money and office equipment in the business.

Step 4 What do the rules say? According to the rules of debit and credit, an increase in assets (Cash and Office Equipment) is a debit. An increase in Capital is a credit. Note that the total dollar amount of debits will equal the total dollar amount of credits when the T accounts are updated in column 5.

Step 5 What does the T account look like? The amount for Cash and Office Equipment is entered on the debit side. The amount for Mia Wong, Capital, goes on the credit side.

A transaction that involves more than one debit or more than one credit is called a **compound entry.** This first transaction of Mia Wong's law firm is a compound entry; it involves a debit of $6,000 to Cash and a debit of $200 to Office Equipment (as well as a credit of $6,200 to Mia Wong, Capital).

Double-entry bookkeeping system: The total of all debits is equal to the total of all credits.

The name for this double-entry analysis of transactions, where two or more accounts are affected and the total of debits and credits is equal, is **double-entry bookkeeping.** This double-entry system helps in checking the recording of business transactions.

As we continue, the explanations will be brief, but do not forget to apply the five steps in analyzing and recording each business transaction.

Transaction B Aug. 29: Law practice bought office equipment for cash, $500.

1 Accounts Affected	2 Category	3 ↓ ↑	4 Rules of Dr. and Cr.	5 T Account Update
Office Equipment	Asset	↑	Dr.	Office Equipment 121 (A) 200 | **(B) 500** |
Cash	Asset	↓	Cr.	Cash 111 (A) 6,000 | **500 (B)**

Analysis of Transaction B

Step 1 The law firm paid $500 cash for the office equipment it received. The accounts involved in the transaction are Cash and Office Equipment.

Step 2 The accounts belong to these categories: Office Equipment is an asset; Cash is an asset.

Step 3 The asset Office Equipment is increasing. The asset Cash is decreasing; it is being reduced to buy the office equipment.

Step 4 An increase in the asset Office Equipment is a debit; a decrease in the asset Cash is a credit.

Step 5 When the amounts are placed in the T accounts, the amount for Office Equipment goes on the debit side and the amount for Cash on the credit side.

Transaction C Aug. 30: Bought more office equipment on account, $300.

1 Accounts Affected	2 Category	3 ↓ ↑	4 Rules of Dr. and Cr.	5 T Account Update
Office Equipment	Asset	↑	Dr.	Office Equipment 121 (A) 200 | (B) 500 | **(C) 300** |
Accounts Payable	Liability	↑	Cr.	Accounts Payable 211 | **300 (C)**

Analysis of Transaction C

Step 1 The law firm receives office equipment $300 by promising to pay in the future. An obligation or liability, Accounts Payable, is created.

Step 2 Office Equipment is an asset. Accounts Payable is a liability.

Step 3 The asset Office Equipment is increasing; the liability Accounts Payable is increasing because the law firm is increasing what it owes.

Step 4 An increase in the asset Office Equipment is a debit. An increase in the liability Accounts Payable is a credit.

Step 5 Enter the amount for Office Equipment on the debit side of the T account. The amount for the Accounts Payable goes on the credit side.

Transaction D Sept. 1–30: Provided legal services for cash, $2,000.

1 Accounts Affected	2 Category	3 ↓ ↑	4 Rules of Dr. and Cr.	5 T Account Update
Cash	Asset	↑	Dr.	Cash 111: Dr. (A) 6,000; (D) **2,000** / Cr. 500 (B)
Legal Fees	Revenue	↑	Cr.	Legal Fees 411: Cr. **2,000 (D)**

Analysis of Transaction D

Step 1 The firm earned revenue from legal services and received $2,000 in cash.

Step 2 Cash is an asset. Legal Fees are revenue.

Step 3 Cash, an asset, is increasing. Legal Fees, or revenue, are also increasing.

Step 4 An increase in Cash, an asset, is debited. An increase in Legal Fees, or revenue, is credited.

Step 5 Enter the amount for Cash on the debit side of the T account. Enter the amount for Legal Fees on the credit side.

Transaction E Sept. 1–30: Provided legal services on account, $3,000.

1 Accounts Affected	2 Category	3 ↓ ↑	4 Rules of Dr. and Cr.	5 T Account Update
Accounts Receivable	Asset	↑	Dr.	Accounts Receivable 112: Dr. (E) **3,000**
Legal Fees	Revenue	↑	Cr.	Legal Fees 411: Cr. 2,000 (D); **3,000 (E)**

Analysis of Transaction E

Step 1 The law practice has earned revenue of $3,000 but has not yet received payment (cash). The amounts owed by these clients are called Accounts Receivable. Revenue is earned at the time the legal services are provided, whether payment is received then or will be received some time in the future.

Step 2 Accounts Receivable is an asset. Legal Fees are revenue.

Step 3 Accounts Receivable is increasing because the law practice increased the amount owed to it for legal fees earned but not yet paid. Legal Fees, or revenue, are increasing.

Step 4 An increase in the asset Accounts Receivable is a debit. An increase in Revenue is a credit.

Step 5 Enter the amount for Accounts Receivable on the debit side of the T account. The amount for Legal Fees goes on the credit side.

Transaction F Sept. 1–30: Received $900 cash from clients for services rendered previously on account.

1 Accounts Affected	2 Category	3 ↓ ↑	4 Rules of Dr. and Cr.	5 T Account Update
Cash	Asset	↑	Dr.	Cash 111 (A) 6,000 | 500 (B) (D) 2,000 | (F) **900** |
Accounts Receivable	Asset	↓	Cr.	Accounts Receivable 112 (E) 3,000 | **900** (F)

Analysis of Transaction F

Step 1 The law firm collects $900 in cash from previous revenue earned. Because the revenue is recorded at the time it is earned, and not when the collection is received in this transaction we are concerned only with the collection, which affects the Cash and Accounts Receivable accounts.

Step 2 Cash is an asset. Accounts Receivable is an asset.

Step 3 Because clients are paying what is owed, Cash (asset) is increasing and the amount owed (Accounts Receivable) is decreasing (the total amount owed by clients to Wong is going down). This transaction results in a shift in assets, more Cash for less Accounts Receivable.

Step 4 An increase in Cash, an asset, is a debit. A decrease in Accounts Receivable, an asset, is a credit.

Step 5 Enter the amount for Cash on the debit side of the T account. The amount for Accounts Receivable goes on the credit side.

Transaction G Sept. 1–30: Paid salaries expense, $700.

1 Accounts Affected	2 Category	3 ↓ ↑	4 Rules of Dr. and Cr.	5 T Account Update
Salaries Expense	Expense	↑	Dr.	Salaries Expense 511 (G) **700** |
Cash	Asset	↓	Cr.	Cash 111 (A) 6,000 | 500 (B) (D) 2,000 | **700** (G) (F) 900 |

Analysis of Transaction G

Step 1 The law firm pays $700 of salaries expense by cash.

Step 2 Salaries Expense is an expense. Cash is an asset.

Step 3 The Salaries Expense of the law firm is increasing, which results in a decrease in Cash.

Step 4 An increase in Salaries Expense, an expense, is a debit. A decrease in Cash, an asset, is a credit.

Step 5 Enter the amount for Salaries Expense on the debit side of the T account. The amount for Cash goes on the credit side.

Transaction H Sept. 1–30: Paid rent expense, $400.

1 Accounts Affected	2 Category	3 ↓ ↑	4 Rules of Dr. and Cr.	5 T Account Update
Rent Expense	Expense	↑	Dr.	Rent Expense 512 (H) 400 |
Cash	Asset	↓	Cr.	Cash 111 (A) 6,000 | 500 (B) (D) 2,000 | 700 (G) (F) 900 | 400 (H)

Analysis of Transaction H

Step 1 The law firm's rent expenses of $400 are paid in cash.

Step 2 Rent is an expense. Cash is an asset.

Step 3 The Rent Expense increases the expenses, and the payment for the Rent Expense decreases the cash.

Step 4 An increase in Rent Expense, an expense, is a debit. A decrease in Cash, an asset, is a credit.

Step 5 Enter the amount for Rent Expense on the debit side of the T account. Place the amount for Cash on the credit side.

Transaction I Sept. 1–30: Received a bill for Advertising Expense (to be paid next month), $200.

1 Accounts Affected	2 Category	3 ↓ ↑	4 Rules of Dr. and Cr.	5 T Account Update
Advertising Expense	Expense	↑	Dr.	Advertising Expense 513 (I) 200 |
Accounts Payable	Liability	↑	Cr.	Accounts Payable 211 | 300 (C) | 200 (I)

Analysis of Transaction I

Step 1 The advertising bill in the amount of $200 has come in and payment is due but has not yet been made. Therefore, the accounts involved here are Advertising Expense and Accounts Payable; the expense has created a liability.

Step 2 Advertising Expense is an expense. Accounts Payable is a liability.

Step 3 Both the expense and the liability are increasing.

Step 4 An increase in an expense is a debit. An increase in a liability is a credit.

Step 5 Enter the amount for Advertising Expense on the debit side of the T account. Enter the amount for Accounts Payable on the credit side.

Transaction J Sept. 1–30: Wong withdrew cash for personal use, $100.

1 Accounts Affected	2 Category	3 ↓ ↑	4 Rules of Dr. and Cr.	5 T Account Update
Mia Wong, Withdrawals	Withdrawals	↑	Dr.	Mia Wong, Withdrawals, 312 (J) **100** |
Cash	Asset	↓	Cr.	Cash 111 (A) 6,000 | 500 (B) (D) 2,000 | 700 (G) (F) 900 | 400 (H) | **100** (J)

Analysis of Transaction J

Step 1 Mia Wong withdraws $100 cash from business for *personal* use. This withdrawal is not a business expense.

Step 2 This transaction affects the Withdrawals and Cash accounts.

Step 3 Mia has increased what she has withdrawn from the business for personal use. The business cash decreased.

Withdrawals are always increased by debits.

Step 4 An increase in Withdrawals is a debit. A decrease in Cash is a credit. (*Remember:* Withdrawals go on the statement of owner's equity; expenses go on the income statement.)

Step 5 Enter the amount for Mia Wong, Withdrawals on the debit side of the T account. The amount for Cash goes on the credit side.

Summary of Transactions for Mia Wong

Assets = Liabilities + Owner's Equity

Cash = Accounts + Capital − Withdrawals + Revenue − Expenses

Assets

Cash 111	
(A) 6,000	500 (B)
(D) 2,000	700 (G)
(F) 900	400 (H)
	100 (J)

Accounts Receivable 112	
(E) 3,000	900 (F)

Office Equipment 121	
(A) 200	
(B) 500	
(C) 300	

= Liabilities

Accounts Payable 211	
	300 (C)
	200 (I)

+ Owner's Equity

Mia Wong, Capital 311	
	6,200 (A)

−

Mia Wong, Withdrawals 312	
(J) 100	

+

Legal Fees 411	
	2,000 (D)
	3,000 (E)

−

Salaries Expense 511	
(G) 700	

−

Rent Expense 512	
(H) 400	

−

Advertising Expense 513	
(I) 200	

LEARNING UNIT 2-2 REVIEW

AT THIS POINT you should be able to

- State the rules of debit and credit.
- List the five steps of a transaction analysis.
- Show how to fill out a transaction analysis chart.
- Explain double-entry bookkeeping.

Accounting Cycle Tutorial

Self-Review Quiz 2-2

King Company uses the following accounts from its chart of accounts: Cash (111), Accounts Receivable (112), Equipment (121), Accounts Payable (211), Jamie King, Capital (311), Jamie King, Withdrawals (312), Professional Fees (411), Utilities Expense (511), and Salaries Expense (512).

Record the following transactions into transaction analysis charts.

a. Jamie King invested in the business $1,000 cash and equipment worth $700 from his personal assets.
b. Billed clients for services rendered, $12,000.
c. Utilities bill due but unpaid, $150.
d. Withdrew cash for personal use, $120.
e. Paid salaries expense, $250.

For additional help go to www.pearsonhighered.com/slater

Solution to Self-Review Quiz 2-2

a.

1 Accounts Affected	2 Category	3 ↓ ↑	4 Rules of Dr. and Cr.	5 T Account Update
Cash	Asset	↑	Dr.	Cash 111 (A) 1,000 |
Equipment	Asset	↑	Dr.	Equipment 121 (A) 700 |
Jamie King, Capital	Capital	↑	Cr.	Jamie King, Capital 311 | 1,700 (A)

b.

1 Accounts Affected	2 Category	3 ↓ ↑	4 Rules of Dr. and Cr.	5 T Account Update
Accounts Receivable	Asset	↑	Dr.	Accounts Receivable 112 (B) 12,000 |
Professional Fees	Revenue	↑	Cr.	Professional Fees 411 | 12,000 (B)

c.

1 Accounts Affected	2 Category	3 ↓ ↑	4 Rules of Dr. and Cr.	5 T Account Update
Utilities Expense	Expense	↑	Dr.	Utilities Expense 511 (C) **150** |
Accounts Payable	Liability	↑	Cr.	Accounts Payable 211 | **150** (C)

d.

1 Accounts Affected	2 Category	3 ↓ ↑	4 Rules of Dr. and Cr.	5 T Account Update
Jamie King, Withdrawals	Withdrawals	↑	Dr.	Jamie King, Withdrawals 312 (D) **120** |
Cash	Asset	↓	Cr.	Cash 111 (A) 1,000 | **120** (D)

e.

1 Accounts Affected	2 Category	3 ↓ ↑	4 Rules of Dr. and Cr.	5 T Account Update
Salaries Expense	Expense	↑	Dr.	Salaries Expense 512 (E) **250** |
Cash	Asset	↓	Cr.	Cash 111 (A) 1,000 | 120 (D) | **250** (E)

NEED HELP?

Let's review first: Make up a note card of the rules of debit and credit from Table 2.1. You will notice that assets, withdrawals, and expenses increase when you put amounts on the left, or debit, side of these accounts. The accounting system balances because liabilities, capital, and revenue increase when you put amounts on the right, or credit, side of these accounts. The increase side of any account will represent its normal balance. Think of a chart of accounts as a roadmap to all account titles a company will use. ALL ACCOUNTS AFFECTED MUST COME FROM THE CHART OF ACCOUNTS.

Transaction A: In column 1 all titles must come from the chart of accounts. The order listed does not matter as long as the sum of the left side equals the sum of the right side. In this transaction we see that accounts affected include cash, equipment, and Jamie King, Capital.

Cash and equipment are assets, while capital is categorized as capital. Remember that the six category choices are as follows:

assets
liabilities
capital
withdrawals
revenue
expenses

The cash and equipment in business are increasing (thus arrows up) and because the owner supplied them Jamie King, Capital rights are increasing. Assets are increased by putting amounts on the debit side and capital is increased by putting amounts on the credit side.

Transaction B: Here we do the work but do not get the money. We see from the chart of accounts that revenue is called Professional Fees and customers owing money is called Accounts Receivable. Revenue for King Co. is going up and customers owe the company more money. Increase in an asset is a debit and increase in revenue is a credit.

Transaction C: Here we record utilities expense before it is paid. The expenses have increased for King Co. and it has increased what it owes the utility company. An increase in an expense is a debit and an increase in a liability is a credit. Here an expense has created a liability.

Transaction D: This is not a business expense since this is a personal withdrawal of cash by the owner. King, Withdrawals are increasing since King is taking the withdrawal but the business is lowering its cash from the withdrawal. An increase in withdrawal is a debit and a decrease in cash is a credit. Note the "dr" in the middle of "withdrawal." A withdrawal always increases by a debit.

Transaction E: In this transaction the business has another expense increasing and is paying for it in cash. The end result is that expenses increase on the debit side and cash, which is an asset, decreases on the credit side. Remember that we record expenses when they happen whether they are paid or not. Here they were paid. In transaction C they were not paid.

Summary: The mind process charts are a great way to organize your information before deciding on what to debit or credit. Column 1 must come from the chart of accounts. In the category column you have six choices: assets, liabilities, capital, revenue, withdrawals, and expenses. The arrows tell you if the business accounts are increasing or decreasing. Note in column 5 that if an account is repeated a running summary of all transactions is accumulated in the account.

Learning Unit 2-3 The Trial Balance and Preparation of Financial Statements

Let us look at all the transactions we have discussed, arranged by T accounts and recorded using the rules of debit and credit. This grouping of accounts is much easier to use than the expanded accounting equation because all the transactions that affect a particular account are in one place.

Summary of Transactions of Mia Wong

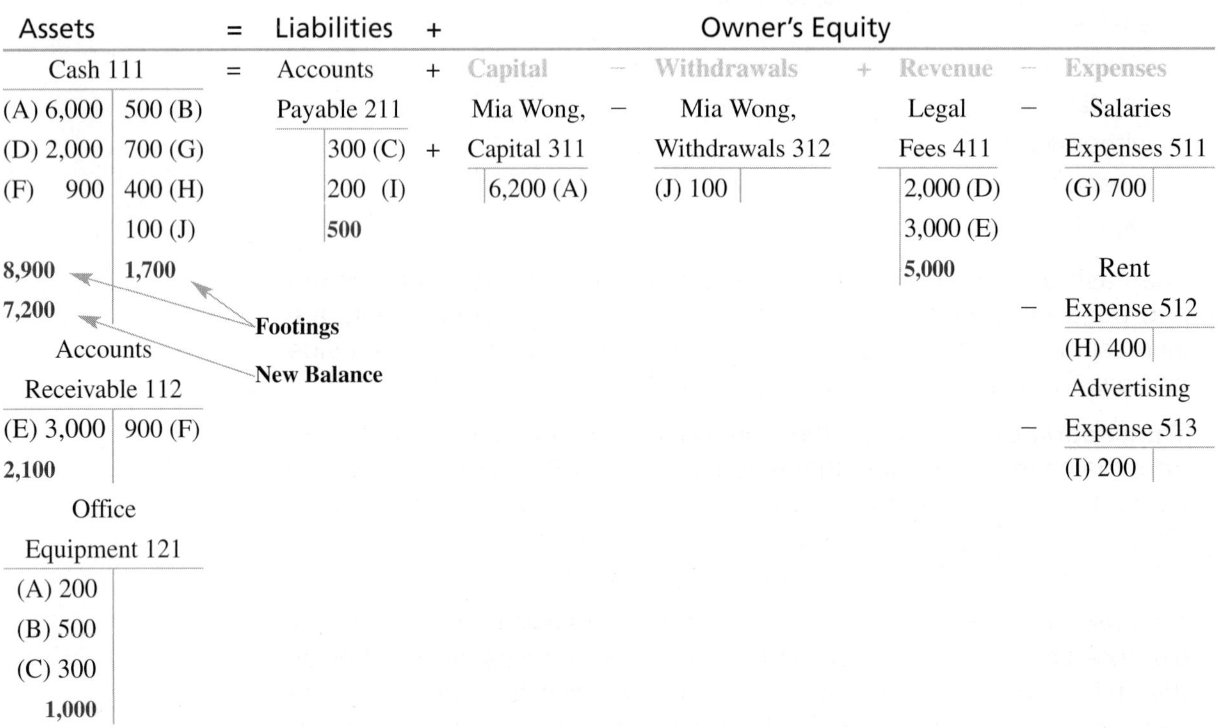

Assets = Liabilities + Owner's Equity

Cash 111 = Accounts Payable 211 + Capital: Mia Wong, Capital 311 − Withdrawals: Mia Wong, Withdrawals 312 + Revenue: Legal Fees 411 − Expenses: Salaries Expenses 511

Cash 111

Dr.	Cr.
(A) 6,000	500 (B)
(D) 2,000	700 (G)
(F) 900	400 (H)
	100 (J)
8,900	**1,700**
7,200	

Footings (8,900 and 1,700)

New Balance (7,200)

Accounts Receivable 112

Dr.	Cr.
(E) 3,000	900 (F)
2,100	

Office Equipment 121

Dr.	Cr.
(A) 200	
(B) 500	
(C) 300	
1,000	

Accounts Payable 211

Dr.	Cr.
	300 (C)
	200 (I)
	500

Mia Wong, Capital 311

Dr.	Cr.
	6,200 (A)

Mia Wong, Withdrawals 312

Dr.	Cr.
(J) 100	

Legal Fees 411

Dr.	Cr.
	2,000 (D)
	3,000 (E)
	5,000

Salaries Expenses 511

Dr.	Cr.
(G) 700	

− **Rent Expense 512**

Dr.	Cr.
(H) 400	

− **Advertising Expense 513**

Dr.	Cr.
(I) 200	

As we saw in Learning Unit 2-2, when all the transactions are recorded in the accounts, the total of all the debits should be equal to the total of all the credits. (If they are not, the accountant must go back and find the error by checking the numbers and adding every column again.)

LO3 The Trial Balance

> As mentioned earlier, the ending balance of Cash, $7,200, is a *normal balance* because it is on the side that increases the asset account.

Footings are used to obtain the totals of each side of every T account that has more than one entry. The footings are used to find the ending balance. The ending balances are used to prepare a **trial balance.** The trial balance is not a financial statement, although it is used to prepare financial statements. The trial balance lists all the accounts with their balances in the same order as they appear in the chart of accounts. It proves the accuracy of the ledger. For example, look at the preceding Cash account. The footing for the debit side is $8,900, and the footing for the credit side is $1,700. Because the debit side is larger, we subtract $1,700 from $8,900 to arrive at an *ending debit balance* of $7,200. Now look at the Rent Expense account. It doesn't need a footing because it has only one entry. The amount itself is the ending balance. When the ending balance has been found for every account, we should be able to show that the total of all debits equals the total of all credits.

In the ideal situation, businesses would take a trial balance every day. The large number of transactions most businesses conduct each day makes this impractical. Instead, trial balances are prepared periodically.

Keep in mind that the figure for capital might not be the beginning figure if any additional investment has taken place during the period. You can tell by looking at the capital account in the ledger.

A more detailed discussion of the trial balance is provided in the next chapter. For now, notice the heading, how the accounts are listed, the debits in the left column, the credits in the right, and that the total of debits is equal to the total of credits.

A trial balance of Mia Wong's accounts is shown in Figure 2.2.

MIA WONG, ATTORNEY-AT-LAW TRIAL BALANCE SEPTEMBER 30, 200X		
	Dr.	Cr.
Cash	7200 00	
Accounts Receivable	2100 00	
Office Equipment	1000 00	
Accounts Payable		500 00
Mia Wong, Capital		6200 00
Mia Wong, Withdrawals	100 00	
Legal Fees		5000 00
Salaries Expense	700 00	
Rent Expense	400 00	
Advertising Expense	200 00	
Totals	11700 00	11700 00

FIGURE 2.2 Trial Balance for Mia Wong's Law Firm

Because this statement is not a formal one, it doesn't need dollar signs; the single and double lines under subtotals and final totals, however, are still used for clarity.

Preparing Financial Statements

LO4

The trial balance is used to prepare the financial statements. The diagram in Figure 2.3 on the following page shows how financial statements can be prepared from a trial balance. Statements do not have debit or credit columns. The left column is used only to subtotal numbers.

Accounting Cycle Tutorial

LEARNING UNIT 2-3 REVIEW

AT THIS POINT you should be able to

- Explain the role of footings.
- Prepare a trial balance from a set of accounts.
- Prepare financial statements from a trial balance.

In QuickBooks and Peachtree, financial statements are prepared simply by selecting the report you want and changing the date to the current period.

Self-Review Quiz 2-3

For additional help go to www.pearsonhighered.com/slater

As the bookkeeper of Pam's Hair Salon, you are to prepare from the accounts that follow on June 30, 200X (1) a trial balance as of June 30, (2) an income statement for the month ended June 30, (3) a statement of owner's equity for the month ended June 30, and (4) a balance sheet as of June 30, 200X.

Cash 111	
4,500	300
2,000	100
1,000	1,200
300	1,300
	2,600

Accounts Payable 211	
300	700

Salon Fees 411	
	3,500
	1,000

Accounts Receivable 121	
1,000	300

Pam Jay, Capital 311	
	4,000*

Rent Expense 511	
1,200	

Salon Equipment 131	
700	

Pam Jay, Withdrawals 321	
100	

Salon Supplies Expense 521	
1,300	

Salaries Expense 531	
2,600	

*No additional investments.

FIGURE 2.3 Steps in Preparing Financial Statements from a Trial Balance

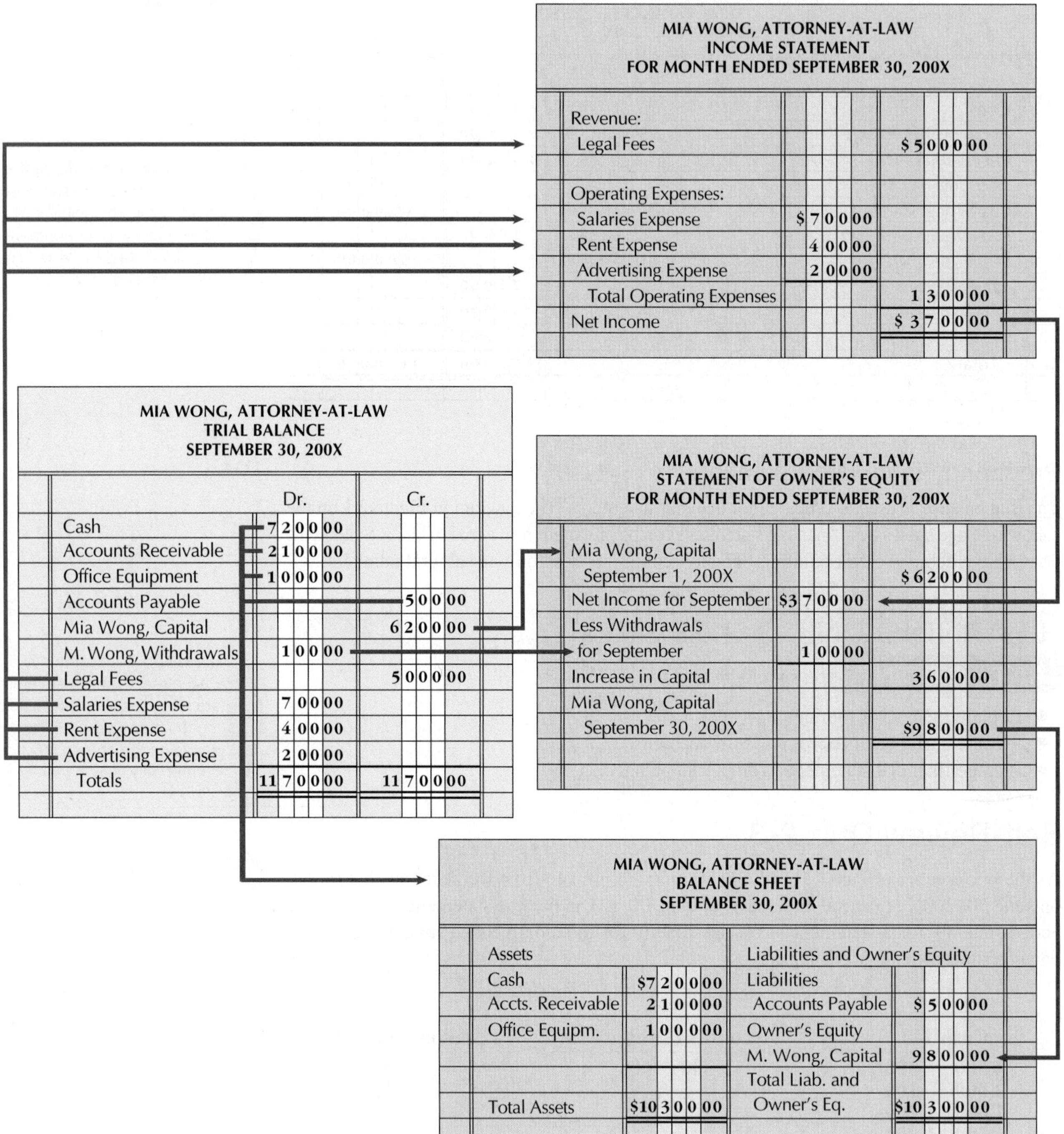

MIA WONG, ATTORNEY-AT-LAW
TRIAL BALANCE
SEPTEMBER 30, 200X

	Dr.	Cr.
Cash	7200 00	
Accounts Receivable	2100 00	
Office Equipment	1000 00	
Accounts Payable		500 00
Mia Wong, Capital		6200 00
M. Wong, Withdrawals	100 00	
Legal Fees		5000 00
Salaries Expense	700 00	
Rent Expense	400 00	
Advertising Expense	200 00	
Totals	11700 00	11700 00

MIA WONG, ATTORNEY-AT-LAW
INCOME STATEMENT
FOR MONTH ENDED SEPTEMBER 30, 200X

Revenue:		
Legal Fees		$5000 00
Operating Expenses:		
Salaries Expense	$700 00	
Rent Expense	400 00	
Advertising Expense	200 00	
Total Operating Expenses		1300 00
Net Income		$3700 00

MIA WONG, ATTORNEY-AT-LAW
STATEMENT OF OWNER'S EQUITY
FOR MONTH ENDED SEPTEMBER 30, 200X

Mia Wong, Capital		
September 1, 200X		$6200 00
Net Income for September	$3700 00	
Less Withdrawals		
for September	100 00	
Increase in Capital		3600 00
Mia Wong, Capital		
September 30, 200X		$9800 00

MIA WONG, ATTORNEY-AT-LAW
BALANCE SHEET
SEPTEMBER 30, 200X

Assets		Liabilities and Owner's Equity	
Cash	$7200 00	Liabilities	
Accts. Receivable	2100 00	Accounts Payable	$500 00
Office Equipm.	1000 00	Owner's Equity	
		M. Wong, Capital	9800 00
		Total Liab. and	
Total Assets	$10300 00	Owner's Eq.	$10300 00

Solution to Self-Review Quiz 2-3

FIGURE 2.4

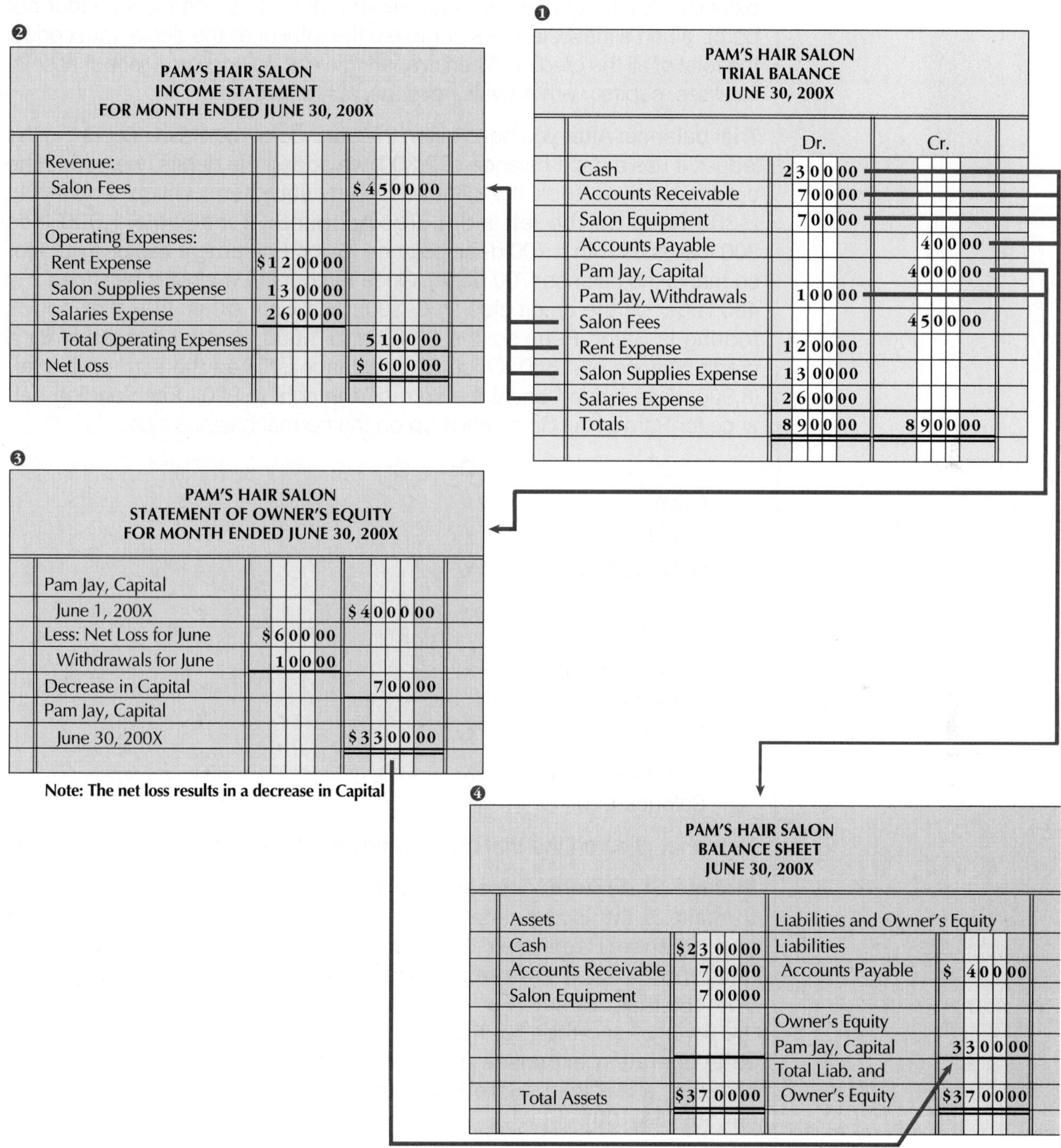

❶ PAM'S HAIR SALON
TRIAL BALANCE
JUNE 30, 200X

	Dr.	Cr.
Cash	2 3 0 0 00	
Accounts Receivable	7 0 0 00	
Salon Equipment	7 0 0 00	
Accounts Payable		4 0 0 00
Pam Jay, Capital		4 0 0 0 00
Pam Jay, Withdrawals	1 0 0 00	
Salon Fees		4 5 0 0 00
Rent Expense	1 2 0 0 00	
Salon Supplies Expense	1 3 0 0 00	
Salaries Expense	2 6 0 0 00	
Totals	8 9 0 0 00	8 9 0 0 00

❷ PAM'S HAIR SALON
INCOME STATEMENT
FOR MONTH ENDED JUNE 30, 200X

Revenue:		
Salon Fees		$ 4 5 0 0 00
Operating Expenses:		
Rent Expense	$ 1 2 0 0 00	
Salon Supplies Expense	1 3 0 0 00	
Salaries Expense	2 6 0 0 00	
Total Operating Expenses		5 1 0 0 00
Net Loss		$ 6 0 0 00

❸ PAM'S HAIR SALON
STATEMENT OF OWNER'S EQUITY
FOR MONTH ENDED JUNE 30, 200X

Pam Jay, Capital		
June 1, 200X		$ 4 0 0 0 00
Less: Net Loss for June	$ 6 0 0 00	
Withdrawals for June	1 0 0 00	
Decrease in Capital		7 0 0 00
Pam Jay, Capital		
June 30, 200X		$ 3 3 0 0 00

Note: The net loss results in a decrease in Capital

❹ PAM'S HAIR SALON
BALANCE SHEET
JUNE 30, 200X

Assets		Liabilities and Owner's Equity	
Cash	$ 2 3 0 0 00	Liabilities	
Accounts Receivable	7 0 0 00	Accounts Payable	$ 4 0 0 00
Salon Equipment	7 0 0 00		
		Owner's Equity	
		Pam Jay, Capital	3 3 0 0 00
		Total Liab. and	
Total Assets	$ 3 7 0 0 00	Owner's Equity	$ 3 7 0 0 00

NEED HELP?

Let's review first: The trial balance is a list of accounts and their ending balances. Each account will have either a debit or credit balance (but not both). When a trial balance is complete the total of all the debits must equal the total of all the credits. When preparing a trial balance you list out assets, liabilities, capital, withdrawals, revenue, and expenses.

Trial balance: After you have taken the balance of the Cash account in the ledger, it has a debit balance of 2,300 (we added the debits, we added the credits, and we took the difference between them, which resulted in 2,300 more on the left side). For Accounts Receivable 1,000 less 300 leaves us with a 700 debit balance. Salon Equipment has one number so that is the balance (700 debit). Once Accounts Payable is balanced it is 400 larger on the credit side (700–300). The only other title that needs footing is Salon Fees so the 3,500 and 1,000 are added together for a credit balance of 4,500. Once each balance is listed the sum on the left (8,900) does indeed equal the sum on the right (8,900). Each ending balance for Pam's Hair Salon ends up on the normal balance side.

	Dr.	Cr.
Cash	x	
Acc. Rec.	x	
Salon Equip.	x	
Accounts Pay.		x
Pam Jay, Cap.		x
Pam Jay, Withd.	x	
Salon Fees		x
Rent Expense	x	
Salon Supp. Exp.	x	
Salaries Exp.	x	

Note that titles on the trial balance are not indented.

Income Statement: Once the trial balance is complete the first report to make is the income statement, which is made up of only revenue and expense. Remember that there are no debits or credits on financial reports. All we are taking are the ending balances of each title from the trial balance. For the income statement, we list salon fees as the revenue and then list the three expense titles in the inside column. Total operating expenses are then subtracted from the salon fees to arrive at a net loss. Here revenue is less than operating expenses ($4,500–$5,100).

Statement of Owner's Equity: The second report to prepare is the statement of owner's equity, which shows how to calculate a new figure for capital. Note that in this case the net loss of $600 is ADDED to the $100 of withdrawals, resulting in a decrease of $700 to capital. The new figure for capital is $3,300 ($4,000–$700).

Balance Sheet: The third report is the balance sheet, which lists out each asset, liability, and the new figure for capital. This report shows that as of June 30 total assets is $3,700 and total liabilities and owner's equity is $3,700. Remember that the ending figure for capital comes from the statement of owner's equity.

Summary: The trial balance is a list of ending balances of ledger accounts. These balances are used to prepare the three financial reports. Financial reports have no debits or credits. The inside columns are used to subtotal numbers. Revenue and expenses go on the income statement. Withdrawals and either net income or net loss go on the statement of owner's equity to calculate a new figure for capital. The balance sheet is a list of assets, liabilities, and the new amount for ending capital. Remember that the trial balance has debit or credits, not the financial reports.

CHAPTER ASSIGNMENTS

All Classroom Demonstration Exercises, Exercises, Problems, and the Continuing Problem in this chapter can be found within MyAccountingLab, an online homework and practice environment. Your instructor may ask you to complete this material using MyAccountingLab.

DEMONSTRATION PROBLEM

The chart of accounts of Mel's Delivery Service includes the following: Cash, 111; Accounts Receivable, 112; Office Equipment, 121; Delivery Trucks, 122; Accounts Payable, 211; Mel Free, Capital, 311; Mel Free, Withdrawals, 312; Delivery Fees Earned, 411; Advertising Expense, 511; Gas Expense, 512; Salaries Expense, 513; and Telephone Expense, 514. The following transactions resulted for Mel's Delivery Service during the month of July:

Transaction A: Mel invested $10,000 in the business from his personal savings account.

Transaction B: Bought delivery trucks on account, $17,000.

Transaction C: Advertising bill received but unpaid, $700.

Transaction D: Bought office equipment for cash, $1,200.

Transaction E: Received cash for delivery services rendered, $15,000.

Transaction F: Paid salaries expense, $3,000.

Transaction G: Paid gas expense for company trucks, $1,250.

Transaction H: Billed customers for delivery services rendered, $4,000.

Transaction I: Paid telephone bill, $300.

Transaction J: Received $3,000 as partial payment of transaction H.

Transaction K: Mel paid home telephone bill from company checkbook, $150.

ASSIGNMENT

As Mel's newly employed accountant, you must do the following:

1. Set up T accounts in a ledger.
2. Record transactions in the T accounts. (Place the letter of the transaction next to the entry.)
3. Foot and take the balance of each account where appropriate.
4. Prepare a trial balance at the end of July.
5. Prepare from the trial balance, in proper form, (a) an income statement for the month of July, (b) a statement of owner's equity, and (c) a balance sheet as of July 31, 200X.

Solution to Demonstration Problem

1,2,3. GENERAL LEDGER

Cash 111

Dr.	Cr.
(A) 10,000	1,200 (D)
(E) 15,000	3,000 (F)
(J) 3,000	1,250 (G)
	300 (I)
	150 (K)
28,000	5,900
22,100	

Accts. Payable 211

Dr.	Cr.
	17,000 (B)
	700 (C)
	17,700

Advertising Expense 511

Dr.	Cr.
(C) 700	

Accts. Receivable 112

Dr.	Cr.
(H) 4,000	3,000 (J)
1,000	

Mel Free, Capital 311

Dr.	Cr.
	10,000 (A)

Gas Expense 512

Dr.	Cr.
(G) 1,250	

Office Equipment 121

Dr.	Cr.
(D) 1,200	

Mel Free, Withdrawals 312

Dr.	Cr.
(K) 150	

Salaries Expense 513

Dr.	Cr.
(F) 3,000	

Delivery Trucks 122

Dr.	Cr.
(B) 17,000	

Delivery Fees Earned 411

Dr.	Cr.
	15,000 (E)
	4,000 (H)
	19,000

Telephone Expense 514

Dr.	Cr.
(I) 300	

Solution Tips to Recording Transactions

Account	Category	↑ ↓	Rules
A. Cash	A	↑	Dr.
Mel Free, Capital	Cap.	↑	Cr.
B. Delivery Trucks	A	↑	Dr.
Accts. Payable	L	↑	Cr.
C. Advertising Expense	Exp.	↑	Dr.
Accts. Payable	L	↑	Cr.
D. Office Equipment	A	↑	Dr.
Cash	A	↓	Cr.
E. Cash	A	↑	Dr.
Del. Fees Earned	Rev.	↑	Cr.
F. Salaries Expense	Exp.	↑	Dr.
Cash	A	↓	Cr.
G. Gas Expense	Exp.	↑	Dr.
Cash	A	↓	Cr.
H. Acc. Receivable	A	↑	Dr.
Del. Fees Earned	Rev.	↑	Cr.
I. Tel. Expense	Exp.	↑	Dr.
Cash	A	↓	Cr.

J. Cash	A	↑	Dr.
Accts. Receivable	A	↓	Cr.

K. Mel Free, Withd.	Withd.	↑	Dr.
Cash	A	↓	Cr.

Mel's Delivery Service
Trial Balance
July 31, 200X

	Dr.	*Cr.*
Cash	22,100	
Accounts Receivable	1,000	
Office Equipment	1,200	
Delivery Trucks	17,000	
Accounts Payable		17,700
Mel Free, Capital		10,000
Mel Free, Withdrawals	150	
Delivery Fees Earned		19,000
Advertising Expense	700	
Gas Expense	1,250	
Salaries Expense	3,000	
Telephone Expense	300	
TOTALS	46,700	46,700

Solution Tips to Taking the Balance of an Account and Preparation of a Trial Balance

3. Footings:

Cash	Add left side, $28,000. Add right side, $5,900. Take difference, $22,100, and stay on side that is larger.
Accounts Payable	Add $17,000 + $700 and stay on same side. Total is $17,700.

4. Trial balance is a list of the ledger's ending balances. The list is in the same order as the chart of accounts. Each title has only one number listed either as a debit or credit balance.

FIGURE 2.5 Financial Reports

5a.

MEL'S DELIVERY SERVICE INCOME STATEMENT FOR MONTH ENDED JULY 31, 200X		
Revenue:		
Delivery Fees Earned		$19 000 00
Operating Expenses:		
Advertising Expense	$ 700 00	
Gas Expense	1 250 00	
Salaries Expense	3 000 00	
Telephone Expense	300 00	
Total Operating Expenses		5 250 00
Net Income		$13 750 00

b.

MEL'S DELIVERY SERVICE STATEMENT OF OWNER'S EQUITY FOR MONTH ENDED JULY 31, 200X		
Mel Free, Capital		
July 1, 200X		$10 000 00
Net Income for July	$13 750 00	
Less Withdrawals for July	150 00	
Increase in Capital		$13 600 00
Mel Free, Capital		
July 31, 200X		$23 600 00

c.

MEL'S DELIVERY SERVICE BALANCE SHEET JULY 31, 200X			
Assets		Liabilities and Owner's Equity	
Cash	$22 100 00	Liabilities	
Accounts Receivable	1 000 00	Accounts Payable	$17 700 00
Office Equipment	1 200 00		
Delivery Trucks	17 000 00		
		Owner's Equity	
		Mel Free, Capital	23 600 00
		Total Liab. and	
Total Assets	$41 300 00	Owner's Equity	$41 300 00

Solution Tips to Prepare Financial Statements from a Trial Balance

Trial Balance

		Dr.	Cr.
Balance Sheet	Assets	X	
	Liabilities		X
Statement of Equity	Capital		X
	Withdrawals	X	
Income Statement	Revenues		X
	Expenses	X	
		XX	XX

Net income of $13,750 on the income statement goes on the statement of owner's equity.

Ending capital of $23,600 on the statement of owner's equity goes on the balance sheet as the new figure for capital.

Note: Financial statements do not show debits or credits. The inside column is used for subtotaling.

SUMMARY OF KEY POINTS

LEARNING UNIT 2-1

1. A T account is a simplified version of a standard account.
2. A ledger is a group of accounts.
3. A debit is the left-hand position (side) of an account, and a credit is the right-hand position (side) of an account.
4. A footing is the total of one side of an account. The ending balance is the difference between the footings.

LEARNING UNIT 2-2

1. A chart of accounts lists the account titles and their numbers for a company.
2. The transaction analysis chart is a teaching device, not to be confused with standard accounting procedures.
3. A compound entry is a transaction involving more than one debit or credit.

LEARNING UNIT 2-3

1. In double-entry bookkeeping, the recording of each business transaction affects two or more accounts, and the total of debits equals the total of credits.
2. A trial balance is a list of the ending balances of all accounts, listed in the same order as on the chart of accounts.
3. Any additional investments during the period result in the Capital balance on the trial balance not being the beginning figure for the Capital account.
4. *No* debit or credit columns are used in the three financial statements.

KEY TERMS

Account An accounting device used in bookkeeping to record increases and decreases of business transactions relating to individual assets, liabilities, capital, withdrawals, revenue, expenses, and so on.

Chart of accounts A numbering system of accounts that lists the account titles and account numbers to be used by a company.

Compound entry A transaction involving more than one debit or credit.

Credit The right-hand side of any account. A number entered on the right side of any account is said to be credited to an account.

Debit The left-hand side of any account. A number entered on the left side of any account is said to be debited to an account.

Double-entry bookkeeping An accounting system in which the recording of each transaction affects two or more accounts and the total of the debits is equal to the total of the credits.

Ending balance The difference between footings in a T account.

Footings The totals of each side of a T account.

Ledger A group of accounts that records data from business transactions.

Normal balance of an account The side of an account that increases by the rules of debit and credit.

Standard account A formal account that includes columns for date, explanation, posting reference, debit, and credit.

T account A skeleton version of a standard account, used for demonstration purposes.

Trial balance A list of the ending balances of all the accounts in a ledger. The total of the debits should equal the total of the credits.

BLUEPRINT: PREPARING FINANCIAL STATEMENTS FROM A TRIAL BALANCE

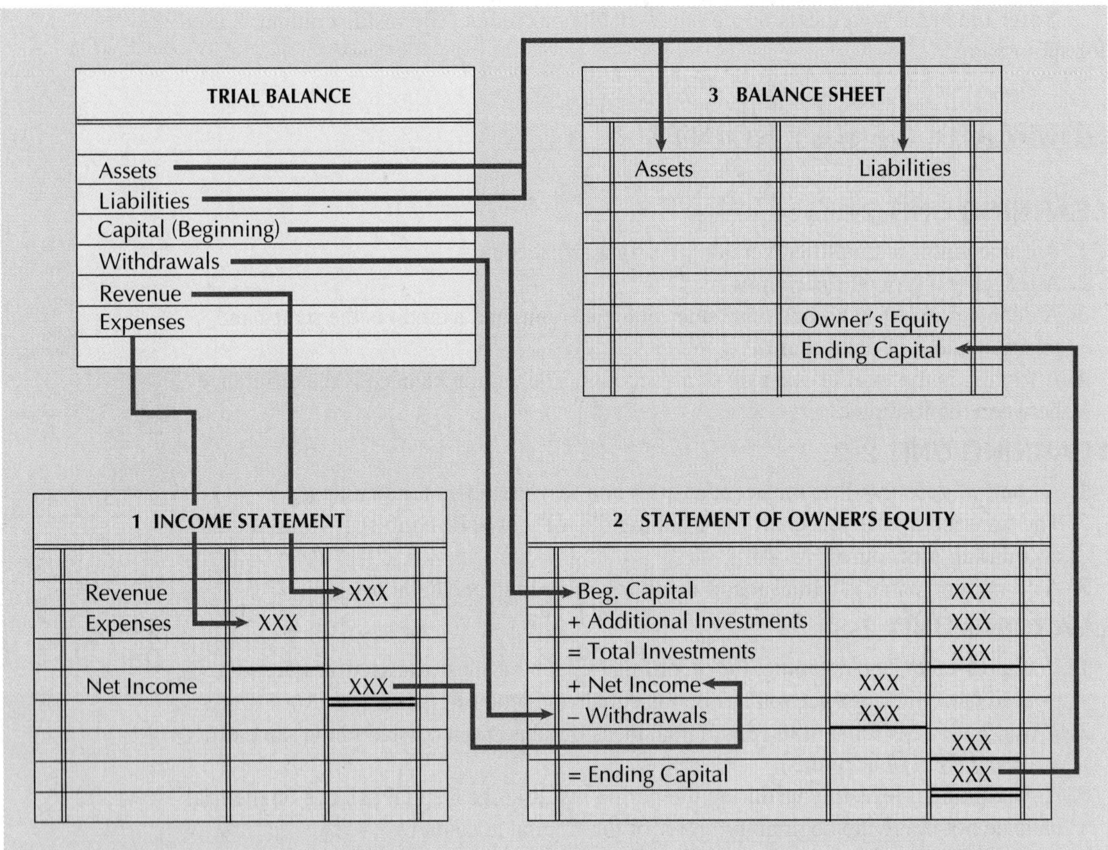

QUESTIONS, CLASSROOM DEMONSTRATION EXERCISES, EXERCISES, AND PROBLEMS

Discussion and Critical Thinking Questions/Ethical Case

1. Define a ledger.
2. Why is the left-hand side of an account called a debit?
3. Footings are used in balancing all accounts. True or false? Please explain.
4. What is the end product of the accounting process?
5. What do we mean when we say that a transaction analysis chart is a teaching device?
6. What are the five steps of the transaction analysis chart?
7. Explain the concept of double-entry bookkeeping.

8. A trial balance is a formal statement. True or false? Please explain.
9. Why are there no debit or credit columns on financial statements?
10. Compare the financial statements prepared from the expanded accounting equation with those prepared from a trial balance.
11. Audrey Flet, the bookkeeper of ALN Co. was scheduled to leave on a three-week vacation at 5:00 on Friday. She couldn't get the company's trial balance to balance. At 4:30, she decided to put in fictitious figures to make it balance. Audrey told herself she would fix it when she got back from her vacation. Was Audrey right or wrong to do this? Why?

Classroom Demonstration Exercises

SET A

The T Account *LO1, 2 (5 min)*

1. From the following, foot and balance each account.

Cash 110

9/5	12,000	9/7	800
9/9	6,000		

Matt Nason, Capital 311

		6/9	6,000
		9/3	4,000
		9/7	1,000

Transaction Analysis *LO2 (5 min)*

2. Complete the following:

Account	Category	↑	↓	Normal Balance
A. Accounts Payable				
B. Taxable Fees Earned				
C. Accounts Receivable				
D. M. Blanc, Capital				
E. M. Blanc, Withdrawals				
F. Prepaid Advertising				
G. Rent Expense				

Transaction Analysis *LO2 (5 min)*

3. Record the following transaction into the transaction analysis chart: Provided grooming fees for $2,500, receiving $600 cash with the remainder to be paid next month.

Accounts Affected	Category	↓	↑	Rules of Dr. and Cr.	T Accounts

Trial Balance *LO4 (5 min)*

4. Rearrange the following titles in the order they would appear on a trial balance:

J. Joy, Withdrawals	Hair Salon Fees Earned
Accounts Receivable	Selling Expense
Cash	Salary Expense
J. Joy, Capital	Advertising Expense
Office Equipment	Accounts Payable

LO3 (10 min) **Trial Balance/Financial Statements**

5. From the following trial balance, identify on which statement each title will appear:
   - Income statement (IS)
   - Statement of owner's equity (OE)
   - Balance sheet (BS)

BERNIE CO.
TRIAL BALANCE
NOV. 30, 200X

		Dr.	*Cr.*
A. ________	Cash	500	
B. ________	Computer	200	
C. ________	Computer Equipment	600	
D. ________	Accounts Payable		900
E. ________	L. Bean, Capital		240
F. ________	L. Bean, Withdrawals	250	
G. ________	Legal Fees Earned		1,000
H. ________	Consulting Fees Earned		500
I. ________	Wage Expense	300	
J. ________	Supplies Expense	700	
K. ________	Internet Advertising Expense	90	
	TOTALS	2,640	2,640

SET B

LO1, 2 (5 min) **The T Account**

1. From the following, foot and balance each account.

Cash 110

5/8	**3,000**	**5/11**	**1,000**
5/12	**9,000**		

A. Slate, Capital 311

		4/9	**8,000**
		4/12	**4,000**
		5/2	**9,000**

LO2 (5 min) **Transaction Analysis**

2. Complete the following:

Account	Category	↑	↓	Normal Balance
A. Digital Cameras				
B. Prepaid Rent				
C. Accounts Payable				
D. A. Sung, Capital				
E. A. Sung, Withdrawals				
F. Legal Fees				
G. Salary Expense				

LO2 (5 min) **Transaction Analysis**

3. Record the following transaction into the transaction analysis chart: Provided legal fees for $4,000, receiving $3,000 cash with the remainder to be collected next month.

Accounts Affected	Category	↓	↑	Rules of Dr. and Cr.	T Accounts

Trial Balance *LO4 (5 min)*

4. Rearrange the following titles in the order they would appear on a trial balance:

Selling Expense	Legal Fees
Accounts Receivable	D. Cope, Withdrawals
Accounts Payable	Rent Expense
D. Cope, Capital	Advertising Expense
Computer Equipment	Cash

Trial Balance/Financial Statements *LO5 (10 min)*

5. From the following trial balance, identify on which statement each title will appear:

- Income statement (IS)
- Statement of owner's equity (OE)
- Balance sheet (BS)

HEATH CO.
TRIAL BALANCE
SEPT. 30, 200X

		Dr.	Cr.
A. ________	Cash	390	
B. ________	Supplies	100	
C. ________	Office Equipment	200	
D. ________	Accounts Payable		100
E. ________	D. Heath, Capital		450
F. ________	D. Heath, Withdrawals	160	
G. ________	Fees Earned		290
H. ________	Hair Salon Fees		300
I. ________	Salaries Expense	130	
J. ________	Rent Expense	120	
K. ________	Advertising Expense	40	
	TOTALS	1,140	1,140

Exercises

MyAccountingLab

2-1. From the following, prepare a chart of accounts, using the same numbering system used in this chapter. *LO1 (10 min)*

Panasonic HD Television	Legal Fees
Salary Expense	L. Jones, Capital
Accounts Payable	Cash
Accounts Receivable	Advertising Expense
Repair Expense	L. Jones, Withdrawals

2-2. Record the following transaction into the transaction analysis chart: Sandy Pointer bought a new piece of computer equipment for $19,000, paying $3,000 down and charging the rest. *LO2 (5 min)*

2-3. Complete the following table. For each account listed on the left, fill in what category it belongs to, whether increases and decreases in the account are *LO2 (5 min)* marked on the debit or credit sides, and on which financial statement the account appears. A sample is provided.

Accounts Affected	Category	↑	↓	Appears on Which Financial Statements
Computer Supplies	Asset	Dr.	Cr.	Balance Sheet
Legal Fees Earned				
P. Rey, Withdrawals				
Accounts Payable				
Salaries Expense				
Auto				

LO2 (20 min)

2-4. Given the following accounts, complete the table by inserting appropriate numbers next to the individual transaction to indicate which account is debited and which account is credited.

1. Cash
2. Accounts Receivable
3. Equipment
4. Accounts Payable
5. B. Baker, Capital
6. B. Baker, Withdrawals
7. Plumbing Fees Earned
8. Salaries Expense
9. Advertising Expense
10. Supplies Expenses

Transaction		Rules Dr.	Rules Cr.
Example: **A.**	Paid salaries expense.	**8**	**1**
B.	Bob paid personal utilities bill from the company checkbook.		
C.	Advertising bill received but unpaid.		
D.	Received cash from plumbing fees.		
E.	Paid supplies expense.		
F.	Bob invested in additional equipment for the business.		
G.	Billed customers for plumbing services rendered.		
H.	Received one-half the balance from transaction G.		
I.	Bought equipment on account.		

LO4 (20 min)

2-5. From the trial balance of Hall's Cleaners on the following page (Fig. 2.6), prepare the following:

- Income statement
- Statement of owner's equity
- Balance sheet

MyAccountingLab

Group A Problems

LO2 (20 min)

2A-1. The following transactions occurred in the opening and operation of Bill's Delivery Service.

a. Bill O'Brien opened the delivery service by investing $21,000 from his personal savings account.

FIGURE 2.6

HALL'S CLEANERS
TRIAL BALANCE
JULY 31, 200X

	Dr.	Cr.
Cash	550 00	
Equipment	692 00	
Accounts Payable		455 00
J. Hall, Capital		800 00
J. Hall, Withdrawals	198 00	
Cleaning Fees		458 00
Salaries Expense	160 00	
Utilities Expense	113 00	
Totals	1713 00	1713 00

b. Purchased used Delivery Trucks on account, $9,000.
c. Rent expense due but unpaid, $900.
d. Received cash for Delivery Fees Earned, $1,400.
e. Billed a client on account, $150.
f. Bill withdrew cash for personal use, $400.

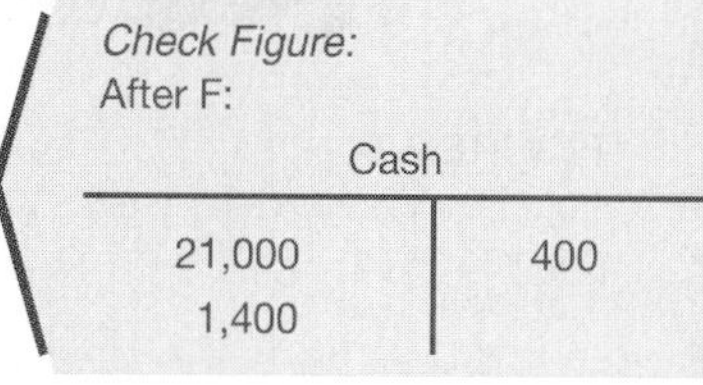

Check Figure:
After F:
Cash
21,000
1,400
400

Complete the transaction analysis chart in the *Study Guide and Working Papers*. The chart of accounts includes Cash; Accounts Receivable; Delivery Trucks; Accounts Payable; Bill O'Brien, Capital; Bill O'Brien, Withdrawals; Delivery Fees Earned; and Rent Expense.

2A-2. Bernie Pillows opened a consulting company, and the following transactions resulted: *LO2 (20 min)*

a. Bernie invested $20,000 in the consulting agency.
b. Bought office equipment on account, $5,000.
c. Agency received cash for consulting work that it completed for a client, $900.
d. Bernie paid a personal bill from the company checkbook, $90.
e. Paid advertising expense for the month, $400.
f. Rent expense for the month due but unpaid, $1,400.
g. Paid $1,000 as partial payment of what was owed from transaction B.

Check Figure:
After G:

Cash			
(A)	20,000	90	(D)
(C)	900	400	(E)
		1,000	(G)

As Bernie's accountant, analyze and record the transactions in T account form. Set up the T accounts and label each entry with the letter of the transaction.

Chart of Accounts

Assets	**Revenue**
Cash 111	Consulting Fees Earned 411
Office Equipment 121	
Liabilities	**Expenses**
Accounts Payable 211	Advertising Expense 511
	Rent Expense 512
Owner's Equity	
Bernie Pillows, Capital 311	
Bernie Pillows, Withdrawals 312	

2A-3. From the following T accounts of Barry's Cleaning Service, (a) record, foot and take the balances of the accounts in the *Study Guide and Working Papers* where appropriate, and (b) prepare a trial balance in proper form for May 31, 200X. *LO3 (20 min)*

Check Figure:
Trial Balance Total $16,100

Cash 111

Dr.	Cr.
(A) 7,000	(D) 200
(G) 3,500	(E) 200
	(F) 400
	(H) 200
	(I) 900

Accounts Payable 211

Dr.	Cr.
(D) 200	(C) 1,300

Cleaning Fees Earned 411

Dr.	Cr.
	(B) 8,000

Accounts Receivable 112

Dr.	Cr.
(B) 8,000	(G) 3,500

Barry Joy, Capital 311

Dr.	Cr.
	(A) 7,000

Rent Expense 511

Dr.	Cr.
(F) 400	

Office Equipment 121

Dr.	Cr.
(C) 1,300	
(H) 200	

Barry Joy, Withdrawals 312

Dr.	Cr.
(I) 900	

Utilities Expense 512

Dr.	Cr.
(E) 200	

LO4 (40 min)

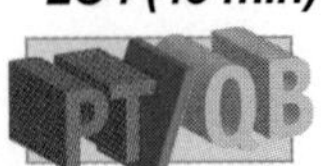

2A-4. From the trial balance of Gracie Lantz, Attorney-at-Law (Fig. 2.7), prepare (a) an income statement for the month of May, (b) a statement of owner's equity for the month ended May 31, and (c) a balance sheet as of May 31, 200X.

FIGURE 2.7

Check Figure:
Total Assets $6,400

GRACIE LANTZ, ATTORNEY-AT-LAW
TRIAL BALANCE
MAY 31, 200X

	Dr.	Cr.
Cash	5 0 0 0 00	
Accounts Receivable	6 5 0 00	
Office Equipment	7 5 0 00	
Accounts Payable		4 3 0 0 00
Salaries Payable		6 7 5 00
G. Lantz, Capital		1 2 7 5 00
G. Lantz, Withdrawals	3 0 0 00	
Revenue from Legal Fees		1 3 5 0 00
Utilities Expense	3 0 0 00	
Rent Expense	4 5 0 00	
Salaries Expense	1 5 0 00	
Totals	7 6 0 0 00	7 6 0 0 00

LO2, 3, 4 (60 min)

2A-5. The chart of accounts for Angel's Delivery Service is as follows:

Check Figure:
Total Trial Balance $38,100

Chart of Accounts

Assets	Revenue
Cash 111	Delivery Fees Earned 411
Accounts Receivable 112	**Expenses**
Office Equipment 121	Advertising Expense 511
Delivery Trucks 122	Gas Expense 512
Liabilities	Salaries Expense 513
Accounts Payable 211	Telephone Expense 514
Owner's Equity	
Alice Angel, Capital 311	
Alice Angel, Withdrawals 312	

Angel's Delivery Service completed the following transactions during the month of March:

Transaction A: Alice Angel invested $16,000 in the delivery service from her personal savings account.

Transaction B: Bought delivery trucks on account, $18,000.

Transaction C: Bought office equipment for cash, $600.

Transaction D: Paid advertising expense, $250.

Transaction E: Collected cash for delivery services rendered, $2,600.

Transaction F: Paid drivers' salaries, $900.

Transaction G: Paid gas expense for trucks, $1,200.

Transaction H: Performed delivery services for a customer on account, $800.

Transaction I: Telephone expense due but unpaid, $700.

Transaction J: Received $300 as partial payment of transaction H.

Transaction K: Alice withdrew cash for personal use, $300.

As Alice's newly employed accountant, you must

1. Set up T accounts in a ledger.
2. Record transactions in the T accounts. (Place the letter of the transaction next to the entry.)
3. Foot and take the balances of the T accounts where appropriate.
4. Prepare a trial balance at the end of March.
5. Prepare from the trial balance, in proper form, (a) an income statement for the month of March, (b) a statement of owner's equity, and (c) a balance sheet as of March 31, 200X.

Group B Problems

MyAccountingLab

2B-1. Bill O'Brien decided to open a delivery service. Record the following transactions into the transaction analysis charts: *LO2 (20 min)*

Transaction A: Bill invested $2,500 in the delivery service from her personal savings account.

Transaction B: Purchased a used delivery truck on account, $900.

Transaction C: Rent expense due but unpaid, $250.

Transaction D: Performed delivery services for cash, $1,200.

Transaction E: Billed clients for deliveries rendered, $700.

Transaction F: Bill paid his home heating bill from the company checkbook, $275.

Check Figure:
After F:

Cash			
(A)	2,500	275	(F)
(D)	1,200		

The chart of accounts for the shop includes Cash; Accounts Receivable; Delivery Truck; Accounts Payable; Bill O'Brien, Capital; Bill O'Brien, Withdrawals; Shuttle Fees Earned; and Rent Expense.

2B-2. Bernie Pillow established a new consulting company. Record the following transactions for Bernie in T account form. Label each entry with the letter of the transaction. *LO2 (20 min)*

Transaction A: Bernie invested $20,000 in the consulting company from his personal bank account.

Transaction B: Bought office equipment on account, $6,000.

Transaction C: Company rendered consulting to Jensen Corp. and received cash, $1,200.

Transaction D: Bernie withdrew cash for personal use, $200.

Check Figure:
After G:

Cash			
(A)	20,000	200	(D)
(C)	1,200	600	(E)
		400	(G)

Transaction E: Paid advertising expense, $600.
Transaction F: Rent expense due but unpaid, $500.
Transaction G: Paid $400 in partial payment of transaction B.

The chart of accounts includes Cash, 111; Office Equipment, 121; Accounts Payable, 211; Bernie Pillows, Capital, 311; Bernie Pillows, Withdrawals, 312; Consulting Fees Earned, 411; Advertising Expense, 511; and Rent Expense, 512.

LO3 (20 min)

2B-3. From the following T accounts of Barry's Cleaning Service, (a) foot and take the balances of the accounts in the *Study Guide and Working Papers* where appropriate and (b) prepare a trial balance for May 31, 200X.

Cash 111	
(A) 10,000	(C) 4,000
(F) 4,000	(D) 310
(G) 2,000	(E) 50
	(H) 600

Accounts Receivable 112	
(G) 2,000	

Office Equipment 121	
(B) 2,000	
(C) 4,000	

Check Figure:
Trial Balance Total $20,000

Accounts Payable 211	
	(B) 2,000

Barry Joy, Capital 311	
	(A) 10,000

Barry Joy, Withdrawals 312	
(H) 600	

Cleaning Fees Earned 411	
	(F) 4,000
	(G) 4,000

Rent Expense 511	
(D) 310	

Utilities Expense 512	
(E) 50	

LO4 (40 min)

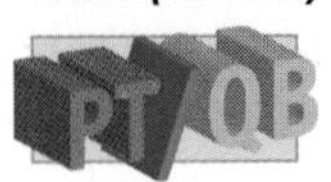

2B-4. From the trial balance of Gracie Lantz, Attorney-at-Law (Fig. 2-8), prepare (a) an income statement for the month of May, (b) a statement of owner's equity for the month ended May 31, and (c) a balance sheet as of May 31, 200X.

FIGURE 2.8

Check Figure:
Total Assets $10,800

GRACIE LANTZ, ATTORNEY-AT-LAW
TRIAL BALANCE
MAY 31, 200X

	Debit	Credit
Cash	6 0 0 0 00	
Accounts Receivable	2 4 0 0 00	
Office Equipment	2 4 0 0 00	
Accounts Payable		2 0 0 00
Salaries Payable		6 0 0 00
G. Lantz, Capital		4 0 0 0 00
G. Lantz, Withdrawals	2 0 0 0 00	
Revenue from Legal Fees		8 8 0 0 00
Utilities Expense	1 0 0 00	
Rent Expense	3 0 0 00	
Salaries Expense	4 0 0 00	
Totals	13 6 0 0 00	13 6 0 0 00

LO2, 3, 4 (60 min)

2B-5. The chart of accounts of Angel's Delivery Service includes the following: Cash, 111; Accounts Receivable, 112; Office Equipment, 121; Delivery Trucks, 122; Accounts Payable, 211; Alice Angel, Capital, 311; Alice Angel, Withdrawals, 312; Delivery Fees Earned, 411; Advertising Expense, 511; Gas Expense, 512; Salaries Expense, 513; and Telephone Expense, 514. The following transactions resulted for Angel's Delivery Service during the month of March:

Check Figure:
Trial Balance Total $84,300

Transaction A: Alice invested $40,000 in the business from her personal savings account.

Transaction B: Bought delivery trucks on account, $25,000.

Transaction C: Advertising bill received but unpaid, $800.

Transaction D: Bought office equipment for cash, $2,500.

Transaction E: Received cash for delivery services rendered, $13,000.

Transaction F: Paid salaries expense, $1,850.

Transaction G: Paid gas expense for company trucks, $750.

Transaction H: Billed customers for delivery services rendered, $5,500.

Transaction I: Paid telephone bill, $400.

Transaction J: Received $1,600 as partial payment of transaction H.

Transaction K: Alice paid her home telephone bill from company checkbook, $88.

As Alice's newly employed accountant, you must

1. Set up T accounts in a ledger.
2. Record transactions in the T accounts. (Place the letter of the transaction next to the entry.)
3. Foot the T accounts where appropriate.
4. Prepare a trial balance at the end of March.
5. Prepare from the trial balance, in proper form, (a) an income statement for the month of March, (b) a statement of owner's equity, and (c) a balance sheet as of March 31, 200X.

ON-THE-JOB-TRAINING

T-1. Andy Leaf is a careless bookkeeper. He is having a terrible time getting his trial balance to balance. Andy has asked for your assistance in preparing a correct trial balance. The following is the incorrect trial balance:

LO4 (20 min)

RANCH COMPANY
TRIAL BALANCE
JUNE 30, 200X

	Dr.	Cr.
Cash	510 00	
Accounts Receivable		635 00
Office Equipment	360 00	
Accounts Payable	110 00	
Wages Payable	10 00	
H. Clo, Capital	635 00	
H. Clo, Withdrawals	1440 00	
Professional Fees		2240 00
Rent Expense		240 00
Advertising Expense	25 00	
Totals	3090 00	3115 00

FIGURE 2.9 Incorrect Trial Balance

Facts you have discovered:

- Debits to the Cash account were $2,640; credits to the Cash account were $2,150.
- Amy Hall paid $15 but was not updated in Accounts Receivable.
- A purchase of office equipment for $5 on account was never recorded in the ledger.
- Revenue was understated in the ledger by $180.

Show how these errors affected the ending balances for the accounts involved and explain how the trial balance will indeed balance once they are corrected.

Tell Ranch Company how it can avoid this problem in the future. Write your recommendations.

LO3, 4 (20 min)

T-2. Cookie Mejias, owner of Mejias Company, asked her bookkeeper how each of the following situations will affect the totals of the trial balance and individual ledger accounts:

1. An $850 payment for a desk was recorded as a debit to Office Equipment, $85, and a credit to Cash, $85.
2. A payment of $300 to a creditor was recorded as a debit to Accounts Payable, $300, and a credit to Cash, $100.
3. The collection on an Accounts Receivable for $400 was recorded as a debit to Cash, $400, and a credit to C. Mejias, Capital, $400.
4. The payment of a liability for $400 was recorded as a debit to Accounts Payable, $40, and a credit to Supplies, $40.
5. A purchase of equipment of $800 was recorded as a debit to Supplies, $800, and a credit to Cash, $800.
6. A payment of $95 to a creditor was recorded as a debit to Accounts Payable, $95, and a credit to Cash, $59.

What did the bookkeeper tell her? Which accounts were overstated, and which were understated? Which were correct? Explain in writing how mistakes can be avoided in the future.

FINANCIAL REPORT PROBLEM

LO4 (5 min)

Reading the Kellogg's Report

Go to Appendix A and find the balance sheet of Kellogg's. Did Kellogg's Accounts Payable go up or down from 2005 to 2006? What does this change mean? Into what category does Accounts Payable fall by rules of debit and credit? Which side of the T account would make it increase?

INTERNET PROJECT

Staples

Go to the Web and search: Annual Report Staples 2008.
Click on Investors Relations.
List out the latest news Staples is providing to its investors.
Order a free annual report.

CONTINUING PROBLEM

MyAccountingLab

LO2, 3, 4 (60 min)

Sanchez Computer Center

The Sanchez Computer Center created its chart of accounts as follows:

Chart of Accounts as of July 1, 200X

Assets		**Revenue**	
1000	Cash	4000	Service Revenue
1020	Accounts Receivable	**Expenses**	
1030	Supplies	5010	Advertising Expense
1080	Computer Shop Equipment	5020	Rent Expense
1090	Office Equipment	5030	Utilities Expense
Liabilities		5040	Phone Expense
2000	Accounts Payable	5050	Supplies Expense
Owner's Equity		5060	Insurance Expense
3000	Freedman, Capital	5070	Postage Expense
3010	Freedman, Withdrawals		

You will use this chart of accounts to complete the Continuing Problem.

The following problem continues from Chapter 1. The balances as of July 31 have been brought forward in your *Study Guide and Working Papers*.

Assignment

1. Set up T accounts in a ledger.
2. Record transactions k through s in the appropriate T accounts.
3. Foot and take the balances of the T accounts where appropriate.
4. Prepare a trial balance at the end of August.
5. Prepare from the trial balance an income statement, statement of owner's equity, and a balance sheet for the two months ending with August 31, 200X.

k. Received the phone bill for the month of July, $155.
l. Paid $150 (check #8099) for insurance for the month.
m. Paid $200 (check #8100) of the amount due from transaction d in Chapter 1.
n. Paid advertising expense for the month, $1,400 (check #8101).
o. Billed a client (Jeannine Sparks) for services rendered, $850.
p. Collected $900 for services rendered.
q. Paid the electric bill in full for the month of July (check #8102, transaction h, Chapter 1).
r. Paid cash (check #8103) for $50 in stamps.
s. Purchased $200 worth of supplies from Computer Connection on credit.

SUBWAY Case

DEBITS ON THE LEFT . . .

LO2 (20 min)

When Stan took the big leap from being an employee to a Subway owner, the thing that terrified him most was *not* the part about managing people—that was one of his strengths as a marketing manager. Why, at Xellent Media, 40 sales reps reported to him! No, Stan was terrified of having to manage the accounts. Subway restaurant owners have so many accounts to deal with: food costs, payroll, rent, utilities, supplies, advertising, promotion, and, biggest of all, cash. It's critical for them to keep debits and credits straight. If not, both they and Subway could lose a lot of money, quickly.

Even though Stan got some intense training in accounting and bookkeeping at Subway University, he still felt shaky about doing his own books. When he confided his fears to Mariah Washington, his field consultant, she suggested he hire an accountant. "You need to play to your strengths," said Mariah, and she told Stan, "More and more owners are using accountants, and almost all owners of multiple franchises do. In fact, some accountants actually specialize in handling Subway accounts for these multirestaurant owners."

Even though Stan decided to hire his cousin, Lila, to do his accounting, he still needs to feed her the right data so she can calculate his T accounts. Like many small business owners, Stan enters data into an accounting software program such as QuickBooks or Peachtree, which he then uploads to his accountant, who edits it and reviews it for accuracy. Several times in the beginning Stan mistakenly debited both cash and supplies when he paid for orders of paper cups, bread dough, and other supplies.

Lila urged Stan to review the rules for recording debits and credits. She even told him to practice for a while using a paper ledger. "On the computer debits and credits are not as visible as they are with your paper system. Since you only enter the payables, the computer does the other side of the balance sheet. So you have to bone up on debits and credits to ensure that your Peachtree data are correct."

Discussion Questions

1. Why is the cash account so important in Stan's business?
2. Why do you think that most owners of the larger shops use accountants to do their books instead of doing the accounting themselves?
3. Is the difference between debits and credits important to Subway restaurant owners who don't do their own books?

3

Beginning the Accounting Cycle

DID YOU KNOW? In 2006 Property and Equipment represented 55% of the total assets of Continental Airlines. Visit *www.continental.com* to find more information about Continental.

LEARNING OBJECTIVES

1. Journalizing: analyzing and recording business transactions into a journal.
2. Posting: transferring information from a journal to a ledger.
3. Preparing a trial balance.

Companies like Continental have to perform certain accounting procedures. The normal accounting procedures that are performed over a period of time are called the **accounting cycle.** The accounting cycle takes place in a period of time called an **accounting period.** An accounting period is the period of time covered by the income statement. Although it can be any time period up to one year (e.g., one month or three months), most businesses use a one-year accounting period. The year can be either a **calendar year** (January 1 through December 31) or a **fiscal year.**

A fiscal year is an accounting period that runs for any 12 consecutive months, so it can be the same as a calendar year. Big Dollar and Aeropostale, Inc., end their accounting period on January 31. A business can choose any fiscal year that is convenient. For example, some retailers may decide to end their fiscal year when inventories and business activity are at a low point, such as after the Christmas season. This period is called a **natural business year.** Using a natural business year allows the business to count its year-end inventory when it is easiest to do so.

Businesses would not be able to operate successfully if they only prepared financial reports at the end of their calendar or fiscal year. For more timely information, most businesses prepare **interim reports** on a monthly, quarterly, or semiannual basis.

In this chapter, as well as in Chapters 4 and 5, we follow Brenda Clark's new business, Clark's Word Processing Services. We follow the normal accounting procedures that the business performs over a period of time. Clark has chosen to use a fiscal period of January 1 to December 31, which also is the calendar year.

LO1 Learning Unit 3-1 Analyzing and Recording Business Transactions into a Journal: Steps 1 and 2 of the Accounting Cycle

The General Journal

Chapter 2 taught us how to analyze and record business transactions into T accounts, or ledger accounts. Recording a debit in an account on one page of the ledger and recording the corresponding credit on a different page of the ledger, however, can make it difficult to find errors. It would be much easier if all the business's transactions were located in the same place. That is the function of the **journal** or **general journal.** Transactions are entered in the journal in chronological order (January 1, 8, 15, etc.), and then this recorded information is used to update the ledger accounts. In computerized accounting, a journal may be recorded on disk or tape.

A business uses a journal to record transactions in chronological order. A ledger accumulates information from a journal. The journal and the ledger are in two different books.

We will use a general journal, the simplest form of a journal, to record the transactions of Clark's Word Processing Services. A transaction [debit(s) + credit(s)] that has been analyzed and recorded in a journal is called a **journal entry.** The process of recording the journal entry into the journal is called **journalizing.**

The journal is called the **book of original entry** because it contains the first formal information about the business transactions. The ledger is known as the **book of final entry** because the information the journal contains will be transferred to the ledger. Like the ledger, the journal may be a bound or loose-leaf book. Each of the journal pages looks like the one in Figure 3.1. The pages of the journal are numbered consecutively from page 1. Keep in mind that the journal and the ledger are separate books.

Relationship between the Journal and the Chart of Accounts The accountant must refer to the business's chart of accounts for the account name that is to be used in the journal. Every company has its own "unique" chart of accounts.

The following chart of accounts for Clark's Word Processing Services lists the accounts used in the business. By the end of Chapter 5, we will have discussed each of these accounts.

Note that we will continue to use transaction analysis charts as a teaching aid in the journalizing process.

CLARK'S WORD PROCESSING SERVICES GENERAL JOURNAL				
				Page 1
Date	Account Titles and Description	PR	Dr.	Cr.

FIGURE 3.1 The General Journal

Clark's Word Processing Services
Chart of Accounts

Assets (100–199)		**Owner's Equity (300–399)**	
111	Cash	311	Brenda Clark, Capital
112	Accounts Receivable	312	Brenda Clark, Withdrawals
114	Office Supplies	313	Income Summary
115	Prepaid Rent	**Revenue (400–499)**	
121	Word Processing Equipment	411	Word Processing Fees
122	Accumulated Depreciation,	**Expenses (500–599)**	
	Word Processing Equipment	511	Office Salaries Expense
Liabilities (200–299)		512	Advertising Expense
211	Accounts Payable	513	Telephone Expense
212	Salaries Payable	514	Office Supplies Expense
		515	Rent Expense
		516	Depreciation Expense,
			Word Processing Equipment

Journalizing the Transactions of Clark's Word Processing Services Certain formalities must be followed in making journal entries:

- The debit portion of the transaction always is recorded first.
- The credit portion of a transaction is indented a ½ inch and placed below the debit portion.
- The explanation of the journal entry follows immediately after the credit and 1 inch from the date column.
- A one-line space follows each transaction and explanation. This makes the journal easier to read, and there is less chance of mixing transactions.
- Finally, as always, the total amount of debits must equal the total amount of credits. The same format is used for each of the entries in the journal.
- Each transaction must affect at least two different accounts.

MAY 1, 200X: BRENDA CLARK BEGAN THE BUSINESS BY INVESTING $10,000 IN CASH			
1 Accounts Affected	2 Category	3 ↓ ↑	4 Rules of Dr. and Cr.
Cash	Asset	↑	Dr.
Brenda Clark, Capital	Capital	↑	Cr.

FIGURE 3.2 Owner Investment

For now the PR (posting reference) column is blank; we discuss it later.

CLARK'S WORD PROCESSING SERVICES GENERAL JOURNAL					
					Page 1
Date		Account Titles and Description	PR	Dr.	Cr.
200X May	1	Cash		10 000 00	
		Brenda Clark, Capital			10 000 00
		Initial investment of cash by owner			

Let's now look at the structure of this journal entry (Fig. 3.2). The entry contains the following information:

1. Year of the journal entry	200X
2. Month of the journal entry	May
3. Day of the journal entry	1
4. Name(s) of accounts debited	Cash
5. Name(s) of accounts credited	Brenda Clark, Capital
6. Explanation of transaction	Investment of cash
7. Amount of debit(s)	$10,000
8. Amount of credit(s)	$10,000

MAY 1: PURCHASED WORD PROCESSING EQUIPMENT FROM BEN CO. FOR $6,000, PAYING $1,000 AND PROMISING TO PAY THE BALANCE WITHIN 30 DAYS

Note that in this compound entry we have one debit and two credits, but the total amount of debits equals the total amount of credits.

1 Accounts Affected	2 Category	3 ↓ ↑	4 Rules of Dr. and Cr.
Word Processing Equipment	Asset	↑	Dr.
Cash	Asset	↓	Cr.
Accounts Payable	Liability	↑	Cr.

This transaction affects three accounts. When a journal entry has more than two accounts, it is called a **compound journal entry.**

In this entry, only the day is entered in the date column because the year and month were entered at the top of the page from the first transaction. This information doesn't need to be repeated until a new page is needed or a change of months occurs.

FIGURE 3.3 Purchase of Equipment

Date		Account Titles and Description	PR	Dr.	Cr.
	1	Word Processing Equipment		6 000 00	
		Cash			1 000 00
		Accounts Payable			5 000 00
		Purchase of equipment from Ben Co.			

MAY 1: RENTED OFFICE SPACE, PAYING $1,200 IN ADVANCE FOR THE FIRST THREE MONTHS			
1 Accounts Affected	2 Category	3 ↓ ↑	4 Rules of Dr. and Cr.
Prepaid Rent	Asset	↑	Dr.
Cash	Asset	↓	Cr.

Rent paid in advance is an asset.

In this transaction Clark gains an asset called prepaid rent and gives up an asset, cash. The prepaid rent does not become an expense until it expires.

FIGURE 3.4 Rent Paid in Advance

	1	Prepaid Rent		1200 00	
		Cash			1200 00
		Rent paid in advance—3 mos.			

MAY 3: PURCHASED OFFICE SUPPLIES FROM NORRIS CO. ON ACCOUNT, $600			
1 Accounts Affected	2 Category	3 ↓ ↑	4 Rules of Dr. and Cr.
Office Supplies	Asset	↑	Dr.
Accounts Payable	Liability	↑	Cr.

Supplies become an expense when used up.

Remember, supplies are an asset when they are purchased. Once they are used up or consumed in the operation of business, they become an expense.

FIGURE 3.5 Purchased Supplies on Account

	3	Office Supplies		600 00	
		Accounts Payable			600 00
		Purchase of supplies on account			
		from Norris			

MAY 7: COMPLETED SALES PROMOTION PIECES FOR A CLIENT AND IMMEDIATELY COLLECTED $3,000			
1 Accounts Affected	2 Category	3 ↓ ↑	4 Rules of Dr. and Cr.
Cash	Asset	↑	Dr.
Word Processing Fees	Revenue	↑	Cr.

FIGURE 3.6 Services Rendered

	7	Cash		3000 00	
		Word Processing Fees			3000 00
		Cash received for services rendered			

MAY 13: PAID OFFICE SALARIES, $650			
1 Accounts Affected	2 Category	3 ↓ ↑	4 Rules of Dr. and Cr.
Office Salaries Expense	Expense	↑	Dr.
Cash	Asset	↓	Cr.

FIGURE 3.7 Paid Salaries

Date	Account Titles and Description	Dr.	Cr.
13	Office Salaries Expense	650 00	
	Cash		650 00
	Payment of office salaries		

Remember, expenses are recorded when they are incurred, no matter when they are paid.

MAY 18: ADVERTISING BILL FROM AL'S NEWS CO. COMES IN BUT IS NOT PAID, $250			
1 Accounts Affected	2 Category	3 ↓ ↑	4 Rules of Dr. and Cr.
Advertising Expense	Expense	↑	Dr.
Accounts Payable	Liability	↑	Cr.

FIGURE 3.8 Advertising Bill

Date	Account Titles and Description	Dr.	Cr.
18	Advertising Expense	250 00	
	Accounts Payable		250 00
	Bill in but not paid from Al's News		

Keep in mind that as withdrawals increase, owner's equity decreases.

MAY 20: BRENDA CLARK WROTE A CHECK ON THE BANK ACCOUNT OF THE BUSINESS TO PAY HER HOME MORTGAGE PAYMENT OF $625			
1 Accounts Affected	2 Category	3 ↓ ↑	4 Rules of Dr. and Cr.
Brenda Clark, Withdrawals	Withdrawals	↑	Dr.
Cash	Asset	↓	Cr.

FIGURE 3.9 Personal Withdrawal

Date	Account Titles and Description	Dr.	Cr.
20	Brenda Clark, Withdrawals	625 00	
	Cash		625 00
	Personal withdrawal of cash		

Reminder: Revenue is recorded when it is earned, no matter when the cash is actually received.

MAY 22: BILLED MORRIS COMPANY FOR A SOPHISTICATED WORD PROCESSING JOB, $5,000			
1 Accounts Affected	2 Category	3 ↓ ↑	4 Rules of Dr. and Cr.
Accounts Receivable	Asset	↑	Dr.
Word Processing Fees	Revenue	↑	Cr.

			PR	Dr.	Cr.
	22	Accounts Receivable		5 0 0 0 00	
		Word Processing Fees			5 0 0 0 00
		Billed Morris Co. for fees earned			

FIGURE 3.10 Fees Earned

MAY 27: PAID OFFICE SALARIES, $650

1 Accounts Affected	2 Category	3 ↓ ↑	4 Rules of Dr. and Cr.
Office Salaries Expense	Expense	↑	Dr.
Cash	Asset	↓	Cr.

FIGURE 3.11 Paid Salaries

CLARK'S WORD PROCESSING SERVICES
GENERAL JOURNAL

Page 2

Date		Account Titles and Description	PR	Dr.	Cr.
200X May	27*	Office Salaries Expense		6 5 0 00	
		Cash			6 5 0 00
		Payment of office salaries			

*Note that this is a new page, so the year and month are repeated.

MAY 28: PAID HALF THE AMOUNT OWED FOR WORD PROCESSING EQUIPMENT PURCHASED MAY 1 FROM BEN CO., $2,500

1 Accounts Affected	2 Category	3 ↓ ↑	4 Rules of Dr. and Cr.
Accounts Payable	Liability	↓	Dr.
Cash	Asset	↓	Cr.

FIGURE 3.12 Partial Payment

			PR	Dr.	Cr.
	28	Accounts Payable		2 5 0 0 00	
		Cash			2 5 0 0 00
		Paid half the amount owed Ben Co.			

MAY 29: RECEIVED AND PAID TELEPHONE BILL, $220

1 Accounts Affected	2 Category	3 ↓ ↑	4 Rules of Dr. and Cr.
Telephone Expense	Expense	↑	Dr.
Cash	Asset	↓	Cr.

FIGURE 3.13 Paid Telephone

			PR	Dr.	Cr.
	29	Telephone Expense		2 2 0 00	
		Cash			2 2 0 00
		Paid telephone bill			

This concludes the journal transactions of Clark's Word Processing Services.

LEARNING UNIT 3-1 REVIEW

AT THIS POINT you should be able to

- Define an accounting cycle.
- Define and explain the relationship of the accounting period to the income statement.
- Compare and contrast a calendar year to a fiscal year.
- Explain the term *natural business year.*
- Explain the function of interim reports.
- Define and state the purpose of a journal.
- Compare and contrast a book of original entry to a book of final entry.
- Differentiate between a chart of accounts and a journal.
- Journalize a business transaction.
- Explain a compound entry.

Self-Review Quiz 3-1

For additional help go to www.pearsonhighered.com/slater

The following are the transactions of Lowe's Repair Service. Journalize the transactions in proper form. The chart of accounts includes Cash; Accounts Receivable; Prepaid Rent; Repair Supplies; Repair Equipment; Accounts Payable; A. Lowe, Capital; A. Lowe, Withdrawals; Repair Fees Earned; Salaries Expense; Advertising Expense; and Supplies Expense.

200X		
June	1	A. Lowe invested $7,000 cash and $5,000 of repair equipment in the business.
	1	Paid two months' rent in advance, $1,200.
	4	Bought repair supplies from Melvin Co. on account, $600. (These supplies have not yet been consumed or used up.)
	15	Performed repair work, received $600 in cash, and had to bill Doe Co. for remaining balance of $300.
	18	A. Lowe paid his home telephone bill, $50, with a check from the company.
	20	Advertising bill for $400 from Jones Co. received but payment not due yet. (Advertising has already appeared in the newspaper.)
	24	Paid salaries, $1,400.

Solution to Self-Review Quiz 3-1

FIGURE 3.14 Transactions Journalized

LOWE'S REPAIR SERVICE
GENERAL JOURNAL

Page 1

Date		Account Titles and Description	PR	Dr.	Cr.
200X					
June	1	Cash		7 0 0 0 00	
		Repair Equipment		5 0 0 0 00	
		A. Lowe, Capital			12 0 0 0 00
		Owner investment			
	1	Prepaid Rent		1 2 0 0 00	
		Cash			1 2 0 0 00
		Rent paid in advance—2 mos.			
	4	Repair Supplies		6 0 0 00	
		Accounts Payable			6 0 0 00
		Purchase on account from Melvin Co.			
	15	Cash		6 0 0 00	
		Accounts Receivable		3 0 0 00	
		Repair Fees Earned			9 0 0 00
		Performed repairs for Doe Co.			
	18	A. Lowe, Withdrawals		5 0 00	
		Cash			5 0 00
		Personal withdrawal			
	20	Advertising Expense		4 0 0 00	
		Accounts Payable			4 0 0 00
		Advertising bill from Jones Co.			
	24	Salaries Expense		1 4 0 0 00	
		Cash			1 4 0 0 00
		Paid salaries			

NEED HELP?

Let's review first: When recording transactions into a general journal the debit(s) will be against the date column and the credit(s) will be indented. These titles will come from the chart of accounts. The explanation line will then be indented below the last credit entry. The sum of the left side (Dr.) must equal the sum of the right side (Cr.) for each transaction.

Here are the mind process charts for each transaction. Be sure to remember that the accounts affected come from the chart of accounts. You have six categories: assets, liabilities, capital, withdrawals, revenues, and expenses. You must ask yourself what the company is getting and how it is getting it. Remember to think of expenses and withdrawals as increasing, resulting in a decrease to owner's equity.

June 1	Cash	Asset	↑	Dr.
	Repair Equip.	Asset	↑	Dr.
	A. Lowe, Cap.	Capital	↑	Cr.

Debits are listed first against the date column and credits are indented. This is an investment by the owner. The month is written because the month starts a new page.

1	Prepaid Rent	Asset	↑	Dr.
	Cash	Asset	↓	Cr.

This is a shift in assets, more rent paid in advance by cash. Note that the month is not repeated.

4	Repair Supplies	Asset	↑	Dr.
	Accounts Payable	Liability	↑	Cr.

This is an example of buy now and pay later. Supplies will not be an expense until they are used up.

15	Cash	Asset	↑	Dr.
	Acc. Receiv.	Asset	↑	Dr.
	Rep. Fees Earn.	Revenue	↑	Cr.

Here we did the work and got some money as well as some promises that the customer will pay later. Note how the two debits are against the date column and the credit is indented.

18	A. Lowe, Withd.	Withdr.	↑	Dr.
	Cash	Asset	↓	Cr.

The owner increases her withdrawals for personal use and the end result is that the business has less cash.

20	Advertising Exp.	Expense	↑	Dr.
	Accounts Pay.	Liability	↑	Cr.

An expense has been incurred but is not paid for. This expense has created a liability. Think of expenses as always increasing.

24	Salaries Exp.	Expense	↑	Dr.
	Cash	Asset	↓	Cr.

Here the expense is increasing and it is being paid for in cash.

LO2 Learning Unit 3-2 Posting to the Ledger: Step 3 of the Accounting Cycle

The general journal serves a particular purpose: It puts every transaction the business does in one place. It cannot do certain things, though. For example, if you were asked to find the balance of the cash account from the general journal, you would have to go through the entire journal and look for only the cash entries. Then you would have to add up the debits and credits for the Cash account and determine the difference between the two.

What we really need to do to find balances of accounts is to transfer the information from the journal to the ledger. This process is called **posting.** In the ledger we accumulate an ending balance for each account so that we can prepare financial statements.

Accounts Payable					Account No. 211	
					Balance	
Date		Explanation	Post. Ref.	Debit	Credit	Debit	Credit
200X							
May	1		GJ1		5000 00		5000 00
	3		GJ1		600 00		5600 00
	18		GJ1		250 00		5850 00
	28		GJ2	2500 00			3350 00

FIGURE 3.15 Four-Column Account

$5,000 Cr. + $600 Cr. = $5,600 Cr.
Cr. + Cr. = Cr.
Dr. + Dr. = Dr.

In Chapter 2 we used the T account form to make our ledger entries. T accounts are simple, but they are not used in the real business world; they are only used for demonstration purposes. In practice, accountants often use a **four-column account** form that includes a column for the business's running balance. Figure 3.15 shows a standard four-column account. We use this format in the text from now on.

Posting is automatic when using QuickBooks and Peachtree software programs. When you select Save in a transaction, the accounts are immediately updated.

Posting

Now let's look at how to post the transactions of Clark's Word Processing Services from its journal. The diagram in Figure 3.16 shows how to post the cash line from the journal to the ledger. The steps in the posting process are numbered and illustrated in the figure.

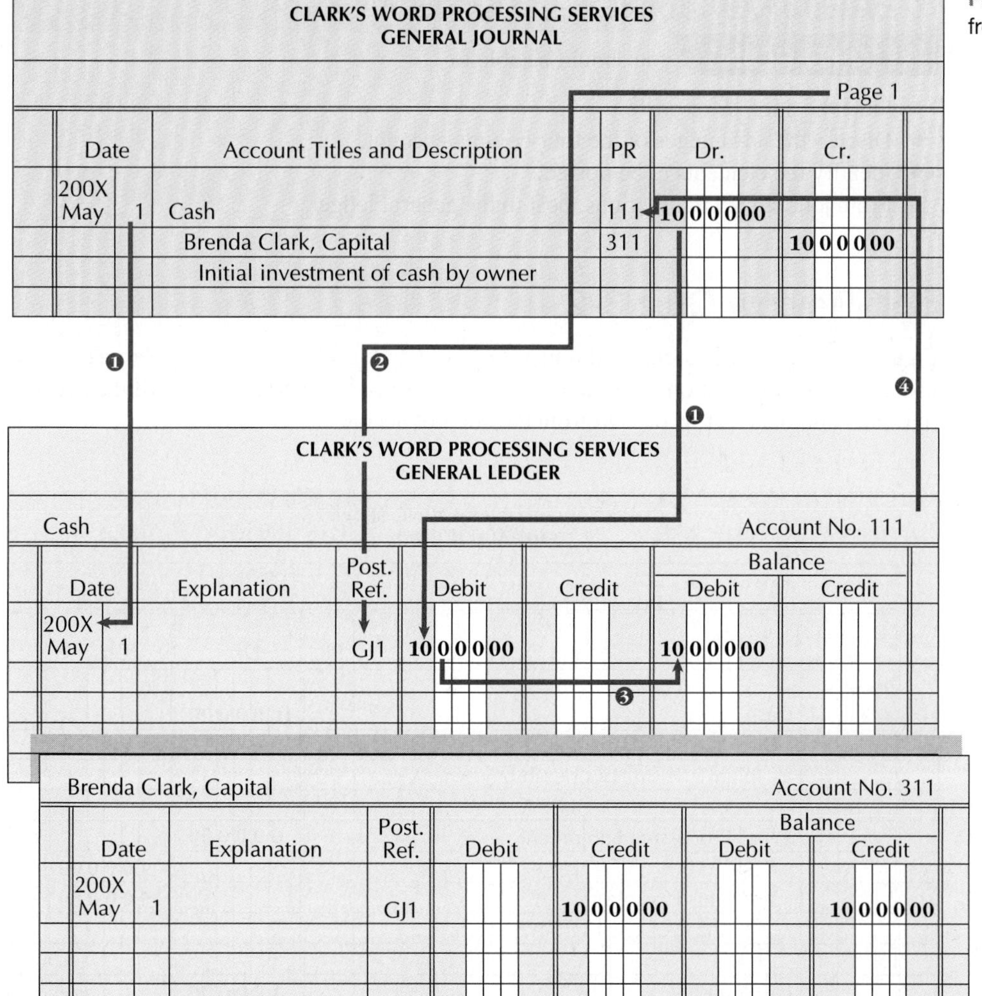

CLARK'S WORD PROCESSING SERVICES
GENERAL JOURNAL

Page 1

Date		Account Titles and Description	PR	Dr.	Cr.
200X					
May	1	Cash	111	10000 00	
		Brenda Clark, Capital	311		10000 00
		Initial investment of cash by owner			

CLARK'S WORD PROCESSING SERVICES
GENERAL LEDGER

Cash						Account No. 111	
						Balance	
Date		Explanation	Post. Ref.	Debit	Credit	Debit	Credit
200X							
May	1		GJ1	10000 00		10000 00	

Brenda Clark, Capital						Account No. 311	
						Balance	
Date		Explanation	Post. Ref.	Debit	Credit	Debit	Credit
200X							
May	1		GJ1		10000 00		10000 00

FIGURE 3.16 How to Post from Journal to Ledger

Step 1 In the Cash account in the ledger, record the date (May 1, 200X) and the amount of the entry ($10,000).

Step 2 Record the page number of the journal "GJ1" in the posting reference (PR) column of the Cash account.

Step 3 Calculate the new balance of the account. To keep a running balance in each account, as you would in your personal checkbook, take the present balance in the account on the previous line and add or subtract the transaction as necessary to arrive at your new balance.

Step 4 Record the account number of Cash (111) in the posting reference (PR) column of the journal. This listing is known as **cross-referencing.**

The same sequence of steps occurs for each line in the journal. In a manual system like Clark's, the debits and credits in the journal may be posted in the order they were recorded, or all the debits may be posted first and then all the credits. If Clark's used a computer system, the program menu would post at the press of a button.

Using Posting References The posting references are helpful. In the journal, the PR column tells us which transactions have or have not been posted and also to which accounts they were posted. In the ledger, the posting reference leads us back to the original transaction in its entirety, so we can see why the debit or credit was recorded and what other accounts were affected. (It leads us back to the original transaction by identifying the journal and the page in the journal from which the information came.)

LEARNING UNIT 3-2 REVIEW

Accounting Cycle Tutorial

AT THIS POINT you should be able to

- State the purpose of posting.
- Discuss the advantages of the four-column account.
- Identify the elements to be posted.
- From journalized transactions, post to the general ledger.

Self-Review Quiz 3-2

Figure 3.17 shows the journalized transactions of Clark's Word Processing Services. Your task is to post information to the ledger. The ledger in your workbook has all the account titles and numbers that were used from the chart of accounts.

FIGURE 3.17 Journalized Entries

CLARK'S WORD PROCESSING SERVICES
GENERAL JOURNAL

Page 1

Date		Account Titles and Description	PR	Dr.	Cr.
200X May	1	Cash		10 0 0 0 00	
		Brenda Clark, Capital			10 0 0 0 00
		Initial investment of cash by owner			
	1	Word Processing Equipment		6 0 0 0 00	
		Cash			1 0 0 0 00
		Accounts Payable			5 0 0 0 00
		Purchase of equip. from Ben Co.			
	1	Prepaid Rent		1 2 0 0 00	
		Cash			1 2 0 0 00
		Rent paid in advance (3 months)			

FIGURE 3.17 *(continued)*

CLARK'S WORD PROCESSING SERVICES
GENERAL JOURNAL

Page 1

Date		Account Titles and Description	PR	Dr.	Cr.
	3	Office Supplies		60000	
		Accounts Payable			60000
		Purchase of supplies on acct. from Norris			
	7	Cash		300000	
		Word Processing Fees			300000
		Cash received for services rendered			
	13	Office Salaries Expense		65000	
		Cash			65000
		Payment of office salaries			
	18	Advertising Expense		25000	
		Accounts Payable			25000
		Bill received but not paid from Al's News			
	20	Brenda Clark, Withdrawals		62500	
		Cash			62500
		Personal withdrawal of cash			
	22	Accounts Receivable		500000	
		Word Processing Fees			500000
		Billed Morris Co. for fees earned			

FIGURE 3.17 *(continued)*

CLARK'S WORD PROCESSING SERVICES
GENERAL JOURNAL

Page 2

Date		Account Titles and Description	PR	Dr.	Cr.
200X May	27	Office Salaries Expense		65000	
		Cash			65000
		Payment of office salaries			
	28	Accounts Payable		250000	
		Cash			250000
		Paid half the amount owed Ben Co.			
	29	Telephone Expense		22000	
		Cash			22000
		Paid telephone bill			

Solution to Self-Review Quiz 3-2

FIGURE 3.18 Posting From Journal to the Ledger Using PR Columns

CLARK'S WORD PROCESSING SERVICES
GENERAL JOURNAL

Page 1

Date		Account Titles and Description	PR	Dr.	Cr.
200X May	1	Cash	111	10 000 00	
		Brenda Clark, Capital	311		10 000 00
		Initial investment of cash by owner			
	1	Word Processing Equipment	121	6 000 00	
		Cash	111		1 000 00
		Accounts Payable	211		5 000 00
		Purchase of equip. from Ben Co.			
	1	Prepaid Rent	115	1 200 00	
		Cash	111		1 200 00
		Rent paid in advance (3 months)			
	3	Office Supplies	114	600 00	
		Accounts Payable	211		600 00
		Purchase of supplies on acct. from Norris			
	7	Cash	111	3 000 00	
		Word Processing Fees	411		3 000 00
		Cash received from services rendered			
	13	Office Salaries Expense	511	650 00	
		Cash	111		650 00
		Payment of office salaries			
	18	Advertising Expense	512	250 00	
		Accounts Payable	211		250 00
		Bill received but not paid from Al's News			
	20	Brenda Clark, Withdrawals	312	625 00	
		Cash	111		625 00
		Personal withdrawal of cash			
	22	Accounts Receivable	112	5 000 00	
		Word Processing Fees	411		5 000 00
		Billed Morris Co. for fees earned			

FIGURE 3.18 *(continued)*

CLARK'S WORD PROCESSING SERVICES
GENERAL JOURNAL

Page 2

Date		Account Titles and Description	PR	Dr.	Cr.
200X May	27	Office Salaries Expense	511	650 00	
		Cash	111		650 00
		Payment of office salaries			
	28	Accounts Payable	211	2500 00	
		Cash	111		2500 00
		Paid half the amount owed Ben Co.			
	29	Telephone Expense	513	220 00	
		Cash	111		220 00
		Paid telephone bill			

FIGURE 3.19 Partial General Ledger

CLARK'S WORD PROCESSING SERVICES
PARTIAL GENERAL LEDGER

Cash — Account No. 111

Date		Explanation	Post. Ref.	Debit	Credit	Balance Debit	Balance Credit
200X May	1		GJ1	10000 00		10000 00	
	1		GJ1		1000 00	9000 00	
	1		GJ1		1200 00	7800 00	
	7		GJ1	3000 00		10800 00	
	13		GJ1		650 00	10150 00	
	20		GJ1		625 00	9525 00	
	27		GJ2		650 00	8875 00	
	28		GJ2		2500 00	6375 00	
	29		GJ2		220 00	6155 00	

Accounts Receivable — Account No. 112

Date		Explanation	Post. Ref.	Debit	Credit	Balance Debit	Balance Credit
200X May	22		GJ1	5000 00		5000 00	

Office Supplies — Account No. 114

Date		Explanation	Post. Ref.	Debit	Credit	Balance Debit	Balance Credit
200X May	3		GJ1	600 00		600 00	

FIGURE 3.19 *(continued)*

Prepaid Rent — Account No. 115

Date		Explanation	Post. Ref.	Debit	Credit	Balance Debit	Balance Credit
200X May	1		GJ1	1 2 0 0 00		1 2 0 0 00	

Word Processing Equipment — Account No. 121

Date		Explanation	Post. Ref.	Debit	Credit	Balance Debit	Balance Credit
200X May	1		GJ1	6 0 0 0 00		6 0 0 0 00	

Accounts Payable — Account No. 211

Date		Explanation	Post. Ref.	Debit	Credit	Balance Debit	Balance Credit
200X May	1		GJ1		5 0 0 0 00		5 0 0 0 00
	3		GJ1		6 0 0 00		5 6 0 0 00
	18		GJ1		2 5 0 00		5 8 5 0 00
	28		GJ2	2 5 0 0 00			3 3 5 0 00

Brenda Clark, Capital — Account No. 311

Date		Explanation	Post. Ref.	Debit	Credit	Balance Debit	Balance Credit
200X May	1		GJ1		10 0 0 0 00		10 0 0 0 00

Brenda Clark, Withdrawals — Account No. 312

Date		Explanation	Post. Ref.	Debit	Credit	Balance Debit	Balance Credit
200X May	20		GJ1	6 2 5 00		6 2 5 00	

Word Processing Fees — Account No. 411

Date		Explanation	Post. Ref.	Debit	Credit	Balance Debit	Balance Credit
200X May	7		GJ1		3 0 0 0 00		3 0 0 0 00
	22		GJ1		5 0 0 0 00		8 0 0 0 00

FIGURE 3.19 *(continued)*

Office Salaries Expense — Account No. 511

Date		Explanation	Post. Ref.	Debit	Credit	Balance Debit	Balance Credit
200X May	13		GJ1	650 00		650 00	
	27		GJ2	650 00		1300 00	

Advertising Expense — Account No. 512

Date		Explanation	Post. Ref.	Debit	Credit	Balance Debit	Balance Credit
200X May	18		GJ1	250 00		250 00	

Telephone Expense — Account No. 513

Date		Explanation	Post. Ref.	Debit	Credit	Balance Debit	Balance Credit
200X May	29		GJ2	220 00		220 00	

NEED HELP?

Let's review first: The PR column of the journal will show to which account information has been posting. The PR column in the ledger accounts show from which page of the journal the information came. When updating ledger accounts, two debits added equals a debit balance. Two credits added would be a credit balance. If you have a debit and a credit, take the difference between them; whichever side is larger is the balance (be it a debit or credit).

Partial General Ledger:

Cash: There are nine postings from the journal to the cash account. GJ1 means that posting came from the general journal, page 1. In the second line the credit of 1,000 is subtracted from the debit balance in line 1 (10,000) to show a new balance of 9,000 in line 2. In line 3 the 1,200 credit is then subtracted from the 9,000 debit for a current balance of 7,800. Normally the balance is on the side that causes it to increase. Thus cash is normally a debit balance.

Accounts Payable: In this account the first three postings were credits from the general journal. Note that the month is written only once. Since all three are credits we add each together, arriving at a credit balance of 5,850. On May 28 a debit of 2,500 is posted and we take the difference between a 5,850 credit balance and a 2,500 debit balance to arrive at a 3,350 ending credit balance.

Office Salaries Expense: Note that here we have two debit postings, so they are added together to arrive at a 1,300 debit balance.

Summary: Posting is copying from the journal to the ledger. The ledger will accumulate information in the form of debits and credits. The last line in the balance column will show whether it is a debit or credit balance. The general journal does not show a running balance like the ledger accounts do.

LO3

Learning Unit 3-3 Preparing the Trial Balance: Step 4 of the Accounting Cycle

Did you note in Quiz 3-2 how each account had a running balance figure? Did you know the normal balance of each account in Clark's ledger? As we discussed in Chapter 2, the list of the individual accounts with their balances taken from the ledger is called a **trial balance.**

The trial balance shown in Figure 3.20 was developed from the ledger accounts of Clark's Word Processing Services that were posted and balanced in Quiz 3-2. If the information is journalized or posted incorrectly, the trial balance will not be correct.

TRIAL BALANCE

Debits	Credits
Assets	*Liabilities*
Expenses	*Revenue*
Withdrawals	*Capital*

The trial balance will not show everything:

- The capital figure on the trial balance may not be the beginning capital figure. For instance, if Brenda Clark had made additional investments during the period, the additional investment would have been journalized and posted to the Capital account. The only way to tell if the capital balance on the trial balance is the original balance is to check the ledger Capital account to see whether any additional investments were made. This confirmation of beginning capital will be important when we make financial reports.

FIGURE 3.20 Trial Balance

CLARK'S WORD PROCESSING SERVICE
TRIAL BALANCE
MAY 31, 200X

	Debit	Credit
Cash	6 1 5 5 00	
Accounts Receivable	5 0 0 0 00	
Office Supplies	6 0 0 00	
Prepaid Rent	1 2 0 0 00	
Word Processing Equipment	6 0 0 0 00	
Accounts Payable		3 3 5 0 00
Brenda Clark, Capital		10 0 0 0 00
Brenda Clark, Withdrawals	6 2 5 00	
Word Processing Fees		8 0 0 0 00
Office Salaries Expense	1 3 0 0 00	
Advertising Expense	2 5 0 00	
Telephone Expense	2 2 0 00	
Totals	21 3 5 0 00	21 3 5 0 00

The trial balance lists the accounts in the same order as in the ledger. The $6,155 figure of cash came from the ledger.

- Even careful cross-referencing does not guarantee that transactions have been properly recorded. For example, the following errors would remain undetected: (1) a transaction that may have been omitted in the journalizing process, (2) a transaction incorrectly analyzed and recorded in the journal, and (3) a journal entry journalized or posted twice.

The totals of a trial balance can balance and yet be incorrect.

What to Do If a Trial Balance Doesn't Balance

The trial balance of Clark's Word Processing Services shows that the total of debits is equal to the total of credits. What happens, however, if the trial balance is in balance but the correct amount is not recorded in each ledger account? Accuracy in the journalizing and posting process will help ensure that no errors are made.

Even if you find an error, the first rule is "don't panic." Everyone makes mistakes, and accepted ways of correcting them are available. Once an entry has been made in ink, correcting an error in it must always show that the entry has been changed and who changed it. Sometimes the change has to be explained.

Some Common Mistakes

If the trial balance does not balance, the cause could be something relatively simple. Here are some common errors and how they can be fixed:

Correcting the trial balance: What to do if your trial balance doesn't balance.

- If the difference (the amount you are off) is 10, 100, 1,000, and so forth, it is probably a mathematical error in addition.
- If the difference is equal to an individual account balance in the ledger, the amount could have been omitted. It is also possible the figure was not posted from the general journal.
- Divide the difference by 2, then check to see whether a debit should have been a credit, or vice versa, in the ledger or trial balance. Example: $150 difference ÷ 2 = $75 means you may have placed $75 as a debit to an account instead of a credit, or vice versa.
- If the difference is evenly divisible by 9, a **slide** or transposition may have occurred. A slide is an error resulting from adding or deleting zeros in writing numbers. For example, $4,175.00 may have been copied as $41.75. A **transposition** is the accidental rearrangement of digits of a number. For example, $4,175 might have been accidentally written as $4,157.
- Compare the balances in the trial balance with the ledger accounts to check for copying errors.
- Recompute balances in each ledger account.
- Trace all postings from journal to ledger.

If you cannot find the error after taking all these steps, take a coffee break. Then start all over again.

Making a Correction Before Posting

Before posting, error correction is straightforward. Simply draw a line through the incorrect entry, write the correct information above the line, and write your initials near the change. Keep in mind that computer systems use their own methods for making corrections.

Correcting an Error in an Account Title Figure 3.21 shows an error and its correction in an account title:

FIGURE 3.21 Account Error

		1	Word Processing Equipment		6 0 0 0 00	
			Cash			1 0 0 0 00
			Accounts Payable amp ~~Accounts Receivable~~			5 0 0 0 00
			Purchase of equipment from Ben Co.			

Correcting a Numerical Error Numbers are handled the same way as account titles, as the next change from 520 to 250 in Figure 3.22 shows:

FIGURE 3.22 Number Error

	18	Advertising Expense	250 00	
		Accounts Payable		amp ~~520 00~~ 250 00
		Bill from Al's News		

Correcting an Entry Error If a number has been entered in the wrong column, a straight line is drawn through it. The number is then written in the correct column, as shown in Figure 3.23:

FIGURE 3.23 Correcting Entry

	1	Word Processing Equipment	6000 00	
		Cash		1000 00
		Accounts Payable	amp ~~5000 00~~	5000 00
		Purchase of equip. from Ben Co.		

Making a Correction After Posting

It is also possible to correct an amount that is correctly entered in the journal but posted incorrectly to the ledger of the proper account. The first step is to draw a line through the error and write the correct figure above it. The next step is changing the running balance to reflect the corrected posting. Here, too, a line is drawn through the balance and the corrected balance is written above it. Both changes must be initialed, as shown in Figure 3.24.

FIGURE 3.24 Correction After Posting

Word Processing Fees							Account No. 411
Date		Explanation	Post. Ref.	Debit	Credit	Balance Debit	Balance Credit
200X May	7		GJ1		2500 00		2500 00
	22		GJ1		~~100 00~~ 4100 00 amp		~~2600 00~~ 6600 00 amp

Correcting an Entry Posted to the Wrong Account

Drawing a line through an error and writing the correction above it is possible when a mistake has occurred within the proper account, but when an error involves a posting to the wrong account, the journal must include a correction accompanied by an explanation. In addition, the correct information must be posted to the appropriate ledgers.

Suppose, for example, as a result of tracing postings from journal entries to ledgers you find that a $180 telephone bill was incorrectly debited as an advertising expense. The following illustration shows how this correction is done.

Step 1 The journal entry is corrected and the correction is explained (Fig. 3.25):

FIGURE 3.25 Corrected Entry for Telephone

GENERAL JOURNAL					Page 3
Date		Account Titles and Description	PR	Dr.	Cr.
200X May	29	Telephone Expense	513	180 00	
		Advertising Expense	512		180 00
		To correct error in which			
		Advertising Exp. was debited			
		for charges to Telephone Exp.			

Step 2 The Advertising Expense ledger account is corrected (Fig. 3.26):

FIGURE 3.26 Ledger Update for Advertising

Advertising Expense						Account No. 512	
						Balance	
Date		Explanation	Post. Ref.	Debit	Credit	Debit	Credit
200X May	18		GJ1	175 00		175 00	
	23		GJ1	180 00		355 00	
	29	Correcting entry	GJ3		180 00	175 00	

Step 3 The Telephone Expense ledger is corrected (Fig. 3.27):

FIGURE 3.27 Ledger Update for Telephone

Telephone Expense						Account No. 513	
						Balance	
Date		Explanation	Post. Ref.	Debit	Credit	Debit	Credit
200X May	29		GJ3	180 00		180 00	

LEARNING UNIT 3-3 REVIEW

AT THIS POINT you should be able to

- Prepare a trial balance with a ledger, using four-column accounts.
- Analyze and correct a trial balance that doesn't balance.
- Correct journal and posting errors.

Self-Review Quiz 3-3

1.

MEMO

To: *Al Vincent*
From: *Professor Jones*
Re: *Trial Balance*

You have submitted to me an incorrect trial balance (Fig. 3.28). Could you please rework and turn in to me before next Friday?
Note: Individual amounts look OK.

For additional help go to www.pearsonhighered.com/slater

FIGURE 3.28 Incorrect Trial Balance

A. RICE TRIAL BALANCE OCTOBER 31, 200X		
	Dr.	Cr.
Cash		8 0 6 0 00
Operating Expenses		1 7 0 0 00
A. Rice, Withdrawals		4 0 0 00
Service Revenue		5 4 0 0 00
Equipment	5 0 0 0 00	
Accounts Receivable	3 5 4 0 00	
Accounts Payable	2 0 0 0 00	
Supplies	3 0 0 00	
A. Rice, Capital		11 6 0 0 00

2. An $8,000 debit to Office Equipment was mistakenly journalized and posted on June 9, 200X, to Office Supplies. Prepare the appropriate journal entry to correct this error.

Solution to Self-Review Quiz 3-3

1.

FIGURE 3.29 Correct Trial Balance

A. RICE TRIAL BALANCE OCTOBER 31, 200X		
	Dr.	Cr.
Cash	8 0 6 0 00	
Accounts Receivable	3 5 4 0 00	
Supplies	3 0 0 00	
Equipment	5 0 0 0 00	
Accounts Payable		2 0 0 0 00
A. Rice, Capital		11 6 0 0 00
A. Rice, Withdrawals	4 0 0 00	
Service Revenue		5 4 0 0 00
Operating Expenses	1 7 0 0 00	
Totals	19 0 0 0 00	19 0 0 0 00

2.

FIGURE 3.30 Correcting Entry

GENERAL JOURNAL					Page 4
Date		Account Titles and Description	PR	Dr.	Cr.
200X June	9	Office Equipment		8 0 0 0 0 0	
		Office Supplies			8 0 0 0 0 0
		To correct error in which office supplies			
		had been debited for purchase of			
		office equipment			

NEED HELP?

Let's review first: Items in a trial balance are listed in the same order as in the ledger or chart of accounts. Expect each account to have its normal balance (either a debit or credit). No title in the trial list balance can have both a debit and credit balance.

List the ending balance of each ledger account (last number listed in the balance columns) and list them in the order of the ledger. They should follow this pattern:

Assets	Dr.
Liabilities	Cr.
Capital	Cr.
Withdrawals	Dr.
Revenues	Cr.
Expenses	Dr.

When complete, the total of all debits will equal the total of the credits. In this case the total is 19,000.

Summary: The trial balance lists the accounts in the same order as the ledger. Be sure to refer to the learning unit for what to do if the trial balance does not balance. It could be a posting mistake or just a math error.

CHAPTER ASSIGNMENTS

All Classroom Demonstration Exercises, Exercises, Problems, and the Continuing Problem in this chapter can be found within MyAccountingLab, an online homework and practice environment. Your instructor may ask you to complete this material using MyAccountingLab.

MyAccountingLab

DEMONSTRATION PROBLEM: STEPS 1–4 OF THE ACCOUNTING CYCLE

In March, Abby's Employment Agency had the following transactions:

200X		
Mar.	1	Abby Todd invested $5,000 cash in the new employment agency.
	4	Bought equipment for cash, $200.
	5	Earned employment fee commission, $200, but payment from Blue Co. will not be received until June.
	6	Paid wages expense, $300.
	7	Abby paid her home utility bill from the company checkbook, $75.
	9	Placed Rick Wool at VCR Corporation, receiving $1,200 cash.
	15	Paid cash for supplies, $200.
	28	Telephone bill received but not paid, $180.
	29	Advertising bill received but not paid, $400.

The chart of accounts includes Cash, 111; Accounts Receivable, 112; Supplies, 131; Equipment, 141; Accounts Payable, 211; A. Todd, Capital, 311; A. Todd, Withdrawals, 321; Employment Fees Earned, 411; Wage Expense, 511; Telephone Expense, 521; and Advertising Expense, 531.

Your task is to

a. Set up a ledger based on the chart of accounts.
b. Journalize (all page 1) and post transactions.
c. Prepare a trial balance for March 31.

Solution to Demonstration Problem

a.

FIGURE 3.31 General Ledger

Cash 111

Date		PR	Dr.	Cr.	Balance Dr.	Balance Cr.
200X Mar.	1	GJ1	5,000		5,000	
	4	GJ1		200	4,800	
	6	GJ1		300	4,500	
	7	GJ1		75	4,425	
	9	GJ1	1,200		5,625	
	15	GJ1		200	5,425	

Accounts Receivable 112

Date		PR	Dr.	Cr.	Balance Dr.	Balance Cr.
200X Mar.	5	GJ1	200		200	

Supplies 131

Date		PR	Dr.	Cr.	Balance Dr.	Balance Cr.
200X Mar.	15	GJ1	200		200	

Equipment 141

Date		PR	Dr.	Cr.	Balance Dr.	Balance Cr.
200X Mar.	4	GJ1	200		200	

Accounts Payable 211

Date		PR	Dr.	Cr.	Balance Dr.	Balance Cr.
200X Mar.	28	GJ1		180		180
	29	GJ1		400		580

A. Todd, Capital 311

Date		PR	Dr.	Cr.	Balance Dr.	Balance Cr.
200X Mar.	1	GJ1		5,000		5,000

A. Todd, Withdrawals 321

Date		PR	Dr.	Cr.	Balance Dr.	Balance Cr.
200X Mar.	7	GJ1	75		75	

Employment Fees Earned 411

Date		PR	Dr.	Cr.	Balance Dr.	Balance Cr.
200X Mar.	5	GJ1		200		200
	9	GJ1		1,200		1,400

Wage Expense 511

Date		PR	Dr.	Cr.	Balance Dr.	Balance Cr.
200X Mar.	6	GJ1	300		300	

Telephone Expense 521

Date		PR	Dr.	Cr.	Balance Dr.	Balance Cr.
200X Mar.	28	GJ1	180		180	

Advertising Expense 531

Date		PR	Dr.	Cr.	Balance Dr.	Balance Cr.
200X Mar.	29	GJ1	400		400	

b.

ABBY'S EMPLOYMENT AGENCY					Page 1
Date		Account Titles and Description	PR	Dr.	Cr.
200X Mar.	1	Cash	111	5 0 0 0 00	
		A. Todd, Capital	311		5 0 0 0 00
		Owner investment			
	4	Equipment	141	2 0 0 00	
		Cash	111		2 0 0 00
		Bought equipment for cash			
	5	Accounts Receivable	112	2 0 0 00	
		Employment Fees Earned	411		2 0 0 00
		Fees on account from Blue Co.			
	6	Wage Expense	511	3 0 0 00	
		Cash	111		3 0 0 00
		Paid wages			
	7	A. Todd, Withdrawals	321	7 5 00	
		Cash	111		7 5 00
		Personal withdrawals			
	9	Cash	111	1 2 0 0 00	
		Employment Fees Earned	411		1 2 0 0 00
		Cash fees			
	15	Supplies	131	2 0 0 00	
		Cash	111		2 0 0 00
		Bought supplies for cash			
	28	Telephone Expense	521	1 8 0 00	
		Accounts Payable	211		1 8 0 00
		Telephone bill owed			
	29	Advertising Expense	531	4 0 0 00	
		Accounts Payable	211		4 0 0 00
		Advertising bill received			

FIGURE 3.32 Journal Entries and Post References

Solution Tips to Journalizing

1. When journalizing, the PR column is not filled in.
2. Write the name of the debit against the date column. Indent credits and list them below debits. Be sure total debits for each transaction equal total credits.
3. Skip a line between each transaction.

This analysis is what should be going through your head before determining debit or credit.

The Analysis of the Journal Entries

March 1	Cash	A	↑	Dr.	$5,000
	A. Todd, Capital	Capital	↑	Cr.	$5,000
4	Equipment	A	↑	Dr.	$ 200
	Cash	A	↓	Cr.	$ 200
5	Accts. Receivable	A	↑	Dr.	$ 200
	Empl. Fees Earned	Rev.	↑	Cr.	$ 200
6	Wage Expense	Exp.	↑	Dr.	$ 300
	Cash	A	↓	Cr.	$ 300
7	A. Todd, Withdrawals	Withd.	↑	Dr.	$ 75
	Cash	A	↓	Cr.	$ 75
9	Cash	A	↑	Dr.	$1,200
	Empl. Fees Earned	Rev.	↑	Cr.	$1,200
15	Supplies	A	↑	Dr.	$ 200
	Cash	A	↓	Cr.	$ 200
28	Telephone Expense	Exp.	↑	Dr.	$ 180
	Accounts Payable	L	↑	Cr.	$ 180
28	Advertising Expense	Exp.	↑	Dr.	$ 400
	Accounts Payable	L	↑	Cr.	$ 400

Solution Tips to Posting

The PR column in the ledger cash account tells you from which page journal information came. After the ledger cash account is posted, account number 111 is put in the PR column of the journal for cross-referencing.

Note how we keep a running balance in the cash account. A $5,000 debit balance and a $200 credit entry result in a new debit balance of $4,800.

FIGURE 3.33

ABBY'S EMPLOYMENT AGENCY
TRIAL BALANCE
MARCH 31, 200X

	Dr.	Cr.
Cash	5 4 2 5 00	
Accounts Receivable	2 0 0 00	
Supplies	2 0 0 00	
Equipment	2 0 0 00	
Accounts Payable		5 8 0 00
A. Todd, Capital		5 0 0 0 00
A. Todd, Withdrawals	7 5 00	
Employment Fees Earned		1 4 0 0 00
Wage Expense	3 0 0 00	
Telephone Expense	1 8 0 00	
Advertising Expense	4 0 0 00	
Totals	6 9 8 0 00	6 9 8 0 00

Solution Tip to Trial Balance

The trial balance lists the ending balance of each title in the order in which they appear in the ledger. The total of 6,980 on the left equals 6,980 on the right.

SUMMARY OF KEY POINTS

LEARNING UNIT 3-1

1. The accounting cycle is a sequence of accounting procedures that are usually performed during an accounting period.
2. An accounting period is the time period for which the income statement is prepared. The time period can be any period up to one year.
3. A calendar year is from January 1 to December 31. The fiscal year is any 12-month period. A fiscal year could be a calendar year but does not have to be.
4. Interim statements are statements that are usually prepared for a portion of the business's calendar or fiscal year (e.g., a month or a quarter).
5. A general journal is a book that records transactions in chronological order. Here debits and credits are shown together on one page. It is the book of original entry.
6. The ledger is a collection of accounts where information is accumulated from the postings of the journal. The ledger is the book of final entry.
7. Journalizing is the process of recording journal entries.
8. The chart of accounts provides the specific titles of accounts to be entered in the journal.
9. When journalizing, the post reference (PR) column is left blank.
10. A compound journal entry occurs when more than two accounts are affected in the journalizing process of a business transaction.

LEARNING UNIT 3-2

1. Posting is the process of transferring information from the journal to the ledger.
2. The journal and ledger contain the same information but in a different form.
3. The four-column account aids in keeping a running balance of an account.
4. The normal balance of an account will be located on the side that increases it according to the rules of debit and credit. For example, the normal balances of liabilities occur on the credit side.
5. The mechanical process of posting requires care in transferring to the appropriate account the dates, post references, and amounts.

LEARNING UNIT 3-3

1. A trial balance can balance but be incorrect. For example, an entire journal entry may not have been posted.
2. If a trial balance doesn't balance, check for errors in addition, omission of postings, slides, transpositions, copying errors, and so on.
3. Specific procedures should be followed in making corrections in journals and ledgers.

KEY TERMS

Accounting cycle For each accounting period, the process that begins with the recording of business transactions or procedures into a journal and ends with the completion of a post-closing trial balance.

Accounting period The period of time for which an income statement is prepared.

Book of final entry Book that receives information about business transactions from a book of original entry (a journal). Example: a ledger.

Book of original entry Book that records the first formal information about business transactions. Example: a journal.

Calendar year January 1 to December 31.

Compound journal entry A journal entry that affects more than two accounts.

Cross-referencing Adding to the PR column of the journal the account number of the ledger account that was updated from the journal.

Fiscal year The 12-month period a business chooses for its accounting year.

Four-column account A running balance account that records debits and credits and has a column for an ending balance (debit or credit). It replaces the standard two-column account we used earlier.

General journal The simplest form of a journal, which records information from transactions in chronological order as they occur. This journal links the debit and credit parts of transactions together.

Interim reports Financial statements that are prepared for a month, quarter, or some other portion of the fiscal year.

Journal A listing of business transactions in chronological order. The journal links on one page the debit and credit parts of transactions.

Journal entry The transaction (debits and credits) that is recorded into a journal once it is analyzed.

Journalizing The process of recording a transaction entry into the journal.

Natural business year A business's fiscal year that ends at the same time as a slow seasonal period begins.

Posting The transferring, copying, or recording of information from a journal to a ledger.

Slide The error that results in adding or deleting zeros in the writing of a number. Example: 79,200 → 7,920.

Transposition The accidental rearrangement of digits of a number. Example: 152 → 125.

Trial balance An informal listing of the ledger accounts and their balances in the ledger to aid in proving the equality of debits and credits.

BLUEPRINT OF FIRST FOUR STEPS OF ACCOUNTING CYCLE

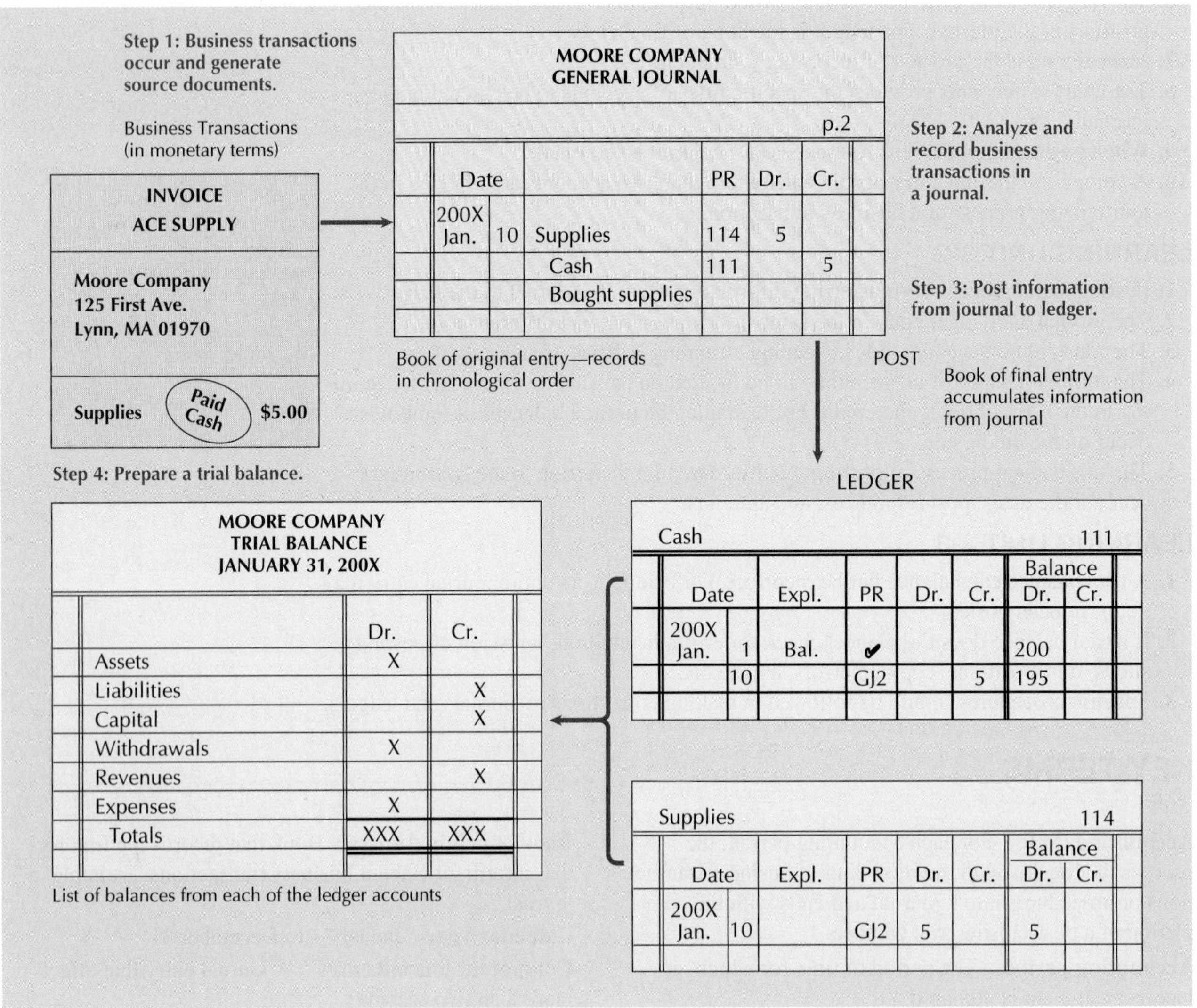

QUESTIONS, CLASSROOM DEMONSTRATION EXERCISES, EXERCISES, AND PROBLEMS

Discussion Questions and Critical Thinking/Ethical Case

1. Explain the concept of the accounting cycle.
2. An accounting period is based on the balance sheet. Agree or disagree?
3. Compare and contrast a calendar year versus a fiscal year.
4. What are interim statements?
5. Why is the ledger called the book of final entry?
6. How do transactions get "linked" in a general journal?
7. What is the relationship of the chart of accounts to the general journal?
8. What is a compound journal entry?
9. Posting means updating the journal. Agree or disagree? Please comment.
10. The side that decreases an account is the normal balance. True or false?
11. The PR column of a general journal is the last item to be filled in during the posting process. Agree or disagree?
12. Discuss the concept of cross-referencing.
13. What is the difference between a transposition and a slide?
14. Jay Simons, the accountant of See Co., would like to buy a new software package for his general ledger. He couldn't do it because all funds were frozen for the rest of the fiscal period. Jay called his friend at Joor Industries and asked whether he could copy its software. Comment on why it is or isn't okay for Jay to make such a request.

Classroom Demonstration Exercises

MyAccountingLab

SET A

General Journal

LO1 (5 min)

1. Complete the following from the general journal of Moore Co.:
   a. Year of journal entry ____________
   b. Month of journal entry ____________
   c. Day of journal entry ____________
   d. Name(s) of accounts debited ____________
   e. Name(s) of accounts credited ____________
   f. Explanation of transaction ____________
   g. Amount of debit(s) ____________
   h. Amount of credit(s) ____________
   i. Page of journal ____________

FIGURE 3.34 General Journal

MOORE COMPANY
GENERAL JOURNAL
Page 1

Date		Account Titles and Descriptions	PR	Dr.	Cr.
200X Nov.	18	Cash		9 0 0 0 00	
		Equipment		10 0 0 0 00	
		B. Moore, Capital			19 0 0 0 00
		Initial Investment by Owner			

LO2 (5 min) **General Journal**

2. Provide the explanation for each of the general journal entries in Figure 3.35.

FIGURE 3.35 Journal Entries

GENERAL JOURNAL					Page 4
Date		Account Titles and Descriptions	PR	Debit	Credit
200X June	10	Cash		17000 00	
		Computer Equipment		26000 00	
		B. Blue, Capital			43000 00
		(A)			
	16	Cash		40 00	
		Accounts Receivable		70 00	
		Legal Fees Earned			110 00
		(B)			
	18	Salary Expense		40 00	
		Accounts Payable			40 00
		(C)			

LO2 (5 min) **Posting and Balancing**

3. Balance this four-column account. What function does the PR column serve? When will Account 111 be used in the journalizing and posting process?

		Cash			Acct. 111 Balance	
Date	**Explanation**	**PR**	**Dr.**	**Cr.**	**Dr.**	**Cr.**
200X						
May 8		GJ 1	19			
16		GJ 1	9			
20		GJ 2		6		
22		GJ 3	2			

LO4 (15 min) **The Trial Balance**

4. The following trial balance (Fig. 3.36) was prepared *incorrectly.*

a. Rearrange the accounts in proper order.

FIGURE 3.36

LEE CO. TRIAL BALANCE OCTOBER 31, 200X		
	Dr.	Cr.
D. Lee, Capital	30 00	
Equipment	112 00	
Rent Expense		17 00
Advertising Expense		3 00
Accounts Payable		108 00
Taxi Fees	16 00	
Cash	17 00	
D. Lee, Withdrawals	—	5 00
Totals	175 00	133 00

b. Calculate the total of the trial balance. (Small numbers are used intentionally so that you can do the calculations in your head.) Assume each account has a normal balance.

Correcting Entry *LO3 (5 min)*

5. On June 1, 2009, a telephone expense for $210 was debited to Repair Expense. On June 10, 2010, this error was found. Prepare the corrected journal entry. When would a correcting entry *not* be needed?

SET B

General Journal *LO1 (5 min)*

1. Complete the following from the general journal of Ranger Co. (Fig. 3.37):

a. Year of journal entry ____________
b. Month of journal entry ____________
c. Day of journal entry ____________
d. Name(s) of accounts debited ____________
e. Name(s) of accounts credited ____________
f. Explanation of transaction ____________
g. Amount of debit(s) ____________
h. Amount of credit(s) ____________
i. Page of journal ____________

FIGURE 3.37 General Journal

RANGER COMPANY
GENERAL JOURNAL
Page 1

Date		Account Titles and Descriptions	PR	Dr.	Cr.
200X Oct.	15	Cash		6 0 0 0 00	
		Equipment		4 0 0 00	
		L. Swan, Capital			6 4 0 0 00
		Initial Investment by Owner			

General Journal *LO2 (5 min)*

2. Provide the explanation for each of the general journal entries in Figure 3.38.

FIGURE 3.38 Journal Entries

GENERAL JOURNAL
Page 4

Date		Account Titles and Descriptions	PR	Debit	Credit
200X July	9	Cash		8 0 0 0 00	
		Office Equipment		5 0 0 0 00	
		J. Walsh, Capital			13 0 0 0 00
		(A)			
	15	Cash		3 0 00	
		Accounts Receivable		6 0 00	
		Hair Fees Earned			9 0 00
		(B)			
	20	Advertising Expense		4 0 00	
		Accounts Payable			4 0 00
		(C)			

LO2 (5 min) **Posting and Balancing**

3. Balance this four-column account. What function does the PR column serve? When will Account 111 be used in the journalizing and posting process?

		Cash			Acct. 111 Balance	
Date	**Explanation**	**PR**	**Dr.**	**Cr.**	**Dr.**	**Cr.**
200X						
June 4		GJ 1	15			
5		GJ 1	6			
9		GJ 2		4		
10		GJ 3	1			

LO4 (15 min) **The Trial Balance**

4. The following trial balance (Fig. 3.39) was prepared *incorrectly.*

FIGURE 3.39

LEE CO.
TRIAL BALANCE
OCTOBER 31, 200X

	Dr.	Cr.
D. Lee, Capital	17 00	
Equipment	12 00	
Rent Expense		4 00
Advertising Expense		3 00
Accounts Payable		8 00
Taxi Fees	16 00	
Cash	17 00	
D. Lee, Withdrawals	—	5 00
Totals	62 00	20 00

a. Rearrange the accounts in proper order.

b. Calculate the total of the trial balance. (Small numbers are used intentionally so that you can do the calculations in your head.) Assume each account has a normal balance.

LO3 (5 min) **Correcting Entry**

5. On May 1, 2009, a telephone expense for $210 was debited to Repair Expense. On June 12, 2010, this error was found. Prepare the corrected journal entry. When would a correcting entry *not* be needed?

MyAccountingLab

Exercises

LO1 (10 min) **3-1.** Prepare journal entries for the following transactions that occurred during October:

200X	
Oct. 1	Janet Wills invested $70,000 cash and $6,000 of equipment into her new business.
3	Purchased building for $40,000 on account.
12	Purchased a truck from Lowell Co. for $16,000 cash.
18	Bought supplies from Lee Co. on account, $900.

3-2. Record the following into the general journal of Reggie's Auto Shop. *LO1 (10 min)*

200X

Jan. 1 Reggie Long invested $16,000 cash in the auto shop.
5 Paid $7,000 for auto equipment.
8 Bought from Lowell Co. auto equipment for $6,000 on account.
14 Received $900 for repair fees earned.
18 Billed Sullivan Co. $900 for services rendered.
20 Reggie withdrew $300 for personal use.

3-3. Post the transactions in Figure 3.40 to the ledger of King Company. The partial ledger of King Company is Cash, 111; Equipment, 121; Accounts Payable, 211; and A. King, Capital, 311. Please use four-column accounts in the posting process. *LO2 (10 min)*

FIGURE 3.40 Journal Entries

Page 4

Date 200X			PR	Dr.	Cr.
April	6	Cash		15 0 0 0 00	
		A. King, Capital			15 0 0 0 00
		Cash investment			
	14	Equipment		9 0 0 0 00	
		Cash			4 0 0 0 00
		Accounts Payable			5 0 0 0 00
		Purchase of equipment			

3-4. From the following transactions for Lowe Company for the month of July, (a) prepare journal entries (assume that it is page 1 of the journal), (b) post to the ledger (use a four-column account), and (c) prepare a trial balance. *LO1, 2, 3 (20 min)*

200X

July 1 Joan Lowe invested $6,000 in the business.
4 Bought from Lax Co. equipment on account, $800.
15 Billed Friend Co. for services rendered, $4,000.
18 Received $5,000 cash for services rendered.
24 Paid salaries expense, $1,800.
28 Joan withdrew $400 for personal use.

A partial chart of accounts includes Cash, 111; Accounts Receivable, 112; Equipment, 121; Accounts Payable, 211; J. Lowe, Capital, 311; J. Lowe, Withdrawals, 312; Fees Earned, 411; and Salaries Expense, 511.

LO3 (15 min) **3-5.** You have been hired to correct the trial balance in Figure 3.41 that has been recorded improperly from the ledger to the trial balance.

FIGURE 3.41 Incorrect Trial Balance

SUNG CO. TRIAL BALANCE MARCH 31, 200X		
	Dr.	Cr.
Accounts Payable	2 0 0 0 00	
A. Sung, Capital		6 5 0 0 00
A. Sung, Withdrawals		3 0 0 00
Services Earned		4 7 0 0 00
Concessions Earned	2 5 0 0 00	
Rent Expense	4 0 0 00	
Salaries Expense	2 5 0 0 00	
Miscellaneous Expense		1 3 0 0 00
Cash	10 0 0 0 00	
Accounts Receivable		1 2 0 0 00
Totals	17 4 0 0 00	14 0 0 0 00

LO3 (10 min) **3-6.** On February 6, 200X, Mike Sullivan made the journal entry in Figure 3.42 to record the purchase on account of office equipment priced at $1,400. This transaction had not yet been posted when the error was discovered. Make the appropriate correction.

FIGURE 3.42 Recording Error

GENERAL JOURNAL					
Date		Account Titles and Description	PR	Dr.	Cr.
200X Feb.	6	Office Equipment		9 0 0 00	
		Accounts Payable			9 0 0 00
		Purchase of office equip. on account			

MyAccountingLab

Group A Problems

LO1 (30 min) **3A-1.** Jack Lang operates Jack's Cleaning Service. As the bookkeeper, you have been requested to journalize the following transactions:

200X

Aug. 1 Paid rent for two months in advance, $9,000.

6 Purchased cleaning equipment on account from Ryan's Supply House, $4,000.

12 Purchased cleaning supplies from Lee's Wholesale for $900 cash.

14 Received $1,900 cash from cleaning fees earned.

20 Jack withdrew $900 for his personal use.

21 Advertising bill received from *Salem News* but unpaid, $400.

25 Paid electrical expense, $90.

28 Paid salaries expense, $700.

29 Performed cleaning work for $2,100, but payment will not be received until January.

30 Paid Ryan's Supply House half the amount owed from Aug. 6 transaction.

Check Figure:
Aug 21
Dr. Advertising expense $400
Cr. Accounts Payable $400

Your task is to journalize the preceding transactions. The chart of accounts for Jack's Cleaning Service is as follows:

Chart of Accounts

Assets		Owner's Equity	
111	Cash	311	Jack Lang, Capital
112	Accounts Receivable	312	Jack Lang, Withdrawals
114	Prepaid Rent	**Revenue**	
116	Cleaning Supplies	411	Cleaning Fees Earned
120	Cleaning Equipment	**Expenses**	
121	Office Equipment	511	Advertising Expense
Liabilities		512	Electrical Expense
211	Accounts Payable	514	Salaries Expense

3A-2. On June 1, 200X, Betty Rice opened Betty's Art Studio. The following transactions occurred in June:

LO 1, 2, 3 (45 min)

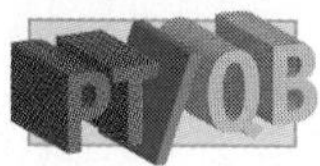

200X		
June	1	Betty Rice invested $12,000 in the art studio.
	1	Paid three months' rent in advance, $1,200.
	3	Purchased $600 of equipment from Aston Co. on account.
	5	Received $900 cash for art-training workshop for teachers.
	8	Purchased $400 of art supplies for cash.
	9	Billed Lester Co. $2,100 for group art lesson for its employees.
	10	Paid salaries of assistants, $600.
	15	Betty withdrew $200 from the business for her personal use.
	28	Paid electrical bill, $140.
	29	Paid telephone bill for June, $210.

Your task is to

a. Set up the ledger based on the following chart of accounts.
b. Journalize (journal is page 1) and post the June transactions.
c. Prepare a trial balance as of June 30, 200X.

Check Figure:
Trial Balance
Total $15,600

The chart of accounts for Betty's Art Studio is as follows:

Chart of Accounts

Assets		Owner's Equity	
111	Cash	311	Betty Rice, Capital
112	Accounts Receivable	312	Betty Rice, Withdrawals
114	Prepaid Rent	**Revenue**	
121	Art Supplies	411	Art Fees Earned
131	Equipment	**Expenses**	
Liabilities		511	Electrical Expense
211	Accounts Payable	521	Salaries Expense
		531	Telephone Expense

LO1, 2, 3 (45 min)

3A-3. The following transactions occurred in June 200X for A. French's Placement Agency:

200X

June 1 A. French invested $9,000 cash in the placement agency.
1 Bought equipment on account from Hook Co., $2,000.
3 Earned placement fees of $1,600, but payment will not be received until July.
5 A. French withdrew $100 for his personal use.
7 Paid wages expense, $300.
9 Placed a client on a local TV show, receiving $600 cash.
15 Bought supplies on account from Lyon Co., $500.
28 Paid telephone bill for June, $160.
29 Advertising bill from Shale Co. received but not paid, $900.

Check Figure:
Trial Balance
Total $14,600

The chart of accounts for A. French Placement Agency is as follows:

Chart of Accounts

Assets		**Owner's Equity**	
111	Cash	311	A. French, Capital
112	Accounts Receivable	312	A. French, Withdrawals
131	Supplies	**Revenue**	
141	Equipment	411	Placement Fees Earned
Liabilities		**Expenses**	
211	Accounts Payable	511	Wage Expense
		521	Telephone Expense
		531	Advertising Expense

Your task is to

a. Set up the ledger based on the chart of accounts.
b. Journalize (page 1) and post the June transactions.
c. Prepare a trial balance as of June 30, 200X.

MyAccountingLab

Group B Problems

LO1 (30 min)

3B-1. In April Jack Lang opened a new cleaning service. Please assist him by journalizing the following business transactions:

200X

Apr. 1 Jack Lang invested $6,000 of cleaning equipment as well as $3,000 cash in the new business.
3 Purchased cleaning supplies on account from Rex Co., $500.
10 Purchased office equipment on account from Ross Stationery, $400.
12 Jack paid his home telephone bill from the company checkbook, $60.
20 Received $600 cash for cleaning services performed.
21 Advertising bill received but not paid, $75.
25 Electrical bill received but not paid, $90.
28 Performed cleaning work for $700, but payment will not be received until May.
29 Paid salaries expense, $400.
30 Paid Ross Stationery half the amount owed from April 10 transaction.

Check Figure:
April 21
Dr. Advertising expense $75
Cr. Accounts payable $75

The chart of accounts for Jack's Cleaning Service includes Cash, 111; Accounts Receivable, 112; Prepaid Rent, 114; Cleaning Supplies, 116; Cleaning Equipment, 120; Office Equipment, 121; Accounts Payable, 211; Jack Lang, Capital, 311; Jack Lang, Withdrawals, 312; Cleaning Fees Earned, 411; Advertising Expense, 511; Electrical Expense, 512; and Salaries Expense, 514.

3B-2. In June the following transactions occurred for Betty's Art Studio:

LO1, 2, 3 (45 min)

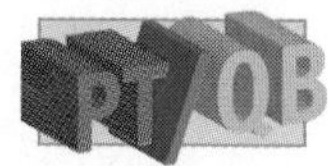

200X		
June	1	Betty Rice invested $6,000 in the art studio.
	1	Paid four months rent in advance, $1,200.
	3	Purchased art supplies on account from A.J.K., $700.
	5	Purchased equipment on account from Reese Company, $900.
	8	Received $1,300 cash for art-training program provided to Northwest Junior College.
	9	Billed Long Co. for art lessons provided, $600.
	10	Betty withdrew $400 from the art studio to buy a new chainsaw for her home.
	15	Paid salaries expense, $400.
	28	Paid telephone bill, $118.
	29	Electric bill received but unpaid, $120.

Check Figure:
Total Trial Balance $9,620

Your task is to

a. Set up a ledger.
b. Journalize (all page 1) and post the June transactions.
c. Prepare a trial balance as of June 30, 200X.

The chart of accounts includes Cash, 111; Accounts Receivable, 112; Prepaid Rent, 114; Art Supplies, 121; Equipment, 131; Accounts Payable, 211; Betty Rice, Capital, 311; Betty Rice, Withdrawals, 312; Art Fees Earned, 411; Electrical Expense, 511; Salaries Expense, 521; and Telephone Expense, 531.

3B-3. In June A. French's Placement Agency had the following transactions:

LO1, 2, 3 (45 min)

200X		
June	1	A. French invested $6,000 in the new placement agency.
	2	Bought equipment for cash, $350.
	3	Earned placement fee commission of $2,100, but payment from Avon Co. will not be received until July.
	5	Paid wages expense, $400.
	7	A. French paid his home utility bill from the company checkbook, $69.
	9	Placed Jay Diamond on a national TV show, receiving $900 cash.
	15	Paid cash for supplies, $350.
	28	Telephone bill received but not paid, $185.
	29	Advertising bill received but not paid, $200.

Check Figure:
Total Trial Balance $9,385

The chart of accounts includes Cash, 111; Accounts Receivable, 112; Supplies, 131; Equipment, 141; Accounts Payable, 211; A. French, Capital, 311; A. French, Withdrawals, 312; Placement Fees Earned, 411; Wage Expense, 511; Telephone Expense, 521; and Advertising Expense, 531.

Your task is to

a. Set up a ledger based on the chart of accounts.
b. Journalize (all page 1) and post transactions.
c. Prepare a trial balance for June 30, 200X.

ON-THE-JOB TRAINING

LO3 (30 min)

T-1. Paul Regan, bookkeeper of Hampton Co., has been up half the night trying to get his trial balance to balance. Figure 3.43 shows his results.

FIGURE 3.43 Incorrect Trial Balance

HAMPTON CO. TRIAL BALANCE JUNE 30, 200X		
	Dr.	Cr.
Office Sales		5720 00
Cash in Bank	3260 00	
Accounts Receivable	5660 00	
Office Equipment	8400 00	
Accounts Payable		4160 00
D. Hole, Capital		11560 00
D. Hole, Withdrawals		700 00
Wage Expense	2600 00	
Rent Expense	940 00	
Utilities Expense	26 00	
Office Supplies	120 00	
Prepaid Rent	180 00	

Ken Small, the accountant, compared Paul's amounts in the trial balance with those in the ledger, recomputed each account balance, and compared postings. Ken found the following errors:

1. A $200 debit to D. Hole, Withdrawals, was posted as a credit.
2. D. Hole, Withdrawals, was listed on the trial balance as a credit.
3. A Note Payable account with a credit balance of $2,400 was not listed on the trial balance.
4. The pencil footings for Accounts Payable were debits of $5,320 and credits of $8,800.
5. A debit of $180 to Prepaid Rent was not posted.
6. Office Supplies bought for $60 was posted as a credit to Office Supplies.
7. A debit of $120 to Accounts Receivable was not posted.
8. A cash payment of $420 was credited to Cash for $240.
9. The pencil footing of the credits to Cash was overstated by $400.
10. The Utilities Expense of $260 was listed in the trial balance as $26.

Assist Paul Regan by preparing a correct trial balance. What advice could you give Ken about Paul? Can you explain the situation to Paul? Put your answers in writing.

LO 3 (20 min)

T-2. Lauren Oliver, an accountant lab tutor, is having a debate with some of her assistants. They are trying to find out how each of the following five unrelated situations would affect the trial balance:

1. A $5 debit to Cash in the ledger was not posted.

2. A $10 debit to Computer Supplies was debited to Computer Equipment.
3. An $8 debit to Wage Expense was debited twice to the account.
4. A $4 debit to Computer Supplies was debited to Computer Sales.
5. A $35 credit to Accounts Payable was posted as a $53 credit.

Could you indicate to Lauren the effect that each situation will have on the trial balance? If a situation will have no effect, indicate that fact. Put in writing how each of these situations could be avoided in the future.

FINANCIAL REPORT PROBLEM

Reading the Kellogg's Annual Report

LO3 (5 min)

Go to Appendix A and find the statement of earnings. Sales are the revenue for a merchandise company. How much did Kellogg's increase sales from 2005 to 2006? What inward flows could result from these net sales?

INTERNET PROJECT

Continental

Go to the Web and search: Annual Report Continental 2008.
Click on Investors Relations.
List out the latest news Continental is providing to its investors.
Order a free annual report.

CONTINUING PROBLEM

MyAccountingLab

Sanchez Computer Center

LO1, 2, 3 (45 min)

Tony's computer center is picking up in business, so he has decided to expand his bookkeeping system to a general journal/ledger system. The balances from August have been forwarded to the ledger accounts.

Assignment

1. Use the chart of accounts in Chapter 2 to record the following transactions in Figures 3.44 through 3.54.

Sanchez Computer Center 8104
385 N. Escondido Blvd.
Escondido CA 92025
September 1, --200X------

Pay
To the
Order of—*Capital Management* -------------------------------------- *$ 1200.00* ------
One thousand two hundred and 00/100

First Union Bank
322 Glen Ave.
Escondido, CA 92025
memo *Prepaid Rent—Aug. Sept. Oct.** -------- *Tony Freedman* --------
0611 062 78 72

FIGURE 3.44 Prepaid Rent

*One check is written for 3 months rent on Sept. 1. That included August rent. For this problem, consider it all prepaid.

FIGURE 3.45 Service Revenue

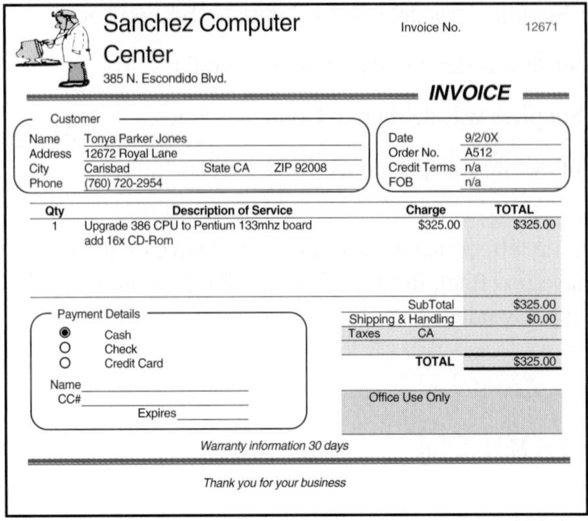

Sanchez Computer Center
385 N. Escondido Blvd.

Invoice No. 12671

INVOICE

Customer
Name Tonya Parker Jones
Address 12672 Royal Lane
City Carlsbad State CA ZIP 92008
Phone (760) 720-2954

Date 9/2/0X
Order No. A512
Credit Terms n/a
FOB n/a

Qty	Description of Service	Charge	TOTAL
1	Upgrade 386 CPU to Pentium 133mhz board add 16x CD-Rom	$325.00	$325.00

SubTotal	$325.00
Shipping & Handling	$0.00
Taxes CA	
TOTAL	$325.00

Payment Details
◉ Cash
○ Check
○ Credit Card
Name
CC#
Expires

Office Use Only

Warranty information 30 days

Thank you for your business

FIGURE 3.46 Service Revenue

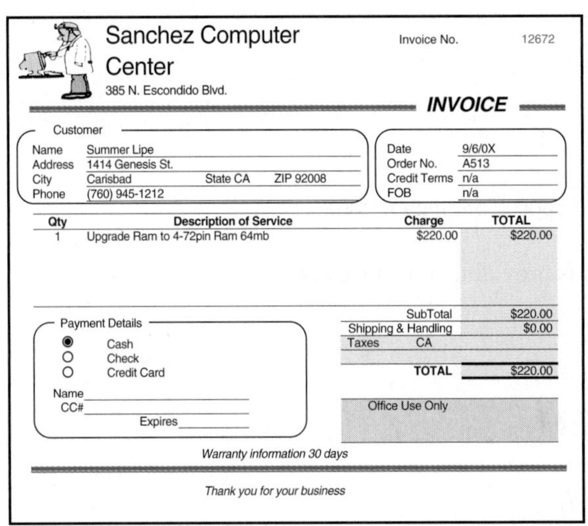

Sanchez Computer Center
385 N. Escondido Blvd.

Invoice No. 12672

INVOICE

Customer
Name Summer Lipe
Address 1414 Genesis St.
City Carlsbad State CA ZIP 92008
Phone (760) 945-1212

Date 9/6/0X
Order No. A513
Credit Terms n/a
FOB n/a

Qty	Description of Service	Charge	TOTAL
1	Upgrade Ram to 4-72pin Ram 64mb	$220.00	$220.00

SubTotal	$220.00
Shipping & Handling	$0.00
Taxes CA	
TOTAL	$220.00

Payment Details
◉ Cash
○ Check
○ Credit Card
Name
CC#
Expires

Office Use Only

Warranty information 30 days

Thank you for your business

FIGURE 3.47 Phone Bill

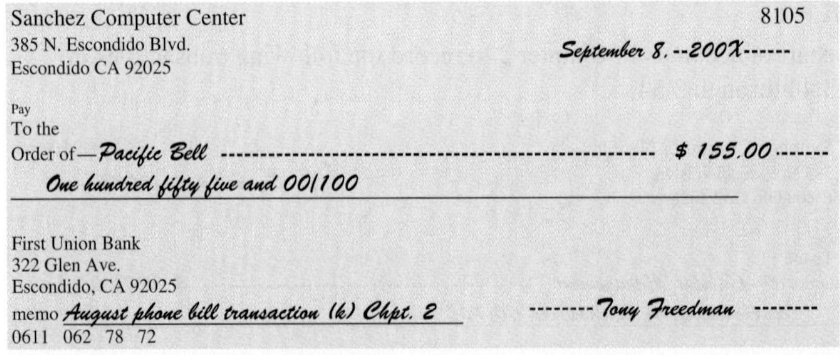

Sanchez Computer Center
385 N. Escondido Blvd.
Escondido CA 92025

8105

September 8, --200X------

Pay
To the
Order of—*Pacific Bell* -- *$ 155.00* ------

One hundred fifty five and 00/100

First Union Bank
322 Glen Ave.
Escondido, CA 92025

memo *August phone bill transaction (k) Chpt. 2*

-------- *Tony Freedman* --------

0611 062 78 72

Refer back to Chapter 2, transaction k.

Jeannine Sparks
1919 Sierra St.
Escondido CA 92025

251

September 12,--200X-----

Pay
To the
Order of—Sanchez Computer Center ------------------------------ $ 850.00 ------

Eight hundred fifty dollars and 00/100

Bank First
322 Cardiff Ave.
Escondido, CA 92025

memo Computer Fixed, Transaction (o) Chpt. 2 ------Jeannine Sparks -------

0611 062 78 72

FIGURE 3.48 Sparks Collection

Refer back to Chapter 2, transaction o.

Sanchez Computer Center
385 N. Escondido Blvd.
Escondido CA 92025

8106

September 15,--200X-----

Pay
To the
Order of—Computer Connection ------------------------------------ $ 200.00 ------

Two hundred dollars and 00/100

First Union Bank
322 Glen Ave.
Escondido, CA 92025

memo Account due from transaction (s) Chpt. 2 ------- Tony Freedman -------

0611 062 78 72

FIGURE 3.49 Paid Computer Connection

Refer back to Chapter 2, transaction s.

Sanchez Computer Center
385 N. Escondido Blvd.
Escondido CA 92025

8107

September 17,--200X------

Pay
To the
Order of—Multi Systems, Inc --------------------------------------- $ 1,200.00 -------

Twelve hundred dollars and 00/100

First Union Bank
322 Glen Ave.
Escondido, CA 92025

Purchase order 200

memo Computer Equipment-Bench Workstations -------- Tony Freedman --------

0611 062 78 72

FIGURE 3.50 Purchased Computer Equipment

FIGURE 3.51 Received Phone Bill

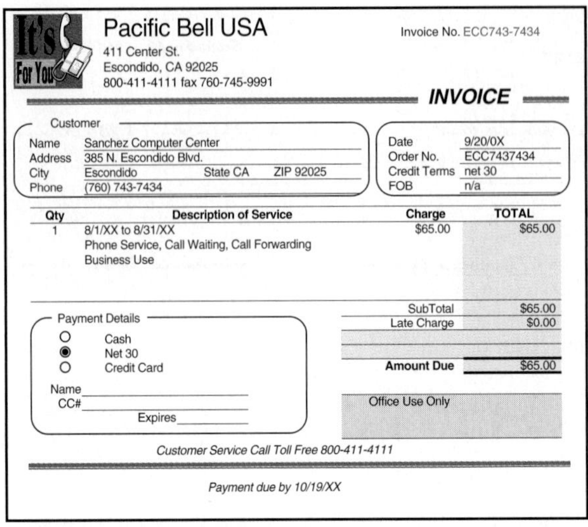

Pacific Bell USA
411 Center St.
Escondido, CA 92025
800-411-4111 fax 760-745-9991

Invoice No. ECC743-7434

INVOICE

Customer
Name Sanchez Computer Center
Address 385 N. Escondido Blvd.
City Escondido State CA ZIP 92025
Phone (760) 743-7434

Date 9/20/0X
Order No. ECC7437434
Credit Terms net 30
FOB n/a

Qty	Description of Service	Charge	TOTAL
1	8/1/XX to 8/31/XX Phone Service, Call Waiting, Call Forwarding Business Use	$65.00	$65.00

Payment Details
O Cash
◉ Net 30
O Credit Card
Name____
CC#____
Expires____

SubTotal	$65.00
Late Charge	$0.00
Amount Due	$65.00

Office Use Only

Customer Service Call Toll Free 800-411-4111

Payment due by 10/19/XX

FIGURE 3.52 Received Electric Bill

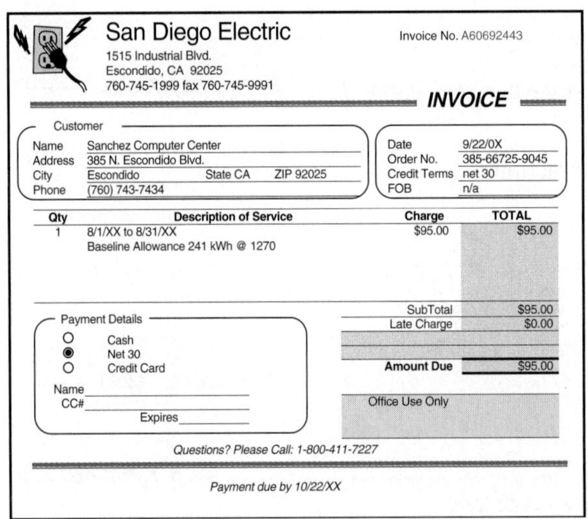

San Diego Electric
1515 Industrial Blvd.
Escondido, CA 92025
760-745-1999 fax 760-745-9991

Invoice No. A60692443

INVOICE

Customer
Name Sanchez Computer Center
Address 385 N. Escondido Blvd.
City Escondido State CA ZIP 92025
Phone (760) 743-7434

Date 9/22/0X
Order No. 385-66725-9045
Credit Terms net 30
FOB n/a

Qty	Description of Service	Charge	TOTAL
1	8/1/XX to 8/31/XX Baseline Allowance 241 kWh @ 1270	$95.00	$95.00

Payment Details
O Cash
◉ Net 30
O Credit Card
Name____
CC#____
Expires____

SubTotal	$95.00
Late Charge	$0.00
Amount Due	$95.00

Office Use Only

Questions? Please Call: 1-800-411-7227

Payment due by 10/22/XX

FIGURE 3.53 Service Revenue

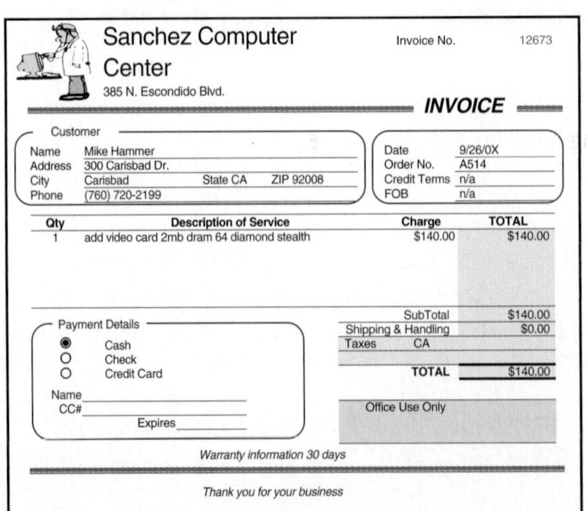

Sanchez Computer Center
385 N. Escondido Blvd.

Invoice No. 12673

INVOICE

Customer
Name Mike Hammer
Address 300 Carisbad Dr.
City Carisbad State CA ZIP 92008
Phone (760) 720-2199

Date 9/26/0X
Order No. A514
Credit Terms n/a
FOB n/a

Qty	Description of Service	Charge	TOTAL
1	add video card 2mb dram 64 diamond stealth	$140.00	$140.00

Payment Details
◉ Cash
O Check
O Credit Card
Name____
CC#____
Expires____

SubTotal	$140.00
Shipping & Handling	$0.00
Taxes CA	
TOTAL	$140.00

Office Use Only

Warranty information 30 days

Thank you for your business

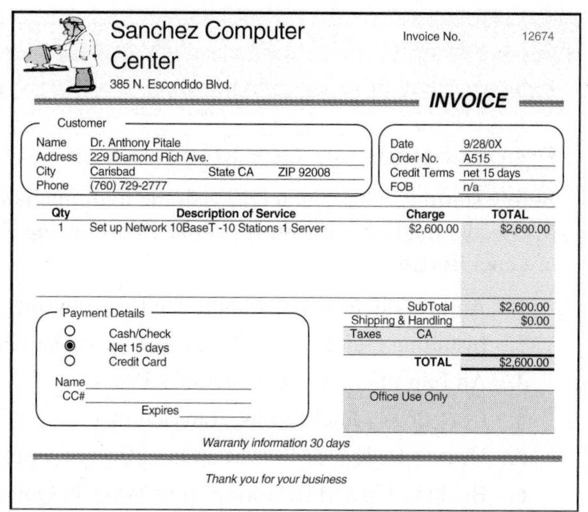
Sanchez Computer Center
385 N. Escondido Blvd.

Invoice No. 12674

INVOICE

Customer
Name Dr. Anthony Pitale
Address 229 Diamond Rich Ave.
City Carlsbad State CA ZIP 92008
Phone (760) 729-2777

Date 9/28/0X
Order No. A515
Credit Terms net 15 days
FOB n/a

Qty	Description of Service	Charge	TOTAL
1	Set up Network 10BaseT -10 Stations 1 Server	$2,600.00	$2,600.00

SubTotal	$2,600.00
Shipping & Handling	$0.00
Taxes CA	
TOTAL	$2,600.00

Payment Details
O Cash/Check
◉ Net 15 days
O Credit Card
Name
CC#
Expires

Office Use Only

Warranty information 30 days

Thank you for your business

FIGURE 3.54 Service Revenue

2. Post all transactions to the general ledger accounts (the Prepaid Rent Account #1025 has been added to the chart of accounts).
3. Prepare a trial balance for September 30, 200X.
4. Prepare the financial statements for the three months ended September 30, 200X.

PEACHTREE COMPUTER WORKSHOP

COMPUTERIZED ACCOUNTING APPLICATION FOR CHAPTER 3

Preparing to use Peachtree Complete Accounting

Before starting this assignment, visit the multimedia library of the MyAccountingLab Web site and read the following PDF documents for your version of Peachtree.

1. An Introduction to Computerized Accounting
2. Installing Peachtree Complete Accounting and Student Data Files
3. An Introduction to Peachtree Complete Accounting
4. Correcting Peachtree Transactions
5. How to Repeat or Restart a Peachtree Assignment
6. Backing Up and Restoring Your Work in Peachtree

Workshop 1:

Journalizing, Posting, General Ledger, Trial Balance, and Chart of Accounts

In this workshop you enter, post, and edit journal entries for the Atlas Company using Peachtree Complete Accounting. You will also print the general journal report, trial balance, and chart of accounts.

Instructions and data files for completing this assignment are in the multimedia library of the MyAccountingLab Web site. Open the ***Workshop 1 Atlas Company*** PDF document for your version of Peachtree and download the ***Atlas Company*** data file for your version of Peachtree.

QUICKBOOKS COMPUTER WORKSHOP

COMPUTERIZED ACCOUNTING APPLICATION FOR CHAPTER 3

Preparing to use QuickBooks Pro

Before starting this assignment, visit the multimedia library of the MyAccountingLab Web site and read the following PDF documents for your version of QuickBooks.

1. An Introduction to Computerized Accounting
2. Installing QuickBooks Pro and Student Data Files
3. An Introduction to QuickBooks Pro
4. Correcting QuickBooks Transactions
5. How to Repeat or Restart a QuickBooks Assignment
6. Backing Up and Restoring Your Work in QuickBooks

Workshop 1:

Journalizing, Posting, General Ledger, Trial Balance, and Chart of Accounts

In this workshop you enter, post, and edit journal entries for the Atlas Company using QuickBooks Pro. You will also print the general journal report, trial balance, and chart of accounts.

Instructions and data files for completing this assignment are in the multimedia library of the MyAccountingLab Web site. Open the ***Workshop 1 Atlas Company*** PDF document for your version of QuickBooks and download the ***Atlas Company*** data file for your version of QuickBooks.

4

The Accounting Cycle Continued

DID YOU KNOW? Black & Decker uses the straight-line method to depreciate its property, plant, and equipment.
Building: 10–50 years
Manufacturing equipment: 3–5 years
Visit *www.blackanddecker.com* to find more information about Black & Decker.

LEARNING OBJECTIVES

1. Adjustments: prepaid rent, office supplies, depreciation on equipment, and accrued salaries.
2. Preparing the adjusted trial balance on the worksheet.
3. Preparing the income statement and balance sheet sections of the worksheet.
4. Preparing financial statements from the worksheet.

QuickBooks and Peachtree programs do not use worksheets. Adjustments are made from preparing the trial balance and are recorded in the general journal.

Each year Black & Decker completes an accounting cycle. In Figure 4.1, steps 1–4 show the parts of the manual accounting cycle that were completed for Clark's Word Processing Services in the previous chapter. This chapter continues the cycle with steps 5–6: the preparation of a worksheet and the three financial statements.

Learning Unit 4-1 Step 5 of the Accounting Cycle: Preparing a Worksheet

An accountant uses a **worksheet** to organize and check data before preparing financial statements necessary to complete the accounting cycle. When an accounting software package is used, a worksheet would not be needed. The most important function of the worksheet is to allow the accountant to find and correct errors before financial statements are prepared. In a way, a worksheet acts as the accountant's scratch pad. No one sees the worksheet once the formal reports are prepared. A sample worksheet is shown in Figure 4.2.

The accounts listed on the far left of the worksheet are taken from the ledger. The rest of the worksheet has five sections: the trial balance, adjustments, adjusted trial balance, income statement, and balance sheet. Each of these sections is divided into debit and credit columns.

The Trial Balance Section

We discussed how to prepare a trial balance in Chapter 2. Some companies prepare a separate trial balance; others, such as Clark's Word Processing Services, prepare the trial balance directly on the worksheet. A trial balance is taken on every account listed in the ledger that has a balance. Additional titles from the ledger are added as they are needed. (We will show how to add account titles later.)

FIGURE 4.1

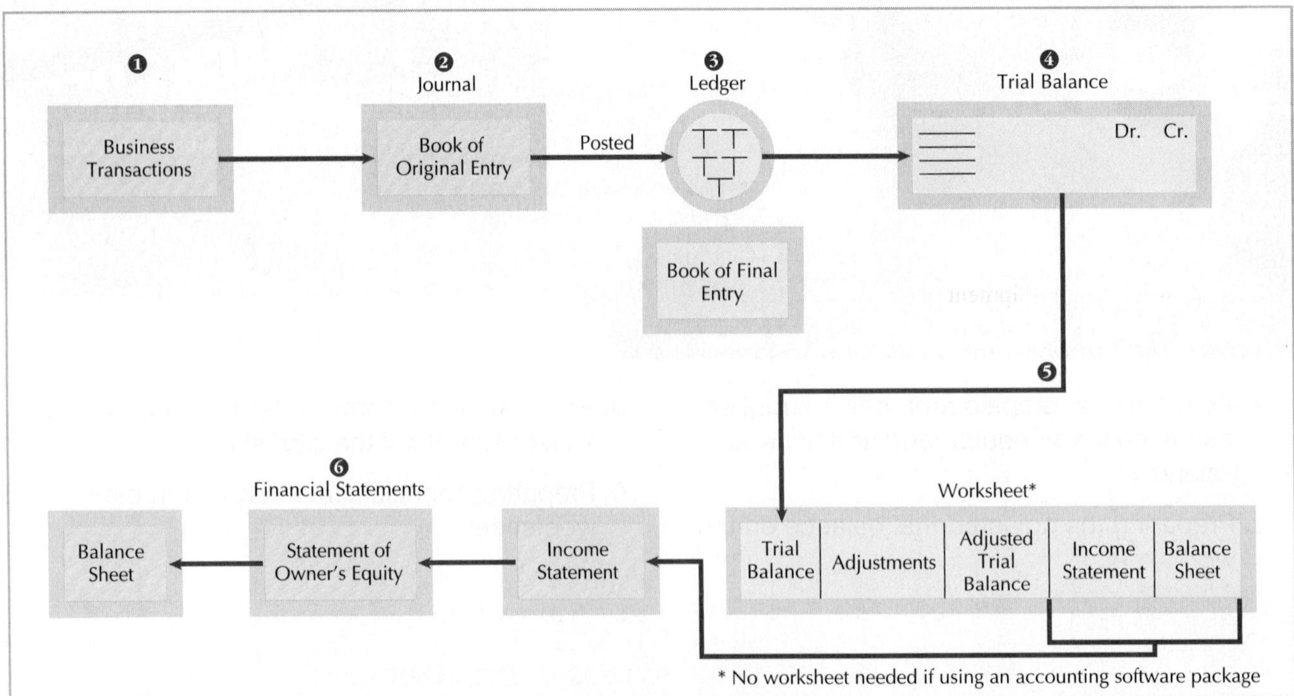

FIGURE 4.2 Sample Worksheet

CLARK'S WORD PROCESSING SERVICES
WORKSHEET
FOR MONTH ENDING MAY 31, 200X

Account Titles	Trial Balance		Adjustments		Adjusted Trial Balance		Income Statement	
	Dr.	Cr.	Dr.	Cr.	Dr.	Cr.	Dr.	Cr.
Cash	6155 00							
Accounts Receivable	5000 00							
Office Supplies	600 00							
Prepaid Rent	1200 00							
Word Processing Equipment	6000 00							
Accounts Payable		3350 00						
Brenda Clark, Capital		10000 00						
Brenda Clark, Withdrawals	625 00							
Word Processing Fees		8000 00						
Office Salaries Expense	1300 00							
Advertising Expense	250 00							
Telephone Expense	220 00							
	21350 00	21350 00						

The Adjustments Section

LO1

Chapters 1–3 discussed transactions that occurred with outside suppliers and companies. In a real business inside transactions also occur during the accounting cycle. These transactions must be recorded, too. At the end of the worksheet process, the accountant will have all of the business's accounts up-to-date and ready to be used to prepare the formal financial reports. The Sarbanes-Oxley Act specifically states the need to have accurate financial reports. By analyzing each of Clark's accounts on the worksheet, the accountant will be able to identify specific accounts that must be **adjusted** to bring them up-to-date. The accountant for Clark's Word Processing Services needs to adjust the following accounts:

Worksheets can be completed on Excel spreadsheets.

A. Office Supplies
B. Prepaid Rent
C. Word Processing Equipment
D. Office Salaries Expense

Let's look at how to analyze and adjust each of these accounts.

A. Adjusting the Office Supplies Account On May 31, the accountant found out that the company had only $100 worth of office supplies on hand. When the company had originally purchased the $600 of office supplies they were considered an asset. As the supplies were used up, they became an expense.

The adjustment for supplies deals with the amount of supplies *used up*.

- Office supplies available: $600 on trial balance.
- Office supplies left or on hand as of May 31: $100 will end up on adjusted trial balance.
- Office supplies used up in the operation of the business for the month of May: $500 is shown in the adjustments column.

Office Supplies Exp. 514

500	

This amount is supplies used up.

Office Supplies 114

600	**500**
100	

↑ This amount is supplies on hand.

As a result, the asset Office Supplies is too high on the trial balance (it should be $100, not $600). At the same time, if we don't show the additional expense of supplies used, the company's *net income* will be too high.

If Clark's accountant does not adjust the trial balance to reflect the change, the company's net income would be too high on the income statement and both sides (Assets and Owner's Equity) of the balance sheet would be too high.

Now let's look at the adjustment for office supplies in terms of the transaction analysis chart.

Will go on income statement

Accounts Affected	Category	↓ ↑	Rules
Office Supplies Expense	Expense	↑	Dr.
Office Supplies	Asset	↓	Cr.

Will go on balance sheet

The Office Supplies Expense account comes from the chart of accounts in Chapter 3. Because it is not listed in the account titles, it must be listed below the trial balance. Let's see how we enter this adjustment on the worksheet in Figure 4.3.

Place $500 in the debit column of the adjustments section on the same line as Office Supplies Expense. Place $500 in the credit column of the adjustments section on the same line as Office Supplies. The numbers in the adjustment column show what is used, *not* what is on hand.

B. Adjusting the Prepaid Rent Account Back on May 1, Clark's Word Processing Services paid three months' rent in advance. The accountant realized that the rent expense would be $400 per month ($1,200 ÷ 3 months = $400).

FIGURE 4.3

Note: Amount "used up" for supplies $500 goes in adjustments column.

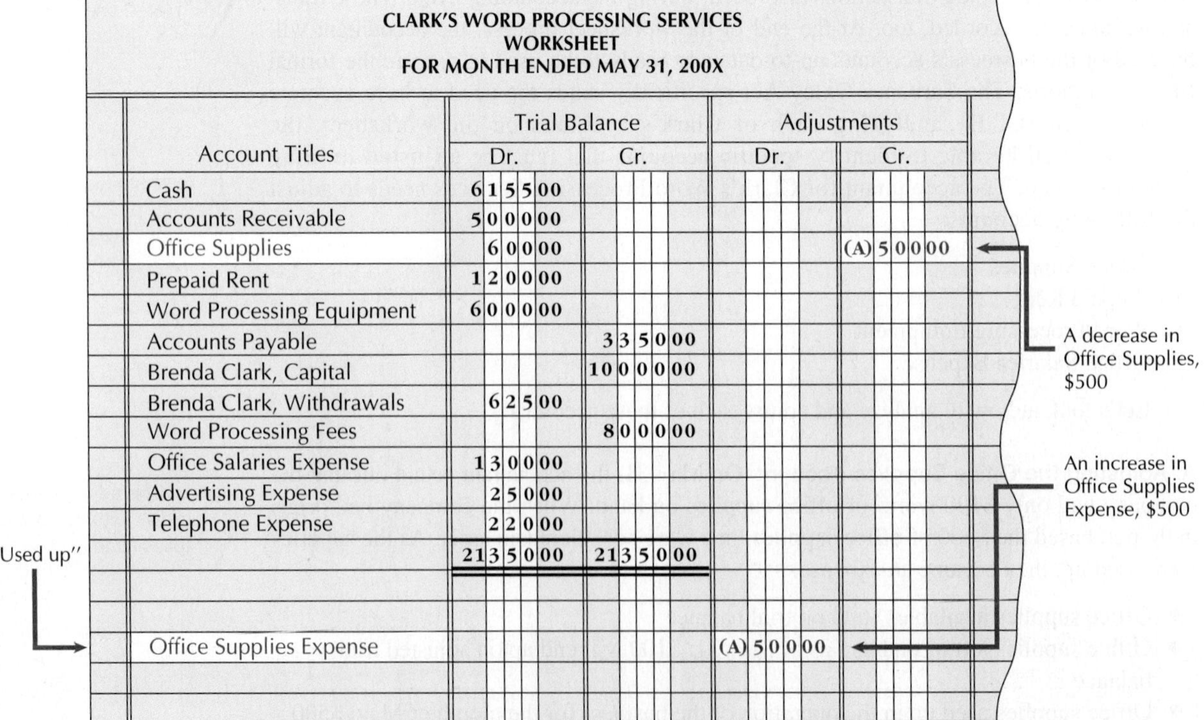

CLARK'S WORD PROCESSING SERVICES
WORKSHEET
FOR MONTH ENDED MAY 31, 200X

Account Titles	Trial Balance Dr.	Trial Balance Cr.	Adjustments Dr.	Adjustments Cr.
Cash	6 1 5 5 00			
Accounts Receivable	5 0 0 0 00			
Office Supplies	6 0 0 00			(A) 5 0 0 00
Prepaid Rent	1 2 0 0 00			
Word Processing Equipment	6 0 0 0 00			
Accounts Payable		3 3 5 0 00		
Brenda Clark, Capital		10 0 0 0 00		
Brenda Clark, Withdrawals	6 2 5 00			
Word Processing Fees		8 0 0 0 00		
Office Salaries Expense	1 3 0 0 00			
Advertising Expense	2 5 0 00			
Telephone Expense	2 2 0 00			
	21 3 5 0 00	21 3 5 0 00		
Office Supplies Expense			(A) 5 0 0 00	

Remember, when rent is paid in advance, it is considered an asset called *prepaid rent.* When the asset, prepaid rent, begins to expire or be used up, it becomes an expense. Now it is May 31, and one month's prepaid rent has become an expense.

How is this type of rent handled? Should the account be $1,200, or is only $800 of prepaid rent left as of May 31? What do we need to do to bring Prepaid Rent to the "true" balance? The answer is that we must increase Rent Expense by $400 and decrease Prepaid Rent by $400 (see Fig. 4.4).

Without this adjustment, the expenses for Clark's Word Processing Services for May will be too low, and the asset Prepaid Rent will be too high. If unadjusted amounts were used in the formal reports, the net income shown on the income statement would be too high, and both sides (Assets and Owner's Equity) would be too high on the balance sheet. In terms of our transaction analysis chart, the adjustment would look like this:

Will go on income statement

Accounts Affected	Category	↓ ↑	Rules
Rent Expense	Expense	↑	Dr.
Prepaid Rent	Asset	↓	Cr.

Will go on balance sheet

Rent Expense 515

Dr.	Cr.
400	

Prepaid Rent 115

Dr.	Cr.
1200	400
800	

Like the Office Supplies Expense account, the Rent Expense account comes from the chart of accounts in Chapter 3.

Figure 4.4 shows how to enter an adjustment to Prepaid Rent.

C. Adjusting the Word Processing Equipment Account for Depreciation The life of the asset affects how it is adjusted. The two accounts we just discussed, Office Supplies and Prepaid Rent, involved things that are used up relatively quickly. Equipment—like word processing equipment—is expected to last much longer. Equipment is

LO2

FIGURE 4.4

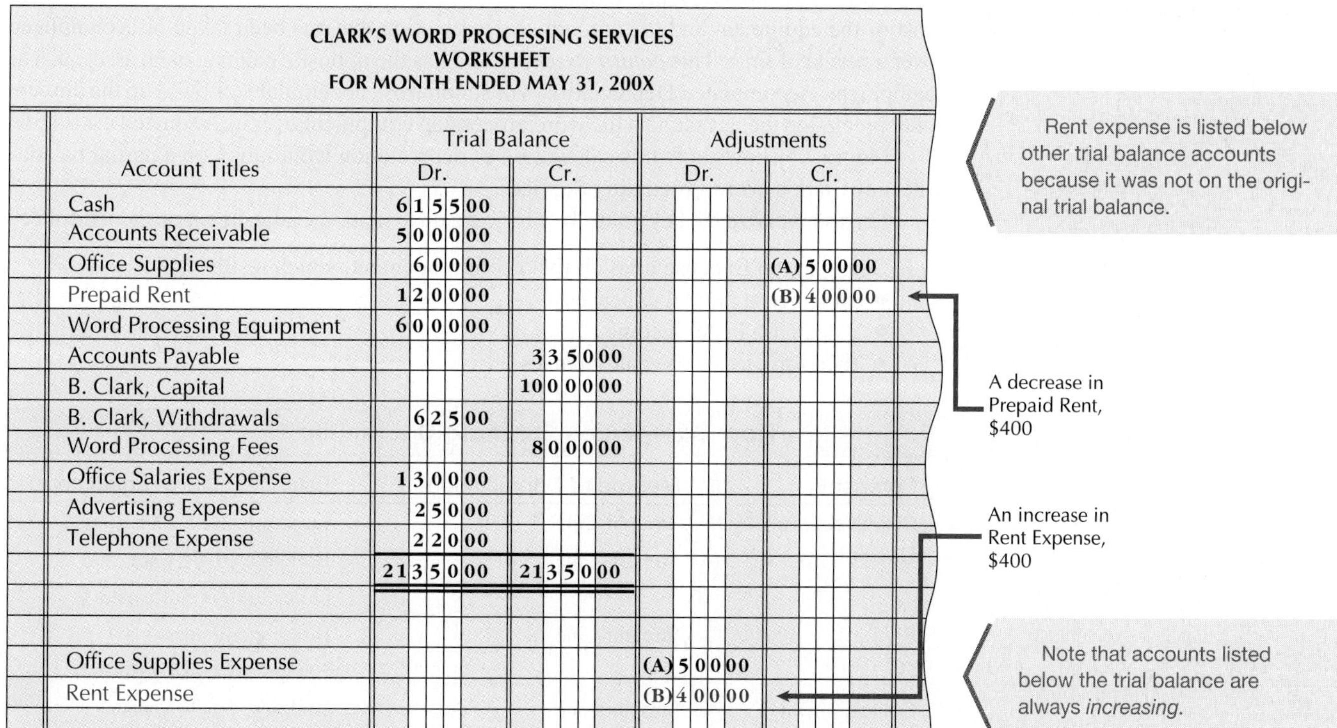

CLARK'S WORD PROCESSING SERVICES
WORKSHEET
FOR MONTH ENDED MAY 31, 200X

Account Titles	Trial Balance Dr.	Trial Balance Cr.	Adjustments Dr.	Adjustments Cr.
Cash	6155 00			
Accounts Receivable	5000 00			
Office Supplies	600 00			(A) 500 00
Prepaid Rent	1200 00			(B) 400 00
Word Processing Equipment	6000 00			
Accounts Payable		3350 00		
B. Clark, Capital		10000 00		
B. Clark, Withdrawals	625 00			
Word Processing Fees		8000 00		
Office Salaries Expense	1300 00			
Advertising Expense	250 00			
Telephone Expense	220 00			
	21350 00	21350 00		
Office Supplies Expense			(A) 500 00	
Rent Expense			(B) 400 00	

Rent expense is listed below other trial balance accounts because it was not on the original trial balance.

Note that accounts listed below the trial balance are always *increasing.*

expected to help produce revenue over a longer period. For that reason accountants treat it differently. The balance sheet reports the **historical cost,** or original cost, of the equipment. The original cost also is reflected in the ledger. The adjustment shows how the cost of the equipment is allocated (spread) over its expected useful life. This spreading is called **depreciation.** To depreciate the equipment, we have to figure out how much its cost goes down each month. Then we have to keep a running total of how that depreciation mounts up over time. The Internal Revenue Service (IRS) issues guidelines, tables, and formulas that must be used to estimate the amount of depreciation. Different methods can be used to calculate depreciation. We will use the simplest method—straight-line depreciation—to calculate the depreciation of Clark's Word Processing Services' equipment. Under the straight-line method, equal amounts are taken over successive periods of time. Table 4-1 shows how some companies estimate life of equipment using the straight-line method.

Original cost of $6,000 for word processing equipment remains *unchanged* after adjustments.

The calculation of depreciation for the year for Clark's Word Processing Services is as follows:

$$\frac{\text{Cost of Equipment} - \text{Residual Value}}{\text{Estimated Years of Usefulness}} = (\text{Trade-In or Salvage Value})$$

According to the IRS, word processing equipment has an expected life of five years. At the end of that time, the property's value is called its "residual value." Think of **residual value** as the estimated value of the equipment at the end of the fifth year. For Clark, the equipment has an estimated residual value of $1,200.

$$\frac{\$6,000 - \$1,200}{5 \text{ Years}} = \frac{\$4,800}{5} = \$960 \text{ Depreciation per Year}$$

Our trial balance is for one month, so we must determine the adjustment for that month:

$$\frac{\$960}{12 \text{ Months}} = \$80 \text{ Depreciation per Month}$$

This $80 is known as depreciation expense, which will be shown on the income statement.

Next, we create a new account to keep a running total of the depreciation amount apart from the original cost of the equipment. The "running total" account is called **Accumulated Depreciation.**

Accumulated Depreciation	
Dr.	Cr.

is a contra-asset account found on the balance sheet.

The Accumulated Depreciation account shows the relationship between the original cost of the equipment and the amount of depreciation that has been taken or accumulated over a period of time. This *contra-asset* account has the opposite balance of an asset such as equipment. Accumulated Depreciation will summarize, accumulate, or build up the amount of depreciation that is taken on the word processing equipment over its estimated useful life.

Figure 4.5 shows how this calculation of depreciation would look on a partial balance sheet of Clark's Word Processing Services.

Let's summarize the key points before going on to mark the adjustment on the worksheet:

1. Depreciation Expense goes on the income statement, which results in
   - an increase in total expenses.
   - a decrease in net income.
   - therefore, less to be paid in taxes.

TABLE 4.1 How Companies Estimate Useful Life

Company	Method of Depreciation	Estimated Life of Equipment
Claire's Stores	Straight-Line	Furniture: 3–25 years
Merck	Straight-Line	Building: 10–50 years Office Equip.: 3–15 years
Big Lots	Straight-Line	Building: 40 years Equipment: 3–15 years
Dollar General	Straight-Line	Building: 39–40 years Furniture: 3–10 years

FIGURE 4.5

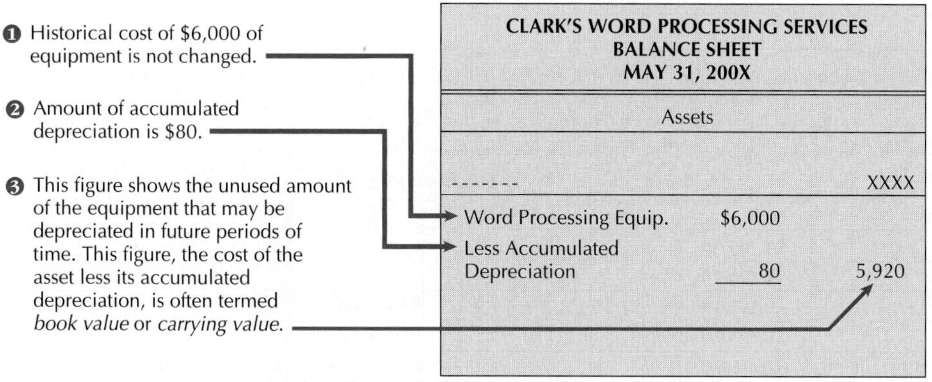
❶ Historical cost of $6,000 of equipment is not changed.
❷ Amount of accumulated depreciation is $80.
❸ This figure shows the unused amount of the equipment that may be depreciated in future periods of time. This figure, the cost of the asset less its accumulated depreciation, is often termed *book value* or *carrying value*.
CLARK'S WORD PROCESSING SERVICES
BALANCE SHEET
MAY 31, 200X
Assets

XXXX
Word Processing Equip. $6,000
Less Accumulated Depreciation 80 5,920

2. Accumulated Depreciation is a contra-asset account found on the balance sheet next to its related equipment account.
3. The original cost of equipment is not reduced; it stays the same until the equipment is sold or removed.
4. Each month the amount in the Accumulated Depreciation account grows larger while the cost of the equipment remains the same.

Now, let's analyze the adjustment on the transaction analysis chart:

Will go on income statement

Accounts Affected	Category	↓ ↑	Rules
Depreciation Expense, Word Processing Equipment	Expense	↑	Dr.
Accumulated Depreciation, Word Processing Equipment	Contra-Asset	↑	Cr.

Will go on balance sheet

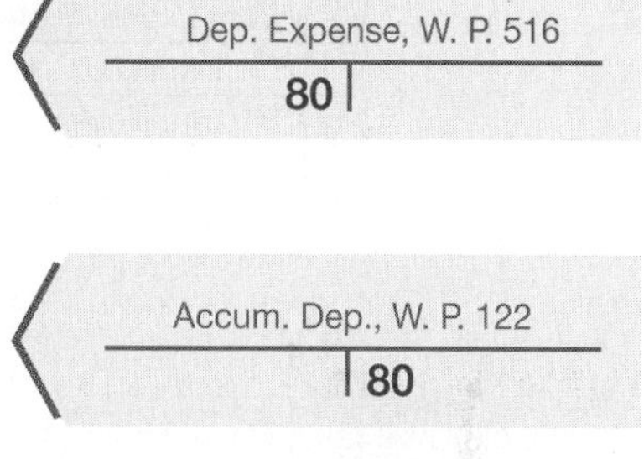
Dep. Expense, W. P. 516
80
Accum. Dep., W. P. 122
80

Remember, the original cost of the equipment never changes: (1) The Equipment account is not included among the affected accounts because the original cost of equipment remains the same, and (2) the original cost does not change. As the accumulated depreciation increases (as a credit), the equipment's **book value** decreases.

Note that the original cost of the equipment on the worksheet has *not* been changed ($6,000).

Figure 4.6 on the following page shows how we enter the adjustment for depreciation of word processing equipment.

Because it is a new business neither account had a previous balance. Therefore, neither is listed in the account titles of the trial balance. We need to list both accounts below Rent Expense in the account titles section. On the worksheet, put $80 in the debit column of the adjustments section on the same line as Depreciation Expense, W. P. Equipment, and put $80 in the credit column of the adjustments section on the same line as Accumulated Depreciation, W. P. Equipment.

Next month, on June 30, $80 would be entered under Depreciation Expense and Accumulated Depreciation would show a balance of $160. Remember, in May, Clark's was a new company so no previous depreciation had been taken.

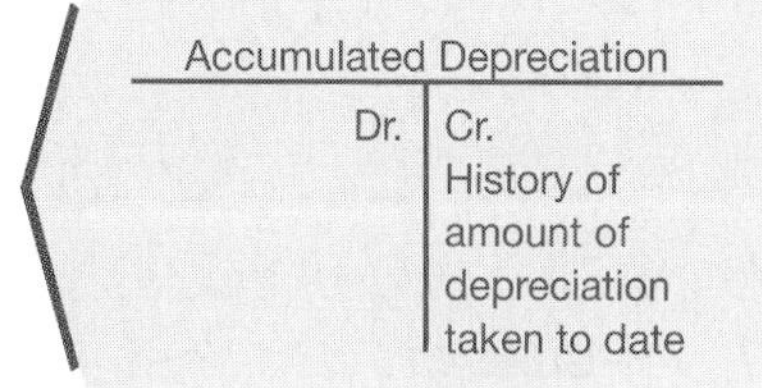
Accumulated Depreciation
Dr.
Cr.
History of amount of depreciation taken to date

Now let's look at the last adjustment for Clark's Word Processing Services.

D. Adjusting the Salaries Accrued Account Clark's Word Processing Services paid $1,300 in Office Salaries Expense (see the trial balance of any previous worksheet in this chapter). The last salary checks for the month were paid on May 27. How can we update this account to show the salary expense as of May 31?

John Murray worked for Clark on May 28, 29, 30, and 31 (see Fig. 4.7 on the following page). His next paycheck is not due until June 3. John earned $350 for these four days. Is the $350 an expense to Clark in May when it was earned, or in June when it is due and is paid?

FIGURE 4.6

CLARK'S WORD PROCESSING SERVICES
WORKSHEET
FOR MONTH ENDED MAY 31, 200X

Account Titles	Trial Balance		Adjustments	
	Dr.	Cr.	Dr.	Cr.
Cash	6155 00			
Accounts Receivable	5000 00			
Office Supplies	600 00			(A) 500 00
Prepaid Rent	1200 00			(B) 400 00
Word Processing Equipment	6000 00			
Accounts Payable		3350 00		
B. Clark, Capital		10000 00		
B. Clark, Withdrawals	625 00			
Word Processing Fees		8000 00		
Office Salaries Expense	1300 00			
Advertising Expense	250 00			
Telephone Expense	220 00			
	21350 00	21350 00		
Office Supplies Expense			(A) 500 00	
Rent Expense			(B) 400 00	
Depreciation Exp., W. P. Equip.			(C) 80 00	
Accum. Deprec., W. P. Equip.				(C) 80 00

An increase in Depreciation Expense, W. P. Equipment.

An increase in Accumulated Depreciation, W. P. Equipment.

An expense can be incurred without being paid as long as it has helped in creating earned revenue for a period of time.

Think back to Chapter 1, where we first discussed revenue and expenses. We noted then that revenue is recorded when it is earned and expenses are recorded when they are incurred, not when they are actually paid. This principle will be discussed further in a later chapter. For now, it is enough to remember that we record revenue and expenses when they occur because we want to match earned revenue with the expenses that resulted in earning those revenues. In this case, by working those four days, John Murray created some revenue for Clark in May. Therefore, the Office Salaries Expense must be shown in May—the month the revenue was earned.

The results are as follows:

- Office Salaries Expense is increased by $350. This unpaid and unrecorded expense for salaries for which payment is not yet due is called **accrued salaries payable.** In effect, we now show the true expense for salaries ($1,650 instead of $1,300):

Office Salaries Expense	
1,300	
350	

FIGURE 4.7

May

Sunday	Monday	Tuesday	Wednesday	Thursday	Friday	Saturday
						1
2	3	4	5	6	7	8
9	10	11	12	13	14	15
16	17	18	19	20	21	22
23	24	25	26	27	28	29
30	31					

- Salaries Payable is also increased by $350. Clark's created a liability called Salaries Payable, which means that the firm owes money for salaries. When the firm pays John Murray, it will reduce its liability Salaries Payable as well as decrease its cash.

In terms of the transaction analysis chart, the following would be done:

Accounts Affected	Category	↓ ↑	Rules
Office Salaries Expense	Expense	↑	Dr.
Salaries Payable	Liability	↑	Cr.

Office Salaries Exp. 511	
1,300	
350	

Salaries Payable 212	
	350

How the adjustment for accrued salaries is entered is shown in Figure 4.8.

FIGURE 4.8

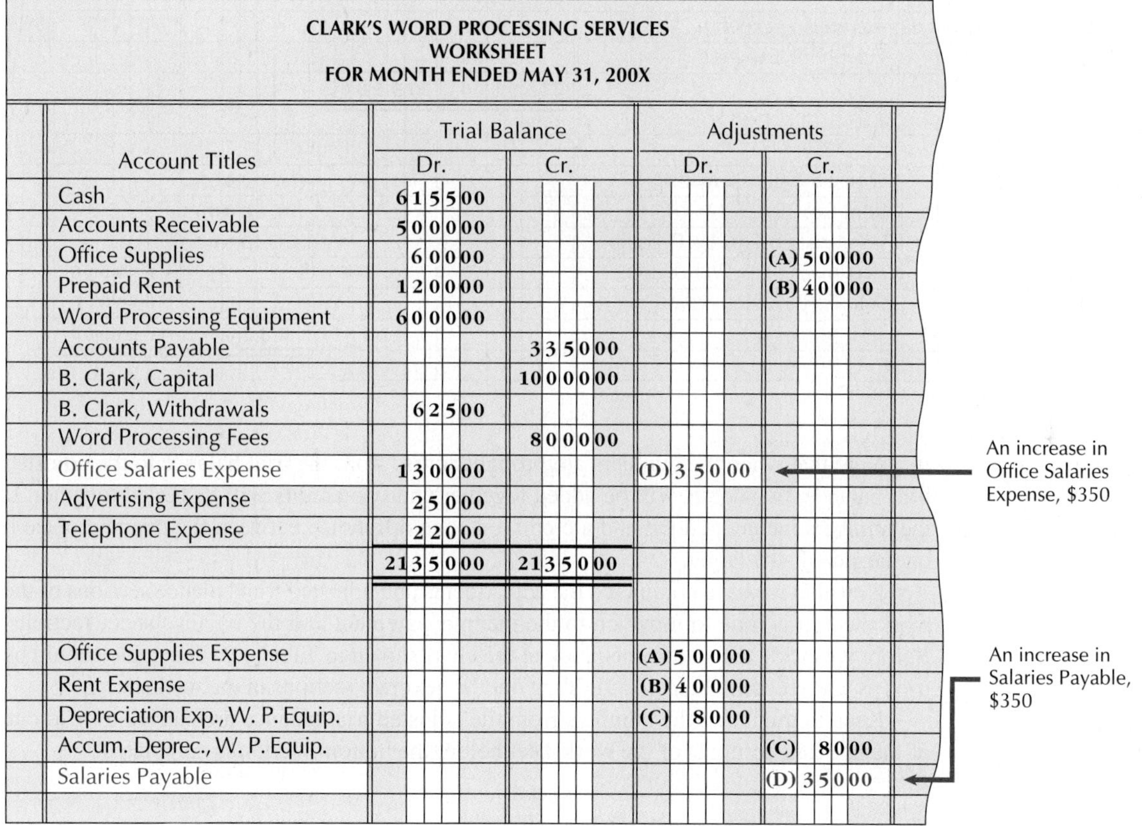

CLARK'S WORD PROCESSING SERVICES
WORKSHEET
FOR MONTH ENDED MAY 31, 200X

Account Titles	Trial Balance Dr.	Trial Balance Cr.	Adjustments Dr.	Adjustments Cr.
Cash	6155 00			
Accounts Receivable	5000 00			
Office Supplies	600 00			(A) 500 00
Prepaid Rent	1200 00			(B) 400 00
Word Processing Equipment	6000 00			
Accounts Payable		3350 00		
B. Clark, Capital		10000 00		
B. Clark, Withdrawals	625 00			
Word Processing Fees		8000 00		
Office Salaries Expense	1300 00		(D) 350 00	
Advertising Expense	250 00			
Telephone Expense	220 00			
	21350 00	21350 00		
Office Supplies Expense			(A) 500 00	
Rent Expense			(B) 400 00	
Depreciation Exp., W. P. Equip.			(C) 80 00	
Accum. Deprec., W. P. Equip.				(C) 80 00
Salaries Payable				(D) 350 00

The account Office Salaries Expense is already listed in the account titles, so $350 is placed in the debit column of the adjustments section on the same line as Office Salaries Expense. However, because the Salaries Payable is not listed in the account titles, it is added below the trial balance after Accumulated Depreciation, W. P. Equipment. The amount $350 is also placed in the credit column of the adjustments section on the same line as Salaries Payable.

Now that we have finished all the adjustments that we intended to make we total the adjustments section, as shown in Figure 4.9 on the following page.

The Adjusted Trial Balance Section

The adjusted trial balance is the next section on the worksheet. To fill it out we must summarize the information in the trial balance and adjustments sections, as shown in Figure 4.10.

Even when using computerized accounting, the user would still prepare an adjusted trial balance.

FIGURE 4.9 The Adjustments Section of the Worksheet

CLARK'S WORD PROCESSING SERVICES
WORKSHEET
FOR MONTH ENDED MAY 31, 200X

Account Titles	Trial Balance Dr.	Trial Balance Cr.	Adjustments Dr.	Adjustments Cr.
Cash	6155 00			
Accounts Receivable	5000 00			
Office Supplies	600 00			(A) 500 00
Prepaid Rent	1200 00			(B) 400 00
Word Processing Equipment	6000 00			
Accounts Payable		3350 00		
B. Clark, Capital		10000 00		
B. Clark, Withdrawals	625 00			
Word Processing Fees		8000 00		
Office Salaries Expense	1300 00		(D) 350 00	
Advertising Expense	250 00			
Telephone Expense	220 00			
	21350 00	21350 00		
Office Supplies Expense			(A) 500 00	
Rent Expense			(B) 400 00	
Depreciation Exp., W. P. Equip.			(C) 80 00	
Accum. Deprec., W. P. Equip.				(C) 80 00
Salaries Payable				(D) 350 00
			1330 00	1330 00

Note that when the numbers are brought across from the trial balance to the adjusted trial balance, two debits will be added together and two credits will be added together. If the numbers include a debit and a credit, take the difference between the two and place it on the side that is larger.

Now that we have completed the adjustments and adjusted trial balance sections of the worksheet, it is time to move on to the income statement and the balance sheet sections. Before we tackle the statements, look at the chart shown in Table 4.2. This table should be used as a reference to help you in filling out the next two sections of the worksheet.

Keep in mind that the numbers from the adjusted trial balance are carried over to one of the last four columns of the worksheet before the bottom section is completed.

LO3 The Income Statement Section

As shown in Figure 4.11, the income statement section lists only revenue and expenses from the adjusted trial balance. Note that Accumulated Depreciation and Salaries Payable do not go on the income statement. Accumulated Depreciation is a contra-asset found on the balance sheet. Salaries Payable is a liability found on the balance sheet.

The revenue ($8,000) and all the individual expenses are listed in the income statement section. The revenue is placed in the credit column of the income statement section because it has a credit balance. The expenses have debit balances so they are placed in the debit column of the income statement section. The following steps must be taken after the debits and credits are placed in the correct columns:

> The difference between $3,100 Dr. and $8,000 Cr. indicates a Net Income of $4,900. Do not think of the Net Income as a Dr. or Cr. The $4,900 is placed in the debit column to balance both columns to $8,000. Actually, the credit side is larger by $4,900.

Step 1 Total the debits and credits.

Step 2 Calculate the balance between the debit and credit columns and place the difference on the smaller side.

Step 3 Total the columns.

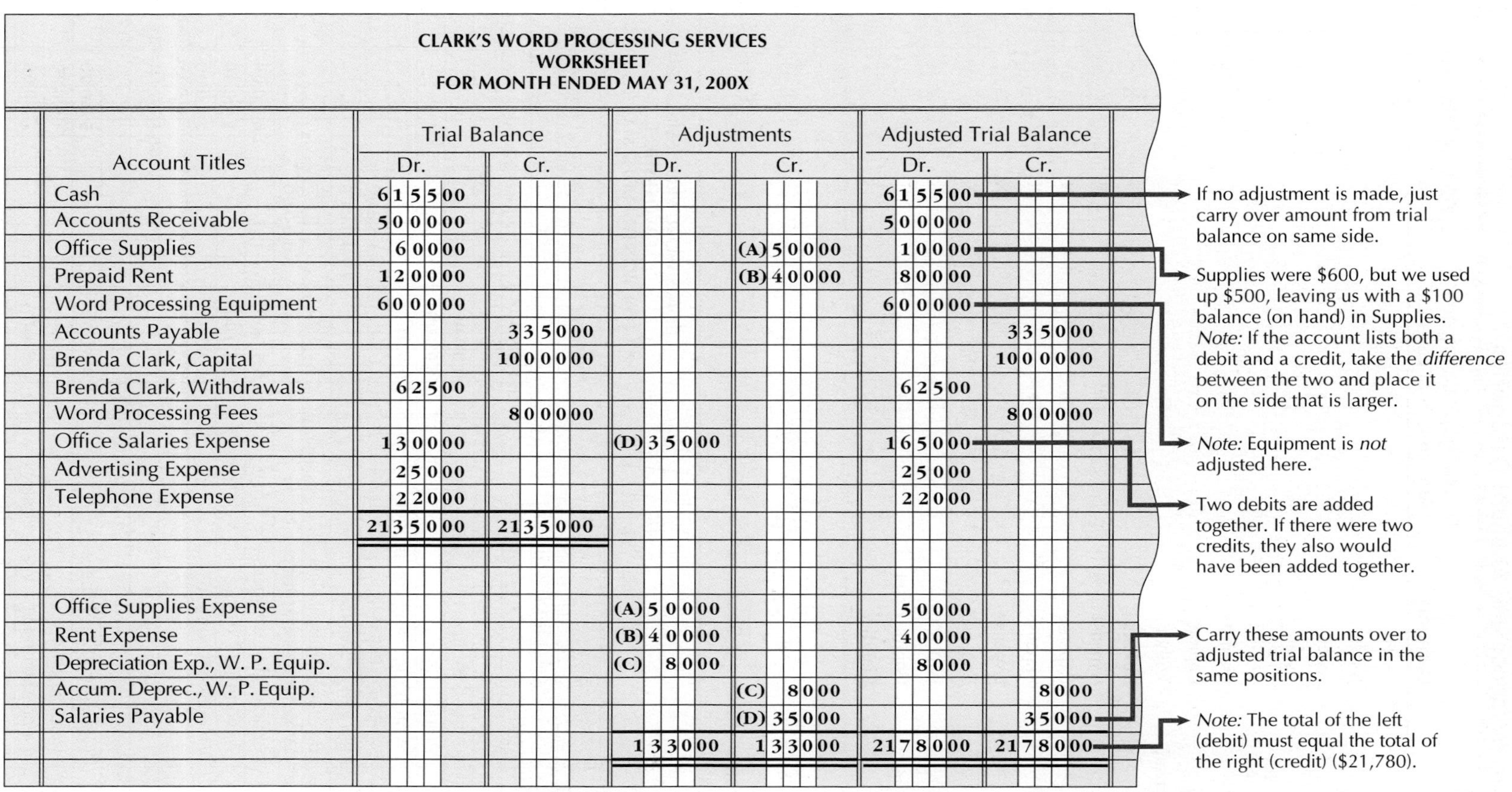

CLARK'S WORD PROCESSING SERVICES
WORKSHEET
FOR MONTH ENDED MAY 31, 200X

Account Titles	Trial Balance Dr.	Trial Balance Cr.	Adjustments Dr.	Adjustments Cr.	Adjusted Trial Balance Dr.	Adjusted Trial Balance Cr.
Cash	6155 00				6155 00	
Accounts Receivable	5000 00				5000 00	
Office Supplies	600 00			(A) 500 00	100 00	
Prepaid Rent	1200 00			(B) 400 00	800 00	
Word Processing Equipment	6000 00				6000 00	
Accounts Payable		3350 00				3350 00
Brenda Clark, Capital		10000 00				10000 00
Brenda Clark, Withdrawals	625 00				625 00	
Word Processing Fees		8000 00				8000 00
Office Salaries Expense	1300 00		(D) 350 00		1650 00	
Advertising Expense	250 00				250 00	
Telephone Expense	220 00				220 00	
	21350 00	21350 00				
Office Supplies Expense			(A) 500 00		500 00	
Rent Expense			(B) 400 00		400 00	
Depreciation Exp., W. P. Equip.			(C) 80 00		80 00	
Accum. Deprec., W. P. Equip.				(C) 80 00		80 00
Salaries Payable				(D) 350 00		350 00
			1330 00	1330 00	21780 00	21780 00

If no adjustment is made, just carry over amount from trial balance on same side.
Supplies were $600, but we used up $500, leaving us with a $100 balance (on hand) in Supplies. Note: If the account lists both a debit and a credit, take the difference between the two and place it on the side that is larger.
Note: Equipment is not adjusted here.
Two debits are added together. If there were two credits, they also would have been added together.
Carry these amounts over to adjusted trial balance in the same positions.
Note: The total of the left (debit) must equal the total of the right (credit) ($21,780).

FIGURE 4.10 The Adjusted Trial Balance Section of the Worksheet

TABLE 4.2 Normal Balances and Account Categories

Account Titles	Category	Normal Balance on Adjusted Trial Balance	Income Statement Dr.	Income Statement Cr.	Balance Sheet Dr.	Balance Sheet Cr.
Cash	Asset	Dr.			X	
Accounts Receivable	Asset	Dr.			X	
Office Supplies	Asset	Dr.			X	
Prepaid Rent	Asset	Dr.			X	
Word Proc. Equip.	Asset	Dr.			X	
Accounts Payable	Liability	Cr.				X
Brenda Clark, Capital	Capital	Cr.				X
Brenda Clark, Withdrawals	Withdrawal	Dr.			X	
Word Proc. Fees	Revenue	Cr.		X		
Office Salaries Exp.	Expense	Dr.	X			
Advertising Expense	Expense	Dr.	X			
Telephone Expense	Expense	Dr.	X			
Office Supplies Exp.	Expense	Dr.	X			
Rent Expense	Expense	Dr.	X			
Dep. Exp., W. P. Equip.	Expense	Dr.	X			
Acc. Dep., W. P. Equip.	Contra-Asset	Cr.				X
Salaries Payable	Liability	Cr.				X

FIGURE 4.11 The Income Statement Section of the Worksheet

CLARK'S WORD PROCESSING SERVICES
WORKSHEET
FOR MONTH ENDED MAY 31, 200X

Account Titles	Adjusted Trial Balance Dr.	Adjusted Trial Balance Cr.	Income Statement Dr.	Income Statement Cr.
Cash	6155 00			
Accounts Receivable	5000 00			
Office Supplies	100 00			
Prepaid Rent	800 00			
Word Processing Equipment	6000 00			
Accounts Payable		3350 00		
B. Clark, Capital		10000 00		
B. Clark, Withdrawals	625 00			
Word Processing Fees		8000 00		8000 00
Office Salaries Expense	1650 00		1650 00	
Advertising Expense	250 00		250 00	
Telephone Expense	220 00		220 00	
Office Supplies Expense	500 00		500 00	
Rent Expense	400 00		400 00	
Depreciation Exp., W. P. Equip.	80 00		80 00	
Accum. Deprec., W. P. Equip.		80 00		
Salaries Payable		350 00		
	21780 00	21780 00	3100 00	8000 00
Net Income			4900 00	
			8000 00	8000 00

$8,000
−3,100
$4,900 → Net Income

The worksheet in Figure 4.11 shows that the label Net Income is added in the account title column on the same line as $4,900. When the figures result in a net income it will be placed in the debit column of the income statement section of the worksheet. A net loss is placed in the credit column. The $8,000 total indicates that the two columns are in balance.

The Balance Sheet Section

To fill out the balance sheet section of the worksheet the following are carried over from the adjusted trial balance section: assets, contra-assets, liabilities, capital, and withdrawals. Because the beginning figure for Capital* is used on the worksheet, the Net Income is brought over to the credit column of the balance sheet so both columns balance.

Remember: The ending figure for capital is not on the worksheet.

Let's now look at the completed worksheet in Figure 4.12 to see how the balance sheet section is completed. Note how the Net Income of $4,900 is brought over to the credit column of the worksheet. The figure for Capital is also in the credit column while the figure for Withdrawals is in the debit column. By placing the net income in the credit column both sides total $18,680. If a net loss were to occur it would be placed in the debit column of the balance sheet column.

Now that we have completed the worksheet, we can go on to the three financial reports. But first let's summarize our progress.

LEARNING UNIT 4-1 REVIEW

AT THIS POINT you should be able to

- Define and explain the purpose of a worksheet.
- Explain the need as well as the process for adjustments.
- Explain the concept of depreciation.
- Explain the difference between depreciation expense and accumulated depreciation.
- Prepare a worksheet from a trial balance and adjustment data.

Accounting Cycle Tutorial

Self-Review Quiz 4-1

From the accompanying trial balance and adjustment data in Figure 4.13, complete a worksheet for P. Logan Co. for the month ended Dec. 31, 200X. (You can use the blank fold-out worksheet located at the end of the textbook.)

Note: The numbers used on this quiz may seem impossibly small, but we have done that on purpose, so that at this point you don't have to worry about arithmetic, just about preparing the worksheet correctly.

Adjustment Data

a. Depreciation Expense, Store Equipment, $1.
b. Insurance Expired, $2.
c. Supplies on hand, $1.
d. Salaries owed but not paid to employees, $3.

For additional help go to www.pearsonhighered.com/slater

*We assume no additional investments during the period.

Original cost of \$6,000 is *not* adjusted — "Used up" — "On hand"

CLARK'S WORD PROCESSING SERVICES
WORKSHEET
FOR MONTH ENDED MAY 31, 200X

Account Titles	Trial Balance Dr.	Trial Balance Cr.	Adjustments Dr.	Adjustments Cr.	Adjusted Trial Balance Dr.	Adjusted Trial Balance Cr.	Income Statement Dr.	Income Statement Cr.	Balance Sheet Dr.	Balance Sheet Cr.
Cash	615500				615500				615500	
Accounts Receivable	500000				500000				500000	
Office Supplies	60000			(A) 50000	10000				10000	
Prepaid Rent	120000			(B) 40000	80000				80000	
Word Processing Equipment	600000				600000				600000	
Accounts Payable		335000				335000				335000
B. Clark, Capital		1000000				1000000				1000000
B. Clark, Withdrawals	62500				62500				62500	
Word Processing Fees		800000				800000		800000		
Office Salaries Expense	130000		(D) 35000		165000		165000			
Advertising Expense	25000				25000		25000			
Telephone Expense	22000				22000		22000			
	2135000	2135000								
Office Supplies Expense			(A) 50000		50000		50000			
Rent Expense			(B) 40000		40000		40000			
Depreciation Exp., W. P. Equip.			(C) 8000		8000		8000			
Accum. Deprec., W. P. Equip.				(C) 8000		8000				8000
Salaries Payable				(D) 35000		35000				35000
			133000	133000	2178000	2178000	310000	800000	1868000	1378000
Net Income							490000			490000
							800000	800000	1868000	1868000

contra-asset

FIGURE 4.12

FIGURE 4.13

P. LOGAN COMPANY
TRIAL BALANCE
DECEMBER 31, 200X

	Dr.	Cr.
Cash	1500	
Accounts Receivable	300	
Prepaid Insurance	300	
Store Supplies	500	
Store Equipment	600	
Accumulated Depreciation, Store Equipment		400
Accounts Payable		200
P. Logan, Capital		1400
P. Logan, Withdrawals	300	
Revenue from Clients		2500
Rent Expense	200	
Salaries Expense	800	
	4500	4500

Solution to Self-Review Quiz 4-1

Don't adjust this line! Store Equipment always contains the historical cost.

Amount used up

Note that supplies on hand end up on the adjusted trial balance

P. LOGAN COMPANY
WORKSHEET
FOR MONTH ENDED DECEMBER 31, 200X

Account Titles	Trial Balance Dr.	Trial Balance Cr.	Adjustments Dr.	Adjustments Cr.	Adjusted Trial Balance Dr.	Adjusted Trial Balance Cr.	Income Statement Dr.	Income Statement Cr.	Balance Sheet Dr.	Balance Sheet Cr.
Cash	15 00				15 00				15 00	
Accounts Receivable	3 00				3 00				3 00	
Prepaid Insurance	3 00			(B) 2 00	1 00				1 00	
Store Supplies	5 00			(C) 4 00	1 00				1 00	
Store Equipment	6 00				6 00				6 00	
Accum. Depr., Store Equipment		4 00		(A) 1 00		5 00				5 00
Accounts Payable		2 00				2 00				2 00
P. Logan, Capital		14 00				14 00				14 00
P. Logan, Withdrawals	3 00				3 00				3 00	
Revenue from Clients		25 00				25 00		25 00		
Rent Expense	2 00				2 00		2 00			
Salaries Expense	8 00		(D) 3 00		11 00		11 00			
	45 00	45 00								
Depr. Exp., Store Equipment			(A) 1 00		1 00		1 00			
Insurance Expense			(B) 2 00		2 00		2 00			
Supplies Expense			(C) 4 00		4 00		4 00			
Salaries Payable				(D) 3 00		3 00				3 00
			10 00	10 00	49 00	49 00	20 00	25 00	29 00	24 00
Net Income							5 00			5 00
							25 00	25 00	29 00	29 00

Note that Accumulated Depreciation is listed in trial balance because the company is not new. Store Equipment has already been depreciated $4.00 from an earlier period.

FIGURE 4.14

NEED HELP?

Let's review first: When completing a worksheet we list the original trial balance, add adjustments, complete an adjusted trial balance, and then decide which titles go on the income statement and balance sheet. Since we do not have columns for statement of owner's equity, withdrawals and net income will be placed on the balance sheet columns to arrive at a new figure for capital. Remember, it is the old figure for capital that is placed on the worksheet.

Account title column: Any item not listed on the original trial balance will be listed below the trial balance. This will happen when we make adjustments. Note that when we list each title below the trial balance it will be increasing in value.

Adjustment column:

A. Depreciation:

In this adjustment Accumulated Depreciation is already listed on the trial balance so we only have to add Depreciation Expense below the trial balance. Here is the mind process chart for this adjustment:

Dep. Expense, St. Equip.	Expense	↑	Dr. $1
Acc. Deprec., St. Equip.	Contra-asset	↑	Cr. $1

Note that the original cost of Store Equipment of $6 is not touched.

B. Insurance Expired:

In this adjustment Prepaid Insurance is already listed on the trial balance so we only have to add Insurance Expense below the trial balance. Here is the mind process chart for this adjustment:

Insurance Expense	Expense	↑	Dr. $2
Prepaid Insurance	Asset	↓	Cr. $2

Expired means used up and thus we use the amount of $2.

C. Supplies On Hand:

In this adjustment we have to calculate the amount of supplies used up. We take the beginning amount of supplies of $5 less the amount on hand of $1 to equal the amount used up of $4. This is the amount of the adjustment. Since we have Office Supplies listed on the trial balance we only have to add Supplies Expense below the trial balance. Here is the mind process chart for this adjustment:

Supplies Expense	Expense	↑	Dr. $4
Office Supplies	Asset	↓	Cr. $4

D. Salaries Owed:

In this adjustment we have Salaries Expense already listed on the trial balance. Here we have to add Salaries Payable below the trial balance. The following mind process chart shows the new expense that has been incurred but has not been paid:

Salaries Expense	Expense	↑	Dr. $3
Salaries Payable	Liability	↑	Cr. $3

The sum of all the debits on the adjustments equals the sum of the credits.

Adjusted Trial Balance Columns: Accounts that were not adjusted or added below the trial balance have their balances carried over to the adjusted trial balance. Accounts that were adjusted will have their combined balances carried over to the adjusted trial balance.

For example, Salaries Expense is adjusted by adding the debit balance of $8 and the adjustment of $3 to equal an $11 debit balance on the adjusted trial balance. Every account in the adjusted trial balance will end up on the Income Statement or Balance Sheet columns of the worksheet.

Income Statement Columns: From the adjusted trial balance all revenues and expenses Accounts are listed. Note that when we total the debit and credit columns they do not equal each other until we calculate the difference between revenues and expenses. In this case, the ($5) difference will be added to the debit column of the income statement section so both columns will total $25.

Balance Sheet Columns: From the adjusted trial balance assets and withdrawals will end up in the debit column. The old figures for capital, liabilities, and contra assets are in the credit column. Note that the totals of the columns will not balance until a net income of $5 is placed under the $24. This is done because we use the old figure for capital on the worksheet and there is no column on the worksheet for the statement of owner's equity.

Summary: On the worksheet items accounts listed below the trial balance are increasing. Adjustments for supplies must be used up. The original cost of equipment is never touched in the adjustment process. Capital is the old balance on the worksheet. Net income is the difference between revenue and expenses and is carried over to the credit column of the balance sheet. Net losses would be in opposite columns. Income Statement Columns and Balance Sheet Columns will be out of balance by amount of Net Income.

LO4

Learning Unit 4-2 Step 6 of the Accounting Cycle: Preparing the Financial Statements from the Worksheet

In a computerized system, such as QuickBooks or Peachtree, preparing the financial statements becomes as easy as selecting the statement from the Report menu and setting the date to the correct period.

The formal financial statements can be prepared from the worksheet completed in Learning Unit 4-1. Before beginning, we must check that the entries on the worksheet are correct and in balance. To ensure the accuracy of the figures, we double-check that (1) all entries are recorded in the appropriate column, (2) the correct amounts are entered in the proper places, (3) the addition is correct across the columns (i.e., from the trial balance to the adjusted trial balance to the financial statements), and (4) the columns are added correctly.

Preparing the Income Statement

The first statement to be prepared for Clark's Word Processing Services is the income statement. When preparing the income statement it is important to remember the following:

1. Every figure on the formal statement is on the worksheet. Figure 4.15 on the following page shows where each of these figures goes on the income statement.
2. No debit or credit columns appear on the formal statement.
3. The inside column on financial statements is used for subtotaling.
4. Withdrawals do not go on the income statement; they go on the statement of owner's equity.

Take a moment to look at the income statement in Figure 4.15. Note where items go from the income statement section of the worksheet onto the formal statement.

Preparing the Statement of Owner's Equity

Figure 4.16 is the statement of owner's equity for Clark's. The figure shows where the information comes from on the worksheet. It is important to remember that if additional investments were made, the figure on the worksheet for Capital would not be the beginning figure for Capital. Checking the ledger account for Capital will tell you whether the amount is correct. Note how Net Income and Withdrawals aid in calculating the new figure for Capital.

Preparing the Balance Sheet

In preparing the balance sheet (Fig. 4.17), remember that the balance sheet section totals on the worksheet ($18,680) do *not* match the totals on the formal balance sheet ($17,975). This information is grouped differently on the formal statement. First, in the formal report Accumulated Depreciation ($80) is subtracted from Word Processing Equipment, reducing the balance. Second, Withdrawals ($625) are subtracted from Owner's Equity, reducing the balance further. These two reductions (−$80 − $625 = −$705) represent the difference between the worksheet and the formal version of the balance sheet ($17,975 − $18,680 = −$705). Figure 4.17 shows how to prepare the balance sheet from the worksheet.

LEARNING UNIT 4-2 REVIEW

AT THIS POINT you should be able to

- Prepare the three financial statements from a worksheet.
- Explain why totals of the formal balance sheet don't match totals of balance sheet columns on the worksheet.

Self-Review Quiz 4-2

From the worksheet for P. Logan, please prepare (1) an income statement for December, (2) a statement of owner's equity, and (3) a balance sheet for December 31, 200X. No additional investments took place during the period.

For additional help go to www.pearsonhighered.com/slater

Account Titles	Income Statement Dr.	Income Statement Cr.
Cash		
Accounts Receivable		
Office Supplies		
Prepaid Rent		
Word Processing Equipment		
Accounts Payable		
Brenda Clark, Capital		
Brenda Clark, Withdrawals		
Word Processing Fees		8 0 0 0 00
Office Salaries Expense	1 6 5 0 00	
Advertising Expense	2 5 0 00	
Telephone Expense	2 2 0 00	
Office Supplies Expense	5 0 0 00	
Rent Expense	4 0 0 00	
Depreciation Expense, W. P. Equip.	8 0 00	
Accum. Deprec., W. P. Equip.		
Salaries Payable		
	3 1 0 0 00	8 0 0 0 00
Net Income	4 9 0 0 00	
	8 0 0 0 00	8 0 0 0 00

CLARK'S WORD PROCESSING SERVICES
INCOME STATEMENT
FOR MONTH ENDED MAY 31, 200X

Revenue:		
Word Processing Fees		$8 0 0 0 00
Operating Expenses:		
Office Salaries Expense	$1 6 5 0 00	
Advertising Expense	2 5 0 00	
Telephone Expense	2 2 0 00	
Office Supplies Expense	5 0 0 00	
Rent Expense	4 0 0 00	
Depreciation Expense, W. P. Equipment	8 0 00	
Total Operating Expenses		3 1 0 0 00
Net Income		$4 9 0 0 00

FIGURE 4.15 From Worksheet to Income Statement

CLARK'S WORD PROCESSING SERVICES
STATEMENT OF OWNER'S EQUITY
FOR MONTH ENDED MAY 31, 200X

Brenda Clark, Capital, May 1, 200X		$10 0 0 0 00
Net Income for May	$4 9 0 0 00	
Less Withdrawals for May	6 2 5 00	
Increase in Capital		4 2 7 5 00
Brenda Clark, Capital, May 31, 200X		$14 2 7 5 00

From income statement Net Income on worksheet (or from formal report just prepared)

Balance Sheet Dr. column on worksheet

This figure is not on the worksheet. It is calculated here and used to prepare the balance sheet. Note that no additional investments were made during May.

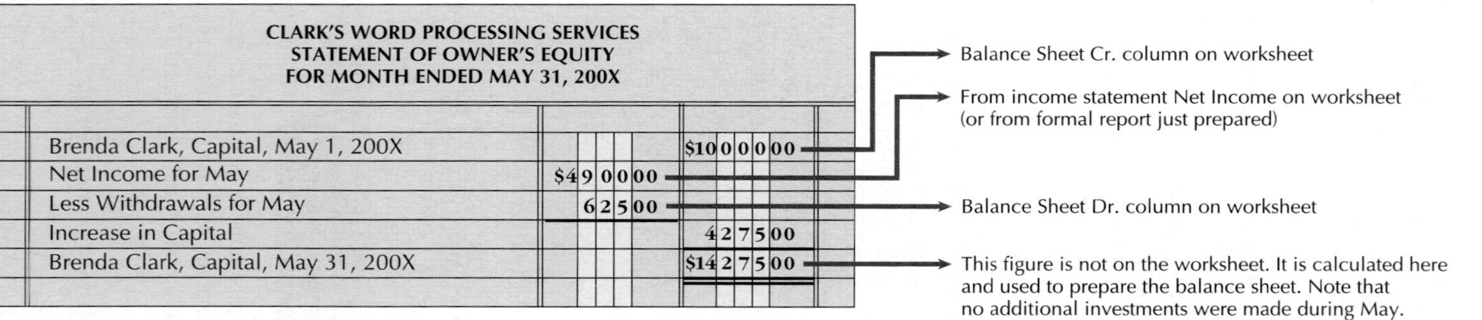

FIGURE 4.16 Completing a Statement of Owner's Equity

FIGURE 4.17 From Worksheet to Balance Sheet

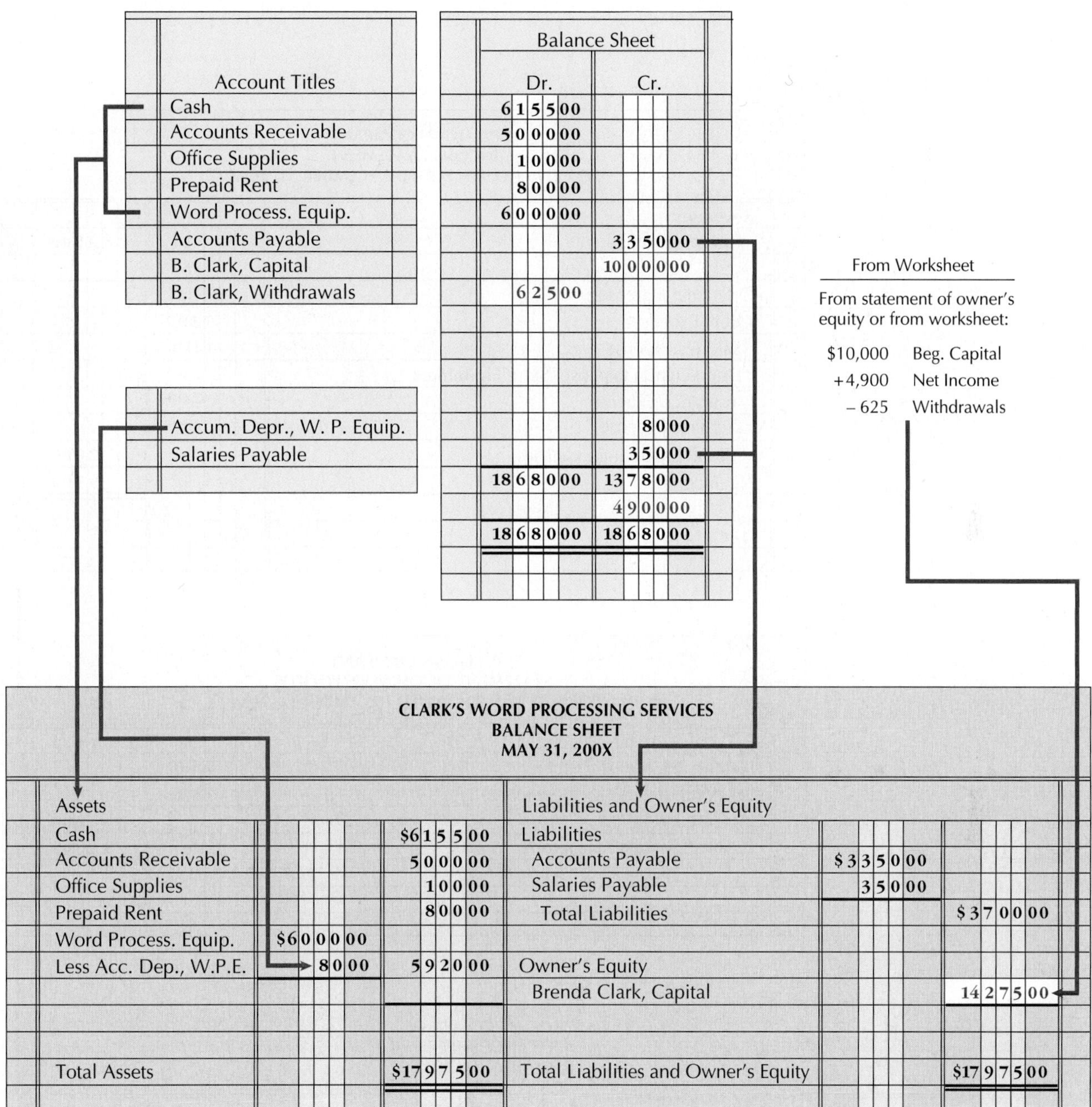

Account Titles	Balance Sheet Dr.	Balance Sheet Cr.
Cash	6155 00	
Accounts Receivable	5000 00	
Office Supplies	100 00	
Prepaid Rent	800 00	
Word Process. Equip.	6000 00	
Accounts Payable		3350 00
B. Clark, Capital		10000 00
B. Clark, Withdrawals	625 00	
Accum. Depr., W. P. Equip.		80 00
Salaries Payable		350 00
	18680 00	13780 00
		4900 00
	18680 00	18680 00

CLARK'S WORD PROCESSING SERVICES
BALANCE SHEET
MAY 31, 200X

Assets			Liabilities and Owner's Equity		
Cash		$6155 00	Liabilities		
Accounts Receivable		5000 00	Accounts Payable	$3350 00	
Office Supplies		100 00	Salaries Payable	350 00	
Prepaid Rent		800 00	Total Liabilities		$3700 00
Word Process. Equip.	$6000 00				
Less Acc. Dep., W.P.E.	80 00	5920 00	Owner's Equity		
			Brenda Clark, Capital		14275 00
Total Assets		$17975 00	Total Liabilities and Owner's Equity		$17975 00

Solution to Self-Review Quiz 4-2

FIGURE 4.18

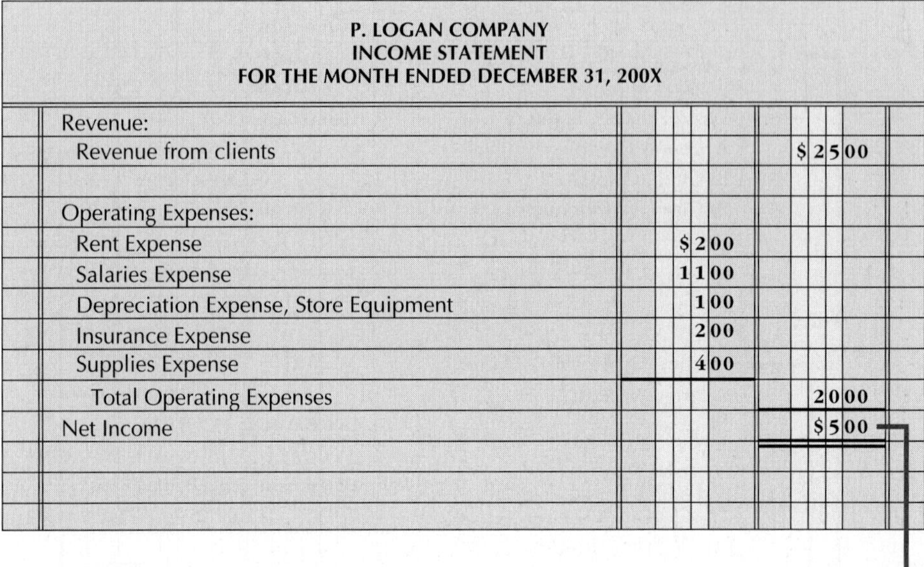

P. LOGAN COMPANY
INCOME STATEMENT
FOR THE MONTH ENDED DECEMBER 31, 200X

Revenue:		
Revenue from clients		$2500
Operating Expenses:		
Rent Expense	$200	
Salaries Expense	1100	
Depreciation Expense, Store Equipment	100	
Insurance Expense	200	
Supplies Expense	400	
Total Operating Expenses		2000
Net Income		$500

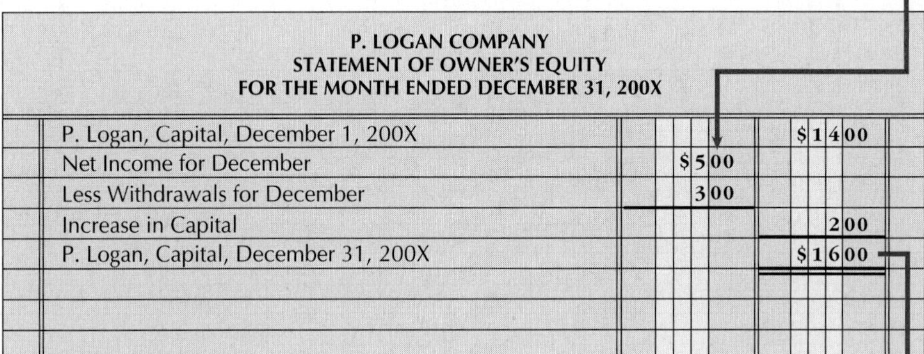

P. LOGAN COMPANY
STATEMENT OF OWNER'S EQUITY
FOR THE MONTH ENDED DECEMBER 31, 200X

P. Logan, Capital, December 1, 200X		$1400
Net Income for December	$500	
Less Withdrawals for December	300	
Increase in Capital		200
P. Logan, Capital, December 31, 200X		$1600

P. LOGAN COMPANY
BALANCE SHEET
DECEMBER 31, 200X

Assets			Liabilities and Owner's Equity		
Cash		$1500	Liabilities		
Accounts Receivable		300	Accounts Payable	$200	
Prepaid Insurance		100	Salaries Payable	300	
Store Supplies		100	Total Liabilities		$500
Store Equipment	$600		Owner's Equity		
Less Acc. Dep., St. Eq.	500	100	P. Logan, Capital		1600
			Total Liabilities and		
Total Assets		$2100	Owner's Equity		$2100

NEED HELP?

Let's review first: There are no debits or credits on the formal financial statements. The three financial statements are made from the last four columns of the worksheet.

Income Statement: The income statement is made up of revenues and expenses. Use the inside column for subtotaling. All numbers found on the income statement are also found on the worksheet.

Statement of Owner's Equity: The net income of $5 is used from the income statement to update the statement of owner's equity. Note that the $14 is the old figure from the worksheet. The increase in capital of $2 is not found on the worksheet. Logan's ending figure of $16 is not found on the worksheet.

Balance Sheet: Logan's ending figure of $16 from the statement of owner's equity is used as the capital figure on the balance sheet. Note under assets how the inside column is used to calculate store equipment less accumulated depreciation. Note that the totals of $21 from the balance sheet are not found on the worksheet. When the financial report is prepared there are no debits or credits.

Summary: The worksheet was prepared in terms of debits and credits, not the formal financial statements. The inside column of the financial statements is for subtotaling. The worksheet used the old figure for Capital while the balance sheet uses the figure from the statement of owner's equity for the new figure of Capital. Many of the numbers on the statement of owner's equity and balance sheet will not be found on the worksheet since there are no debits or credits on formal financial statements.

CHAPTER ASSIGNMENTS

All Classroom Demonstration Exercises, Exercises, Problems, and the Continuing Problem in this chapter can be found within MyAccountingLab, an online homework and practice environment. Your instructor may ask you to complete this material using MyAccountingLab.

DEMONSTRATION PROBLEM: STEPS 5 AND 6 OF THE ACCOUNTING CYCLE

From the following trial balance and additional data complete (1) a worksheet and (2) the three financial statements (numbers are intentionally small so you may concentrate on the theory).

FROST COMPANY
TRIAL BALANCE
DECEMBER 31, 200X

	Dr.	Cr.
Cash	14	
Accounts Receivable	4	
Prepaid Insurance	5	
Plumbing Supplies	3	
Plumbing Equipment	7	
Accumulated Depreciation, Plumbing Equipment		5
Accounts Payable		1
J. Frost, Capital		12
J. Frost, Withdrawals	3	
Plumbing Fees		27
Rent Expense	4	
Salaries Expense	5	
Totals	45	45

Adjustment Data

1. Insurance Expired, $3.
2. Plumbing Supplies on Hand, $1.
3. Depreciation Expense, Plumbing Equipment, $1.
4. Salaries owed but not paid to employees, $2.

Solution Tips to Building a Worksheet

1. Adjustments

a.

Insurance Expense	Expense	↑	Dr.	$3
Prepaid Insurance	Asset	↓	Cr.	$3

Expired means used up

b.

Plumbing Supplies Expense	Expense	↑	Dr.	$2
Plumbing Supplies	Asset	↓	Cr.	$2

$3 − 1 = $2 *used up*

Solution to Worksheet

Original cost not adjusted — "Used up" — "On hand"

FROST COMPANY
WORKSHEET
FOR MONTH ENDED DECEMBER 31, 200X

Account Titles	Trial Balance Dr.	Trial Balance Cr.	Adjustments Dr.	Adjustments Cr.	Adjusted Trial Balance Dr.	Adjusted Trial Balance Cr.	Income Statement Dr.	Income Statement Cr.	Balance Sheet Dr.	Balance Sheet Cr.
Cash	1400				1400				1400	
Accounts Receivable	400				400				400	
Prepaid Insurance	500			(A) 300	200				200	
Plumbing Supplies	300			(B) 200	100				100	
Plumbing Equipment	700				700				700	
Accum. Depr., Plumb. Equip.		500		(C) 100		600				600
Accounts Payable		100				100				100
J. Frost, Capital		1200				1200				1200
J. Frost, Withdrawals	300				300				300	
Plumbing Fees		2700				2700		2700		
Rent Expense	400				400		400			
Salaries Expense	500		(D) 200		700		700			
	4500	4500								
Insurance Expense			(A) 300		300		300			
Plumbing Supplies Expense			(B) 200		200		200			
Depr. Exp. Plumb. Equip.			(C) 100		100		100			
Salaries Payable				(D) 200		200				200
			800	800	4800	4800	1700	2700	3100	2100
Net Income							1000			1000
							2700	2700	3100	3100

FIGURE 4.19

c.

Depreciation Expense, Plumbing Equipment	Expense	↑	Dr.	$1
Contra-Asset Accumulated Depreciation, Plumbing Equipment	Contra-Asset	↑	Cr.	$1

The original cost of equipment of $7 is not "touched."

d.

Salaries Expense	Expense	↑	Dr.	$2
Salaries Payable	Liability	↑	Cr.	$2

2. Last four columns of worksheet prepared from adjusted trial balance.
3. Capital of $12 is the old figure. Net income of $10 (revenue − expenses) is brought over to same side as capital on the balance sheet Cr. column to balance columns.

FROST COMPANY
INCOME STATEMENT
FOR MONTH ENDED DECEMBER 31, 200X

Revenue:		
Plumbing Fees		$27
Operating Expenses:		
Rent Expense	$4	
Salaries Expense	7	
Insurance Expense	3	
Plumbing Supplies Expense	2	
Depreciation Expense, Plumbing Equipment	1	
Total Operating Expenses		17
Net Income		$10

FROST COMPANY
STATEMENT OF OWNER'S EQUITY
FOR MONTH ENDED DECEMBER 31, 200X

J. Frost, Capital, Dec. 1, 200X		$12
Net Income for December	$10	
Less Withdrawals for December	3	
Increase in Capital		7
J. Frost, Capital, Dec. 31, 200X		$19

FROST COMPANY
BALANCE SHEET
DECEMBER 31, 200X

Assets			**Liabilities and Owner's Equity**		
Cash		$14	Liabilities		
Accounts Receivable		4	Accounts Payable	$1	
Prepaid Insurance		2	Salaries Payable	2	
Plumbing Supplies		1	Total Liabilities		$3
Plumbing Equipment	$7				
Less Accumulated Dep.	6	1	Owner's Equity		
			J. Frost, Capital		19
			Total Liabilities and		
Total Assets		$22	Owner's Equity		$22

Solution Tips for Preparing Financial Statements from a Worksheet

Inside columns of the three financial statements are used for subtotaling. No debits or credits appear on the formal statements.

	Statements
Income Statement	From Income Statement columns of worksheet for revenue and expenses.
Statement of Owner's Equity	Beginning figure for Capital from Balance Sheet worksheet Cr. column. Net Income from Income Statement. Withdrawal figure from Balance Sheet worksheet Dr. column.
Balance Sheet	Assets from Balance Sheet worksheet Dr. column. Liabilities and Accumulated Depreciation from Balance Sheet worksheet Cr. Column. New figure for Capital from statement of owner's equity.

Note how Plumbing Equipment $7 and Accumulated Depreciation $6 are rearranged on the formal balance sheet. The Total Assets of $22 is not on the worksheet. Remember, no debits or credits appear on formal statements.

SUMMARY OF KEY POINTS

LEARNING UNIT 4-1

1. The worksheet is not a formal statement.
2. Adjustments update certain accounts so that they will be up to their latest balance before financial statements are prepared. Adjustments are the result of internal transactions.
3. Adjustments will affect both the income statement and the balance sheet.
4. Accounts listed *below* the account titles on the trial balance of the worksheet are *increasing.*
5. The original cost of a piece of equipment is not adjusted; historical cost is not lost.
6. Depreciation is the process of spreading the original cost of the asset over its expected useful life.
7. Accumulated depreciation is a contra-asset on the balance sheet that summarizes, accumulates, or builds up the amount of depreciation that an asset has accumulated.
8. Book value is the original cost less accumulated depreciation.
9. Accrued salaries are unpaid and unrecorded expenses that are accumulating but for which payment is not yet due.
10. Revenue and expenses go on income statement sections of the worksheet. Assets, contra-assets, liabilities, capital, and withdrawals go on balance sheet sections of the worksheet.

LEARNING UNIT 4-2

1. The formal statements prepared from a worksheet do not have debit or credit columns.
2. Revenue and expenses go on the income statement. Beginning capital plus net income less withdrawals (or, beginning capital minus net loss less withdrawals) go on the statement of owner's equity. Be sure to check the capital account in the ledger to see whether any additional investments took place. Assets, contra-assets, liabilities, and the new figure for capital go on the balance sheet.

KEY TERMS

Accrued salaries payable Salaries that are earned by employees but unpaid and unrecorded during the period (and thus need to be recorded by an adjustment) and will not come due for payment until the next accounting period.

Accumulated Depreciation A contra-asset account that summarizes or accumulates the amount of depreciation that has been taken on an asset.

Adjusting The process of calculating the latest up-to-date balance of each account at the end of an accounting period.

Book value Cost of equipment less accumulated depreciation.

Depreciation The allocation (spreading) of the cost of an asset (such as an auto or equipment) over its expected useful life.

Historical cost The actual cost of an asset at time of purchase.

Residual value Estimated value of an asset after all the allowable depreciation has been taken.

Worksheet A columnar device used by accountants to aid them in completing the accounting cycle—often called a spreadsheet. It is not a formal report.

BLUEPRINT OF STEPS 5 AND 6 OF THE ACCOUNTING CYCLE

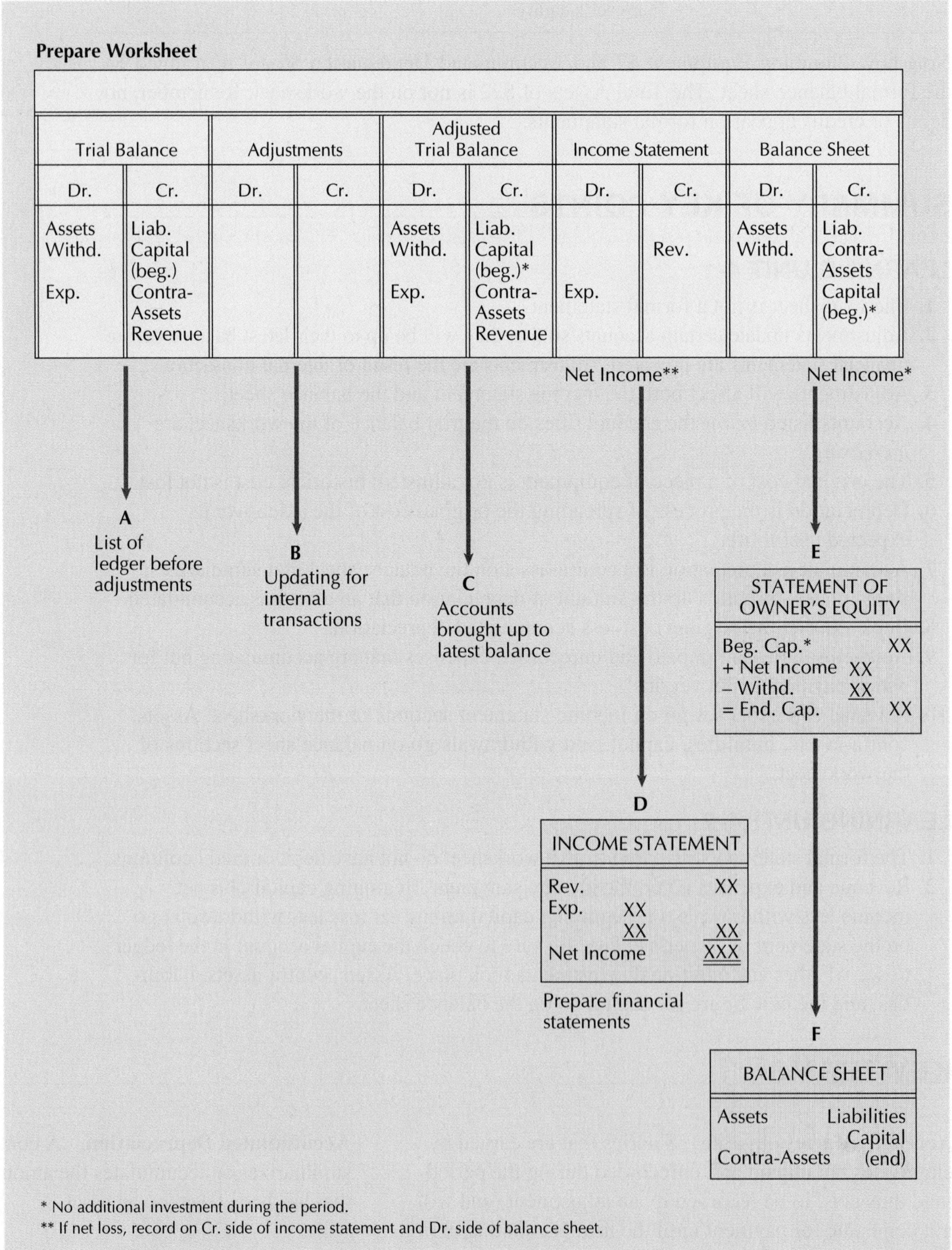

* No additional investment during the period.

** If net loss, record on Cr. side of income statement and Dr. side of balance sheet.

QUESTIONS, CLASSROOM DEMONSTRATION EXERCISES, EXERCISES, AND PROBLEMS

Discussion Questions and Critical Thinking/Ethical Case

1. Worksheets are required in every company's accounting cycle. Please agree or disagree and explain why.
2. What is the purpose of adjusting accounts?
3. What is the relationship of internal transactions to the adjusting process?
4. Explain how an adjustment can affect both the income statement and balance sheet. Please give an example.
5. Why do we need the Accumulated Depreciation account?
6. Depreciation expense goes on the balance sheet. True or false. Why?
7. Each month Accumulated Depreciation grows while Equipment goes up. Agree or disagree? Defend your position.
8. Define the term *accrued salaries.*
9. Why don't the formal financial statements contain debit or credit columns?
10. Explain how the financial statements are prepared from the worksheet.
11. Janet Fox, president of Angel Co., went to a tax seminar. One of the speakers at the seminar advised the audience to put off showing expenses until next year because doing so would allow them to take advantage of a new tax law. When Janet returned to the office, she called in her accountant, Frieda O'Riley. She told Frieda to forget about making any adjustments for salaries in the old year so more expenses could be shown in the new year. Frieda told her that putting off these expenses would not follow generally accepted accounting procedures. Janet said she should do it anyway. You make the call. Write your specific recommendations to Frieda.

Classroom Demonstration Exercises

MyAccountingLab

SET A

Adjustment for Supplies *LO1 (5 min)*

1. *Before Adjustment*

Office Supplies		Office Supplies Expense	
700			

Given: At year end, an inventory of Office Supplies showed $50.

a. How much is the adjustment for Office Supplies?
b. Draw a transaction analysis box for this adjustment.
c. What will the balance of Office Supplies be on the adjusted trial balance?

Adjustment for Prepaid Rent *LO1 (10 min)*

2. *Before Adjustment*

Prepaid Rent		Rent Expense	
1,200			

Given: At year end, rent expired is $700.

a. How much is the adjustment for Prepaid Rent?
b. Draw a transaction analysis box for this adjustment.
c. What will be the balance of Prepaid Rent on the adjusted trial balance?

Adjustment for Depreciation *LO1 (10 min)*

3. *Before Adjustment*

Equip.		Acc. Dep., Equip.		Dep. Exp., Equip.	
9,000			2,000		

Given: At year end, depreciation on Equipment is $2,000.

a. Which of these three T accounts is not affected?

b. Which account is a contra-asset?

c. Draw a transaction analysis box for this adjustment.

d. What will be the balance of these three accounts on the adjusted trial balance?

LO1 (10 min) **Adjustment for Accrued Salaries**

4. *Before Adjustment*

Salaries Expense		Salaries Payable	
1,400			

Given: Accrued Salaries, $300.

a. Draw a transaction analysis box for this adjustment.

b. What will be the balance of these two accounts on the adjusted trial balance?

LO 2, 3 (15 min) **Worksheet**

5. From the following adjusted trial balance titles of a worksheet, identify in which column each account will be listed on the last four columns of the worksheet:

(ID) Income Statement Dr. Column

(IC) Income Statement Cr. Column

(BD) Balance Sheet Dr. Column

(BC) Balance Sheet Cr. Column

		ATB	IS	BS
A. Ex: Legal Fees	~~~	~~~	IC	______
B. Accts. Payable	~~~	~~~	______	______
C. Cash	~~~	~~~	______	______
D. Prepaid Advertising	~~~	~~~	______	______
E. Salaries Payable	~~~	~~~	______	______
F. Dep. Expense	~~~	~~~	______	______
G. V., Capital	~~~	~~~	______	______
H. V., Withdrawals	~~~	~~~	______	______
I. Computer Supplies	~~~	~~~	______	______
J. Rent Expense	~~~	~~~	______	______
K. Supplies Payable	~~~	~~~	______	______
L. Advertising Expense	~~~	~~~	______	______
M. Accum. Depreciation	~~~	~~~	______	______
N. Wages Payable	~~~	~~~	______	______

LO 4 (15 min) **6.** From the following balance sheet (which was made from the worksheet and other financial statements), explain why the lettered numbers were not found on the worksheet. *Hint:* No debits or credits appear on the formal financial statements.

LAZE CO.
BALANCE SHEET
DECEMBER 31, 200X

Assets			**Liabilities and Owner's Equity**		
Cash		$6	Liabilities		
Acc. Receivable		2	Accounts Payable	$2	
Supplies		2	Salaries Payable	1	
Equipment	$10		Total Liabilities		$3 (B)
Less Acc. Dep.	4	6 (A)	Owner's Equity		
			J. Laze, Capital		13
Total Assets		$16	**Total Liabilities and Owner's Equity**		$16

SET B

Adjustment for Supplies

LO1 (5 min)

1. *Before Adjustment*

Computer Supplies		Computer Supplies Expense	
700			

Given: At year end, an inventory of Computer Supplies showed $100.

a. How much is the adjustment for Computer Supplies?

b. Draw a transaction analysis box for this adjustment.

c. What will the balance of Computer Supplies be on the adjusted trial balance?

Adjustment for Prepaid Rent

LO1 (10 min)

2. *Before Adjustment*

Prepaid Rent		Rent Expense	
700			

Given: At year end, rent expired is $300.

a. How much is the adjustment for Prepaid Rent?

b. Draw a transaction analysis box for this adjustment.

c. What will be the balance of Prepaid Rent on the adjusted trial balance?

Adjustment for Depreciation

LO1 (10 min)

3. *Before Adjustment*

Equip.		Acc. Dep., Equip.		Dep. Exp., Equip.	
6,000			1,000		

Given: At year end, depreciation on Equipment is $1,000.

a. Which of these three T accounts is not affected?

b. Which account is a contra-asset?

c. Draw a transaction analysis box for this adjustment.

d. What will be the balance of these three accounts on the adjusted trial balance?

Adjustment for Accrued Salaries

LO1 (10 min)

4. *Before Adjustment*

Salaries Expense		Salaries Payable	
900			

Given: Accrued Salaries, $200.

a. Draw a transaction analysis box for this adjustment.

b. What will be the balance of these two accounts on the adjusted trial balance?

Worksheet

LO2, 3 (15 min)

5. From the following adjusted trial balance titles of a worksheet, identify in which column each account will be listed on the last four columns of the worksheet:

(ID) Income Statement Dr. Column

(IC) Income Statement Cr. Column

(BD) Balance Sheet Dr. Column

(BC) Balance Sheet Cr. Column

		ATB	IS	BS
A. Ex: Supplies	~~~	~~~	____	BD
B. Accts. Receivable	~~~	~~~	____	____
C. Cash	~~~	~~~	____	____
D. Prepaid Rent	~~~	~~~	____	____
E. Equipment	~~~	~~~	____	____
F. Acc. Depreciation	~~~	~~~	____	____
G. B., Capital	~~~	~~~	____	____
H. B., Withdrawals	~~~	~~~	____	____
I. Taxi Fees	~~~	~~~	____	____
J. Advertising Expense	~~~	~~~	____	____
K. Off. Supplies Expense	~~~	~~~	____	____
L. Rent Expense	~~~	~~~	____	____
M. Depreciation Expense	~~~	~~~	____	____
N. Salaries Payable	~~~	~~~	____	____

LO2, 3 (15 min) **6.** From the following balance sheet (which was made from the worksheet and other financial statements), explain why the lettered numbers were not found on the worksheet. *Hint:* No debits or credits appear on the formal financial statements.

H. WELLS
BALANCE SHEET
DECEMBER 31, 200X

Assets			**Liabilities and Owner's Equity**		
Cash		$6	Liabilities		
Acc. Receivable		2	Accounts Payable	$2	
Supplies		2	Salaries Payable	1	
Equipment	$10		Total Liabilities		$3
Less Acc. Dep.	4	6	Owner's Equity		
			H. Wells, Capital		13 (B)
			Total Liabilities and		
Total Assets		$16 (A)	**Owner's Equity**		$16

MyAccountingLab

Exercises

LO4 (5 min) **4-1.** Complete the following table.

Account	Category	Normal Balance	Which Financial Statement(s) Found
Accounts Payable			
Prepaid Rent			
Office Equipment			
Depreciation Expense			
B. Reel, Capital			
B. Reel, Withdrawals			
Wages Payable			
Accumulated Depreciation			

LO1 (10 min) **4-2.** Use transaction analysis charts to analyze the following adjustments:

a. Depreciation on equipment, $600.

b. Rent expired, $400.

4-3. From the following adjustment data, calculate the adjustment amount and record appropriate debits or credits: *LO1 (10 min)*

a. Supplies purchased, $700.
Supplies on hand, $200.

b. Store equipment, $12,000.
Accumulated depreciation before adjustment, $900.
Depreciation expense, $200.

4-4. From the following trial balance (Fig. 4.20) and adjustment data, complete a worksheet for J. Trent as of December 31, 200X: *LO3 (20 min)*

a. Depreciation expense, equipment, $2.00.
b. Insurance expired, $1.00.
c. Store supplies on hand, $4.00.
d. Wages owed, but not paid for (they are an expense in the old year), $5.00.

FIGURE 4.20

J. TRENT
TRIAL BALANCE
DECEMBER 31, 200X

	Dr.	Cr.
Cash	9 00	
Accounts Receivable	2 00	
Prepaid Insurance	7 00	
Store Supplies	6 00	
Store Equipment	7 00	
Accumulated Depreciation, Equipment		2 00
Accounts Payable		4 00
J. Trent, Capital		17 00
J. Trent, Withdrawals	6 00	
Revenue from Clients		24 00
Rent Expense	4 00	
Wage Expense	6 00	
	47 00	47 00

4-5. From the completed worksheet in Exercise 4-4, prepare *LO4 (20 min)*

a. an income statement for December.
b. a statement of owner's equity for December.
c. a balance sheet as of December 31, 200X.

Group A Problems

MyAccountingLab

4A-1. Use the following adjustment data on December 31 to complete a partial worksheet (Fig. 4.21 on the following page) up to the adjusted trial balance. *LO1, 2 (15 min)*

a. Fitness supplies on hand, $600.
b. Depreciation taken on fitness equipment, $700.

4A-2. Update the trial balance for Ling's Landscaping Service (Fig. 4.22 on the following page) for December 31, 200X. *LO2, 3 (30 min)*

Adjustment Data to Update the Trial Balance

a. Rent expired, $600.
b. Landscaping supplies on hand (remaining), $200.
c. Depreciation expense, Landscaping equipment, $300.
d. Wages earned by workers but not paid or due until January, $400.

Your task is to prepare a worksheet for Ling's Landscaping Service for the month of December.

FIGURE 4.21

Check Figure:
Total of adjusted trial balance $35,350

JILL'S FITNESS CENTER TRIAL BALANCE DECEMBER 31, 200X		
	Debit	Credit
Cash in Bank	1000000	
Accounts Receivable	600000	
Fitness Supplies	540000	
Fitness Equipment	920000	
Accumulated Depreciation, Fitness Equipment		700000
J. Walsh, Capital		1435000
J. Walsh, Withdrawals	300000	
Fitness Fees		1330000
Rent Expense	90000	
Advertising Expense	15000	
	3465000	3465000

FIGURE 4.22

Check Figure:
Net Income $654

LING'S LANDSCAPING SERVICE TRIAL BALANCE DECEMBER 31, 200X		
	Dr.	Cr.
Cash in Bank	400000	
Accounts Receivable	70000	
Prepaid Rent	80000	
Landscaping Supplies	74200	
Landscaping Equipment	140000	
Accumulated Depreciation, Landscaping Equipment		106000
Accounts Payable		83600
A. Ling, Capital		325000
Landscaping Revenue		435600
Heat Expense	40000	
Advertising Expense	20000	
Wage Expense	126000	
	950200	950200

FIGURE 4.23

Check Figure:
Net Income $2,140

KEVIN'S MOVING CO. TRIAL BALANCE OCTOBER 31, 200X		
	Dr.	Cr.
Cash	500000	
Prepaid Insurance	250000	
Moving Supplies	120000	
Moving Truck	1100000	
Accumulated Depreciation, Moving Truck		900000
Accounts Payable		276800
K. Hoff, Capital		544200
K. Hoff, Withdrawals	140000	
Revenue from Moving		900000
Wage Expense	371200	
Rent Expense	108000	
Advertising Expense	31800	
	2621000	2621000

4A-3. Update the trial balance for Kevin's Moving Co. (Fig. 4.23) for October 31, 200X. *LO1 (60 min)*

Adjustment Data to Update Trial Balance

a. Insurance expired, $700.
b. Moving supplies on hand, $900.
c. Depreciation on moving truck, $500.
d. Wages earned but unpaid, $250.

Your task is to

1. complete a worksheet for Kevin's Moving Co. for the month of October.
2. prepare an income statement for October, a statement of owner's equity for October, and a balance sheet as of October 31, 200X.

4A-4. The trial balance for Dick's Repair Service appears in Figure 4.24. *LO2, 3, 4 (60 min)*

FIGURE 4.24

Check Figure:
Net Income $1,830

DICK'S REPAIR SERVICE
TRIAL BALANCE
NOVEMBER 30, 200X

	Dr.	Cr.
Cash	3 2 0 0 00	
Prepaid Insurance	4 0 0 0 00	
Repair Supplies	4 6 0 0 00	
Repair Equipment	3 0 0 0 00	
Accumulated Depreciation, Repair Equipment		7 0 0 00
Accounts Payable		5 5 7 0 00
D. Horn, Capital		3 8 0 0 00
Revenue from Repairs		7 0 0 0 00
Wages Expense	1 8 0 0 00	
Rent Expense	3 6 0 00	
Advertising Expense	1 1 0 00	
	17 0 7 0 00	17 0 7 0 00

Adjustment Data to Update Trial Balance

a. Insurance expired, $700.
b. Repair supplies on hand, $3,000.
c. Depreciation on repair equipment, $200.
d. Wages earned but unpaid, $400.

Your task is to

1. complete a worksheet for Dick's Repair Service for the month of November.
2. prepare an income statement for November, a statement of owner's equity for November, and a balance sheet as of November 30, 200X.

Group B Problems

MyAccountingLab

4B-1. Please complete a partial worksheet (Fig. 4.25 on the following page) up to the adjusted trial balance for Jill's Fitness Center using the following adjustment data: *LO1, 2 (15 min)*

a. Fitness supplies on hand, $3,000.
b. Depreciation taken on fitness equipment, $500.

4B-2. Given the trial balance in Figure 4.26 on the following page and adjustment data of Ling's Landscaping Service, your task is to prepare a worksheet for the month of December.

Adjustment Data *LO2, 3 (30 min)*

a. Landscaping supplies on hand, $60.
b. Rent expired, $150.
c. Depreciation on landscaping equipment, $200.
d. Wages earned but unpaid, $115.

FIGURE 4.25

Check Figure:
Total of Adjusted Trial Balance $25,600

JILL'S FITNESS CENTER TRIAL BALANCE DECEMBER 31, 200X		
	Dr.	Cr.
Cash	6000 00	
Accounts Receivable	2000 00	
Fitness Supplies	4200 00	
Fitness Equipment	11000 00	
Accumulated Depreciation, Fitness Equipment		9700 00
J. Walsh, Capital		11000 00
J. Walsh, Withdrawals	1000 00	
Fitness Fees		4400 00
Rent Expense	800 00	
Advertising Expense	100 00	
	25100 00	25100 00

FIGURE 4.26

Check Figure:
Net Income $673

LING'S LANDSCAPING SERVICE TRIAL BALANCE DECEMBER 31, 200X		
	Dr.	Cr.
Cash in Bank	396 00	
Accounts Receivable	284 00	
Prepaid Rent	400 00	
Landscaping Supplies	310 00	
Landscaping Equipment	1000 00	
Accumulated Depreciation, Landscaping Equipment		200 00
Accounts Payable		346 00
A. Ling, Capital		456 00
Landscaping Revenue		4680 00
Heat Expense	632 00	
Advertising Expense	1200 00	
Wage Expense	1460 00	
Total	5682 00	5682 00

LO1 (60 min)

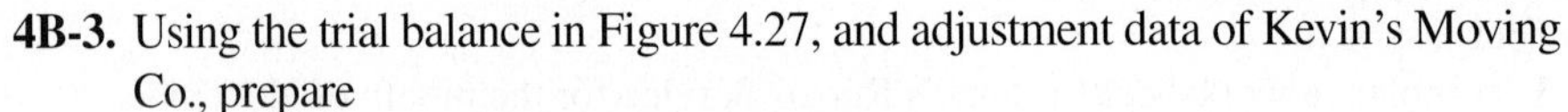

4B-3. Using the trial balance in Figure 4.27, and adjustment data of Kevin's Moving Co., prepare

1. a worksheet for the month of October.
2. an income statement for October, a statement of owner's equity for October, and a balance sheet as of October 31, 200X.

Adjustment Data

a. Insurance expired, $600.
b. Moving supplies on hand, $310.
c. Depreciation on moving truck, $580.
d. Wages earned but unpaid, $410.

LO2, 3, 4 (60 min)

4B-4. As the bookkeeper of Dick's Repair Service, use the information in Figure 4.28, to prepare

1. a worksheet for the month of November.
2. an income statement for November, a statement of owner's equity for November, and a balance sheet as of November 30, 200X.

Adjustment Data

a. Insurance expired, $300.
b. Repair supplies on hand, $170.

c. Depreciation on repair equipment, $250.
d. Wages earned but unpaid, $106.

FIGURE 4.27

KEVIN'S MOVING CO.
TRIAL BALANCE
OCTOBER 31, 200X

	Dr.	Cr.
Cash	3 9 2 0 00	
Prepaid Insurance	3 2 8 8 00	
Moving Supplies	1 4 0 0 00	
Moving Truck	10 6 5 8 00	
Accumulated Depreciation, Moving Truck		3 6 6 0 00
Accounts Payable		1 3 1 2 00
K. Hoff, Capital		17 4 8 2 00
K. Hoff, Withdrawals	4 2 4 0 00	
Revenue from Moving		8 1 6 2 00
Wages Expense	5 7 1 2 00	
Rent Expense	1 0 8 0 00	
Advertising Expense	3 1 8 00	
	30 6 1 6 00	30 6 1 6 00

Check Figure:
Net Loss $1,628

FIGURE 4.28

DICK'S REPAIR SERVICE
TRIAL BALANCE
NOVEMBER 30, 200X

	Dr.	Cr.
Cash	3 2 0 4 00	
Prepaid Insurance	4 0 0 0 00	
Repair Supplies	7 7 0 00	
Repair Equipment	3 1 0 6 00	
Accumulated Depreciation, Repair Equipment		6 5 0 00
Accounts Payable		1 9 0 4 00
D. Horn, Capital		6 2 5 8 00
Revenue from Repairs		5 6 3 4 00
Wages Expense	1 6 0 0 00	
Rent Expense	1 5 6 0 00	
Advertising Expense	2 0 6 00	
	14 4 4 6 00	14 4 4 6 00

Check Figure:
Net Income $1,012

ON-THE-JOB TRAINING

T-1.

LO1 (20 min)

MEMO

To: *Hal Hogan, Bookkeeper*

From: *Pete Tennant, V. P.*

Re: *Adjustments for year ended December 31, 200X*

Hal, here is the information you requested. Please supply me with the adjustments needed ASAP. Also, please put in writing why we need to do these adjustments.

Thanks.

Attached to memo:

a. Insurance data:

Policy No.	Date of Policy Purchase	Policy Length	Cost
100	November 1 of previous year	4 years	$480
200	May 1 of current year	2 years	600
300	September 1 of current year	1 year	240

b. Rent data: Prepaid rent had a $500 balance at the beginning of the year. An additional $400 of rent was paid in advance in June. At year end, $200 of rent had expired.

c. Revenue data: Accrued storage fees of $500 were earned but uncollected and unrecorded at year end.

LO1 (30 min) **T-2.**

Hint: Unearned Rent is a liability on the balance sheet.

On Friday, Harry Swag's boss asks him to prepare a special report, due on Monday at 8:00 A.M. Harry gathers the following material in his briefcase:

			Dec. 31	
			2009	**2008**
Prepaid Advertising			$300	$600
Interest Payable			150	350
Unearned Rent			500	300
Cash paid for:	Advertising	$1,900		
	Interest	1,500		
Cash received for:	Rent	2,300		

As his best friend, could you help Harry show the amounts that are to be reported on the income statement for (a) Advertising Expense, (b) Interest Expense, and (c) Rent Fees Earned. Please explain in writing why Unearned Rent is considered a liability.

FINANCIAL REPORT PROBLEM

LO1 (20 min)

Reading the Kellogg's Annual Report

Go to Appendix A and look at Note 1 under Property. Find out how Kellogg's depreciates its equipment. How is the equipment recorded?

INTERNET PROJECT

Black & Decker

Go to the Web and search: Annual Report Black & Decker 2008.
Click on Investors Relations.
List out the latest news Black & Decker is providing to its investors.
Order a free annual report.

CONTINUING PROBLEM

MyAccountingLab

Sanchez Computer Center

LO2, 3, 4 (45 min)

At the end of September, Tony took a complete inventory of his supplies and found the following:

5 dozen ¼″ screws at a cost of $8.00 a dozen
2 dozen ½″ screws at a cost of $5.00 a dozen
2 cartons of computer inventory paper at a cost of $14 a carton
3 feet of coaxial cable at a cost of $4.00 per foot

After speaking to his accountant, he found that a reasonable depreciation amount for each of his long-term assets is as follows:

Computer purchased July 5, 200X	Depreciation $33 a month
Office equipment purchased July 17, 200X	Depreciation $10 a month
Computer workstations purchased Sept. 17, 200X	Depreciation $20 a month

Tony uses the straight-line method of depreciation and declares no salvage value for any of the assets. If any long-term asset is purchased in the first 15 days of the month, he will charge depreciation for the full month. If an asset is purchased on the 16th of the month, or later, he will not charge depreciation in the month it was purchased.

August and September's rent has now expired.

Assignment

Use your trial balance from the completed problem in Chapter 3 and the adjusting information given here to complete the worksheet for the three months ended September 30, 200X. From the worksheets prepare the financial statements.

SUBWAY Case

WHERE THE DOUGH GOES . . .

LO1, 2, 3 (20 min)

No matter how harried Stan Hernandez feels as the owner of his own Subway restaurant, the aroma of his fresh-baked gourmet breads *always* perks him up. However, the sales generated by Subway's line of gourmet seasoned breads perks Stan up even more. Subway restaurants introduced freshly baked bread in 1983, a practice that made it stand out from other fast-food chains and helped build its reputation for made-to-order freshness. Since then Subway franchisees have introduced many types of gourmet seasoned breads—such as Hearty Italian or Monterey Cheddar—according to a schedule determined by headquarters.

Stan was one month into the "limited-time promotion" for the chain's new Roasted Garlic seasoned bread when his bake oven started faltering. "The temperature controls just don't seem quite right," said his employee and "sandwich artist," Rashid. "It's taking incrementally longer to bake the bread."

"This couldn't happen at a worse time," moaned Stan. "We're baking enough Roasted Garlic bread to keep a whole town of vampires away, but if we don't get it out of the oven fast enough, we'll keep our customers away!"

That very day Stan called his field consultant, Mariah, to discuss what to do about his bake oven. Mariah reminded Stan that his oven trouble illustrated the flip side of buying an existing store from a retired franchisee—having to repair or replace worn or old equipment. After receiving a rather expensive repair estimate and considering the age of the oven, Stan ultimately decided it would make sense for him to purchase a new one. Mariah concurred, "At the rate your sales are going, Stan, you're going to need that roomier new model."

"Wow, do you realize how much this new bake oven is going to cost me?—$3,000!" Stan exclaimed while meeting with his cousin-turned-Subway-accountant, Lila Hernandez. "Yes, it's a lot to lay out, Stan," said Lila, "but you'll be depreciating the cost over a period of 10 years, which will help you at tax time. Let's do the adjustment on your worksheet, so you can see it."

The two of them were sitting in Stan's small office, behind the Subway kitchen, and they pulled up this month's worksheet on Stan's Peachtree program. Lila laughed, "I'm sure glad you started entering your worksheets on Peachtree again! The figures on those old ones were so doodled over and crossed out that I could barely decipher them! We may need your worksheets at tax time."

"Anything for you, *mi prima,*" Stan said. "I may depreciate my bake oven, but my gratitude for your accounting skills only appreciates with time!"

Discussion Questions

1. If you are using a straight-line method of depreciation and Stan's bake oven has a residual value of $1,000, how much depreciation will he account for each year and what would the adjustment be for each month?
2. Where does Lila get the information on the useful life of Stan's bake oven and the estimate for its residual value? Why do you think she gets her information from this particular source?
3. Why is a clear worksheet helpful even after that month's statements have been prepared?

PEACHTREE COMPUTER WORKSHOP

COMPUTERIZED ACCOUNTING APPLICATION FOR CHAPTER 4

Refresher on using Peachtree Complete Accounting

Before starting this assignment, you may want to refresh your memory by reading the following PDF documents found in the multimedia library on the MyAccountingLab Web site. Remember to choose the PDF document for your version of Peachtree.

1. An Introduction to Peachtree Complete Accounting
2. Correcting Peachtree Transactions
3. How to Repeat or Restart a Peachtree Assignment
4. Backing Up and Restoring Your Work in Peachtree

You also should have completed Workshop 1 for the Atlas Company in Chapter 3.

Workshop 2:

Compound Journal Entries, Adjusting Entries, and Financial Reports

In this workshop you will post compound journal entries and adjusting journal entries for Zell Company using Peachtree. You will also print the general journal report, trial balance, income statement, and balance sheet.

Instructions and the data file for completing this assignment are in the multimedia library of the MyAccountingLab Web site. Open the ***Workshop 2 Zell Company*** PDF document for your version of Peachtree and download the ***Zell Company*** data file for your version of Peachtree.

QUICKBOOKS COMPUTER WORKSHOP

COMPUTERIZED ACCOUNTING APPLICATION FOR CHAPTER 4

Refresher on using QuickBooks Pro

Before starting this assignment, you may want to refresh your memory by reading the following PDF documents found in the multimedia library on the MyAccountingLab Web site. Remember to choose the PDF document for your version of QuickBooks.

1. An Introduction to Computerized Accounting
2. Installing QuickBooks Pro and Student Data Files
3. An Introduction to QuickBooks Pro
4. Correcting QuickBooks Transactions
5. How to Repeat or Restart a QuickBooks Assignment
6. Backing Up and Restoring Your Work in QuickBooks. You also should have completed Workshop 1 for the Atlas Company in Chapter 3.

Workshop 2:

Compound Journal Entries, Adjusting Entries, and Financial Reports

In this workshop you will post compound journal entries and adjusting journal entries for Zell Company using Quickbooks. You will also print the general journal report, trial balance, income statement, and balance sheet.

Instructions and the data file for completing this assignment are in the multimedia library of the MyAccountingLab Web site. Open the ***Workshop 2 Zell Company*** PDF document for your version of Quickbooks and download the ***Zell Company*** data file for your version of Quickbooks.

5

The Accounting Cycle Completed

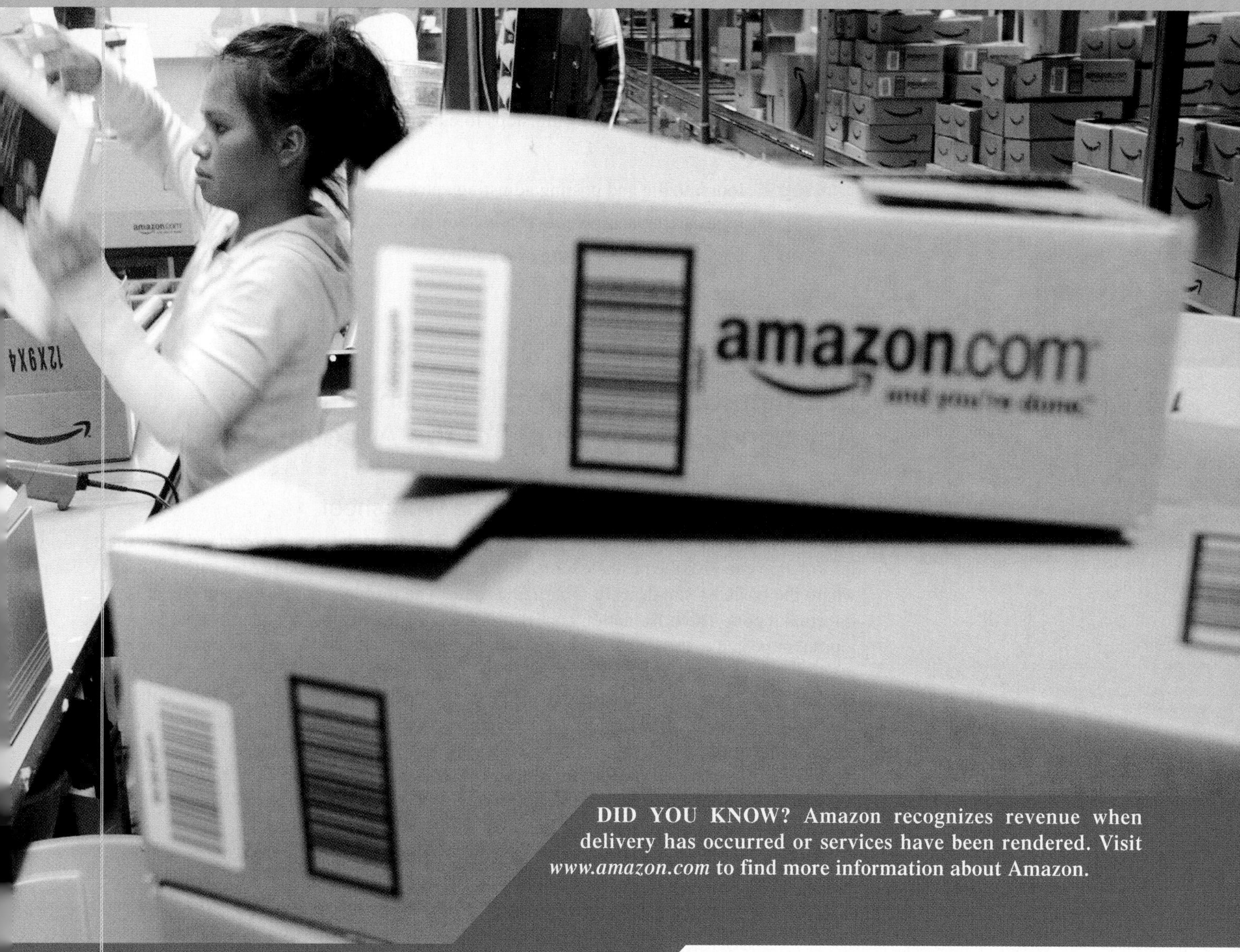

DID YOU KNOW? Amazon recognizes revenue when delivery has occurred or services have been rendered. Visit *www.amazon.com* to find more information about Amazon.

LEARNING OBJECTIVES

1. Journalizing and posting adjusting entries.
2. Journalizing and posting closing entries.
3. Preparing a post-closing trial balance.

In computerized accounting, this process has been completed. Entries are both journalized and posted at the same time.

Each accounting cycle completed by Amazon will end with the preparation of a post-closing trial balance. In Chapters 3 and 4 we completed these steps of the manual accounting cycle for Clark's Word Processing Services:

Step 1 Business transactions occurred and generated source documents.
Step 2 Business transactions were analyzed and recorded into a journal.
Step 3 Information was posted or transferred from journal to ledger.
Step 4 A trial balance was prepared.
Step 5 A worksheet was completed.
Step 6 Financial statements were prepared.

This chapter covers the following steps to complete Clark's accounting cycle for the month of May:

Step 7 Journalizing and posting adjusting entries.
Step 8 Journalizing and posting closing entries.
Step 9 Preparing a post-closing trial balance.

LO1

Learning Unit 5-1 Journalizing and Posting Adjusting Entries: Step 7 of the Accounting Cycle

Recording Journal Entries from the Worksheet

At this point, many ledger accounts are not up-to-date.

The information in the worksheet is up-to-date. The financial reports prepared from that information can give the business's management and other interested parties a good idea of where the business stands as of a particular date. The problem is that the worksheet is an informal report. The information concerning the adjustments has not been placed into the journal or posted to the ledger accounts, which means that the books are not up-to-date and ready for the next accounting cycle to begin. For example, the ledger shows $1,200 of Prepaid Rent, but the balance sheet we prepared in Chapter 4 shows an $800 balance. Essentially, the worksheet is a tool for preparing financial statements. Now we must use the adjustment columns of the worksheet as a basis for bringing the ledger up-to-date. To update the ledger, we use **adjusting journal entries** (see Figs. 5.1, 5.2). Again, the updating must be done before the next accounting period starts. For Clark's Word Processing Services, the next period begins on June 1.

Figure 5.2 shows the adjusting journal entries for Clark's taken from the adjustments section of the worksheet. Once the adjusting journal entries are posted to the ledger, the accounts making up the financial statements that were prepared from the worksheet will equal the updated ledger. (Keep in mind that we are using the same journal and ledger as in the previous chapters.) Let's look at some simplified T accounts to show how Clark's ledger looked before and after the adjustments (A–D) were posted.

Adjustment (A)

	Office Supplies 114		Office Supplies Expense 514	
Before Posting:	600			
After Posting:	600	500	500	

Account Titles	Trial Balance Dr.	Trial Balance Cr.	Adjustments Dr.	Adjustments Cr.
Cash	6155 00			
Accounts Receivable	5000 00			
Office Supplies	600 00			(A) 500 00
Prepaid Rent	1200 00			(B) 400 00
Word Processing Equipment	6000 00			
Accounts Payable		3350 00		
Brenda Clark, Capital		10000 00		
Brenda Clark, Withdrawals	625 00			
Word Processing Fees		8000 00		
Office Salaries Expense	1300 00		(D) 350 00	
Advertising Expense	250 00			
Telephone Expense	220 00			
	21350 00	21350 00		
Office Supplies Expense			(A) 500 00	
Rent Expense			(B) 400 00	
Depreciation Exp., W. P. Equip.			(C) 80 00	
Accum. Deprec., W. P. Equip.				(C) 80 00
Salaries Payable				(D) 350 00
			1330 00	1330 00

FIGURE 5.1 Journalizing and Posting Adjustments from the Adjustments Section of the Worksheet

CLARK'S WORD PROCESSING SERVICES
GENERAL JOURNAL

Page 2

Date		Account Titles and Description	PR	Dr.	Cr.
		Adjusting Entries			
May	31	Office Supplies Expense	514	500 00	
		Office Supplies	114		500 00
	31	Rent Expense	515	400 00	
		Prepaid Rent	115		400 00
	31	Depreciation Expense, W. P. Equip.	516	80 00	
		Accumulated Depreciation, W. P. Equip.	122		80 00
	31	Office Salaries Expense	511	350 00	
		Salaries Payable	212		350 00

FIGURE 5.2 Adjustments A–D in the Adjustments Section of the Worksheet Must Be Recorded in the Journal and Posted to the Ledger

Each adjustment affects both the income statement and balance sheet and never affects cash.

Adjustment (B)

Before Posting:

Prepaid Rent 115	
1,200	

Rent Expense 515	

After Posting:

Prepaid Rent 115	
1,200	400

Rent Expense 515	
400	

Adjustment (C)

Before Posting:

Word Processing Equipment 121	
6,000	

Depreciation Expense, W. P. Equipment 516	

Accumulated Depreciation, W. P. Equipment 122	

After Posting:

Word Processing Equipment 121	
6,000	

Depreciation Expense, W. P. Equipment 516	
80	

Accumulated Depreciation, W. P. Equipment 122	
	80

The first adjustment in (C) shows the same balances for Depreciation Expense and Accumulated Depreciation. However, in subsequent adjustments the Accumulated Depreciation balance will keep getting larger, but the debit to Depreciation Expense and the credit to Accumulated Depreciation will be the same. We will see why in a moment.

Adjustment (D)

Before Posting:

Office Salaries Expense 511	
650	
650	

Salaries Payable 212	

After Posting:

Office Salaries Expense 511	
650	
650	
350	

Salaries Payable 212	
	350

LEARNING UNIT 5-1 REVIEW

AT THIS POINT you should be able to

Accounting Cycle Tutorial

- Define and state the purpose of adjusting entries.
- Journalize adjusting entries from the worksheet.
- Post journalized adjusting entries to the ledger.
- Compare specific ledger accounts before and after posting of the journalized adjusting entries.

Self-Review Quiz 5-1

Turn to the worksheet of P. Logan (Figure 4.14 in Chapter 4) and (1) journalize and post the adjusting entries and (2) compare the adjusted ledger accounts before and after the adjustments are posted. T accounts are provided in your study guide with beginning balances.

Solution to Self-Review Quiz 5-1

Page 2

Date		Account Titles and Description	PR	Dr.	Cr.
		Adjusting Entries			
Dec.	31	Depreciation Expense, Store Equip.	511	1 00	
		Accumulated Depreciation, Store Equip.	122		1 00
	31	Insurance Expense	516	2 00	
		Prepaid Insurance	116		2 00
	31	Supplies Expense	514	4 00	
		Store Supplies	114		4 00
	31	Salaries Expense	512	3 00	
		Salaries Payable	212		3 00

FIGURE 5.3 Journalized Adjusting Entries

For additional help go to www.pearsonhighered.com/slater

Partial Ledger

Before Posting

Depreciation Expense, Store Equipment 511

Dr.	Cr.

Accumulated Depreciation Store Equipment 122

Dr.	Cr.
	4

Prepaid Insurance 116

Dr.	Cr.
3	

Insurance Expense 516

Dr.	Cr.

Store Supplies 114

Dr.	Cr.
5	

Supplies Expense 514

Dr.	Cr.

Salaries Expense 512

Dr.	Cr.
8	

Salaries Payable 212

Dr.	Cr.

After Posting

Depreciation, Expense, Store Equipment 511

Dr.	Cr.
1	

Accumulated Depreciation, Store Equipment 122

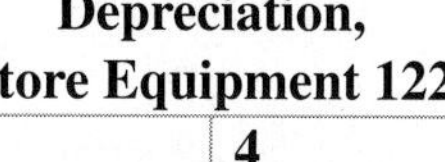

Dr.	Cr.
	4
	1

Prepaid Insurance 116

Dr.	Cr.
3	2

Insurance Expense 516

Dr.	Cr.
2	

Store Supplies 114

Dr.	Cr.
5	4

Supplies Expense 514

Dr.	Cr.
4	

Salaries Expense 512

Dr.	Cr.
8	
3	

Salaries Payable 212

Dr.	Cr.
	3

NEED HELP?

Let's review first: Once the financial statements are prepared from the worksheet our ledger is still not up-to-date. Information about the adjustments on the worksheet have not been journalized or posted to the ledger.

How to update the ledger with adjustments on the worksheet: Using the worksheet of Logan Company, go to the adjustments column and journalize the four adjusting entries. Once the adjustments are journalized they must be posted to the ledger. When the postings are complete, the titles for depreciation expense, accumulated depreciation, insurance expense, prepaid insurance, supplies expense, store supplies, salaries expense, and salaries payable will have the latest, up-to-date balances.

Summary: The ending balances in the ledger after posting adjustments will be the same amounts that were found on the adjusted trial balance.

LO2 Learning Unit 5-2 Journalizing and Posting Closing Entries: Step 8 of the Accounting Cycle

Closing is not a necessary step when using Peachtree or QuickBooks. Net income is calculated after each transaction, and financial statements are current.

To make recording of the next period's transactions easier, a mechanical step, called *closing,* is taken by Clark's accountant. Closing is intended to end—or close off—the revenue, expense, and withdrawal accounts at the end of the accounting period. The information needed to complete closing entries will be found in the income statement and balance sheet sections of the worksheet.

To make it easier to understand this process, we will first look at the difference between temporary (nominal) accounts and permanent (real) accounts.

Here is the expanded accounting equation we used in an earlier chapter:

Assets = Liabilities + Capital − Withdrawals + Revenues − Expenses

Permanent accounts are found on the balance sheet.

Three of the items in that equation—Assets, Liabilities, and Capital—are known as **real** or **permanent accounts** because their balances are carried over from one accounting period to another. The other three items—Withdrawals, Revenues, and Expenses—are called **nominal** or **temporary accounts** because their balances are not carried over from one accounting period to another. Instead, their "balances" are reset at zero at the beginning of each accounting period by closing their balances at the end of the prior period. This process allows us to accumulate new data about revenue, expenses, and withdrawals in the new accounting period. The process of closing summarizes the effects of the temporary accounts on Capital for that period using **closing journal entries.** When the closing process is complete, the accounting equation will be reduced to

Assets = Liabilities + Ending Capital

After all closing entries are journalized and posted to the ledger, all temporary accounts have a zero balance in the ledger. Closing is a step-by-step process.

If you look back to Figure 4.16 in Chapter 4, you will see that we already calculated the new capital on the balance sheet to be $14,275 for Clark's Word Processing Services. Before the mechanical closing procedures are journalized and posted, Clark's Capital account in the ledger is only $10,000 (Chapter 3, Figure 3.19). Let's look now at how to journalize and post closing entries.

How to Journalize Closing Entries

An Income Summary is a temporary account located in the chart of accounts under Owner's Equity. It does not have a normal balance of a debit or a credit.

Four steps are needed in journalizing closing entries:

Step 1 Clear to zero the revenue balance and transfer it to Income Summary. **Income Summary** is a temporary account in the ledger needed for closing. At the end of the closing process, Income Summary will no longer hold a balance.

Revenue ⟶ Income Summary

Step 2 Clear to zero the individual expense balances and transfer them to Income Summary.

Expenses ⟶ Income Summary

Step 3 Clear to zero the balance in Income Summary and transfer it to Capital.

Income Summary ⟶ Capital

Step 4 Clear to zero the balance in Withdrawals and transfer it to Capital.

Withdrawals ⟶ Capital

Figure 5.4 is a visual representation of these four steps. Keep in mind that this information must first be journalized and then posted to the appropriate ledger accounts. The worksheet presented in Figure 5.5 contains all the figures we will need for the closing process.

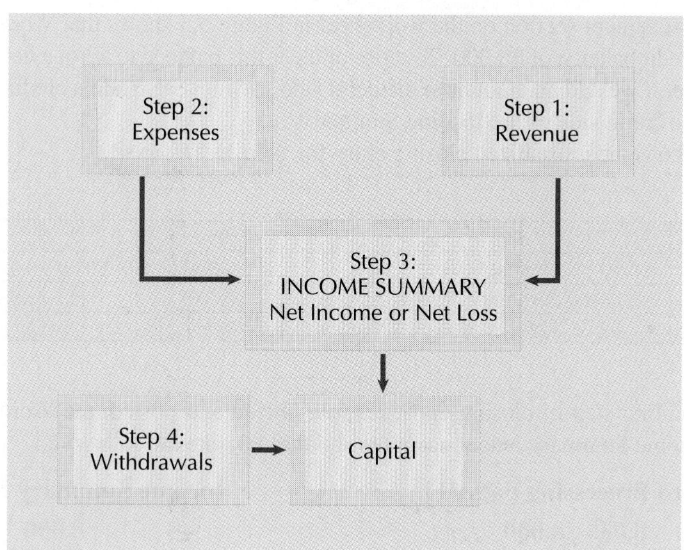

FIGURE 5.4 Four Steps in Journalizing Closing Entries (All numbers can be found on the worksheet in Figure 5.5.)

Don't forget two goals of closing:
1. Clear all temporary accounts in ledger.
2. Update Capital to a new balance that reflects a summary of all the temporary accounts.

FIGURE 5.5 Closing Figures on the Worksheet

Account Titles	Income Statement Dr.	Income Statement Cr.	Balance Sheet Dr.	Balance Sheet Cr.
Cash			6155 00	
Accounts Receivable			5000 00	
Office Supplies			100 00	
Prepaid Rent			800 00	
Word Processing Equipment			6000 00	
Accounts Payable				3350 00
B. Clark, Capital		For Step 1		10000 00
B. Clark, Withdrawals	For Step 2		625 00	
Word Processing Fees		8000 00		
Office Salaries Expense	1650 00		For Step 4	
Advertising Expense	250 00			
Telephone Expense	220 00			
Office Supplies Expense	500 00			
Rent Expense	400 00			
Depreciation Exp., W. P. Equip.	80 00			
Acc. Depreciation, W. P. Equip.		For Step 3		80 00
Salaries Payable				350 00
	3100 00	8000 00	18680 00	13780 00
Net Income	4900 00			4900 00
	8000 00	8000 00	18680 00	18680 00

All numbers used in the closing process can be found on the worksheet. Note that the account Income Summary is not on the worksheet.

Step 1: Clear Revenue Balance and Transfer to Income Summary Here is what is in the ledger before closing entries are journalized and posted:

Word Processing Fees 411	
	8,000

Income Summary 313	

The income statement section on the worksheet in Figure 5.5 shows that Word Processing Fees has a credit balance of $8,000. To close or clear this balance to zero, a debit of $8,000 is needed. But if we add an amount to the debit side, we must also add a credit—so we add $8,000 on the credit side of the Income Summary.

Figure 5.6 is the journalized closing entry for Step 1:

FIGURE 5.6 Closing Revenue to Income Summary

				Dr.	Cr.
May	31	Word Processing Fees	411	8,000.00	
		Income Summary	313		8,000.00

After the first step of closing entries is journalized and posted, the Word Processing Fees and Income Summary ledger accounts should look like the following:

Word Processing Fees 411

Dr.	Cr.
8,000 Closing	8,000 Revenue

Income Summary 313

Dr.	Cr.
	8,000 Revenue

Note that the revenue balance is cleared to zero and transferred to Income Summary, a temporary account also located in the ledger.

Remember, the worksheet is a tool. The accountant realizes that the information about the total of the expenses will be transferred to the Income Summary.

Step 2: Clear Individual Expense Balances and Transfer the Total to Income Summary

The ledger for each expense account is shown here before closing entries are journalized and posted. Each expense is listed on the worksheet in the debit column of the income statement section in Figure 5.5.

Office Salaries Expense 511

Dr.	Cr.
650	
650	
350	

Advertising Expense 512

Dr.	Cr.
250	

Telephone Expense 513

Dr.	Cr.
220	

Office Supplies Expense 514

Dr.	Cr.
500	

Rent Expense 515

Dr.	Cr.
400	

Depreciation Expense, W. P. Equipment 516

Dr.	Cr.
80	

The income statement section of the worksheet lists all the expenses as debits. If we want to reduce each expense to zero, each one must be credited.

Figure 5.7 is the journalized closing entry for Step 2:

FIGURE 5.7 Closing Each Expense to Income Summary

The $3,100 is the total of the expenses on the worksheet.

				Dr.	Cr.
	31	Income Summary	313	3,100.00	
		Office Salaries Expense	511		1,650.00
		Advertising Expense	512		250.00
		Telephone Expense	513		220.00
		Office Supplies Expense	514		500.00
		Rent Expense	515		400.00
		Depreciation Expense, W. P. Equip.	516		80.00

Individual expenses and Income Summary accounts should look like the following after closing entries are journalized and posted:

Office Salaries Expense 511

650	Closing 1,650
650	
350	

Advertising Expense 512

250	Closing 250

Telephone Expense 513

220	Closing 220

Office Supplies Expense 514

500	Closing 500

Rent Expense 515

400	Closing 400

Depreciation Expense, W. P. Equipment 516

80	Closing 80

Income Summary 313

	Expenses	Revenue	
Step 2	3,100	8,000	Step 1

Step 3: Clear Balance in Income Summary (Net Income) and Transfer It to Capital The Income Summary and B. Clark, Capital, accounts look this way before Step 3:

Income Summary 313

3,100	8,000
	4,900

B. Clark, Capital 311

	10,000

Note that the balance of Income Summary (Revenues minus Expenses, or $8,000 − $3,100) is $4,900. We must clear that amount from the Income Summary account and transfer to the B. Clark, Capital, account.

In order to transfer the balance of $4,900 from Income Summary (check the bottom debit column of the income statement section on the worksheet in Fig. 5.5) to Capital, it will be necessary to debit Income Summary for $4,900 (the difference between the revenue and expenses) and credit or increase Capital of B. Clark for $4,900.

Figure 5.8 is the journalized closing entry for Step 3:

	31	Income Summary	313	4 9 0 0 00	
		B. Clark, Capital	311		4 9 0 0 00

FIGURE 5.8 Closing Net Income to B. Clark, Capital

The Income Summary and B. Clark, Capital, accounts will look like the following in the ledger after the closing entries of Step 3 are journalized and posted:

Income Summary 313

Total of Expenses →	3,100	8,000	← Revenue
Debit to close account →	4,900	4,900	← Net Income

B. Clark, Capital 311

	10,000	
	4,900	← Net Income

At the end of these three steps, the Income Summary has a zero balance. If we had a net loss, the end result would be to decrease Capital. The entry would be debit Capital and credit Income Summary for the loss.

Step 4: Clear the Withdrawals Balance and Transfer It to Capital Next, we must close the Withdrawals account. The B. Clark, Withdrawals, and B. Clark, Capital, accounts now look like this:

B. Clark, Withdrawals 312

625	

B. Clark, Capital 311

	10,000
	4,900

To bring the Withdrawals account to a zero balance and summarize its effect on Capital, we must credit Withdrawals and debit Capital.

Remember, withdrawals are a nonbusiness expense and thus are not transferred to Income Summary. The closing entry is journalized as shown in Figure 5.9.

FIGURE 5.9 Closing Withdrawal to B. Clark, Capital

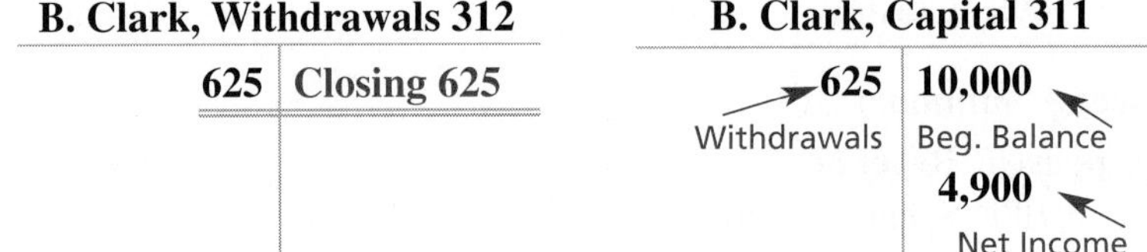

31	B. Clark, Capital	311	625 00	
	B. Clark, Withdrawals	312		625 00

At this point the B. Clark, Withdrawals, and B. Clark, Capital, accounts would look this way in the ledger.

Note that the $10,000 is a beginning balance because no additional investments were made during the period.

B. Clark, Withdrawals 312

Dr.	Cr.
625	Closing 625

B. Clark, Capital 311

Dr.	Cr.
625 (Withdrawals)	10,000 (Beg. Balance)
	4,900 (Net Income)

Now let's look at a summary of the closing entries in Figure 5.10.

FIGURE 5.10 Four Closing Entries

SUMMARY OF CLOSING ENTRIES

Date		Account Titles and Description	PR	Dr.	Cr.	
		Closing Entries				
200X						
May	31	Word Processing Fees	411	8000 00		
		Income Summary	313		8000 00	← Step 1
	31	Income Summary	313	3100 00		
		Office Salaries Expense	511		1650 00	
		Advertising Expense	512		250 00	
		Telephone Expense	513		220 00	← Step 2
		Office Supplies Expense	514		500 00	
		Rent Expense	515		400 00	
		Depreciation Expense, W. P. Equip.	516		80 00	
	31	Income Summary	313	4900 00		
		B. Clark, Capital	311		4900 00	← Step 3
	31	B. Clark, Capital	311	625 00		
		B. Clark, Withdrawals	312		625 00	← Step 4

The following figure shows the complete ledger for Clark's Word Processing Services (see Fig. 5.11). Note how "adjusting" or "closing" is written in the explanation column of individual ledgers, as, for example, in the one for Office Supplies. If the goals of closing have been achieved, only permanent accounts will have balances carried to the next accounting period. All temporary accounts should have zero balances.

FIGURE 5.11 Complete Ledger

CLARK'S WORD PROCESSING SERVICES
GENERAL LEDGER

Cash — Account No. 111

Date		Explanation	Post. Ref.	Debit	Credit	Balance Debit	Balance Credit
200X May	1		GJ1	10 0 0 0 00		10 0 0 0 00	
	1		GJ1		1 0 0 0 00	9 0 0 0 00	
	1		GJ1		1 2 0 0 00	7 8 0 0 00	
	7		GJ1	3 0 0 0 00		10 8 0 0 00	
	15		GJ1		6 5 0 00	10 1 5 0 00	
	20		GJ1		6 2 5 00	9 5 2 5 00	
	27		GJ2		6 5 0 00	8 8 7 5 00	
	28		GJ2		2 5 0 0 00	6 3 7 5 00	
	29		GJ2		2 2 0 00	6 1 5 5 00	

Accounts Receivable — Account No. 112

Date		Explanation	Post. Ref.	Debit	Credit	Balance Debit	Balance Credit
200X May	22		GJ1	5 0 0 0 00		5 0 0 0 00	

Office Supplies — Account No. 114

Date		Explanation	Post. Ref.	Debit	Credit	Balance Debit	Balance Credit
200X May	3		GJ1	6 0 0 00		6 0 0 00	
	31	Adjusting	GJ2		5 0 0 00	1 0 0 00	

(continued on next page)

FIGURE 5.11 *(continued)*

Prepaid Rent — Account No. 115

Date		Explanation	Post. Ref.	Debit	Credit	Balance Debit	Balance Credit
200X May	1		GJ1	1 2 0 0 00		1 2 0 0 00	
	31	Adjusting	GJ2		4 0 0 00	8 0 0 00	

Word Processing Equipment — Account No. 121

Date		Explanation	Post. Ref.	Debit	Credit	Balance Debit	Balance Credit
200X May	1		GJ1	6 0 0 0 00		6 0 0 0 00	

Accumulated Depreciation, Word Processing Equipment — Account No. 122

Date		Explanation	Post. Ref.	Debit	Credit	Balance Debit	Balance Credit
200X May	31	Adjusting	GJ2		8 0 00		8 0 00

Accounts Payable — Account No. 211

Date		Explanation	Post. Ref.	Debit	Credit	Balance Debit	Balance Credit
200X May	1		GJ1		5 0 0 0 00		5 0 0 0 00
	3		GJ1		6 0 0 00		5 6 0 0 00
	18		GJ1		2 5 0 00		5 8 5 0 00
	28		GJ2	2 5 0 0 00			3 3 5 0 00

Salaries Payable — Account No. 212

Date		Explanation	Post. Ref.	Debit	Credit	Balance Debit	Balance Credit
200X May	31	Adjusting	GJ2		3 5 0 00		3 5 0 00

Brenda Clark, Capital — Account No. 311

Date		Explanation	Post. Ref.	Debit	Credit	Balance Debit	Balance Credit
200X May	1		GJ1		10 0 0 0 00		10 0 0 0 00
	31	Closing (Net Income)	GJ2		4 9 0 0 00		14 9 0 0 00
	31	Closing (Withdrawals)	GJ2	6 2 5 00			14 2 7 5 00

Note how this amount is same ending balance as Fig 4.15.

FIGURE 5.11 *(continued)*

Brenda Clark, Withdrawals — Account No. 312

Date		Explanation	Post. Ref.	Debit	Credit	Balance Debit	Balance Credit
200X May	20		GJ1	625 00		625 00	
	31	Closing	GJ2		625 00	—	—

Income Summary — Account No. 313

Date		Explanation	Post. Ref.	Debit	Credit	Balance Debit	Balance Credit
200X May	31	Closing (Revenue)	GJ2		8000 00		8000 00
	31	Closing (Expenses)	GJ2	3100 00			4900 00
	31	Closing (Net Income)	GJ2	4900 00		—	—

Word Processing Fees — Account No. 411

Date		Explanation	Post. Ref.	Debit	Credit	Balance Debit	Balance Credit
200X May	7		GJ1		3000 00		3000 00
	22		GJ1		5000 00		8000 00
	31	Closing	GJ2	8000 00		—	—

Office Salaries Expense — Account No. 511

Date		Explanation	Post. Ref.	Debit	Credit	Balance Debit	Balance Credit
200X May	13		GJ1	650 00		650 00	
	27		GJ2	650 00		1300 00	
	31	Adjusting	GJ2	350 00		1650 00	
	31	Closing	GJ2		1650 00	—	—

Advertising Expense — Account No. 512

Date		Explanation	Post. Ref.	Debit	Credit	Balance Debit	Balance Credit
200X May	18		GJ1	250 00		250 00	
	31	Closing	GJ2		250 00	—	—

(continued on next page)

FIGURE 5.11 *(continued)*

Telephone Expense — Account No. 513

Date		Explanation	Post. Ref.	Debit	Credit	Balance Debit	Balance Credit
200X May	29		GJ2	220 00		220 00	
	31	Closing	GJ2		220 00	—	—

Office Supplies Expense — Account No. 514

Date		Explanation	Post. Ref.	Debit	Credit	Balance Debit	Balance Credit
200X May	31	Adjusting	GJ2	500 00		500 00	
	31	Closing	GJ2		500 00	—	—

Note: Accounts 312 to 516 are temporary and are closed to zero.

Rent Expense — Account No. 515

Date		Explanation	Post. Ref.	Debit	Credit	Balance Debit	Balance Credit
200X May	31	Adjusting	GJ2	400 00		400 00	
	31	Closing	GJ2		400 00	—	—

Depreciation Expense, Word Processing Equipment — Account No. 516

Date		Explanation	Post. Ref.	Debit	Credit	Balance Debit	Balance Credit
200X May	31	Adjusting	GJ2	80 00		80 00	
	31	Closing	GJ2		80 00	—	—

LEARNING UNIT 5-2 REVIEW

AT THIS POINT you should be able to

For additional help go to www.pearsonhighered.com/slater

- Define closing.
- Differentiate between temporary (nominal) and permanent (real) accounts.
- List the four mechanical steps of closing.
- Explain the role of the Income Summary account.
- Explain the role of the worksheet in the closing process.

Self-Review Quiz 5-2

Go to the worksheet for P. Logan in Fig. 4.14 (in Chapter 4). Then (1) journalize and post the closing entries and (2) calculate the new balance for P. Logan, Capital.

Solution to Self-Review Quiz 5-2

FIGURE 5.12 Closing Entries for Logan

		Closing Entries			
Dec.	31	Revenue from Clients	410	25 00	
		Income Summary	312		25 00
	31	Income Summary	312	20 00	
		Rent Expense	518		2 00
		Salaries Expense	512		11 00
		Depreciation Expense, Store Equip.	510		1 00
		Insurance Expense	516		2 00
		Supplies Expense	514		4 00
	31	Income Summary	312	5 00	
		P. Logan, Capital	310		5 00
	31	P. Logan, Capital	310	3 00	
		P. Logan, Withdrawals	311		3 00

Partial Ledger

P. Logan, Capital 310	
3	14
	5
	16

Revenue from Clients 410	
25	25

Supplies Expense 514	
4	4

P. Logan, Withdrawals 311	
3	3

Dep. Exp., Store Equip. 510	
1	1

Insurance Expense 516	
2	2

Income Summary 312	
20	25
5	5

Salaries Expense 512	
11	11

Rent Expense 518	
2	2

P. Logan, (Beginning) Capital		$14
Net Income	$5	
Less Withdrawals	3	
Increase in Capital		2
P. Logan, Capital (ending)		$16

NEED HELP?

Let's review first: Why are closing entries necessary? In the ledger we need to get the new balance in the Capital account. When financial statements were prepared, the ledger for Capital had only the old balance. Also, to get ready for the next accounting period we must close all temporary accounts to zero so they will be ready to collect new data regarding revenues, expenses, and withdrawals. Without the closing process each year, financial statements would run into the next period and financial analysis would be difficult. Keep in mind that the Income Summary account that will be used in the closing process is a temporary account (I like to call it a storage area for revenues and expenses).

Why use four steps to closing?
The four steps to closing when journalized and posted will do the following:

1. Clear all temporary accounts to zero.
2. Update the Capital account in the ledger to its new balance.

Steps to closing:

1. Close revenue account(s) to Income Summary.
2. Close each INDIVIDUAL expense to Income Summary.
3. Remove the balance in Income Summary (net income or net loss) and transfer it to the Capital account.
4. Close any withdrawals directly to Capital.

All the closing entries can be journalized directly from the last four columns of the worksheet. Each individual expense along with the total of expenses is found on the worksheet. Once these four closing entries are journalized and posted, all temporary accounts have a zero balance and P. Logan, Capital, now has an ending balance of $16. This is same amount of ending capital that was used to make the formal balance sheet.

Summary: If you look at the T-account in the solution you will see four numbers in Income Summary. Can you explain them?
20...this represents the total of all the expenses.
25...this represents the total revenue of all the revenues.
5 on the credit side...this is net income (25–20).
5 on the debit side...this comes from the 3rd closing entry, which transfers the balance in Income Summary to Capital.

LO3

Learning Unit 5-3 The Post-Closing Trial Balance: Step 9 of the Accounting Cycle and the Cycle Reviewed

Preparing a Post-Closing Trial Balance

The post-closing trial balance helps prove the accuracy of the adjusting and closing process. It contains the true ending figure for Capital.

The last step in the accounting cycle is the preparation of a **post-closing trial balance,** which lists only permanent accounts in the ledger and their balances after adjusting and closing entries have been posted. This post-closing trial balance aids in checking whether the ledger is in balance. This checking is important because so many new postings go to the ledger from the adjusting and closing process.

The procedure for taking a post-closing trial balance is the same as for a trial balance, except that, because closing entries have closed all temporary accounts, the post-closing trial balances will contain only permanent accounts (balance sheet). Keep in mind, however, that adjustments have occurred. We will walk through this procedure in the Learning Unit 5-3 quiz coming up after we review the accounting cycle.

The Accounting Cycle Reviewed

Table 5.1 lists the steps we completed in the manual accounting cycle for Clark's Word Processing Services for the month of May.

TABLE 5.1 Steps of the Manual Accounting Cycle

Steps	Explanation
1. Collect source documents from business transactions as they occur.	Cash register tape, sales tickets, bills, checks, payroll cards.
2. Analyze and record business transactions into a journal.	Called journalizing.
3. Post or transfer information from journal to ledger.	Copying the debits and credits of the journal entries into the ledger accounts.
4. Prepare a trial balance.	Summarizing each individual ledger account and listing those accounts to test for mathematical accuracy in recording transactions.
5. Prepare a worksheet.	A multicolumn form that summarizes accounting information to complete the accounting cycle.
6. Prepare financial statements.	Income statement, statement of owner's equity, and balance sheet.
7. Journalize and post adjusting entries.	Use figures in the adjustment columns of worksheet.
8. Journalize and post closing entries.	Use figures in the income statement and balance sheet sections of worksheet.
9. Prepare a post-closing trial balance.	Prove the mathematical accuracy of the adjusting and closing process of the accounting cycle.

Remember: No worksheet is needed in a computerized cycle.

Insight Most companies journalize and post adjusting and closing entries only at the end of their fiscal year. A company that prepares interim statements may complete only the first six steps of the cycle. Worksheets allow the preparation of interim reports without the formal adjusting and closing of the books. In this case, footnotes on the interim report will indicate the extent to which adjusting and closing were completed.

Insight To prepare a financial statement for April, the data needed can be obtained by subtracting the worksheet accumulated totals from the end of March from the worksheet prepared at the end of April. In this chapter we chose a month that would show the completion of an entire cycle for Clark's Word Processing Services.

LEARNING UNIT 5-3 REVIEW

AT THIS POINT you should be able to

- Prepare a post-closing trial balance.
- Explain the relationship of interim statements to the accounting cycle.

act
Accounting Cycle Tutorial

Self-Review Quiz 5-3

From the ledger in Fig. 5.11, prepare a post-closing trial balance.

For additional help go to www.pearsonhighered.com/slater

Solution to Self-Review Quiz 5-3

FIGURE 5.13 Post-Closing Trial Balance for Clark's Word Processing Services

CLARK'S WORD PROCESSING SERVICES
POST-CLOSING TRIAL BALANCE
MAY 31, 200X

	Dr.	Cr.
Cash	615500	
Accounts Receivable	500000	
Office Supplies	10000	
Prepaid Rent	80000	
Word Processing Equipment	600000	
Accumulated Depreciation, Word Processing Equip.		8000
Accounts Payable		335000
Salaries Payable		35000
Brenda Clark, Capital		1427500
Totals	1805500	1805500

NEED HELP?

Let's review first: The post-closing trial balance contains only permanent accounts because all temporary accounts have been closed. All temporary accounts are summarized in the Capital account. Remember that Income Summary is a temporary account.

Post-Closing Trial Balance: Once all the closing entries have been journalized and posted we can then prepare a post-closing trial balance. Since only permanent accounts are left after closing, the structure of the post-closing trial balance should look as follows:

Assets ....Dr.
Contra Assets ....Cr.
Liabilities ....Cr.
Ending Capital ......Cr.

Summary: To begin the next accounting cycle only permanent accounts with balances are brought forward. In the new cycle transactions will be journalized and posted. Adjustments will be made and new financial statements will be prepared. By the end of the cycle all temporary accounts will be closed to get a new ending figure for capital in the ledger. The end result will be to prepare a new post-closing trial balance.

CHAPTER ASSIGNMENTS

All Classroom Demonstration Exercises, Exercises, Problems, and the Continuing Problem in this chapter can be found within MyAccountingLab, an online homework and practice environment. Your instructor may ask you to complete this material using MyAccountingLab.

DEMONSTRATION PROBLEM: REVIEWING THE ACCOUNTING CYCLE

From the following transactions for Rolo Co. complete the entire accounting cycle. Use the following chart of accounts:

Assets	**Owner's Equity**
111 Cash	311 Rolo Kern, Capital
112 Accounts Receivable	312 Rolo Kern, Withdrawals
114 Prepaid Rent	313 Income Summary
115 Office Supplies	**Revenue**
121 Office Equipment	411 Fees Earned
122 Accumulated Depreciation,	**Expenses**
Office Equipment	511 Salaries Expense
Liabilities	512 Advertising Expense
211 Accounts Payable	513 Rent Expense
212 Salaries Payable	514 Office Supplies Expense
	515 Depreciation Expense,
	Office Equipment

Note: Accounts 312 to 515 are temporary accounts.

We will use unusually small numbers to simplify calculation and emphasize the theory.

200X		
Jan.	1	Rolo Kern invested $1,200 cash and $100 of office equipment to open Rolo Co.
	1	Paid rent for three months in advance, $300
	4	Purchased office equipment on account, $50
	6	Bought office supplies for cash, $40
	8	Collected $400 for services rendered
	12	Rolo paid his home electric bill from the company checkbook, $20
	14	Provided $100 worth of services to clients who will not pay until next month
	16	Paid salaries, $60
	18	Advertising bill received for $70 but will not be paid until next month

Adjustment Data on January 31

a. Supplies on hand, $6.
b. Rent expired, $100.
c. Depreciation, Office Equipment, $20.
d. Salaries accrued, $50.

Solutions to Demonstration Problem

Journalizing Transactions and Posting to Ledger, Rolo Company

FIGURE 5.14 Journal Entries for Rolo Company

General Journal — Page 1

Date		Account Titles and Description	PR	Dr.	Cr.
200X Jan	1	Cash	111	1200 00	
		Office Equipment	121	100 00	
		R. Kern, Capital	311		1300 00
		Initial Investment			
	1	Prepaid Rent	114	300 00	
		Cash	111		300 00
		Rent Paid in Advance—3 mos.			
	4	Office Equipment	121	50 00	
		Accounts Payable	211		50 00
		Purchased Equipment on Account			
	6	Office Supplies	115	40 00	
		Cash	111		40 00
		Supplies purchased for cash			
	8	Cash	111	400 00	
		Fees Earned	411		400 00
		Services rendered			
	12	R. Kern, Withdrawals	312	20 00	
		Cash	111		20 00
		Personal payment of a bill			
	14	Accounts Receivable	112	100 00	
		Fees Earned	411		100 00
		Services rendered on account			
	16	Salaries Expense	511	60 00	
		Cash	111		60 00
		Paid salaries			
	18	Advertising Expense	512	70 00	
		Accounts Payable	211		70 00
		Advertising bill, but not paid			

Solution Tips to Journalizing and Posting Transactions

Date	Account	Category	↑ ↓	Rules	Amount
Jan 1	Cash	Asset	↑	Dr.	$1,200
	Office Equipment	Asset	↑	Dr.	$ 100
	R. Kern, Capital	Capital	↑	Cr.	$1,300

Date	Account	Category	↑ ↓	Rules	Amount
1	Prepaid Rent	Asset	↑	Dr.	$ 300
	Cash	Asset	↓	Cr.	$ 300

4	Office Equipment	Asset	↑	Dr.	$ 50
	Accounts Payable	Liability	↑	Cr.	$ 50
6	Office Supplies	Asset	↑	Dr.	$ 40
	Cash	Asset	↓	Cr.	$ 40
8	Cash	Asset	↑	Dr.	$ 400
	Fees Earned	Revenue	↑	Cr.	$ 400
12	R. Kern, Withdrawals	Withdrawals	↑	Dr.	$ 20
	Cash	Asset	↓	Cr.	$ 20
14	Accounts Receivable	Asset	↑	Dr.	$ 100
	Fees Earned	Revenue	↑	Cr.	$ 100
16	Salaries Expense	Expense	↑	Dr.	$ 60
	Cash	Asset	↓	Cr.	$ 60
18	Advertising Expense	Expense	↑	Dr.	$ 70
	Accounts Payable	Liability	↑	Cr.	$ 70

Note: All account titles come from the chart of accounts. When journalizing, the PR column of the general journal is blank. It is in the posting process that we update the ledger. The PR column in the ledger accounts tells us from what journal page the information came. After the title in the ledger is posted to, we fill in the PR column of the journal, telling us to what account number the information was transferred.

Completing the Worksheet

See the worksheet in Fig. 5.15 on the following page spread.

Solution Tips to the Trial Balance and Completion of the Worksheet

After the posting process is complete from the journal to the ledger, we take the ending balance in each account and prepare a trial balance on the worksheet (see Fig. 5.15). If a title has no balance, it is not listed on the trial balance. New titles on the worksheet will be added as needed.

Adjustments

Office Supplies Expense	Expense	↑	Dr.	$ 34	($40 − $6)
Office Supplies	Asset	↓	Cr.	$ 34	

Supplies on hand of $6 is not the adjustment. Need to calculate amount used up.

Rent Expense	Expense	↑	Dr.	$100
Prepaid Rent	Asset	↓	Cr.	$100

Do not touch original cost of equipment.

Depr. Exp., Office Equip.	Expense	↑	Dr.	$ 20
Accum. Dep., Office Equip.	Contra-Asset	↑	Cr.	$ 20

Salaries Expense	Expense	↑	Dr.	$ 50
Salaries Payable	Liability	↑	Cr.	$ 50

Note: This information on the worksheet has *not* been updated in the ledger. (Updating happens when we journalize and post adjustments at the end of the cycle.)

Note that the last four columns of the worksheet come from numbers on the adjusted trial balance.

We move the Net Income of $166 to the Balance Sheet credit column because the Capital figure is the old one on the worksheet.

Supplies used up — Supplies on hand

ROLO CO.
WORKSHEET
FOR MONTH ENDED JANUARY 31, 200X

Account Titles	Trial Balance Dr.	Trial Balance Cr.	Adjustments Dr.	Adjustments Cr.	Adjusted Trial Balance Dr.	Adjusted Trial Balance Cr.	Income Statement Dr.	Income Statement Cr.	Balance Sheet Dr.	Balance Sheet Cr.
Cash	1180 00				1180 00				1180 00	
Accounts Receivable	100 00				100 00				100 00	
Prepaid Rent	300 00			(B) 100 00	200 00				200 00	
Office Supplies	40 00			(A) 34 00	6 00				6 00	
Office Equipment	150 00				150 00				150 00	
Accounts Payable		120 00				120 00				120 00
R. Kern, Capital		1300 00				1300 00				1300 00
R. Kern, Withdrawals	20 00				20 00				20 00	
Fees Earned		500 00				500 00		500 00		
Salaries Expense	60 00		(D) 50 00		110 00		110 00			
Advertising Expense	70 00				70 00		70 00			
	1920 00	1920 00								
Office Supplies Expense			(A) 34 00		34 00		34 00			
Rent Expense			(B) 100 00		100 00		100 00			
Depr. Exp., Office Equip.			(C) 20 00		20 00		20 00			
Acc. Dep., Office Equip.				(C) 20 00		20 00				20 00
Salaries Payable				(D) 50 00		50 00				50 00
			204 00	204 00	1990 00	1990 00	334 00	500 00	1656 00	1490 00
Net Income							166 00			166 00
							500 00	500 00	1656 00	1656 00

FIGURE 5.15 Completed Worksheet for Rolo Company

Preparing the Formal Financial Statements

FIGURE 5.16 Income Statement for Rolo Company

ROLO CO. INCOME STATEMENT FOR MONTH ENDED JANUARY 31, 200X		
Revenue:		
Fees Earned		$500 00
Operating Expenses		
Salaries Expense	$110 00	
Advertising Expense	70 00	
Office Supplies Expense	34 00	
Rent Expense	100 00	
Depreciation Expense, Office Equipment	20 00	
Total Operating Expenses		334 00
Net Income		$166 00

FIGURE 5.17 Statement of Owner's Equity for Rolo Company

ROLO CO. STATEMENT OF OWNER'S EQUITY FOR MONTH ENDED JANUARY 31, 200X		
R. Kern, Capital, January 1, 200X		$1300 00
Net Income for January	$166 00	
Less Withdrawals for January	20 00	
Increase in Capital		146 00
R. Kern, Capital, January 31, 200X		$1446 00

FIGURE 5.18 Balance Sheet for Rolo Company

ROLO CO. BALANCE SHEET JANUARY 31, 200X					
Assets			Liabilities & Owner's Equity		
Cash		$1180 00	Liabilities		
Accounts Receivable		100 00	Accounts Payable	$120 00	
Prepaid Rent		200 00	Salaries Payable	50 00	
Office Supplies		6 00	Total Liabilities		$ 170 00
Office Equipment	$150 00		Owner's Equity		
Less Accum. Depr.	20 00	130 00	R. Kern, Capital		1446 00
			Total Liabilities &		
Total Assets		$1616 00	Owner's Equity		$1616 00

Solution Tips to Preparing the Financial Statements

The statements are prepared from the worksheet. (Many of the ledger accounts are not up-to-date.) The income statement (Fig. 5.16) lists revenue and expenses. The Net Income figure of $166 is used to update the statement of owner's equity. The statement of owner's equity (Fig. 5.17) calculates a new figure for Capital, $1,446 (Beginning Capital + Net Income − Withdrawals). This new figure is then listed on the balance sheet (Fig. 5.18) (Assets, Liabilities, and a new figure for Capital).

Journalizing and Posting Adjusting and Closing Entries

See the journal in Figure 5.19.

FIGURE 5.19 Adjusting and Closing Entries Journalized and Posted

General Journal — Page 2

	Date		Account Titles and Description	PR	Dr.	Cr.
			ADJUSTING ENTRIES			
	Jan.	31	Office Supplies Expense	514	3400	
			Office Supplies	115		3400
		31	Rent Expense	513	10000	
			Prepaid Rent	114		10000
		31	Depr. Expense, Office Equipment	515	2000	
			Accum. Depr., Office Equip.	122		2000
		31	Salaries Expense	511	5000	
			Salaries Payable	212		5000
			CLOSING ENTRIES			
Closing: Step 1 →		31	Fees Earned	411	50000	
			Income Summary	313		50000
Step 2 →		31	Income Summary	313	33400	
			Salaries Expense	511		11000
			Advertising Expense	512		7000
			Office Supplies Expense	514		3400
			Rent Expense	513		10000
			Depr. Expense, Office Equip.	515		2000
Step 3 →		31	Income Summary	313	16600	
			R. Kern, Capital	311		16600
Step 4 →		31	R. Kern, Capital	311	2000	
			R. Kern, Withdrawals	312		2000

Solution Tips to Journalizing and Posting Adjusting and Closing Entries

Adjustments

The adjustments from the worksheet are journalized (same journal) and posted to the ledger. Now ledger accounts will be brought up-to-date. Remember, we have already prepared the financial statements from the worksheet. Our goal now is to get the ledger up-to-date.

Closing

Note that Income Summary is a temporary account located in the ledger.

GOALS

1. Wipe out all temporary accounts in the ledger to zero balances.
2. Get a new figure for Capital in the ledger.

Steps in the Closing Process

Step 1 Close revenue to Income Summary.

Step 2 Close individual expenses to Income Summary.

Step 3 Close balance of Income Summary to Capital. (This amount really is the Net Income figure on the worksheet.)

Step 4 Close balance of Withdrawals to Capital.

All the journal closing entries are posted. (No new calculations are needed because all figures are on the worksheet.) The result in the ledger is that all temporary accounts have a zero balance (Fig. 5.20).

FIGURE 5.20 General Ledger for Rolo Company

GENERAL LEDGER

Cash 111

Date	PR	Dr.	Cr.	Balance Dr.	Balance Cr.
1/1	GJ1	1,200		1,200	
1/1	GJ1		300	900	
1/6	GJ1		40	860	
1/8	GJ1	400		1,260	
1/12	GJ1		20	1,240	
1/16	GJ1		60	1,180	

Accounts Receivable 112

Date	PR	Dr.	Cr.	Balance Dr.	Balance Cr.
1/14	GJ1	100		100	

Accumulated Depreciation, Equipment 122

Date	PR	Dr.	Cr.	Balance Dr.	Balance Cr.
1/31Adj.	GJ2		20		20

Accounts Payable 211

Date	PR	Dr.	Cr.	Balance Dr.	Balance Cr.
1/4	GJ1		50		50
1/18	GJ1		70		120

Salaries Payable 212

Date	PR	Dr.	Cr.	Balance Dr.	Balance Cr.
1/31Adj.	GJ2		50		50

FIGURE 5.20 *(continued)*

Prepaid Rent 114

Date	PR	Dr.	Cr.	Balance Dr.	Balance Cr.
1/1	GJ1	300		300	
1/31Adj.	GJ2		100	200	

Office Supplies 115

Date	PR	Dr.	Cr.	Balance Dr.	Balance Cr.
1/6	GJ1	40		40	
1/31Adj	GJ2		34	6	

Office Equipment 121

Date	PR	Dr.	Cr.	Balance Dr.	Balance Cr.
1/1	GJ1	100		100	
1/4	GJ1	50		150	

Fees Earned 411

Date	PR	Dr.	Cr.	Balance Dr.	Balance Cr.
1/8	GJ1		400		400
1/14	GJ1		100		500
1/31 Clos.	GJ2	500		———	

Salaries Expense 511

Date	PR	Dr.	Cr.	Balance Dr.	Balance Cr.
1/16	GJ1	60		60	
1/31 Adj.	GJ2	50		110	
1/31 Clos.	GJ2		110	———	

Advertising Expense 512

Date	PR	Dr.	Cr.	Balance Dr.	Balance Cr.
1/18	GJ1	70		70	
1/31 Clos.	GJ2		70	———	

Rolo Kern, Capital 311

Date	PR	Dr.	Cr.	Balance Dr.	Balance Cr.
1/1	GJ1		1,300		1,300
1/31Clos.	GJ2		166		1,466
1/31Clos.	GJ2	20			1,446

Rolo Kern, Withdrawals 312

Date	PR	Dr.	Cr.	Balance Dr.	Balance Cr.
1/12	GJ1	20		20	
1/31Clos.	GJ2		20	———	

Income Summary 313

Date	PR	Dr.	Cr.	Balance Dr.	Balance Cr.
1/31 Clos.	GJ2		500		500
1/31 Clos.	GJ2	334			166
1/31 Clos.	GJ2	166			———

Rent Expense 513

Date	PR	Dr.	Cr.	Balance Dr.	Balance Cr.
1/31 Adj.	GJ2	100		100	
1/31 Clos.	GJ2		100	———	

Office Supplies Expense 514

Date	PR	Dr.	Cr.	Balance Dr.	Balance Cr.
1/31 Adj.	GJ2	34		34	
1/31 Clos.	GJ2		34	———	

Depreciation Expenses Office Equipment 515

Date	PR	Dr.	Cr.	Balance Dr.	Balance Cr.
1/31 Adj.	GJ2	20		20	
1/31 Clos.	GJ2		20	———	

Solution Tips for the Post-Closing Trial Balance

The post-closing trial balance is a list of the ledger *after* adjusting and closing entries have been completed. Note that the figure for Capital, $1,446, is the new figure.

FIGURE 5.21 Post-Closing Trial Balance for Rolo Company

The post-closing trial balance contains all permanent accounts.

ROLO CO.
POST-CLOSING TRIAL BALANCE
JANUARY 31, 200X

	Dr.	Cr.
Cash	1 1 8 0 00	
Accounts Receivable	1 0 0 00	
Prepaid Rent	2 0 0 00	
Office Supplies	6 00	
Office Equipment	1 5 0 00	
Accum. Dep., Office Equipment		2 0 00
Accounts Payable		1 2 0 00
Salaries Payable		5 0 00
R. Kern, Capital		1 4 4 6 00
TOTAL	1 6 3 6 00	1 6 3 6 00

Accounting Cycle Tutorial
Adjusting & Closing The Books

Beginning Capital	$1,300
+ Net Income	166
− Withdrawals	20
= Ending Capital	$1,446

Next accounting period we will enter new amounts in the Revenues, Expenses, and Withdrawal accounts. For now, the post-closing trial balance is made up of permanent accounts only.

SUMMARY OF KEY POINTS

LEARNING UNIT 5-1

1. After formal financial statements have been prepared, the ledger has still not been brought up-to-date.
2. Information for journalizing adjusting entries comes from the adjustments section of the worksheet.

LEARNING UNIT 5-2

1. Closing is a mechanical process that aids the accountant in recording transactions for the next period.
2. Assets, Liabilities, and Capital are permanent (real) accounts; their balances are carried over from one accounting period to another. Withdrawals, Revenue, and Expenses are temporary (nominal) accounts; their balances are *not* carried over from one accounting period to another.
3. Income Summary is a temporary account in the general ledger and does not have a normal balance. It will summarize revenue and expenses and transfer the balance to Capital. Withdrawals do not go into Income Summary because they are *not* business expenses.
4. All information for closing can be obtained from the worksheet or ledger.
5. When closing is complete, all temporary accounts in the ledger will have a zero balance, and all this information will be updated in the Capital account.
6. Closing entries are usually done only at year-end. Interim reports can be prepared from worksheets that are prepared monthly, quarterly, or some other regular time period.

LEARNING UNIT 5-3

1. The post-closing trial balance is prepared from the ledger accounts after the adjusting and closing entries have been posted.
2. The accounts on the post-closing trial balance are all permanent titles.

KEY TERMS

Adjusting journal entries Journal entries that are needed in order to update specific ledger accounts to reflect correct balances at the end of an accounting period.

Closing journal entries Journal entries that are prepared to (a) reduce or clear all temporary accounts to a zero balance or (b) update Capital to a new balance.

Income Summary A temporary account in the ledger that summarizes revenue and expenses and transfers the balance (net income or net loss) to Capital. This account does not have a normal balance.

Permanent accounts (real) Accounts whose balances are carried over to the next accounting period. Examples: Assets, Liabilities, Capital.

Post-closing trial balance The final step in the accounting cycle that lists only permanent accounts in the ledger and their balances after adjusting and closing entries have been posted.

Temporary accounts (nominal) Accounts whose balances at the end of an accounting period are not carried over to the next accounting period. These accounts—Revenue, Expenses, Withdrawals—help summarize a new or ending figure for Capital to begin the next accounting period. Keep in mind that Income Summary is also a temporary account.

BLUEPRINT OF CLOSING PROCESS FROM THE WORKSHEET

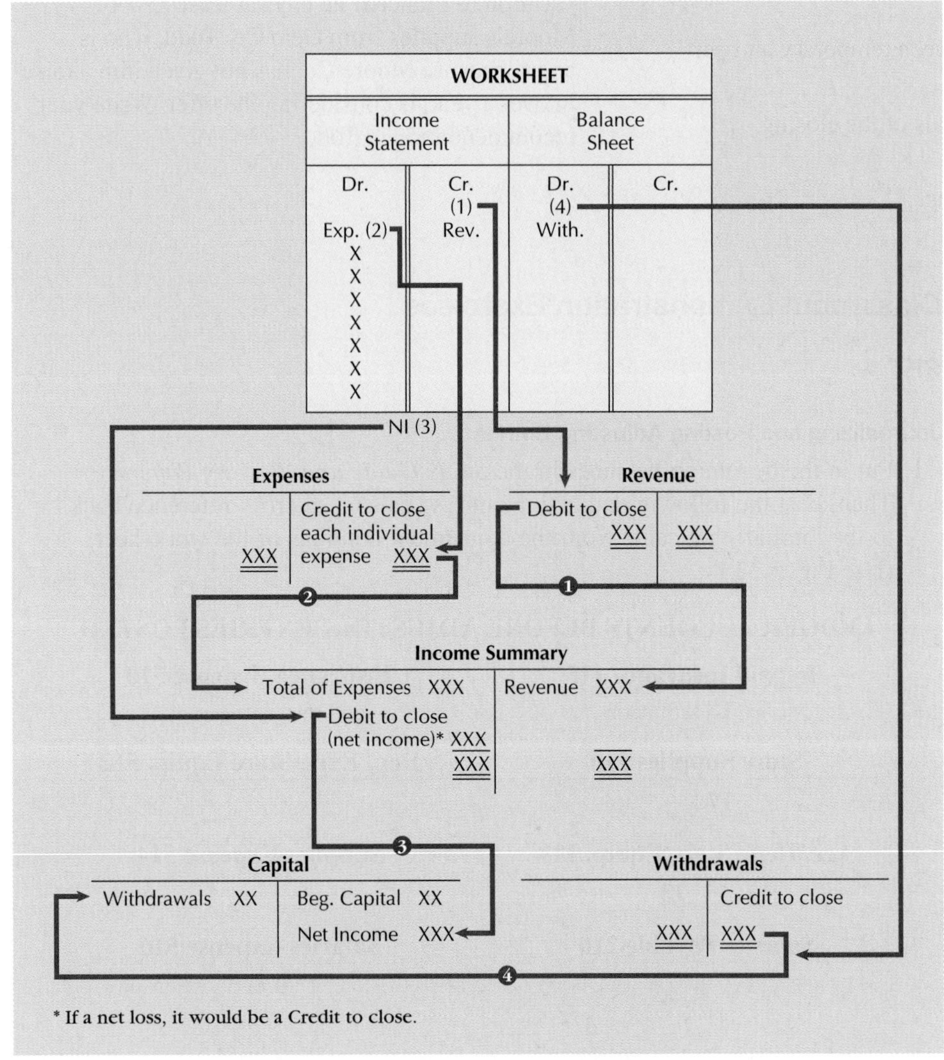

The Closing Steps

1. Close revenue ($) balance to Income Summary.
2. Close each *individual* expense and transfer *total* of all expenses to Income Summary.
3. Transfer balance in Income Summary (net income or net loss) to Capital.
4. Close Withdrawals to Capital.

QUESTIONS, CLASSROOM DEMONSTRATION EXERCISES, EXERCISES, AND PROBLEMS

Discussion and Critical Thinking Questions/Ethical Case

1. When a worksheet is completed, what balances are found in the general ledger?
2. Why must adjusting entries be journalized even though the formal statements have already been prepared?
3. "Closing slows down the recording of next year's transactions." Defend or reject this statement with supporting evidence.
4. What is the difference between temporary and permanent accounts?
5. What are the two major goals of the closing process?
6. List the four steps of closing.
7. What is the purpose of Income Summary and where is it located?
8. How can a worksheet aid the closing process?
9. What accounts are usually listed on a post-closing trial balance?
10. Closing entries are always prepared once a month. Agree or disagree? Why?
11. Todd Silver is the purchasing agent for Moore Co. One of his suppliers, Gem Co., offers Todd a free vacation to France if he buys at least 75% of Moore's supplies from Gem Co. Todd, who is angry because Moore Co. has not given him a raise in over a year, is considering the offer. Write your recommendation to Todd.

MyAccountingLab

Classroom Demonstration Exercises

SET A

LO1 (5 min) **Journalizing and Posting Adjusting Entries**

1. Put in the beginning balances in the *Study Guide and Working Papers*. Then, post the following adjusting entries (be sure to cross-reference back to the journal) that came from the adjustment columns of the worksheet. (Use Fig. 5.22.)

LEDGER ACCOUNTS BEFORE ADJUSTING ENTRIES POSTED

Prepaid Insurance 115		**Insurance Expense 510**	
18			

Store Supplies 116		**Dep. Exp., Store Equip. 512**	
17			

Acc. Dep., Store Equip. 119		**Supplies Expense 514**	
	13		

Salaries Payable 210		**Salaries Expense 516**	
		9	

General Journal					Page 3
Date		Account Titles and Description	PR	Dr.	Cr.
Dec.	31	Insurance Expense		6 00	
		Prepaid Insurance			6 00
	31	Supplies Expense		4 00	
		Store Supplies			4 00
	31	Depr. Exp., Store Equipment		9 00	
		Accum. Depr., Store Equipment			9 00
	31	Salaries Expense		5 00	
		Salaries Payable			5 00

FIGURE 5.22 Journalized Adjusting Entries

Steps of Closing and Journalizing Closing Entries *LO2 (10 min)*

2. Explain the four steps of the closing process given the following:

Dec. 31 ending balance, before closing	
Fees Earned	$200
Rent Expense	100
Advertising Expense	60
J. Rice, Capital	3,000
J. Rice, Withdrawals	15

Journalizing Closing Entries *LO2 (15 min)*

3. From the following accounts, journalize the closing entries (assume December 31).

Mel Blanc, Capital 310

	40

Gas Expense 510

8	

Mel Blanc, Withdr. 312

7	

Advertising Exp. 512

12	

Income Summary 314

Dep. Exp., Taxi 516

5	

Taxi Fees 410

	39

Posting to Income Summary *LO2 (10 min)*

4. Draw a T account of Income Summary and post to it all entries from Question 3 that affect it. Is Income Summary a temporary or permanent account?

Posting to Capital *LO2 (10 min)*

5. Draw a T account for Mel Blanc, Capital, and post to it all entries from Question 3 that affect it. What is the final balance of the Capital account?

SET B

Journalizing and Posting Adjusting Entries *LO1 (5 min)*

1. Put in the beginning balances in the *Study Guide and Working Papers.* Then, post the following adjusting entries (be sure to cross-reference back to the journal) that came from the adjustment columns of the worksheet. (Use Fig. 5.23 on the following page.)

LEDGER ACCOUNTS BEFORE ADJUSTING ENTRIES POSTED

Prepaid Insurance 115	
12	

Insurance Expense 510	

Store Supplies 116	
15	

Dep. Exp., Store Equip. 512	

Acc. Dep., Store Equip. 119	
	12

Supplies Expense 514	

Salaries Payable 210	

Salaries Expense 516	
7	

FIGURE 5.23 Journalized Adjusting Entries

General Journal — Page 3

Date		Account Titles and Description	PR	Dr.	Cr.
Dec.	31	Insurance Expense		4 00	
		Prepaid Insurance			4 00
	31	Supplies Expense		3 00	
		Store Supplies			3 00
	31	Depr. Exp., Store Equipment		7 00	
		Accum. Depr., Store Equipment			7 00
	31	Salaries Expense		4 00	
		Salaries Payable			4 00

LO2 (15 min) **Steps of Closing and Journalizing Closing Entries**

2. From the worksheet in Figure 5.24, explain the four steps of closing. Keep in mind that each *individual* expense normally would be listed in the closing process.

FIGURE 5.24

Worksheet

IS		BS	
Dr.	Cr.	Dr.	Cr.
(2)	Rev. (1)	Withd.	(4)
E X P E N S E S			
NI (3)			

Goals of Closing

1. Temporary accounts in the ledger should have a zero balance.
2. New figure for Capital in closing.

Note: All closing can be done from the worksheet. Income Summary is a temporary account in the ledger.

Journalizing Closing Entries *LO2 (15 min)*

3. From the following accounts, journalize the closing entries (assume December 31).

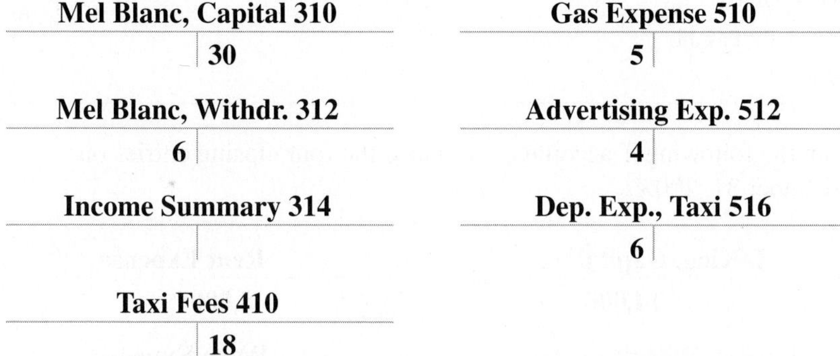

Posting to Income Summary *LO2 (10 min)*

4. Draw a T account of Income Summary and post to it all entries from Question 3 that affect it. Is Income Summary a temporary or permanent account?

Posting to Capital *LO2 (10 min)*

5. Draw a T account for Mel Blanc, Capital, and post to it all entries from Question 3 that affect it. What is the final balance of the Capital account?

Exercises

MyAccountingLab

5-1. From the adjustments section of a worksheet presented in Figure 5.25, prepare adjusting journal entries for the end of December. *LO1 (15 min)*

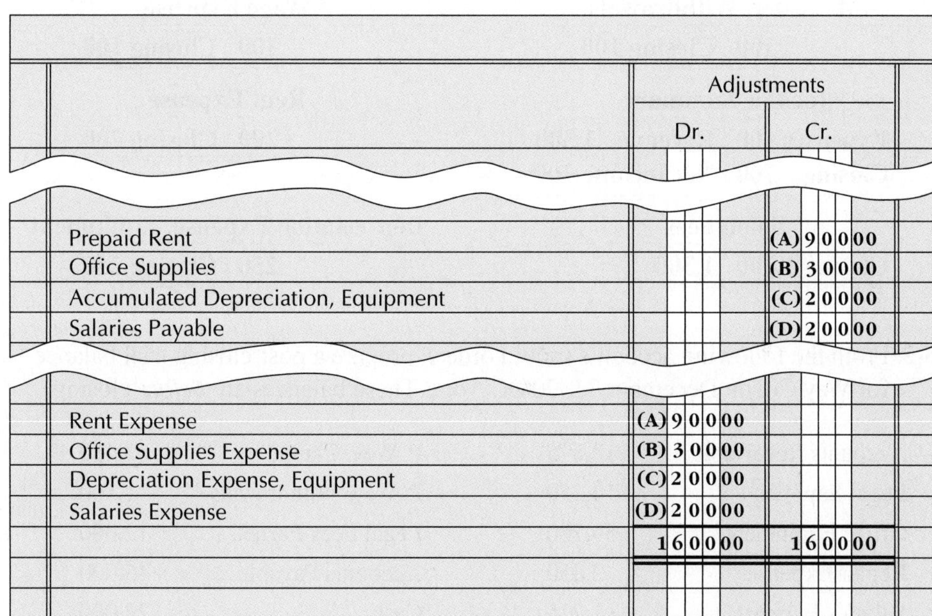

	Adjustments Dr.	Adjustments Cr.
Prepaid Rent		(A) 900 00
Office Supplies		(B) 300 00
Accumulated Depreciation, Equipment		(C) 200 00
Salaries Payable		(D) 200 00
Rent Expense	(A) 900 00	
Office Supplies Expense	(B) 300 00	
Depreciation Expense, Equipment	(C) 200 00	
Salaries Expense	(D) 200 00	
	1600 00	1600 00

FIGURE 5.25 Adjustments on Worksheet

LO1, 2 (10 min) **5-2.** Complete the following table by placing an X in the correct column.

	Temporary	Permanent	Will Be Closed
Ex. Accounts Receivable		X	
1. Income Summary			
2. Jen Rich, Capital			
3. Salary Expense			
4. Jen Rich, Withdrawals			
5. Fees Earned			
6. Accounts Payable			
7. Cash			

LO2 (15 min) **5-3.** From the following T accounts, journalize the four closing entries on December 31, 200X.

J. King, Capital

Dr.	Cr.
	14,000

Rent Expense

Dr.	Cr.
5,000	

J. King, Withdrawals

Dr.	Cr.
4,000	

Wage Expense

Dr.	Cr.
7,000	

Income Summary

Dr.	Cr.

Insurance Expense

Dr.	Cr.
1,200	

Fees Earned

Dr.	Cr.
	33,000

Dep. Expense, Office Equipment

Dr.	Cr.
900	

LO2 (20 min) **5-4.** From the following posted T accounts, reconstruct the closing journal entries for December 31, 200X.

M. Foster, Capital

Dr.	Cr.
Withdrawals 100	2,000 (Dec. 1)
	700 Net income

Insurance Expense

Dr.	Cr.
50	Closing 50

M. Foster, Withdrawals

Dr.	Cr.
100	Closing 100

Wage Expense

Dr.	Cr.
100	Closing 100

Income Summary

Dr.	Cr.
Expenses 600	Revenue 1,300
Closing 700	Net Income 700

Rent Expense

Dr.	Cr.
200	Closing 200

Salon Fees

Dr.	Cr.
Closing 1,300	1,300

Depreciation Expense, Equipment

Dr.	Cr.
250	Closing 250

LO3 (20 min) **5-5.** From the following accounts (not in order), prepare a post-closing trial balance for Wey Co. on December 31, 200X. *Note:* These balances are *before* closing.

Accounts Receivable	$18,875	P. Wey, Capital	63,450
Legal Supplies	14,250	P. Wey, Withdrawals	1,500
Office Equipment	59,700	Legal Fees Earned	12,000
Repair Expense	2,850	Accounts Payable	45,000
Salaries Expense	1,275	Cash	22,000

Group A Problems

MyAccountingLab

5A-1. Given the data in Figure 5.26 for Debbie's Dance Studio:

LO1, 2 (40 min)

FIGURE 5.26 Trial Balance for Debbie's Dance Studio

DEBBIE'S DANCE STUDIO TRIAL BALANCE JUNE 30, 200X		
	Dr.	Cr.
Cash	40,000.00	
Accounts Receivable	7,000.00	
Prepaid Insurance	400.00	
Dance Supplies	1,500.00	
Dance Equipment	13,000.00	
Accumulated Depreciation, Dance Equipment		11,900.00
Accounts Payable		21,000.00
D. Dee, Capital		13,200.00
D. Dee, Withdrawals	800.00	
Dance Fees Earned		19,800.00
Salaries Expense	1,600.00	
Telephone Expense	1,000.00	
Advertising Expense	600.00	
	65,900.00	65,900.00

Check Figure:
Net Income $14,600

Adjustment Data

a. Insurance expired, $300.
b. Dance supplies on hand, $700.
c. Depreciation on dance equipment, $500.
d. Salaries earned by employees but not to be paid until July, $400.

Your task is to

1. Prepare a worksheet.
2. Journalize adjusting and closing entries.

5A-2. Enter the beginning balance in each account in your working papers from the Trial Balance columns of the worksheet (Fig. 5.27 on the following page). From that worksheet, (1) journalize and post adjusting and closing entries after entering the beginning balance in each account in the ledger, and (2) prepare from the ledger a post-closing trial balance for the month of March.

LO1, 2, 3 (35 min)

Check Figure:
Post-closing trial balance $3,504

5A-3. As the bookkeeper of Pete's Plowing, you have been asked to complete the entire accounting cycle for Pete from the following information.

LO1, 2, 3 (150 min)

200X		
Jan.	1	Pete invested $7,000 cash and $6,000 worth of snow equipment into the plowing company.
	1	Paid rent for three months in advance for garage space, $2,000.
	4	Purchased office equipment on account from Ling Corp., $7,200.
	6	Purchased snow supplies for $700 cash.
	8	Collected $15,000 from plowing local shopping centers.
	12	Pete Mack withdrew $1,000 from the business for his own personal use.
	20	Plowed North East Co. parking lots, payment not to be received until March, $5,000.
	26	Paid salaries to employees, $1,800.
	28	Paid Ling Corp. one-half amount owed for office equipment.
	29	Advertising bill received from Bush Co. but will not be paid until March, $900.
	30	Paid telephone bill, $210.

(continued on the following page spread)

POTTER CLEANING SERVICE WORKSHEET FOR MONTH ENDED MARCH 31, 200X										
	Trial Balance		Adjustments		Adjusted Trial Balance		Income Statement		Balance Sheet	
Account Titles	Dr.	Cr.	Dr.	Cr.	Dr.	Cr.	Dr.	Cr.	Dr.	Cr.
Cash	40000				40000				40000	
Prepaid Insurance	52000			(A) 18000	34000				34000	
Cleaning Supplies	14400			(B) 10000	4400				4400	
Auto	272000				272000				272000	
Accum. Depr. Auto		86000		(C) 15000		101000				101000
Accounts Payable		22400				22400				22400
B. Potter, Capital		54000				54000				54000
B. Potter, Withdrawals	46000				46000				46000	
Cleaning Fees		468000				468000		468000		
Salaries Expense	144000		(D) 16000		160000		160000			
Telephone Expense	26400				26400		26400			
Advertising Expense	19600				19600		19600			
Gas Expense	16000				16000		16000			
	630400	630400								
Insurance Expense			(A) 18000		18000		18000			
Cleaning Supplies Expense			(B) 10000		10000		10000			
Depr. Expense Auto			(C) 15000		15000		15000			
Salaries Payable				(D) 16000		16000				16000
			59000	59000	661400	661400	265000	468000	396400	193400
Net Income							203000			203000
							468000	468000	396400	396400

FIGURE 5.27 Worksheet for Potter Cleaning Service

Use the following chart of accounts.

Chart of Accounts

Assets	Owner's Equity
111 Cash	311 Pete Mack, Capital
112 Accounts Receivable	312 Pete Mack, Withdrawals
114 Prepaid Rent	313 Income Summary
115 Snow Supplies	**Revenue**
121 Office Equipment	411 Plowing Fees
122 Accumulated Depreciation, Office Equipment	**Expenses**
123 Snow Equipment	511 Salaries Expense
124 Accumulated Depreciation Snow Equipment	512 Advertising Expense
Liabilities	513 Telephone Expense
211 Accounts Payable	514 Rent Expense
212 Salaries Payable	515 Snow Supplies Expense
	516 Depreciation Expense, Office Equipment
	517 Depreciation Expense, Snow Equipment

Adjustment Data

a. Snow supplies on hand, $400.
b. Rent expired, $600.
c. Depreciation on office equipment, $120: ($7,200 ÷ 5 yr. = $1,440/12 mo. = $120).
d. Depreciation on snow equipment, $100: ($6,000 ÷ 5 yr. = $1,200/12 mo. = $100).
e. Accrued salaries, $190.

Check Figure:
Net Income $15,780

Group B Problems

LO1, 2 (40 min)

5B-1.

MEMO

To: *Matt Kaminsky*
From: *Abby Ellen*
Re: *Accounting Needs*

Please prepare ASAP from the following information (Fig. 5.28 on the following page) (1) a worksheet along with (2) journalized adjusting and closing entries.

Check Figure:
Net Income $3,530

Adjustment Data

a. Insurance expired, $100.
b. Dance supplies on hand, $20.
c. Depreciation on dance equipment, $200.
d. Salaries earned by employees but not due to be paid until July, $490.

LO1, 2 (35 min)

Check Figure:
Post-closing Trial Balance $3,294

5B-2. Enter the beginning balance in each account in your working papers from the Trial Balance columns of the worksheet (Fig. 5.29). From the worksheet (1) journalize and post adjusting and closing entries after entering beginning balances in each account in the ledger, and (2) prepare from the ledger a post-closing trial balance at the end of March.

LO1, 2, 3 (150 min)

5B-3. From the following transactions as well as additional data, please complete the entire accounting cycle for Pete's Plowing (use the preceeding chart of accounts on this page).

FIGURE 5.28 Trial Balance for Debbie's Dance Studio

DEBBIE'S DANCE STUDIO TRIAL BALANCE JUNE 30, 200X		
	Dr.	Cr.
Cash	10150 00	
Accounts Receivable	5000 00	
Prepaid Insurance	700 00	
Dance Supplies	300 00	
Dance Equipment	12950 00	
Accumulated Depreciation, Dance Equipment		4000 00
Accounts Payable		5750 00
D. Dee, Capital		15150 00
D. Dee, Withdrawals	400 00	
Dance Fees Earned		5200 00
Salaries Expense	450 00	
Telephone Expense	70 00	
Advertising Expense	80 00	
	30100 00	30100 00

Check Figure:
Net Income $9,610

200X

Jan.	1	To open the business, Pete invested $8,000 cash and $9,600 worth of snow equipment.
	1	Paid rent for five months in advance, $3,000.
	4	Purchased office equipment on account from Russell Co., $6,000.
	6	Bought snow supplies, $350.
	8	Collected $7,000 for plowing during winter storm emergency.
	12	Pete paid his home telephone bill from the company checkbook, $70.
	20	Billed Eastern Freight Co. for plowing fees earned but not to be received until March, $6,500.
	24	Advertising bill received from Jones Co. but will not be paid until next month, $350.
	26	Paid salaries to employees, $1,800.
	28	Paid Russell Co. one-half of amount owed for office equipment.
	29	Paid telephone bill of company, $165.

Adjustment Data

a. Snow supplies on hand, $200.
b. Rent expired, $600.
c. Depreciation on office equipment, $125: ($6,000/4 yr = $1,500 ÷ 12 = $125).
d. Depreciation on snow equipment, $400: ($9,600 ÷ 2 = $4,800 ÷ 12 = $400).
e. Salaries accrued, $300.

ON-THE-JOB TRAINING

LO3 (15 min)

T-1. Carol Miller needs a loan from the Charles Bank to help finance her business. She submitted to the Charles Bank the following unadjusted trial balance. As the loan officer, you will be meeting with Carol tomorrow. Could you make some specific written suggestions to Carol regarding her loan report? What do you think would be the bank loan officer's concerns?

Cash in Bank	770
Accounts Receivable	1,480
Office Supplies	3,310

(continued on following page spread)

POTTER CLEANING SERVICE
WORKSHEET
FOR MONTH ENDED MARCH 31, 200X

Account Titles	Trial Balance		Adjustments		Adjusted Trial Balance		Income Statement		Balance Sheet	
	Dr.	Cr.	Dr.	Cr.	Dr.	Cr.	Dr.	Cr.	Dr.	Cr.
Cash	1724 00				1724 00				1724 00	
Prepaid Insurance	350 00			(A) 200 00	150 00				150 00	
Cleaning Supplies	800 00			(B) 600 00	200 00				200 00	
Auto	1220 00				1220 00				1220 00	
Accumulated Depreciation, Auto		660 00		(C) 150 00		810 00				810 00
Accounts Payable		674 00				674 00				674 00
B. Potter, Capital		2480 00				2480 00				2480 00
B. Potter, Withdrawals	600 00				600 00				600 00	
Cleaning Fees		3700 00				3700 00		3700 00		
Salaries Expense	2000 00		(D) 175 00		2175 00		2175 00			
Telephone Expense	284 00				284 00		284 00			
Advertising Expense	276 00				276 00		276 00			
Gas Expense	260 00				260 00		260 00			
	7514 00	7514 00								
Insurance Expense			(A) 200 00		200 00		200 00			
Cleaning Supplies Expense			(B) 600 00		600 00		600 00			
Depreciation Expense, Auto			(C) 150 00		150 00		150 00			
Salaries Payable				(D) 175 00		175 00				175 00
			1125 00	1125 00	7839 00	7839 00	3945 00	3700 00	3894 00	4139 00
Net Loss								245 00	245 00	
							3945 00	3945 00	4139 00	4139 00

FIGURE 5.29 Worksheet for Potter Cleaning Service

Equipment	7,606	
Accounts Payable		684
C. Miller, Capital		8,000
Service Fees		17,350
Salaries	11,240	
Utilities Expense	842	
Rent Expense	360	
Insurance Expense	280	
Advertising Expense	146	
Totals	26,034	26,034

LO2 (15 min)

T-2. Janet Smother is the new bookkeeper who replaced Dick Burns, owing to his sudden illness. Janet finds on her desk a note requesting that she close the books and supply the ending Capital figure. Janet is upset because she can only find the following:

a. Revenue and expense accounts all were zero balance.

b. Income Summary

14,360	19,300

c. Owner withdrew $8,000.

d. Owner beginning Capital was $34,400.

Could you help Janet accomplish her assignment? What written suggestions should Janet make to her supervisor so that this situation will not happen again?

FINANCIAL REPORT PROBLEM

LO3 (15 min)

Reading the Kellogg's Annual Report

Go to Appendix A and find Note 1 under Use Estimates in the Accounting Policies section. Why do actual financial reports have different estimates? What is the fiscal year for Kellogg's Company?

INTERNET PROJECT

Amazon

Go to the Web and search: Annual Report Amazon 2008.
Click on Investors Relations.
List out the latest news Amazon is providing to its investors.
Order a free annual report.

MyAccountingLab

CONTINUING PROBLEM

LO1, 2, 3 (60 min)

Sanchez Computer Center

Tony decided to end the Sanchez Computer Center's first year as of September 30, 200X. Following is an updated chart of accounts.

Assets	**Revenue**
1000 Cash	4000 Service Revenue
1020 Accounts Receivable	**Expenses**
1025 Prepaid Rent	5010 Advertising Expense
1030 Supplies	5020 Rent Expense
1080 Computer Shop Equip.	5030 Utilities Expense
1081 Accum. Depr., C.S. Equip.	5040 Phone Expense
1090 Office Equipment	5050 Supplies Expense
1091 Accum. Depr., Office Equip.	5060 Insurance Expense

Liabilities
2000 Accounts Payable
Owner's Equity
3000 T. Freedman, Capital
3010 T. Freedman, Withdrawals
3020 Income Summary
5070 Postage Expense
5080 Depr. Exp., C.S. Equip.
5090 Depr. Exp., Office Equip.

Assignment

1. Journalize the adjusting entries from Chapter 4.
2. Post the adjusting entries to the ledger.
3. Journalize the closing entries.
4. Post the closing entries to the ledger.
5. Prepare a post-closing trial balance.

SUBWAY Case

CLOSING TIME

LO2, 3 (20 min)

"You wait and see," Stan told his new sandwich artist Wanda Kurtz. "Everything will fall into place soon." Wanda had a tough time serving customers quickly enough, and Stan was in the middle of giving her a pep talk when the phone rang.

"I'll let the machine pick up," Stan reassured Wanda, as he proceeded to train her in some crucial POS touch-screen maneuvers.

"Stan!" an urgent voice came over the message machine. "I think you've forgotten something!" Stan picked up the phone and said, "Lila, can I get back to you tomorrow? I'm in the middle of an important talk with Wanda." One of Stan's strong points as an employer was his ability to focus 100 percent on his employees' concerns. Yet, Lila simply would not wait.

"Stan," Lila said impatiently, "you absolutely must get me your worksheet by 12 noon tomorrow so I can close your books. Tomorrow's the 31st of March and we close on the last day of the month!"

"*Ay caramba!*" Stan sighed. "Looks like I'm going to be up till the wee hours," he confided to Wanda when he put down the phone.

Although Subway company policy doesn't require a closing every month, closing the books is a key part of their accounting training for all new franchisees. By closing their books, business owners can clearly measure their net profit and loss for each period separate from all other periods. This practice makes activities such as budgeting and comparing performance with similar businesses (or performance over time) possible.

At 9:00 A.M. the next morning, an exhausted Stan opened up the restaurant and e-mailed his worksheet to Lila. He was feeling quite pleased with himself—that is, until he heard Lila's urgent-sounding voice coming over the message machine 10 minutes later.

"I've been over and over this," said Lila after Stan picked up, "and I can't get it to balance. I know it's hard for you to do this during working hours, but I need you to go back over the figures."

Stan opened up Peachtree and pored over his worksheets. Errors are hard to find when closing the books and, unfortunately, the process doesn't offer a set way to detect errors or any set place to start. Stan chose payroll because it is one of the largest expenses and because of the new hire.

At 11:45 he called Lila who sounded both exasperated and relieved to hear from him. "I think I've got it! It looks like I messed up on adjusting the Salaries Expense account. I looked at the payroll register and compared the total to the Salaries Payable account. It didn't match! When I hired Wanda Kurtz on the 26th, I should have increased both the Salaries Expense and the Salaries Payable lines because she has accrued wages."

"Yes," said Lila, "Salaries Expense is a debit and Salaries Payable is a credit, and you skipped the payable. Great! With this adjusting entry in the general journal, the worksheet will balance."

Stan's sigh of relief turned into a big yawn, and they both laughed. "I guess I just find it easier to hire people and train them than to account for them," said Stan.

Discussion Questions

1. How would the adjustment be made if Wanda Kurtz received $7.00 per hour and worked 25 additional hours? Where do you place her accrued wages?
2. Stan bought three new Subway aprons and hats for Wanda Smith for $20 each but forgot to post it to the Uniforms account. How much will the closing balance be off? In what way will it be off?
3. Put yourself in Stan's shoes: What is the value of doing a monthly closing, no matter how much—or little—business you do?

MINI PRACTICE SET

SULLIVAN REALTY

Reviewing the Accounting Cycle Twice

Est Time 5 hours

This comprehensive review problem requires you to complete the accounting cycle for Sullivan Realty twice. This practice set allows you to review Chapters 1–5 while reinforcing the relationships between all parts of the accounting cycle. By completing two cycles, you will see how the ending June balances in the ledger are used to accumulate data in July.

First, look at the chart of accounts for Sullivan Realty.

Sullivan Realty
Chart of Accounts

Assets	**Revenue**
111 Cash	411 Commissions Earned
112 Accounts Receivable	**Expenses**
114 Prepaid Rent	511 Rent Expense
115 Office Supplies	512 Salaries Expense
121 Office Equipment	513 Gas Expense
122 Accumulated Depreciation, Office Equipment	514 Repairs Expense
123 Automobile	515 Telephone Expense
124 Accumulated Depreciation, Automobile	516 Advertising Expense
Liabilities	517 Office Supplies Expense
211 Accounts Payable	518 Depreciation Expense, Office Equipment
212 Salaries Payable	519 Depreciation Expense, Automobile
Owner's Equity	524 Miscellaneous Expense
311 John Sullivan, Capital	
312 John Sullivan, Withdrawals	
313 Income Summary	

On June 1, 200X, John Sullivan opened a real estate office called Sullivan Realty. The following transactions were completed for the month of June:

200X		
June	1	John Sullivan invested $9,000 cash in the real estate agency along with $4,000 of office equipment.

DEPOSIT TICKET

SULLIVAN REALTY (213)478-3584
8200 SUNSET BOULEVARD
Los Angeles, CA 90028

DATE *June 1 200X*

SIGN HERE IN PRESENCE OF TELLER FOR CASH RET'D FROM DEP.

BAY BANK
Box 1739 Terminal Annex
Los Angeles, CA 90052

CASH	CURRENCY	9,000	00
	COIN		
LIST CHECKS SINGLY			
TOTAL FROM OTHER SIDE			
TOTAL		9,000	00
LESS CASH RECEIVED			
NET DEPOSIT		9,000	00

16-66/1220

A hold for uncollected funds may be placed on funds deposited by check or similar instruments. This could delay your ability to withdraw such funds. The delay if any would not exceed the period of time permitted by law.

⑆122000661⑆1400⑈03857⑈01362⑈

June 1 Rented and paid three months rent in advance to Miller Property Management $3,000.

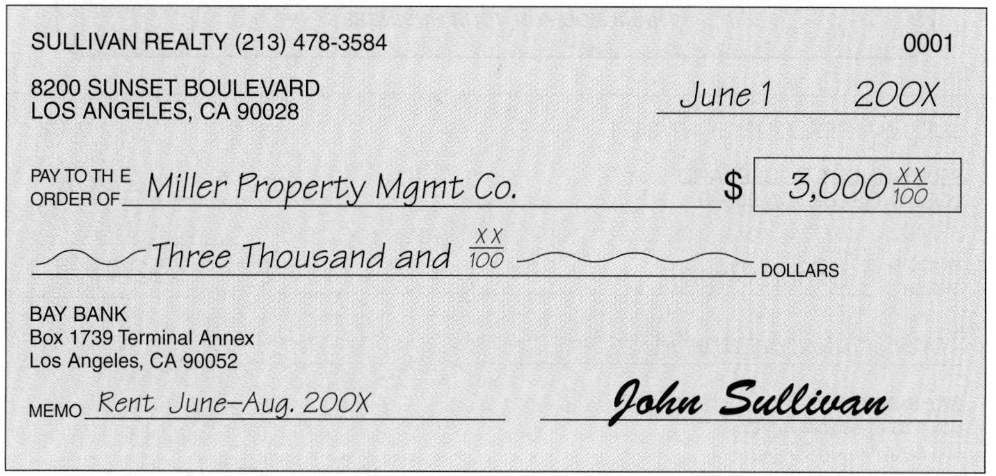

SULLIVAN REALTY (213) 478-3584 0001
8200 SUNSET BOULEVARD
LOS ANGELES, CA 90028

June 1 200X

PAY TO THE ORDER OF *Miller Property Mgmt Co.* $ *3,000 XX/100*

Three Thousand and XX/100 DOLLARS

BAY BANK
Box 1739 Terminal Annex
Los Angeles, CA 90052

MEMO *Rent June–Aug. 200X* *John Sullivan*

June 1 Bought an automobile on account from Volvo West, $14,000.

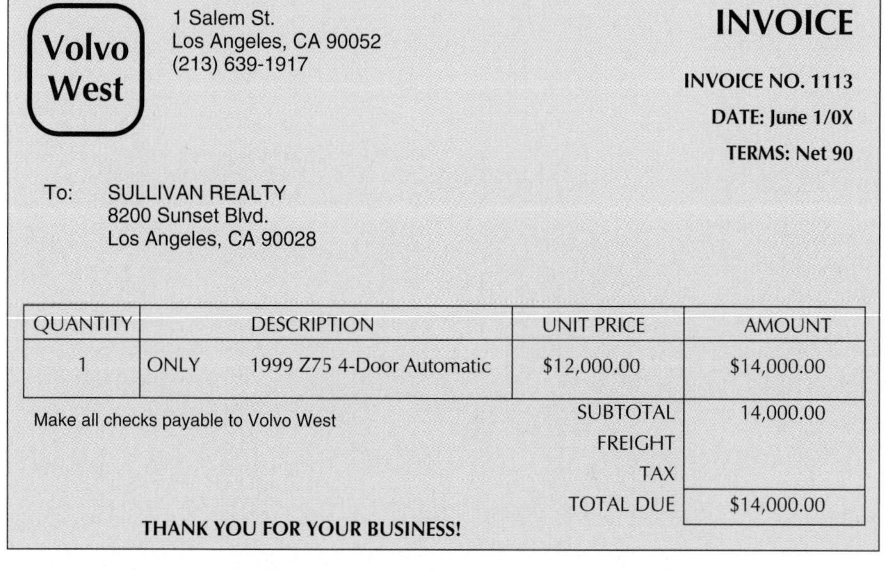

Volvo West
1 Salem St.
Los Angeles, CA 90052
(213) 639-1917

INVOICE

INVOICE NO. 1113
DATE: June 1/0X
TERMS: Net 90

To: SULLIVAN REALTY
8200 Sunset Blvd.
Los Angeles, CA 90028

QUANTITY	DESCRIPTION	UNIT PRICE	AMOUNT
1	ONLY 1999 Z75 4-Door Automatic	$12,000.00	$14,000.00
		SUBTOTAL	14,000.00
		FREIGHT	
		TAX	
		TOTAL DUE	$14,000.00

Make all checks payable to Volvo West

THANK YOU FOR YOUR BUSINESS!

June 4 Purchased office supplies from Office Depot for cash, $300.

Office Depot

1 Ferncroft Rd.
Los Angeles, CA 90052
Phone (213) 631-0288

INVOICE

DATE: June 4/0X
NUMBER: D198795
TERMS: Cash

SOLD TO:	SHIPPED TO:
Sullivan Realty 8200 Sunset Blvd. Los Angeles, CA 90028	Sullivan Realty 8200 Sunset Blvd. Los Angeles, CA 90028

DATE	DESCRIPTION	UNIT PRICE	AMOUNT
Jun 4/0X	Office supplies PAYMENT RECEIVED - - CHK #0002 - THANK YOU		$300.00
		Subtotal	300.00
		Total	$300.00

Business Number: 115555559

PLEASE PAY THE ABOVE

THANK YOU FOR YOUR BUSINESS

SULLIVAN REALTY (213) 478-3584 0002

8200 SUNSET BOULEVARD
LOS ANGELES, CA 90028

June 4 200X

PAY TO THE ORDER OF Office Depot $ 300 XX/100

Three Hundred and XX/100 DOLLARS

BAY BANK
Box 1739 Terminal Annex
Los Angeles, CA 90052

MEMO Office supplies

John Sullivan

June 5 Purchased additional office supplies from Office Depot on account, $150.

Office Depot

1 Ferncroft Rd.
Los Angeles, CA 90052
Phone (213) 631-0288

INVOICE

DATE: June 5/0X
NUMBER: D198825
TERMS: net 60

SOLD TO:	SHIPPED TO:
Sullivan Realty 8200 Sunset Blvd. Los Angeles, CA 90028	Sullivan Realty 8200 Sunset Blvd. Los Angeles, CA 90028

DATE	DESCRIPTION	UNIT PRICE	AMOUNT
Jun 5/0X	Office supplies		$150.00
		Subtotal	150.00
		Total	$150.00

Business Number: 115555559

THANK YOU FOR YOUR BUSINESS

PLEASE PAY THE ABOVE

June 6 Sold a house to Bill Barnes and collected a $6,000 commission.

DEPOSIT TICKET

SULLIVAN REALTY (213)478-3584
8200 SUNSET BOULEVARD
Los Angeles, CA 90028

DATE June 6 200X

SIGN HERE IN PRESENCE OF TELLER FOR CASH RET'D FROM DEP.

BAY BANK
Box 1739 Terminal Annex
Los Angeles, CA 90052

CASH	CURRENCY		
	COIN		
LIST CHECKS SINGLY 250-99		6,000	00
TOTAL FROM OTHER SIDE			
TOTAL			
LESS CASH RECEIVED			
NET DEPOSIT		6,000	00

16-66/1220

A hold for uncollected funds may be placed on funds deposited by check or similar instruments. This could delay your ability to withdraw such funds. The delay if any would not exceed the period of time permitted by law.

⑆122000661⑆1400⑈03857⑈01362⑈

SULLIVAN REALTY COMMISSION REPORT			***Date:*** June 6, 200X	
Name: Bill Barnes				
Date:	***Sales Description***	***Sales No.***	***Commission Amount***	
Jun 6/0X	*Home at 66 Sullivan St.*	*A1001*	*$6,000.00*	*Paid in full.*
C001		***Remarks:***		

June 8 Paid gas bill to Petro Petroleum, $22.

SULLIVAN REALTY (213) 478-3584 0003

8200 SUNSET BOULEVARD
LOS ANGELES, CA 90028

June 8 200X

PAY TO THE ORDER OF Petro Petroleum $ 22 XX/100

Twenty-two and XX/100 DOLLARS

BAY BANK
Box 1739 Terminal Annex
Los Angeles, CA 90052

MEMO Gas Bill – June 6

John Sullivan

June 15 Paid Betty Long, office secretary, $350.

SULLIVAN REALTY (213) 478-3584 0004

8200 SUNSET BOULEVARD
LOS ANGELES, CA 90028

June 15 200X

PAY TO TH E ORDER OF Betty Long $ 350 XX/100

Three Hundred fifty and XX/100 DOLLARS

BAY BANK
Box 1739 Terminal Annex
Los Angeles, CA 90052

MEMO Salary – June 1–15

John Sullivan

June 17 Sold a building lot to West Land Developers and earned a commission, $6,500 payment to be received on July 8.

SULLIVAN REALTY
COMMISSION REPORT ***Date:*** June 17, 200X

Name: West Land Developers

Date:	***Sales Description***	***Sales No.***	***Commission Amount***	
Jun 17/0X	*Lot at 8 Ridge Rd.*	*A1002*	*$6,500.00*	

C002 ***Remarks:*** Payment due July 8, 200X

June 20 John Sullivan withdrew $1,000 from the business to pay personal expenses.

SULLIVAN REALTY (213) 478-3584 0005
8200 SUNSET BOULEVARD
LOS ANGELES, CA 90028

June 20 200X

PAY TO THE ORDER OF John Sullivan $ 1,000 XX/100

One Thousand and XX/100 DOLLARS

BAY BANK
Box 1739 Terminal Annex
Los Angeles, CA 90052

MEMO Withdrawal John Sullivan

June 21 Sold a house to Laura Harrison and collected a $3,500 commission.

DEPOSIT TICKET

SULLIVAN REALTY (213)478-3584
8200 SUNSET BOULEVARD
Los Angeles, CA 90028

DATE June 21 200X

SIGN HERE IN PRESENCE OF TELLER FOR CASH RET'D FROM DEP.

BAY BANK
Box 1739 Terminal Annex
Los Angeles, CA 90052

CASH	CURRENCY		
	COIN		
LIST CHECKS SINGLY 270-88		3,500	00
TOTAL FROM OTHER SIDE			
TOTAL			
LESS CASH RECEIVED			
NET DEPOSIT		3,500	00

16-66/1220

A hold for uncollected funds may be placed on funds deposited by check or similar instruments. This could delay your ability to withdraw such funds. The delay if any would not exceed the period of time permitted by law.

⑆122000661⑆1400⑈03857⑈01362⑈

SULLIVAN REALTY
COMMISSION REPORT

Date: June 21, 200X

Name: Ms. Laura Harrison

Date:	***Sales Description***	***Sales No.***	***Commission Amount***	
Jun 21/0X	*Home at 666 Jersey St.*	*A1003*	*$3,500.00*	*Paid in full.*

C003 ***Remarks:***

June 22 Paid gas bill, $25, to Petro Petroleum.

SULLIVAN REALTY (213) 478-3584 0006

8200 SUNSET BOULEVARD
LOS ANGELES, CA 90028

June 22 200X

PAY TO THE ORDER OF Petro Petroleum $ 25 XX/100

Twenty-five and XX/100 DOLLARS

BAY BANK
Box 1739 Terminal Annex
Los Angeles, CA 90052

MEMO Gas Bill–June 22

John Sullivan

June 24 Paid Volvo West $600 to repair automobile.

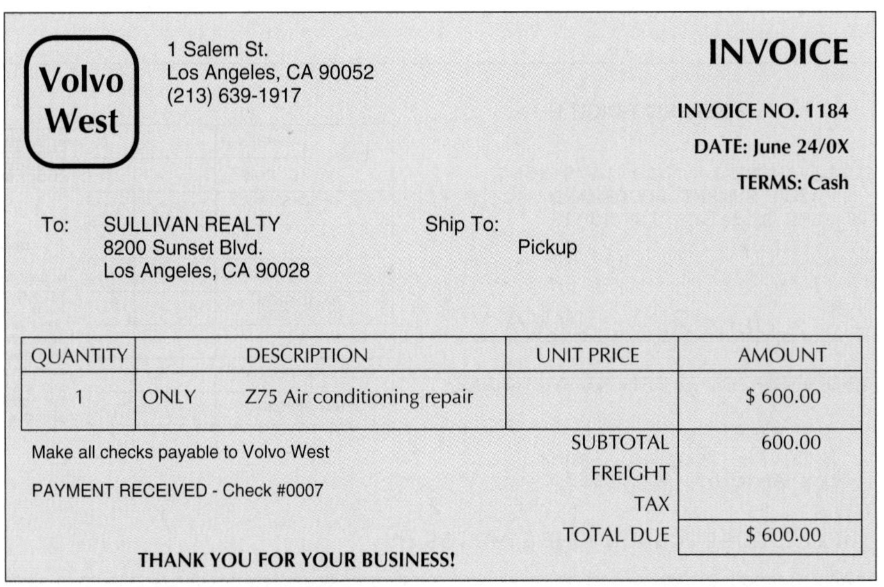

Volvo West

1 Salem St.
Los Angeles, CA 90052
(213) 639-1917

INVOICE

INVOICE NO. 1184
DATE: June 24/0X
TERMS: Cash

To: SULLIVAN REALTY
8200 Sunset Blvd.
Los Angeles, CA 90028

Ship To: Pickup

QUANTITY	DESCRIPTION	UNIT PRICE	AMOUNT
1	ONLY Z75 Air conditioning repair		$ 600.00
		SUBTOTAL	600.00
		FREIGHT	
		TAX	
		TOTAL DUE	$ 600.00

Make all checks payable to Volvo West

PAYMENT RECEIVED - Check #0007

THANK YOU FOR YOUR BUSINESS!

SULLIVAN REALTY (213) 478-3584 0007

8200 SUNSET BOULEVARD
LOS ANGELES, CA 90028

June 24 200X

PAY TO THE ORDER OF Volvo West $ 600 XX/100

Six Hundred and XX/100 DOLLARS

BAY BANK
Box 1739 Terminal Annex
Los Angeles, CA 90052

MEMO Auto Repairs – Inv. 1184

John Sullivan

June 30 Paid Betty Long, office secretary, $350.

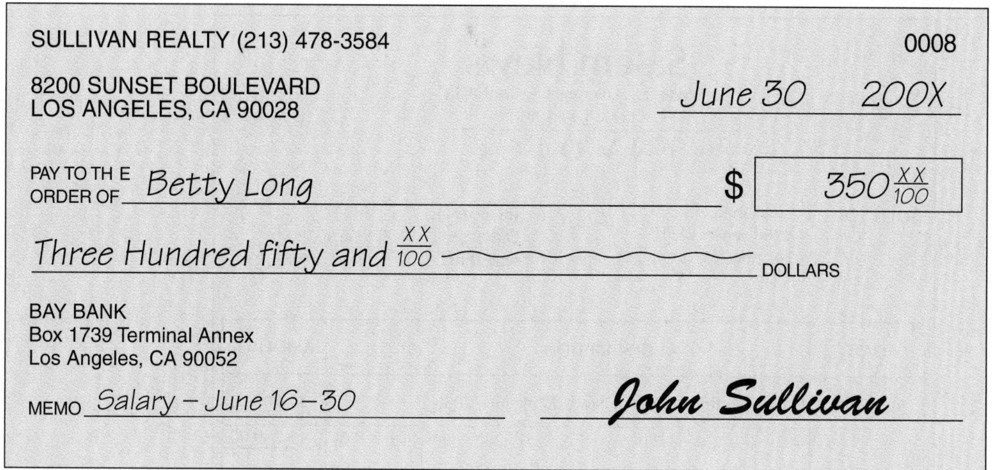

SULLIVAN REALTY (213) 478-3584 0008

8200 SUNSET BOULEVARD
LOS ANGELES, CA 90028

June 30 200X

PAY TO THE ORDER OF Betty Long $ 350 XX/100

Three Hundred fifty and XX/100 DOLLARS

BAY BANK
Box 1739 Terminal Annex
Los Angeles, CA 90052

MEMO Salary – June 16–30 John Sullivan

June 30 Paid Verizon June telephone bill, $510.

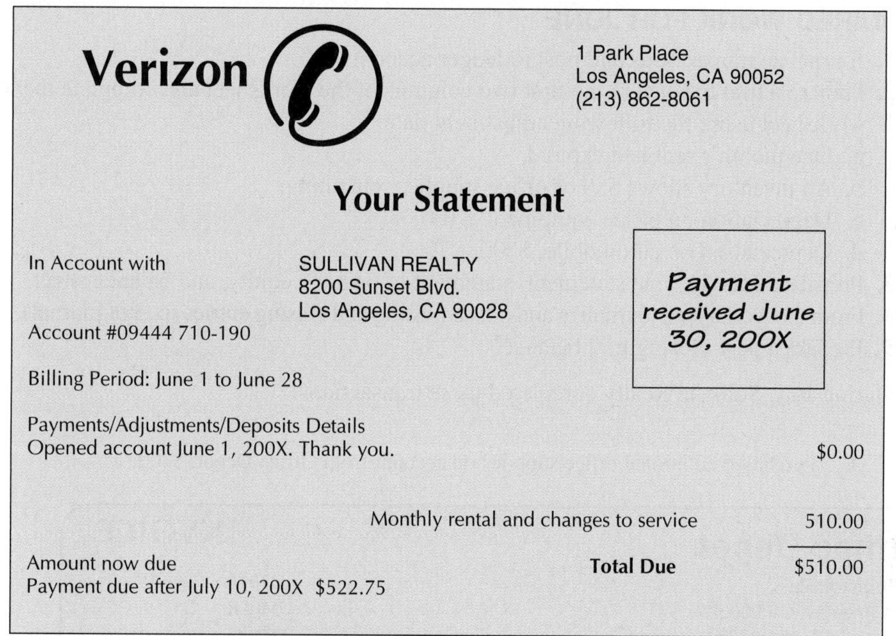

Verizon

1 Park Place
Los Angeles, CA 90052
(213) 862-8061

Your Statement

In Account with SULLIVAN REALTY
8200 Sunset Blvd.
Los Angeles, CA 90028

Account #09444 710-190

Payment received June 30, 200X

Billing Period: June 1 to June 28

Payments/Adjustments/Deposits Details
Opened account June 1, 200X. Thank you. $0.00

Monthly rental and changes to service 510.00

Amount now due
Payment due after July 10, 200X $522.75

Total Due $510.00

SULLIVAN REALTY (213) 478-3584 0009

8200 SUNSET BOULEVARD
LOS ANGELES, CA 90028

June 30 200X

PAY TO THE ORDER OF Verizon $ 510 XX/100

Five Hundred Ten and XX/100 DOLLARS

BAY BANK
Box 1739 Terminal Annex
Los Angeles, CA 90052

MEMO June Phone Bill John Sullivan

June 30 Received advertising bill for June, $1,200, from *Salem News.* The bill is to be paid on July 2.

Salem News
1 Main St., Los Angeles, CA 90052
(213) 744-1000

INVOICE

SOLD TO: Sullivan Realty
8200 Sunset Blvd.
Los Angeles, CA 90028

Invoice No.: 4879
Date: June 30, 200X
Due Date: July 2, 200X

DATE	DESCRIPTION		AMOUNT
June 26/0X	Advertising in Salem News during June 200X		$1,200.00
		SUBTOTAL	1,200.00
		TOTAL	$1,200.00

Business Number 944122338
MAKE ALL CHECKS PAYABLE TO SALEM NEWS

REQUIRED WORK FOR JUNE

Check Figure:
June post closing trial balance $38,893

1. Journalize transactions and post to ledger accounts.
2. Prepare a trial balance in the first two columns of the worksheet and complete the worksheet using the following adjustment data:
   a. One month's rent had expired.
   b. An inventory shows $50 of office supplies remaining.
   c. Depreciation on office equipment, $100.
   d. Depreciation on automobile, $200.
3. Prepare a June income statement, statement of owner's equity, and balance sheet.
4. From the worksheet, journalize and post adjusting and closing entries (p. 3 of journal).
5. Prepare a post-closing trial balance.

During July, Sullivan Realty completed these transactions:

July 1 Purchased additional office supplies on account from Office Depot, $700.

Office Depot
1 Ferncroft Rd.
Los Angeles, CA 90052
Phone (213) 631-0288

INVOICE
DATE: Jul 1/0X
NUMBER: D1996035
TERMS: Net 60

SOLD TO:
Sullivan Realty
8200 Sunset Blvd.
Los Angeles, CA 90028

SHIPPED TO:
Sullivan Realty
8200 Sunset Blvd.
Los Angeles, CA 90028

DATE	DESCRIPTION	UNIT PRICE	AMOUNT
Jul 2/0X	Office supplies		$700.00
		Subtotal	700.00
		Total	$700.00

Business Number: 115555559

PLEASE PAY THE ABOVE

THANK YOU FOR YOUR BUSINESS

July 2 Paid *Salem News* advertising bill for June.

SULLIVAN REALTY (213) 478-3584 0010

8200 SUNSET BOULEVARD
LOS ANGELES, CA 90028

July 2 200X

PAY TO THE ORDER OF Salem News $ 1,200 XX/100

One Thousand Two Hundred and XX/100 DOLLARS

BAY BANK
Box 1739 Terminal Annex
Los Angeles, CA 90052

MEMO Invoice # 4879 John Sullivan

⑆122000661⑆1400⑈03857⑈01362⑈0010

July 3 Sold a house to Melissa King and collected a commission of $6,600.

SULLIVAN REALTY **COMMISSION REPORT**			***Date:*** July 3, 200X	
Name:	Melissa King			
Date:	***Sales Description***	***Sales No.***	***Commission Amount***	
July 3/0X	*Home at 800 Rose Ave.*	*A1004*	*$6,600.00*	*Paid in full.*
C004		***Remarks:***		

DEPOSIT TICKET

SULLIVAN REALTY (213)478-3584
8200 SUNSET BOULEVARD
Los Angeles, CA 90028

DATE July 3 200X

SIGN HERE IN PRESENCE OF TELLER FOR CASH RET'D FROM DEP.

BAY BANK
Box 1739 Terminal Annex
Los Angeles, CA 90052

⑆122000661⑆1400⑈03857⑈01362⑈

CASH	CURRENCY		
	COIN		
LIST CHECKS SINGLY 278-92		6,600	00
TOTAL FROM OTHER SIDE			
TOTAL			
LESS CASH RECEIVED			
NET DEPOSIT		6,600	00

16-66/1220

A hold for uncollected funds may be placed on funds deposited by check or similar instruments. This could delay your ability to withdraw such funds. The delay if any would not exceed the period of time permitted by law.

July 6 Paid gas bill to Petro Petroleum, $29.

SULLIVAN REALTY (213) 478-3584 0011
8200 SUNSET BOULEVARD
LOS ANGELES, CA 90028
July 6 200X

PAY TO THE ORDER OF Petro Petroleum $ 29 XX/100

Twenty-nine and XX/100 DOLLARS

BAY BANK
Box 1739 Terminal Annex
Los Angeles, CA 90052

MEMO Gas Bill – July 6 John Sullivan

July 8 Collected commission from West Land Developers for sale of building lot on June 17.

DEPOSIT TICKET

SULLIVAN REALTY (213)478-3584
8200 SUNSET BOULEVARD
Los Angeles, CA 90028

DATE July 8 200X

SIGN HERE IN PRESENCE OF TELLER FOR CASH RET'D FROM DEP.

CASH	CURRENCY		
	COIN		
LIST CHECKS SINGLY 228-114		6,500	00
TOTAL FROM OTHER SIDE			
TOTAL			
LESS CASH RECEIVED			
NET DEPOSIT		6,500	00

16-66/1220

A hold for uncollected funds may be placed on funds deposited by check or similar instruments. This could delay your ability to withdraw such funds. The delay if any would not exceed the period of time permitted by law.

BAY BANK
Box 1739 Terminal Annex
Los Angeles, CA 90052

⑆1220006 6⑆1400⑈0385 7⑈0136 2⑈

July 12 Paid $300 to Regan Realtors Assoc. to send employees to realtors' workshop.

SULLIVAN REALTY (213) 478-3584 0012
8200 SUNSET BOULEVARD
LOS ANGELES, CA 90028
July 12 200X

PAY TO THE ORDER OF Regan Realtors Assoc. $ 300 XX/100

Three Hundred and XX/100 DOLLARS

BAY BANK
Box 1739 Terminal Annex
Los Angeles, CA 90052

MEMO Workshop Registration John Sullivan

July 15 Paid Betty Long, office secretary, $350.

SULLIVAN REALTY (213) 478-3584 0013

8200 SUNSET BOULEVARD
LOS ANGELES, CA 90028

July 15 200X

PAY TO THE ORDER OF Betty Long $ 350 XX/100

Three Hundred fifty and XX/100 DOLLARS

BAY BANK
Box 1739 Terminal Annex
Los Angeles, CA 90052

MEMO Salary July 1–15

John Sullivan

July 17 Sold a house to Matt Karminsky and earned a commission of $2,400. Commission to be received on August 10.

SULLIVAN REALTY
COMMISSION REPORT

Date: July 17, 200X

Name: Matt Karminsky

Date:	*Sales Description*	*Sales No.*	*Commission Amount*	
July 17/0X	*Home at RR2, Site 3*	*A1010*	*$2,400.00*	
C005		***Remarks:*** Payment due August 10, 200X		

July 18 Sold a building lot to DiBiasi Builders and collected a commission of $7,000.

DEPOSIT TICKET

SULLIVAN REALTY (213)478-3584
8200 SUNSET BOULEVARD
Los Angeles, CA 90028

DATE July 18 200X

SIGN HERE IN PRESENCE OF TELLER FOR CASH RET'D FROM DEP.

BAY BANK
Box 1739 Terminal Annex
Los Angeles, CA 90052

CASH	CURRENCY		
	COIN		
LIST CHECKS SINGLY 269-10		7,000	00
TOTAL FROM OTHER SIDE			
TOTAL			
LESS CASH RECEIVED			
NET DEPOSIT		7,000	00

16-66/1220

A hold for uncollected funds may be placed on funds deposited by check or similar instruments. This could delay your ability to withdraw such funds. The delay if any would not exceed the period of time permitted by law.

⑆122000661⑆1400⑈03857⑈01362⑈

SULLIVAN REALTY
COMMISSION REPORT

Date: July 18, 200X

Name: DiBiasi Builders

Date:	*Sales Description*	*Sales No.*	*Commission Amount*	
July 18/0X	*Building lot at 5004 King St. E*	*A1005*	*$7,000.00*	*Paid in full.*
C006		*Remarks:*		

July 22 Sent a check to Catholic Charities for $40 to help sponsor a local road race to aid the poor. (This amount is not to be considered an advertising expense, but it is a business expense and is posted to Miscellaneous Expense.)

SULLIVAN REALTY (213) 478-3584 0014

8200 SUNSET BOULEVARD
LOS ANGELES, CA 90028

July 22 200X

PAY TO THE ORDER OF *Catholic Charities* $ *40 XX/100*

Forty and XX/100 DOLLARS

BAY BANK
Box 1739 Terminal Annex
Los Angeles, CA 90052

MEMO *Aid to Poor* *John Sullivan*

⑆122000661⑆1400⑈03857⑈0136 2⑈0014

July 24 Paid Volvo West $590 for repairs to automobile due to accident.

Volvo West

1 Salem St.
Los Angeles, CA 90052
(213) 639-1917

INVOICE

INVOICE NO. 2119
DATE: July 24/0X
TERMS: Cash

To: SULLIVAN REALTY
8200 Sunset Blvd.
Los Angeles, CA 90028

QUANTITY	DESCRIPTION	UNIT PRICE	AMOUNT
	Accident Repairs		$ 590.00
Make all checks payable to Volvo West		SUBTOTAL	590.00
PAYMENT RECEIVED - Check #0015		FREIGHT	
		TAX	
		TOTAL DUE	$ 590.00

SULLIVAN REALTY (213) 478-3584 0015
8200 SUNSET BOULEVARD
LOS ANGELES, CA 90028
July 24 200X

PAY TO THE ORDER OF Volvo West $ 590 XX/100

Five Hundred Ninety and XX/100 DOLLARS

BAY BANK
Box 1739 Terminal Annex
Los Angeles, CA 90052

MEMO Auto Repairs – Inv. 2119 John Sullivan

July 28 John Sullivan withdrew $1,800 from the business to pay personal expenses.

SULLIVAN REALTY (213) 478-3584 0016
8200 SUNSET BOULEVARD
LOS ANGELES, CA 90028
July 28 200X

PAY TO THE ORDER OF John Sullivan $ 1,800 XX/100

One Thousand Eight hundred and XX/100 DOLLARS

BAY BANK
Box 1739 Terminal Annex
Los Angeles, CA 90052

MEMO Withdrawal John Sullivan

July 30 Paid Betty Long, office secretary, $350.

SULLIVAN REALTY (213) 478-3584 0017
8200 SUNSET BOULEVARD
LOS ANGELES, CA 90028
July 30 200X

PAY TO THE ORDER OF Betty Long $ 350 XX/100

Three Hundred fifty and XX/100 DOLLARS

BAY BANK
Box 1739 Terminal Annex
Los Angeles, CA 90052

MEMO Salary – July 16–31 John Sullivan

July 30 Paid Verizon telephone bill, $590.

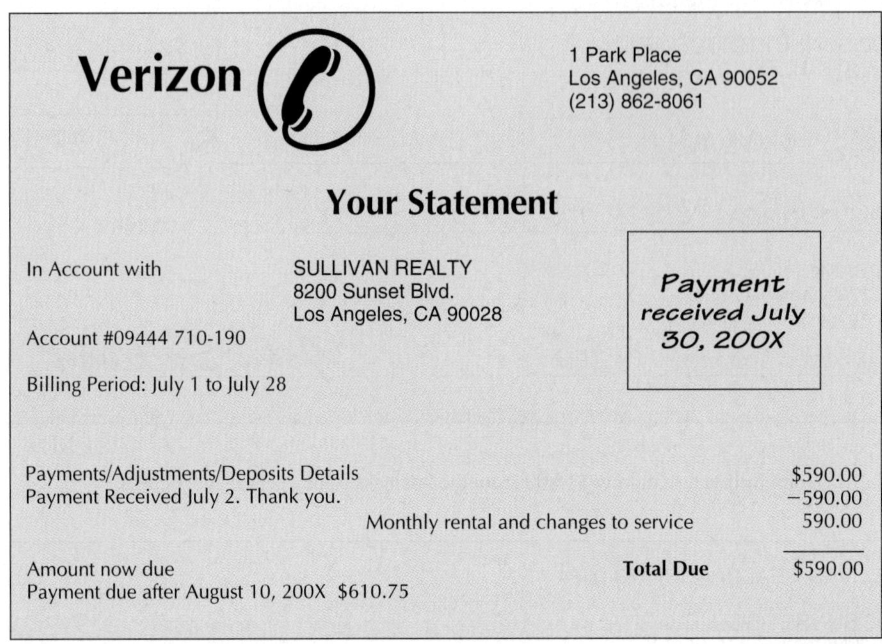

Verizon

1 Park Place
Los Angeles, CA 90052
(213) 862-8061

Your Statement

In Account with SULLIVAN REALTY
8200 Sunset Blvd.
Los Angeles, CA 90028

Account #09444 710-190

Billing Period: July 1 to July 28

Payment received July 30, 200X

Payments/Adjustments/Deposits Details	$590.00
Payment Received July 2. Thank you.	−590.00
Monthly rental and changes to service	590.00
Amount now due **Total Due**	$590.00

Payment due after August 10, 200X $610.75

SULLIVAN REALTY (213) 478-3584 0018

8200 SUNSET BOULEVARD
LOS ANGELES, CA 90028

July 30 200X

PAY TO THE ORDER OF *Verizon* $ *590 XX/100*

Five Hundred Ninety and XX/100 DOLLARS

BAY BANK
Box 1739 Terminal Annex
Los Angeles, CA 90052

MEMO *July Phone Bill* *John Sullivan*

July 30 Advertising bill from *Salem News* for July, $1,400. The bill is to be paid on August 2.

Salem News
1 Main St., Los Angeles, CA 90052
(213) 744-1000

INVOICE

SOLD TO: Sullivan Realty
8200 Sunset Blvd.
Los Angeles, CA 90028

Invoice No.: 5400
Date: July 30, 200X
Due Date: August 2, 200X

DATE	DESCRIPTION		AMOUNT
July 30/0X	Advertising in Salem News during July 200X		$1,400.00
		SUBTOTAL	1,400.00
		TOTAL	$1,400.00

Business Number 944122338
MAKE ALL CHECKS PAYABLE TO SALEM NEWS

REQUIRED WORK FOR JULY

1. Journalize transactions in a general journal (p. 4) and post to ledger accounts.
2. Prepare a trial balance in the first two columns of a blank, fold-out worksheet located at the end of your textbook and complete the worksheet using the following adjustment data:
   a. One month's rent had expired.
   b. An inventory shows $90 of office supplies remaining.
   c. Depreciation on office equipment, $100.
   d. Depreciation on automobile, $200.
3. Prepare a July income statement, statement of owner's equity, and balance sheet.
4. From the worksheet, journalize and post adjusting and closing entries (p. 6 of journal).
5. Prepare a post-closing trial balance.

PEACHTREE COMPUTER WORKSHOP

COMPUTERIZED ACCOUNTING APPLICATION FOR CHAPTER 5

Refresher on using Peachtree Complete Accounting

Before starting this assignment, you may want to refresh your memory by reading the following PDF documents in the multimedia library of the MyAccountingLab Web site. Remember to choose the PDF document for your version of Peachtree.

1. An Introduction to Peachtree Complete Accounting
2. Correcting Peachtree Transactions
3. How to Repeat or Restart a Peachtree Assignment
4. Backing Up and Restoring Your Work in Peachtree

You also should have completed the following workshops:

1. Workshop 1 Atlas Company from Chapter 3
2. Workshop 2 Zell Company from Chapter 4

Workshop 3:

Accounting Cycle Mini Practice Set

In this workshop you will complete the June and July accounting cycles for Sullivan Realty using Peachtree. Tasks include posting journal entries and adjusting journal entries, printing reports and financial statements, and closing the accounting period.

Instructions and the data file for completing this assignment are in the multimedia library of the MyAccountingLab Web site. Open the ***Workshop 3 Sullivan Realty*** PDF document for your version of Peachtree and download the ***Sullivan Realty*** data file for your version of Peachtree.

QUICKBOOKS COMPUTER WORKSHOP

COMPUTERIZED ACCOUNTING APPLICATION FOR CHAPTER 5

Refresher on using QuickBooks Pro

Before starting this assignment, you may want to refresh your memory by reading the following PDF documents in the multimedia library of the MyAccountingLab Web site. Remember to choose the PDF document for your version of QuickBooks.

1. An Introduction to QuickBooks Pro
2. Correcting QuickBooks Transactions
3. How to Repeat or Restart a QuickBooks Assignment
4. Backing Up and Restoring Your Work in QuickBooks

You also should have completed the following workshops:

1. Workshop 1 Atlas Company from Chapter 3
2. Workshop 2 Zell Company from Chapter 4

Workshop 3:

Accounting Cycle Mini Practice Set

In this workshop you will complete the June and July accounting cycles for Sullivan Realty using QuickBooks. Tasks include posting journal entries and adjusting journal entries, printing reports and financial statements, and closing the accounting period.

Instructions and the data file for completing this assignment are in the multimedia library of the MyAccountingLab Web site. Open the ***Workshop 3 Sullivan Realty*** PDF document for your version of QuickBooks and download the ***Sullivan Realty*** data file for your version of QuickBooks.

6

Banking Procedure and Control of Cash

DID YOU KNOW? In 2006 more than 53 million visited the Bankrate.com Web site. Bankrate continually surveys more than 4,800 financial institutions to keep the bank rates on its Web site up-to-date. Visit *www.Bankrate.com* to find more information about Bankrate.

LEARNING OBJECTIVES

1. Depositing, writing, and endorsing checks for a checking account.
2. Reconciling a bank statement.
3. Establishing and replenishing a petty cash fund; setting up an auxiliary petty cash record.
4. Establishing and replenishing a change fund.
5. Handling transactions involving cash short and over.

Bank Rate, Inc., helps you monitor how interest rates change. Be it in business or personal life, you need to make wise financial decisions. In the first five chapters of this book, we analyzed the accounting cycle for businesses that perform personal services (e.g., word processing or legal services). In this chapter we turn our attention to Becca's Jewelry Store, a merchandising company that earns revenue by selling goods (or merchandise) to customers. When Becca's business began to increase, she became concerned that she was not monitoring the business's cash closely. She understood that a business with good **internal control systems** safeguards cash. Cash is the asset that is most easily stolen, lost, or mishandled. Therefore, it is important to protect all cash receipts and to control cash payments so that payments are made only for authorized business purposes.

The internal control policies of a company will depend on things such as number of employees, company size, sources of cash, and usage of the Internet.

After studying the situation carefully, Becca began a series of procedures that were to be followed by all company employees. The new company policies that Becca's Jewelry Store would put into place are as follows:

1. Responsibilities and duties of employees will be divided. For example, the person receiving the cash, whether at the register or by opening the mail, will not record this information into the accounting records. The accountant will not be handling the cash receipts.
2. All cash receipts of Becca's Jewelry Store will be deposited into the bank the same day they arrive.
3. All cash payments will be made by check (except petty cash, which is discussed later in this chapter).
4. Employees will be rotated. This change allows workers to become acquainted with the work of others as well as to prepare for a possible changeover of jobs.
5. Becca Baker will sign all checks after receiving authorization to pay from the departments concerned.
6. At time of payment, all supporting invoices or documents will be stamped paid. The stamp will show when the invoice or document is paid as well as the number of the check used.
7. All checks will be prenumbered. Periodically, the number of the checks that were issued and the numbers of the blank check forms remaining should be verified to make sure that all check numbers are accounted for. This change will control the use of checks and make it difficult to use a check fraudulently without its being revealed at some point.
8. Monthly bank statements will be sent to and reconciled by someone other than the employees who handle, record, or deposit the cash.

LO1 Learning Unit 6-1 Bank Procedures, Checking Accounts, and Bank Reconciliation

Becca knew that a checking account is one of the most useful and common banking services available, but she had many questions and decisions to make. She wanted to know about account options, monthly service charges, check printing charges, minimum balance requirements, interest paid on the account, availability of automatic teller machines (ATMs), and debit cards. Before Becca's Jewelry opened on April 1, 200X, she met with the manager at the Sunshine Bank to discuss opening and using a checking account for the company.

Opening a Checking Account

A signature card is another safeguard.

The bank manager gave Becca a signature card to fill out. The bank uses the **signature card** to verify the authenticity of the signature on all checks. Because Becca would be signing all the checks for her company, she was the only person who needed to sign the card.

After Becca completed the initial paperwork, she received a set of checks and deposit slips. A **deposit slip** is a form that is used when making deposits in a bank or savings and loan association. When filling out a deposit slip, you list the total amount of currency, coins, and checks that you are depositing (see Fig. 6.1). You list each check you are

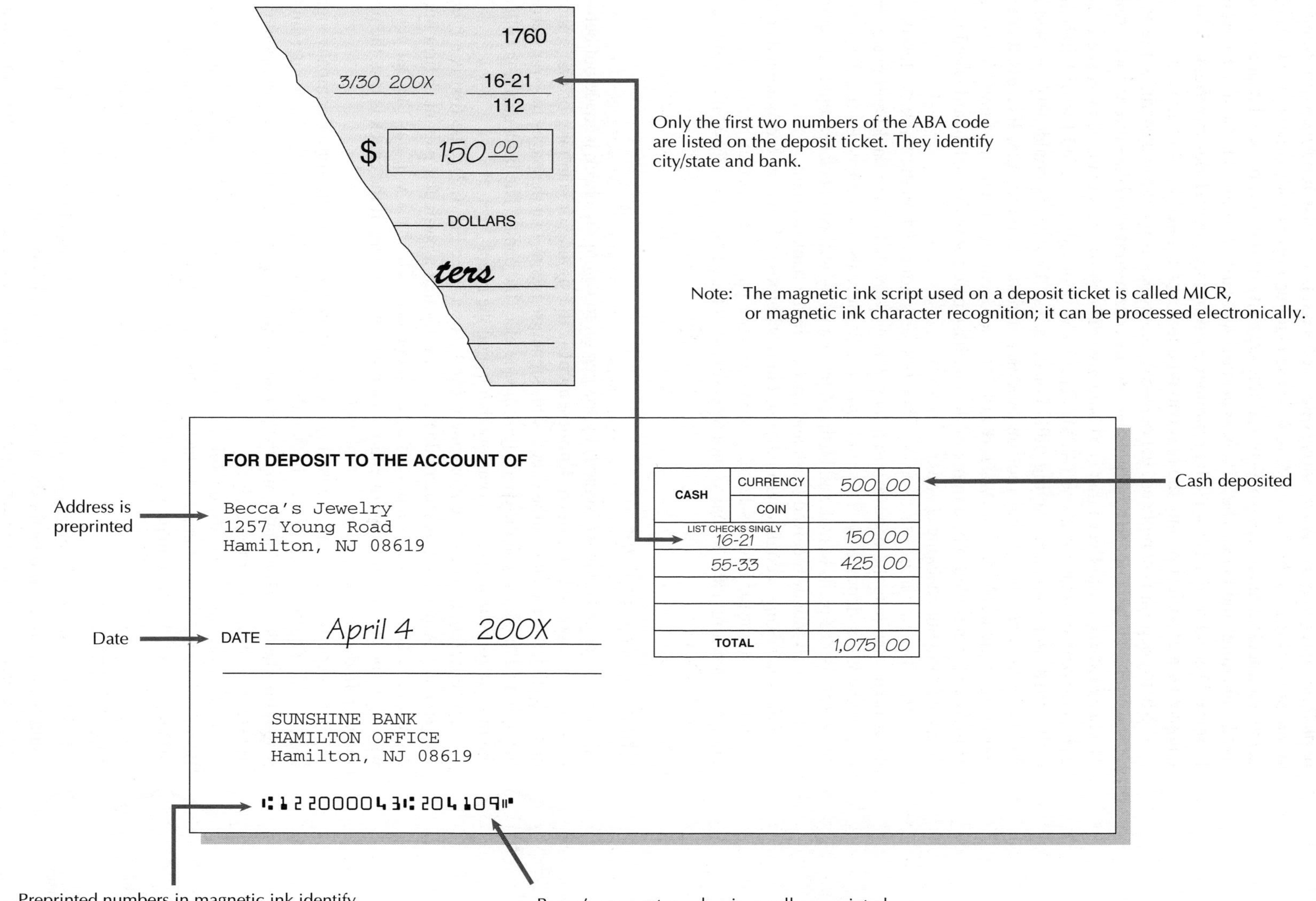
1760
3/30 200X
16-21
112
$ 150 00
DOLLARS
ters
Only the first two numbers of the ABA code are listed on the deposit ticket. They identify city/state and bank.
Note: The magnetic ink script used on a deposit ticket is called MICR, or magnetic ink character recognition; it can be processed electronically.
FOR DEPOSIT TO THE ACCOUNT OF
Address is preprinted
Becca's Jewelry
1257 Young Road
Hamilton, NJ 08619
Date
DATE April 4 200X
SUNSHINE BANK
HAMILTON OFFICE
Hamilton, NJ 08619
CASH
CURRENCY 500 00
COIN
LIST CHECKS SINGLY
16-21 150 00
55-33 425 00
TOTAL 1,075 00
Cash deposited
Preprinted numbers in magnetic ink identify bank number and routing and sorting of check.
Becca's account number is usually preprinted.

FIGURE 6.1 Deposit Ticket

depositing individually. Also, alongside each check you list its American Bankers Association (ABA) code. The ABA code is found in the upper right-corner of each check, below the check number. The 16 identifies the large city or state the bank is located in, and the 21 identifies the bank. The 112 is split into two parts: 1 represents the First Federal Reserve District, and 12 is a routing number used by the Federal Reserve Bank. When completing a deposit slip, only the first two numbers are required.

When a deposit is completed, the depositor receives a copy of the deposit as a receipt or proof of the transaction. The deposit should also be recorded on the current check stub. The bank manager told Becca that she could give the deposits to a bank teller or she could use an automated teller machine (ATM). The ATM could also be used for withdrawing cash, transferring funds, or paying bills. For decades, ATM cards could only be used at ATMs, but in recent years, they took on another function, a debit feature. As a **debit card,** the card carries a VISA or MasterCard logo and can be used anywhere VISA or MasterCard is accepted. The amount of the purchase paid for with a debit card is deducted directly from your checking account.

Often, Becca makes her deposits after business hours when the bank is closed. At those times, she puts the deposit into a locked bag (provided by the bank) and places the bag in the night depository. The bank will credit Becca's account when the deposit is processed. Becca plans to make all business payments by written check (except petty cash) and deposit all money received (cash and checks) in the bank account.

When a bank credits your account, it is increasing the balance.

Many checking accounts earn interest. For our purposes, however, we assume that the checking account for Becca's Jewelry Store does not pay interest. Also, we must assume that the checking account has a monthly service charge but no individual charge for checks written.

Check Endorsement

Checks have to be *endorsed* (signed) by the person to whom the check is made out before they can be deposited or cashed. **Endorsement** is the signing or stamping of one's name on the back left-hand side of the check. This signature means that the payee has transferred the right to deposit or cash the check to someone else (the bank). The bank can then collect the money from the person or company that issued the check.

Endorsements can be made by using a rubber stamp instead of a handwritten signature.

Three different types of endorsement can be used (see Fig. 6.2). The first is a *blank endorsement.* A blank endorsement does not specify that a particular person or firm must endorse it. It can be further endorsed by someone else. The bank will pay the last person who signs the check. This type of endorsement is not very safe. If the check is lost, the person who finds it can sign it and get the money.

The second type of endorsement is a *full endorsement.* The person or company signing (or stamping) the back of the check indicates the name of the company or the person to whom the check is to be paid. Only the person or company named in the endorsement can transfer the check to someone else.

Restrictive endorsements, the third type of endorsement, are the safest for businesses. Becca's Jewelry Store stamps the back of the check so that it must be deposited in the firm's account. This stamp limits any further use of the check.

The regulations require the endorsement to be within the top 1½ inches to speed up the check-clearing process.

The Checkbook

When Becca opened her business's checking account, she received checks. These checks could be used to buy things for the business or to pay bills or salaries.

Drawer: One who writes the check.

Drawee: One who pays money to payee.

Payee: One to whom the check is payable.

A **check** is a written order signed by a **drawer** (the person who writes the check) instructing a **drawee** (the person who pays the check) to pay a specific sum of money to the **payee** (the person to whom the check is payable). Figure 6.3 shows a check issued by Becca's Jewelry Store. Becca Baker is the drawer, Sunshine Bank is the drawee, and Ziegler Wholesalers is the payee.

Look at the check in Figure 6.3. Notice that certain things, such as the company's name and address and the check number, are preprinted. Other things you should notice are (1) the line drawn after $\frac{XX}{100}$ which is to fill up the empty space and ensure that the amount

Types of Check Endorsement

Blank Endorsement

Becca Baker

204109

A signature on the back left side of a check of the person or firm the check is payable to. This check can be *further* endorsed by someone else; the bank will give the money to the last person who signs the check. This type of endorsement is not very safe. If the check is lost, anyone who picks it up can sign it and get the money.

Full Endorsement

Pay to the order of
Sunshine Bank
Becca's Jewelry Store
204109

This type of endorsement is safer than a simple signature, because the person or company signing (or stamping) the back of the check indicates the name of the company or person to whom the check is to be paid. Only the person or company named in the endorsement can transfer the check to someone else.

Restrictive Endorsement

Payable to the order of
Sunshine Bank
for deposit only.
Becca's Jewelry Store
204109

This endorsement is the safest for businesses. Becca's Jewelry Store stamps the back of the check so that it must be deposited in the firm's account. This endorsement limits any further use of the check (it can only be deposited in the specified account).

FIGURE 6.2 Types of Check Endorsement

cannot be changed, and (2) the word *and,* which should be used only to differentiate between dollars and cents.

Figure 6.3 on the following page includes a check stub. The check stub is used to record transactions, and it is kept for future reference. The information found on the stub includes the beginning balance ($3,441), the amount of any deposits ($0), the total amount in the account ($3,441), the amount of the check being written ($580), and the ending balance ($2,861). The check stub should be filled out before the check is written.

If the written amount on the check does not match the amount expressed in figures, Sunshine Bank may pay the amount written in words, return the check unpaid, or contact the drawer to see what was meant.

Many companies use checkwriting machines to type out the information on the check. These machines prevent people from making fraudulent changes on handwritten checks.

During the same time period, in-company records must be kept for all transactions affecting Becca's Jewelry Store's checkbook balance. Figure 6.4 on the following page spread shows these records. Note that the bank deposits ($6,446) minus the checks written ($2,529) give an ending checkbook balance of $3,917.

Banking on the Internet is expanding rapidly.

Monthly Recordkeeping: The Bank's Statement of Account and In-Company Records

Each month, Sunshine Bank will send Becca's Jewelry Store a Statement of Account. This statement reflects all the activity in the account during that period. It begins with the beginning balance of the account at the start of the month, along with the checks the bank has paid and any deposits received (see Fig. 6.5 on the following page spread). Any other charges or additions to the bank balance are indicated by codes found on the statement. All checks that have been paid by the bank are sent back to Becca's Jewelry Store. They are called **cancelled checks** because they have been processed by the bank and are no longer negotiable. The ending balance in Figure 6.5 is $3,592.

Figure 6.5 shows one format for a bank statement. Different banks use different formats.

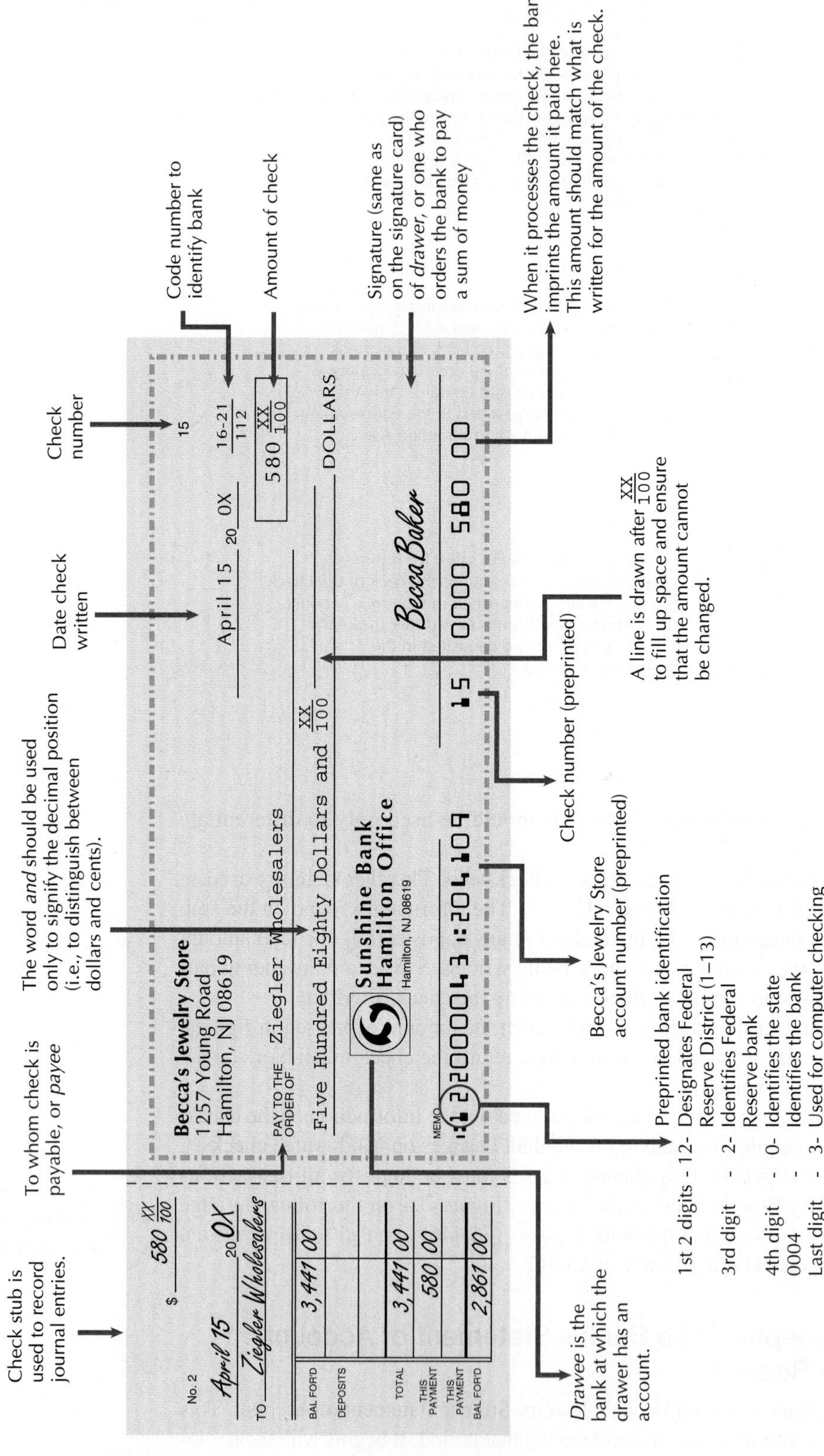

FIGURE 6.3 A Company Check

FIGURE 6.4 Transactions (In-Company Records) Affecting Checkbook Balance

Bank Deposits Made for April

Date of Deposit		Amount	Received From
Apr.	1	$5,000	Becca Baker, Capital
	4	340	Jennifer Leung
	16	89	Mary Figueroa
	27	117	Carl Jones
	28	900	Cash Sales
Total deposits for month:		$6,446	

Checks Written for the Month of April

Date		Check No.	Payment To	Amount	Description
Apr.	2	10	Quality Insurance	$ 500	Insurance paid in advance
	7	11	ABC Wholesalers	400	Merchandise
	9	12	Payroll	800	Salaries
	10	13	Times Newspaper	100	Advertising
	12	14	Verizon	99	Telephone
	15	15	Ziegler Wholesalers	580	Merchandise
	15		ATM Withdrawal	50	Postage
Total Amount of Checks Written:				$2,529	
Checks Deposited				$6,446	
Checks Paid				–2,529	
Balance in Account				$3,917	

FIGURE 6.5 A Bank Statement

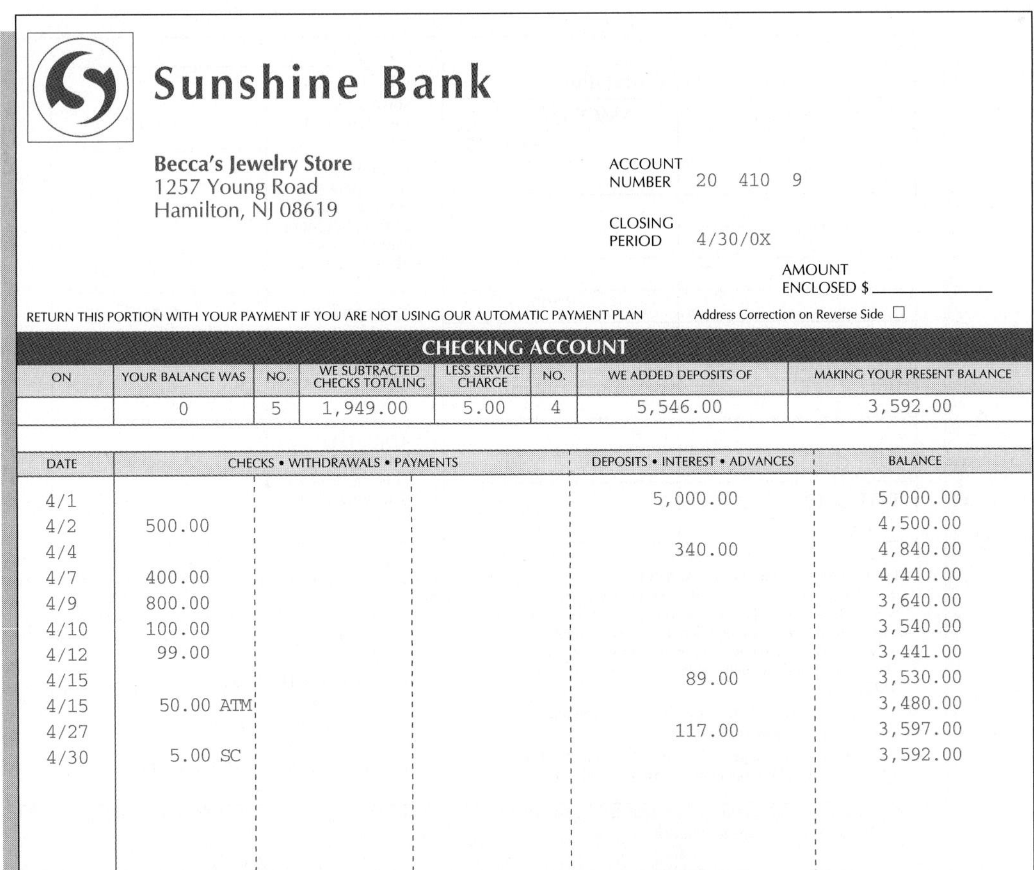

Sunshine Bank

Becca's Jewelry Store
1257 Young Road
Hamilton, NJ 08619

ACCOUNT NUMBER 20 410 9

CLOSING PERIOD 4/30/0X

AMOUNT ENCLOSED $ ______

RETURN THIS PORTION WITH YOUR PAYMENT IF YOU ARE NOT USING OUR AUTOMATIC PAYMENT PLAN

Address Correction on Reverse Side ☐

CHECKING ACCOUNT

ON	YOUR BALANCE WAS	NO.	WE SUBTRACTED CHECKS TOTALING	LESS SERVICE CHARGE	NO.	WE ADDED DEPOSITS OF	MAKING YOUR PRESENT BALANCE
	0	5	1,949.00	5.00	4	5,546.00	3,592.00

DATE	CHECKS • WITHDRAWALS • PAYMENTS			DEPOSITS • INTEREST • ADVANCES	BALANCE
4/1				5,000.00	5,000.00
4/2	500.00				4,500.00
4/4				340.00	4,840.00
4/7	400.00				4,440.00
4/9	800.00				3,640.00
4/10	100.00				3,540.00
4/12	99.00				3,441.00
4/15				89.00	3,530.00
4/15	50.00 ATM				3,480.00
4/27				117.00	3,597.00
4/30	5.00 SC				3,592.00

LO2 The Bank Reconciliation Process

The problem is that the ending bank balance of $3,592 does not agree with the amount in Becca's checkbook, $3,917, or the balance in the cash amount in the ledger, $3,917. Such differences are caused partly by the time a bank takes to process a company's transactions. A company records a transaction when it occurs. A bank cannot record a deposit until it receives that deposit, and it cannot pay a check until the check is presented by the payee. In addition, the bank statement will report fees and transactions that the company did not know about.

Becca's accountant has to find out why there is a $325 difference between the balances and how the records can be brought into balance. The process of reconciling the bank balance on the bank statement versus the company's checkbook balance is called a **bank reconciliation.** Bank reconciliations involve several steps, including calculating the deposits in transit and the outstanding checks. The bank reconciliation usually is done on the back of the **bank statement** (see Fig. 6.6). It can also be done by computer software, however.

Online banking and computer software has made the reconciliation process even easier.

Deposits in Transit In comparing the list of deposits received by the bank with the checkbook, the accountant notices that a deposit made on April 28 for $900 was not on the bank's statement. The accountant realizes that to prepare this statement, the bank only included information about Becca's Jewelry Store up to April 27. This deposit made by Becca was not shown on the monthly bank statement because it arrived at the bank after the statement was printed. Thus, timing becomes a consideration in the reconciliation process. Deposits not yet added to the bank balance are called **deposits in transit.** This deposit needs to be added to the bank balance shown on the bank statement. Becca's checkbook is not affected, because the deposit has already been added to its balance. The bank has no way of knowing that the deposit is coming until it receives it.

Deposits in transit: These unrecorded deposits could result if a deposit were placed in a night depository on the last day of the month.

Outstanding Checks The first thing the accountant does when the bank statement is received is put the checks in numerical order (1, 2, 3, etc.). In doing so, the accountant notices that one payment was not made by the bank and check no. 15 was not returned by the bank.

Check #15 is outstanding.

FIGURE 6.6 Bank Reconciliation Using the Back of the Bank Statement

CHECKS OUTSTANDING	
NUMBER	AMOUNT
15	580 00
TOTAL OF CHECKS OUTSTANDING	580 00

1. Enter balance shown on this statement	3,592 00
2. If you have made deposits since the date of this statement add them to the above balance.	900 00
3. SUBTOTAL	4,492 00
4. Deduct total of checks outstanding	580 00
5. ADJUSTED BALANCE This should agree with your checkbook.	3,912 00*

TO VERIFY YOUR CHECKING BALANCE

1. Sort checks by number or by date issued and compare with your check stubs and prior outstanding list. Make certain all checks paid have been recorded in your checkbook. If any of your checks were not included with this statement, list the numbers and amounts under "CHECKS OUTSTANDING."
2. Deduct the Service Charge as shown on the statement from your checkbook balance.
3. Review copies of charge advices included with this statement and check for proper entry in your checkbook.

IF THE ADJUSTED BALANCE DOES NOT AGREE WITH YOUR CHECKBOOK BALANCE, THE FOLLOWING SUGGESTIONS ARE OFFERED FOR YOUR ASSISTANCE.

- Recheck additions and subtractions in your checkbook and figures to the left.
- Make certain checkbook balances have been carried forward properly.
- Verify deposits recorded on statement against deposits entered in checkbook.
- Compare amount on each checkbook stub.

*Note the $5 service charge is included

Keep in mind that both the bank and the depositor can make mistakes that will not be discovered until the reconciliation process.

Becca's books showed that this check had been deducted from the checkbook balance. The **outstanding check,** however, had not yet been presented to the bank for payment or deducted from the bank balance. When this check does reach the bank, the bank will reduce the amount of the balance.

Checks outstanding are checks drawn by the depositor but not yet presented to the bank for payment by the payee.

Service Charges Becca's accountant also notices a bank service charge of $5. Becca's book balance will be lowered by $5.

Nonsufficient Funds An **NSF (nonsufficient funds)** check is a check that has been returned because the drawer did not have enough money in its account to pay the check. Accountants are continually on the lookout for NSF (nonsufficient funds) checks. An NSF check means less money in the checking account than was thought. Becca will have to (1) lower the checkbook balance and (2) try to collect the amount from the customer. The bank would notify Becca's Jewelry of an NSF (or other deductions) check by a **debit memorandum.** Think of a debit memorandum as a deduction from the depositor's balance.

Debit memorandum:
↓
Deducted from balance

If the bank acts as a collecting agent for Becca's Jewelry, say in collecting notes, it will charge Becca a small fee and the net amount collected will be added to Becca's bank balance. The bank will send to Becca a **credit memorandum** verifying the increase in the depositor's balance.

Credit memorandum: Addition to balance.

A journal entry is also needed to bring the ledger accounts of Cash and Service Charge expense up-to-date. Any adjustment to the checkbook balance results in a journal entry. The entry in Figure 6.7 was made to accomplish this step:

Apr.	30	Service Charge Expense	5 00	
		Cash		5 00
		Bank service charge for April		

FIGURE 6.7 Service Charge Journalized

It is important for Becca to prepare a bank reconciliation when she receives her bank statement every month as part of the cash control procedure. It verifies the amount of cash in her checking account. Another important reason to do a bank reconciliation is that it may uncover irregularities such as employee theft of funds.

Here are step-by-step instructions for preparing a bank reconciliation:

1. **Prepare a list of deposits in transit.** Compare the deposits listed on your bank statement with the bank deposits shown in your checkbook. On your bank reconciliation, list any deposits that have not yet cleared the bank statement. Also, take a look at the bank reconciliation you prepared last month. Did all of last month's deposits in transit clear on this month's bank statement? If not, you should find out what happened.
2. **Prepare a list of outstanding checks.** In your checkbook, mark each check that cleared the bank statement this month. On your bank reconciliation, list all the checks in your checkbook that did not clear. Also, take a look at the bank reconciliation you prepared last month. Did any checks outstanding from last month still not clear the bank? If so, be sure they are on your list of outstanding checks this month. If a check is several months old and still has not cleared the bank, you may want to investigate further.
3. **Record any bank charges or credits.** Take a close look at your bank statement. Are all special charges made by the bank recorded in your books? If not, record them now as if you had just written a check for that amount. By the same token, any credits made to your account by the bank should be recorded as well. Post the entries to your general ledger.
4. **Compute the cash balance per your books.**

5. **Enter bank balance on the reconciliation.** At the top of the bank reconciliation statement, enter the ending balance from the bank statement.
6. **Total the deposits in transit.** Add up the deposits in transit and enter the total on the reconciliation. Add the total deposits in transit to the bank balance to arrive at a subtotal.
7. **Total the outstanding checks.** Add up the outstanding checks, and enter the total on the reconciliation.
8. **Compute the balance per the reconciliation.** Subtract the total outstanding checks from the subtotal in step 6. The result should equal the balance shown in your general ledger.

Before we look at a more comprehensive bank statement, let's look at trends in banking.

Trends in Banking

Adjustments to the checkbook balance must be journalized and posted. These steps keep the depositor's ledger accounts (especially Cash) up-to-date.

This charge could be recorded as a miscellaneous expense.

The Internet is changing how people bank. In the past, banking took place on the main street of your town. The branches were open 9 A.M. to 3 P.M. Monday to Thursday. They were probably open 9 A.M. to 6 P.M. on Friday and possibly 9 A.M. to noon on Saturday. These times were not always convenient for people who worked full time.

Many financial institutions have developed or are developing ways to transfer funds electronically, without the use of paper checks. Such systems are called **electronic funds transfers (EFT).** Most EFTs are established to save money and avoid theft.

Financial institutions use powerful computer networks to automate millions of daily transactions. Today, banks are able to use computer technology to give you the option of bypassing the time-consuming, paper-based aspects of traditional banking so that you can manage your finances more quickly and efficiently.

The first step toward online banking, **automatic teller machines (ATMs),** were first installed into banks about 40 years ago. For the first time, customers could make deposits, withdraw money, and obtain account balances without having to stand in line during the times that the bank was open. Customers are able to use an ATM in banks, supermarkets, malls, and possibly even at your college student center.

Call centers were the next major step forward for banks. Customers could now telephone the center using either a toll-free number or local number and find out information about their accounts without leaving their home.

The latest development in banking is Internet or online banking. Most of the large banks offer fully secure, fully functional online banking for free or for a small fee. Some smaller banks offer limited access; for instance, you may be able to view your account balance and history but may not be able to initiate transactions online. As more banks succeed online and more customers use their sites, fully functional online banking will probably become as common as ATMs.

With a debit card and personal identification number (PIN), you can use an ATM to withdraw cash, make deposits, or transfer funds between accounts. Some ATMs charge a fee if you are not a member of the ATM network or are making a transaction at a remote location.

Retail purchases can also be made with a debit card. You enter your PIN or sign for the purchase. Some banks that issue debit cards are charging customers a fee for a debit card purchase made with a PIN. Although a debit card looks like a credit card, the money for the purchase is transferred from your bank account to the store's account. The purchase will be shown on your bank account statement.

Immediately call the card issuer when you suspect a debit card may be lost or stolen. Most companies have toll-free numbers and a 24-hour service to deal with such emergencies. Although federal law limits your liability for a stolen credit card to $50, your liability for unauthorized use of your ATM or debit card can be much greater—depending on how quickly you report the loss. Also, it is important to remember that when you use a debit card, federal law does not give you the right to stop payment. You must resolve the problem with the seller.

If you don't mind foregoing the teller window and the lobby cookie, a virtual bank or e-bank, such as Virtual Bank or Giant Bank, may save you real money. Virtual banks are banks without bricks. They exist entirely online and offer much of the same range of services and adhere to the same regulations as your corner bank. Virtual banks pass the money that they save on overhead, such as buildings and tellers, along to you in the form of higher yields and lower fees. Banking is available everywhere, all the time. Your finances are at your fingertips.

Advantages of Online Banking Customers who use online banking services enjoy many advantages. They can do almost everything from the comfort of their own homes at convenient times and without standing in long lines.

- *Convenience:* Unlike your corner site, online banks never close. They are available 24 hours a day, seven days a week.
- *Availability:* If you are out of state or even out of the country when a money problem arises, you can log on instantly to your online bank and take care of business, 24/7.
- *Transaction speed:* Online bank sites generally execute and confirm transactions as quickly or even faster than ATM processing speeds.
- *Efficiency:* You can access and manage all of your bank accounts, including IRAs and CDs, from one secure site.
- *Effectiveness:* Many online banking sites now offer sophisticated tools to help you manage all of your assets more effectively. Most of these tools are compatible with money managing programs such as Quicken and Microsoft Money.

Disadvantages of Online Banking Although online banking has many advantages, it also has disadvantages.

- *Start-up may take time:* In order to register for your bank's online program, you will probably have to provide some personal identification and sign a form at a branch bank.
- *Learning curve:* Banking sites can be difficult to navigate at first. Plan to invest time to read the tutorials in order to become comfortable in your virtual lobby.
- *Bank site changes:* Even the largest banks periodically upgrade their online programs, adding new features in unfamiliar places. In some cases, you may need to reenter account information.
- *The trust thing:* For many people, the biggest hurdle to online banking is learning to trust it. Did my transaction go through? Did I push the transfer button once or twice? Best bet: Always print the transaction receipt and keep it with your bank records until it shows up on your personal site or your bank statement.

When problems arise, it is usually much easier to sort them out face to face rather than having to use e-mail or the telephone. Perhaps the biggest problem with online banking is security. It is important to keep passwords safe and to be aware of fake e-mails arriving in your inbox. These e-mails pretend to be from your bank and attempt to obtain information from you. This kind of fraud is called **phishing.**

Fraudulent practices can happen at cash registers when you make a purchase or at restaurants when you pay with a credit card and the waiter is out of your sight. Skimming at ATMs can be much more damaging because of the number of accounts and the amount of money that can be quickly accessed. Card-based purchases—online, debit, and credit—are convenient for consumers. For example, tens of thousands of ATMs are swipe-based. The large number of ATMs contributes to the skimming problem. In a way, we've become victims of the convenience we demand.

Here are some tips to help you avoid becoming a skimming victim.

- Keep your PIN safe. Don't give it to anyone.
- Watch out for people who try to "help" you at an ATM.
- Look at the ATM before using it. If it doesn't look right, don't use it.
- If an ATM has any unusual signage, don't use it. No bank would hang a sign that says, "Swipe your ATM here before inserting it in the card reader" or something to that effect.
- If your card is not returned after the transaction or after pressing cancel, immediately contact the institution that issued the card.
- Check your statement to be sure no unusual withdrawals appear on it.

Check Truncation (Safekeeping) Some banks do not return cancelled checks to the depositor but use a procedure called **check truncation** or **safekeeping.** The bank holds a cancelled check for a specific period of time (usually 90 days) and then keeps a microfilm copy handy and destroys the original check. In Texas, for example, some credit unions and savings and loan institutions do not send back checks. Instead, the check date, number, and amount are listed on the bank statement. If the customer needs a copy of a check, the bank will provide the check or a photocopy for a small fee. (Photocopies are accepted as evidence in Internal Revenue Service tax returns and audits.)

Truncation cuts down on the amount of "paper" that is returned to customers and thus provides substantial cost savings. It is estimated that more than 80 million checks are written each day in the United States.

Example of a More Comprehensive Bank Statement The bank reconciliation of Becca's Jewelry was not as complicated as it is for many companies, even using today's computer technology. Let's look at a reconciliation for Matty's Supermarket (Figs. 6.8 and 6.9), which is based on the following:

Matty's checkbook balance		$13,176.84
Bank balance		23,726.04
Leased space to Subway		8,456.00
Leased space to Dunkin' Donuts		3,616.12
The rental payment is transferred by electronic transfer		
Matty pays a health insurance payment each month by electronic transfer		1,444.00
Deposits in transit 5/30		6,766.52
Checks outstanding		
ck # 738	$1,144.00	
739	1,277.88	
740	332.00	
741	812.56	
742	1,834.12	
Check # 734 was overstated in company's books		1,440.00

Note in Figure 6.9 on the following page spread that each adjustment to Matty's checkbook is the reconciliation process that would result in general journal entries.

FIGURE 6.8 Bank Statement for Matty's Supermarket

Ranger Bank
1 Left St.
Marblehead, MA 01945

ACCOUNT STATEMENT

Matty's Supermarket
20 Sullivan St.
Lynn, MA 01917

Checking Account: 775800061

Checking Account Summary as of 6/30/0X

Beginning Balance	Total Deposits	Total Withdrawals	Service Charge	Ending Balance
$26,224.48	$17,410.56	$19,852.00	$57.00	$23,726.04

Checking Accounts Transactions

Deposits	Date	Amount
Deposit	6/05	4,000.00
Deposit	6/05	448.00
Deposit	6/09	778.40
EFT leasing: Dunkin' Donuts	6/18	3,616.12
EFT leasing: Subway	6/27	8,456.00
Interest	6/30	112.04

Charges	Date	Amount
Service charge: Check printing	6/30	57.00
EFT: Blue Cross/Blue Shield	6/21	1,444.00
NSF	6/21	208.00

Checks

Number	Date	Amount
401	6/07	400.00
733	6/13	12,000.00
734	6/13	600.00
735	6/11	400.00
736	6/18	400.00
737	6/30	4,400.00

Daily Balance

Date	Balance	Date	Balance
5/28	26,224.48	6/18	21,059.00
6/05	30,464.48	6/21	19,615.00
6/07	29,664.48	6/28	28,071.00
6/09	30,442.88	6/30	23,726.04
6/11	30,042.88		
6/13	17,442.88		

LEARNING UNIT 6-1 REVIEW

AT THIS POINT you should be able to

- Define and explain the need for deposit tickets.
- Explain where the American Bankers Association transit number is located on the check and what its purpose is.
- List as well as compare and contrast the three common types of check endorsement.
- Explain the structure of a check.
- Define and state the purpose of a bank statement.
- Explain deposits in transit, checks outstanding, service charge, and NSF.
- Explain the difference between a debit memorandum and a credit memorandum.
- Explain how to do a bank reconciliation.
- Explain electronic funds transfer and check truncation.
- Explain the advantages and disadvantages of online banking.

FIGURE 6.9 Bank Reconciliation for Matty's Supermarket

MATTY'S SUPERMARKET Bank Reconciliation as of June 30, 200X					
Checkbook balance			**Bank balance**		
Matty's checkbook balance		$13,176.84	Bank balance		$23,726.04
Add:			Add:		
EFT leasing: Dunkin' Donuts	$ 3,616.12		Deposits in transit, 5/30		6,766.52
					$30,492.56
EFT leasing: Subway	8,456.00				
Interest	112.04				
Error: Overstated check no. 734	1,440.00	13,624.16			
		$26,801.00			
Deduct:			Deduct:		
Service charge	$ 57.00		Outstanding checks:		
NSF check	208.00		No. 738	$1,144.00	
EFT health insurance payment	1,444.00	1,709.00	No. 739	1,277.88	
			No. 740	332.00	
			No. 741	812.56	
			No. 742	1,834.12	5,400.56
Reconciled balance		$25,092.00	Reconciled balance		$25,092.00

Self-Review Quiz 6-1

Indicate, by placing an X under it, the heading that describes the appropriate action for each of the following situations:

Situation	Add to Bank Balance	Deduct from Bank Balance	Add to Checkbook Balance	Deduct from Checkbook Balance
1. Check printing charge				
2. Deposits in transit				
3. NSF check				
4. A $75 check was written and recorded by the company as $85				
5. Proceeds of a note collected by the bank				
6. Check outstanding				
7. Forgot to record ATM withdrawal				
8. Forgot to record direct deposit of a payroll check				

Solution to Self-Review Quiz 6-1

Situation	Add to Bank Balance	Deduct from Bank Balance	Add to Checkbook Balance	Deduct from Checkbook Balance
1				X
2	X			
3				X

Situation	Add to Bank Balance	Deduct from Bank Balance	Add to Checkbook Balance	Deduct from Checkbook Balance
4			X	
5			X	
6		X		
7				X
8			X	

Deposits in transit are added to the bank balance, whereas checks outstanding are subtracted from the bank balance.

Learning Unit 6-2 The Establishment of Petty Cash and Change Funds

LO3

Petty Cash is an asset on the balance sheet.

Becca realized how time-consuming and expensive it would be to write checks for small amounts to pay for postage, small supplies, and so forth, so she set up a **petty cash fund.** Similarly, she established a *change fund* to make cash transactions more convenient. This unit explains how to manage petty cash and change funds.

Setting Up the Petty Cash Fund

The check for $60 is drawn to the order of the custodian and is cashed, and the proceeds are turned over to John Sullivan, the custodian.

The petty cash fund is an account dedicated to paying small day-to-day expenses. These petty cash expenses are recorded in an auxiliary record and later summarized, journalized, and posted. Becca estimated that the company would need a fund of $60 to cover small expenditures during the month of May. This petty cash was not expected to last longer than one month. She gave one of her employees responsibility for overseeing the fund. This person is called the *custodian.*

Becca named her office manager, John Sullivan, as custodian. In other companies, the cashier or secretary may be in charge of petty cash. Check no. 6 was drawn to the order of the custodian and cashed to establish the fund. John keeps the petty cash fund in a small tin box in the office safe.

Petty Cash is an asset that is established by writing a new check. The Petty Cash account is debited only once unless a greater or lesser amount of petty cash is needed on a regular basis.

Shown here is the transaction analysis chart for the establishment of a $60 petty cash fund, which would be journalized on May 1, 200X, as shown in Figure 6.10.

Accounts Affected	Category	↑ ↓	Rules
Petty Cash	Asset	↑	Dr.
Cash (checks)	Asset	↓	Cr.

Note that the new asset called Petty Cash, which was created by writing check no. 6, reduced the asset Cash. In reality, the total assets stay the same; what has occurred is a shift from the asset Cash (check no. 6) to a new asset account called Petty Cash.

The Petty Cash account is not debited or credited again if the size of the fund is not changed. If the $60 fund is used up quickly, the fund should be increased. If the fund is too large, the Petty Cash account should be reduced. We take a closer look at this issue when we discuss replenishment of petty cash.

Making Payments from the Petty Cash Fund

John Sullivan has the responsibility for filling out a **petty cash voucher** for each cash payment made from the petty cash fund. The petty cash vouchers are numbered in sequence.

FIGURE 6.10 Establishing Petty Cash

GENERAL JOURNAL — Page 1

Date		Account Title and Description	PR	Dr.	Cr.
200X May	1	Petty Cash		6000	
		Cash			6000
		Establishment			

Note that when the voucher (shown in Fig. 6.11) is completed, it will include

- the voucher number (which will be in sequence),
- the date,
- the person or organization to whom the payment was made,
- the amount of payment,
- the reason for payment: in this case, cleaning,
- the signature of the person who approved the payment,
- the signature of the person who received the payment from petty cash, and
- the account to which the expense will be charged.

FIGURE 6.11 Petty Cash Voucher

Petty Cash Voucher No. 1
Date: May 2, 200X   Amount: $3.00
Paid To: Al's Cleaning
For: Cleaning

Approved By: *John Sullivan*
Payment Received By: *Al Smith*

Debit Account No.: 619

The completed vouchers are placed in the petty cash box. No matter how many vouchers John Sullivan fills out, the total of (1) the vouchers in the box and (2) the cash on hand should equal the original amount of petty cash with which the fund was established ($60).

Assume that at the end of May the following items are documented by petty cash vouchers in the petty cash box as having been paid by John Sullivan:

200X		
May	2	Cleaning package, $3.00.
	5	Postage stamps, $9.00.
	8	First-aid supplies, $15.00.
	9	Delivery expense, $6.00.
	14	Delivery expense, $15.00.
	27	Postage stamps, $6.00.

John records this information in the **auxiliary petty cash record** shown in Figure 6.12. It is not a required record but an aid to John, an auxiliary record that is not essential but is quite helpful as part of the petty cash system. You may want to think of the auxiliary petty cash record as an optional worksheet. Let's look at how to replenish the petty cash fund.

How to Replenish the Petty Cash Fund

No postings are done from the auxiliary book because it is not a journal. At some point the summarized information found in the auxiliary petty cash record is used as a basis for a journal entry in the general journal and eventually posted to appropriate ledger accounts to reflect up-to-date balances.

A new check is written in the replenishment process, which is payable to the custodian and is cashed by John, and the cash is placed in the petty cash box.

This $54 of expenses (see Fig. 6.12) is recorded in the general journal (Fig. 6.13) and a new check, no. 17, for $54 is cashed and returned to John Sullivan. In replenishment, old expenses are updated in the journal and ledger to show where money has gone. The order is auxiliary before replenishment. The petty cash box now once again reflects $60 cash.

FIGURE 6.12 Auxiliary Petty Cash Record

Date		Voucher No.	Description	Receipts	Payments	Category of Payments: Postage Expense	Delivery Expense	Sundry: Account	Amount
200X May	1		Establishment	60 00					
	2	1	Cleaning		3 00			Cleaning	3 00
	5	2	Postage		9 00	9 00			
	8	3	First Aid		15 00			Misc.	15 00
	9	4	Delivery		6 00		6 00		
	14	5	Delivery		15 00		15 00		
	27	6	Postage		6 00	6 00			
			Total	60 00	54 00	15 00	21 00		18 00

The old vouchers that were used are stamped to indicate that they have been processed and the fund replenished.

Note that in the replenishment process the debits are a summary of the totals (except sundry, because individual items are different) of expenses or other items from the auxiliary petty cash record. Posting these specific expenses will ensure that the expenses will not be understated on the income statement. The credit to Cash allows us to draw a check for $54 to put money back in the petty cash box. The $60 in the box now agrees with the Petty Cash account balance. The end result is that our petty cash box is filled, and we have justified for which accounts the petty cash money was spent. Think of replenishment as a single, summarizing entry.

Remember that if at some point the petty cash fund is to be greater than $60, a check can be written that will increase Petty Cash and decrease Cash. If the Petty Cash account balance is to be reduced, we can credit or reduce Petty Cash. For our present purpose, however, Petty Cash will remain at $60.

FIGURE 6.13 Establishment and Replenishment of Petty Cash Fund

GENERAL JOURNAL — Page 1

Date		Account Title and Description	PR	Dr.	Cr.
200X May	1	Petty Cash		60 00	
		Cash			60 00
		Establishment			
	31	Postage Expense		15 00	
		Delivery Expense		21 00	
		Cleaning Expense		3 00	
		Miscellaneous Expense		15 00	
		Cash			54 00
		Replenishment			

Petty cash is an asset. →

Note that the Petty Cash account is not listed in replenishment unless we raise or lower it. To raise it we would debit it; to lower it we would credit it. →

The auxiliary petty cash record after replenishment would look as shown in Figure 6.14 (keep in mind no postings are made from the auxiliary). Figure 6.15 may help you put the sequence together.

Before concluding this unit, let's look at how Becca will handle setting up a change fund and problems with cash shortages and overages.

FIGURE 6.14 Auxiliary Petty Cash Record with Replenishment

AUXILIARY PETTY CASH RECORD

Date		Voucher No.	Description	Receipts	Payments	Category of Payments			
						Postage Expense	Delivery Expense	Sundry	
								Account	Amount
200X May	1		Establishment	60 00					
	2	1	Cleaning		3 00			Cleaning	3 00
	5	2	Postage		9 00	9 00			
	8	3	First Aid		15 00			Misc.	15 00
	9	4	Delivery		6 00		6 00		
	14	5	Delivery		15 00		15 00		
	27	6	Postage		6 00	6 00			
			Total	60 00	54 00	15 00	21 00		18 00
			Ending Balance		6 00				
				60 00	60 00				
			Ending Balance	6 00					
	31		Replenishment	54 00					
	31		Balance (New)	60 00					

LO4 Setting Up a Change Fund and Insight into Cash Short and Over

If a company such as Becca's Jewelry expects to have many cash transactions occurring, it may be a good idea to establish a **change fund.** This fund is placed in the cash register drawer and used to make change for customers who pay cash. Becca decides to put $120 in the change fund, made up of various denominations of bills and coins. Let's look at a transaction analysis chart and the journal entry (Fig. 6.16) for this sort of procedure.

Accounts Affected	Category	↑ ↓	Rules
Change Fund	Asset	↑	Dr.
Cash	Asset	↓	Cr.

Beg. change fund
+ Cash register total
= Cash should have on hand
− Counted cash
= Shortage or overage of cash

At the close of the business day, Becca will place the amount of the change fund back in the safe in the office. She will set up the change fund (the same $120) in the appropriate denominations for the next business day. She will deposit in the bank the *remainder* of the cash taken in for the day.

In the next section, we look at how to record errors that are made in making change, called **cash short and over.**

LO5 **Cash Short and Over** In a local pizza shop the total sales for the day did not match the amount of cash on hand. Errors often happen in making change. To record and summarize the differences in cash, an account called *Cash Short and Over* is used. This account

FIGURE 6.15 Which Transactions Involve Petty Cash and How to Record Them

Date		Description	New Check Written	Petty Cash Voucher Prepared	Recorded in Auxiliary Petty Cash Record	
200X May	1	Establishment of petty cash for $60	X		X	Dr. Petty Cash / Cr. Cash
	2	Paid salaries, $2,000	X			Has nothing to do with petty cash (amounts too great)
	10	Paid $10 from petty cash for Band-Aids		X	X	No journal entries
	19	Paid $8 from petty cash for postage		X	X	No journal entries
	24	Paid light bill, $200	X			
	29	Replenishment of petty cash to $60	X		X	Dr. individual expenses / Cr. Cash

In this step the old expenses are listed in the general journal and a new check is written to replenish. All old vouchers are removed from the petty cash box.

Date		Account	PR	Dr.	Cr.
Apr.	1	Change Fund		120 00	
		Cash			120 00
		Establish change fund			

FIGURE 6.16 Change Fund Established

records both overages (too much money) and shortages (not enough money). Let's first look at the account (in T account form).

Cash Short and Over	
Dr. **shortage**	**Cr.** **overage**

All shortages will be recorded as debits and all overages will be recorded as credits. This account is temporary. If the ending balance of the account is a debit (a shortage), it is considered a miscellaneous expense that would be reported on the income statement. If the balance of the account is a credit (an overage), it is considered as other income reported on the income statement. Let's look at how the Cash Short and Over account could be used to record shortages or overages in sales as well as in the petty cash process.

Example 1: Shortages and Overages in Sales On December 5 a pizza shop rang up sales of $560 for the day but only had $530 in cash.

Accounts Affected	Category	↑ ↓	Rules
Cash	Asset	↑	Debit $530
Cash Short and Over	Misc. Exp.	↑	Debit $30
Sales	Revenue	↑	Credit $560

The journal entry would be as shown in Figure 6.17.

FIGURE 6.17 Cash Shortage

Dec. 5	Cash	530 00	
	Cash Short and Over	30 00	
	Sales		560 00
	Cash shortage		

Note that the shortage of $30 is a debit and would be recorded on the income statement as a miscellaneous expense.

What would the entry look like if the pizza shop showed a $50 overage?

Accounts Affected	Category	↑ ↓	Rules
Cash	Asset	↑	Debit $610
Cash Short and Over	Other Income	↑	Credit $50
Sales	Revenue	↑	Credit $560

The journal entry would be as shown in Figure 6.18.

FIGURE 6.18 Cash Overage

Dec. 5	Cash	610 00	
	Cash Short and Over		50 00
	Sales		560 00
	Cash overage		

Note that the Cash Short and Over account would be reported as other income on the income statement. Now let's look at how to use this Cash Short and Over account to record petty cash transactions.

Example 2: Cash Short and Over in Petty Cash A local computer company established petty cash for $200. On November 30, the petty cash box had $160 in vouchers as well as $32 in coin and currency. What would be the journal entry to replenish petty cash? Assume the vouchers were made up of $90 for postage and $70 for supplies expense.

If you add up the vouchers and cash in the box, cash is short by $8.

NOTE:
The account Petty Cash is not used since the level in petty cash is not raised or lowered.

Accounts Affected	Category	↑ ↓	Rules
Postage Expense	Expense	↑	Debit $90
Supplies Expense	Expense	↑	Debit $70
Cash Short and Over	Misc. Expense	↑	Debit $8
Cash	Asset	↓	Credit $168

The journal entry is shown in Figure 6.19.

FIGURE 6.19 Petty Cash Replenished with Shortage

Nov. 30	Postage Expense	90 00	
	Supplies Expense	70 00	
	Cash Short and Over	8 00	
	Cash		168 00

In the case of an overage, the Cash Short and Over would be a credit as other income. The solution to Self-Review Quiz 6-2 shows how a fund shortage would be recorded in the auxiliary record.

LEARNING UNIT 6-2 REVIEW

AT THIS POINT you should be able to

- State the purpose of a petty cash fund.
- Prepare a journal entry to establish a petty cash fund.
- Prepare a petty cash voucher.
- Explain the relationship of the auxiliary petty cash record to the petty cash process.
- Prepare a journal entry to replenish Petty Cash to its original amount.
- Explain why individual expenses are debited in the replenishment process.
- Explain how a change fund is established.
- Explain how Cash Short and Over could be a miscellaneous expense.

Self-Review Quiz 6-2

As the custodian of the petty cash fund, it is your task to prepare entries to establish the fund on October 1 as well as to replenish the fund on October 31. Please keep an auxiliary petty cash record.

200X		
Oct.	1	Establish petty cash fund for $90, check no. 8.
	5	Voucher 11, delivery expense, $21.
	9	Voucher 12, delivery expense, $15.
	10	Voucher 13, office repair expense, $24.
	17	Voucher 14, general expense, $12.
	30	Replenishment of petty cash fund, $78, check no. 108. (Check would be payable to the custodian.)

How to calculate shortage: $21 + $15 + $24 + $12 = $72 of vouchers. Replenished with $78 check. Thus there was a $6 shortage. Note how cash short and over was entered in the auxiliary petty cash record.

Solution to Self-Review Quiz 6-2

GENERAL JOURNAL					Page 6
Date		Account Title and Description	PR	Dr.	Cr.
200X Oct.	1	Petty Cash		90 00	
		Cash			90 00
		Establishment, Check 8			
	31	Delivery Expense		36 00	
		General Expense		12 00	
		Office Repair Expense		24 00	
		Cash Short and Over		6 00	
		Cash			78 00
		Replenishment, Check 108			

FIGURE 6.20
Establishment and Replenishment of Petty Cash

FIGURE 6.21 Auxiliary Petty Cash Record

AUXILIARY PETTY CASH RECORD

Date		Voucher No.	Description	Receipts	Payments	Category of Payments: Delivery Expense	General Expense	Sundry: Account	Sundry: Amount
200X Oct.	1		Establishment	90 00					
	5	11	Delivery		21 00	21 00			
	9	12	Delivery		15 00	15 00			
	10	13	Repairs		24 00			Office	
								Repair	24 00
	17	14	General		12 00		12 00		
	25		Fund Shortage		6 00			Cash Short and Over	6 00
			Totals	90 00	78 00	36 00	12 00		30 00
			Ending Balance		12 00				
					90 00				
	30		Ending Balance	12 00					
	31		Replenishment	78 00					
Nov.	1		New Balance	90 00					

CHAPTER ASSIGNMENTS

SUMMARY OF KEY POINTS

LEARNING UNIT 6-1

1. Restrictive endorsement limits any further negotiation of a check.
2. Check stubs are filled out before a check is written.
3. The payee is the person to whom the check is payable. The drawer is the one who orders the bank to pay a sum of money. The drawee is the bank with which the drawer has an account.
4. The process of reconciling the bank balance with the company's balance is called the bank reconciliation. The timing of deposits, when the bank statement was issued, and so forth often result in differences between the bank balance and the checkbook balance.
5. Deposits in transit are added to the bank balance.
6. Checks outstanding are subtracted from the bank balance.
7. NSF means that a check has nonsufficient funds to be credited (deposited) to a checking account; therefore, the amount is not included in the bank balance and thus the checking account balance is lowered.
8. When a bank debits your account, it is deducting an amount from your balance. A credit to the account is an increase to your balance.
9. All adjustments to the checkbook balance require journal entries.
10. The Internet has expanded online banking options.

LEARNING UNIT 6-2

1. Petty Cash is an asset found on the balance sheet.
2. The auxiliary petty cash record is an auxiliary book; thus no postings are done from this book. Think of it as an optional worksheet.
3. When a petty cash fund is established, the amount is entered as a debit to Petty Cash and a credit to Cash.
4. At the time of replenishment of the petty cash fund, all expenses are debited (by category) and a credit to Cash (a new check) results. This replenishment, when journalized and posted, updates the ledger from the journal.
5. The only time the Petty Cash account is used is to establish the fund initially or to bring the fund to a higher or lower level. If the petty cash level is deemed sufficient, all replenishments will debit specific expenses and credit Cash (new check written). The asset Petty Cash account balance will remain unchanged.
6. A change fund is an asset that is used to make change for customers.
7. Cash Short and Over is an account that is either a miscellaneous expense or miscellaneous income, depending on whether the ending balance is a shortage or overage.

KEY TERMS

ATM Automatic teller machine that allow for depositing, withdrawal, and advance banking transactions.

Auxiliary petty cash record A supplementary record for summarizing petty cash information.

Bank reconciliation The process of reconciling the checkbook balance with the bank balance given on the bank statement.

Bank statement A report sent by a bank to a customer indicating the previous balance, individual checks processed, individual deposits received, service charges, and ending bank balance.

Cancelled check A check that has been processed by a bank and is no longer negotiable.

Cash Short and Over The account that records cash shortages and overages. If the ending balance is a debit, it is recorded on the income statement as a miscellaneous expense; if it is a credit, it is recorded as other income.

Change fund Fund made up of various denominations that are used to make change for customers.

Check A form used to indicate a specific amount of money that is to be paid by the bank to a named person or company.

Check truncation (safekeeping) Procedure whereby checks are not returned to the drawer with the bank statement but are instead kept at the bank for a certain amount of time before being first transferred to microfilm and then destroyed.

Credit memorandum Increase in depositor's balance.

Debit card A card similar to a credit card except that the amount of a purchase is deducted directly from the customer's bank account.

Debit memorandum Decrease in depositor's balance.

Deposit slip A form provided by a bank for use in depositing money or checks into a checking account.

Deposits in transit Deposits that were made by customers of a bank but did not reach, or were not processed by, the bank before the preparation of the bank statement.

Drawee Bank that drawer has an account with.

Drawer Person who writes a check.

Electronic funds transfer (EFT) An electronic system that transfers funds without the use of paper checks.

Endorsement *Blank:* Could be further endorsed. *Full:* Restricts further endorsement to only the person or company named. *Restrictive:* Restricts any further endorsement.

Internal control system Procedures and methods to control a firm's assets as well as monitor its operations.

NSF (nonsufficient funds) Notation indicating that a check has been written on an account that lacks sufficient funds to back it up.

Outstanding checks Checks written by a company or person that were not received or not processed by the bank before the preparation of the bank statement.

Payee The person or company to whom the check is payable.

Petty cash fund Fund (source) that allows payment of small amounts without the writing of checks.

Petty cash voucher A petty cash form to be completed when money is taken out of petty cash.

Phishing Fake e-mails that attempt to obtain information about online banking customers.

Signature card A form signed by a bank customer that the bank uses to verify signature authenticity on all checks.

BLUEPRINT: A BANK RECONCILIATION

Checkbook Balance	Bank Balance
+ EFT (electronic funds transfer)	+ Deposits in transit
+ Interest earned	− Outstanding checks
+ Notes collected	± Bank errors
+ Direct deposits	
− ATM withdrawals	
− Check redeposits	
− NSF check	
− Online fees	
− Automatic withdrawals	
− Overdrafts	
− Service charges	
− Stop payments	
± Book errors*	
CM—adds to balance	
DM—deducts from balance	

* If a $60 check is recorded as 50, we must decrease checkbook balance by $10.

QUESTIONS, CLASSROOM DEMONSTRATION EXERCISES, EXERCISES, AND PROBLEMS

Discussion and Critical Thinking Questions/Ethical Case

1. What is the purpose of internal control?
2. What is the advantage of having preprinted deposit tickets?
3. Explain the difference between a blank endorsement and a restrictive endorsement.
4. Explain the difference between payee, drawer, and drawee.
5. Why should check stubs be filled out first, before the check itself is written?
6. A bank statement is sent twice a month. True or false? Please explain.
7. Explain the end product of a bank reconciliation.
8. Why are checks outstanding subtracted from the bank balance?
9. An NSF check results in a bank issuing the depositor a credit memorandum. Agree or disagree? Please support your response.
10. Why do adjustments to the checkbook balance in the reconciliation process need to be journalized?
11. What is EFT?
12. What are the major advantages and disadvantages of online banking?
13. What is meant by check truncation or safekeeping?
14. Petty cash is a liability. Agree or disagree? Explain.
15. Explain the relationship of the auxiliary petty cash record to the recording of the cash payment.
16. At the time of replenishment, why are the totals of individual expenses debited?
17. Explain the purpose of a change fund.
18. Explain how Cash Short and Over can be a miscellaneous expense.
19. Sean Nah, the bookkeeper of Revell Co., received a bank statement from Lone Bank. Sean noticed a $250 mistake made by the bank in the company's favor. Sean called his supervisor, who said that as long as it benefits the company, he should not tell the bank about the error. You make the call. Write your specific recommendations to Sean.

Classroom Demonstration Exercises

SET A

Bank Reconciliation *LO2 (10 min)*

1. Indicate what effect each situation will have on the bank reconciliation process.

1. Add to bank balance.
2. Deduct from bank balance.
3. Add to checkbook balance.
4. Deduct from checkbook balance.

_____ **a.** Check no. 150 was outstanding for $100.
_____ **b.** $300 deposit in transit.
_____ **c.** $162 NSF check.
_____ **d.** A $15 check was written and recorded as $25.
_____ **e.** Bank collected a $1,000 note less $50 collection fee.
_____ **f.** $14 bank service charge.

Journal Entries in Reconciliation Process *LO2 (5 min)*

2. Which of the transactions in Exercise 1 would require a journal entry?

Bank Reconciliation *LO2 (10 min)*

3. From the following, construct a bank reconciliation for Ace Co. as of June 30, 200X.

Checkbook balance	$1,869.60
Bank statement balance	1,951.20
Deposits in transit	271.20
Outstanding checks	427.80
Bank service charge	13.80
NSF check	61.20

Petty Cash *LO3 (10 min)*

4. Indicate what effect each situation will have.

1. New check written.
2. Recorded in general journal.
3. Petty cash voucher prepared.
4. Recorded in auxiliary petty cash record.

_____ **a.** Established petty cash.
_____ **b.** Paid $1,000 bill.
_____ **c.** Paid $2 for Band-Aids from petty cash.
_____ **d.** Paid $3 for stamps from petty cash.
_____ **e.** Paid electric bill, $250.
_____ **f.** Replenished petty cash.

Replenishment of Petty Cash *LO3 (15 min)*

5. Petty cash was originally established for $20. During the month, $5 was paid out for Band-Aids and $6 for stamps. During replenishment, the custodian discovered that the balance in petty cash was $8. Record, using a general journal entry, the replenishment of petty cash back to $20.

LO3 (10 min) **Increasing Petty Cash**

6. In Exercise 5, if the custodian decided to raise the level of petty cash to $30, what would be the journal entry to replenish (use a general journal entry)?

SET B

LO2 (10 min) **Bank Reconciliation**

1. Indicate what effect each situation will have on the bank reconciliation process.

1. Add to bank balance.
2. Deduct from bank balance.
3. Add to checkbook balance.
4. Deduct from checkbook balance.

_____ **a.** $15 bank service charge.
_____ **b.** $725 deposit in transit.
_____ **c.** $36 NSF check.
_____ **d.** A $78 check was written and recorded as $87.
_____ **e.** Bank collected a $5,000 note less $50 collection fee.
_____ **f.** Check no. 113 was outstanding for $360.

LO2 (5 min) **2.** Which of the transactions in Exercise 1 would require a journal entry?

LO2 (10 min) **3.** From the following, construct a bank reconciliation for Ace Co. as of June 30, 200X.

Checkbook balance	$28,724
Bank statement balance	29,840
Outstanding check	3,454
Deposit in transit	1,714
NSF check	600
Bank service charge	24

LO3 (10 min) **4.** Indicate what effect each situation will have.

1. New check written.
2. Recorded in general journal.
3. Petty cash voucher prepared.
4. Recorded in auxiliary petty cash record.

_____ **a.** Established petty cash fund for $200.
_____ **b.** Paid telephone bill, $135.
_____ **c.** Paid $10 to employee A for $10 turnpike tolls from petty cash.
_____ **d.** Paid $7.80 for stamps from petty cash.
_____ **e.** Replenished petty cash.
_____ **f.** Increased original petty cash fund to $300.

LO3 (15 min) **5.** Petty cash was original established for $60. During the month, $10 was paid out for parking costs, $15 was paid out for postage, and $25 was paid out for emergency purchase of office supplies. Record, using a general journal entry, the replenishment of the petty cash back to $60.

LO3 (10 min) **6.** In Exercise 5, if the custodian decided to raise the level of petty cash to $100, what would be the journal entry to replenish?

Exercises

6-1. From the following information, construct a bank reconciliation for Bing Co. as of July 31, 200X. Then prepare journal entries if needed. *LO2 (15 min)*

Checkbook balance	$1,500	Outstanding checks	$678
Bank statement balance	1,200	Bank service charge	40
Deposits (in transit)	900	NSF; Mia Kaminsky's check in payment of account was returned for insufficient funds.	38

6-2. In general journal form, prepare journal entries to establish a petty cash fund on July 1 and replenish it on July 31. *LO3 (15 min)*

200X		
July	1	A $100 petty cash fund is established.
	31	At end of the month, $12 cash plus the following paid vouchers exist: donations expense, $20; postage expense, $18; office supplies expense, $25; miscellaneous expense, $25.

6-3. If in Exercise 6-2 cash on hand is $11, prepare the entry to replenish the petty cash on July 31. *LO3 (15 min)*

6-4. If in Exercise 6-2 cash on hand is $13, prepare the entry to replenish the petty cash on July 31. *LO3 (15 min)*

6-5. At the end of the day the clerk for Pete's Variety Shop noticed an error in the amount of cash he should have. Total cash sales from the sales tape were $1,200, whereas the total cash in the register was $1,156. Pete keeps a $30 change fund in his shop. Prepare an appropriate general journal entry to record the cash sale as well as reveal the cash shortage. *LO5 (15 min)*

Group A Problems

6A-1. Lee.com received a bank statement from Ranch Bank indicating a bank balance of $8,000. Based on Lee.com's check stubs, the ending checkbook balance was $9,000. Your task is to prepare a bank reconciliation for Lee.com as of July 31, 200X, from the following information (journalize entries as needed): *LO2 (20 min)*

Check Figure: Reconciled Balance $8,690

a. Checks outstanding: no. 122, $800; no. 130, $710.
b. Deposits in transit, $2,200.
c. Lee.com forgot to record a $1,260 equipment purchase made with a debit card.
d. Bank service charges, $50.
e. Ranch Bank collected a note for Lee.com, $1010, less a $10 collection fee.

6A-2. From the following bank statement, please (1) complete the bank reconciliation for Rick's Deli found on the reverse of the bank statement on the following page and (2) journalize the appropriate entries as needed. *LO2 (20 min)*

Check Figure: Reconciled Balance $5,270

a. A deposit of $2,000 is in transit.
b. Rick's Deli has an ending checkbook balance of $5,600.
c. Checks outstanding: no. 111, $600; no. 119, $1,200; no. 121, $330.
d. Jim Rice's check for $300 bounced due to lack of sufficient funds.

Lowell National Bank
Rio Mean Brand
Bugna, Texas

Rick's Deli
8811 2nd St,
Bugna, Texas

Old Balance	Checks in Order of Payment		Deposits	Date	New Balance
6,000				2/2	6,000
	90.00	210.00		2/3	5,700
	150.00		300.00	2/10	5,850
	600.00		600.00	2/15	5,850
	300.00	NSF	300.00	2/20	5,850
	1,200.00		1,200.00	2/24	5,850
	600.00	30.00 SC	180.00	2/28	5,400

LO3 (30 min)

Check Figure: Cash Replenishment $76

6A-3. The following transactions occurred in April for Merry Co.:

200X		
April	1	Issued check no. 14 for $100 to establish a petty cash fund.
	5	Paid $15 from petty cash for postage, voucher no. 1.
	8	Paid $20 from petty cash for office supplies, voucher no. 2.
	15	Issued check no. 15 to Reliable Corp. for $200 from past purchases on account.
	17	Paid $18 from petty cash for office supplies, voucher no. 3.
	20	Issued check no. 16 to Roger Corp., $600 for past purchases on account.
	24	Paid $14 from petty cash for postage, voucher no. 4.
	26	Paid $9 from petty cash for local church donation, voucher no. 5 (a miscellaneous payment).
	28	Issued check no. 17 to Roy Kloon to pay for office equipment, $700.
	30	Replenish petty cash, check no. 18.

Your tasks are to

1. Record the appropriate entries in the general journal as well as the auxiliary petty cash record as needed.
2. Be sure to replenish the petty cash fund on April 30 (check no. 18).

LO3, 4, 5 (40 min)

Check Figure: Cash Replenishment $106

6A-4. From the following, record the transactions into Logan's auxiliary petty cash record and general journal as needed:

200X		
Oct.	1	A check was drawn (no. 444) payable to Roberta Floss, petty cashier, to establish a $150 petty cash fund.
	5	Paid $24 for postage stamps, voucher no. 1.
	9	Paid $12 for delivery charges on goods for resale, voucher no. 2.
	12	Paid $8 for donation to a church (miscellaneous expense), voucher no. 3.
	14	Paid $9 for postage stamp, voucher no. 4.
	17	Paid $18 for delivery charges on goods for resale, voucher no. 5.
	27	Purchased computer supplies from petty cash for $18; voucher no. 6.
	28	Paid $14 for postage, voucher no. 7.
	29	Drew check no. 618 to replenish petty cash and a $3 shortage.

Group B Problems

6B-1. As the bookkeeper of Lee.com, you received the bank statement from Ranch Bank indicating a balance of $9,750. The ending checkbook balance was $10,290. Prepare the bank reconciliation for Lee.com as of July 31, 200X, and prepare journal entries as needed based on the following:

LO2 (20 min)

Check Figure: Reconciled Balance $11,050

a. Deposits in transit, $2,875.
b. Bank service charges, $25.
c. Checks outstanding: no. 111, $485; no. 115, $1,650.
d. Ranch Bank collected a note for Lee.com, $1,100, plus $110 interest.
e. NSF check $525.
f. Lee.com's records indicate that check no. 107, written on Aug. 15, was issued for $900 to pay the month's rent. However, the cancelled check and the listing on the bank statement shows the actual check was $800.
g. The bank made an error by deducting a check for $560 issued by another business.

6B-2. Based on the following, please (1) complete the bank reconciliation for Rick's Deli found on the reverse of the bank statement and (2) journalize the appropriate entries as needed.

LO2 (20 min)

a. Checks outstanding: no. 110, $80; no. 116, $160; no. 118, $52.
b. A deposit of $416 is in transit.
c. The checkbook balance of Rick's Deli shows an ending balance of $798.
d. Jim Rice's check for $40 bounced due to lack of sufficient funds.

Lowell National Bank
Rio Mean Brand
Bugna, Texas

Rick's Deli
8811 2nd St,
Bugna, Texas

Check Figure: Reconciled Balance $756

Old Balance	Checks in Order of Payment		Deposits	Date	New Balance
718.00				4/2	718.00
	12.00	36.00		4/3	670.00
	20.00		40.00	4/10	690.00
	80.00		80.00	4/15	690.00
	40.00	NSF	40.00	4/20	690.00
	160.00		160.00	4/24	690.00
	80.00	2.00 SC	24.00	4/28	632.00

6B-3. From the following transactions, (1) record the entries as needed in the general journal of Merry Co. as well as the auxiliary petty cash record and (2) replenish the petty cash fund on April 30 (check no. 8).

LO3 (30 min)

200X		
Apr.	1	Issued check no. 4 for $60 to establish a petty cash fund.
	5	Paid $9 from petty cash for postage, voucher no. 1.
	8	Paid $12 from petty cash for office supplies, voucher no. 2.
	15	Issued check no. 5 to Reliable Corp. for $400 for past purchases on account.
	17	Paid $7 from petty cash for office supplies, voucher no. 3.
	20	Issued check no. 6 to Roger Corp. $300 for past purchases on account.

Check Figure: Cash Replenishment $46

(continued on next page)

24 Paid $6 from petty cash for postage, voucher no. 4.
26 Paid $12 from petty cash for local church donation, voucher no. 5 (a miscellaneous payment).
28 Issued check no. 7 to Roy Kloon to pay for office equipment, $800.
30 Replenish petty cash, check no. 8.

LO3, 4, 5 (40 min)

6B-4. From the following, record the transactions into Logan's auxiliary petty cash record and general journal (p. 2) as needed:

200X

Oct. 1 Roberta Floss, the petty cashier, cashed a check, no. 444, to establish a $90 petty cash fund.
5 Paid $16 for postage stamps, voucher no. 1.
9 Paid $14 for delivery charges on goods for resale, voucher no. 2.
12 Paid $6 for donation to a church (miscellaneous expense), voucher no. 3.
14 Paid $10 for postage stamps, voucher no. 4.
17 Paid $7 for delivery charges on goods for resale, voucher no. 5.
27 Purchased computer supplies from petty cash for $9, voucher no. 6.
28 Paid $3 for postage, voucher no. 7.
29 Drew check no. 618 to replenish petty cash and a $4 shortage.

Check Figure:
Cash Replenishment $69

ON-THE-JOB TRAINING

LO3 (15 min)

T-1. Claire Montgomery, the bookkeeper of Angel Co., has appointed Mike Kaminsky as the petty cash custodian. The following transactions occurred in November:

200X

Nov. 25 Check no. 441 was written and cashed to establish a $50 petty cash fund.
27 Paid $8.50 delivery charge for goods purchased for resale.
29 Purchased office supplies for $12 from petty cash.
30 Purchased postage stamps for $15 from petty cash.

Check Figure:
Cash Replenishment $40.50

On December 3, Mike received the following internal memo:

MEMO

To: *Mike Kaminsky*
From: *Claire Montgomery*
Re: *Petty Cash*

Mike, I'll need $5 for postage stamps. By the way, I noticed that our petty cash account seems to be too low. Let's increase its size to $100.

Could you help Mike replenish petty cash on December 3 by providing him with a general journal entry? Support your answer and indicate in writing whether Claire was correct.

LO2 (30 min)

T-2. Lee Company has the policy of depositing all receipts and making all payments by check. On receiving the bank statement, Bill Free, a new bookkeeper, is quite upset that the balance in Cash in the ledger is $4,209.50, whereas the ending bank balance is $4,440.50. Bill is convinced the bank has made an error. Based on the following facts, is Bill's concern warranted? What other written suggestions could you offer Bill in the bank reconciliation process?

a. The November 30 cash receipts, $611, had been placed in the bank's night depository after banking hours and consequently did not appear on the bank statement as a deposit.

b. Two debit memorandums and a credit memorandum were included with the returned check. None of the memorandums had been recorded at the time of the reconciliation. The first debit memorandum had a $130 NSF check written by Abby Ellen. The second was a $6.50 debit memorandum for service charges. The credit memorandum was for $494 and represented the proceeds less a $6 collection fee from a $500 non-interest-bearing note collected for Lee Company by the bank.

c. It was also found that checks no. 942 for $71.50 and no. 947 for $206.50, both written and recorded on November 28, were not among the cancelled checks returned.

d. Bill found that check no. 899 was correctly drawn for $1,094, in payment for a new cash register. This check, however, had been recorded as though it were for $1,148.

e. The October bank reconciliation showed two checks outstanding on September 30, no. 621 for $152.50 and no. 630 for $179.30. Check no. 630 was returned with the November bank statement, but check no. 621 was not.

FINANCIAL REPORT PROBLEM

Reading the Kellogg's Annual Report

LO2 (15 min)

Go to Appendix A of the Kellogg's annual report. How do you think Kellogg's reconciles its bank statement? Manually or with computers? Support your position.

INTERNET PROJECT

Bankrate

Go to the Web and search: Annual Report Bankrate 2008.
Click on Investors Relations.
List out the latest news Bankrate is providing to its investors.
Order a free annual report.

CONTINUING PROBLEM

Sanchez Computer Center

LO2, 3, 4 (60 min)

The books have been closed for the first year of business for Sanchez Computer Center. The company ended up with a marginal profit for the first three months in operation. Tony expects faster growth as he enters a busy season.

Following is a list of transactions for the month of October. Petty Cash account #1010 and Miscellaneous Expense account #5100 have been added to the chart of accounts.

Oct.	1	Paid rent for November, December, and January, $1,200 (check no. 8108).
	2	Established a petty cash fund for $100.
	4	Collected $3,600 from a cash customer for building five systems.
	5	Collected $2,600, the amount due from A. Pitale's invoice no. 12674, customer on account.
	6	Purchased $25 worth of stamps using petty cash voucher no. 101.
	7	Withdrew $2,000 (check no. 8109) for personal use.

(*continued on next page*)

8	Purchased $22 worth of supplies using petty cash voucher no. 102.
12	Paid the newspaper carrier $10 using petty cash voucher no. 103.
16	Paid the amount due on the September phone bill, $65 (check no. 8110).
17	Paid the amount due on the September electric bill, $95 (check no. 8111).
22	Performed computer services for Taylor Golf; billed the client $4,200 (invoice no. 12675).
23	Paid $20 for computer paper using petty cash voucher no. 104.
30	Took $15 out of petty cash for lunch, voucher no. 105.
31	Replenished the petty cash. Coin and currency in drawer total $8.00.

Because Tony was so busy trying to close his books, he forgot to reconcile his last three months of bank statements. A list of all deposits and checks written for the past three months (each entry is identified by chapter, transaction date, or transaction letter) and the bank statements for July through September are provided. The statement for October won't arrive until the first week of November.

Assignment

1. Record the transactions in general journal or petty cash format.
2. Post the transactions to the general ledger accounts.
3. Prepare a trial balance.
4. Compare the Computer Center's deposits and checks with the bank statements and complete a bank reconciliation as of September 30, 200X.

Sanchez Computer Center Summary of Deposits and Checks

Chapter	Transaction	Payor/Payee	Amount
		Deposits	
1	a	Tony Freedman	$4,500
1	f	Cash customer	250
1	i	Taylor Golf	1,200
1	g	Cash customer	200
2	p	Cash customer	900
3	Sept. 2	Tonya Parker Jones	325
3	Sept. 6	Summer Lipe	220
3	Sept. 12	Jeannine Sparks	850
3	Sept. 26	Mike Hammer	140

Chapter	Transaction	Check #	Payor/Payee	Amount
		Checks		
1	b	8095	Multi Systems, Inc.	$1,200
1	c	8096	Office Furniture, Inc.	600
1	e	8097	Capital Management	400
1	j	8098	Tony Freedman	100
2	l	8099	Insurance Protection, Inc.	150
2	m	8100	Office Depot	200
2	n	8101	Computer Edge Magazine	1,400
2	q	8102	San Diego Electric	85
2	r	8103	U.S. Postmaster	50

3	Sept. 1	8104	Capital Management	1,200
3	Sept. 8	8105	Pacific Bell USA	155
3	Sept. 15	8106	Computer Connection	200
3	Sept. 16	8107	Multi Systems, Inc.	1,200

Bank Statement

First Union Bank 322 Glen Ave. Escondido, CA 92025

Sanchez Computer Center Statement Date: July 22, 200X

Checks Paid:			Deposits and Credits:	
Date paid	Number	Amount	Date received	Amount
7-4	8095	1,200.00	7-1	4,500.00
7-7	8096	600.00	7-10	250.00
7-15	8097	400.00	7-20	1,200.00
			7-21	200.00
Total 3 checks paid for $2,200.00			Total Deposits	$6,150.00

Ending balance on July 22—
$3,950.00

Received statement July 29, 200X.

Bank Statement

First Union Bank 322 Glen Ave. Escondido, CA 92025

Sanchez Computer Center Statement Date: August 21, 200X

Checks Paid:			Deposits and Credits:	
Date paid	Number	Amount	Date received	Amount
8-2	8098	100.00	8-12	900.00
8-3	8099	150.00		
8-10	8100	200.00		
8-15	8101	1,400.00		
8-20	8102	85.00		
Total 5 checks paid for $1,935.00			Total Deposits	$900.00
Beginning balance on July 22— $3,950.00			Ending balance on August 21— $2,915.00	

Received statement August 27, 200X.

Bank Statement

First Union Bank 322 Glen Ave. Escondido, CA 92025

Sanchez Computer Center Statement Date: September 20, 200X

Checks Paid:			Deposits and Credits:	
Date paid	Number	Amount	Date received	Amount
9-2	8103	50.00	9-4	325.00
9-6	8104	1,200.00	9-7	220.00
9-12	8105	155.00	9-14	850.00
Total 3 checks paid for $1,405.00			Total Deposits	$1,395.00
Beginning balance on August 21 $2,915.00			Ending balance on September 20 $2,905.00	

Received statement September 29, 200X.

SUBWAY Case

COUNTING DOWN THE CASH *LO1, 2, 3, 4 (20 min)*

Subway now requires all of its franchisees to submit their weekly sales and inventory reports electronically using new point-of-sale (POS) touch-screen cash registers. With the new POS registers, clerks use a touch screen to punch in the number and type of items bought. Franchisees can quickly reconfigure prices and products to match new promotions. Not only is this POS method faster than using the old cash registers but it also allows franchisees to view every transaction as it occurs—from their own back office computers or even from home. Also, individual POS terminals within the restaurant are linked, so franchisees are able to see consolidated data quickly.

The transition to electronic reporting and networked POS terminals, however, has not been without bumps, as Stan can testify. About six months before the deadline for all Subway franchisees to "go electronic," Stan attended a heated meeting on the topic at his local chapter of the North American Association of Subway Franchisees (NAASF). The NAASF is an independent organization of franchisees that serves as an advisory council on Subway policies and issues of common concern. Everyone seemed to be talking at once.

"I just don't trust these machines. What am I supposed to do when the system crashes?" complained one man.

"Yeah, and I don't like the idea of a bunch of kids knowing more about how to run the software than I do," said one older franchisee.

"Don't be so quick to assume that our sandwich artists will love POS," said one woman. "I overheard one of my employees say to another, 'POS means **P**eeking **O**ver **S**houlders.' These young kids we hire have more reason to be resistant than we do!"

"I'll say they do!" rejoined Jay Harden, the president of Stan's local NAASF. "Employee theft is one of the largest problems we face as franchisees. I, for one, really welcome the cash control we get with POS."

Stan had to agree with Jay. Training staff to record every sale and record it correctly is a critical component of a cash business such as Subway. In Stan's view, the POS machines would only make that training easier. Cash control is built into the new system, which also provides the owners with information that will help them spot problems—such as employee theft—and track trends. Of course, thought Stan, the chore of counting down the cash at the end of a shift remained. No matter what type of computer program you install, cash still must be counted down and rectified with the register tape at the end of each shift.

As the voices rang louder around him, Stan thought about what had happened that day when Ellen closed out her cash register drawer. He had spent hours figuring out a discrepancy between the cash in the drawer and the register tape. Ellen had forgotten to void a mistaken entry for $99.99. Stan had first suspected that she had made a huge error in counting change.

Thinking of errors in counting brought him back to the topic of the meeting. Stan raised his hand to speak.

"One thing that concerns me is the potential for accounting errors. I still have to key in data from the POS into my Peachtree accounting software. Every time I have to reenter data, the potential for error multiplies."

"That shows some foresight, Stan," said Jay Harden. "We're actually exploring computer programs that will feed the data directly from the POS into our accounting programs." Even some of the technophobes and POS skeptics in the group had to agree it would be a great idea.

Discussion Questions

1. What is an advisory council? Why do you think franchisees need one?
2. Why do you think some small business owners fear computerization?
3. How would Stan catch a discrepancy in the Cash account? How would he record a loss?
4. Why does Subway invest time, money, and effort in investigating new cash handling systems such as its new POS terminals?

7

Calculating Pay and Payroll Taxes: The Beginning of the Payroll Process

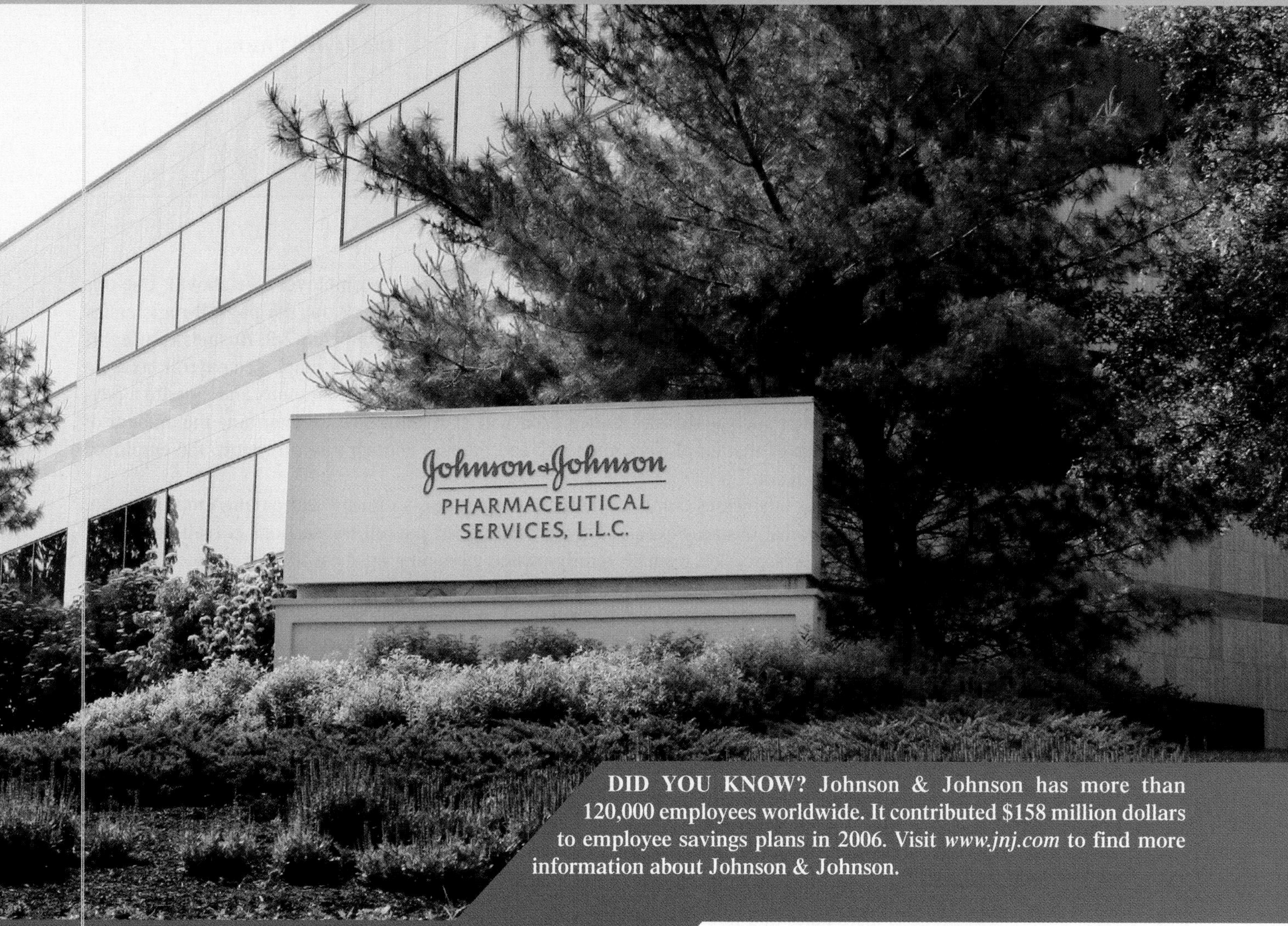

DID YOU KNOW? Johnson & Johnson has more than 120,000 employees worldwide. It contributed $158 million dollars to employee savings plans in 2006. Visit *www.jnj.com* to find more information about Johnson & Johnson.

LEARNING OBJECTIVES

1. Calculating gross pay, employee payroll tax deductions for federal income tax withholding, state income tax withholding, FICA (OASDI, Medicare), and net pay.
2. Calculating employer taxes for FICA (OASDI, Medicare), FUTA, SUTA, and workers' compensation insurance.
3. Preparing a payroll register.
4. Maintaining an employee earnings record.

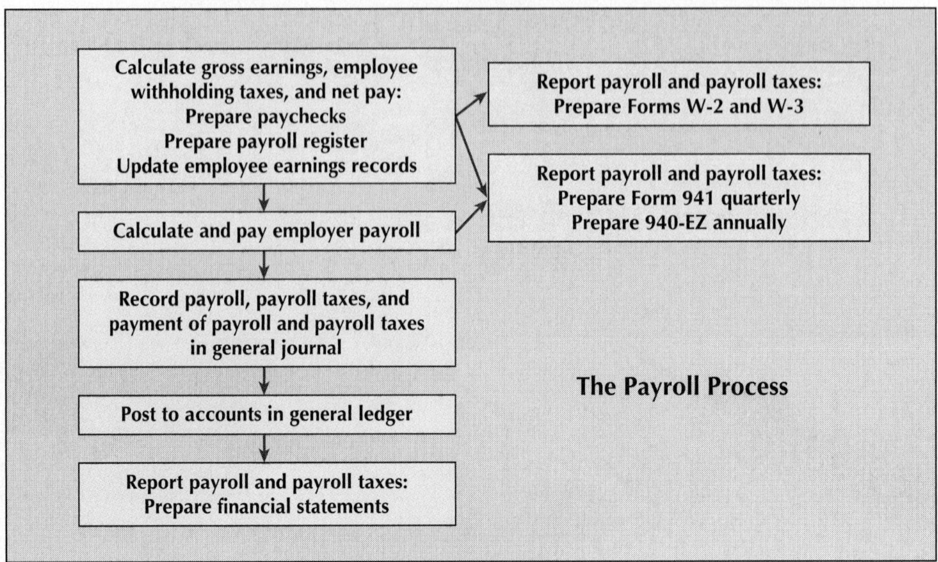

In this chapter we will look at the payroll process for the employer (see above). Use this chart as a reference tool when reading the chapter. Check out the payroll register for Travelwithus.com in Figure 7.3 at the beginning of Learning Unit 7-2. Businesses use this document to calculate employees' pay and the deductions for employee payroll taxes on that pay. In this chapter you will learn how to compute these amounts and prepare a payroll register such as the one shown. You will also learn how to determine the amount of payroll taxes that employers must pay and prepare another payroll report, the employee earnings record.

Most businesses can't run without employees, so hiring and paying employees are pretty typical business events. The accounting for payroll transactions is really the same whether a business is a small, family-owned gardening business in your town or a nationwide retail department store. Either way, it's important to know how to calculate, pay, record, and report payroll and payroll taxes in this payroll process.

Federal, state, and maybe even local laws regulate the payroll process. A business may be fined substantial penalties and interest for failing to follow these laws properly. For example, a business may be fined $50 per statement up to a maximum of $100,000 per year for failing to give its employees their W-2 form, Wage and Tax Statement. Because of this, there are many companies, such as ADP, Paychex, and Ceridian, that will handle payroll for a fee. However, it is often less costly for the business to do these tasks itself.

In this chapter we take a close look at the employees of Travelwithus.com, a new Internet-based company that makes travel arrangements for its customers, to see how a payroll is figured and recorded. Travelwithus.com specializes in two types of travel, cruises and business travel. We look at how its payroll is affected by federal, state, and local taxes and how the accountant at Travelwithus.com handles payroll transactions for the company.

LO1 Learning Unit 7-1 Calculation of Gross Earnings, Employee Withholding Taxes, and Net Pay

Katherine Kurtz is the accountant for Travelwithus.com who calculates and records each payroll for the company. Several parts of Katherine's job are especially important. First, Katherine must be accurate in everything she does, because any mistake she makes in working with the payroll may affect both the employee and the company. Second, Katherine needs to be on time when working on the company's payroll so that employees get their paychecks as expected and governments receive payroll taxes when due. Third, Katherine must at all times obey the appropriate federal, state, and local laws governing payroll matters. Fourth, because processing payroll involves personal employee information such as pay rates and marital status, Katherine always needs to keep payroll data confidential.

Gross Earnings

To begin the payroll process, Katherine must first calculate the earnings for Travelwithus.com employees. To make the correct calculations, Katherine must know how each employee has been classified for payroll purposes. As a rule, a company will classify every employee either as "hourly" or "salaried." If an employee is an hourly employee, that employee only will be paid for the hours he or she worked. Employees classified as salaried employees receive a fixed dollar amount for the hours worked.

Travelwithus.com classified three of its six employees as hourly. For these three employees, Katherine must compute the hours they worked during a specific time period known as a pay period; the number of hours determines how much each has earned. For payroll purposes, **pay periods** are defined as daily, weekly, biweekly (every two weeks), semimonthly (twice each month), monthly, quarterly, or annually. A pay period can start on any day of the week and must end after the specified period of time has passed. Most companies use weekly, biweekly, semimonthly, or monthly pay periods when calculating their payrolls.

Companies can use different pay periods for different groups of employees. Travelwithus.com chose a biweekly pay period for its hourly employees and a monthly pay period for its salaried employees. The biweekly pay period starts on Monday and ends two weeks later on a Sunday. Hourly employees actually receive their paychecks on the following Friday because it takes Katherine a few days to calculate all of the amounts involved in paying an hourly payroll. The monthly pay period starts on the first day of the calendar month and ends on the last day of that month. Salaried employees will be paid on the last day of the month. Because they receive a fixed amount of pay, Katherine is able to calculate these payroll amounts much faster than the hourly ones and can even start these calculations before the month ends.

Now that Katherine knows the pay period for Travelwithus.com's hourly employees, she calculates their total or **gross earnings.** Gross earnings are calculated by adding the regular earnings for an employee for the period to any overtime earnings the employee has earned for that period.

Overtime earnings must be computed according to federal law. The federal law that governs overtime earnings is called the **Fair Labor Standards Act** and is sometimes referred to as the **Federal Wage and Hour Law.** An employer must follow the Fair Labor Standards Act if it is involved in **interstate commerce,** in other words, if it is doing business in more than one state. For most employers, this law says that an hourly employee must be paid at least one and a half times his or her regular pay rate for any hours he or she works over 40 in one workweek. A **workweek,** according to the law, is a seven-day (or 168-hour) period that can start at any time, but once the starting time for the week is determined, it must stay the same for each week.

It is important to know that some states also have payroll laws that need to be followed in determining pay. For example, California requires employers to pay overtime pay to hourly employees who have worked more than 8 hours in any day, even if they work less than 40 hours total for that week. Employers must follow both sets of laws, and in this case, Travelwithus.com would pay overtime if an employee works more than 8 hours in one day and if an employee works more than 40 hours in one week.

Hourly employees of Travelwithus.com have two workweeks in each biweekly pay period. Travelwithus.com's hourly workweek starts on Monday morning at 12:01 A.M. each week and ends seven days later on Sunday evening at 12:00 midnight. Thus, Katherine must calculate overtime pay for any employee who worked more than 40 hours in each week of this two-week period.

Stephanie Higuera is one of the three hourly employees working for Travelwithus.com. Travelwithus.com's most recent biweekly pay period began on Monday, October 16, at 12:01 A.M. and ended on Sunday, October 29 at 12:00 midnight. The first week of this period ended on Sunday, October 22, and during this week Stephanie worked 44 hours. During the second week that ended on October 29, Stephanie worked 38 hours.

How much should she be paid? Katherine will answer this question by first calculating both Stephanie's regular hours and her overtime hours. According to the federal law, Katherine must look at each week separately. Stephanie worked 44 hours during the first week, which means that she worked 40 regular hours and 4 overtime hours. Because she worked fewer than 40 hours in the second week, all of these hours are regular hours.

Week No.	Week Ending	Regular Hours	Overtime Hours	Total Hours
1	October 22	40	4	44
2	October 29	38	0	38
Total		78	4	82

Stephanie earns $11.40 for each hour she works, so Katherine computes Stephanie's pay as follows:

$11.40 regular rate × 1.5 = $17.10 overtime rate
78 regular hours × $11.40 regular rate = *$889.20 regular earnings*
4 overtime hours × $17.10 overtime rate = *68.40 overtime earnings*
$889.20 regular earnings + $68.40 overtime earnings = *$957.60 gross earnings*

Or, Katherine could figure Stephanie's pay this way: SAME

$11.40 regular rate × 0.5 = $5.70 extra pay for each overtime hour
82 total hours × $11.40 regular rate = *$934.80 earnings at the regular rate*
4 overtime hours × $5.70 extra pay for each overtime hour = *22.80 extra earnings*
$934.80 earnings at the regular rate + $22.80 extra earnings = *$957.60 gross earnings*

Notice that either way, Katherine computed exactly the same amount of gross earnings. The advantage of using the first method is that it clearly shows the amount of extra money that Stephanie earned from working overtime. The advantage of the second is that it shows the effect of being paid at a higher, overtime rate for those extra hours worked.

Julia Regan also works for Travelwithus.com. She, however, is a salaried employee, and earns $4,875 per month. As a salaried (exempt) employee, she is not eligible for overtime pay, and Katherine will list her total earnings for the month of October as $4,875. To be considered a salaried employee, Julia must qualify as a salaried employee according to the specifics of the Fair Labor Standards Act. Thus, Travelwithus.com can't decide to classify employees as salaried just to avoid paying the overtime pay; these employees must be salaried persons according to this law.

Federal Income Tax Withholding

After Katherine determines Stephanie's and Julia's gross earnings, she figures out how much each of them will actually receive in their paychecks after several different taxes have been withheld. These taxes are called payroll taxes, and must be paid by the employees. Employees pay these amounts by having them taken out, or withheld, from their paychecks. Their employer then sends them to the Internal Revenue Service (IRS), state governments, and maybe even local governments so they count against the amount of federal, state, and possible local income taxes that the employees will owe for the year.

In this way, Stephanie and Julia pay their taxes on a "pay as you go basis." In other words, when Stephanie and Julia complete their federal income tax returns at the end of the year, they will deduct the amount of income tax withheld during the year from the total amount owed for the year. How and when Travelwithus.com turns these amounts over to the federal, state, and local governments will be discussed in Chapter 8. Katherine computes the amount of taxes to be withheld based on each employee's gross earnings for the pay period.

Katherine starts figuring out how much to withhold from each employee's pay by looking at the W-4 that he or she completed. The IRS **Form W-4, Employee's Withholding Allowance Certificate,** is completed by every employee and provides information that will be used to determine the amount of **federal income tax (FIT) withholdings** for the period. Figure 7.1 on the following page is Stephanie's W-4 form. Notice that it shows Stephanie's marital status and total number of **allowances** she claims for federal income tax purposes. Usually, an employee may claim one allowance for himself or herself, one for his or her spouse, and one for each of his or her dependents, such as a child. Employees who want more withheld from their paychecks can claim fewer allowances than they really have. However, they are not allowed to claim more allowances than they really have to avoid underpaying taxes owed, which may also result in them owing the government amounts for penalties and interest.

To look up the amount of federal income tax that needs to be withheld from Stephanie's paycheck, Katherine uses Stephanie's marital status and the number of claimed allowances listed on her Form W-4. She also uses Stephanie's gross earnings for the pay period and the length of the pay period. The amount of federal income tax that needs to be withheld is listed in a **wage bracket table** that is in the IRS publication called **Circular E,** *Employer's Tax Guide*, also known as Publication 15. Check out one of the tables from the Circular that's shown in Figure 7.2. Notice from the heading "SINGLE Persons—BIWEEKLY Payroll Period" that this table applies to single persons who are paid biweekly. Wage bracket tables are prepared according to marital status and pay period; Circular E has a similar table for married persons who are paid biweekly, as well as tables for single and married persons who are paid daily, weekly, monthly, semimonthly, monthly, quarterly, and annually. Also notice that the table has rows for different ranges of gross pay, starting from lower amounts of pay in the top rows of the table to higher amounts in the bottom rows.

Katherine determines the amount of federal income taxes that need to be withheld from Stephanie's paycheck by first locating the correct table in Circular E. She finds the table for single persons who are paid biweekly. Then, she locates the row that says "At least $940 but less than $960." Stephanie's gross pay for this pay period is $957.60, so this row applies to her. Katherine traces this row to the column for one withholding allowance, and finds that the amount of withholding tax is $92. Based on Stephanie's gross earnings of $957.60 and her one claimed allowance, Katherine will withhold $92 in federal income taxes from Stephanie's pay.

What if Stephanie had earned $960 instead of 957.60? Would the amount of federal income tax withheld be the same? No, Katherine would have withheld $95. To see this, check out the heading for the columns showing the wages. Notice that it says, "If the wages are—." Katherine will look at the rows of wage ranges, stopping when she sees the line that says, "At least $940 but less than $960." If Stephanie's gross wages are exactly $960—not less than $960—Katherine must go to the next line, which says, "At least $960 but less than $980" and withhold the amount in the column for one withholding allowance, which is $95.

State Income Tax Withholding

Most states also charge their residents an income tax based on the amount of money they earn from their employers. In 2008, only Alaska, Florida, Nevada, South Dakota, Texas, Washington, and Wyoming did not. (Technically, Tennessee also does not have a state income tax; it is only imposed on interest and dividends.) So, in addition to withholding federal income taxes, Katherine may also have to determine amounts for **state income tax (SIT) withholding.** Fortunately for Katherine, the process for withholding state income tax is much the same as it is for withholding federal income tax. In many states, withholding amounts are based on the same information that is listed in the employee's W-4, although some states do have their own versions of this form that are used instead. Employers use

Cut here and give Form W-4 to your employer. Keep the top part for your records.

Form **W-4**
Department of the Treasury
Internal Revenue Service

Employee's Withholding Allowance Certificate

▶ **Whether you are entitled to claim a certain number of allowances or exemption from withholding is subject to review by the IRS. Your employer may be required to send a copy of this form to the IRS.**

OMB No. 1545-0074
200X

1 Type or print your first name and middle initial. Stephanie A.	Last name Higuera	2 Your social security number 123 45 6789
Home address (number and street or rural route) 1014 Inverness Way		3 ☒ Single ☐ Married ☐ Married, but withhold at higher Single rate. **Note.** If married, but legally separated, or spouse is a nonresident alien, check the "Single" box.
City or town, state, and ZIP code Southside, MA 01945		4 **If your last name differs from that shown on your social security card, check here. You must call 1-800-772-1213 for a new card.** ▶ ☐

5 Total number of allowances you are claiming (from line **H** above **or** from the applicable worksheet on page 2) . . . **5** 1

6 Additional amount, if any, you want withheld from each paycheck . . . . **6** $

7 I claim exemption from withholding for 2006, and I certify that I meet **both** of the following conditions for exemption.
- Last year I had a right to a refund of **all** federal income tax withheld because I had **no** tax liability **and**
- This year I expect a refund of **all** federal income tax withheld because I expect to have **no** tax liability.

If you meet both conditions, write "Exempt" here . . . . ▶ **7**

Under penalties of perjury, I declare that I have examined this certificate and to the best of my knowledge and belief, it is true, correct, and complete.

Employee's signature
(Form is not valid
unless you sign it.) ▶ Stephanie A. Higuera **Date** ▶ January 3, 200X

8 Employer's name and address (Employer: Complete lines 8 and 10 only if sending to the IRS.)	**9** Office code (optional)	**10** Employer identification number (EIN)

For Privacy Act and Paperwork Reduction Act Notice, see page 2. Cat. No. 10220Q Form **W-4** (200X)

FIGURE 7.1 Completed Form W-4

state publications similar to the federal Publication 15 to figure the amount to be withheld for state income taxes. However, because the 43 states can differ significantly in the way they calculate income tax, we will keep our discussion simple by assuming that state income tax is a fixed percentage of employee earnings.

Other Income Tax Withholding

We pointed out previously that employees would have state income taxes withheld from their paychecks if they live in one of the 43 states that charges such a tax. In addition, many cities and counties tax employee earnings. Sometimes the tax will be a percentage of gross earnings much like federal income tax, or it may be a fixed dollar amount that the employer will withhold from every pay period. These cities and counties have their own rules regarding payroll tax deposits and tax reports for this type of withholding tax.

FIGURE 7.2 Wage Bracket Tables: Single Persons—Biweekly Payroll Period

SINGLE Persons—BIWEEKLY Payroll Period

(For Wages Paid in 2008)

If the wages are–		And the number of withholding allowances claimed is—										
At least	But less than	0	1	2	3	4	5	6	7	8	9	10
		The amount of income tax to be withheld is—										
$800	$820	$92	$71	$51	$31	$17	$4	$0	$0	$0	$0	$0
820	840	95	74	54	34	19	6	0	0	0	0	0
840	860	98	77	57	37	21	8	0	0	0	0	0
860	880	101	80	60	40	23	10	0	0	0	0	0
880	900	104	83	63	43	25	12	0	0	0	0	0
900	920	107	86	66	46	27	14	0	0	0	0	0
920	940	110	89	69	49	29	16	2	0	0	0	0
940	960	113	92	72	52	32	18	4	0	0	0	0
960	980	116	95	75	55	35	20	6	0	0	0	0
980	1,000	119	98	78	58	38	22	8	0	0	0	0
1,000	1,020	122	101	81	61	41	24	10	0	0	0	0
1,020	1,040	125	104	84	64	44	26	12	0	0	0	0
1,040	1,060	128	107	87	67	47	28	14	1	0	0	0
1,060	1,080	131	110	90	70	50	30	16	3	0	0	0
1,080	1,100	134	113	93	73	53	33	18	5	0	0	0
1,100	1,120	137	116	96	76	56	36	20	7	0	0	0
1,120	1,140	140	119	99	79	59	39	22	9	0	0	0
1,140	1,160	143	122	102	82	62	42	24	11	0	0	0
1,160	1,180	146	125	105	85	65	45	26	13	0	0	0
1,180	1,200	149	128	108	88	68	48	28	15	1	0	0
1,200	1,220	152	131	111	91	71	51	30	17	3	0	0
1,220	1,240	155	134	114	94	74	54	33	19	5	0	0
1,240	1,260	158	137	117	97	77	57	36	21	7	0	0
1,260	1,280	161	140	120	100	80	60	39	23	9	0	0
1,280	1,300	164	143	123	103	83	63	42	25	11	0	0
1,300	1,320	167	146	126	106	86	66	45	27	13	0	0
1,320	1,340	172	149	129	109	89	69	48	29	15	2	0
1,340	1,360	177	152	132	112	92	72	51	31	17	4	0
1,360	1,380	182	155	135	115	95	75	54	34	19	6	0
1,380	1,400	187	158	138	118	98	78	57	37	21	8	0
1,400	1,420	192	161	141	121	101	81	60	40	23	10	0
1,420	1,440	197	164	144	124	104	84	63	43	25	12	0
1,440	1,460	202	168	147	127	107	87	66	46	27	14	0
1,460	1,480	207	173	150	130	110	90	69	49	29	16	2
1,480	1,500	212	178	153	133	113	93	72	52	32	18	4
1,500	1,520	217	183	156	136	116	96	75	55	35	20	6
1,520	1,540	222	188	159	139	119	99	78	58	38	22	8
1,540	1,560	227	193	162	142	122	102	81	61	41	24	10
1,560	1,580	232	198	165	145	125	105	84	64	44	26	12
1,580	1,600	237	203	170	148	128	108	87	67	47	28	14
1,600	1,620	242	208	175	151	131	111	90	70	50	30	16
1,620	1,640	247	213	180	154	134	114	93	73	53	33	18
1,640	1,660	252	218	185	157	137	117	96	76	56	36	20
1,660	1,680	257	223	190	160	140	120	99	79	59	39	22
1,680	1,700	262	228	195	163	143	123	102	82	62	42	24
1,700	1,720	267	233	200	166	146	126	105	85	65	45	26
1,720	1,740	272	238	205	171	149	129	108	88	68	48	28
1,740	1,760	277	243	210	176	152	132	111	91	71	51	31
1,760	1,780	282	248	215	181	155	135	114	94	74	54	34
1,780	1,800	287	253	220	186	158	138	117	97	77	57	37
1,800	1,820	292	258	225	191	161	141	120	100	80	60	40
1,820	1,840	297	263	230	196	164	144	123	103	83	63	43
1,840	1,860	302	268	235	201	167	147	126	106	86	66	46
1,860	1,880	307	273	240	206	172	150	129	109	89	69	49
1,880	1,900	312	278	245	211	177	153	132	112	92	72	52
1,900	1,920	317	283	250	216	182	156	135	115	95	75	55
1,920	1,940	322	288	255	221	187	159	138	118	98	78	58
1,940	1,960	327	293	260	226	192	162	141	121	101	81	61
1,960	1,980	332	298	265	231	197	165	144	124	104	84	64
1,980	2,000	337	303	270	236	202	169	147	127	107	87	67
2,000	2,020	342	308	275	241	207	174	150	130	110	90	70
2,020	2,040	347	313	280	246	212	179	153	133	113	93	73
2,040	2,060	352	318	285	251	217	184	156	136	116	96	76
2,060	2,080	357	323	290	256	222	189	159	139	119	99	79
2,080	2,100	362	328	295	261	227	194	162	142	122	102	82

$2,100 and over Use Table 2(a) for a **SINGLE person** on page 38. Also see the instructions on page 36.

Employee Withholding for Social Security Taxes

In addition to withholding federal, and probably, state income tax, Katherine must also compute and withhold Social Security tax from Travelwithus.com employees. Social Security tax is also known as **FICA** because it was created by a 1935 federal law called the **Federal Insurance Contribution Act.** The law became effective in 1937. Ever since then, employers have been required to withhold amounts from employees' pay and turn them over to the federal government. The government then uses these amounts to make the following payments:

- Monthly retirement benefits for persons over 62 years old
- Medical benefits for persons over 65 years old
- Benefits for persons who have become disabled
- Benefits for families of deceased workers who were covered by this law

Before the amount of taxes withheld from employees' pay can be calculated, we need to know a few things about the Social Security (or FICA) tax. First, the tax is really two taxes. One tax is called the old-age, survivor's, and disability insurance (OASDI) tax and the other is known as Medicare (or HI, which stands for health insurance). Usually people talk about the two taxes as though they were one, but it is key to know that they are actually separate because each tax is calculated differently. Also know that OASDI puts a limit on the amount of tax that an employee must pay by setting a maximum dollar amount of earnings that can be taxed, and this amount is called the wage base. The same is not true of Medicare; all wages earned are subject to the Medicare tax. The OASDI and Medicare tax rates and the OASDI wage base amount are all set by the federal government; they can, and typically do, increase a little in each **calendar year.** The amounts for 2008 are as follows:

Tax	2008 Tax Rate	2008 Wage Base*
OASDI	6.2%	$102,000
Medicare	1.45%	None

Katherine begins to calculate the amount of Social Security tax that needs to be withheld from Stephanie's pay by looking at Stephanie's current and year-to-date (YTD) gross earnings. She needs to know the amount of earnings from the current pay period so that she can calculate the current amount of taxes. However, she also needs to know the YTD earnings so that she can see whether Stephanie has reached the maximum amount of OASDI tax yet, or if Stephanie will reach it in this pay period. So far in this calendar year, Stephanie has earned a total of $19,471.20. This amount includes the $957.60 that she has earned for the most recent, biweekly pay period.

Katherine calculates Stephanie's OASDI and Medicare taxes as follows:

$957.60 gross earnings × 6.2% OASDI tax rate = $59.37 OASDI tax

$957.60 gross earnings × 1.45% Medicare tax rate = $13.89 Medicare tax

Because Stephanie has earned less than the wage base limit of $102,000, all of her earnings for the current pay period are taxable. But what if Stephanie had earned more this year so far? Suppose she had earned $101,340 before this pay period. With her current earnings of $957.60, she would have earned a total of $102,297.60 for the year-to-date, which is more than the wage base limit of $102,000. In that case, Katherine would have calculated the amount of OASDI tax to be withheld from Stephanie's pay by first calculating the amount of taxable earnings for the current period:

Stephanie's YTD earnings before this pay period	$101,340.00
Plus: Stephanie's current earnings	957.60
Stephanie's YTD earnings after this pay period	$102,297.60

* The OASDI wage base in 2009 is $106,800.

Less: 2008 OASDI tax wage base limit	102,000.00
Stephanie's earnings above the limit, and thus, not taxable	$297.60
Stephanie's current earnings	$957.60
Less: Stephanie's earnings above the limit, and thus, not taxable	297.60
Stephanie's current OASDI taxable earnings	$660.00

Now Katherine would calculate the amount of OASDI tax as follows:

$660.00 current taxable earnings × 6.2% OASDI tax rate = $40.92 OASDI tax

Stephanie has now reached the maximum amount of taxable wages (**taxable earnings**), which means she is done paying OASDI tax for the calendar year. What if Stephanie had already earned $102,000 or more before the current pay period? In that case, none of Stephanie's current gross earnings would be subject to OASDI tax. In other words, Stephanie would already have paid her maximum OASDI tax for the year by paying tax on the money she made up to this $102,000 wage base limit. What about next year? Both Social Security taxes are calculated on a calendar year basis, and Stephanie would have to start paying the OASDI tax again until she reaches the maximum for that year.

What about the Medicare tax? Would the current amount tax that Stephanie needs to pay for this tax change too? No, because the Medicare tax does not limit the amount of earnings that can be taxed, all of Stephanie's earnings will be taxable. In other words, even if Stephanie had already earned $102,000 this year, all of her current earnings of $957.60 would be taxable and she would still have $13.89 withheld from her current paycheck for the Medicare tax.

Other Withholdings

Sometimes employees have additional amounts withheld from their paychecks for various reasons. For example, they may choose to buy **medical insurance** for themselves and maybe even their spouse and dependents through an insurance plan offered by their employer. Sometimes the employer pays the premium for this insurance coverage, or at least pays for the part of the premium that covers the employee. Even if the employer pays some of the premium, however, it is common for the employee to pay the rest. The employee pays this premium by having it withheld from his or her pay, just as the employee pays income and Social Security taxes by having these amounts withheld by the employer. Travelwithus.com currently offers this opportunity to its employees, and the cost to the hourly employee is $33 for each pay period.

Net Pay

Katherine's next step in the payroll accounting process is to calculate the amount of pay that Stephanie will actually receive as her paycheck, and this amount is called **net pay.** At this point, Katherine has computed all of the amounts necessary to determine Stephanie's net pay. Now she simply needs to combine them as follows:

Gross earnings for the current, biweekly pay period:		$957.60
Deductions for employee withholding taxes:		
Federal income tax	$92.00	
State income tax	76.61	
OASDI tax	59.37	
Medicare tax	13.89	
Medical insurance	33.00	
Total deductions		274.87
Net pay		$682.73

LEARNING UNIT 7-1 REVIEW

AT THIS POINT you should be able to

- Explain the purpose of the Fair Labor Standards Act (i.e., the Federal Wage and Hour Law).
- Calculate regular, overtime, and total gross pay.
- Complete a W-4 form.
- Discuss the term *claiming an allowance*.
- Use a wage-bracket tax table to determine the amount of federal income tax withholding.
- Define the purpose of the Social Security (FICA) taxes, OASDI, and Medicare.
- Calculate withholdings for OASDI and Medicare taxes.
- Calculate net pay.

Self-Review Quiz 7-1

Tony Kagaragis is an hourly software engineer who is paid biweekly. He earns $23.00 per hour. In the first week of the most recent pay period, he worked 39 hours, and during the second week of the period he worked 46 hours. Please calculate his regular, overtime, and gross earnings.

Solutions to Self-Review Quiz 7-1

1. $23.00 regular rate × 79 regular hours = $1,817.00 regular earnings
2. $23.00 regular rate × 1½ = $34.50 overtime rate × 6 overtime hours = $207.00 overtime earnings
3. $1,817.00 + $207.00 = $2,024.00 gross earnings

LO3 Learning Unit 7-2 Preparing a Payroll Register and Employee Earning Record

At this point, Katherine Kurtz, the accountant for Travelwithus.com, knows how much each of the three hourly employees earned for the most recent biweekly pay period and how many dollars of taxes need to be withheld from their paychecks. She now needs to enter this information into the accounting records for the company. Two primary records are used in accounting systems to keep track of payroll information for a company. The first of these records is a worksheet, known as a payroll register, which shows all information related to an entire pay period. The second record is called the employee earnings record and is used to keep track of an individual employee's payroll history for an entire calendar year.

The Payroll Register

Katherine enters information about the current payroll period for hourly employees in a **payroll register.** The register includes each employee's gross earnings, employee withholding taxes, net pay, taxable earnings, cumulative earnings, and the accounts to be charged for the salary and wage expense for that pay period. Travelwithus.com will actually have two registers, a biweekly one for its hourly employees and a monthly one for its salaried personnel. Figure 7.3 shows the completed, payroll register for the hourly payroll covering the biweekly pay period from October 16 through October 29.

TRAVELWITHUS.COM INC.
HOURLY EMPLOYEE PAYROLL REGISTER
OCTOBER 16 – 29

Employee / Social Security No.	Allowances and Marital Status	Previous Earnings (YTD)	Current Earnings: Regular Hours	Regular Rate	Regular Amount	Overtime Hours	Overtime Rate	Overtime Amount	Gross	Current Earnings (YTD)
Higuera, Stephanie	S-1	1851360	78	1140	88920	4	1710	6840	95760	1947120
123-45-6789										
Sui, Annie	S-0	212100	80	1515	121200	4	2273	9090	130290	342390
123-45-6788										
Taylor, Harold	S-2	1904370	78	1210	94380	4	1815	7260	101640	2006010
123-45-6787										
TOTALS					304500			23190	327690	4295520

Marital Status and No. of allowances are from Employee's W-4.
Previous YTD earnings = the employee's total earnings for the year before this pay period.
Regular Hours x Regular Rate = Regular Amount.
Overtime Hours x Overtime Rate = Overtime Amount.
Regular Amount + Overtime Amount = Gross Current Earnings.
Previous YTD Earnings + Gross Current Earnings = Current YTD Earnings.

Taxable Earnings, FUTA/SUTA = Gross Current Earnings < FUTA/SUTA limit of $7,000.
Taxable Earnings, OASDI = GrossCurrent Earnings < OASDI Limit of $102,000.
FIT = FIT from wage Bracket Table in Circular E.
SIT = Gross Current Earnings x 8%.
FICA, OASDI = Taxable Earnings, OASDI x 6.2%.
FICA, Medicare =Gross Current Earnings x 1.45%.
Medical Insurance = $33 per employee.
Net Pay = Gross Current Earnings – FIT – SIT – OASDI – Medicare – Medical Insurance.

TRAVELWITHUS.COM INC.
HOURLY EMPLOYEE PAYROLL REGISTER
OCTOBER 16 – 29

Employee / Social Security No.	Taxable Earnings: FUTA/SUTA	Taxable Earnings: OASDI	Deductions: FIT	SIT	FICA: OASDI	FICA: Medicare	Medical Insurance	Net Pay	Check No.	Account Charged: Business Scheduling Expense	Cruise Scheduling Expense
Higuera, Stephanie	—	95760	9200	7661	5937	1389	3300	68273	820	95760	
123-45-6789											
Sui, Annie	130290	130290	16700	10423	8078	1889	3300	89900	821		130290
123-45-6788											
Taylor, Harold	—	101640	8100	8131	6302	1474	3300	74333	822		101640
123-45-6787											
TOTALS	130290	327690	34000	26215	20317	4752	9900	232506		95760	231930

FIGURE 7.3 Payroll Register

LO4

The Employee Earnings Record

After Katherine prepares the payroll register for the period, and in order to comply with all applicable employment laws and regulations, she also completes a payroll record known as the **individual employee earnings record.** This record provides a summary of each employee's earnings, withholding taxes, net pay, and cumulative earnings during each calendar year, as shown in Figure 7.4. Katherine uses the information summarized in this record to prepare quarterly and annual payroll tax reports. Thus, the employee earnings record is split into calendar quarters, with each quarter being 13 weeks long.

LEARNING UNIT 7-2 REVIEW

AT THIS POINT you should be able to

- Explain and prepare a payroll register.
- Explain the purpose of the taxable earnings columns of the register and explain how they relate to the cumulative earnings column.
- Update an individual employee earnings record.

Self-Review Quiz 7-2

Mike Chen is an hourly employee who is paid biweekly. He is paid overtime at a rate of 1½ times his hourly rate for any hours he works over 40 in a workweek. Mike worked many overtime hours this year to develop a Web site for his employer, and as of December 10 his cumulative earnings total $100,778.06. For the pay period ending on December 24, Mike's gross earnings are $1,940.85. Calculate Mike's net pay based on the following facts:

- Mike is single and claims three withholding allowances per his Form W-4. Use the tax table in Figure 7.2 to find Mike's federal income tax withholding amount.
- The state income tax rate is 8% with no wage base limit.
- The OASDI tax rate is 6.2% with a wage base limit of $102,000 for the year; the Medicare rate is 1.45% with no wage base limit.
- Mike pays $44.00 for medical insurance for the pay period.

Solutions to Self-Review Quiz 7-2

1. Federal income tax = $226.00 (Look at the "At least $1,940" line and trace it into the "3" withholding allowance column.)
2. State income tax is $155.27 ($1,940.85 × .08)
3. FICA OASDI tax is $75.76 ($102,000 − $100,778.06 = $1,221.94 taxable; $1,221.94 × .062)
4. FICA Medicare tax is $28.14 ($1,940.85 × .0145)
5. Mike Chen's net pay is $1,411.68 ($1,940.85 – $226.00 − $155.27 − $75.76 – $28.14 – $44.00)

LO2

Learning Unit 7-3 Employer Payroll Tax Expense

Employer Withholding for Social Security Taxes

As we discussed, employees pay payroll taxes including federal income tax, Social Security taxes, probably state income tax, and maybe even a city or county income tax. It surprises some employees to find that their employers pay payroll taxes, too. As a matter of fact, employers pay exactly the same amount of Social Security taxes for each employee as the employee pays. In addition to paying Social Security taxes for each employee, employers also pay unemployment taxes that are used to provide unemployed workers with benefits while they are looking for work.

As Travelwithus.com's accountant, Katherine calculates the amount of Social Security taxes that the company must pay as an employer much the same way that she calculated

TRAVELWITHUS.COM INC.
EMPLOYEE EARNINGS RECORD
Stephanie Higuera Social Security No. 123-45-6789

Pay Period	Hours		Earnings			Deductions					Net Pay	Check No.	YTD Earnings
								FICA		Medical Insurance			
	Regular	Overtime	Regular	Overtime	Gross	FIT	SIT	OASDI	Medicare				
10/2 - 10/15	80	0	91200	000	91200	8600	7296	5654	1322	3300	65027	806	1851360
10/16 - 10/29	78	4	88920	6840	95760	9200	7661	5937	1389	3300	68273	820	1947120
10/30 - 11/12	76	0	86640	000	86640	8000	6931	5372	1256	3300	61781	825	2033760
11/13 - 11/26	80	2	91200	3420	94620	9200	7570	5866	1372	3300	67312	839	2128380
11/27 - 12/10	80	4	91200	6840	98040	9800	7843	6078	1422	3300	69597	844	2226420
12/11 - 12/24	80	0	91200	000	91200	8600	7296	5654	1322	3300	64828	858	2317620
12/25 - 12/31	48	0	54720	000	54720	3200	4378	3393	793	3300	39656	863	2372340
4th Quarter Totals			595080	17100	612180	56600	48975	37954	8876	23100	436474		
YTD Totals			2314200	58140	2372340	224186	189787	147085	34399	85800	1691083		

FIGURE 7.4 Employee Earnings Record

them for each employee. She first determines the amount of current gross earnings for all employees that fall below the wage base limit of $102,000. She looks at the OASDI Taxable Earnings total in the payroll register for the current period. She then multiplies this total by the OASDI tax rate of 6.2% to determine the OASDI tax that Travelwithus.com must pay:

$3,276.90 gross earnings × 6.2% OASDI tax rate = $203.17 OASDI tax

Katherine then calculates Travelwithus.com's Medicare tax by taking the current gross earnings for all employees and multiplying this total by the Medicare tax rate of 1.45%. Remember that the amount of Medicare tax for each employee is not subject to any limit; every dollar that an employee earns is taxed at the Medicare tax rate of 1.45%.

$3,276.90 gross earnings × 1.45% Medicare tax rate = $47.52 Medicare tax

The way Katherine computes these taxes differs in only one way compared to how she computed them for each employee. Because Katherine is now calculating Travelwithus.com's share of these taxes, Katherine uses current gross earnings for the company in total instead of using each employee's current gross earnings as she did when she was determining the amount to withhold from each employee's paycheck.

FUTA and SUTA

In addition to paying its employer share of FICA taxes, Travelwithus.com must also pay unemployment taxes. Unemployment tax, or unemployment insurance as it is sometimes called, was created by the same 1935 law that created Social Security. This federal law requires all 50 states, the District of Columbia, and U.S. territories to run unemployment compensation programs that are approved and monitored by the federal government. Unemployment taxes are paid by employers based on wages paid to employees. Federal Unemployment Tax Act (FUTA) taxes pay the costs of administering the federal and state programs, but do not pay benefits to employees. State Unemployment Tax Act (SUTA) taxes pay the benefits to unemployed persons.

Currently, employers pay FUTA tax at a rate of 6.2% on wages earned by each employee up to a wage base limit of $7,000. However, the federal government allows employers to take a tax credit for SUTA tax against this tax, up to a maximum credit of 5.4%.

FUTA tax rate	6.2%
Less: Normal FUTA tax credit	5.4%
Net FUTA tax rate	0.8%

Employers are allowed to take this credit as long as they have paid all amounts that they owe for SUTA taxes, and paid them on time. In other words, the federal law essentially says to employers, "Comply with your state's unemployment tax laws and your total tax will not exceed a maximum of 6.2%: 0.8% to the federal government and a state rate that will vary up to maximum of 5.4%." Remember that employers alone are responsible for paying FUTA tax; it is never withheld from the earnings of employees.

Katherine calculates FUTA tax by referring to the FUTA Taxable Earnings total in the current payroll register. This column tells her how much, in total, Travelwithus.com's employees have earned this period that falls below the FUTA wage base limit of $7,000. She uses this amount to calculate the FUTA tax by multiplying it by the net FUTA tax rate as follows:

$1,302.90 FUTA taxable earnings × 0.8% FUTA tax rate = $10.42 FUTA tax

Because states run their own unemployment programs, each state may use a different SUTA wage base limit. These amounts are based on the needs of the unemployment funds in each state. In 2005 the wage base limits for states ranged from $7,000 to $34,000. Different states have different SUTA tax rates for the same reason that the wage base limits vary; they are based on the needs of the unemployment funds in each state.

Additionally, the SUTA tax rate can vary from employer to employer within a state. In any state, an employer's SUTA tax rate will be based on how many dollars it contributes to the state unemployment fund and the dollar amount of claims that its employees make against that fund.

In other words, the rate is tied to the employer's employment history. The more frequently an employer lays off its employees, the more unemployment benefits the state will have to pay, and the higher the tax rate for that employer. In other words, employers who rarely lay off their workers will be charged a lower SUTA rate than employers who lay off workers often. In this way, the SUTA tax rate motivates employers to stabilize their workforce.

Travelwithus.com's current SUTA rate is 5.4% and the wage base limit for the state in which it is located is $7,000. Katherine calculates Travelwithus.com's SUTA tax similar to the way she calculated its FUTA tax. She first looks at the SUTA Taxable Earnings total in the current payroll register to see how much, in total, Travelwithus.com's employees earned this period below the SUTA wage base limit of $7,000. She then calculates the SUTA tax by multiplying this amount by the SUTA tax rate as follows:

$1,302.90 SUTA taxable earnings × 5.4% SUTA tax rate = $70.36

Workers' Compensation Insurance

Workers' compensation insurance insures employees against losses they may incur due to accidental injury or death while on the job. Each employer must purchase this insurance either through an insurance broker or state agency. In most states, this tax is paid completely by the employer, not the employee.

Travelwithus.com's premium for this insurance is based on its total estimated gross payroll, and the rate is calculated for each $100 of weekly payroll. By estimating payroll before the beginning of the year, the insurance company can determine the amount of the premium to charge Travelwithus.com. If actual payroll for the year turns out to differ from estimated payroll, then the insurance company will either credit Travelwithus.com for any overpayment or bill it for any underpayment. The rate for Travelwithus.com is based on the type of work that its employees perform as well as the amount and extent of any on-the-job injuries that its employees experience.

Travelwithus.com has two groups of employees: travel schedulers and managers. It estimated that it would have $50,000 of gross payroll for its schedulers in the next year, and its rate is $1.80 for every $100 of this payroll. The company also estimated that it will incur $190,000 of payroll for managers, and its rate for this group is $.22 for every $100 of payroll. Travelwithus.com then calculated its premium as follows:

Workers' compensation premium for schedulers:	*$50,000/$100 = 500 × $1.80 =*	*$ 900.00*
Workers' compensation premium for managers:	*$190,000/$100 = 1,900 × $.22 =*	*418.00*
Total workers' compensation premium =		*$1,318.00*

Suppose, however, that at the end of the year, Travelwithus.com's scheduler payroll totaled $57,977.14 and its manager payroll totaled $220,648.16. The actual premiums for the year would be calculated in the following manner:

Workers' compensation premium for schedulers:	*$57,977.14/$100 = 580 × $1.80 =*	*$1,044.00*
Workers' compensation premium for managers:	*$220,648.16/$100 = 2,206 × $.22 =*	*485.32*
Total workers' compensation premium =		*$1,529.32*

Travelwithus.com would then owe an additional amount of premium:

Workers' compensation premium based on actual gross payroll	*$1,529.32*
Workers' compensation premium based on estimated gross payroll	*1,318.00*
Additional workers' compensation premium owed =	*$ 211.32*

LEARNING UNIT 7-3 REVIEW

AT THIS POINT you should be able to

- Explain the use of the taxable earnings column of the payroll register in calculating the employer's payroll tax expense.
- Calculate the employer's payroll taxes of OASDI, Medicare, FUTA, and SUTA.
- Explain the difference between FUTA and SUTA taxes.
- Understand the purpose of workers' compensation insurance.
- Calculate the estimated premium for workers' compensation insurance.

Self-Review Quiz 7-3

Given the following, calculate the employer FICA OASDI, FICA Medicare, FUTA, and SUTA for Farmington Co. for the weekly payroll of July 8. Assume the following:

- FUTA tax is paid at the net rate of 0.8% on the first $7,000 of earnings.
- SUTA tax is paid at a rate of 5.6% on the first $7,000 of earnings.
- FICA tax rate for Social Security is 6.2% on $102,000, and Medicare is 1.45% on all earnings.

Employee	Cumulative Pay Before This Week's Payroll	Gross Pay for Week
Bill Jones	$6,000	$800
Julie Warner	$6,600	$400
Al Brooks	$7,900	$700

Solutions to Self-Review Quiz 7-3

1. FICA OASDI = $1,900 × .062 = $117.80
2. FICA Medicare = $1,900 × .0145 = $27.55
3. FUTA = $1,200 × .008 = $9.60
4. SUTA = $1,200 × .056 = $67.20

CHAPTER ASSIGNMENTS

SUMMARY OF KEY POINTS

LEARNING UNIT 7-1

1. The Fair Labor Standards Act states that hourly workers will receive a minimum of one and a half times their regular hourly rate of pay for all hours they work over 40 hours during a workweek.
2. Salaried employees are employees who are classified as salaried according to the provisions of the Fair Labor Standards Act. These employees receive a fixed amount of pay for each pay period.
3. For the rules of the Fair Labor Standards Act to apply to an employer, the employer must be involved in interstate commerce. Most companies today are involved in interstate commerce.
4. Employees and employers pay equal amounts of Social Security tax. Note that Social Security, or FICA tax, is made up of two taxes: OASDI and Medicare. The OASDI tax is based on a tax rate and wage base amount that is set for each calendar year.

The OASDI tax rate for 2008 is 6.2% and the wage base limit for this year is $102,000. Medicare has no wage base limit, so an employee and employer will pay this tax on all of an employee's earnings during the calendar year, at a rate of 1.45% for 2008.

5. Federal income tax withholding amounts are listed in tax tables found in IRS Circular E, *Employer's Tax Guide*, also known as Publication 15.
6. Gross earnings minus deductions equals net pay.

LEARNING UNIT 7-2

1. The two primary accounting records used to keep track of payroll amounts are the payroll register and employee earnings record. The payroll register shows gross earnings, deductions, net pay, and taxable earnings for a payroll period. The employee earnings record shows the gross earnings, deductions, and net pay for an employee for an entire calendar year.
2. The taxable earnings columns of the payroll register do not show the tax. They show the amount of earnings to be taxed for unemployment taxes, OASDI, and Medicare. The individual employee earnings records are updated soon after the payroll register is prepared.

LEARNING UNIT 7-3

1. The payroll tax expense for an employer is made up of FICA OASDI, FICA Medicare, FUTA, and SUTA.
2. The maximum amount of credit given for state unemployment taxes paid against the FUTA tax is 5.4%. This figure is known as the normal FUTA tax credit. The normal FUTA tax credit typically results in employers paying 0.8% for FUTA tax.
3. Employers pay workers' compensation insurance premiums based on estimated payroll. At the end of the year, estimated payroll is compared to actual payroll, and the employer either pays any additional premium or receives a credit for any overpayment of premium.

KEY TERMS

Allowances (also called *exemptions*) Certain dollar amounts of a person's income tax that will be considered nontaxable for income tax withholding purposes.

Calendar year A one-year period beginning on January 1 and ending on December 31. Employers must use a calendar year for payroll purposes, even if the employer uses a fiscal year for financial statements and for any other reason.

Circular E An IRS tax publication of tax tables.

Fair Labor Standards Act (Federal Wage and Hour Law) A law the majority of employers must follow that contains rules stating the minimum hourly rate of pay and the maximum number of hours a worker will work before being paid time and a half for overtime hours worked. This law also has other rules and regulations that employers must follow for payroll purposes.

Federal income tax (FIT) withholding Amount of federal income tax withheld by the employer from the employee's gross pay; the amount withheld is determined by the employee's gross pay, the pay period, the number of allowances claimed by the employee on the W-4 form, and the marital status indicated on the W-4 form.

FICA (Federal Insurance Contributions Act) Part of the Social Security Act of 1935, this law taxes both the employer and employee up to a certain maximum rate and wage base for OASDI tax purposes. It also taxes both the employer and employee for Medicare purposes, but this tax has no wage base maximum.

Form W-4 (Employee's Withholding Allowance Certificate) A form filled out by employees and used by employers to supply needed information about the number of allowances claimed, marital status, and so forth. The form is used for payroll purposes to determine federal income tax withholding from an employee's paycheck.

Gross earnings (gross pay) Amount of pay received before any deductions.

Individual employee earnings record An accounting document that summarizes the total amount of wages paid and the deductions for the calendar year. It aids in preparing governmental reports. A new record is prepared for each employee each year.

Interstate commerce A test that is applied to determine whether an employer must follow the rules of the Fair Labor Standards Act. If an employer communicates or does business with another business in some other state, it is usually considered to be involved in interstate commerce.

Medical insurance Health care insurance for which premiums may be paid through a deduction from an employee's paycheck.

Net pay Gross earnings, less deductions. Net pay, or take-home pay, is what the worker actually takes home.

Pay or payroll period A length of time used by an employer to calculate the amount of an employee's earnings. Pay periods can be daily, weekly, biweekly (once every two weeks), semimonthly (twice each month), monthly, quarterly, or annual.

Payroll register A multicolumn form that can be used to record payroll data.

State income tax (SIT) withholding Amount of state income tax withheld by the employer from the employee's gross pay.

Taxable earnings Shows amount of earnings subject to a tax. The tax itself is not shown.

Wage bracket table One of various charts in IRS Circular E that provide information about deductions for federal income tax based on earnings and data supplied on the W-4 form.

Workers' compensation insurance A benefit plan required by federal regulations in which employers must purchase insurance to protect their employees against losses due to injury or death incurred while on the job.

Workweek A seven-day (168-hour) period used to determine overtime hours for employees. A workweek can begin on any given day, but must end seven days later.

BLUEPRINT FOR RECORDING TRANSACTIONS IN A PAYROLL REGISTER

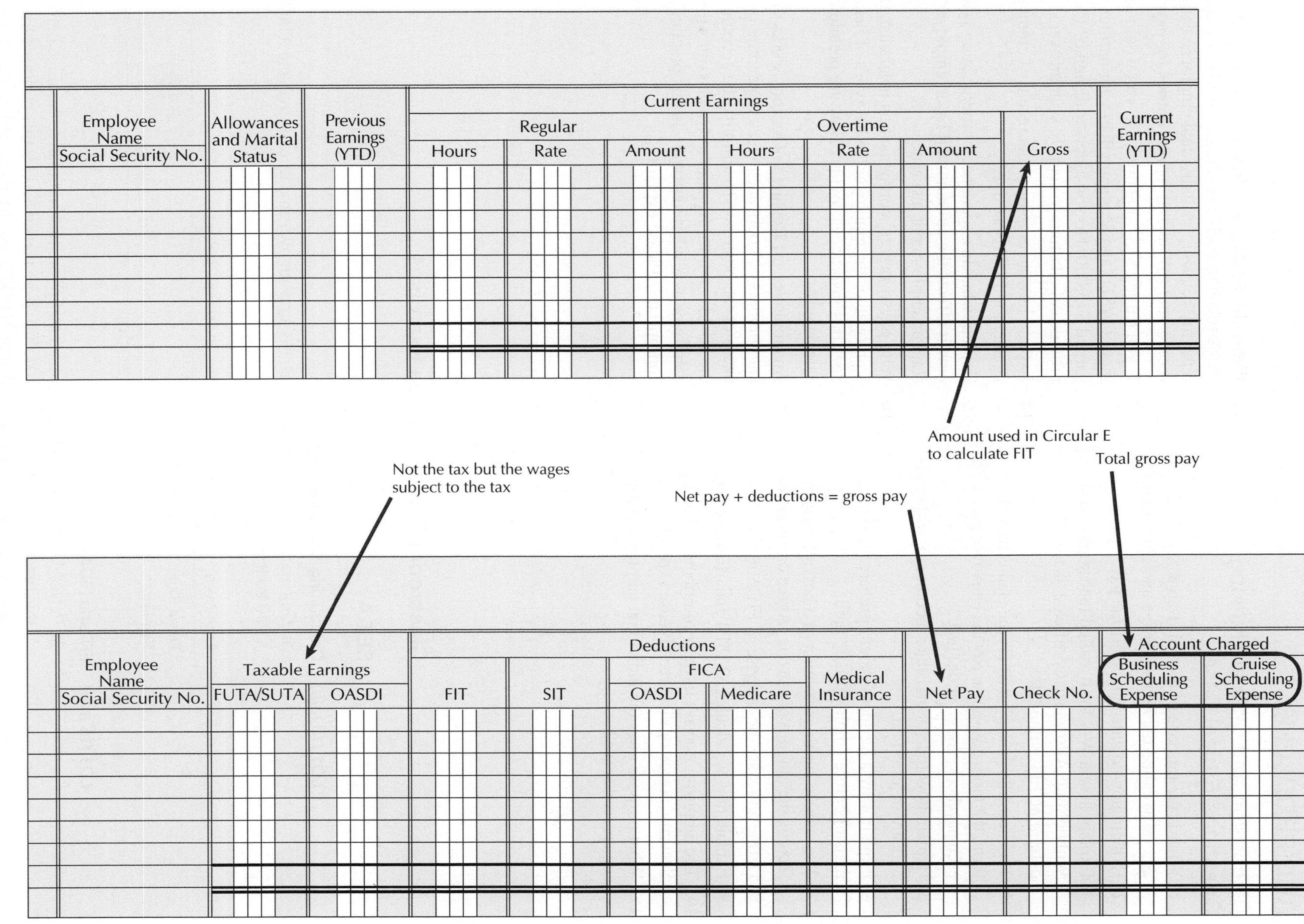

Employee Name / Social Security No.	Allowances and Marital Status	Previous Earnings (YTD)	Current Earnings: Regular Hours	Regular Rate	Regular Amount	Overtime Hours	Overtime Rate	Overtime Amount	Gross	Current Earnings (YTD)

Employee Name / Social Security No.	Taxable Earnings: FUTA/SUTA	Taxable Earnings: OASDI	Deductions: FIT	SIT	FICA: OASDI	FICA: Medicare	Medical Insurance	Net Pay	Check No.	Account Charged: Business Scheduling Expense	Account Charged: Cruise Scheduling Expense

QUESTIONS, CLASSROOM DEMONSTRATION EXERCISES, EXERCISES, AND PROBLEMS

Discussion and Critical Thinking Questions/Ethical Case

1. What is the purpose of the Fair Labor Standards Act (also called the Federal Wage and Hour Law)?
2. Explain how to calculate overtime pay.
3. Explain how a W-4 form, called the Employee's Withholding Allowance Certificate, is used to determine FIT withheld.
4. The more allowances an employee claims on a W-4 form, the more take-home pay the employee gets with each paycheck. Agree or disagree?
5. Explain how federal and state income tax withholdings are determined.
6. Explain why a business should prepare a payroll register before employees are paid.
7. The taxable earnings column of a payroll register records the amount of tax due. Agree or disagree?
8. Define and state the purpose of FICA taxes.
9. Explain how to calculate OASDI and Medicare taxes.
10. The employer doesn't have to contribute to Social Security. Agree or disagree? Please explain.
11. What purpose does the individual employee earnings record serve?
12. Please draw a diagram showing how the following items relate to each other: (a) a weekly payroll, (b) a payroll register, (c) individual employee earnings record, and (d) general journal entries for payroll.
13. If you earned $130,000 this year, you would pay more OASDI and Medicare than your partner who earned $75,000. Do you agree or disagree? Please provide calculations to support your answer.
14. Explain how an employer can receive a credit against the FUTA tax due.
15. Explain what an experience or merit rating is and how it affects the amount paid by an employer for state unemployment insurance.
16. Who pays workers' compensation insurance, the employee or the employer? What types of benefits does this insurance provide? How are premiums calculated?
17. An employee for Repairs to Go, Inc., works different numbers of hours each week depending on the needs of the business. To simplify the accounting, the bookkeeper for Repairs to Go classifies this employee as a salaried person. Is this practice appropriate? Please explain.

Classroom Demonstration Exercises

SET A

LO1 (10 min) **Calculating Gross Earnings**

1. Calculate the total wages earned (assume an overtime rate of time and a half over 40 hours).

Employee	Hourly Rate	No. of Hours Worked
Dawn Slow	$10	39
Ben Fritz	$12	50

LO1 (15 min) **FIT and FICA**

2. Peter Martin, single, claiming one exemption, has cumulative earnings before this biweekly pay period of $101,000. If he is paid $2,000 this period, what will his deductions be for FIT and FICA (OASDI and Medicare)? Use the tables and rates in this text.

Net Pay *LO1 (15 min)*

3. From Exercise 2, calculate Peter's net pay. The state income tax rate is 5% and health insurance is $40.

Payroll Register *LO3 (10 min)*

4. Match the following:
   1. Total gross pay
   2. A deduction
   3. Net pay
   _____ a. Office Salary Expense
   _____ b. FICA OASDI Payable
   _____ c. FICA Medicare Payable
   _____ d. Federal Income Tax Payable
   _____ e. Medical Insurance Payable
   _____ f. Wages and Salaries Payable

Employer and Employee Taxes *LO2 (10 min)*

5. Identify which of the following taxes are paid by the employee (EE) and which are paid by the employer (ER):
   _____ a. FICA Medicare
   _____ b. FIT
   _____ c. FUTA
   _____ d. SUTA

SET B

Calculating Gross Earnings *LO1 (10 min)*

1. Calculate the total wages earned (assume an overtime rate of time and a half over 40 hours).

Employee	Hourly Rate	No. of Hours Worked
Tom Suarez	$14	37
Jim Martin	$12	48

FIT and FICA *LO1 (10 min)*

2. Cindy Hwang, single, claiming two exemptions, has cumulative earnings before this biweekly pay period of $101,000. If she is paid $1,800 this period, what will her deductions be for FIT and FICA (OASDI and Medicare)? Use the tables and rates in this text.

Net Pay *LO1 (10 min)*

3. From Exercise 2, calculate Cindy's net pay. The state income tax rate is 6% and health insurance is $30.

Payroll Register *LO3 (10 min)*

4. Match the following:
   1. Total gross pay
   2. A deduction
   3. Net pay
   _____ a. Store Wage Expense
   _____ b. FICA OASDI Payable
   _____ c. FICA Medicare Payable
   _____ d. State Income Tax Payable
   _____ e. Medical Insurance Payable
   _____ f. Wages and Salaries Payable

LO2 (10 min) **Employer and Employee Taxes**

5. Identify which of the following taxes are paid by the employee (EE) and which are paid by the employer (ER):

_____ **a.** FICA OASDI
_____ **b.** FICA Medicare
_____ **c.** SIT
_____ **d.** SUTA

Exercises

LO1 (15 min) **7-1.** Calculate the total wages earned for each employee assuming an overtime rate of time and a half over 40 hours.

Employee	Hourly Rate	No. of Hours Worked
Carmen Amador	$9	39
Jill West	$12	44
Fred Aster	$14	46

LO1, 3 (20 min) **7-2.** Compute the net pay for each employee using the federal income tax withholding table in Figure 7.2. Assume the FICA OASDI tax is 6.2% on a wage base limit of $102,000; Medicare is 1.45% on all earnings, the payroll is paid biweekly, and no state income tax applies.

Employee	Status	Allowances	Cumulative Pay	This Week's Pay
Alvin Pang	Single	1	$60,000	$1,690
Angelina Potts	Single	0	$64,300	$1,600

LO2 (20 min) **7-3.** From the following information, calculate the payroll tax expense for Baker Company for the payroll of August 9:

Employee	Cumulative Earnings Before Weekly Payroll	Gross Pay for the Week
J. Kline	$3,500	$900
A. Met	6,600	750
D. Ring	7,900	300

The FICA tax rate for OASDI is 6.2% on the first $102,000 earned, and Medicare is 1.45% on all earnings. Federal unemployment tax is 0.8% on the first $7,000 earned by each employee. The experience or merit rating for Baker is 5.6% on the first $7,000 of employee earnings for state unemployment purposes.

LO2 (15 min) **7-4.** Refer to Exercise 7-3 and assume that the state changed Baker's experience/merit rating to 4.9%. What effect would this change have on the total payroll tax expense?

LO2 (15 min) **7-5.** Refer to Exercise 7-3. If D. Ring earned $2,000 for the week instead of $300, what effect would this change have on the total payroll tax expense?

LO2 (20 min) **7-6.** The total wage expense for Howell Co. was $160,000. Of this total, $30,000 was above the OASDI wage base limit and not subject to this tax. All earnings are subject to Medicare tax, and $60,000 was above the federal and state unemployment wage base limits and not subject to unemployment taxes. Please calculate the total payroll tax expense for Howell Co. given the following rates and wage base limits:

a. FICA tax rate: OASDI, 6.2% with a wage base limit of $102,000; Medicare, 1.45% with no wage base limit

b. State unemployment tax rate: 5.9% with a wage base limit of $7,000

c. Federal unemployment tax rate (after credit): 0.8% with a wage base limit of $7,000

7-7. At the end of the first quarter of 200X, you are asked to determine the FUTA tax liability for Oscar Company. The FUTA tax rate is 0.8% on the first $7,000 each employee earns during the year (assuming 13 weeks). *LO2 (20 min)*

Employee	Gross Pay Per Week
J. Kane	$700
A. Ling	800
P. Made	600
C. Slove	500

7-8. From the following data, estimate the annual premium for workers' compensation insurance: *LO4 (10 min)*

Type of Work	Estimated Payroll	Rate per $100
Office	$30,000	$ .21
Repairs	84,000	1.70

Group A Problems

7A-1. From the following information, please complete the chart for gross earnings for the week. (Assume an overtime rate of time and a half over 40 hours.) *LO1 (20 min)*

Employee	Hourly Rate	No. of Hours Worked	Gross Earnings
Joe Vasquez	$9	45	
Lisa Ferris	$10	40	
Nancy Patt	$12	42	
Dave Johnson	$13	50	

Check Figure:
Dave Johnson: $715 Gross Earnings

7A-2. March Company has five salaried employees. Your task is to use the following information to calculate net pay for each employee: *LO1, 3 (30 min)*

Employee	Allowance and Marital Status	Cumulative Earnings Before This Payroll	Biweekly Salary	Department
Dunn, Dylan	S-1	$42,000	$1,100	Customer Service
Fein, Marc	S-1	30,000	900	Office
Kraft, Alison	S-2	59,200	1,300	Office
Mae, Audrey	S-3	101,080	2,090	Customer Service
Zimmer, Lionel	S-0	29,000	810	Customer Service

Assume the following:

1. FICA OASDI is 6.2% on $102,000; FICA Medicare is 1.45% on all earnings.
2. Each employee contributes $30 biweekly for medical insurance.
3. State income tax is 6% of gross pay.
4. FIT is calculated from Figure 7.2.

Check Figure:
Total Net Pay $4,579.73

LO1, 3 (40 min)

7A-3. The bookkeeper of Izumi Co. gathered the following data from individual employee earnings records and daily time cards. Your task is to complete a payroll register on December 12.

Employee	Allowance and Marital Status	Cumulative Earnings Before This Payroll	Daily Time M	T	W	T	F	Hourly Rate of Pay	FIT
Fine, Pam	M-1	$64,100	5	11	9	8	8	$16	$52
Hale, Don	S-0	15,000	8	10	9	9	4	15	76
Pope, Ria	M-3	66,000	8	10	10	10	10	18	72
Vent, Jane	S-1	19,000	8	8	8	8	8	20	104

Check Figure:
Total Net Pay $2,346.50

Assume the following:

1. FICA OASDI is 6.2% on $102,000; FICA Medicare is 1.45% on all earnings.
2. Federal income tax has been calculated from a weekly table for you.
3. Each employee contributes $30 weekly for health insurance.
4. Overtime is paid at a rate of time and a half over 40 hours.
5. Fine and Pope work in the office; the other employees work in sales.

LO1, 2, 3, 4 (40 min)

7A-4. You gathered the following data from time cards and individual employee earnings records. Your tasks are as follows:

1. On December 5, 200X, prepare a payroll register for this biweekly payroll.
2. Calculate the employer taxes of FICA OASDI, FICA Medicare, FUTA, and SUTA.

Employee	Allowance and Marital Status	Cumulative Earnings Before This Payroll	Biweekly Salary	Check No.	Department
Abers, John	S-3	$37,200	$1,550	30	Production
Gomez, Nicki	S-1	48,000	2,000	31	Office
Moreno, Jeff	S-2	64,800	2,070	32	Production
Sung, Paul	S-1	4,600	800	33	Office

Check Figure:
Total Net Pay $4,748.86

Assume the following:

1. FICA OASDI: 6.2% on $102,000; FICA Medicare: 1.45% on all earnings.
2. Federal income tax is calculated from Figure 7.2.
3. State income tax is 5% of gross pay.
4. Union dues are $12 biweekly.
5. The SUTA rate is 5.4% and the FUTA rate is 0.8% on earnings below $7,000.

Group B Problems

LO1 (20 min)

7B-1. From the following information, please complete the chart for gross earnings for the week. (Assume an overtime rate of time and a half over 40 hours.)

Employee	Hourly Rate	No. of Hours Worked	Gross Earnings
Joe Vasquez	$5	40	
Edna Kane	$10	47	
Dick Wall	$12	36	
Pat Green	$14	55	

Check Figure:
Pat Green: Gross Pay $875

7B-2. March Company employs five salaried employees. Your task is to use the following information to calculate net pay for each employee: *LO1, 3 (30 min)*

Employee	Allowance and Marital Status	Cumulative Earnings Before This Payroll	Biweekly Salary	Department
Kool, Alice	S-1	$45,150	$1,290	Sales
Lose, Bob	S-1	22,575	800	Office
Moore, Linda	S-2	59,300	1,240	Office
Relt, Rusty	S-3	101,100	1,300	Sales
Veel, Larry	S-0	21,875	860	Sales

Assume the following:

1. FICA OASDI is 6.2% on $102,000; FICA Medicare: 1.45% on all earnings.
2. Each employee contributes $25 biweekly for union dues.
3. State income tax is 6% of gross pay.
4. FIT is calculated from Figure 7.2.

Check Figure: Total Net Pay $4,102.41

7B-3. The bookkeeper of Pearl Co. gathered the following data from individual employee earnings records and daily time cards. Your task is to complete a payroll register on December 12. *LO1, 3 (40 min)*

Employee	Allowance and Marital Status	Cumulative Earnings Before This Payroll	Daily Time M	T	W	T	F	Hourly Rate of Pay	FIT
Boy, Pete	M-1	$64,900	12	11	7	7	7	$16	$62
Heat, Donna	S-0	19,000	8	9	9	9	5	16	82
Pyle, Ray	M-3	102,350	10	10	10	10	5	20	75
Vent, Joan	S-1	13,500	6	8	8	8	8	19	84

Check Figure: Total Net Pay $2,470.73

Assume the following:

1. FICA OASDI is 6.2% on $102,000; FICA Medicare is 1.45% on all earnings.
2. Federal income tax has been calculated from a weekly table for you.
3. Each employee contributes $25 weekly for health insurance.
4. Heat and Vent work in the office; the other employees work in sales.

7B-4. You gathered the following data from time cards and individual employee earnings records. Your tasks are as follows: *LO1, 2, 3, 4 (40 min)*

1. On December 5, 200X, prepare a payroll register for this biweekly payroll.
2. Calculate the employer taxes of FICA OASDI, FICA Medicare, FUTA, and SUTA.

Employee	Allowance and Marital Status	Cumulative Earnings Before This Payroll	Biweekly Salary	Check No.	Department
Aulson, Andy	S-3	$30,000	$ 800	30	Factory
Flynn, Jacki	S-1	50,000	1,100	31	Office
Moore, Jeff	S-2	60,000	1,050	32	Factory
Sullivan, Alison	S-1	65,000	1,200	33	Office

Assume the following:

Check Figure:
Total Net Pay $3,220.02

1. FICA OASDI is 6.2% on $102,000; FICA Medicare is 1.45% on all earnings.
2. Federal income tax is calculated from Figure 7.2.
3. State income tax is 5% of gross pay.
4. Union dues are $10 biweekly.
5. The SUTA rate is 5.6%, and the FUTA rate is 0.8% on earnings below $7,000.

ON-THE-JOB TRAINING

LO1, 2, 4 (60 min)

T-1. Bert Ryan owns Small Company, a sole proprietorship. During the current pay period, his two employees, Jim Roy and Janice Alter, worked 48 hours and 56 hours, respectively. The reason for these extra hours is that both Jim and Janice worked their regular 40-hour workweek, plus Jim worked 8 extra hours on Sunday and Janice worked 8 extra hours on Saturday and Sunday. Their contract with Small Co. is that they are each paid an hourly rate of $8 per hour with all hours over 40 to be time and a half and double time on Sunday. Bert, the owner, feels he is also entitled to a salary because he works as many hours. He plans to pay himself $425. As the accountant for Small Co., (1) calculate the gross pay for Jim and Janice, and (2) write a letter to Bert Ryan with your recommendations regarding his salary.

LO1, 2, 4 (40 min)

T-2. Marcy Moore works for Moose Company during the day and GTA Company at night. Both her employers deduct FICA taxes for OASDI and Medicare. At year-end, Marcy has earned $96,600 at her job at Moose Company and $12,000 at GTA.

At a party she meets Bill Barnes, an accountant, who tells her she has paid too much Social Security tax and that she is entitled to a refund or credit on the tax return she files for the year. Bill suggests that she call the Internal Revenue Service's toll-free number and ask for taxpayer assistance. Assume Social Security of 6.2% on $102,000 and Medicare of 1.45% on all Marcy's earnings during the year.

As Marcy's friend, (1) check to see whether she has actually overpaid any FICA tax, and (2) write a brief note to her and show her your calculations to support your answer.

FINANCIAL REPORT PROBLEM

LO1, 2 (10 min)

Reading the Kellogg's Annual Report

Go to Appendix A of the Kellogg's Annual Report and calculate from Note 15 how much Accrued Salaries and Wages has increased from 2005 to 2006.

INTERNET PROJECT

Johnson & Johnson

Go to the Web and Search: Annual Report Johnson & Johnson 2008.
Click on Investors Relations.
List out the latest news Johnson & Johnson is providing to its investors.
Order a free annual report.

CONTINUING PROBLEM

LO1, 2, 3 (60 min)

Sanchez Computer Center

In preparing for next year, Tony Freedman hired two hourly employees to assist with some troubleshooting and repair work.

Assignment

1. Record the following transactions in the general journal and post them to the general ledger.
2. Prepare a payroll register for the three pay periods.
3. Prepare a trial balance as of November 30, 200X.

Assume the following transactions:

a. The following accounts have been added to the chart of accounts: Wage Expense #5110, FICA OASDI Payable #2020, FICA Medicare Payable #2030, FIT Payable #2040, State Income Tax Payable #2050, and Wages Payable #2010.

b. Assume FICA OASDI is taxed at 6.2% up to $76,200 in earnings, and Medicare at 1.45% on all earnings. Note that this figure is not the current wage-base limit for Social Security, but will be used for this problem.

c. State income tax is 2% of gross pay.

d. None of the employees has federal income tax taken out of his or her pay.

e. Each employee earns $10 an hour and is paid 1½ times salary for hours worked in excess of 40 weekly.

Nov.	1	Billed Vita Needle Company $6,800, invoice no. 12675, for services rendered.
	3	Billed Accu Pac, Inc., $3,900, invoice no. 12676, for services rendered.
	5	Purchased new shop benches for $1,400 on account from System Design Furniture.
	7	Paid employee wages: Lance Kumm, 38 hours, and Anthony Hall, 42 hours. (This transaction will be recorded as part of the Chapter 8 problem.)
	9	Received the phone bill, $150.
	12	Collected $500 of the amount due from Taylor Golf.
	14	Paid employee wages: Lance Kumm, 25 hours, and Anthony Hall, 36 hours. (This transaction will be recorded as part of the Chapter 8 problem.)
	18	Collected $800 of the amount due from Taylor Golf.
	20	Purchased a fax machine for the office from Multi Systems, Inc., on credit, $450.00.
	21	Paid employee wages: Lance Kumm, 26 hours, and Anthony Hall, 35 hours. (This transaction will be recorded as part of the Chapter 8 problem.)

**Note:* Transactions on the 7th, 14th, and 21st will be required in the Chapter 8 general journal.

SUBWAY Case

PAYROLL RECORDS: A FULL-TIME JOB?

LO1, 2, 3, 4 (30 min)

Like every Subway restaurant owner, Stan needs to keep a master file of important employee information. This file contains every employee's name, address, phone number, Social Security number, rate of pay, hours worked per week, and W-4 form.

Stan employs two part-time "sandwich artists" and no full-time managers—yet. If his sales continue to be high, he'll need to hire someone to manage operations so that he can spend more time analyzing the financials—with Lila's help—and growing his business. Most restaurants hire primarily part-timers with a core of full-time employees, but the numbers vary from restaurant to restaurant. Benefits vary too. Stan, for instance, plans to offer health and dental benefits when he hires a manager. He knows what a great incentive these benefits are, with health costs so high. He pays his sandwich artists, Rashid and Ellen, the minimum wage because they both have less than a year's experience. However, he's talking to Mariah Washington about creating some incentives to keep them motivated. If Rashid and Ellen are with him for a full year, they'll see a nice raise in their biweekly paychecks. Both the frequency of pay and the tax rates vary by state and sometimes by city or county.

Stan must record all this vital information and report it to the various state, local, and federal authorities. In addition, Stan includes total payroll expenses on the weekly sales and inventory report, which he submits electronically to headquarters from his point-of-sale (POS) screen.

Scheduling workers and keeping payroll records are the bane of Stan's existence. These tasks are so incredibly time-consuming. He was pleased to hear, then, at the last meeting of his local North American Association of Subway Franchisees (NAASF) that the new POS terminals will soon offer an electronic scheduling package.

"Wow! That will really help," said Stan cheerfully to another franchisee. "No more different colors of ink just to keep track of who will work when! Now I can plan around Rashid and Ellen's exam schedules without a hassle. Scheduling might just become my favorite module in the new system."

"Sure," said Javier Gonzalez, another owner. "Now you can concentrate on payroll records. What fun!"

"Ay. Que lata," Stan groaned. What a drag!

Discussion Questions

1. What payroll records does Stan need to keep for his Subway restaurant?
2. What other information might Stan want in order to schedule working hours for each employee?
3. How does the payroll register help Stan prepare the payroll? (Consult the process outlined at the beginning of the chapter.)

8

Paying, Recording, and Reporting Payroll and Payroll Taxes: The Conclusion of the Payroll Process

DID YOU KNOW? Coca-Cola is more than 120 years old and is still the best-selling beverage brand. A new coolLift delivery system has resulted in a four-day workweek for many employees, along with less manual labor. Visit *www.thecoca-colacompany.com* to find more information about Coca-Cola.

LEARNING OBJECTIVES

1. Recording payroll and payroll taxes.
2. Recording the payroll and the paying of the payroll taxes.
3. Recording employer taxes for FICA OASDI, FICA HI, FUTA, SUTA, and workers' compensation insurance.
4. Paying FUTA, SUTA, and workers' compensation insurance.
5. Preparing Forms W-2, W-3, 941, and 940.

Balance Sheet

ASSETS

Cash 111

XXX	

Cash account used for paying payroll taxes

Payroll Cash 112

XXX	

Cash account used only for writing paychecks

Prepaid WC Insurance 121

XXX	

Account used only for the prepaid workers' compensation insurance premium

LIABILITIES

Wages and Salaries Payable 202

	XXX

Wages and salaries due to employees

FICA OASDI Payable 203

	XXX

Employee and employer's share of FICA OASDI due to the IRS

FICA Medicare Payable 204

	XXX

Employee and employer's share of FICA Medicare due to the IRS

FIT Payable 205

	XXX

Federal income tax withheld and due to the IRS

SIT Payable 206

	XXX

State income tax withheld and due to the state government

FUTA Tax Payable 207

	XXX

Federal unemployment tax due to the IRS

SUTA Tax Payable 208

	XXX

State unemployment tax due to the state government

Medical Insurance Payable 209

	XXX

Medical insurance premium withheld and due to the health insurance carrier

Income Statement

EXPENSES

Business Scheduling Expense 601

XXX	

Wage and salary expense of employees scheduling business travel

Cruise Scheduling Expense 602

XXX	

Wage and salary expense of employees scheduling cruises

Payroll Tax Expense 603

XXX	

Employer's expense for its share of FICA OASDI, its share of FICA Medicare, FUTA, and SUTA

WC Insurance Expense 604

XXX	

Employer's expense for workers' compensation insurance

Coca-Cola has many thousands of employees world wide. With the aid of computers, the accounting department of Coca-Cola must monitor as well as complete in a timely manner its employer tax responsibilities. In Chapter 7 we learned how to calculate gross earnings, employee withholding taxes, net pay, and employer payroll taxes. We now look at how businesses pay, record, and report these amounts. The journal entries necessary to record all of the payroll transactions for Travelwithus.com appear in the next section. Use the preceding T accounts as a reference guide. They will be covered as part of our discussion on completing the payroll process.

Learning Unit 8-1 Recording Payroll and Payroll Tax Expense and Paying the Payroll

At this point in the payroll process, Katherine Kurtz, the accountant for Travelwithus.com, has calculated gross earnings, deductions for employee withholding taxes, and net pay for each of Travelwithus.com's employees. She entered these amounts into two accounting records for Travelwithus.com called the payroll register and the employee earnings record. She also computed the amount of payroll taxes that Travelwithus.com must pay as an employer. At this point, Katherine must record these payroll amounts in the accounts of Travelwithus.com by making journal entries in the general journal and posting these entries to accounts in the general ledger. By entering these amounts into Travelwithus.com's accounting system, Travelwithus.com's financial statements will include these payroll transactions.

Recording Payroll

LO1

Before we discuss how payroll transactions are recorded, let's first review the accounts that we will be using and the rules for increasing and decreasing these accounts:

Accounts Affected	Category	↑ ↓	Rules	Financial Statement
Business Scheduling Expense	Expense	↑	Dr.	Income Statement
Cruise Scheduling Expense	Expense	↑	Dr.	Income Statement
Payroll Tax Expense	Expense	↑	Dr.	Income Statement
Workers' Compensation Insurance Expense	Expense	↑	Dr.	Income Statement
Payroll Cash	Asset	↑	Dr.	Balance Sheet
Prepaid Workers' Compensation Insurance	Asset	↑	Dr.	Balance Sheet
FICA OASDI Payable	Liability	↑	Cr.	Balance Sheet
FICA Medicare Payable	Liability	↑	Cr.	Balance Sheet
FIT Payable	Liability	↑	Cr.	Balance Sheet
SIT Payable	Liability	↑	Cr.	Balance Sheet
FUTA Payable	Liability	↑	Cr.	Balance Sheet
SUTA Payable	Liability	↑	Cr.	Balance Sheet
Medical Insurance Payable	Liability	↑	Cr.	Balance Sheet
Wages and Salaries Payable	Liability	↑	Cr.	Balance Sheet

Katherine needs to record the expense of wages and salaries, and the information needed to make these journal entries comes from the hourly and salaried payroll registers. Figure 8.1 on the following page shows the hourly payroll register for the current payroll period. Katherine locates this register and uses totals from it to make the following journal entry:

GENERAL JOURNAL

Date			PR	Dr.	Cr.
200X					
Oct.	29	Business Scheduling Expense		957 60	
		Cruise Scheduling Expense		2319 30	
		FIT Payable			340 00
		SIT Payable			262 15
		FICA OASDI Payable			203 17
		FICA Medicare Payable			47 52
		Medical Insurance Payable			99 00
		Wages and Salaries Payable			2325 06
		To record payroll for the pay period ending October 29, 200X			

TRAVELWITHUS.COM INC.
HOURLY EMPLOYEE PAYROLL REGISTER
OCTOBER 16 – 29

Employee / Social Security No.	Allowances and Marital Status	Previous Earnings (YTD)	Current Earnings: Regular Hours	Regular Rate	Regular Amount	Overtime Hours	Overtime Rate	Overtime Amount	Gross	Current Earnings (YTD)
Higuera, Stephanie	S-1	1851360	78	1140	88920	4	1710	6840	95760	1947120
123-45-6789										
Sui, Annie	S-0	212100	80	1515	121200	4	22725	9090	130290	342390
123-45-6788										
Taylor, Harold	S-2	1904370	78	1210	94380	4	1815	7260	101640	2006010
123-45-6787										
TOTALS					304500			23190	327690	4295520

TRAVELWITHUS.COM INC.
HOURLY EMPLOYEE PAYROLL REGISTER
OCTOBER 16 – 29

Employee / Social Security No.	Taxable Earnings: FUTA/SUTA	Taxable Earnings: OASDI	Deductions: FIT	SIT	FICA: OASDI	FICA: Medicare	Medical Insurance	Net Pay	Check No.	Account Charged: Business Scheduling Expense	Cruise Scheduling Expense
Higuera, Stephanie	—	95760	9200	7661	5937	1389	3300	68273	820	95760	
123-45-6789											
Sui, Annie	130290	130290	16700	10423	8078	1889	3300	89900	821		130290
123-45-6788											
Taylor, Harold	—	101640	8100	8131	6302	1474	3300	74333	822		101640
123-45-6787											
TOTALS	130290	327690	34000	26215	20317	4752	9900	232506		95760	231930

FIGURE 8.1 Payroll Register

A couple things may be surprising about the journal entry. First, notice that the gross earnings, not the net pay, are recorded as expenses for the two different departments that the employees worked in. This total amount of earnings is the real expense to Travelwithus.com. Employees will actually only receive the lower, net pay; the difference relates to deductions that the employees must "pay" to the federal and state governments in the form of withholdings for the different kinds of taxes and insurance.

Also notice that the amounts of taxes withheld are recorded in "Payable" accounts, which means that they are liabilities of Travelwithus.com. How can Travelwithus.com be liable for these taxes if the taxes are paid by employees? The answer is that Travelwithus.com collects these amounts by withholding them from the paychecks of its employees and then turns them over to the federal and, in this case, state governments. In other words, Travelwithus.com is the intermediary in this process. Until it does pay these amounts to the governments, Travelwithus.com owes these taxes to the governments. The same is true of the medical insurance premiums that the employees pay; the company collects them and then pays them to the insurance company.

Recording Payroll Tax Expense

Katherine's next task is to record the employer payroll taxes for Travelwithus.com, and the entry to record the taxes for the current hourly payroll follows:

GENERAL JOURNAL

Date			PR	Dr.	Cr.
200X					
Oct.	29	Payroll Tax Expense		331 47	
		FICA OASDI Payable			203 17
		FICA Medicare Payable			47 52
		FUTA Payable			10 42
		SUTA Payable			70 36
		To record payroll tax expense for the pay period ending October 29, 200X			

Notice that FICA OASDI, FICA Medicare, FUTA, and SUTA were recorded in separate liability accounts because they are different taxes and, except for the FICA taxes, are paid to different government agencies. Also note that the amount of all of these taxes are added together and recorded as one amount for Travelwithus.com's **payroll tax expense**. These amounts are an expense to Travelwithus.com because they represent the cost of the payroll taxes that it must pay as an employer.

Paying the Payroll and Recording the Payment

LO2

Katherine next must record the payment of payroll to Travelwithus.com's employees:

GENERAL JOURNAL

Date			PR	Dr.	Cr.
200X					
Nov.	3	Wages and Salaries Payable		2325 06	
		Payroll Cash			2325 06
		To record the payment of hourly payroll for the pay period ending October 29, 200X			

Travelwithus.com, like most companies, uses a special checking account for paying its payroll. This account is called Payroll Cash and only paychecks are written from this account. A company with a substantial number of employees might want to use an extra account just for payroll for a number of reasons. First, having a separate account just for paychecks provides much better internal control over the funds deposited to pay employees. Also, because only payroll checks are written from this account, it is easier to reconcile it to the bank statement each month and determine whether someone has not cashed his or her paycheck for some reason. Finally, the business can still manage its cash effectively even with this extra bank account; the business simply deposits the total net pay amount in this account and thus has enough money to pay every paycheck without leaving extra in the account that could be used for other purposes.

The paychecks that Travelwithus.com gives to its employees are, like the paychecks of most companies, attached to pay stubs that show the employee's gross earnings, deductions for employee withholding taxes, and net pay. Stephanie Higuera's current paycheck and stub look like this:

Travelwithus.com Inc.

Employee	Social Security	Check	Net Pay	Pay Date	Marital Status	Allowances
Stephanie Higuera	123-45-6789	820	$682.73	11/03/200X	S	1

Earnings	Current			Deductions		
	Pay Rate	Hours	Earnings	Item	Current	YTD
Regular Earnings	11.40	78	889.20	FIT	92.00	2,066.00
Overtime Earnings	17.10	4	68.40	SIT	76.61	1,557.70
Current Gross Earnings			957.60	OASDI	59.37	1,207.21
				Medicare	13.89	282.33
				Medical insurance	33.00	693.00
				Total	274.87	5,806.24

Travelwithus.com Inc.
504 Washington Blvd.
Salem, MA 01970

11-325/1210

No. 820

November 3, 200X

PAY TO THE ORDER OF Stephanie Higuera $682.73

Six hundred eighty two and 73/100 DOLLARS

BC Bank of Commerce

MEMO October 16–29 payroll

Julia Regan

LEARNING UNIT 8-1 REVIEW

AT THIS POINT you should be able to

- Explain how to use the payroll register to record the payroll.
- Journalize the payroll.
- Journalize the employer's payroll tax expense.
- Journalize the payment of a payroll.

Self-Review Quiz 8-1

Given the following information, prepare the general journal entry to record the payroll tax expense for Bill Co. for the weekly payroll of Oct 29. Assume the following:

- SUTA tax is paid at a rate of 5.6% on the first $7,000 of earnings.
- FUTA tax is paid at the net rate of .8% on the first $7,000 of earnings.
- FICA tax rate for OASDI is 6.2% on $102,000, and Medicare is 1.45% on all earnings.

Employee	Cumulative Pay Before This Week's Payroll	Gross Pay for the Week
Bill Jones	$6,000	$800
Julie Warner	$6,600	$400
Al Brooks	$7,900	$700

Solution to Self-Review Quiz 8-1

GENERAL JOURNAL

Date		Account	PR	Dr.	Cr.
200X					
Oct.	29	Payroll Tax Expense		222 15	
		FICA OASDI Payable			117 80
		FICA Medicare Payable			27 55
		FUTA Payable			9 60
		SUTA Payable			67 20
		To record payroll tax expense for the pay period ending July 8, 200X			

FICA OASDI = $1,900 × .062 = $117.80

FICA Medicare = $1,900 × .0145 = $ 27.55

FUTA = $1,200 × .008 = $ 9.60

SUTA = $1,200 × .056 = $ 67.20

Remember that OASDI and Medicare are employer payroll taxes even though employees pay these taxes, too.

Learning Unit 8-2 Paying Fit and Fica Taxes and Completing the Employer's Quarterly Federal Tax Return, Form 941

As we discussed in Chapter 7, both employers and employees pay payroll taxes. Employees pay these amounts not by writing checks to the different levels of government, but by having the amounts of these taxes taken out, or withheld, from the amount of pay that they actually receive. Employers withhold these amounts, report them and the related earnings to federal, state, and sometimes local governments, and then turn them over to those levels of government. Let's now discuss how Travelwithus.com carries out these responsibilities.

For Travelwithus.com, the process began when the business opened. When opening a business, every employer must get a federal identification number. This number is also called an **employer identification number (EIN)**, and is like a Social Security number for businesses in the sense that it identifies businesses to the government. To get an EIN, an employer fills out **Form SS-4**, much like individuals fill out Form SS-5 get a Social Security number. Travelwithus.com will use its EIN, 58-1213479, to report employee earnings and payroll taxes.

Travelwithus.com must next determine when its payroll taxes are due to the government, and due dates vary according to the type of tax being paid.

LO3 Paying FIT and FICA Taxes

As required by law, Travelwithus.com withholds federal income tax from employees' paychecks, along with Social Security (OASDI) and Medicare taxes as established by the **Federal Insurance Contribution Act** or **FICA.** As the employer, Travelwithus.com reports and pays these taxes to the federal government. The **Federal Unemployment Tax Act (FUTA)** tax is the unemployment tax that employers pay to the federal government, which is paid and reported separately. To see how Travelwithus.com reports the FIT and FICA taxes to the federal government, let's look at its payroll information for the last **calendar quarter** of the year, which covers October, November, and December.

To comply with federal law, Travelwithus.com must do two things: First, it must determine when FIT and FICA taxes need to be paid to the federal government and make this payment on time. Second, it must report these taxes on **Form 941, the Employer's Quarterly Federal Tax Return.** Figure 8.2 contains a worksheet that Katherine prepared from payroll registers to make sure that these two tasks happen the way they should.

FIGURE 8.2 Form 941 Worksheet

TRAVELWITHUS.COM INC.
Form 941 Taxes
4th Quarter

Payroll Period		Pay Check Date	Earnings	FIT	Taxable FICA Wages for OASDI	Taxable FICA Wages for Medicare	FICA OASDI EE + ER*	FICA Medicare EE + ER	Total Tax	Cumulative Tax
October	2–15	Oct. 20	3,680.75	393.84	3,680.75	3,680.75	456.41	106.74	956.99	956.99
October	16–29	Nov. 3	3,276.90	340.00	3,276.90	3,276.90	406.34	95.04	841.38	1,798.37
October	31	Oct. 31	18,387.33	3,493.59	18,387.33	18,387.33	2,280.03	533.23	6,306.85	8,105.22
Oct./Nov.	30–12	Nov. 17	3,276.90	352.00	3,276.90	3,276.90	406.34	95.03	853.37	8,958.59
November	13–26	Dec. 1	3,870.02	414.09	3,870.02	3,870.02	479.88	112.23	1,006.20	9,964.79
November	30	Nov. 30	18,387.33	3,493.59	18,387.33	18,387.33	2,280.03	533.23	6,306.85	16,271.64
Nov./Dec.	27–10	Dec. 15	3,340.60	357.44	3,340.60	3,340.60	414.23	96.88	868.55	17,140.19
December	11–24	Dec. 29	3,214.50	343.95	3,214.50	3,214.50	398.60	93.22	835.77	17,975.96
December	25–31	Dec. 29	1,578.90	168.94	1,578.90	1,578.90	195.78	45.79	410.51	18,386.47
December	31	Dec. 29	18,387.33	3,493.59	16,887.33	18,387.33	2,094.03	533.23	6,120.85	24,507.32
4th Quarter Totals			77,400.56	12,851.03	75,900.56	77,400.56	9,411.67	2,244.62	24,507.32	24,507.32
			(a)	(b)	(c)	(d)	(e)	(f)	(g)	(h)

*EE stands for employee; ER stands for employer

Notice a few things about this worksheet. First, look at the payroll period dates and see that some cover two-week periods and others show the last day of the month. Remember that the two types of dates relate to the two types of payroll that Travelwithus.com has, hourly and salaried. Next, observe that the quarter is 13 weeks long. By putting 13 weeks into each quarter, companies report all 52 weeks of a calendar year. Also, FIT and FICA are shown in separate columns because the IRS wants those amounts reported separately. Finally, notice that for the December 31 monthly payroll not all of the wages earned are taxable for OASDI because an employee has reached the $102,000 wage base limit by this point in the year.

The total amount of taxes due must be deposited in what is called an authorized depository in Travelwithus.com's area of the country, or in a Federal Reserve Bank. Authorized depositories are banks that have been authorized by the Federal Reserve System to accept payroll deposits from their own checking account customers. A Federal Reserve Bank can accept payroll tax deposits from any business, no matter where the business keeps its checking account.

Types of Payroll Tax Depositors To determine when payroll taxes are due, for payroll tax deposit purposes employers are usually classified as either monthly or semiweekly depositors. Rarely a company will owe less than $2,500 in total taxes, but in this case the taxes may be deposited quarterly. A **monthly depositor** is an employer who only has to deposit **Form 941 taxes** (federal income tax withholdings, OASDI, and Medicare) on the 15th day of every month. **Semiweekly depositors** must deposit their Form 941 taxes once or twice each week, depending on when payroll is paid. These classifications last for an entire calendar year, and employers are reevaluated every year.

Employers are classified according to the dollar amount of the Form 941 taxes that they have paid in the past. The IRS developed a rule known as the **look-back period** rule to determine how to classify an employer for payroll tax deposits. Under this rule, the IRS looks back to a one-year time period that begins on July 1 and ends the following June 30 of the previous year. If during this look-back period an employer paid less than $50,000 of Form 941 taxes, then it is classified as a monthly depositor. Alternately, if the employer paid $50,000 or more during this period, then it is considered a semiweekly depositor. New companies are automatically classified as monthly depositors until they have been in business long enough to have a look-back period that can be used to classify them. Figure 8.3 shows how the look-back period works.

Travelwithus.com is a semiweekly depositor because it made more than $50,000 of FIT and FICA deposits during the most recent look-back period.

Rules for Monthly Depositors If an employer is classified as a monthly depositor, the FIT and both the employee and employer OASDI and Medicare taxes accumulated during any month must be deposited by the 15th day of the next month. If the 15th is a Saturday, Sunday, or bank holiday, then the deposit must be made on the next **banking day.**

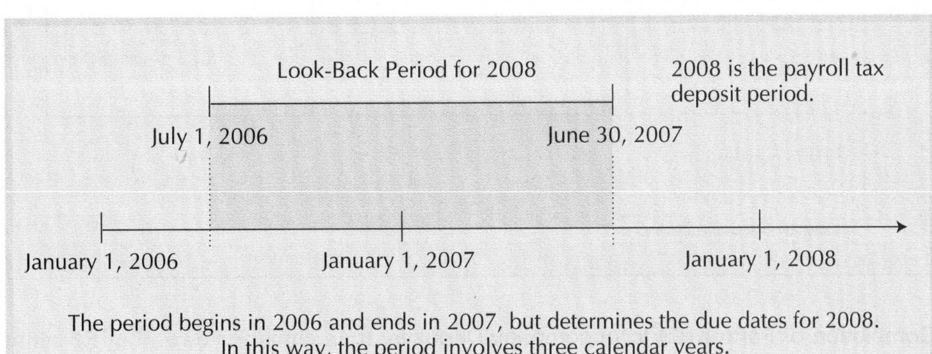
Look-Back Period for 2008
2008 is the payroll tax deposit period.
July 1, 2006
June 30, 2007
January 1, 2006
January 1, 2007
January 1, 2008
The period begins in 2006 and ends in 2007, but determines the due dates for 2008.
In this way, the period involves three calendar years.

FIGURE 8.3 Look-Back Illustration

Rules for Semiweekly Depositors If an employer is classified as a semiweekly depositor, as a general rule it always has three banking days to make its payroll tax deposit. However, semiweekly depositors like Travelwithus.com may have to make up to two payroll tax deposits every week, depending on when they pay their employees. According to the IRS, for this purpose, each week begins on Wednesday and ends on the following Tuesday. This week is broken into two parts, Wednesday through Friday, and Saturday through Tuesday. If the company's payday is a Wednesday, Thursday, or Friday, the payroll tax deposit is due on the following Wednesday. If the company's payday is a Saturday, Sunday, Monday, or Tuesday, the payroll tax deposit is due on the following Friday.

Thus, if an employer pays its employees on a Thursday and a Monday, it must make two payroll tax deposits, one on Wednesday for the Thursday payday, and one on Friday for the Monday payday. If a bank holiday occurs between a payday and the day when the payroll tax deposit is due, the employer gets an extra day to make the deposit. So, a deposit due on a Wednesday will be due on Thursday, or a Friday deposit will be due on the following Monday.

The diagram in Figure 8.4 shows how these rules work:

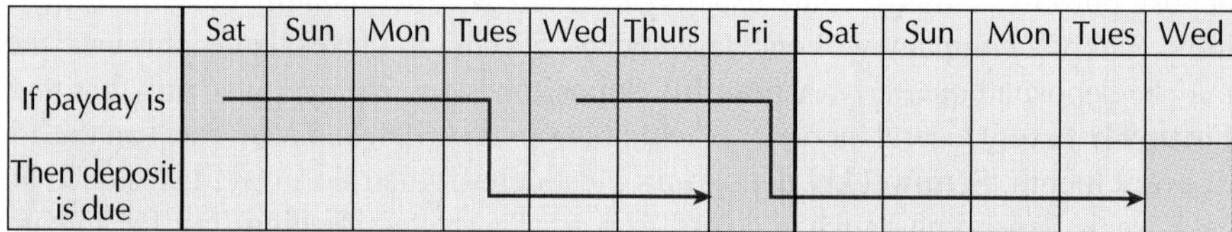

Sat
Sun
Mon
Tues
Wed
Thurs
Fri
Sat
Sun
Mon
Tues
Wed
If payday is
Then deposit is due

FIGURE 8.4 Semiweekly Deposit Rules Illustration

See Figure 8.5 to see how the rules apply to Travelwithus.com. Remember that Travelwithus.com's hourly payroll is always paid on a Friday. Because Travelwithus.com is a semiweekly payroll tax depositor, its Form 941 payroll tax deposits for its hourly payroll are due on the following Wednesday. Because its hourly payroll is paid on a biweekly, or every other week, basis, Travelwithus.com will need to make a deposit every other Wednesday. However, if we look at week 52, the payday for this week is Friday, December 29, which is two days before New Year's Day. Under the law, January 1 is a federal holiday, so Katherine must apply the rule regarding a holiday that falls between a payday and a tax deposit day and will make the Form 941 tax deposit not on Wednesday but on Thursday, January 4, of the next year.

Travelwithus.com also has a salaried payroll, and this payroll is paid on the last day of the month. In October, the last day of the month is a Tuesday, so Travelwithus.com will make its Form 941 tax deposit for this payroll on the following Friday.

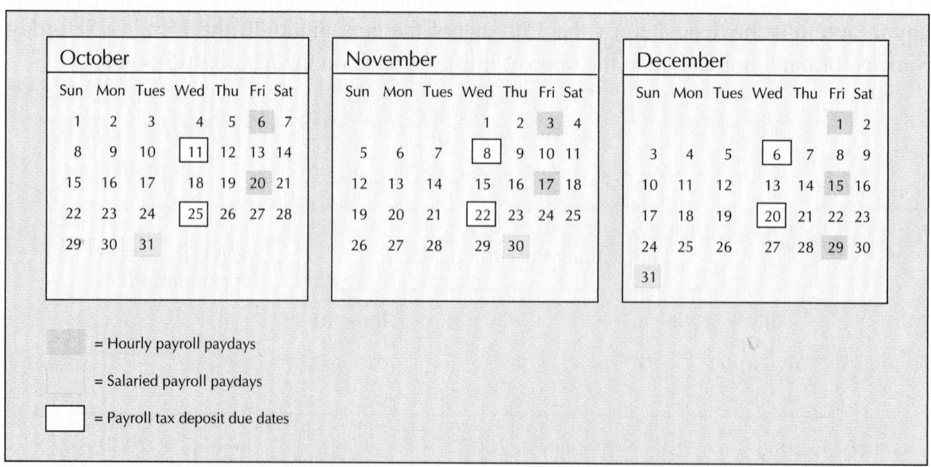

FIGURE 8.5 Third Quarter Payroll Calendar for Travelwithus.com

Completion of Form 8109 to Accompany Deposits If an employer owes the IRS more than $200,000 of deposits in a year in total, then the IRS requires it to pay Form 941 taxes by the Electronic Federal Tax Payment System (EFTPS). If the amount owed is less than

$200,000 as it is for Travelwithus.com, then the IRS allows the employer to pay Form 941 taxes by check. The IRS then also requires employers to use **Form 8109, Federal Tax Deposit Coupon,** to make these deposits. This form is much like a deposit slip used to make deposits into bank accounts, and goes with the check that Travelwithus.com deposits. Remember that by depositing the amount of Form 941 taxes with an authorized financial institution, Travelwithus.com is "paying" these taxes to the IRS.

Katherine received a book of 8109 coupons when she got the EIN for Travelwithus.com. Figure 8.6 on the following page shows a completed Form 8109 for Travelwithus.com. Notice that Katherine completed this coupon for the tax deposit that needed to be made to cover the 941 taxes for the October 16–29 hourly pay period that was paid on November 3. Also notice that the dollar amount at the top of the form, $841.38, is the same as the amount found in the total tax column for the pay period in Figure 8.2. The "941" bubble in the "Type of Tax" section is filled in, as is the "4th Quarter" bubble in the "Tax Period" portion of the coupon. By darkening these bubbles, Travelwithus.com tells the IRS what kind of tax is being reported and to which quarter the deposit applies.

The last task that Katherine must perform is to record the payment of the FIT and FICA taxes. The journal entry that she makes looks like this:

GENERAL JOURNAL

Date			PR	Dr.	Cr.
200X					
Nov.	8	FICA OASDI Payable		406 34	
		FICA Medicare Payable		95 04	
		FIT Payable		340 00	
		Cash			841 38
		To record payment of FIT and FICA			
		taxes for pay period ending			
		October 29, 200X			

To get a better idea of how payroll tax amounts appear in the accounting system of Travelwithus.com, let's check out its general ledger for the FICA OASDI Payable and FICA Medicare Payable accounts:

FICA OASDI Payable — Account No. 203

Date		PR	Dr.	Cr.	Cr. Bal.
200X					
Oct.	15	GJ28		456 41	456 41
	25	GJ28	456 41		0
	29	GJ29		406 34	406 34
	31	GJ29		2280 03	2686 37
Nov.	3	GJ29	2280 03		406 34
	8	GJ30	406 34		0

FICA Medicare Payable — Account No. 204

Date		PR	Dr.	Cr.	Cr. Bal.
200X					
Oct.	15	GJ28		106 74	106 74
	25	GJ28	106 74		0
	29*	GJ29		95 04	95 04
	31	GJ29		533 23	628 27
Nov.	3	GJ29	533 23		95 04
	8	GJ30	95 04		0

*This represents both the employee and employer deductions.

Notice several things about the ledger accounts. First, the entries on October 29 crediting the FICA OASDI Payable and FICA Medicare Payable accounts came from the general journal entries on this date because the payroll and payroll taxes were recorded on this date. These amounts represent both the employee and employer's shares of OASDI and Medicare. Also notice that the entries on November 8 debiting FICA OASDI for $406.34 and FICA Medicare for $95.04 came from the general journal. They are part of the payment that Travelwithus.com deposited with the Form 941 taxes. To summarize, journal entries crediting these accounts record tax liabilities, and journal entries debiting these accounts record payments of these taxes.

FIGURE 8.6 Completed Form 8109

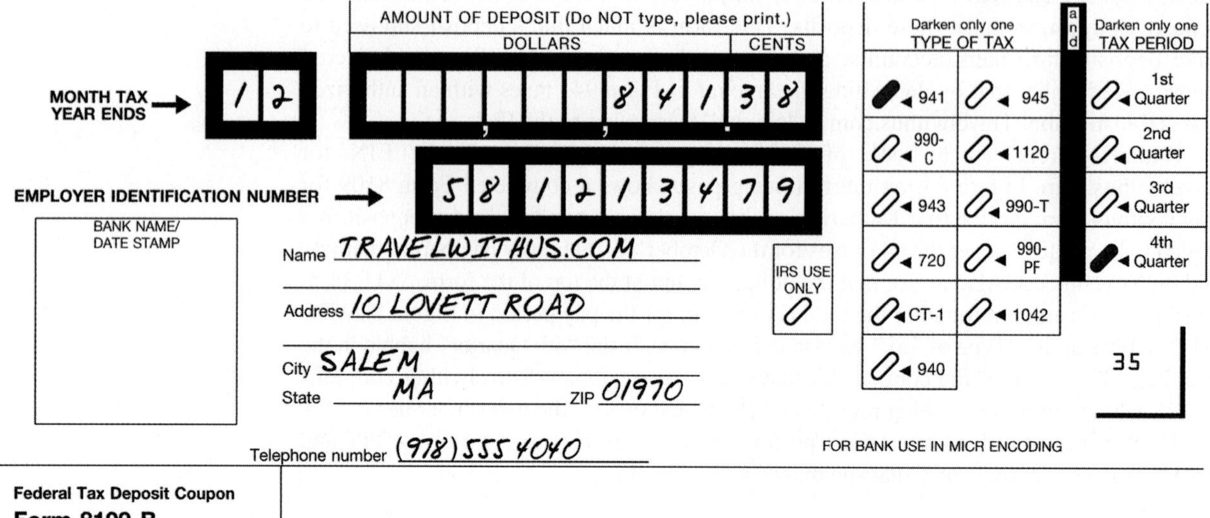

MONTH TAX YEAR ENDS 1 2

AMOUNT OF DEPOSIT (Do NOT type, please print.)

DOLLARS 841 CENTS 38

EMPLOYER IDENTIFICATION NUMBER 58 1213479

BANK NAME/ DATE STAMP

Name TRAVELWITHUS.COM

Address 10 LOVETT ROAD

City SALEM

State MA ZIP 01970

Telephone number (978) 555 4040

IRS USE ONLY

Darken only one TYPE OF TAX: 941 (darkened), 945, 990-C, 1120, 943, 990-T, 720, 990-PF, CT-1, 1042, 940

Darken only one TAX PERIOD: 1st Quarter, 2nd Quarter, 3rd Quarter, 4th Quarter (darkened)

35

FOR BANK USE IN MICR ENCODING

Federal Tax Deposit Coupon
Form 8109-B

SEPARATE ALONG THIS LINE AND SUBMIT TO DEPOSITARY WITH PAYMENT **OMB NO. 1545-0257**

Note: *Except for the name, address, and telephone number, entries must be made in pencil.* ***Use soft lead*** *(for example, a #2 pencil) so that the entries can be read more accurately by optical scanning equipment. The name, address, and telephone number may be completed other than by hand.* ***You cannot use photocopies of the coupons to make your deposits. Do not*** *staple, tape, or fold the coupons.*

Purpose of form. Use Form 8109-B to make a tax deposit **only** in the following two situations:

1. You have not yet received your resupply of preprinted deposit coupons (Form 8109); or

2. You are a new entity and have already been assigned an employer identification number (EIN), but you have not received your initial supply of preprinted deposit coupons (Form 8109). If you have not received your EIN, see ***Exceptions*** below.

Note: *If you do not receive your resupply of deposit coupons and a deposit is due or you do not receive your initial supply within 5–6 weeks of receipt of your EIN, call 1-800-829-4933.*

How to complete the form. Enter your name as shown on your return or other IRS correspondence, address, and EIN in the spaces provided. **Do not** make a name or address change on this form (see **Form 8822,** Change of Address). If you are required to file a Form 1120, 990-C, 990-PF (with net investment income), 990-T, or 2438, enter the month in which your tax year ends in the MONTH TAX YEAR ENDS boxes. For example, if your tax year ends in January, enter 01; if it ends in December, enter 12. Make your entries for EIN and MONTH TAX YEAR ENDS (if applicable) as shown in **Amount of deposit** below.

Exceptions. If you have applied for an EIN, have not received it, and a deposit must be made, **do not** use Form 8109-B. Instead, send your payment to the IRS address where you file your return. Make your check or money order payable to the United States Treasury and show on it your name (as shown on **Form SS-4,** Application for Employer Identification Number), address, kind of tax, period covered, and date you applied for an EIN. **Do not** use Form 8109-B to deposit delinquent taxes assessed by the IRS. Pay those taxes directly to the IRS. See **Circular E,** Employer's Tax Guide, for information on depositing by electronic funds transfer.

Amount of deposit. Enter the amount of the deposit in the space provided. Enter the amount legibly, forming the characters as shown below:

1 2 3 4 5 6 7 8 9 0

Hand print money amounts without using dollar signs, commas, a decimal point, or leading zeros. If the deposit is for whole dollars only, enter "00" in the CENTS boxes. For example, a deposit of $7,635.22 would be entered like this:

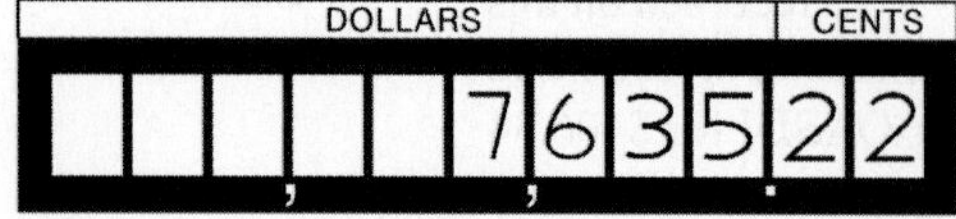

DOLLARS 7635 CENTS 22

Caution: *Darken one space each in the TYPE OF TAX and TAX PERIOD columns as explained below. Darken the space to the left of the applicable tax form and tax period. Darkening the wrong space may delay proper crediting of your account.*

Types of Tax

Form 941 Employer's Quarterly Federal Tax Return (includes Forms **941-M, 941-PR,** and **941-SS**)

Form 943 Employer's Annual Tax Return for Agricultural Employers

Form 945 Annual Return of Withheld Federal Income Tax

Form 720 Quarterly Federal Excise Tax Return

Form CT-1 Employer's Annual Railroad Retirement Tax Return

Form 940 Employer's Annual Federal Unemployment (FUTA) Tax Return (includes Form **940-PR**)

Form 1120 U.S. Corporation Income Tax Return (includes Form **1120** series of returns and Form **2438**)

Form 990-C Farmers' Cooperative Association Income Tax Return

Form 990-T Exempt Organization Business Income Tax Return

Form 990-PF Return of Private Foundation or Section 4947(a)(1) Nonexempt Charitable Trust Treated as a Private Foundation

Form 1042 Annual Withholding Tax Return for U.S. Source Income of Foreign Persons

Marking the Proper Tax Period

Payroll taxes and withholding. For Forms 941, 940, 943, 945, CT-1, and 1042, if your liability was incurred during:

- January 1 through March 31, darken the 1st quarter space
- April 1 through June 30, darken the 2nd quarter space
- July 1 through September 30, darken the 3rd quarter space
- October 1 through December 31, darken the 4th quarter space

Note: *If the liability was incurred during one quarter and deposited in another quarter, darken the space for the quarter in which the tax liability was incurred. For example, if the liability was incurred in March and deposited in April, darken the 1st quarter space.*

Excise taxes. For Form 720, follow the instructions above for Forms 941, 940, etc. For Form 990-PF, with net investment income, follow the instructions below for Form 1120, 990-C, etc.

Income Taxes (Form 1120, 990-C, 990-T, and 2438). To make an estimated tax deposit for any quarter of the current tax year, **darken only the 1st quarter space.**

Example 1. If your tax year ends on December 31, 2007, and a deposit for 2007 is being made between January 1 and December 31, 2007, darken the 1st quarter space.

Department of the Treasury
Internal Revenue Service

Cat. No. 61042S

Form **8109-B**

Completing the Employer's Quarterly Federal Tax Return, Form 941

The IRS requires all employers to complete tax returns reporting FICA OASDI, FICA Medicare, and FIT taxes. If these taxes total less than $2,500 for a calendar year, then employers will prepare **Form 944, Employer's Annual Federal Tax Return.** This form is due from employers by January 31 of the following year. Employers will complete this return only if the IRS notifies them that it is the form that they must use. If, however, taxes total more than $2,500 for a calendar year, then employers must instead complete Form 941, Employer's Quarterly Federal Tax Return, and submit it to the IRS for every quarter in a calendar year. Katherine Kurtz, the accountant for Travelwithus.com, used the worksheet in Figure 8.2 to prepare Form 941 for the last quarter of the year because Travelwithus.com's taxes exceeded $2,500.

The top section of Travelwithus.com's fourth quarter Form 941 in Figure 8.7 on the following page identifies the taxpayer, Travelwithus.com, and lists its address, the date that the quarter ended, and its EIN. Refer back to the worksheet in Figure 8.2 and use the letters below the column totals to follow amounts from this worksheet to the Form 941. Line-by-line instructions for completing the Form 941 are as follows:

Part 1: *Answering questions that relate to the current quarter.*

Line 1: This line is used to show how many employees were paid during the quarter.

2: This line is used to report total gross earnings for the quarter, which is $77,400.56 per column (a) of the worksheet.

3: Total income tax withheld is $12,851.03, which comes from column (b).

4: No entry is needed here; this line is only used for special situations.

5a, Column 1: The wages subject to FICA OASDI tax are the total taxable earnings of $75,900.56, which match column (c). The amount on this line is different from the line 2 amount because one employee reached the OASDI wage base limit of $102,000.

5a, Column 2: Katherine multiples the amount on line 5a, Column 1, by 12.4%, which is the 6.2% rate for employees and the 6.2% rate for employers, to get the tax of $9,411.67 entered here. Notice that this amount matches column (e) of the worksheet.

5b: This line is used to report taxable tips that employees might have received. Travelwithus.com employees did not receive any tips, so this line is left blank.

5c, Column 1: The wages subject to Medicare tax are the total taxable earnings of $77,400.56, which match column (d). The amount on this line is the same as the line 2 amount because the Medicare tax has no wage base limit.

5c, Column 2: Katherine multiplies the amount on line 5c, Column 1, by 2.9%, which is the 1.45% rate for employees and the 1.45% rate for employers, to get the tax of $2,244.62 entered here. Notice that this amount matches column (f) of the worksheet.

5d: The total of OASDI tax of $9,411.67 and Medicare tax of $2,244.62 is $11,656.29.

6: This line is used to report the total income tax, OASDI tax, and Medicare tax withheld of $24,507.32. It is the sum of lines 3 and 5d. Notice that it matches column (g).

7a–h: These lines are used to report special tax adjustments. None apply to Travelwithus.com, so these lines are left blank.

8: This line reports total tax after adjustments, so it is the same as line 6.

9: If Travelwithus.com advanced any earned income credit to its employees, it would deduct these amounts on this line.

FIGURE 8.7 Completed Form 941

Form **941 for 200X: Employer's Quarterly Federal Tax Return** 9901

(Rev. January 2005) Department of the Treasury — Internal Revenue Service OMB No. 1545-0029

Employer identification number 5 8 – 1 2 1 3 4 7 9

Name *(not your trade name)* TRAVELWITH US.COM

Trade name *(if any)*

Address 10 LOVETT ROAD

Number Street Suite or room number

SALEM MA 01970

City State ZIP code

Report for this Quarter ...
(Check one.)

- [ ] 1: January, February, March
- [ ] 2: April, May, June
- [ ] 3: July, August, September
- [X] 4: October, November, December

Read the separate instructions before you fill out this form. Please type or print within the boxes.

Part 1: Answer these questions for this quarter.

1 Number of employees who received wages, tips, or other compensation for the pay period including: *Mar. 12* (Quarter 1), *June 12* (Quarter 2), *Sept. 12* (Quarter 3), *Dec. 12* (Quarter 4)		1	6
2 Wages, tips, and other compensation		2	77400.56
3 Total income tax withheld from wages, tips, and other compensation		3	12851.03
4 If no wages, tips, and other compensation are subject to social security or Medicare tax			☐ Check and go to line 6.
5 Taxable social security and Medicare wages and tips:			
	Column 1	*Column 2*	
5a Taxable social security wages	75900.56 × .124 =	9411.67	
5b Taxable social security tips	. × .124 =	.	
5c Taxable Medicare wages & tips	77400.56 × .029 =	2244.62	
5d Total social security and Medicare taxes (*Column 2*, lines 5a + 5b + 5c = line 5d)		5d	11656.29
6 Total taxes before adjustments (lines 3 + 5d = line 6)		6	24507.32
7 Tax adjustments (If your answer is a negative number, write it in brackets.):			
7a Current quarter's fractions of cents		.	
7b Current quarter's sick pay		.	
7c Current quarter's adjustments for tips and group-term life insurance		.	
7d Current year's income tax withholding (Attach Form 941c)		.	
7e Prior quarters' social security and Medicare taxes (Attach Form 941c)		.	
7f Special additions to federal income tax (reserved use)		.	
7g Special additions to social security and Medicare (reserved use)		.	
7h Total adjustments (Combine all amounts: lines 7a through 7g.)		7h	.
8 Total taxes after adjustments (Combine lines 6 and 7h.)		8	24507.32
9 Advance earned income credit (EIC) payments made to employees		9	.
10 Total taxes after adjustment for advance EIC (lines 8 – 9 = line 10)		10	24507.32
11 Total deposits for this quarter, including overpayment applied from a prior quarter		11	24507.32
12 Balance due (lines 10 – 11 = line 12) Make checks payable to the *United States Treasury*		12	.
13 Overpayment (If line 11 is more than line 10, write the difference here.)		.	Check one ☐ Apply to next return. ☐ Send a refund.

Next ➔

For Privacy Act and Paperwork Reduction Act Notice, see the back of the Payment Voucher. Cat. No. 17001Z Form **941** (Rev. 1-2005)

FIGURE 8.7 *(continued)*

9902

Name *(not your trade name)* TRAVELWITHUS.COM	**Employer identification number** 58 - 1213479

Part 2: Tell us about your deposit schedule for this quarter.

If you are unsure about whether you are a monthly schedule depositor or a semiweekly schedule depositor, see *Pub. 15 (Circular E)*, section 11.

14 [M][A] Write the state abbreviation for the state where you made your deposits OR write "MU" if you made your deposits in *multiple* states.

15 Check one: ☐ Line 10 is less than $2,500. Go to Part 3.

☐ You were a monthly schedule depositor for the entire quarter. Fill out your tax liability for each month. Then go to Part 3.

Tax liability:	
Month 1	.
Month 2	.
Month 3	.
Total	. Total must equal line 10.

☒ You were a semiweekly schedule depositor for any part of this quarter. Fill out *Schedule B (Form 941): Report of Tax Liability for Semiweekly Schedule Depositors,* and attach it to this form.

Part 3: Tell us about your business. If a question does NOT apply to your business, leave it blank.

16 If your business has closed and you do not have to file returns in the future . . . . ☐ Check here, and

enter the final date you paid wages [/ /].

17 If you are a seasonal employer and you do not have to file a return for every quarter of the year . . ☐ Check here.

Part 4: May we contact your third-party designee?

Do you want to allow an employee, a paid tax preparer, or another person to discuss this return with the IRS? See the instructions for details.

☐ Yes. Designee's name [ ]

Phone ( ) – Personal Identification Number (PIN) [ ][ ][ ][ ][ ]

☒ No.

Part 5: Sign here

Under penalties of perjury, I declare that I have examined this return, including accompanying schedules and statements, and to the best of my knowledge and belief, it is true, correct, and complete.

X Sign your name here *Katherine C. Kurtz*

Print name and title KATHERINE C. KURTZ, CONTROLLER

Date 1 / 31 / 0X Phone (978) 555 - 4040

Part 6: For paid preparers only ***(optional)***

Preparer's signature [ ]

Firm's name [ ]

Address [ ] EIN [ ]

[ ] ZIP code [ ]

Date / / Phone ( ) – SSN/PTIN [ ]

☐ Check if you are self-employed.

10: This line is the difference between lines 8 and 9.

11: This line shows the total of the Form 941 deposits that Travelwithus.com made for the last quarter, $24,507.32. This amount includes the last deposit that Travelwithus.com made for the quarter on Thursday, January 4, because it applies to the December 31 biweekly and monthly payrolls.

12 and 13: Travelwithus.com's deposits exactly total the Form 941 taxes for the quarter, which means it does not have any balance due, nor has it overpaid its taxes.

Part 2: *Providing information about the deposit schedule.*

Line 14: Katherine indicates the abbreviation of the state in which Travelwithus.com has made its deposits.

Line 15: As a semiweekly depositor, Travelwithus.com checks this box and completes and attaches Schedule B: Report of Tax Liability for Semiweekly Schedule Depositors. By showing each day of the quarter, this schedule requires employers to present tax liability amounts on a day-by-day basis. The IRS requires employers to complete this schedule because, by comparing the dates of the tax liabilities to the dates that the deposits were made, it easily allows them to determine whether deposits were made on time. (Schedule B is not shown here.) The amounts for each day are added together to show the total for each month, and these monthly totals together should equal the total liability on line 10.

Part 3: *Indicating specific situations that relate to the business.*

Lines 16 and 17: If a business has not closed and is not a seasonal employer, these lines do not apply. Katherine leaves them blank.

Part 4: *Indicating whether the business would like to be contacted by the IRS regarding this return.* Katherine checks "No."

Part 5: *Signing the return.* Katherine signs the return on behalf of Travelwithus.com.

LEARNING UNIT 8-2 REVIEW

AT THIS POINT you should be able to

- Explain the purpose of Form SS-4.
- Explain which taxes are reported on Form 941.
- Understand how employers are classified as payroll tax depositors.
- Summarize Form 941 payroll tax deposit rules for monthly depositors.
- Summarize Form 941 payroll tax deposit rules for semiweekly depositors.
- Prepare and explain the purpose of Form 8109.
- Record the general journal entry to pay FIT, FICA OASDI, and FICA Medicare when a payroll tax deposit is made.
- Understand how the general journal entries recording FICA OASDI and FICA Medicare and the payment of these taxes are posted into the general ledger.
- Complete a Form 941, Employer's Quarterly Federal Tax Return, from a worksheet.

Self-Review Quiz 8-2

Carol Ann's Import Chalet is a business that employs five full-time employees and four part-time employees. The accountant for Carol Ann's determined that the business is a monthly depositor. The accountant prepared a worksheet showing the following payroll tax liabilities for the month of October:

Date	OASDI EE + ER	Medicare EE + ER	FIT
10/7	$486.56	$169.05	$829.00
10/14	$632.15	$165.01	$901.00
10/21	$579.43	$131.05	$734.00
10/28	$389.99	$142.24	$765.00
Totals	$2,088.13	$607.35	$3,229.00

1. What is the dollar amount of the Form 941 tax deposit that must be made and when must it be made according to the monthly deposit rule? Use Figure 8.5 for the date.
2. Now assume that Carol Ann is classified as a semiweekly depositor. Please calculate the amount of each Form 941 tax deposit and its due date by completing the following table (use Figure 8.5 for the dates):

Date	Date of Deposit	Amount of Deposit
10/7	?	?
10/14	?	?
10/21	?	?
10/28	?	?

The tax for Form 941 is
FICA OASDI: employee and employer
FICA Medicare: employee and employer
FIT: employee only

Solutions to Self-Review Quiz 8-2

1. As a monthly depositor, Carol Ann's deposit date is Wednesday, November 15. The total amount of the deposit is $5,924.48 ($2,088.13 + $607.35 + $3,229.00).
2. As a semiweekly depositor, Carol Ann's deposit schedule is completed as follows:

Date	Date of Deposit	Amount of Deposit	
10/7	10/13	$1,484.61	($486.56 + $169.05 + $829.00)
10/14	10/20	$1,698.16	
10/21	10/27	$1,444.48	
10/28	11/3	$1,297.23*	

*Note that this deposit will be made in November according to the calendar dates found in Figure 8.5.

Learning Unit 8-3 Preparing Forms W-2 and W-3, Paying FUTA Tax and Completing the Employer's Annual Unemployment Tax Return, Form 940, and Paying SUTA Tax and Workers' Compensation Insurance

Preparing Form W-2: Wage and Tax Statement

LO5

The Internal Revenue Service requires that employers complete Form W-2, Wage and Tax Statement, a multipart form, each calendar year. The IRS requires Travelwithus.com to give or mail copies of Form W-2 to each person who worked for the company in the past year. These forms must be distributed by January 31 of the following year. Employees use the amount on this form to prepare their income tax returns and calculate the amount of income tax they owe. They must attach one copy of the form to their federal income tax return, and other copies are attached to any state or local income tax returns that they may be required to file.

Figure 8.8 shows the W-2 that Stephanie Higuera received from Travelwithus.com. Travelwithus.com prepares the W-2s by using information from Stephanie's employee earnings record. Note that OASDI wages and taxes are shown separately from the amounts reported for Medicare wages and taxes because of the wage base limit for the OASDI tax that does not apply to the Medicare tax.

If an employee stopped working for Travelwithus.com during the year, he or she may ask for a W-2 before the year ends. Travelwithus.com must provide the W-2 within 30 days of the last paycheck or the date of the request, whichever is later. Travelwithus.com must also give copies of the W-2s for all employees to the Social Security Administration and state and local governments. It will also keep a copy for its own records.

FIGURE 8.8 Completed Form W-2

a Control number 22222	Void ☐	For Official Use Only ► OMB No. 1545-0008	
b Employer identification number (EIN) 58-1213479		1 Wages, tips, other compensation 23 723.40	2 Federal income tax withheld 2 241.86
c Employer's name, address, and ZIP code TRAVELWITHUS.COM 10 LOVETT ROAD SALEM, MA 01970		3 Social security wages 23 723.40	4 Social security tax withheld 1470.85
		5 Medicare wages and tips 23 723.40	6 Medicare tax withheld 343.99
		7 Social security tips	8 Allocated tips
d Employee's social security number 123-45-6789		9 Advance EIC payment	10 Dependent care benefits
e Employee's first name and initial STEPHANIE A.	Last name HIGUERA	Suff.	11 Nonqualified plans	12a See instructions for box 12
1014 INVERNESS WAY SOUTHSIDE, MA 01945		13 Statutory employee ☐ Retirement plan ☐ Third-party sick pay ☐	12b
		14 Other	12c
f Employee's address and ZIP code			12d

15 State	Employer's state ID number	16 State wages, tips, etc.	17 State income tax	18 Local wages, tips, etc.	19 Local income tax	20 Locality name
MA	621-8966-4	23 723.40	1897.87			

Form **W-2** **Wage and Tax Statement** 200X

Department of the Treasury—Internal Revenue Service

For Privacy Act and Paperwork Reduction Act Notice, see back of Copy D.

Copy A For Social Security Administration — Send this entire page with Form W-3 to the Social Security Administration; photocopies are **not** acceptable.

Cat. No. 10134D

Do Not Cut, Fold, or Staple Forms on This Page — Do Not Cut, Fold, or Staple Forms on This Page

Preparing Form W-3: Transmittal of Income and Tax Statements

The IRS also requires Travelwithus.com to prepare its **Form W-3, Transmittal of Wage and Tax Statements.** Employers such as Travelwithus.com send this form to the Social Security Administration along with copies of the W-2s for all employees (see Fig. 8.9). Form W-3 reports the total amounts of wages, tips, and compensation paid to employees, the total OASDI and Medicare taxes withheld, and some other information. The information used to complete Form W-3 came from a summary of the individual employee earnings records that Katherine prepared soon after the year ended. (See Fig. 8.10.)

FIGURE 8.9 Completed Form W-3

DO NOT STAPLE

a Control number	33333	For Official Use Only ► OMB No. 1545-0008	
b Kind of Payer: 941 [X] Military [ ] 943 [ ] 944 [ ] CT-1 [ ] Hshld. emp. [ ] Medicare govt. emp. [ ] Third-party sick pay [ ]		1 Wages, tips, other compensation 286 425.30	2 Federal income tax withheld 48 063.67
		3 Social security wages 284 925.30	4 Social security tax withheld 17655.37
c Total number of Forms W-2 6	d Establishment number	5 Medicare wages and tips 286 425.30	6 Medicare tax withheld 4153.17
e Employer identification number (EIN) 58-1213479		7 Social security tips	8 Allocated tips
f Employer's name TRAVELWITHUS.COM		9 Advance EIC payments	10 Dependent care benefits
		11 Nonqualified plans	12 Deferred compensation
10 LOVETT ROAD SALEM, MA 01970 g Employer's address and ZIP code		13 For third-party sick pay use only	
		14 Income tax withheld by payer of third-party sick pay	
h Other EIN used this year			
15 State MA Employer's state ID number 621-8966-4		16 State wages, tips, etc. 286 425.30	17 State income tax 22914.02
		18 Local wages, tips, etc.	19 Local income tax
Contact person KATHERINE C. KURTZ		Telephone number (978)555 4040	For Official Use Only
Email address KKURTZ@TRAVELWITH.US		Fax number (978)555 4040	

Under penalties of perjury, I declare that I have examined this return and accompanying documents, and, to the best of my knowledge and belief, they are true, correct, and complete.

Signature ► *Katherine C. Kurtz* Title ► CONTROLLER Date ► 2/28/200X

Form **W-3 Transmittal of Wage and Tax Statements** 200X Department of the Treasury Internal Revenue Service

Send this entire page with the entire Copy A page of Form(s) W-2 to the Social Security Administration. Photocopies are not acceptable.

Do not send any payment (cash, checks, money orders, etc.) with Forms W-2 and W-3.

Employers send Form W-2 and Form W-3 to the Social Security Administration for FICA tax purposes. The Social Security Administration, under a special agreement with the IRS, makes all information found on individual W-2 forms electronically available to the IRS so that it can check the accuracy of the employer's 941 forms and individual employees' federal income tax returns.

Paying FUTA Tax

LO4

If the total FUTA tax owed for the calendar year is less than $500, an employer must pay the tax to the IRS by the end of January of the next year. If the total amount owed is more than $500, then it is due by the end of the month following the end of the calendar quarter. If the employer is required to make Form 941 tax payments by EFTPS, then it must also deposit FUTA tax by this method; if not, the deposit can be made by check accompanied with Form 8109, Federal Tax Deposit Coupon, at a Federal Reserve Bank or authorized depository.

By the end of the year, all of Travelwithus.com's employees earned more than the $7,000 wage base limit, so its total FUTA tax will be calculated as follows:

6 employees × $7,000 FUTA taxable earnings × 0.8%* FUTA tax rate = $336 FUTA tax

*Normal FUTA Tax credit 6.2%–5.4%.

FIGURE 8.10 W-3 Worksheet

TRAVELWITHUS.COM INC.
W-3 Amounts
YTD Totals

Employee	Total Earnings	FICA Taxable Earnings		FICA Tax		FIT
		OASDI	Medicare	OASDI	Medicare	
Goldman, Ernie	103500 00	102000 00	103500 00	6324 00	1500 75	20097 00
Higuera, Stephanie	23723 40	23723 40	23723 40	1470 85	343 99	2241 86
Kurtz, Katherine	66448 16	66448 16	66448 16	4119 79	963 50	12625 15
Regan, Julia	58500 00	58500 00	58500 00	3627 00	848 25	9945 00
Sui, Annie	8287 14	8287 14	8287 14	513 80	120 16	1077 33
Taylor, Harold	25966 60	25966 60	25966 60	1609 93	376 52	2077 33
Total	286425 30	284925 30	286425 30	17665 37	4153 17	48063 67

Because this amount is less than $500, Katherine does not need to make a deposit during the year and will deposit the taxes by the end of January of the following year. She then makes the following journal entry to record the payment of FUTA tax.

GENERAL JOURNAL

Date			PR	Dr.	Cr.
200X					
Jan.	31	FUTA Payable		336 00	
		Cash			336 00
		To record payment of the 200X FUTA tax			

Completing the Employer's Annual Federal Unemployment (FUTA) Tax Return, Form 940

Businesses must complete **Form 940, Employer's Annual Federal Unemployment (FUTA) Tax Return.** Employers must file Form 940 by January 31 of the following year; however, if all taxes owed for the year were deposited by January 31, then the business has until February 10 to file its return.

To make sure that Travelwithus.com makes its FUTA deposits on time, Katherine keeps track of the amount of FUTA tax owed. Katherine prepared the worksheet in Figure 8.11 to determine the amount of FUTA taxes that Travelwithus.com owes for the first quarter of the year. Notice that she calculates the FUTA tax on the total wages because reporting the FUTA tax for each individual employee is not required. Also notice that Annie Sui has no earnings for the first quarter and therefore no earnings that are taxable for FUTA purposes because she was hired after the quarter began. Finally, notice that Ernie Goldman, Katherine Kurtz, and Julia Regan's first quarter earnings are greater than their FUTA taxable earnings because they earned more than $7,000 during the first quarter, and only the first $7,000 of earnings is taxable.

Although Travelwithus.com's other payroll amounts have been shown for the last quarter of the year, showing FUTA tax calculations for this quarter would not be very helpful. Almost all employees will have made more than the $7,000 FUTA limit by the start of the fourth quarter, and Travelwithus.com would only owe FUTA taxes for one employee, Annie Sui, who was hired just before the fourth quarter began.

At the end of the calendar year, Katherine prepares the Form 940 in Figure 8.12. Line-by-line instructions follow:

Part 1:

Line 1a: This line is used to show the state in which payments are made if only one state is involved.

1b is used by employers who pay state unemployment in more than one state.

Part 2: *Reporting taxable wages and FUTA tax.*

Line 3: Katherine shows the total wages and salaries paid during the year, $286,425.30, as shown on the W-3 worksheet.

4: This line is used to show any payments that are exempt from FUTA taxes, and does not apply to Travelwithus.com.

5: This line shows the amount of wages and salaries above the $7,000 limit, which is $244,425.30. Because the six employees all reached the $7,000 limit, the total limit is $42,000. Total wages and salaries of $286,425.30 minus taxable wages and salaries of $42,000 equals $244,425.30.

6: Katherine adds the total of lines 4 and 5 and gets $244,425.30.

7: Katherine subtracts line 6 from line 3 to determine the taxable amount of wages and salaries, $42,000.

8: Katherine multiplies line 7, $42,000, by the FUTA tax rate of .008 to get the total FUTA tax of $336.00 for the year.

Part 3 is used to determine adjustments to the FUTA tax calculated in line 8, if any.

Part 4 is used to calculate your FUTA tax.

12: This is the amount of FUTA tax less any adjustments made in Part 3. Travelwithus.com did not have any adjustments.

13: This line shows the amount of FUTA tax that Travelwithus.com paid for the year.

14 and 15: Travelwithus.com paid exactly the right amount of FUTA tax for the year; therefore, no balance is due and no overpayment was made.

Part 5: *Showing the tax liability by quarter.*

Katherine divides the total FUTA tax for the year into the quarters where the tax liability originated. Notice that the amount of FUTA tax for the first quarter matches the amount that Katherine calculated on the FUTA tax worksheet in Figure 8.11.

FIGURE 8.11 FUTA Worksheet

TRAVELWITHUS.COM INC.
FUTA Taxes
1st Quarter

Employee	1st Quarter Earnings	FUTA Taxable Earnings	FUTA Tax Rate	FUTA Tax
Goldman, Ernie	23,925.00	7,000.00		
Higuera, Stephanie	5,928.00	5,928.00		
Kurtz, Katherine	16,612.04	7,000.00		
Regan, Julia	14,625.00	7,000.00		
Sui, Annie	—	—		
Taylor, Harold	5,325.59	5,325.59		
Total	66,415.63	32,253.59	0.008	258.03

FIGURE 8.12 Completed Form 940

Form **940 for 200X: Employer's Annual Federal Unemployment (FUTA) Tax Return** 850108

Department of the Treasury — Internal Revenue Service OMB No. 1545-0028

(EIN) Employer identification number 5 8 – 1 2 1 3 4 7 9

Name *(not your trade name)*

Trade name *(if any)* TRAVELWITHUS.COM

Address 10 LOVETT ROAD
Number Street Suite or room number

SALEM MA 01970
City State ZIP code

Type of Return (Check all that apply.)

- ☐ **a.** Amended
- ☐ **b.** Successor employer
- ☐ **c.** No payments to employees in 2008
- ☐ **d.** Final: Business closed or stopped paying wages

Read the separate instructions before you fill out this form. Please type or print within the boxes.

Part 1: Tell us about your return. If any line does NOT apply, leave it blank.

1 **If you were required to pay your state unemployment tax in ...**

1a **One state only,** write the state abbreviation . . . . 1a M A

- OR -

1b **More than one state** (You are a multi-state employer) . . . . . 1b ☐ Check here. Fill out Schedule A.

Skip line 2 for 2008 and go to line 3.

2 If you paid wages in a state that is subject to CREDIT REDUCTION . . . . 2 ☐ Check here. Fill out Schedule A (Form 940), Part 2.

Part 2: Determine your FUTA tax before adjustments for 2008. If any line does NOT apply, leave it blank.

3 **Total payments to all employees** 3 $286,425.30

4 **Payments exempt from FUTA tax** . . . . . 4 0 .

Check all that apply: 4a ☐ Fringe benefits 4c ☐ Retirement/Pension 4e ☐ Other
4b ☐ Group-term life insurance 4d ☐ Dependent care

5 **Total of payments made to each employee in excess of $7,000** 5 244,425.30

6 **Subtotal** (line 4 + line 5 = line 6) 6 244,425.30

7 **Total taxable FUTA wages** (line 3 – line 6 = line 7) 7 42,000.00

8 **FUTA tax before adjustments** (line 7 × .008 = line 8) 8 336.00

Part 3: Determine your adjustments. If any line does NOT apply, leave it blank.

9 **If ALL of the taxable FUTA wages you paid were excluded from state unemployment tax, multiply line 7 by .054** (line 7 × .054 = line 9). Then go to line 12 . . . . . 9 0 .

10 **If SOME of the taxable FUTA wages you paid were excluded from state unemployment tax, OR you paid ANY state unemployment tax late** (after the due date for filing Form 940), fill out the worksheet in the instructions. Enter the amount from line 7 of the worksheet onto line 10 . . 10 0 .

Skip line 11 for 2008 and go to line 12.

11 If credit reduction applies, enter the amount from line 3 of Schedule A (Form 940) . . . . 11 .

Part 4: Determine your FUTA tax and balance due or overpayment for 2008. If any line does NOT apply, leave it blank.

12 **Total FUTA tax after adjustments** (lines 8 + 9 + 10 + 11 = line 12) 12 336.00

13 **FUTA tax deposited for the year, including any payment applied from a prior year** 13 336.00

14 **Balance due** (If line 12 is more than line 13, enter the difference on line 14.)

- If line 14 is more than $500, you must deposit your tax.
- If line 14 is $500 or less, you may pay with this return. For more information on how to pay, see the separate instructions . . . . . 14 .

15 **Overpayment** (If line 13 is more than line 12, enter the difference on line 15 and check a box below.) . . . . . 15 .

Check one: ☐ Apply to next return. ☐ Send a refund.

▶ You **MUST** fill out both pages of this form and **SIGN** it.

Next ➔

For Privacy Act and Paperwork Reduction Act Notice, see the back of Form 940-V, Payment Voucher. Cat. No. 11234O Form **940** (2008)

FIGURE 8.12 (continued)

Name *(not your trade name)*	**Employer identification number (EIN)** 58-1213479

Part 5: Report your FUTA tax liability by quarter only if line 12 is more than $500. If not, go to Part 6.

16 **Report the amount of your FUTA tax liability for each quarter; do NOT enter the amount you deposited. If you had no liability for a quarter, leave the line blank.**

16a **1st quarter** (January 1 – March 31) . . . . **16a** [ ]

16b **2nd quarter** (April 1 – June 30) . . . . **16b** [ ]

16c **3rd quarter** (July 1 – September 30) . . . . **16c** [ ]

16d **4th quarter** (October 1 – December 31) . . . . **16d** [ ]

17 **Total tax liability for the year** (lines 16a + 16b + 16c + 16d = line 17) **17** [ ] **Total must equal line 12.**

Part 6: May we speak with your third-party designee?

Do you want to allow an employee, a paid tax preparer, or another person to discuss this return with the IRS? See the instructions for details.

☐ **Yes.** Designee's name and phone number [ ] ( ) –

Select a 5-digit Personal Identification Number (PIN) to use when talking to IRS [ ][ ][ ][ ][ ]

☐ **No.**

Part 7: Sign here. You MUST fill out both pages of this form and SIGN it.

Under penalties of perjury, I declare that I have examined this return, including accompanying schedules and statements, and to the best of my knowledge and belief, it is true, correct, and complete, and that no part of any payment made to a state unemployment fund claimed as a credit was, or is to be, deducted from the payments made to employees. Declaration of preparer (other than taxpayer) is based on all information of which preparer has any knowledge.

X Sign your name here Katherine C. Kurtz

Print your name here: KATHERINE C. KURTZ

Print your title here: Controller

Date: 2/10/200X

Best daytime phone: ( ) –

Paid preparer's use only Check if you are self-employed . . . ☐

Preparer's name		Preparer's SSN/PTIN	
Preparer's signature		Date	/ /
Firm's name (or yours if self-employed)		EIN	
Address		Phone	( ) –
City	State	ZIP code	

Paying SUTA Tax

State Unemployment Tax Act (SUTA) taxes are paid to the government of the state in which a business is located and are typically due by the end of the month following each calendar quarter. Employers also usually are required to complete a state unemployment tax report, much like they complete Form 940. Using the first quarter earnings, Katherine calculates the SUTA tax due for the first quarter as follows:

$32,253.59 SUTA taxable earnings × 5.4% SUTA tax rate = $1,741.69

The journal entry to record the payment of SUTA follows:

GENERAL JOURNAL

Date			PR	Dr.	Cr.
200X					
April	30	SUTA Payable		1741 69	
		Cash			1741 69
		To record payment of the SUTA			
		tax for the quarter ending March 31,			
		200X			

Paying Workers' Compensation Insurance

Remember from Chapter 7 that the premium for **workers' compensation insurance** is paid at the beginning of the year based on estimated gross payroll for the year, and the journal entry to record this payment is as follows:

GENERAL JOURNAL

Date			PR	Dr.	Cr.
200X					
Jan.	5	Prepaid Workers' Compensation Insurance		1318 00	
		Cash			1318 00
		To record payment of the workers'			
		compensation insurance premium			
		for 200X			

Like any prepaid amount, this amount will gradually be transferred from the Prepaid Workers' Compensation Insurance account, an asset, to the Workers' Compensation Insurance Expense account in the month-end adjusting entries for 200X.

At the end of the year, if Travelwithus.com owes an additional premium because actual gross payroll was higher than estimated gross payroll, the payment of the additional premium would be recorded as follows:

GENERAL JOURNAL

Date			PR	Dr.	Cr.
200X					
Dec.	31	Workers' Compensation Insurance Expense		211 32	
		Cash			211 32
		To record payment of the additional			
		workers' compensation insurance			
		premium for 200X			

LEARNING UNIT 8-3 REVIEW

AT THIS POINT you should be able to

- Prepare a Form W-2 and a Form W-3.
- Explain the difference between a Form W-2 and a Form W-3.
- Prepare Form 940.
- Explain when FUTA and SUTA taxes are paid.
- Explain when workers' compensation insurance premiums are paid.
- Record the payment of FUTA, SUTA, and workers' compensation insurance amounts.

Self-Review Quiz 8-3

Are the following statements true or false?

1. Employees must receive W-4s by January 31 of the following year.
2. Form W-3 is sent to the Social Security Administration yearly.
3. A Form 940 can only be prepared by a business that employs workers in only one state.
4. The Employer's Annual Federal Unemployment Tax Return reports the employer's FICA and FIT tax liabilities.
5. A FUTA tax liability of $500 must be paid 10 days after the quarter ends.
6. Premiums for workers' compensation insurance may be adjusted based on actual payroll figures.

Solutions to Self-Review Quiz 8-3

1. False. W-2 forms must be sent to each employee by January 31 of the following year. The W-4 form is filled out by a new employee and is used for calculating federal and state income taxes.
2. True.
3. False. Form 940 can be prepared by a business that employs workers in one or more states.
4. False. The Employee's Annual Federal Unemployment Tax Return, Form 940, reports the FUTA tax liability. Form 941 reports the FICA and FIT tax liabilities.
5. False. A FUTA tax liability of $500 must be paid one month after the quarter ends.
6. True.

Remember that the employee completes a W-4 when hired. The employer completes a W-2 for the employee at the end of the year.

CHAPTER ASSIGNMENTS

SUMMARY OF KEY POINTS

LEARNING UNIT 8-1

1. The payroll register provides the data for journalizing the payroll in the general journal.
2. Deductions for payroll withholding taxes represent liabilities of the employer until paid.
3. The Accounts Charged columns of the payroll register indicate which accounts will be debited to record the total wages and salaries expense when a journal entry is prepared.
4. The accounts FICA OASDI Payable and FICA Medicare Payable accumulate the tax liabilities of both the employer and the employee for OASDI and Medicare taxes.

5. The payroll tax expense is recorded at the same time that the payroll is recorded.
6. Paying a payroll results in debiting Wages and Salaries Payable and crediting Cash or Payroll Cash.

LEARNING UNIT 8-2

1. Federal Form 941 is prepared and filed no later than one month after the calendar quarter ends. It reports the amount of FIT, OASDI, and Medicare tax withheld from employees and the OASDI and Medicare taxes due from the employer for the calendar quarter.
2. FIT, OASDI, and Medicare taxes are known as Form 941 taxes.
3. The total amount of Form 941 taxes paid by a business during a specific period of time determines how often the business will have to make its payroll tax deposits. This time period is called a look-back period.
4. Businesses will normally make their payroll tax deposits to pay their Form 941 taxes either monthly or semiweekly.
5. Different deposit rules apply to monthly and semiweekly depositors and these rules determine when deposits are due.
6. Form 941 payroll tax deposits must be made using Form 8109, known as the Federal Tax Deposit Coupon, unless they are made by EFTPS.

LEARNING UNIT 8-3

1. Information to prepare W-2 forms can be obtained from the individual employee earnings records.
2. Form W-3 is used by the Social Security Administration in verifying that taxes have been withheld as reported on individual employee W-2 forms.
3. Form 940 is prepared by January 31, after the end of the previous calendar year. This form can be filed by February 10 if all required deposits have been made by January 31.
4. If the amount of FUTA taxes is equal to or more than $500 during any calendar quarter, the deposit must be made no later than one month after the quarter ends. If the amount is less than $500, no deposit is required until the liability reaches the $500 point or until the year ends, when any tax due must be paid by January 31 of the following year.
5. The premium for workers' compensation insurance based on estimated payroll for the year is paid at the beginning of the year by the employer to protect against potential losses to its employees due to accidental death or injury incurred while on the job.

KEY TERMS

Banking day A banking day is any day that a bank is open to the public for business. Generally, a banking day will end at 2:00 or 3:00 P.M. local time. Banking business transacted after this time is usually considered to be the next day's business. Saturdays, Sundays, and federal holidays are usually not considered banking days.

Calendar quarter A three-month, 13-week time period. Four calendar quarters occur during a calendar year that runs from January 1 through December 31. The first quarter is January through March, the second is April through June, the third is July through September, and the fourth is October through December.

Employer identification number (EIN) A number assigned by the IRS that is used by an employer when recording and paying payroll and income taxes.

Federal Insurance Contribution Act (FICA) Part of the Social Security law that requires employees and employers to pay OASDI taxes and Medicare taxes.

Federal Unemployment Tax Act (FUTA) A tax paid by employers to the federal government. The current rate is 0.8% on the first $7,000 of earnings of each employee after the normal FUTA tax credit is applied.

Form SS-4 The form filled out by an employer to get an EIN. The form is sent to the IRS, which assigns the number to the business.

Form W-2, Wage and Tax Statement A form completed by the employer at the end of the calendar year to provide a summary of gross earnings and deductions to each employee. At least two copies go to the employee, one copy to the IRS, one copy to any state where employee income taxes have been withheld, one copy to the Social Security Administration, and one copy into the records of the business.

Form W-3, Transmittal of Income and Tax Statement A form completed by the employer to verify the number of W-2s and amounts withheld as shown on them. This form is sent to the Social Security Administration data processing center along with copies of each employee's W-2 forms.

Form 8109, Federal Tax Deposit Coupon A coupon that is completed and sent along with payments of tax deposits relating to Forms 940, 941, or 944. This form can also be used to deposit other types of taxes a business may owe the federal government.

Form 940, Employer's Annual Federal Unemployment Tax Return This form is used by employers at the end of the calendar year to report the amount of unemployment tax due for the year. If more than $500 is cumulatively owed in a quarter, it should be paid quarterly, one month after the end of the quarter. Normally, the report is due January 31 after the calendar year, or February 10 if an employer has already made all deposits.

Form 941, Employer's Quarterly Federal Tax Return A tax report that a business will complete after the end of each calendar quarter indicating the total FICA (OASDI and Medicare) taxes owed plus the amount of FIT withheld from employees' pay for the quarter. If federal tax deposits have been made on time, the total amount deposited should equal the amount due on Form 941. Any difference results in a payment due or a refund.

Form 941 taxes Another term used to describe FIT, OASDI, and Medicare. This name comes from the form used to report these taxes.

Form 944, Employer's Annual Federal Tax Return The new, other version of the form used by employers to report FICA (OASDI and Medicare) taxes owed and the amount of FIT withheld from an employee's pay. This version will be filed by January 31 following the end of the year and can be used by employers who owe $2,500 or less for theses taxes and who have been told by the IRS that they must file this form.

Look-back period A period of time used to determine whether a business should make its Form 941 tax deposits on a monthly or semiweekly basis. The IRS defined this period as July 1 through June 30 of the year prior to the year in which Form 941 tax deposits will be made.

Monthly depositor A business classified as a monthly depositor will make its payroll tax deposits only once each month for the amount of Form 941 taxes due from the prior month.

Payroll tax expense The cost to employers includes the total of the employer's FICA OASDI, FICA Medicare, FUTA, and SUTA taxes.

Semiweekly depositor A business classified as a semiweekly depositor may make its payroll tax deposits up to twice in one week, depending on when payroll is paid.

State Unemployment Tax Act (SUTA) A tax usually paid only by employers to the state for employee unemployment insurance.

Workers' compensation insurance Insurance paid, in advance, by an employer to protect its employees against loss due to accidental death or injury incurred during employment.

BLUEPRINT: FORM 941 TAX DEPOSIT RULES

Ten Frequently Asked Questions and Answers About Depositing OASDI, Medicare, and FIT to the Government

Here is a summary of questions and answers to help you understand the payroll tax deposit rules for Form 941 taxes:

1. **What are Form 941 taxes?** The term *Form 941 taxes* is used to describe the amount of FIT, OASDI, and Medicare paid by employees and the amount of OASDI and Medicare taxes that are matched and paid by an employer. The total of these taxes is known as Form 941 taxes because it is reported on Form 941 each quarter.

2. **When does an employer deposit Form 941 taxes?** How often an employer deposits Form 941 taxes depends on how the employer is classified for this purpose. The IRS usually classifies an employer as either a monthly or semiweekly depositor based on the amount of Form 941 taxes paid during a time period known as a look-back period.
3. **When is a look-back period?** A look-back period is a fiscal year that begins on July 1 and ends on June 30 of the year before the calendar year when the deposits will be made. For example, for the 2008 calendar year, an employer's look-back period will begin on July 1, 2006, and end on June 30, 2007.
4. **What is the dollar amount used to classify an employer for Form 941 tax deposits?** The key dollar amount used to determine whether an employer is a monthly or semiweekly depositor is $50,000 in Form 941 taxes. Two rules apply here:
   a. If the total amount deposited in Form 941 taxes is less than $50,000 during the look-back period, the employer is considered a monthly tax depositor.
   b. If the total amount deposited in Form 941 taxes is $50,000 or more during the look-back period, the employer is considered a semiweekly tax depositor.
5. **How do employers deposit Form 941 taxes?** Unless it makes its deposits by EFTPS, an employer fills out a Form 8109, Federal Tax Deposit Coupon, and gives this form with a check to a bank authorized to receive payroll tax deposits or to a Federal Reserve Bank. Usually, authorized banks will only take checks written from an account maintained at that same bank. Therefore, an employer usually cannot make a Form 941 deposit at Bank A using a check written from an account maintained at Bank B. A Federal Reserve Bank will accept a check from any U.S. bank for payroll tax deposit purposes.
6. **When do monthly depositors make their deposits?** A monthly depositor will figure the total amount of Form 941 taxes owed in a calendar month and then pay this amount by the 15th of the next month. If an employer owes $3,125 in Form 941 taxes for the month of June, it will deposit this same amount no later than July 15 of the same year.
7. **When do semiweekly depositors make their deposits?** The rules for making deposits are a little more complicated for a semiweekly depositor. The depositor may have to make up to two Form 941 deposits each week. When a tax deposit is due depends on when the employees are paid. To keep the rules consistent, the IRS has taken a calendar week and divided it into two payday time periods. It is easiest to think of a two-week period of time when discussing these periods: Wednesday through Friday of week 1, and Saturday of week 1 through Tuesday of week 2.

   Two deposit rules apply to these two time periods. We can call these rules the Wednesday and Friday rules.
   a. Wednesday rule: If employees are paid during the Wednesday through Friday of week 1 period, the tax deposit will be due on Wednesday of week 2.
   b. Friday rule: If employees are paid anytime from Saturday of week 1 through Tuesday of week 2, the tax deposit will be due on Friday of week 2.

   These rules mean that the payroll tax deposit will be due three banking days after the payday time period ends. For the Wednesday rule, the deposit is due three banking days after Friday of week 1, on the following Wednesday in week 2. For the Friday rule, the deposit is due three banking days after Tuesday of week 2, on Friday of week 2. The following illustration shows how this timing works.

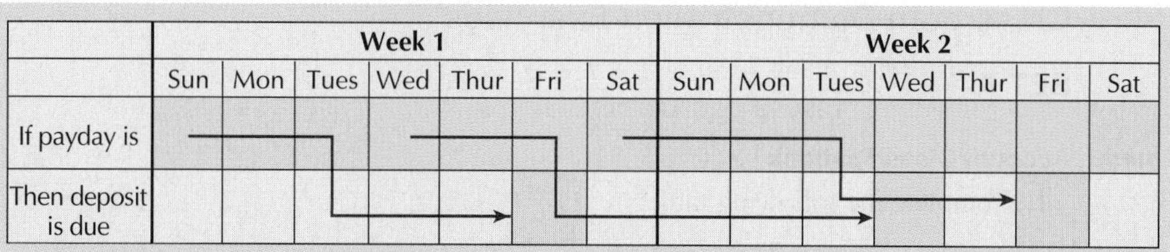

	Week 1							Week 2						
	Sun	Mon	Tues	Wed	Thur	Fri	Sat	Sun	Mon	Tues	Wed	Thur	Fri	Sat
If payday is														
Then deposit is due														

8. **What is a banking day?** The term *banking day* refers to any day that a bank is open to the public for business. Saturdays, Sundays, and legal holidays are not banking days.

9. **How do legal holidays affect payroll tax deposits?** If a legal holiday occurs after the last day of a payday time period, the employer will get one extra day to make its Form 941 tax deposit as follows:
   - **a.** For monthly depositors: If the 15th of the month is a Saturday, Sunday, or legal holiday, the deposit will be due and payable on the next banking day.
   - **b.** For semiweekly depositors: A deposit due on Wednesday will be due on Thursday of the same week, and a Friday deposit will be due on Monday of the following week. Remember that the employer will always have three banking days after the last day of either payday time period to make its payroll tax deposit.

10. **What happens if an employer is late with its Form 941 tax deposit?** If a Form 941 tax deposit is not made the day it should be deposited, the employer may be assessed a fine for lateness and may even be charged interest, depending on how late the deposit is.

QUESTIONS, CLASSROOM DEMONSTRATION EXERCISES, EXERCISES, AND PROBLEMS

Discussion and Critical Thinking Questions/Ethical Case

1. What taxes are recorded when recording Payroll Tax Expense?
2. What is a calendar year?
3. An employer must always use a calendar year for payroll purposes. Agree or disagree?
4. Why does payroll information center on 13-week quarters?
5. How is an employer classified as a monthly or semiweekly depositor for Form 941 tax purposes?
6. What is the purpose of Form 8109?
7. How often is Form 941 completed?
8. Under what circumstance(s) does the amount on line 15 of Form 941 match the amount found on line 10?
9. Bill Smith leaves his job on July 9. He requests a copy of his W-2 form when he leaves. His boss tells him to wait until January of next year. Please discuss whether Bill's boss is correct in making this statement.
10. Why would one employer prepare a Form 940 completing Part 1 line 1a, but another would prepare a Form 940 Part 1 line 1 b?
11. Employer A has a FUTA tax liability of $67.49 on March 31 of the current year. When does the employer have to make the deposit for this liability?
12. Employer B has a FUTA tax liability of $553.24 on January 31 of the current year. When does the employer have to make the deposit for this liability?
13. Who completes Form W-4? Form W-2? Form W-3? When is each form completed?
14. Why is the year-end adjusting entry needed for workers' compensation insurance?
15. Happy Carpet Cleaning, Inc., collects FIT, OASDI, and Medicare from its employees by withholding these taxes from its employees' pay. However, Happy does not pay these amounts to the federal government until the end of the calendar year so that it can maximize its cash during the year. Because it will be paying these amounts to the government, it believes that this practice does not affect its employees. Please comment on this practice.

Classroom Demonstration Exercises

SET A

LO1 (10 min) **Account Classifications**

1. Complete the following table:

Accounts Affected	Category	↑ ↓	Rules
a. Payroll Tax Expense			
b. FICA OASDI Payable			
c. SIT Payable			
d. SUTA Payable			
e. Prepaid Workers' Compensation Insurance			

LO1, 2, 3 (10 min) **Look-Back Periods**

2. Label the following look-back periods for 200C by months.

A	B	C	D
200A		200B	

LO1, 2, 3 (15 min) **Monthly versus Semiweekly Depositor**

3. In December 200B, Lin is trying to find out whether she is a monthly or semiweekly depositor for FICA (OASDI and Medicare) and federal income tax for 200C. Please advise based on the following taxes owed:

200A	Quarter 3	$28,000
	Quarter 4	12,000
200B	Quarter 1	3,000
	Quarter 2	10,000

LO1, 2, 3 (15 min) **Paying the Tax**

4. Complete the following table:

Depositor	4-Quarter Look-Back Period Tax Liability	Payroll Paid	Tax Paid by
Monthly	$28,000	November	a.
Semiweekly	$66,000	On Wednesday	b.
		On Thursday	c.
		On Friday	d.
		On Saturday	e.
		On Sunday	f.
		On Monday	g.

LO1, 2, 3 (15 min) **Payroll Account**

5. Indicate which of the following items apply to the following account titles.

1. An asset
2. A liability
3. An expense

4. Appears on the income statement
5. Appears on the balance sheet
_____ **a.** FICA OASDI Payable
_____ **b.** Office Salaries Expense
_____ **c.** Federal Income Tax Payable
_____ **d.** FICA Medicare Payable
_____ **e.** Wages and Salaries Payable

SET B

Account Classifications

LO1 (10 min)

1. Complete the following table:

Accounts Affected	Category	↑ ↓	Rules
a. Store Wage Expense			
b. Federal Income Tax Payable			
c. FICA Medicare Payable			
d. Medical Insurance Payable			
e. Payroll Cash			

Look-Back Periods

LO1, 2, 3 (10 min)

2. Label the following look-back periods for 200E by months.

A	B	C	D
200C		200D	

Monthly versus Semiweekly Depositor

LO1, 2, 3 (15 min)

3. In December 200B, Heather tries to find out whether she is a monthly or semiweekly depositor for FICA (OASDI and Medicare) and federal income tax for 200C. Please advise based on the following taxes owed:

200A	Quarter 3	$11,000
	Quarter 4	2,000
200B	Quarter 1	3,000
	Quarter 2	10,000

Paying the Tax

LO1, 2, 3 (15 min)

4. Complete the following table:

Depositor	4-Quarter Look-Back Period Tax Liability	Payroll Paid	Tax Paid by
Monthly	$36,000	October	a.
Semiweekly	$56,000	On Wednesday	b.
		On Thursday	c.
		On Friday	d.
		On Saturday	e.
		On Sunday	f.
		On Monday	g.

LO1, 2, 3 (15 min) **Payroll Account**

5. Indicate which of the following items apply to the following account titles.

1. An asset
2. A liability
3. An expense
4. Appears on the income statement
5. Appears on the balance sheet

_____ **a.** FICA OASDI Payable
_____ **b.** Store Wage Expense
_____ **c.** State Income Tax Payable
_____ **d.** FICA Medicare Payable
_____ **e.** Wages and Salaries Payable

Exercises

LO1, 2 (10 min) **8-1.** Complete the table.

Item	Category	Normal Balance	Account Appears on Which Financial Statements?
Medical Insurance Payable			
Wages and Salaries Payable			
Office Salaries Expense			
Market Wages Expense			
FICA OASDI Payable			
Federal Income Tax Payable			
State Income Tax Payable			

LO1, 2 (20 min) **8-2.** The following amounts were taken from the weekly payroll register for the Wu Lee Company on October 9, 200X. Using the same account title headings used in this chapter, please prepare the general journal entry to record the payroll for the Wu Lee Company for October 9.

Plant Wages Expense	$7,158.00
Office Salaries Expense	3,194.00
Deduction for FICA OASDI	592.30
Deduction for FICA Medicare	150.10
Deduction for federal income tax	2,225.68
Deduction for state income tax	517.60
Deduction for union dues	960.00

LO1, 2, 3 (20 min) **8-3.** Use the information from Exercise 8-2 and the following information to prepare the general journal entry to record the payroll tax expense for the weekly payroll of October 9, 200X:

Wages below the FUTA tax wage base limit	$900.00
FUTA tax rate	.8%
Wages below the SUTA tax wage base limit	$900.00
SUTA tax rate	5.4%

LO1, 2, 3 (20 min) **8-4.** At the end of February 200X, the total amount of OASDI, $590, and Medicare, $210, was withheld as tax deductions from the employees of Wheat Fields Inc. Federal income tax of $2,950 was also deducted from their paychecks. Wheat Fields is classified as a monthly depositor of Form 941 taxes. Indicate when this payroll tax deposit is due and provide a general journal entry to record the payment.

8-5. The following payroll journal entry was prepared by Palmdale Company from its payroll register. Which columns of the payroll register have the data come from? How do the taxable earnings columns of the payroll register relate to this entry? *LO1, 2 (15 min)*

GENERAL JOURNAL

Date			PR	Dr.	Cr.
200X					
Oct.	15	Customer Service Expense		1250 00	
		FIT Payable			137 50
		SIT Payable			75 00
		FICA OASDI Payable			77 50
		FICA Medicare Payable			18 13
		Payroll Cash			941 87
		To record payroll			

8-6. Carol's Grocery Store made the following Form 941 payroll tax deposits during the look-back period of July 1, 200A, through June 30, 200B: *LO1, 2, 3 (20 min)*

Quarter Ended	Amount Paid in 941 Taxes
September 30, 200A	$15,783.26
December 31, 200A	13,893.22
March 31, 200B	13,601.94
June 30, 200B	14,021.01

Should Carol's Grocery Store make Form 941 tax deposits monthly or semiweekly for 200C?

8-7. If Carol's Grocery Store downsized its operation during the second quarter of 200B and, as a result, paid only $6,121.93 in Form 941 taxes for the quarter that ended on June 30, 200B, should Carol's Grocery make its Form 941 payroll tax deposits monthly or semiweekly for 200C? *LO1, 2, 3 (15 min)*

8-8. From the following T accounts, record the following: (a) the July 3 payment for FICA (OASDI and Medicare) and federal income taxes, (b) the July 30 payment of SUTA tax, and (c) the July 30 deposit of any FUTA tax that may be required. *LO1, 2, 3 (15 min)*

FICA OASDI Payable 203

	June 30 400 (EE) 400 (ER)

FICA Medicare Payable 204

	June 30 100 (EE) 100 (ER)

FIT Payable 205

	June 30 3,005

FUTA Tax Payable 206

	June 30 143

SUTA Tax Payable 207

	June 30 612

Group A Problems

LO1, 2, 3 (30 min)

8A-1. For the biweekly pay period ending on April 10 at Susie's Pet Store, the following partial payroll summary was taken from the individual employee earnings records. Use it to

1. Complete the table. Use the federal income tax withholding table in Figure 7.2 to figure the amount of income tax withheld.
2. Prepare a journal entry to record the payroll tax expense for Susie's. Please show the calculations for FICA taxes.

Check Figure:
Payroll Tax Expense $691.33

			FICA		
Employee	Allowance and Marital Status	Gross	OASDI	Medicare	Federal Income Tax
Eddie Janway	S-1	$1,050			
Jan Kunz	S-0	900			
Julia Long	S-2	1,000			
Mike Roald	S-0	1,260			
Tom Valens	S-2	1,580			

Assume the FICA tax rate for OASDI is 6.2% up to $102,000 in earnings (no one earned this much as of April 10), and Medicare is 1.45% on all earnings. The state unemployment tax rate is 5.1% on the first $7,000 of earnings, and the federal unemployment tax rate is .8% of the first $7,000 of earnings. (Only Tom Valens earned more than $7,000 as of April 10.) In cases where the amount of FICA tax calculates to one-half cent, round up to the next cent.

LO1, 2, 3 (50 min)

8A-2. The following is the monthly payroll of White Company, owned by Dean White. Employees are paid on the last day of each month.

JANUARY

			FICA		
Employee	Monthly Earnings	YTD Earnings	OASDI	Medicare	Federal Income Tax
Sam Koy	$1,950	$1,950	$120.90	$ 28.28	$ 258.00
Joy Lane	3,200	3,200	198.40	46.40	361.00
Amy Hess	3,800	3,800	235.60	55.10	500.00
	$8,950	$8,950	$554.90	$129.78	$1,119.00

FEBRUARY

			FICA		
Employee	Monthly Earnings	YTD Earnings	OASDI	Medicare	Federal Income Tax
Sam Koy	$2,100	$ 4,050	$130.20	$ 30.45	$ 302.00
Joy Lane	3,350	6,550	207.70	48.58	325.00
Amy Hess	3,775	7,575	234.05	54.74	426.00
	$9,225	$18,175	$571.95	$133.77	$1,053.00

MARCH

Employee	Monthly Earnings	YTD Earnings	FICA OASDI	FICA Medicare	Federal Income Tax
Sam Koy	$2,100	$ 6,150	$130.20	$ 30.45	$ 586.00
Joy Lane	2,500	9,050	155.00	36.25	558.00
Amy Hess	4,100	11,675	254.20	59.45	545.00
	$8,700	$26,875	$539.40	$126.15	$1,689.00

Check Figure: Deposit of SUTA Tax $1,148.55

White Company is located at 2 Square Street, Marblehead, Massachusetts 01945. Its employer identification number is 29-3458822. The FICA tax rate for Social Security is 6.2% up to $102,000 in earnings during the year, and Medicare is 1.45% on all earnings. The SUTA tax rate is 5.7% on the first $7,000. The FUTA tax rate is .8% on the first $7,000 of earnings. White Company is classified as a monthly depositor for Form 941 taxes.

Your tasks are to

1. Journalize the entries to record the employer's payroll tax expense for each pay period in the general journal.
2. Journalize entries for the payment of each tax liability in the general journal.

8A-3. Ed Ward, the accountant for White Company, must complete Form 941 for the first quarter of the current year. Ed gathered the needed data as presented in Problem 8A-2. Suddenly called away to an urgent budget meeting, Ed requested that you assist him by preparing the Form 941 for the first quarter. Please note that the difference in the tax liability, a few cents, should be adjusted on line 7a; this difference is due to the rounding of FICA tax amounts.

LO1, 2, 3 (50 min)

Check Figure: Total Liability for Quarter $7,972.90

8A-4. The following is the monthly payroll for the last three months of the year for Henson's Sporting Goods Shop, 2 Boat Road, Lynn, Massachusetts 01945. The shop is a sole proprietorship owned and operated by Bill Henson. The employer ID number for Henson's Sporting Goods is 28-9311893.

LO1, 2, 3 (60 min)

The employees at Henson's are paid once each month on the last day of the month. Pam Adams is the only employee who has contributed the maximum into Social Security. None of the other employees will reach the social security wage-base limit by the end of the year. Assume the rate for social security to be 6.2% with a wage-base maximum of $102,000, and the rate for Medicare to be 1.45% on all earnings. Henson's is classified as a monthly depositor for Form 941 payroll tax deposit purposes.

Check Figure: Dec. 31 Payroll Tax Expense $882.37

Your tasks are to

1. Journalize the entries to record the employer's payroll tax expense for each period in the general journal.
2. Journalize the payment of each tax liability in the general journal.
3. Complete Form 941 for the fourth quarter of the current year.

OCTOBER

Employee	Monthly Earnings	YTD Earnings	FICA OASDI	FICA Medicare	Federal Income Tax
Pam Adams	$ 2,850	$ 95,850	$176.70	$ 41.33	$ 530.00
Jim Lee	3,490	40,150	216.38	50.61	427.00
Dave Oswald	3,800	43,900	235.60	55.10	536.00
	$10,140	$179,900	$628.68	$147.04	$1,493.00

NOVEMBER

			FICA		
Employee	Monthly Earnings	YTD Earnings	OASDI	Medicare	Federal Income Tax
Pam Adams	$ 3,030	$ 98,880	$187.86	$ 43.94	$ 597.00
Jim Lee	3,870	44,020	239.94	56.12	468.00
Dave Oswald	3,750	47,650	232.50	54.38	559.00
	$10,650	$190,550	$660.30	$154.44	$1,624.00

DECEMBER

			FICA		
Employee	Monthly Earnings	YTD Earnings	OASDI	Medicare	Federal Income Tax
Pam Adams	$ 4,250	$103,130	$193.44	$ 61.63	$ 867.00
Jim Lee	3,800	47,820	235.60	55.10	479.00
Dave Oswald	4,400	52,050	272.80	63.80	704.00
	$12,450	$203,000	$701.84	$180.53	$2,050.00

LO4, 5 (20 min)

Check Figure: Total Exempt Payments $182,000

8A-5. Using the information from Problem 8A-4, please complete a Form 940 for Henson's Sporting Goods for the current year. Additional information needed to complete the form is as follows:

a. SUTA rate: 5.7%
b. State reporting number: 025-319-2
c. No FUTA tax deposits were made for this year.
d. Henson's three employees for the year all earned over $7,000.

Group B Problems

LO1, 2, 3 (30 min)

Check Figure: Payroll Tax Expense $536.11

8B-1. For the biweekly pay period ending on April 8 at Kane's Hardware, the following partial payroll summary is taken from the individual employee earnings records. Use it to

1. Complete the table. Use the federal income tax withholding table in Figure 7.2 to figure the amount of income tax withheld.
2. Prepare a journal entry to record the payroll tax expense for Kane's. Please show the calculations for FICA taxes.

			FICA		
Employee	Allowance and Marital Status	Gross	OASDI	Medicare	Federal Income Tax
Al Jones	S-1	$ 820			
Janice King	S-2	890			
Alice Long	S-0	850			
Jill Reese	S-1	1,100			
Jeff Vatack	S-2	1,340			

Assume the FICA tax rate for OASDI is 6.2% up to $102,000 in earnings (no one has earned this much as of April 8), and Medicare is 1.45% on all earnings. The state unemployment tax rate is 5.2% on the first $7,000 of earnings, and the federal unemployment tax rate is .8% of the first $7,000 of earnings. (Only Jill Reese and Jeff Vatack have earned more than $7,000 as of April 8.) In cases where the amount of FICA tax calculates to one-half cent, round up to the next cent.

8B-2. The following is the monthly payroll of Hogan Company, owned by Dean Hogan. Employees are paid on the last day of each month. Employees are paid on the last day of each month.

LO1, 2, 3 (50 min)

Check Figure:
Deposit of SUTA tax $1,189.59

JANUARY

			FICA		
Employee	Monthly Earnings	YTD Earnings	OASDI	Medicare	Federal Income Tax
Sam Koy	$1,850	$1,850	$114.70	$ 26.83	$222.00
Joy Lane	3,000	3,000	186.00	43.50	343.00
Amy Hess	3,590	3,590	222.58	52.06	396.00
	$8,440	$8,440	$523.28	$122.39	$961.00

FEBRUARY

			FICA		
Employee	Monthly Earnings	YTD Earnings	OASDI	Medicare	Federal Income Tax
Sam Koy	$2,200	$ 4,050	$136.40	$ 31.90	$ 293.00
Joy Lane	2,900	5,900	179.80	42.05	325.00
Amy Hess	3,775	7,365	234.05	54.74	426.00
	$8,875	$17,315	$550.25	$128.69	$1,044.00

MARCH

			FICA		
Employee	Monthly Earnings	YTD Earnings	OASDI	Medicare	Federal Income Tax
Sam Koy	$ 2,820	$ 6,870	$174.84	$ 40.89	$ 405.00
Joy Lane	4,000	9,900	248.00	58.00	535.00
Amy Hess	4,300	11,665	266.60	62.35	556.00
	$11,120	$28,435	$689.44	$161.24	$1,496.00

Hogan Company is located at 2 Roundy Road, Marblehead, Massachusetts 01945. Its employer identification number is 29-3458821. The FICA tax rate for Social Security is 6.2% up to $102,000 in earnings during the year, and Medicare is 1.45% on all earnings. The SUTA tax rate is 5.7% on the first $7,000. The FUTA tax rate is .8% on the first $7,000 of earnings. Hogan Company is classified as a monthly depositor for Form 941 taxes.

Your tasks are to

1. Journalize the entries to record the employer's payroll tax expense for each pay period in the general journal.
2. Journalize entries for the payment of each tax liability in the general journal.

LO1, 2, 3 (50 min)

Check Figure:
Liability for Quarter $7,851.58

8B-3. Ed Ward, the accountant for Hogan Company, must complete Form 941 for the first quarter of the current year. Ed gathered the needed data as presented in Problem 8B-2. Suddenly called away to an urgent budget meeting, Ed requested that you assist him by preparing the Form 941 for the first quarter. Please note that the difference in the tax liability, a few cents, should be adjusted on line 7a; this difference is due to the rounding 319of FICA tax amounts.

LO1, 2, 3 (60 min)

8B-4. The following is the monthly payroll for the last three months of the year for Henson's Sporting Goods Shop, 1 Roe Road, Lynn, Massachusetts 01945. The shop is a sole proprietorship owned and operated by Bill Henson. The employer ID number for Henson's Sporting Goods is 28-9311892.

The employees at Henson's are paid once each month on the last day of the month. Pete Avery is the only employee who has contributed the maximum into Social Security. None of the other employees will reach the Social Security wage-base limit by the end of the year. Assume the rate for Social Security to be 6.2% with a wage-base maximum of $102,000, and the rate for Medicare to be 1.45% on all earnings. Henson's is classified as a monthly depositor for Form 941 payroll tax deposit purposes.

Your tasks are to

1. Journalize the entries to record the employer's payroll tax expense for each period in the general journal.
2. Journalize the payment of each tax liability in the general journal.
3. Complete Form 941 for the fourth quarter of the current year.

OCTOBER

			FICA		
Employee	Monthly Earnings	YTD Earnings	OASDI	Medicare	Federal Income Tax
Pete Avery	$ 2,950	$ 97,000	$182.90	$ 42.78	$ 530.00
Janet Lee	3,590	41,075	222.58	52.06	427.00
Sue Lyons	3,800	44,000	235.60	55.10	536.00
	$10,340	$182,075	$641.08	$149.94	$1,493.00

NOVEMBER

			FICA		
Employee	Monthly Earnings	YTD Earnings	OASDI	Medicare	Federal Income Tax
Pete Avery	$ 3,000	$100,000	$186.00	$ 43.50	$ 552.00
Janet Lee	3,650	44,725	226.30	52.93	439.00
Sue Lyons	3,710	47,710	230.02	53.80	503.00
	$10,360	$192,435	$642.32	$150.23	$1,494.00

DECEMBER

Employee	Monthly Earnings	YTD Earnings	FICA OASDI	FICA Medicare	Federal Income Tax
Pete Avery	$ 4,250	$104,250	$124.00	$ 61.63	$ 857.00
Janet Lee	3,850	48,575	238.70	55.83	490.00
Sue Lyons	3,900	51,610	241.80	56.55	559.00
	$12,000	$204,435	$604.50	$174.01	$1,906.00

Check Figure:
Dec. 31 Payroll Tax Expense $778.51

8B-5. Using the information from Problem 8B-4, please complete a Form 940 for Henson's Sporting Goods for the current year. Additional information needed to complete the form is as follows:

LO4, 5 (20 min)

a. SUTA rate: 5.7%
b. State reporting number: 025-319-2
c. No FUTA tax deposits were made for this year.
d. Henson's three employees for the year all earned over $7,000.

Check Figure:
Line 4 Total Exempt Payments $183,435

ON-THE-JOB TRAINING

LO1, 2, 3, 4 (60 min)

T-1. Sunshine School Supplies is a leading manufacturer of back-to-school kits and other items used by students in elementary and middle schools. Each summer Sunshine needs additional help to assemble, pack, and ship school items sold in stores around the country. Sunshine's company policy has been to hire 30 additional workers for 12 weeks during the summer. Each employee works 40 hours per week and earns $6.50 per hour. At the end of August these additional workers are laid off.

Sunshine's state unemployment rate has risen to 5.4% with no experience/merit rating allowed due to these layoffs in the last few years.

Miriam Holtz, who is the president of Sunshine, asks for your help to find a way to reduce Sunshine's 5.4% state unemployment rate. When Miriam called the state department of labor and employment, she was told that Sunshine's unemployment rate could drop to 4.1% if it stopped laying off workers.

Miriam has thought about using temporary employment agency workers during the summer months as a way to obtain the help the company needs and at the same time stop the seasonal layoffs.

Miriam asks you to evaluate whether this idea would be good for Sunshine. She gives you the following facts to use in analyzing this idea:

1. Five hundred workers who are permanent employees of Sunshine each earn in excess of $7,000 by September of each year.
2. A temporary employment agency told Miriam it would charge Sunshine $7.00 per hour for each worker it supplied during the summer.
3. The current federal unemployment tax rate is .8% up to the first $7,000 each employee earns during a year.
4. The current SUTA wage-base limit is the first $7,000 each employee earns during a year.
5. Sunshine pays a FICA tax rate of 6.2% for social security and 1.45% for Medicare. The Social Security wage-base limit is $102,000; there is no wage-base limit for Medicare.

Please write a short memo to Miriam Holtz that shows your analysis of two options: (1) continue to hire 30 additional workers for the summer and then lay them off, or (2) have the temporary employment agency provide 30 additional workers for the summer.

In your memo be sure to show the financial effect of both options in terms of the tax calculations on employee earnings for SUTA, FUTA, and FICA. For option 1, be sure to include the SUTA and FUTA tax effects for both the permanent and temporary workers. At the end of your memo please provide Miriam with your conclusion so she can make a good decision for her company.

LO3, 4, 5 (20 min) **T-2.** Cathy Johnson was recently hired as a bookkeeper for the Pet World Dog Toy Company. She just graduated from the local community college with an associates degree in business. Although she took several accounting courses at school, she was unable to take the school's payroll accounting course.

Cathy is confused about payroll tax forms and their purpose. She wants to learn more about the forms the business must prepare and send in to the government.

You are the accountant for Pet World. Your boss has asked you to help teach Cathy about the forms and why they are used. The boss feels it is best to give Cathy a brief written summary about the following forms:

1. Form 941
2. Form 940
3. Form 8109
4. Form W-2
5. Form W-3

Please write a brief report to Cathy to help her understand the following points about these payroll tax forms:

a. The purpose of each form
b. What is reported on each form
c. When each form is sent to the government
d. Where the amounts found on each form come from in the accounting system

FINANCIAL REPORT PROBLEM

LO4 (20 min)

Reading the Kellogg's Annual Report

Go to Appendix A of the Kellogg's Annual Report and find Note 9: Expenses. How much did Kellogg's spend to fund the 401(k) plans and similar saving plans?

INTERNET PROJECT

Coca-Cola

Go to the Web and search: Annual Report Coca-Cola 2008.
Click on Investors Relations.
List out the latest news Coca-Cola is providing to its investors.
Order a free annual report.

CONTINUING PROBLEM

LO1, 2, 3, 4 (40 min)

Sanchez Computer Center

As December comes to an end, Tony Freedman wants to take care of his payroll obligations. He will complete Form 941 for the fourth quarter of the current year and Form 940 for federal unemployment taxes. Tony will make the necessary deposits and payments associated with his payroll.

Assignment

1. Using the information in the Chapter 7 problem, record the November payrolls and the payment of the payrolls in the general journal.
2. Using the information in the Chapter 7 problem, record the payroll tax expense for the fourth quarter in the general journal. Use December 31 as the date of the journal entry to record the payroll tax expense for the entire quarter.
3. Record the payment of each tax liability in the general journal. Sanchez Computer Center is classified as a quarterly depositor. The company wishes to pay all payroll taxes on December 31 even if no deposits are required.
4. Prepare Form 941 for the fourth quarter. Sanchez Computer Center's employer identification number is 35-4132588.
5. Complete Form 940 for Sanchez Computer Center. The FUTA tax ceiling is $7,000, and the SUTA tax ceiling is $7,000 in cumulative wages for each employee. The Sanchez Computer Center's FUTA rate is .8% and the SUTA rate is 2.7%. The state reporting number is 025-025-2.

Hint: Sometimes the amount of social security taxes paid by the employee for the quarter will not equal the employee's tax liability because of rounding. Any overage or difference should be reported on line 7a of Form 941.

HOLD THE LETTUCE, WITHHOLD THE TAXES

LO1, 2, 3, 4 (30 min)

"As an employer, Stan, what are your tax responsibilities?" asked Angel Tavarez, president of the Los Palmos Kiwanis club. They were at one of the luncheons sponsored by the club every month, and Stan had been asked to join a discussion on the Role of Small Business in the local economy. Fortunately, Angel had told the panelists the questions in advance, so Stan had his answers ready.

"Well, of course, I pay city, state, and U.S. government taxes myself. I also have to file city, state, and federal withholding taxes for each of my two employees. I have to withhold state unemployment taxes, as well as FICA, which is another name for OASDI and Medicare taxes, for each of them. I pay workers' compensation, too," said Stan.

"That's strange," said a voice from the audience. "My brother-in-law has a Subway restaurant in the southern part of the state, and he doesn't pay any city taxes. What's going on here?"

"Naturally, the situation is slightly different for Subway owners in different cities in our state—and across the country," said Stan confidently. "Not all cities have city income taxes. Different states have different regulations about workers' comp as well."

"Oh, right," said the voice, sounding embarrassed.

"So, Stan, how often do you have to pay taxes?" asked Angel Tavarez, shifting the topic diplomatically.

Stan picked up a piece of chalk and drew four large circles on the blackboard. Then he wrote the word "ASPIRIN" in each of the circles. A murmur of "Huh" and "What" went around the room.

"The average employee working for a company pays taxes once a year on April 15 and has one big tax headache. As an employer," Stan said, "I file tax returns on a quarterly basis, so I have four big tax headaches a year! Rather than filling out the 1040-EZ, I complete the Form 941, the Employer's Quarterly Federal Return, to report and pay payroll taxes to the IRS. Yet, while the form is due quarterly, I actually need to deposit the tax money into a Federal Reserve

Bank once a month. In addition, I have to file the 940 at the end of each year to pay my federal and state unemployment taxes. Then, for each employee...."

"Stan," Angel interrupted, "I'm afraid time is running out for your segment of the panel discussion. We'll move on to Pamela Pudelle, who is going to tell us about advertising her new pet-grooming parlor."

Later, during the reception, Stan tapped Angel on the shoulder, "Sorry I went over my time limit," he said. "You didn't really go over," said Angel, "but you were getting a little too technical for the audience." While Stan was sorry to have let the discussion veer off course, he felt a little burst of pride: Who would have thought a year ago that he would be willing—and able—to expound about the tax burden of a small business owner!

Discussion Questions

1. What are the taxes called "Form 941 taxes"?
2. Why is Stan classified as a monthly depositor of Form 941 taxes?
3. Assume Stan owed $2,069.90 in Form 941 taxes for March. When would it be due? What would happen if that day were a Sunday?

PEACHTREE COMPUTER WORKSHOP

COMPUTERIZED ACCOUNTING APPLICATION FOR CHAPTER 8

Refresher on using Peachtree Complete Accounting

Before starting this assignment, you may want to refresh your memory by reading the following PDF documents in the multimedia library of the MyAccountingLab Web site. Remember to choose the PDF document for your version of Peachtree.

1. An Introduction to Peachtree Complete Accounting
2. Correcting Peachtree Transactions
3. How to Repeat or Restart a Peachtree Assignment
4. Backing Up and Restoring Your Work in Peachtree

You also should have completed the following workshops:

1. Workshop 1 Atlas Company from Chapter 3
2. Workshop 2 Zell Company from Chapter 4
3. Workshop 3 Sullivan Realty from Chapter 5

Workshop 4:

Payroll Mini Practice Set

In this workshop you will prepare January, February, and March payroll for Pete's Market using Peachtree. Tasks include entering payroll data, producing paychecks, and remitting payroll taxes. You will also print payroll reports.

Instructions and the data file for completing this assignment are in the multimedia library of the MyAccountingLab Web site. Open the ***Workshop 4 Pete's Market*** PDF document for your version of Peachtree and download the ***Pete's Market*** data file for your version of Peachtree.

QUICKBOOKS COMPUTER WORKSHOP

COMPUTERIZED ACCOUNTING APPLICATION FOR CHAPTER 8

Refresher on using QuickBooks Pro

Before starting this assignment, you may want to refresh your memory by reading the following PDF documents in the multimedia library of the MyAccountingLab Web site. Remember to choose the PDF document for your version of QuickBooks.

1. An Introduction to QuickBooks Pro
2. Correcting QuickBooks Transactions
3. How to Repeat or Restart a QuickBooks Assignment
4. Backing Up and Restoring Your Work in QuickBooks

You also should have completed the following workshops:

1. Workshop 1 Atlas Company from Chapter 3
2. Workshop 2 Zell Company from Chapter 4
3. Workshop 3 Sullivan Realty from Chapter 5

Workshop 4:

Payroll Mini Practice Set

In this workshop you will prepare January, February, and March payroll for Pete's Market using QuickBooks. Tasks include entering payroll data, producing paychecks, and remitting payroll taxes. You will also print payroll reports.

Instructions and the data file for completing this assignment are in the multimedia library of the MyAccountingLab Web site. Open the ***Workshop 4 Pete's Market*** PDF document for your version of QuickBooks and download the ***Pete's Market*** data file for your version of QuickBooks.

9 Sales and Cash Receipts

DID YOU KNOW? Rebates, reimbursements for markdowns from vendors, are recognized as a reduction to cost of sales when the inventory is sold. Visit *www.biglots.com* to find more information about Big Lots.

LEARNING OBJECTIVES

1. Recording and posting sales transactions.
2. Preparing, journalizing, and posting a credit memorandum.
3. Recording and posting cash receipts transactions.
4. Recording to the accounts receivable subsidiary ledger.
5. Preparing a schedule of accounts receivable.

When you shop in Big Lots, a merchandise company, you will see a wide variety of products in the store. Let's first look at Chou's Toy Shop to get an overview of merchandise terms and journal entries. After that, we take an in-depth look at how Art's Wholesale Clothing Company keeps its books.

Learning Unit 9-1 Chou's Toy Shop: Seller's View of a Merchandise Company

Sales are recorded on an invoice (on account) or a receipt (cash) in the Customer module of QuickBooks and Peachtree.

Chou's Toy Shop, owned by Chou Li, is a **retailer.** It buys toys, games, bikes, and similar items from manufacturers and wholesalers and resells these goods (or **merchandise**) to its customers. The shelving, display cases, and so forth are called "fixtures" or "equipment." These items are not for resale.

Gross Sales

Each cash or charge sale made at Chou's Toy Shop is rung up at the register. Suppose the shop had $3,000 in sales on July 18. Of that amount, $1,800 was cash sales and $1,200 was charges. The account that recorded those sales would be

Gross sales:
Revenue earned from sale of merchandise to customers.

Sales (Gross)	
Dr.	Cr.
	3,000 ← Revenue account with a credit balance

This account is a revenue account with a credit balance and will be found on the income statement. Figure 9.1 shows the journal entry for the day. *Note:* We talk about sales tax later.

Accounts Affected	Category	↑ ↓	Rules	T Account Update
Cash	Asset	↑	Dr.	**Cash** Dr. 1,800
Accounts Receivable	Asset	↑	Dr.	**Accounts Receivable** Dr. 1,200
Sales	Revenue	↑	Cr.	**Sales** Cr. 3,000

Sales Returns and Allowances

It would be great for Chou if all the customers were completely satisfied, but that rarely is the case. On July 19, Michelle Reese brought back a doll she bought on account for $50. She told Chou that the doll was defective and that she wanted either a price reduction or a

FIGURE 9.1 Recording Cash and Charge Sales for the Day

July	18	Cash	1 8 0 0 00	
		Accounts Receivable	1 2 0 0 00	
		Sales		3 0 0 0 00
		Sales for July 18		

new doll. They agreed on a $10 price reduction. Michelle now owes Chou $40. The account called **Sales Returns and Allowances (SRA)** would record this information.

Sales Returns and Allowances

Contra-revenue account with a debit balance →	Dr.	Cr.
	10	

This account is a contra-revenue account with a debit balance. It will be recorded on the income statement. Figure 9.2 shows how the journal entry would look.

Accounts Affected	Category	↑ ↓	Rules	T Account Update
Sales Returns and Allowances	Contra-revenue	↑	Dr.	**Sales Ret. & Allow.** Dr. 10 | Cr.
Accounts Receivable, Michelle Reese	Asset	↓	Cr.	**Accounts Receivable** Dr. 1,200 | Cr. 10

Look at how the sales returns and allowances increase.

				Dr.	Cr.
July	19	Sales Returns and Allowances		10 00	
		Accounts Receivable, Michelle Reese			10 00
		Issued credit memorandum			

FIGURE 9.2 Issuing a Credit Memorandum in the General Journal

Sales Discount

Chou gives a 2% **sales discount** to customers who pay their bills early. He wants his customers to know about this policy, so he posted the following sign at the cash register:

When setting up a new customer in QuickBooks and Peachtree, be sure to include the credit terms. When payment is made the program will calculate the discount if that information is available.

SALES DISCOUNT POLICY

2/10, n/30	*2% discount is allowed off price of bill if paid within the first 10 days or full amount is due within 30 days.*
n/10, EOM	*No discount. Full amount of bill is due within 10 days after the end of the month.*

Note that the **discount period** is the time when a discount is granted. The discount period is less time than the **credit period,** which is the length of time allowed to pay the amount owed on the bill.

If Michelle pays her $40 bill early, she will get an $.80 discount. This information is recorded in the **Sales Discount account** as follows:

Sales Discount

Contra-revenue account with a debit balance →	Dr.	Cr.
	.80	

Michelle's discount is calculated as follows:

$$.02 \times \$40 = \$.80$$

Michelle pays her bill on July 24. She is entitled to the discount because she paid her bill within 10 days. Figure 9.3 shows how Chou would record this payment on his books.

Accounts Affected	Category	↑ ↓	Rules	T Account Update
Cash	Asset	↑	Dr.	**Cash** **Dr.** | **Cr.** **39.20** |
Sales Discount	Contra-revenue	↑	Dr.	**Sales Discount** **Dr.** | **Cr.** **.80** |
Accounts Receivable	Asset	↓	Cr.	**Accounts Receivable** **Dr.** | **Cr.** **1,200** | 40

Gross Sales
- Sales discount
- SRA
= Net sales

FIGURE 9.3 Recording Sales Discount

Date		Account	Dr.	Cr.
July	24	Cash	39 20	
		Sales Discount	80	
		Accounts Receivable, Michelle Reese		40 00
		Payment from Sale on Account		

Although Michelle pays $39.20, her Accounts Receivable is credited for the full amount, $40.

In the examples so far we have not shown any transactions with sales tax. Note that the actual or **net sales** for Chou would be **gross sales** less sales returns and allowances less any sales discounts. Let's look at how Chou would record his monthly sales if sales tax were charged.

Sales Tax Payable

Sales taxes are special functions in accounting software that usually must be turned on and set up. When set up correctly, the program will automatically calculate the amount of sales tax to be charged or to be returned when issuing a credit memorandum.

None of the preceding examples shows state sales tax. Still, like it or not, Chou must collect that tax from his customers and send it to the state. Sales tax represents a liability to Chou. The amount Chou must pay to the state is recorded in the **Sales Tax Payable account.**

Assume the state Chou's is located in charges a 5% sales tax. Remember that Chou's sales on July 18 were $3,000. Chou must figure out the sales tax on the purchases. For this purpose, let's assume only two sales were made on that date: the cash sale ($1,800) and the charge sale ($1,200).

The sales tax on the cash purchase is calculated as follows:

$$\$1,800 \times .05 = \$90 \text{ Tax}$$
$$\$1,800 + \$90 \text{ tax} = \$1,890 \text{ Cash}$$

Here is how the sales tax on the charge sale is computed:

$$\$1,200 \times .05 = \$60 \text{ Tax} + \$1,200 \text{ Charge} = \$1,260 \text{ Accounts Receivable}$$

It would be recorded as shown in Figure 9.4.

Accounts Affected	Category	↑ ↓	Rules	T Account Update
Cash	Asset	↑	Dr.	**Cash** Dr. 1,890 | Cr.
Accounts Receivable	Asset	↑	Dr.	**Accounts Receivable** Dr. 1,260 | Cr.
Sales Tax Payable	Liability	↑	Cr.	**Sales Tax Payable** Dr. | Cr. 90, 60
Sales	Revenue	↑	Cr.	**Sales** Dr. | Cr. 3,000

Date		Account	Dr.	Cr.
July	18	Cash	1 8 9 0 00	
		Accounts Receivable	1 2 6 0 00	
		Sales Tax Payable		1 5 0 00
		Sales		3 0 0 0 00
		July 18 Sales		

FIGURE 9.4 Sales with Sales Tax

In Learning Unit 9-2, we will look in detail at Art's Wholesale Company.

LEARNING UNIT 9-1 REVIEW

AT THIS POINT you should be able to

- Explain the purpose of a contra-revenue account.
- Explain how to calculate net sales.
- Define, journalize, and explain gross sales, sales returns and allowances, and sales discounts.
- Journalize an entry for sales tax payable.

Self-Review Quiz 9-1

Respond true or false to the following:

1. Sales Returns and Allowances is a contra-asset account.
2. Sales Discount has a normal balance of a debit.
3. Sales Tax Payable is a liability.
4. Sales Discount is a contra-asset.
5. Accounts Receivable is a revenue.

Solutions to Self-Review Quiz 9-1

1. False
2. True
3. True
4. False
5. False

Sales: Revenue	↑	Cr.
SRA: Contra-revenue	↑	Dr.
SD: Contra-revenue	↑	Dr.

LO1 Learning Unit 9-2* Recording and Posting Sales Transactions on Account for Art's Wholesale Clothing Company: Introduction to Subsidiary Ledgers and Credit Memorandum

Art's Wholesale Clothing Company, as a **wholesaler,** buys merchandise from suppliers and sells the items to retailers, who in turn sell it to individual consumers.

The following transactions occurred in April for Art's Wholesale Clothing Company:

200X		
April	3	Sold on account merchandise to Hal's Clothing, $800; terms 2/10, n/30.
	6	Sold on account merchandise to Bevan's Company, $1,600; terms 2/10, n/30.
	12	Credit memo #1 to Bevan's Company for returned merchandise, $600.
	18	Sold on account merchandise to Roe Company, $2,000; terms 2/10, n/30.
	24	Sold on account merchandise to Roe Company, $500; terms 2/10, n/30.
	28	Sold on account merchandise to Mel's Department Store, $900; terms 2/10, n/30.
	29	Sold on account merchandise to Mel's Department Store, $700; terms 2/10, n/30.

Let's look closer at the April 3 transaction of Art selling to Hal's Clothing. Figure 9.5 shows the actual bill on the **sales invoice** for this sale:

April 3 Sold account merchandise to Hal's Clothing, $800. Terms 2/10, n/30.

The Analysis

Accounts Affected	Category	↑ ↓	Rules	Amount
Accounts Receivable, Hal's Clothing	Asset	↑	Dr.	$800
Sales	Revenue	↑	Cr.	$800

The general journal is shown in Figure 9.6.

FIGURE 9.5 Sales Invoice

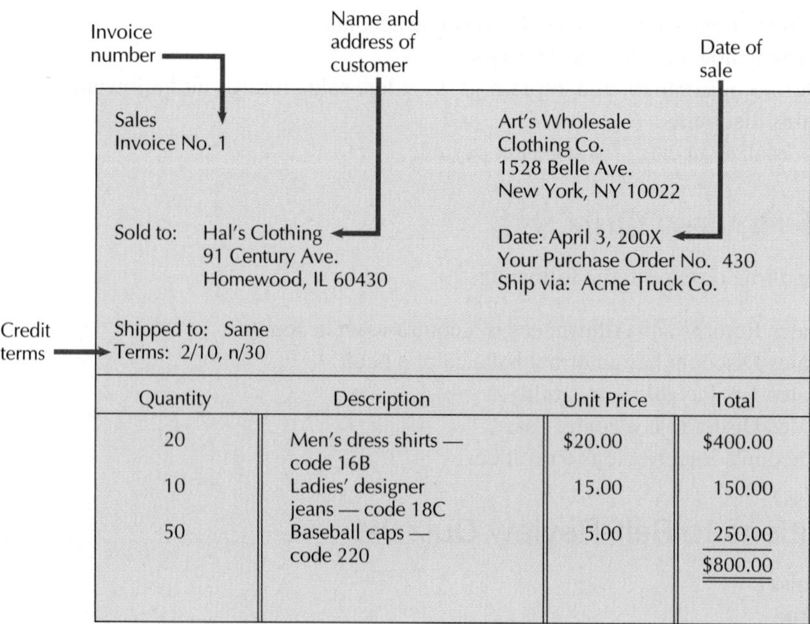

Sales
Invoice No. 1

Art's Wholesale
Clothing Co.
1528 Belle Ave.
New York, NY 10022

Sold to: Hal's Clothing
91 Century Ave.
Homewood, IL 60430

Date: April 3, 200X
Your Purchase Order No. 430
Ship via: Acme Truck Co.

Shipped to: Same
Terms: 2/10, n/30

Quantity	Description	Unit Price	Total
20	Men's dress shirts — code 16B	$20.00	$400.00
10	Ladies' designer jeans — code 18C	15.00	150.00
50	Baseball caps — code 220	5.00	250.00
			$800.00

*At the end of Chapter 10, Appendix A shows an alternative method that uses a special journal to record transactions. Your instructor will let you know if this will be covered in your course.

ART'S WHOLESALE CLOTHING COMPANY GENERAL JOURNAL				Page 2
Date	Account Titles and Description	PR	Dr.	Cr.
200X				
April 3	Accounts Receivable, Hal's Clothing		800 00	
	Sales			800 00
	Sale on account to Hal's			

FIGURE 9.6 Merchandise Sold and Accounts Receivable

Accounts Receivable Subsidiary Ledgers

So far in this text, the only title we have used for recording amounts owed to the seller has been Accounts Receivable. Art could have replaced the Accounts Receivable title in the general ledger with the following list of customers who owe him money:

- Accounts Receivable, Bevans Company
- Accounts Receivable, Hal's Clothing
- Accounts Receivable, Mel's Department Store
- Accounts Receivable, Roe Company

As you can see, this system would not be manageable if Art had 1,000 credit customers. To solve this problem, Art sets up a separate **accounts receivable subsidiary ledger.** Such a special ledger, often simply called a **subsidiary ledger,** contains a single type of account, such as credit customers. An account is opened for each customer, and the accounts are arranged alphabetically.

The diagram in Figure 9.7 shows how the accounts receivable subsidiary ledger fits in with the general ledger. To clarify the difference in updating the general ledger versus the subsidiary ledger, we will *post* to the general ledger and *record* to the subsidiary ledger. The word *post* refers to information that is moved from the journal to the general ledger; the word *record* refers to information that is transferred from the journal into the individual customer's account in the subsidiary ledger.

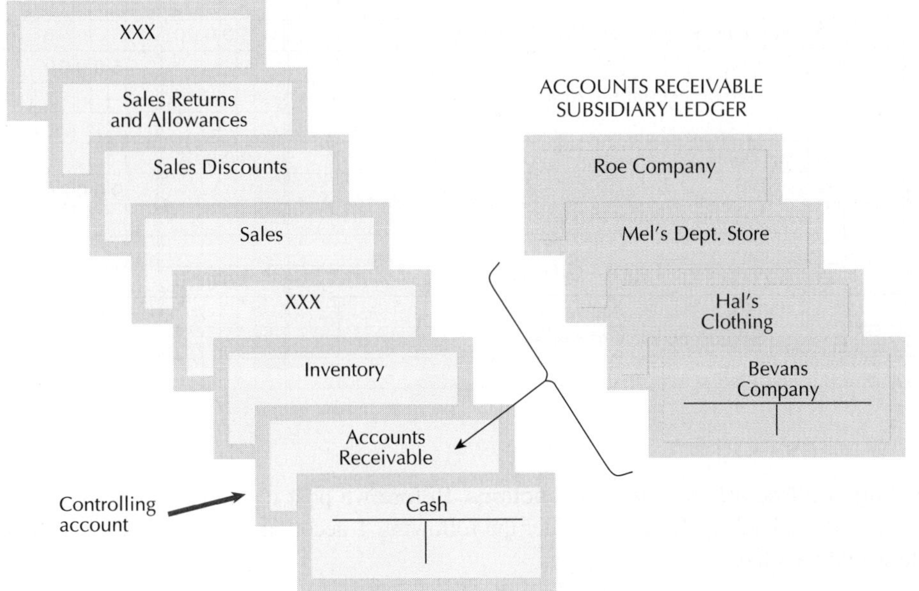

FIGURE 9.7 Partial General Ledger of Art's Wholesale Clothing Company and Accounts Receivable Subsidiary Ledger

Proving: At the end of the month, the sum of the accounts receivable subsidiary ledger will equal the ending balance in accounts receivable, the controlling account in the general ledger.

The general ledger is not in the same book as the accounts receivable subsidiary ledger.

The accounts receivable subsidiary ledger, or any other subsidiary ledger, can be in the form of a card file, a binder notebook, or computer tapes or disks. It will not have page numbers. The accounts receivable subsidiary ledger is organized alphabetically based on customers' names and addresses; new customers can be added and inactive customers deleted.

When using an accounts receivable subsidiary ledger, the account title Accounts Receivable in the general ledger is called the **controlling account—Accounts Receivable** because it summarizes or controls the accounts receivable subsidiary ledger. At the end of the month the total of the individual accounts in the accounts receivable ledger will equal the ending balance in Accounts Receivable in the general ledger.

Figure 9.8 shows how the general journal looks for Art before posting and recording this months sales transactions on account.

FIGURE 9.8 Before Posting and Recording Sales Transactions

ART'S WHOLESALE CLOTHING COMPANY
GENERAL JOURNAL — **Page 2**

Date		Account Titles and Description	PR	Dr.	Cr.
200X					
Apr.	3	Accounts Receivable, Hal's Clothing		80000	
		Sales			80000
		Sale on account to Hal's			
	6	Accounts Receivable, Bevan's Company		160000	
		Sales			160000
		Sale on account to Bevan's			
	12	Sales Returns and Allowances		60000	
		Accounts Receivable, Bevan's Company			60000
		Issued credit memo no. 1			
	18	Accounts Receivable, Roe Company		200000	
		Sales			200000
		Sale on account to Roe			
	24	Accounts Receivable, Roe Company		50000	
		Sales			50000
		Sale on account to Roe			
	28	Accounts Receivable, Mel's Dept. Store		90000	
		Sales			90000
		Sale on account to Mel's			
	29	Accounts Receivable, Mel's Dept. Store		70000	
		Sales			70000
		Sale on account to Mel's			

Posting and Recording Sales Transactions Before we post to the general ledger and record to the subsidiary ledger, consider the following T accounts, which show what each title would look like.

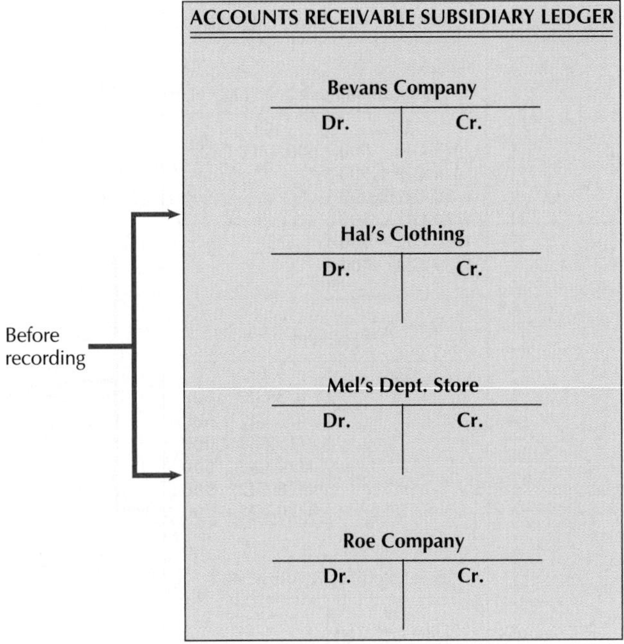

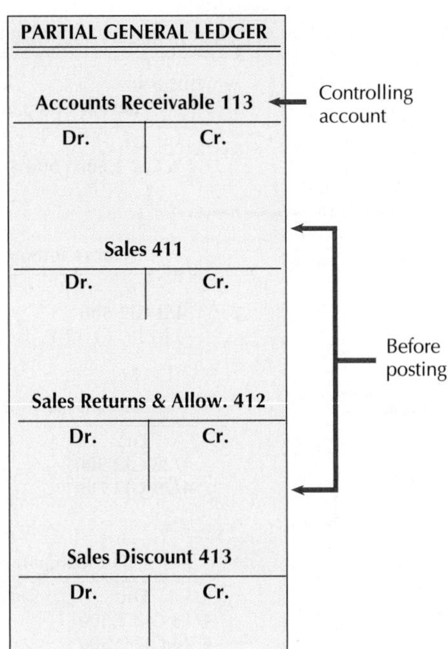

Figure 9.9 shows how the April 3 transaction is posted and recorded.

For this transaction we *post* to the general ledger Accounts Receivable and Sales accounts. Note how the account numbers of 113 and 411 are entered into the PR column of general journal. We must also *record* to Hal's Clothing in the accounts receivable subsidiary ledger. It is placed on the debit side because Hal owed Art the money. When the subsidiary ledger is updated, a (✓) is placed in the PR column of the general journal. The following is how the accounts receivable subsidiary ledger and partial general ledger

FIGURE 9.9 Transaction for April 3 Posted and Recorded

GENERAL JOURNAL — Page 2

Date		Account Titles and Description	PR	Dr.	Cr.
200X					
April	3	Accounts Receivable, Hal's Clothing	113/✓	800 00	
		Sales	411		800 00
		Sale on account to Hal's			

PARTIAL ACCOUNTS RECEIVABLE SUBSIDIARY LEDGER

Hal's Clothing

Dr.	Cr.
4/3 GJ2 800	

PARTIAL GENERAL LEDGER

Accounts Receivable 113

Dr.	Cr.
4/3 GJ2 800	

Sales 411

Dr.	Cr.
	800 4/3 GJ2

(continued on next page)

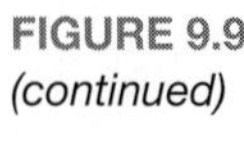

FIGURE 9.9
(continued)

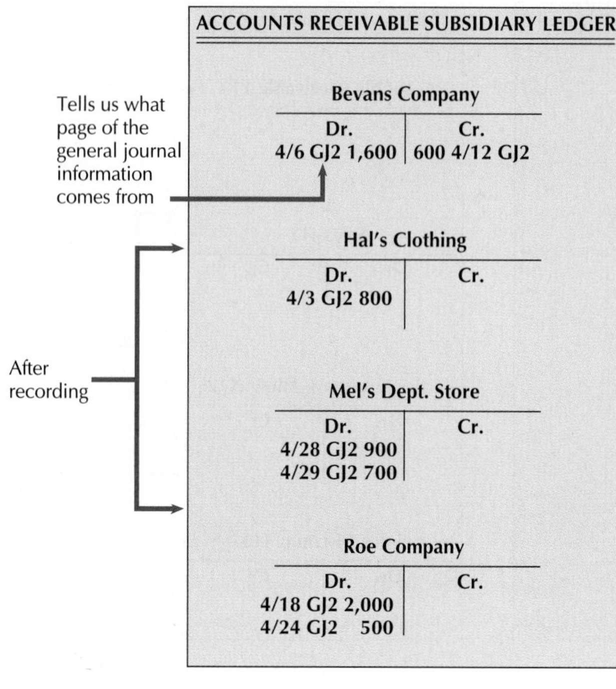

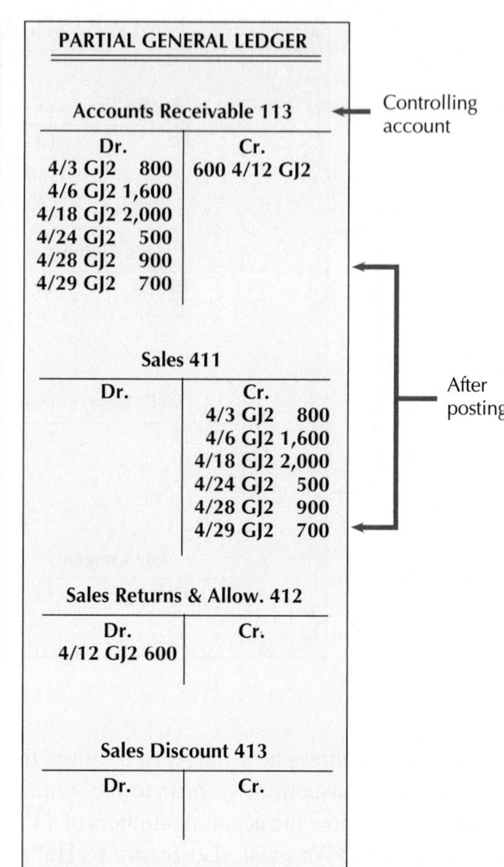

would look after postings. Before concluding this unit, let's look closely at the April 12 transaction when Art issues a credit memorandum to Bevan. We will analyze the transaction and show how to post and record it.

LO2 The Credit Memorandum

Companies usually handle sales returns and allowances by means of a **credit memorandum.** Credit memoranda inform customers that the amount of the goods returned or the amount allowed for damaged goods has been subtracted (credited) from the customer's ongoing account with the company.

A sample credit memorandum from Art's Wholesale Clothing Company appears in Figure 9.10. It shows that on April 12, Credit Memorandum No. 1 was issued to Bevans Company for defective merchandise that had been returned.

FIGURE 9.10

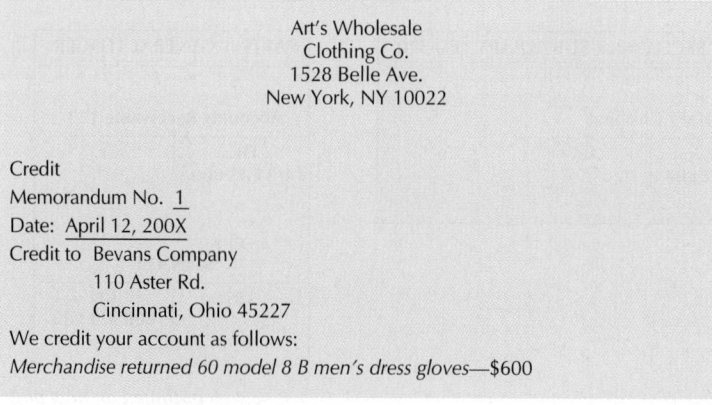

Art's Wholesale
Clothing Co.
1528 Belle Ave.
New York, NY 10022

Credit
Memorandum No. 1
Date: April 12, 200X
Credit to Bevans Company
110 Aster Rd.
Cincinnati, Ohio 45227
We credit your account as follows:
Merchandise returned 60 model 8 B men's dress gloves—$600

Let's look at a transaction analysis chart before we journalize, record, and post this transaction.

Accounts Affected	Category	↑ ↓	Rules
Sales Returns and Allowances	Contra-revenue account	↑	Dr.
Accounts Receivable, Bevans Co.	Asset	↓	Cr.

Journalizing, Recording, and Posting the Credit Memorandum

The credit memorandum results in two postings to the general ledger and one recording to the accounts receivable subsidiary ledger (see Fig. 9.11).

Remember: Sales discounts are not taken on returns.

Page 1

Date		Account Titles and Description	PR	Dr.	Cr.
200X					
Apr.	12	Sales Returns and Allowances	412	600 00	
		Accounts Receivable, Bevans Co.	113/✓		600 00
		Issued credit memo no.1			

412 A debit of $600 is recorded in Sales Returns and Allowances, account no. 412 in the general ledger. When the amount is recorded, the account number is placed in the PR column of the journal.

113 The credit of $600 is also posted to Accounts Receivable in the controlling account in the general ledger. Then, the account number (113) is placed in the PR column of the journal.

✔ The check indicates that $600 has been recorded as a credit to the account of Bevans Company in the accounts receivable subsidiary ledger.

FIGURE 9.11 Postings and Recordings for the Credit Memorandum into the Subsidiary and General Ledgers

Note in the PR column next to Accounts Receivable, Bevans Co., a diagonal line separates the account number 113 above and a ✓ below. This notation shows that the amount of $600 has been credited to Accounts Receivable in the controlling account in the general ledger *and* credited to the account of Bevans Company in the accounts receivable subsidiary ledger.

LEARNING UNIT 9-2 REVIEW

AT THIS POINT you should be able to

- Define and state the purposes of the accounts receivable subsidiary ledger.
- Define and state the purpose of the controlling account, Accounts Receivable.
- Journalize, record, or post sales on account to a general journal and its related accounts receivable and general ledgers.
- Explain, journalize, post, and record a credit memorandum.

Self-Review Quiz 9-2

Journalize, post to the general ledger, and record to accounts receivable subsidiary ledger the following transactions of Bernie Company.

200X		
May	10	Sold merchandise on account to Ring Company, $600; terms 2/10, n/30.
	18	Sold merchandise on account to Lee Corp., $900; terms 2/10, n/30.
	25	Issued credit memo #1 to Ring Company for returned merchandise, $200.

Solution to Self-Review Quiz 9-2

BERNIE COMPANY
GENERAL JOURNAL
Page 4

Date		Account Titles and Description	PR	Dr.	Cr.
200X					
May	10	Accounts Receivable, Ring Clothing	141/✓	600 00	
		Sales	310		600 00
		Sale on account to Ring Co.			
	18	Accounts Receivable, Lee Corp.	141/✓	900 00	
		Sales	310		900 00
		Sale on account to Lee Corp.			
	25	Sales Returns and Allowances	312	200 00	
		Accounts Receivable, Ring Co.	141/✓		200 00
		Issued credit memo no. 1			

ACCOUNTS RECEIVABLE SUBSIDIARY LEDGER

Lee Corp.

Dr.	Cr.
5/18 GJ4 900	

Ring Co.

Dr.	Cr.
5/10 GJ4 600	200 5/25 GJ4

PARTIAL GENERAL LEDGER

Accounts Receivable 141

Dr.	Cr.
5/10 GJ4 600	200 5/25 GJ4
5/18 GJ4 900	

Sales 310

Dr.	Cr.
	600 5/10 GJ4
	900 5/18 GJ4

Sales Returns & Allow. 312

Dr.	Cr.
5/25 GJ4 200	

LO3 Learning Unit 9-3 Recording and Posting Cash Receipt Transactions for Art's Wholesale: Schedule of Accounts Receivable

The following cash receipts transactions occurred for Art's Wholesale Clothing in April:

200X		
Apr.	1	Art Newner invested $8,000 in the business.
	4	Received check from Hal's Clothing for payment of invoice no. 1, less 2% discount.
	15	Cash sales for first half of April, $900.
	16	Received check from Bevans Company in settlement of invoice no. 2, less returns and 2% discount.
	22	Received check from Roe Company for payment of invoice no. 3, less 2% discount.
	27	Sold store equipment, $500.
	30	Cash sales for second half of April, $1,200.

Figure 9.12 provides a closer look at how the April 4 transaction would be journalized.

Accounts Affected	Category	↑ ↓	Rules	T Account Update
Cash	Asset	↑	Dr.	**Cash** Dr. 784 | Cr.
Sales Discount	Contra-revenue	↑	Dr.	**Sales Discount** Dr. 16 | Cr.
Accounts Receivable, Hal's Clothing	Asset	↓	Cr.	**Acc. Rec.** Dr. 800 | Cr. 800; **Hal's Clothing** Dr. 800 | Cr. 800

Hal's Clothing is located in the accounts receivable subsidiary ledger.

Apr.	4	Cash		784 00	
		Sales Discount		16 00	
		Accounts Receivable, Hal's Clothing			800 00

FIGURE 9.12 Recording Sales Discount in General Journal

Figure 9.13 shows the complete set of April cash receipts transactions for Art's Wholesale journalized for the month, followed by a complete posting to the general ledger and recordings to the accounts receivable ledger. (Remember from the past unit that we posted all the sales on account information.)

FIGURE 9.13 Journalized Cash Receipts Transactions

GENERAL JOURNAL — Page 2

Date		Account Titles and Description	PR	Dr.	Cr.
200X					
Apr.	1	Cash	111	8 000 00	
		Art Newner, Capital	311		8 000 00
		Owner Investment			
	4	Cash	111	784 00	
		Sales Discount	413	16 00	
		Accounts Receivable, Hal's Clothing	113/✓		800 00
		Hal's paid invoice no. 1			
	15	Cash	111	900 00	
		Sales	411		900 00
		Cash sales for first half of April			
	16	Cash	111	980 00	
		Sales Discount	413	20 00	
		Accounts Receivable, Bevan's Company	113/✓		1 000 00
		Bevan paid invoice no. 2			
	22	Cash	111	1 960 00	
		Sales Discount	413	40 00	
		Accounts Receivable, Roe Co.	113/✓		2 000 00
		Roe paid invoice no. 3			

(continued on next page)

FIGURE 9.13
(continued)

27	Cash	111	500 00	
	Store Equipment	121		500 00
	Sold store equipment			
30	Cash	111	1200 00	
	Sales	411		1200 00
	Cash sales for second half of April			

LO4

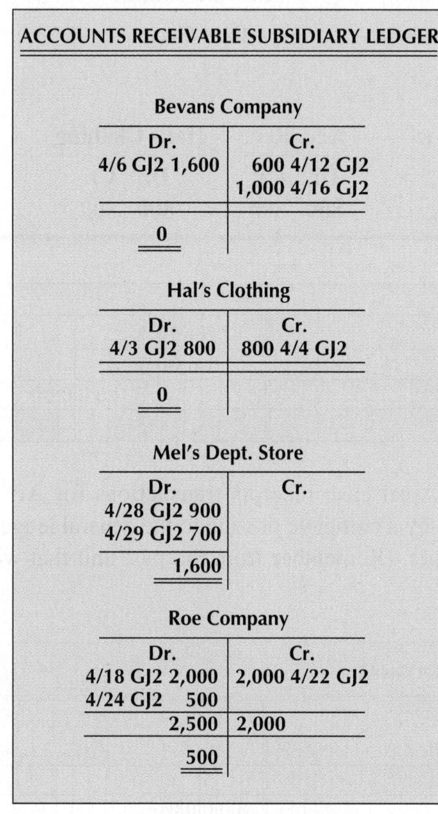

ACCOUNTS RECEIVABLE SUBSIDIARY LEDGER
Bevans Company
Dr.
Cr.
4/6 GJ2 1,600
600 4/12 GJ2
1,000 4/16 GJ2
0
Hal's Clothing
Dr.
Cr.
4/3 GJ2 800
800 4/4 GJ2
0
Mel's Dept. Store
Dr.
Cr.
4/28 GJ2 900
4/29 GJ2 700
1,600
Roe Company
Dr.
Cr.
4/18 GJ2 2,000
2,000 4/22 GJ2
4/24 GJ2 500
2,500
2,000
500

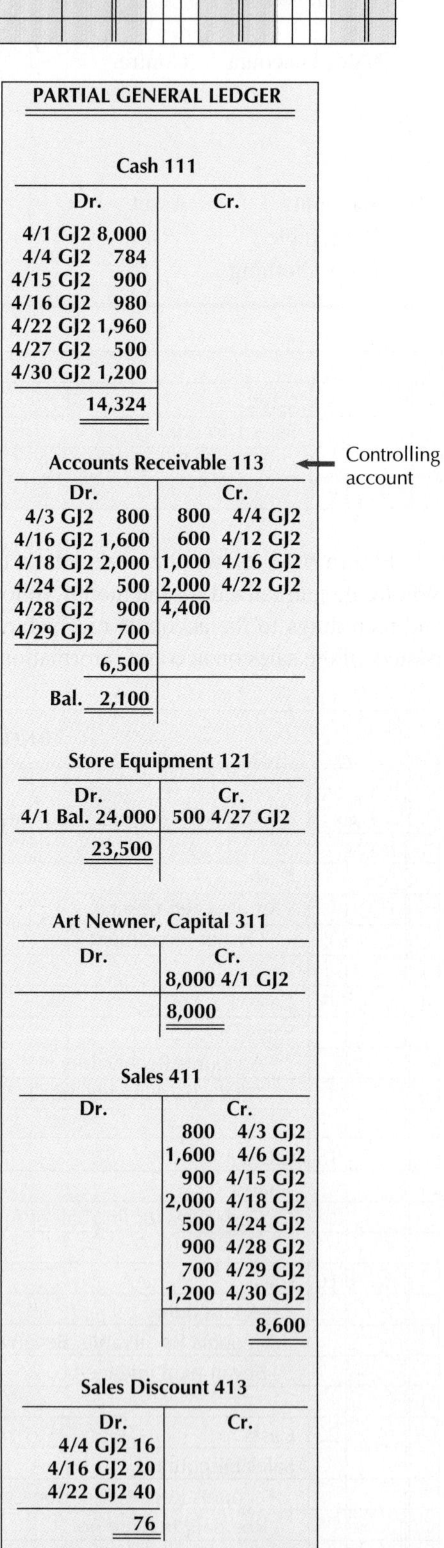

PARTIAL GENERAL LEDGER
Cash 111
Dr.
Cr.
4/1 GJ2 8,000
4/4 GJ2 784
4/15 GJ2 900
4/16 GJ2 980
4/22 GJ2 1,960
4/27 GJ2 500
4/30 GJ2 1,200
14,324
Accounts Receivable 113
Controlling account
Dr.
Cr.
4/3 GJ2 800
800 4/4 GJ2
4/16 GJ2 1,600
600 4/12 GJ2
4/18 GJ2 2,000
1,000 4/16 GJ2
4/24 GJ2 500
2,000 4/22 GJ2
4/28 GJ2 900
4,400
4/29 GJ2 700
6,500
Bal. 2,100
Store Equipment 121
Dr.
Cr.
4/1 Bal. 24,000
500 4/27 GJ2
23,500
Art Newner, Capital 311
Dr.
Cr.
8,000 4/1 GJ2
8,000
Sales 411
Dr.
Cr.
800 4/3 GJ2
1,600 4/6 GJ2
900 4/15 GJ2
2,000 4/18 GJ2
500 4/24 GJ2
900 4/28 GJ2
700 4/29 GJ2
1,200 4/30 GJ2
8,600
Sales Discount 413
Dr.
Cr.
4/4 GJ2 16
4/16 GJ2 20
4/22 GJ2 40
76

Schedule of Accounts Receivable

LO5

The **schedule of accounts receivable** is an alphabetical list of the companies that have an outstanding balance in the accounts receivable subsidiary ledger. This total should be equal to the balance of the Accounts Receivable controlling account in the general ledger at the end of the month.

Let's examine the schedule of accounts receivable for Art's Wholesale Clothing Company in Figure 9.14.

FIGURE 9.14 Schedule of Accounts Receivable

ART'S WHOLESALE CLOTHING COMPANY SCHEDULE OF ACCOUNTS RECEIVABLE APRIL 30, 200X	
Mel's Dept. Store	$1 6 0 0 00
Roe Company	5 0 0 00
Total Accounts Receivable	$2 1 0 0 00

Schedule is listed in alphabetical order.

The balance of the controlling account, Accounts Receivable ($2,100), in the general ledger does indeed equal the sum of the individual customer balances in the accounts receivable ledger ($2,100) as shown in the schedule of accounts receivable. The schedule of accounts receivable can help forecast potential cash inflows as well as possible credit and collection decisions.

LEARNING UNIT 9-3 REVIEW

AT THIS POINT you should be able to

- Journalize cash receipts transactions.
- Record and post cash receipts transactions to the accounts receivable subsidiary ledger and general ledger.
- Prepare a schedule of accounts receivable.

Self-Review Quiz 9-3

Journalize, post to the general ledger, and record to the accounts receivable subsidiary ledger the following transactions of Mabel Corporation, given the following balances.

Accounts Receivable Subsidiary Ledger

Name	*Balance*	*Invoice No.*
Irene Welch	$500	1
Janis Fross	200	2

Partial General Ledger

	Acct. No.	*Balance*
Cash	110	$600
Accounts Receivable	120	700
Store Equipment	130	600
Sales	410	700
Sales Discount	420	

200X

May	1	Received check from Irene Welch for invoice no. 1, less 2% discount.
	8	Cash sales collected, $200.
	15	Received check from Janis Fross for invoice no. 2, less 2% discount.
	19	Sold store equipment at cost, $300.

Solution to Self-Review Quiz 9-3

MABEL CORPORATION
GENERAL JOURNAL **Page 3**

Date			PR	Dr.	Cr.
200X					
May	1	Cash	110	490 00	
		Sales Discount	420	10 00	
		Accounts Receivable, Irene Welch	120/✓		500 00
		Received payment from Irene Welch			
	8	Cash	110	200 00	
		Sales	410		200 00
		Cash sale			
	15	Cash	110	196 00	
		Sales Discount	420	4 00	
		Accounts Receivable, Janis Fross	120/✓		200 00
		Received payment from Janis Fross			
	19	Cash	110	300 00	
		Store Equipment	130		300 00
		Sold store equipment			

ACCOUNTS RECEIVABLE SUBSIDIARY LEDGER

Janis Fross

Dr.	Cr.
Bal. 200	200

Irene Welch

Dr.	Cr.
Bal. 500	500 5/1 GJ3

PARTIAL GENERAL LEDGER

Cash 110

Dr.	Cr.
Bal. 600	
5/1 GJ3 490	
5/8 GJ3 200	
5/15 GJ3 196	
5/19 GJ3 300	

Accounts Receivable 120

Dr.	Cr.
Bal. 700	500 5/1 GJ3
	200 5/15 GJ3

Store Equipment 130

Dr.	Cr.
Bal. 600	300 5/19 GJ3

Sales 410

Dr.	Cr.
	700 Bal.
	200 5/8 GJ3

Sales Discount 420

Dr.	Cr.
5/1 GJ3 10	
5/15 GJ3 4	

CHAPTER ASSIGNMENTS

SUMMARY OF KEY POINTS

LEARNING UNIT 9-1

1. Sales Returns and Allowances and Sales Discount are contra-revenue accounts.
2. Net Sales = Gross Sales − Sales Returns and Allowances − Sales Discounts.
3. Discounts are not taken on sales tax, freight, or goods returned. The discount period is shorter than the credit period.
4. Sales Tax Payable is a liability account.

LEARNING UNIT 9-2

1. The normal balance of the accounts receivable subsidiary ledger is a debit balance.
2. A (✓) in the PR of the general journal means the subsidiary ledger has been updated.
3. The accounts receivable subsidiary ledger, organized in alphabetical order, is not in the same book as Accounts Receivable, the controlling account in the general ledger.
4. When a credit memorandum is issued, the result is that Sales Returns and Allowances increases and Accounts Receivable decreases. When we record this entry into the general journal, we assume all parts of the transaction will be posted to the general ledger and recorded in the subsidiary ledger.

LEARNING UNIT 9-3

1. At the end of the month, the total of all customers' ending balances in the accounts receivable subsidiary ledger should be equal to the ending balance in Accounts Receivable, the controlling account in the general ledger.
2. The schedule of accounts receivable is an alphabetical list of companies with an outstanding balance.

KEY TERMS

Accounts receivable subsidiary ledger A book or file that contains, in alphabetical order, the individual records of amounts owed by various credit customers.

Controlling account—Accounts Receivable The Accounts Receivable account in the general ledger, after postings are complete, shows a firm the total amount of money owed to it. This figure is broken down in the accounts receivable subsidiary ledger, where it indicates specifically who owes the money.

Credit memorandum A piece of paper sent by the seller to a customer who has returned merchandise previously purchased on credit. The credit memorandum indicates to the customer that the seller is reducing the amount owed by the customer.

Credit period Length of time allowed for payment of goods sold on account.

Discount period A period shorter than the credit period when a discount is available to encourage early payment of bills.

Gross sales The revenue earned from sale of merchandise to customers.

Merchandise Goods brought into a store for resale to customers.

Net sales Gross sales less sales returns and allowances less sales discounts.

Retailers Merchants who buy goods from wholesalers for resale to customers.

Sales discount Amount a customer is allowed to deduct from bill total for paying a bill during the discount period.

Sales Discount account A contra-revenue account that records cash discounts granted to customers for payments made within a specific period of time.

Sales invoice A bill sent to customer(s) reflecting a sale on credit.

Sales Returns and Allowances (SRA) account A contra-revenue account that records price adjustments and allowances granted on merchandise that is defective and has been returned.

Sales Tax Payable account An account in the general ledger that accumulates the amount of sales tax owed. It has a credit balance.

Schedule of accounts receivable A list of the customers, in alphabetical order, that have an outstanding balance in the accounts receivable ledger (or the accounts receivable subsidiary ledger). This total should be equal to the balance of the Accounts Receivable controlling account in the general ledger at the end of the month.

Subsidiary ledger A ledger that contains accounts of a single type. Example: The accounts receivable subsidiary ledger records all credit customers.

Wholesalers Merchants who buy goods from suppliers and manufacturers for sale to retailers.

BLUEPRINT: TRANSFERRING INFORMATION FROM THE GENERAL JOURNAL

Post → General Ledger (account #)

Record → Subsidiary Ledger (✓)

Issuing a Credit Memo without Sales Tax Recorded in a General Journal

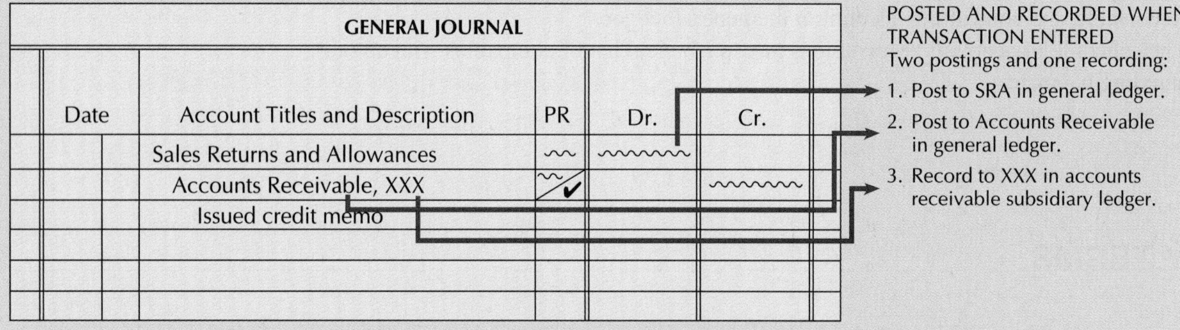

GENERAL JOURNAL
Date
Account Titles and Description
PR
Dr.
Cr.
Sales Returns and Allowances
Accounts Receivable, XXX
Issued credit memo
POSTED AND RECORDED WHEN TRANSACTION ENTERED
Two postings and one recording:
1. Post to SRA in general ledger.
2. Post to Accounts Receivable in general ledger.
3. Record to XXX in accounts receivable subsidiary ledger.

Issuing a Credit Memo with Sales Tax Recorded in a General Journal

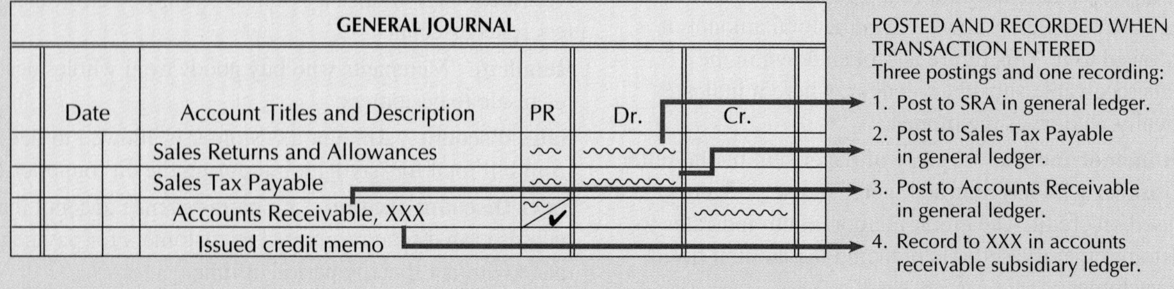

QUESTIONS, CLASSROOM DEMONSTRATION EXERCISES, EXERCISES, AND PROBLEMS

Discussion and Critical Thinking Questions /Ethical Case

1. Explain the purpose of a contra-revenue account.
2. What is the normal balance of Sales Discount?
3. Give two examples of contra-revenue accounts.
4. What is the difference between a discount period and a credit period?
5. Explain the terms:
   a. 2/10, n/30.
   b. n/10, EOM.
6. What category is Sales Discount in?
7. Compare and contrast the Controlling Account—Accounts Receivable to the accounts receivable subsidiary ledger.
8. Why is the accounts receivable subsidiary ledger organized in alphabetical order?
9. When is a (✓) used?
10. What is an invoice? What purpose does it serve?
11. Why is sales tax a liability to the business?
12. Sales discounts are taken on sales tax. Agree or disagree? Explain why.
13. When a seller issues a credit memorandum (assume no sales tax), what accounts will be affected?
14. Amy Jak is the National Sales Manager of Land.com. To get sales up to the projection for the old year, Amy asked the accountant to put the first two weeks' sales in January back into December. Amy told the accountant that this secret would only be between them. Should Amy move the new sales into the old sales year? You make the call. Write down your specific recommendations to Amy.

Classroom Demonstration Exercises

SET A

Overview *LO1 (5 min)*

1. Complete the following table for Sales, Sales Returns and Allowances, and Sales Discounts.

Accounts Affected	Category	↑ ↓	Temporary or Permanent

Calculating Net Sales *LO1 (5 min)*

2. Given the following, calculate net sales:

Gross Sales	$40
Sales Returns and Allowances	9
Sales Discounts	4

General Journal *LO1, 3, 4 (10 min)*

3. Match the following activities to the three business transactions (more than one number can be used).
   1. Record to the accounts receivable subsidiary ledger.
   2. Recorded in the general journal.
   3. Posted to the general ledger.
   a. ______ Sold merchandise on account to Ree Co., invoice no. 1, $50.
   b. ______ Sold merchandise on account to Flynn Co., invoice no. 2, $1,000.
   c. ______ Issued credit memorandum no. 1 to Flynn Co. for defective merchandise, $25.

LO2 (10 min) **Credit Memorandum**

4. Draw a transactional analysis box for the following transaction: Issued credit memorandum to Met.com for defective merchandise, $200.

Journalize Transactions

LO1, 2, 3 (15 min) **5.** Journalize the following transactions:

a. Sold merchandise on account to Ally Co., invoice no. 10, $40.
b. Received check from Moore Co., $100, less 2% discount.
c. Cash Sales, $100.
d. Issued credit memorandum no. 2 to Ally Co. for defective merchandise, $20.

LO5 (15 min) **6.** From the following, prepare a schedule of accounts receivable for Blue Co. for May 31, 200X.

Accounts Receivable Subsidiary Ledger

Bon Co.

	Dr.	Cr.	
5/6 GJ1	100		

Peke Co.

	Dr.	Cr.	
5/20 GJ1	30	10	5/27 GJ1

Green Co.

	Dr.	Cr.	
5/9 GJ1	10		

General Ledger

Accounts Receivable

	Dr.	Cr.	
5/31 GJ1	140	10	5/31 GJ1

SET B

LO1 (5 min) **Overview**

1. Complete the following table for Accounts Receivable, Sales Tax Payable, and Sales Discounts.

Accounts Affected	Category	↑ ↓	Temporary or Permanent

LO1 (5 min) **Calculating Net Sales**

2. Given the following, calculate net sales:

Gross Sales	$70
Sales Returns and Allowances	15
Sales Discounts	12

LO1, 3, 4 (10 min) **Sales Journal and General Journal**

3. Match the following to the three journal entries (more than one number can be used).

1. Record to the accounts receivable subsidiary ledger.
2. Recorded in the general journal.
3. Posted to the general ledger.

a. ______ Sold merchandise on account to Ree Co., invoice no. 1, $60.
b. ______ Sold merchandise on account to Flynn Co., invoice no. 2, $90.
c. ______ Issued credit memorandum no. 1 to Flynn Co. for defective merchandise, $30.

Credit Memorandum *LO2 (10 min)*

4. Draw a transactional analysis box for the following transaction: Issued credit memorandum to Met.com for defective merchandise, $100.

Sales and Cash Receipts

5. Journalize the following transactions: *LO1, 2, 3 (15 min)*

a. Sold merchandise on account to Ally Co., invoice no. 10, $30.
b. Received check from Moore Co., $70, less 20% discount.
c. Cash Sales, $400.
d. Issued credit memorandum no. 2 to Ally Co. for defective merchandise, $10.

6. From the following, prepare a schedule of accounts receivable for Blue Co. for May 31, 200X. *LO5 (15 min)*

Accounts Receivable Subsidiary Ledger

Bon Co.

	Dr.	Cr.	
5/6 GJ1	90		

Peke Co.

	Dr.	Cr.	
5/20 GJ1	20	10	5/27 GJ1

Green Co.

	Dr.	Cr.	
5/9 GJ1	30		

General Ledger

Accounts Receivable

	Dr.	Cr.	
5/31 GJ1	140	10	5/31 GJ1

Exercises

9-1. From the general journal in Figure 9.15 record to the accounts receivable subsidiary ledger and post to the general ledger accounts as appropriate. *LO1, 4 (10 min)*

General Journal

Date			PR	Dr.	Cr.
200X					
April	18	Accounts Receivable, Amazon.com		600 00	
		Sales			600 00
		Sold merchandise to Amazon			
	19	Accounts Receivable, Bill Valley Co.		900 00	
		Sales			900 00
		Sold merchandise to Bill Valley			

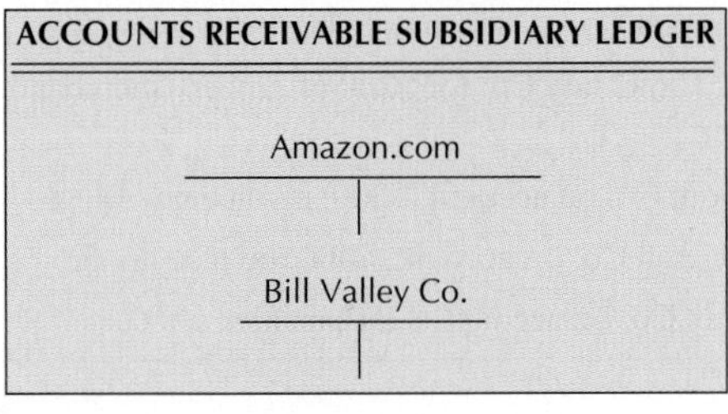

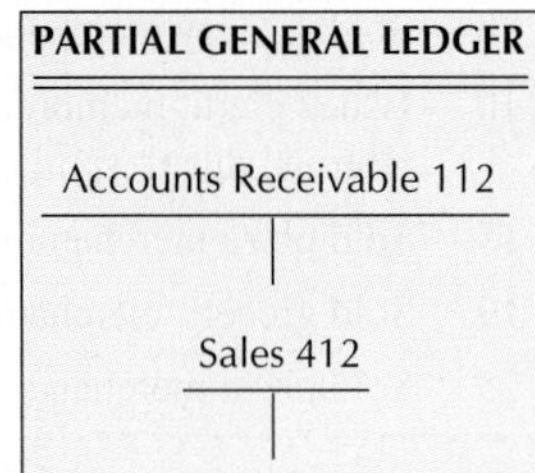

FIGURE 9.15 General Journal, Subsidiary Ledger, and Partial General Ledger

LO1, 2, 4 (10 min)

9-2. Journalize, record, and post when appropriate the following transactions into the general journal (all sales carry terms of 2/10, n/30):

200X		
May	16	Sold merchandise on account to Ronald Co., invoice no. 1, $1,000.
	18	Sold merchandise on account to Bass Co., invoice no. 2, $1,700.
	20	Issued credit memorandum no. 1 to Bass Co. for defective merchandise, $700.

Use the following account numbers: Accounts Receivable, 112; Sales, 411; Sales Returns and Allowances, 412.

LO3, 4 (10 min)

9-3. From Exercise 9-2, journalize the receipt of a check from Ronald Co. for payment of invoice no. 1 on May 24.

LO4, 5 (20 min)

9-4. From the following transactions for Edna Co., journalize, record, post, and prepare a schedule of accounts receivable when appropriate. You will have to set up your own accounts receivable subsidiary ledger and partial general ledger as needed. All sales terms are 2/10, n/30.

200X		
June	1	Edna Cares invested $3,000 in the business.
	1	Sold merchandise on account to Boston Co., invoice no. 1, $700.
	2	Sold merchandise on account to Gary Co., invoice no. 2, $900.
	3	Cash sale, $200.
	8	Issued credit memorandum no. 1 to Boston for defective merchandise, $200.
	10	Received check from Boston for invoice no. 1, less returns and discount.
	15	Cash sale, $400.
	18	Sold merchandise on account to Boston Co., invoice no. 3, $600.

LO2 (10 min)

9-5. From the following facts calculate what Ann Frost paid Blue Co. for the purchase of a dining room set. Sale terms are 2/10, n/30.

a. Sales ticket price before tax, $4,000, dated April 5.
b. Sales tax, 7%.
c. Returned one defective chair for credit of $400 on April 8.
d. Paid bill on April 13.

Group A Problems

LO1, 2, 4, 5 (40 min)

9A-1. Joan Lunden has opened Pizza and More, a wholesale grocery and pizza company. The following transactions occurred in June:

200X		
June	1	Sold grocery merchandise to Cindy Co. on account, $700, invoice no. 1.
	4	Sold pizza merchandise to Groom Co. on account, $800, invoice no. 2.
	8	Sold grocery merchandise to French Co. on account, $900, invoice no. 3.
	10	Issued credit memorandum no. 1 to Cindy Co. for $200 of grocery merchandise returned due to spoilage.
	15	Sold pizza merchandise to Groom Co. on account, $300, invoice no. 4.
	19	Sold grocery merchandise to French Co. on account, $400, invoice no. 5.
	25	Sold pizza merchandise to Cindy Co. on account, $250, invoice no. 6.

Check Figure:
Schedule of accounts receivable $3,150

Required

1. Journalize the transactions.
2. Record to the accounts receivable subsidiary ledger and post to the general ledger as appropriate.
3. Prepare a schedule of accounts receivable for the end of June.

9A-2. The following transactions of Ted's Auto Supply occurred in November (your working papers have balances as of November 1 for certain general ledger and accounts receivable ledger accounts): ***LO1, 2, 4, 5 (50 min)***

200X		
Nov.	1	Sold auto parts merchandise to R. Volan on account, $1,000, invoice no. 60, plus 5% sales tax.
	5	Sold auto parts merchandise to J. Seth on account, $800, invoice no. 61, plus 5% sales tax.
	8	Sold auto parts merchandise to Lance Corner on account, $9,000, invoice no. 62, plus 5% sales tax.
	10	Issued credit memorandum no. 12 to R. Volan for $500 for defective auto parts merchandise returned from Nov. 1 transaction. (Be careful to record the reduction in Sales Tax Payable as well.)
	12	Sold auto parts merchandise to J. Seth on account, $600, invoice no. 63, plus 5% sales tax.

Check Figure:
Schedule of accounts receivable $13,045

Required

1. Journalize the transactions.
2. Record to the accounts receivable subsidiary ledger and post to the general ledger as appropriate.
3. Prepare a schedule of accounts receivable for the end of November.

9A-3. Mark Peaker owns Peaker's Sneaker Shop. (In your working papers balances as of May 1 are provided for the accounts receivable and general ledger accounts.) The following transactions occurred in May: ***LO1, 2, 3, 4, 5 (70 min)***

200X		
May	1	Mark Peaker invested an additional $12,000 in the sneaker store.
	3	Sold $700 of merchandise on account to B. Dale, sales ticket no. 60; terms 1/10, n/30.
	4	Sold $500 of merchandise on account to Ron Lester, sales ticket no. 61; terms 1/10, n/30.
	9	Sold $200 of merchandise on account to Jim Zon, sales ticket no. 62; terms 1/10, n/30.
	10	Received cash from B. Dale in payment of May 3 transaction, sales ticket no. 60, less discount.
	20	Sold $3,000 of merchandise on account to Pam Pry, sales ticket no. 63; terms 1/10, n/30.
	22	Received cash payment from Ron Lester in payment of May 4 transaction, sales ticket no. 61.
	23	Collected cash sales, $3,000.
	24	Issued credit memorandum no. 1 to Pam Pry for $2,000 of merchandise returned from May 20 sales on account.
	26	Received cash from Pam Pry in payment of May 20, sales ticket no. 63. (Don't forget about the credit memo and discount.)
	28	Collected cash sales, $7,000.
	30	Sold sneaker rack equipment for $300 cash. (Beware.)

Check Figure:
Schedule of accounts receivable $5,700

(continued on next page)

	30	Sold merchandise priced at $4,000, on account to Ron Lester, sales ticket no. 64; terms 1/10, n/30.
	31	Issued credit memorandum no. 2 to Ron Lester for $700 of merchandise returned from May 30 transaction, sales ticket no. 64.

Required

1. Journalize the transactions.
2. Record to the accounts receivable subsidiary ledger and post to the general ledger as needed.
3. Prepare a schedule of accounts receivable for the end of May.

LO1, 2, 3, 4, 5 (75 min)

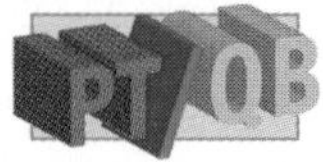

9A-4. Bill Murray opened Bill's Cosmetic Market on April 1. A 6% sales tax is calculated and added to all cosmetic sales. Bill offers no sales discounts. The following transactions occurred in April:

Check Figure:
Schedule of accounts receivable $1,643

200X		
Apr.	1	Bill Murray invested $8,000 in the Cosmetic Market from his personal savings account.
	5	From the cash register tapes, lipstick cash sales were $5,000, plus sales tax.
	5	From the cash register tapes, eye shadow cash sales were $2,000, plus sales tax.
	8	Sold lipstick on account to Alice Koy Co., $300, sales ticket no. 1, plus sales tax.
	9	Sold eye shadow on account to Marika Sanchez Co., $1,000, sales ticket no. 2, plus sales tax.
	15	Issued credit memorandum no. 1 to Alice Koy Co. for $150 for lipstick returned. (Be sure to reduce Sales Tax Payable for Bill.)
	19	Marika Sanchez Co. paid half the amount owed from sales ticket no. 2, dated April 9.
	21	Sold lipstick on account to Jeff Tong Co., $300, sales ticket no. 3, plus sales tax.
	24	Sold eye shadow on account to Rusty Neal Co., $800, sales ticket no. 4, plus sales tax.
	25	Issued credit memorandum no. 2 to Jeff Tong Co. for $200 for lipstick returned from sales ticket no. 3, dated April 21.
	29	Cash sales taken from the cash register tape showed the following: **1.** Lipstick: $1,000 + $60 sales tax collected. **2.** Eye shadow: $3,000 + $180 sales tax collected.
	29	Sold lipstick on account to Marika Sanchez Co., $400, sales ticket no. 5, plus sales tax.
	30	Received payment from Marika Sanchez Co. of sales ticket no. 5, dated April 29.

Required

1. Journalize the transactions.
2. Record to the accounts receivable subsidiary ledger and post to the general ledger when appropriate.
3. Prepare a schedule of accounts receivable for the end of April.

Group B Problems

LO1, 2, 4, 5 (40 min)

9B-1. The following transactions occurred for Pizza and More for the month of June:

200X		
June	1	Sold grocery merchandise to Cindy Co. on account, $800, invoice no. 1.
	4	Sold pizza merchandise to Groom Co. on account, $550, invoice no. 2.

	8	Sold grocery merchandise to French Co. on account, $900, invoice no. 3.
	10	Issued credit memorandum no. 1 to Cindy Co. for $160 of grocery merchandise returned due to spoilage.
	15	Sold pizza merchandise to Groom Co. on account, $700, invoice no. 4.
	19	Sold grocery merchandise to French Co. on account, $250, invoice no. 5.

Required

1. Journalize the transactions.
2. Record to the accounts receivable subsidiary ledger and post to the general ledger as appropriate.
3. Prepare a schedule of accounts receivable for the end of June.

Check Figure:
Schedule of accounts receivable $3,040

9B-2. In November the following transactions occurred for Ted's Auto Supply (your working papers have balances as of November 1 for certain general ledger and accounts receivable ledger accounts): ***LO1, 2, 4, 5 (50 min)***

200X		
Nov.	1	Sold merchandise to R. Volan on account, $4,000, invoice no. 70, plus 5% sales tax.
	5	Sold merchandise to J. Seth on account, $1,600, invoice no. 71, plus 5% sales tax.
	8	Sold merchandise to Lance Corner on account, $15,000, invoice no. 72, plus 5% sales tax.
	10	Issued credit memorandum no. 14 to R. Volan for $2,000 for defective merchandise returned from Nov. 1 transaction. (Be sure to record the reduction in Sales Tax Payable as well.)
	12	Sold merchandise to J. Seth on account, $1,400, invoice no. 73, plus 5% sales tax.

Required

1. Journalize the transactions.
2. Record to the accounts receivable subsidiary ledger and post to the general ledger as appropriate.
3. Prepare a schedule of accounts receivable for the end of November.

Check Figure:
Schedule of accounts receivable $22,600

9B-3. (In your working papers, all the beginning balances needed are provided for the accounts receivable subsidiary and general ledgers.) The following transactions occurred for Peaker's Sneaker Shop: ***LO1, 2, 3, 4, 5 (70 min)***

200X		
May	1	Mark Peaker invested an additional $14,000 in the sneaker store.
	3	Sold $2,000 of merchandise on account to B. Dale, sales ticket no. 60; terms 1/10, n/30.
	4	Sold $900 of merchandise on account to Ron Lester, sales ticket no. 61; terms 1/10, n/30.
	9	Sold $600 of merchandise on account to Jim Zon, sales ticket no. 62; terms 1/10, n/30.
	10	Received cash from B. Dale in payment of May 3 transaction, sales ticket no. 60, less discount.
	20	Sold $4,000 of merchandise on account to Pam Pry, sales ticket no. 63; terms 1/10, n/30.
	22	Received cash payment from Ron Lester in payment of May 4 transaction, sales ticket no. 61.

(continued on next page)

23	Collected cash sales, $6,000.
24	Issued credit memorandum no. 1 to Pam Pry for $500 of merchandise returned from May 20 sales on account.
26	Received cash from Pam Pry in payment of May 20 sales ticket no. 63. (Don't forget about the credit memo and discount.)
28	Collected cash sales, $12,000.
30	Sold sneaker rack equipment for $200 cash.
30	Sold $6,000 of merchandise on account to Ron Lester, sales ticket no. 64, terms 1/10, n/30.
31	Issued credit memorandum no. 2 to Ron Lester for $800 of merchandise returned from May 30 transaction, sales ticket no. 64.

Check Figure:
Schedule of accounts receivable $8,000

Required

1. Journalize the transactions.
2. Record and post as appropriate.
3. Prepare a schedule of accounts receivable for the end of May.

LO1, 2, 3, 4, 5 (75 min)

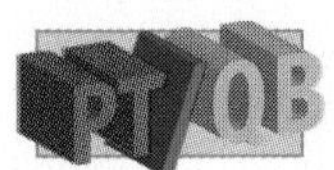

9B-4. Bill's Cosmetic Market began operating in April. A 6% sales tax is calculated and added to all cosmetic sales. Bill offers no discounts. The following transactions occurred in April:

200X		
Apr.	1	Bill Murray invested $10,000 in the Cosmetic Market from his personal account.
	5	From the cash register tapes, lipstick cash sales were $5,000, plus sales tax.
	5	From the cash register tapes, eye shadow cash sales were $3,000, plus sales tax.
	8	Sold lipstick on account to Alice Koy Co., $400, sales ticket no. 1, plus sales tax.
	9	Sold eye shadow on account to Marika Sanchez Co., $900, sales ticket no. 2, plus sales tax.
	15	Issued credit memorandum no. 1 to Alice Koy Co. for lipstick returned, $200. (Be sure to reduce Sales Tax Payable for Bill.)
	19	Marika Sanchez Co. paid half the amount owed from sales ticket no. 2, dated April 9.
	21	Sold lipstick on account to Jeff Tong Co., $600, sales ticket no. 3, plus sales tax.
	24	Sold eye shadow on account to Rusty Neal Co., $1,000, sales ticket no. 4, plus sales tax.
	25	Issued credit memorandum no. 2 to Jeff Tong Co. for $300, for lipstick returned from sales ticket no. 3, dated April 21.
	29	Cash sales taken from the cash register tape showed the following: **1.** Lipstick: $4,000 + $240 sales tax collected. **2.** Eye shadow: $2,000 + $120 sales tax collected.
	29	Sold lipstick on account to Marika Sanchez Co., $700, sales ticket no. 5, plus sales tax.
	30	Received payment from Marika Sanchez Co. of sales ticket no. 5, dated April 29.

Check Figure:
Schedule of accounts receivable $2,067

Required

1. Journalize, record, and post as appropriate.
2. Prepare a schedule of accounts receivable for the end of April.

ON-THE-JOB TRAINING

T-1. Pete O'Brady has been hired by Logan Company to help reconstruct the general journal, which was recently destroyed in a fire. The owner of Logan Company has supplied him with the following data. Please ignore dates, invoice numbers, and so forth and enter the entries into the reconstructed general journal. What written recommendation should Pete make so reconstruction will not be needed in the future? ***LO1, 2, 3, 4, 5 (60 min)***

ACCOUNTS RECEIVABLE SUBSIDIARY LEDGER

P. Bond

	Dr.	Cr.	
Bal.	100	150	GJ
GJ	150	Entitled to 2% discount	

M. Raff

	Dr.	Cr.
Bal.	200	
GJ	100	

J. Smooth

	Dr.	Cr.	
Bal.	300	1,000	GJ
GJ	2,000	1,000	GJ ← Entitled to 1% discount
GJ	1,000	500	GJ

R. Venner

	Dr.	Cr.
Bal.	200	400
GJ	400	

PARTIAL GENERAL LEDGER

Cash

Dr.	Cr.
5,000	
147	
400	
5,000	
1,000	
990	
200	

Accounts Receivable

	Dr.	Cr.	
Bal.	800	1,000	GJ
	150	500	GJ
	100	150	GJ
	400		
	2,000	400	
	1,000	1,000	

Shelving Equipment

	Dr.	Cr.	
Bal.	200	200	GJ

M. Rang, Capital

Dr.	Cr.
	1,000 Bal.
	5,000 ← Additional investment this month

(continued on next page)

Sales

	Dr.	Cr.	
		800	Bal.
		150	GJ
		100	GJ
		400	GJ
		2,000	GJ
		1,000	GJ
		5,000	Cash Sales

Sales Discount

	Dr.	Cr.
GJ	3	
	10	

Sales Returns and Allowances

	Dr.	Cr.
GJ	1,000	
GJ	500	

LO2, 3, 4, 5 (45 min)

T-2. The bookkeeper of Joy Company records credit sales and returns in a general journal. The bookkeeper did the following:

1. Recorded an $18 credit sale as $180 in the general journal.
2. Correctly recorded a $40 sale in the general journal but posted it to B. Blue's account as $400 in the accounts receivable ledger.
3. Made an additional error in determining the balance of J. B. Window Co. in the accounts receivable ledger.
4. Posted a sales return from B. Katz Co. that was recorded in the general journal to the Sales Returns and Allowance account and the Accounts Receivable account but forgot to record it to the B. Katz Co. subsidiary ledger accounts.
5. Added the total of the general journal incorrectly.
6. Posted a sales return to the Accounts Receivable account but not to the Sales Returns and Allowances account. The Accounts Receivable ledger was recorded correctly.

Could you inform the bookkeeper in writing as to when each error will be discovered?

FINANCIAL REPORT PROBLEM

LO1 (15 min)

Reading the Kellogg's Annual Report

Go to Appendix A, Note 1, Revenue Recognition, and find out what account records the promotional package inserts.

INTERNET PROJECT

Big Lots

Go to the Web and search: Annual Report Big Lots 2008.
Click on Investors Relations.
List out the latest news Big Lots is providing to its investors.
Order a free annual report.

CONTINUING PROBLEM

Sanchez Computer Center

LO1, 2, 3, 4, 5 (60 min)

To assist you in recording these transactions for the month of January, at the end of this problem is the schedule of accounts receivable as of December 31 and an updated chart of accounts with the current balance listed for each account.

Assignment

1. Journalize the transactions.
2. Record in the accounts receivable subsidiary ledger and post to the general ledger as appropriate. A partial general ledger is included in the *Working Papers.*
3. Prepare a schedule of accounts receivable as of January 31, 200X.

The January transactions are as follows:

Jan.	1	Sold $700 worth of merchandise to Taylor Golf on credit, sales invoice no. 5000; terms 2/10, n/30.
	10	Sold $3,000 worth of merchandise on account to Anthony Pitale, sales invoice no. 5001; terms 2/10, n/30.
	11	Received $3,000 from Accu Pac, Inc., toward payment of its balance; no discount allowed.
	12	Collected $2,000 cash sales.
	19	Sold $4,000 worth of merchandise on account to Vita Needle, sales invoice no. 5002; terms 4/10, n/30.
	20	Collected balance in full from invoice no. 5001, Anthony Pitale.
	29	Issued credit memorandum to Taylor Golf for $400 worth of merchandise returned, invoice no. 5000.
	29	Collected full payment from Vita Needle, invoice no. 5002.

Schedule of Accounts Receivable
Sanchez Computer Center
December 31, 200X

Taylor Golf	$ 2,900.00
Vita Needle	6,800.00
Accu Pac	3,900.00
Total Amount Due	$13,600.00

Chart of Accounts and Current Balances as of 12/31/0X

Account #	Account Name	Debit Balance	Credit Balance
1000	Cash	$3,336.65	
1010	Petty Cash	100	
1020	Accounts Receivable	13,600	
1025	Prepaid Rent	1,600	
1030	Supplies	132	
1040	Merchandise Inventory	0	
1080	Computer Shop Equipment	3,800	
1081	Accumulated Dep., C.S. Equip.		$ 99
1090	Office Equipment	1,050	

(continued on next page)

1091	Accumulated Dep., Office Equip.		20
2000	Accounts Payable		2,050
2010	Wages Payable		0
2020	FICA—Social Security Payable		0
2030	FICA—Medicare Payable		0
2040	FIT Payable		0
2050	SIT Payable		0
2060	FUTA Payable		0
2070	SUTA Payable		0
3000	Freedman, Capital		7,406
3010	Freedman, Withdrawals	2,015	
3020	Income Summary		0
4000	Service Revenue		18,500
4010	Sales		0
4020	Sales Returns and Allowances	0	
4030	Sales Discounts	0	
5010	Advertising Expense	0	
5020	Rent Expense	0	
5030	Utilities Expense	0	
5040	Phone Expense	150	
5050	Supplies Expense	0	
5060	Insurance Expense	0	
5070	Postage Expense	25	
5080	Dep. Exp., C.S. Equipment	0	
5090	Dep. Exp., Office Equipment	0	
5100	Miscellaneous Expense	10	
5110	Wage Expense	2,030	
5120	Payroll Tax Expense	226.35	
5130	Interest Expense	0	
5140	Bad Debt Expense	0	
6000	Purchases	0	
6010	Purchases Returns and Allowances		0
6020	Purchases Discounts		0
6030	Freight In	0	

10 Purchases and Cash Payments

DID YOU KNOW? Trade promotions from companies like Del Monte are amounts paid to retailers for temporary price reductions, circular advertisements, and favorable stock locations. Trade promotions reduce sales and are recorded as accrued liabilities. Visit *www.delmonte.com* to find more information about Del Monte.

LEARNING OBJECTIVES

1. Recording and posting purchase transactions.
2. Recording to accounts payable subsidiary ledger.
3. Preparing, journalizing, and posting a debit memorandum.
4. Recording and posting cash payment transactions.
5. Preparing a schedule of accounts payable.
6. Journalizing transactions for a perpetual accounting system.

LO1

Learning Unit 10-1 Chou's Toy Shop: Buyer's View of a Merchandise Company

Purchases

Purchases of merchandise on account are recorded on a purchase order in Peachtree and QuickBooks.

When you go into your local supermarket do you ever wonder how a store records all of the merchandise it purchases from a company like Del Monte? First, let's look at Chou's Toy Shop. Chou brings merchandise into his toy store for resale to customers. The account that records the cost of this merchandise is called **Purchases.** Suppose Chou buys $4,000 worth of Barbie dolls on account from Mattel Manufacturing on July 6. The Purchases account records all merchandise bought for resale.

Purchases is a cost.
The rules work the same as an expense.

Purchases	
Dr.	Cr.
4,000	

This account has a debit balance and is classified as a cost. Purchases represent costs that are directly related to bringing merchandise into the store for resale to customers. The July 6 entry would be analyzed and journalized as in Figure 10.1.

If Chou's purchased a new display case for the store, it would not show up in the Purchases account. The case is considered equipment that is not for resale to customers.

Accounts Affected	Category	↑ ↓	Rules	T Account Update
Purchases	Cost	↑	Dr.	Purchases: Dr. 4,000
Accounts Payable, Mattel	Liability	↑	Cr.	Acc. Payable: Cr. 4,000; Mattel: Cr. 4,000

FIGURE 10.1 Purchased Merchandise on Account

			Dr.	Cr.
July	6	Purchases	400000	
		Accounts Payable, Mattel		400000
		Purchases on account		

Keep in mind we would have to record to Mattel in the accounts payable subsidiary ledger. We talk about the subsidiary ledger in Learning Unit 10-2.

Purchases Returns and Allowances

Chou noticed that some of the dolls he received were defective, and he notified the manufacturer of the defects. On July 9, Mattel issued a credit memorandum indicating that Chou would get a $500 reduction from the original selling price. Chou then agreed to keep the dolls. The account that records a decrease to a buyer's cost is a contra-cost account called **Purchases Returns and Allowances.** The account lowers the cost of purchases.

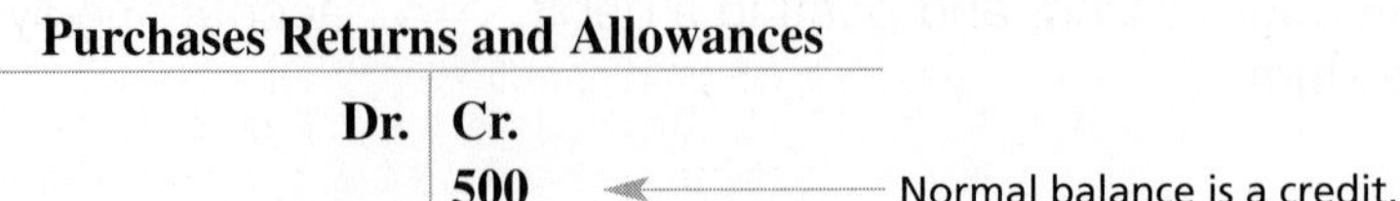

Let's analyze this reduction to cost and prepare a general journal entry (Fig. 10.2).

Accounts Affected	Category	↑ ↓	Rules	T Account Update
Accounts Payable, Mattel	Liability	↓	Dr.	**Acc. Payable** Dr. 500 | Cr. 4,000; **Mattel** Dr. 500 | Cr. 4,000
Purchases Returns and Allowances	Contra-cost	↑	Cr.	**Purchases Ret. & Allow.** Dr. | Cr. 500

				Dr.	Cr.
July	9	Accounts Payable, Mattel		500 00	
		Purchases Returns and Allowances			500 00
		Received credit memorandum			

FIGURE 10.2 Credit Memorandum Received

When posted to general ledger accounts as well as recorded to Mattel in the accounts payable subsidiary ledger, Chou owes $500 less.

Purchases Discount Now let's look at the analysis and journal entry when Chou pays Mattel. Mattel offers a 2% cash discount if the invoice is paid within 10 days. To take advantage of this cash discount, Chou sent a check to Mattel on July 15. The discount is taken after the allowance.

Remember: For Mattel, it is a sales discount, whereas for Chou it is a purchases discount.

$4,000
− 500 allowance
$3,500 × .02 = $70 purchases discount

The account that records this discount is called **Purchases Discount.** It, too, is a contra-cost account because it lowers the cost of purchases.

Remember: Purchases are debits; purchases discounts are credits.

Purchases Discount

Dr.	Cr.
	70

← Normal balance is a credit.

Let's analyze (on top of next page) and prepare (below) a general journal entry (Fig. 10.3).

				Dr.	Cr.
July	15	Accounts Payable, Mattel		3500 00	
		Purchases Discount			70 00
		Cash			3430 00
		Paid Mattel balance owed			

FIGURE 10.3 Purchase Discount Journalized

Accounts Affected	Category	↑ ↓	Rules	T Account Update
Accounts Payable, Mattel	Liability	↓	Dr.	**Acc. Payable** Dr. / Cr.: **500** / **4,000**; 3,500 — **Mattel** Dr. / Cr.: **500** / **4,000**; 3,500
Purchases Discount	Contra-cost	↑	Cr.	**Purchases Discount** Dr. / Cr.: — / 70
Cash	Asset	↓	Cr.	**Cash** Dr. / Cr.: — / 3,430

After the journal entry is posted and recorded to Mattel, the result will show that Chou saved $70 and totally reduced what he owed to Mattel. The actual—or net—cost of his purchase is $3,430, calculated as follows:

Purchases	$4,000
− Purchases Returns and Allowances	500
− Purchases Discounts	70
= Net Purchases	$3,430

F.O.B. Destination: Seller pays freight to point of destination.

F.O.B. Shipping Point: Buyer pays freight from seller's shipping point.

Freight charges are not taken into consideration in calculating net purchases. Still, they are important. If the seller is responsible for paying the shipping cost until the goods reach their destination, the freight charges are **F.O.B. destination.** (F.O.B. stands for "free on board" the carrier.) For example, if a seller located in Boston sold goods F.O.B. destination to a buyer in New York, the seller would have to pay the cost of shipping the goods to the buyer.

If the buyer is responsible for paying the shipping costs, the freight charges are **F.O.B. shipping point.** In this situation, the seller will sometimes prepay the freight charges as a matter of convenience and will add it to the invoice of the purchaser, as in the following example:

Bill amount ($800 + $80 prepaid freight)	$880
Less 5% cash discount (.05 × $800)	40
Amount to be paid by buyer	$840

Purchases discounts are not taken on freight. The discount is based on the purchase price.

If the seller ships goods F.O.B. shipping point, legal ownership (title) passes to the buyer *when the goods are shipped.* If goods are shipped by the seller F.O.B. destination, title will change *when goods have reached their destination.* (See Exhibit 10.1 on top of next page.)

LEARNING UNIT 10-1 REVIEW

AT THIS POINT you should be able to

- Explain and calculate purchases, purchases returns and allowances, and purchases discounts.
- Calculate net purchases.
- Explain why purchases discounts are not taken on freight.
- Compare and contrast F.O.B. destination with F.O.B. shipping point.

EXHIBIT 10.1

FOB shipping point		FOB destination	

FOB shipping point: title changes hands at the shipping point, and buyer owns the goods while they are in transit. So, the buyer pays the shipping costs.		**FOB destination:** title changes hands at the destination point, and seller owns the goods while they are in transit. So, the seller, not the buyer, pays the shipping costs.	

Self-Review Quiz 10-1

Respond true or false to the following:

1. Net purchases = Purchases − Purchases Returns and Allowances − Purchases Discount.
2. Purchases is a contra-cost.
3. F.O.B. destination means the seller covers shipping cost and retains title until goods reach their destination.
4. Purchases discounts are not taken on freight.
5. Purchases Discount is a contra-cost account.

Solutions to Self-Review Quiz 10-1

1. True
2. False
3. True
4. True
5. True

Learning Unit 10-2 Recording and Posting Purchases Transactions on Account for Art's Wholesale Clothing Company: Introduction to Subsidiary Ledgers and Debit Memorandum

200X		
April	3	Purchased merchandise on account $5,000 and freight $50 from Abby Blake Co.; terms 2/10, n/60.
	4	Purchased equipment on account $4,000 from Joe Francis Co.
	6	Purchased merchandise on account $800 from Thorpe Co.; terms 1/10, n/30.
	7	Purchased merchandise on account $980 from John Sullivan Co.; terms n/10, EOM.
	9	Art's issued debit memo #1 $200 to Thorpe for defective merchandise.
	12	Purchased merchandise on account $600 from Abby Blake Co.; terms 1/10, n/30.
	25	Purchased $500 of supplies on account from John Sullivan Co.

Let's look at the steps Art's Wholesale Clothing Company took when it ordered goods from Abby Blake Company on April 3.

Authorized personnel initiate purchase requisition.

Step 1: Prepare a Purchase Requisition at Art's Wholesale Clothing Company The inventory clerk notes a low inventory level of ladies' jackets for resale, so the clerk sends a **purchase requisition** to the purchasing department. A duplicate copy is sent to the accounting department. A third copy remains with the department that initiated the request to be used as a check on the purchasing department.

Four copies of purchase order: (1) (original) to supplier, (2) to accounting department, (3) to department that initiated purchase requisition, and (4) to file of purchasing department.

Step 2: Purchasing Department of Art's Wholesale Clothing Company Prepares a Purchase Order After checking various price lists and suppliers' catalogs, the purchasing department fills out a form called a **purchase order.** This form gives Abby Blake Company the authority to ship the ladies' jackets ordered by Art's Wholesale Clothing Company (see Fig. 10.4).

Step 3: Sales Invoice Prepared by Abby Blake Company Abby Blake Company receives the purchase order and prepares a sales invoice. The sales invoice for the seller is the **purchase invoice** for the buyer. A sales invoice is shown in Figure 10.5.

The invoice shows that the goods will be shipped **F.O.B.** Englewood Cliffs. Thus, Art's Wholesale Clothing Company is responsible for paying the shipping costs.

The sales invoice also shows a freight charge. Thus, Abby Blake prepaid the shipping costs as a matter of convenience. Art's will repay the freight charges when it pays the invoice.

Step 4: Receiving the Goods When goods are received, Art's Wholesale inspects the shipment and completes a **receiving report.** The receiving report verifies that the exact merchandise that was ordered was received in good condition.

FIGURE 10.4 Purchase Order

PURCHASE ORDER NO. 1
ART'S WHOLESALE CLOTHING COMPANY
1528 BELLE AVE.
NEW YORK, NY 10022

Purchased From: Abby Blake Company
12 Foster Road
Englewood Cliffs, NJ 07632

Date: April 1, 200X
Shipped VIA: Freight Truck
Terms: 2/10, n/60
FOB: Englewood Cliffs

Quantity	Description	Unit Price	Total
100	Ladies' Jackets Code 14-0	$50	$5,000

Art's Wholesale
By: Bill Joy

Purchase order number must appear on all invoices.

FIGURE 10.5 Sales Invoice

SALES INVOICE NO. 228
ABBY BLAKE COMPANY
12 FOSTER ROAD
ENGLEWOOD, CLIFFS, NJ 07632

Sold To: Art's Wholesale
Clothing Co.
1528 Belle Ave.
New York, NY 10022

Date: April 3, 200X
Shipped VIA: Freight Truck
Terms: 2/10, n/60
Your Order No: 1
FOB: Englewood Cliffs

Quantity	Description	Unit Price	Total
100	Ladies' Jackets Code 14-0	$50	$5,000
	Freight		50
			$5,050

Step 5: Verifying the Numbers Before the invoice is approved for recording and payment, the accounting department must check the purchase order, invoice, and receiving report to make sure that all are in agreement and that no steps have been omitted. The form used for checking and approval is an **invoice approval form** (see Fig. 10.6).

INVOICE APPROVAL FORM Art's Wholesale Clothing Co.	
Purchase Order #	______
Requisition check	______
Purchase Order check	______
Receiving Report check	______
Invoice check	______
Approved for Payment	______

FIGURE 10.6 Invoice Approval Form

Keep in mind that Art's Wholesale Clothing Company does not record this purchase until the *invoice is approved for recording and payment.* Abby Blake Company records this transaction in its records when the sales invoice is prepared, however.

Let's look closer at the April 3 transaction.

200X

April 3 Purchased merchandise on account $5,000 plus freight $50 from Abby Blake Co.

THE ANALYSIS

Accounts Affected	Category	↑ ↓	Rules of Dr. and Cr.
Purchases	Cost	↑	Dr. $5,000
Freight-In	Expense	↑	Dr. $50
Accounts Payable, Abby Blake Co.	Liability	↑	Cr. $5,050

Buyer			Seller		
Purchase	Dr.	Cost	Sale	Cr.	Revenue
PRA	Cr.	Contra-cost	SRA	Dr.	Contra-revenue
PD	Cr.	Contra-cost	SD	Dr.	Contra-revenue

Figure 10.7 shows how the general journal would look.

				Page 2
April	3	Purchases	5 0 0 0 00	
		Freight-In	5 0 00	
		Accounts Payable, Abby Blake Co.		5 0 5 0 00
		Purchased merchandise on account		
		from Abby Blake		

FIGURE 10.7 Merchandise Purchase, Plus Freight Cost

Accounts Payable Subsidiary Ledger

LO2

In the last chapter we saw the accounts receivable subsidiary ledger. It listed customers owing Art's money from sales on account. Now we look at Art's, the buyer, and an **accounts payable subsidiary ledger.** See Figure 10.8 on the following page.

Note that the normal balance is a credit for Accounts Payable and its subsidiary ledger whereas in the last chapter Accounts Receivable had a debit normal balance.

Accounts Payable is the controlling account in the ledger and at the end of the month the sum of the individual amount owed to the creditors should equal the balance in Accounts Payable at the end of the month.

Figure 10.9 on the following page shows how the general journal looks for Art's before posting and recording this month's purchases on account.

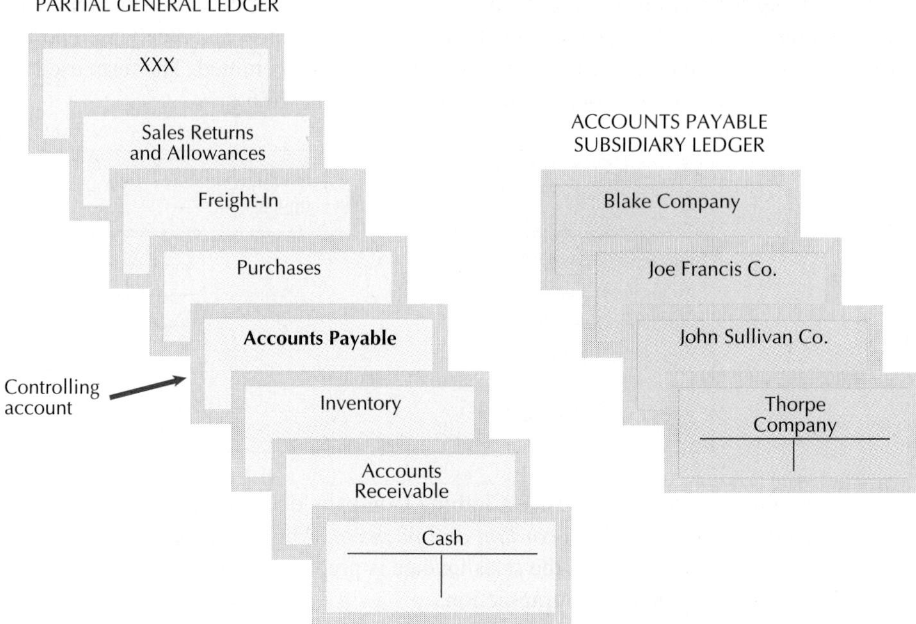

FIGURE 10.8 Partial General Ledger of Art's Wholesale Clothing Company and Accounts Payable Subsidiary Ledger

FIGURE 10.9

GENERAL JOURNAL

Page 2

Date		Account Titles and Description	PR	Dr.	Cr.
200X					
April	3	Purchases		500000	
		Freight-In		5000	
		Accounts Payable, Abby Blake Co.			505000
		Purchased merchandise on account, Blake			
	4	Equipment		400000	
		Accounts Payable, Joe Francis			400000
		Purchased equipment on account, Francis			
	6	Purchases		80000	
		Accounts Payable, Thorpe Company			80000
		Purchased merchandise on account, Thorpe			
	7	Purchases		98000	
		Accounts Payable, John Sullivan Co.			98000
		Purchased merchandise on account, Sullivan			
	9	Accounts Payable, Thorpe Company		20000	
		Purchases Returns and Allowances			20000
		Debit memo no. 1			
	12	Purchases		60000	
		Accounts Payable, Abby Blake Co.			60000
		Purchased merchandise on account, Blake			
	25	Supplies		50000	
		Accounts Payable, John Sullivan Co.			50000
		Purchased supplies on account, Sullivan			

Posting and Recording Purchases Transactions Before we post to the general ledger and record to the subsidiary ledger, let's first examine the T accounts and what each one would look like.

(Before Recordings)

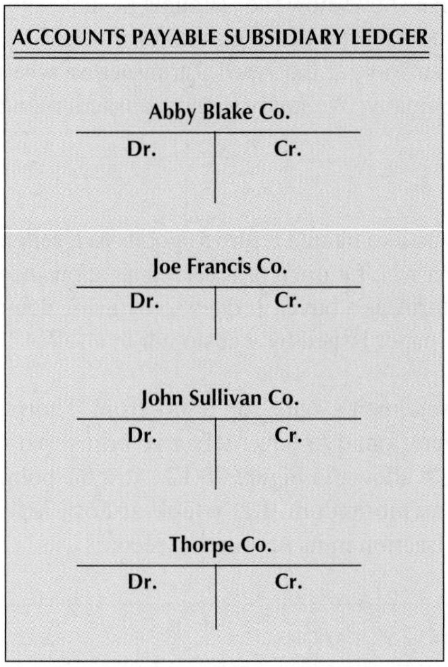

ACCOUNTS PAYABLE SUBSIDIARY LEDGER

Abby Blake Co.	
Dr.	Cr.

Joe Francis Co.	
Dr.	Cr.

John Sullivan Co.	
Dr.	Cr.

Thorpe Co.	
Dr.	Cr.

(Before Postings)

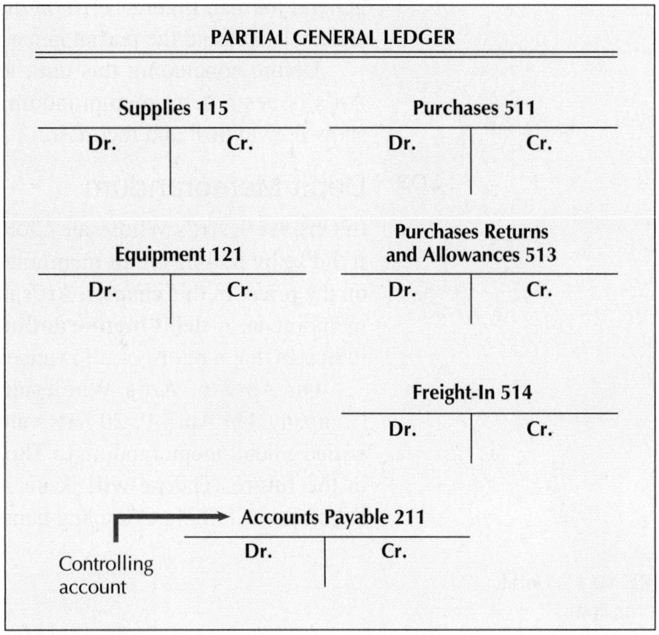

PARTIAL GENERAL LEDGER

Supplies 115	
Dr.	Cr.

Purchases 511	
Dr.	Cr.

Equipment 121	
Dr.	Cr.

Purchases Returns and Allowances 513	
Dr.	Cr.

Freight-In 514	
Dr.	Cr.

Controlling account →

Accounts Payable 211	
Dr.	Cr.

Now let's look at how to post and record the April 3 transaction.

FIGURE 10.10

GENERAL JOURNAL — Page 2

Date		Account Titles and Description	PR	Dr.	Cr.
200X					
April	3	Purchases	511	5 0 0 0 00	
		Freight-In	514	5 0 00	
		Accounts Payable, Abby Blake Co.	211 ✓		5 0 5 0 00
		Purchased merchandise on account, Blake			

PARTIAL ACCOUNTS PAYABLE SUBSIDIARY LEDGER

Abby Blake Co.	
Dr.	Cr.
	5,050 GJ2 4/3

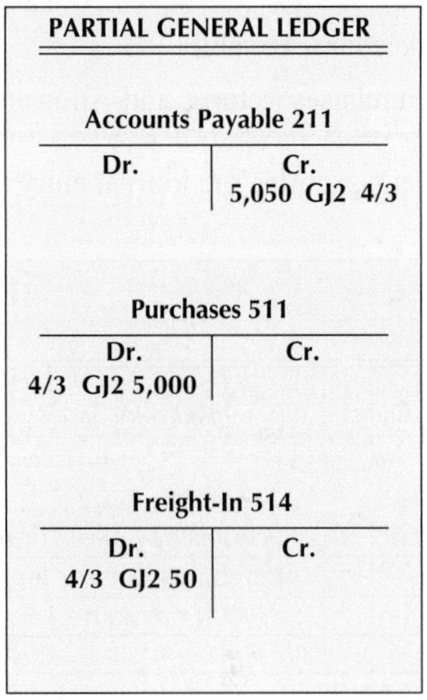

PARTIAL GENERAL LEDGER

Accounts Payable 211	
Dr.	Cr.
	5,050 GJ2 4/3

Purchases 511	
Dr.	Cr.
4/3 GJ2 5,000	

Freight-In 514	
Dr.	Cr.
4/3 GJ2 50	

For this transaction we post to the general ledger accounts Purchases, Freight-In, and Accounts Payable. Note how the account numbers 511, 514, and 211 are entered into the PR column of the general journal. We must also *record* to Abby Blake Co. in the accounts payable subsidiary ledger. Note that it is placed on the credit side because we owe Abby the money. When the subsidiary ledger is updated, a (✓) is placed in the PR column of the general journal. Figure 10.10 on the preceding page shows how the accounts payable subsidiary ledger and the partial general ledger would look after postings and recordings.

Before concluding this unit, let's take a closer look at the April 9 transaction when Art's issues a debit memorandum to Thorpe Company. We analyze the transaction and show how to post and record it.

LO3 Debit Memorandum

In Chapter 9, Art's Wholesale Clothing Company had to handle returned goods as a seller. It did so by issuing credit memoranda to customers who returned or received an allowance on the price. In this chapter, Art's must handle returns as a buyer. It does so by using debit memoranda. A **debit memorandum** is a piece of paper issued by a customer to a seller. It indicates that a return or allowance has occurred.

On April 6, Art's Wholesale had purchased men's hats for $800 from Thorpe Company. On April 9, 20 hats valued at $200 were found to have defective brims. Art's issued a debit memorandum to Thorpe Company, as shown in Figure 10.11. At some point in the future, Thorpe will issue Art's a credit memorandum. Let's look at how Art's Wholesale Clothing Company handles such a transaction in its accounting records.

FIGURE 10.11 Debit Memorandum

DEBIT MEMORANDUM No. 1

Art's Wholesale
Clothing Company
1528 Belle Ave.
New York, NY 10022

TO: Thorpe Company April 9, 200X
3 Access Road
Beverly, MA 01915

WE DEBIT your account as follows:

Quantity		Unit Cost	Total
20	Men's Hats Code 827 – defective brims	$10	$200

A debit memo shows that Art's does not owe as much money.

Journalizing and Posting the Debit Memo First, let's look at a transactional analysis chart.

Result of debit memo: debits or reduces Accounts Payable. On seller's books, accounts affected would include Sales Returns and Allowances and Accounts Receivable.

Accounts Affected	Category	↑ ↓	Rules
Accounts Payable	Liability	↓	Dr.
Purchases Returns and Allowances	Contra-cost	↑	Cr.

Next, let's examine the journal entry for the debit memorandum (Fig. 10.12).

FIGURE 10.12 Debit Memorandum Journalized and Posted

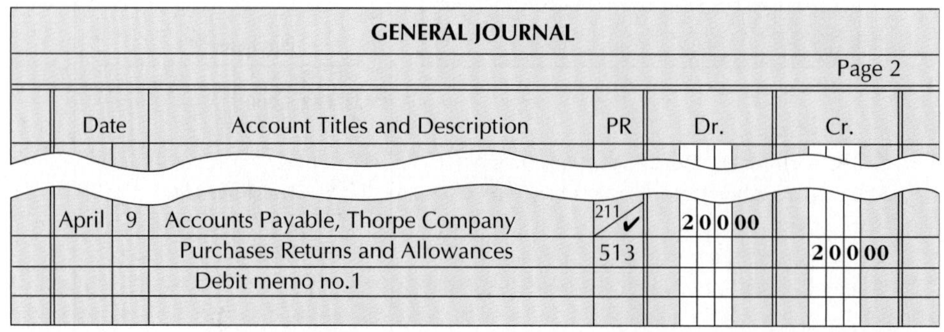

GENERAL JOURNAL

Page 2

Date		Account Titles and Description	PR	Dr.	Cr.
April	9	Accounts Payable, Thorpe Company	211/✓	200 00	
		Purchases Returns and Allowances	513		200 00
		Debit memo no.1			

The two postings and one recording are

1. 211: Post to Accounts Payable as a debit in the general ledger account no. 211. When done, place in the PR column the account number, 211, above the diagonal on the same line as Accounts Payable in the journal.
2. ✓: Record to Thorpe Co. in the accounts payable subsidiary ledger to show that Art's doesn't owe Thorpe as much money. When done, place a ✓ in the journal in the PR column below the diagonal line on the same line as Accounts Payable in the journal.
3. 513: Post to Purchases Returns and Allowances as a credit in the general ledger (account no. 513). When done, place the account number, 513, in the PR column of the journal on the same line as Purchases Returns and Allowances. (If equipment was returned that was not merchandise for resale, we would credit Equipment and not Purchases Returns and Allowances.)

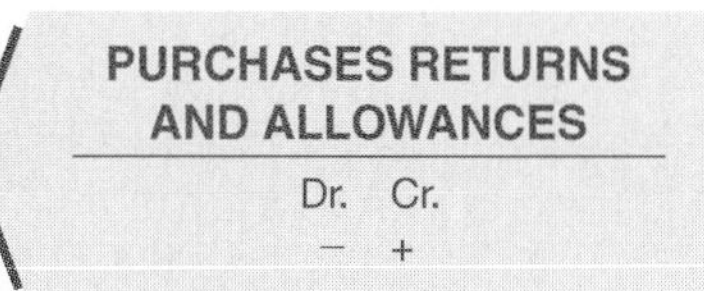

The following are the completed Accounts Payable Subsidiary Ledger and general ledger for Art's.

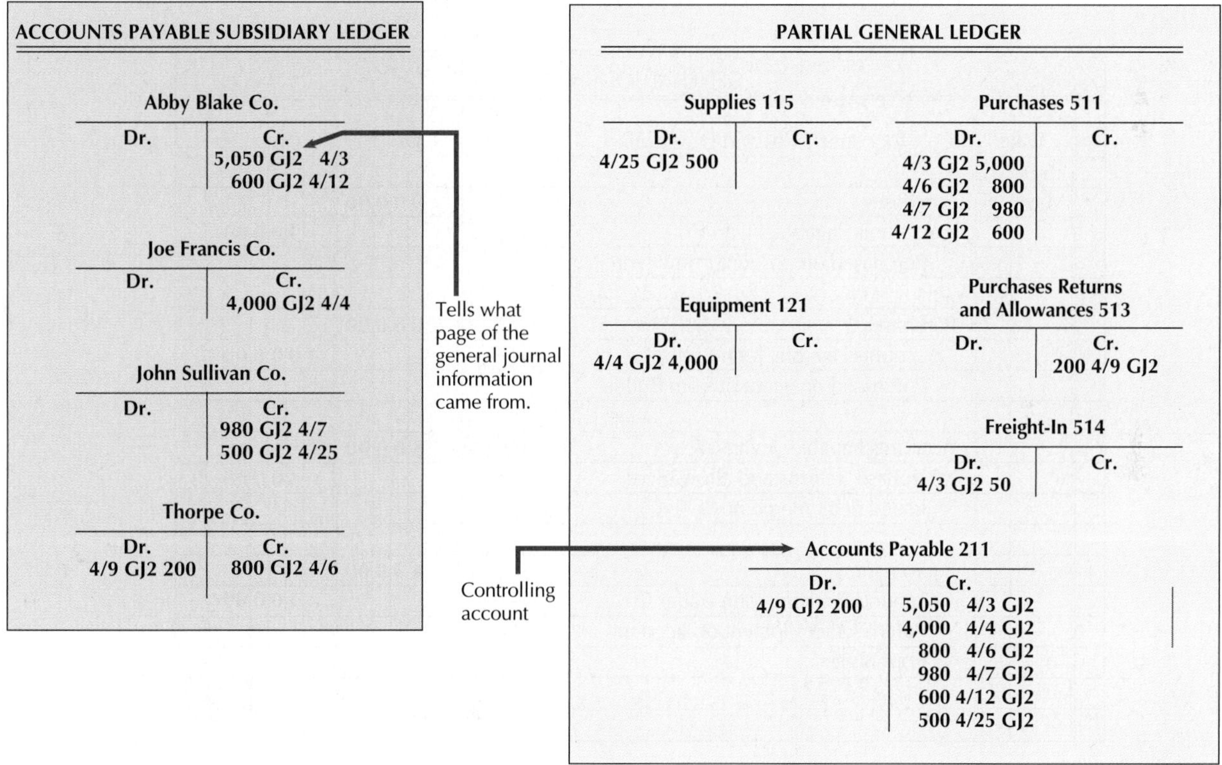

LEARNING UNIT 10-2 REVIEW

AT THIS POINT you should be able to

- Explain the relationship between a purchase requisition, a purchase order, and a purchase invoice.
- Explain why a typical invoice approval form may be used.
- Journalize transactions for purchase and cash payments.
- Explain how to record to the accounts payable subsidiary ledger and post to the general ledger from a general journal.
- Explain a debit memorandum and be able to journalize an entry resulting from its issuance.

Self-Review Quiz 10-2

Journalize and post the following transactions:

200X		
May	5	Bought merchandise on account from Flynn Co., invoice no. 512, dated May 6, $900; terms 1/10, n/30.
	7	Bought merchandise from John Butler Company, invoice no. 403, dated May 7, $1,000; terms n/10 EOM.
	13	Issued debit memo no. 1 to Flynn Co. for merchandise returned, $300, from invoice no. 512.
	17	Purchased $400 of equipment on account from John Butler Company, invoice no. 413, dated May 18.

Solution to Self-Review Quiz 10-2

GENERAL JOURNAL — Page 1

Date		Account Titles and Description	PR	Dr.	Cr.
200X					
May	5	Purchases	512	900 00	
		Accounts Payable, Flynn Co.	212/✓		900 00
		Purchased on account from Flynn			
	7	Purchases	512	1000 00	
		Accounts Payable, John Butler Co.	212/✓		1000 00
		Purchased on account from Butler			
	13	Accounts Payable, Flynn Co.	212/✓	300 00	
		Purchases returns and allowances	513		300 00
		Issued debit memo no. 1			
	17	Equipment	121	400 00	
		Accounts Payable, John Butler Co.	212/✓		400 00
		Purchased equipment on account			
		from Butler			

ACCOUNTS PAYABLE SUBSIDIARY LEDGER

John Butler Co.

Dr.	Cr.
	1,000 5/7 GJ1
	400 5/17 GJ1

Flynn Co.

Dr.	Cr.
5/13 GJ1 300	900 5/5 GJ1

PARTIAL GENERAL LEDGER

Equipment 121

Dr.	Cr.
5/17 GJ1 400	

Purchases 512

Dr.	Cr.
5/5 GJ1 900	
5/7 GJ1 1,000	

Accounts Payable 212

Dr.	Cr.
5/13 GJ1 300	900 5/5 GJ1
	1,000 5/7 GJ1
	400 5/17 GJ1

Purchases Returns and Allowances 513

Dr.	Cr.
	300 5/13 GJ1

Learning Unit 10-3 Recording and Posting Cash Payments Transactions for Art's Wholesale: Schedule of Accounts Payable

LO4

The following cash payment transactions occurred for Art's Wholesale Clothing Company in April.

200X		
Apr.	2	Issued check no. 1 to Pete Blum for insurance paid in advance, $900.
	7	Issued check no. 2 to Joe Francis Company in payment of its April 4 invoice no. 388.
	9	Issued check no. 3 to Rick Flo Co. for merchandise purchased for cash, $800.
	12	Issued check no. 4 to Thorpe Company in payment of its April 6 invoice no. 414, less the return and 1% discount.
	28	Issued check no. 5, $700, for salaries paid.

Figure 10.13 provides a closer look at how the April 12 transaction would be journalized.

Accounts Affected	Category	↑ ↓	Rules	T Account Update
Cash	Asset	↓	Cr.	**Cash** — Dr. / Cr. 594
Purchases Discount	Contra-cost	↑	Cr.	**Purchases Discount** — Dr. / Cr. 6
Account Payable, Thorpe Co.	Liability	↓	Dr.	**Accounts Payable** — Dr. 600 / Cr. 600; **Thorpe Co.** — Dr. 600 / Cr. 600

				Dr.	Cr.
April	12	Accounts Payable, Thorpe Co.		600 00	
		Purchases Discount			6 00
		Cash			594 00
		Paid invoice no. 414			

FIGURE 10.13

Figure 10.14 on the following pages shows the complete set of cash payments transactions journalized for the month, followed by a complete posting to the general ledger and recordings to the accounts payable subsidiary ledger (remember from the past unit that we posted all the purchases on account).

LO5

Schedule of Accounts Payable Now let's prove that the sum of the accounts payable subsidiary ledger at the end of the month is equal to the **controlling account,** Accounts Payable, at the end of April for Art's Wholesale Clothing Company. To do so, creditors

FIGURE 10.14

GENERAL JOURNAL — Page 2

Date		Account Titles and Description	PR	Dr.	Cr.
200X					
April	2	Prepaid Insurance	116	900 00	
		Cash	111		900 00
		Paid for insurance in advance			
	7	Accounts Payable, Joe Francis Co.	211/✔	4000 00	
		Cash	111		4000 00
		Paid invoice no. 388			
	9	Purchases	511	800 00	
		Cash	111		800 00
		Cash purchases			
	12	Accounts Payable, Thorpe Co.	211/✔	600 00	
		Purchases Discount	512		6 00
		Cash	111		594 00
		Paid invoice no. 414			
	28	Salaries Expense	611	700 00	
		Cash	111		700 00
		Paid salaries			

(*continued on next page*)

with an ending balance in Art's accounts payable subsidiary ledger must be listed in the schedule of accounts payable (see Fig. 10.15). At the end of the month, the total owed ($7,130) in Accounts Payable, the controlling account in the general ledger, should equal the sum owed the individual creditors that are listed on the schedule of accounts payable. If it doesn't, the journalizing, posting, and recording must be checked to ensure that they are complete. Also, the balances of each title should be checked.

LEARNING UNIT 10-3 REVIEW

AT THIS POINT you should be able to

- Journalize, post, and record cash payments transactions.
- Prepare a schedule of accounts payable.

Self-Review Quiz 10-3

For the following transactions, journalize, post to the general ledger, and record to the accounts payable subsidiary ledger.

Accounts Payable Subsidiary Ledger

Name	Balance	Invoice No.
Bob Finkelstein	$300	488
Al Jeep	200	410

(*continued on following page spread*)

FIGURE 10.14
(continued)

ACCOUNTS PAYABLE SUBSIDIARY LEDGER

Abby Blake Co.

Dr.	Cr.
	5,050 4/3 GJ1
	600 4/12 GJ1

Joe Francis Co.

Dr.	Cr.
4/7 GJ2 4,000	4,000 4/4 GJ1

John Sullivan Co.

Dr.	Cr.
	980 4/7 GJ2
	500 4/25 GJ2

Thorpe Co.

Dr.	Cr.
4/9 GJ1 200	800 4/6 GJ2
4/12 GJ1 600	

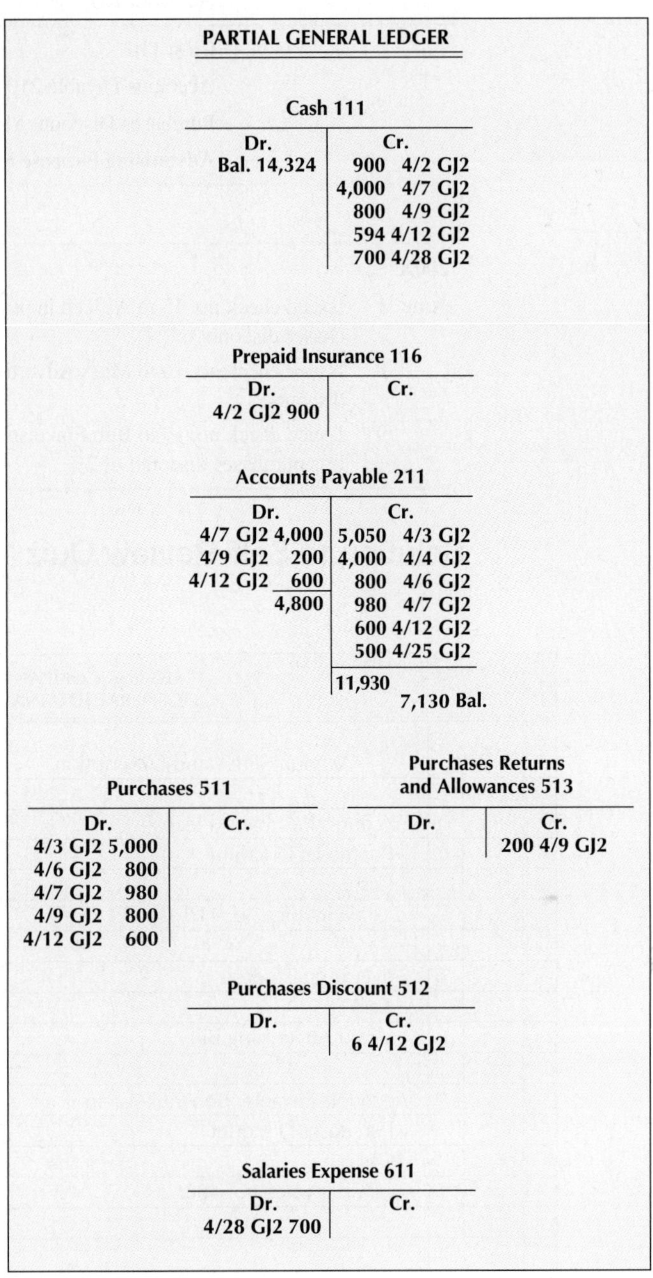

PARTIAL GENERAL LEDGER
Cash 111
Dr.
Cr.
Bal. 14,324
900 4/2 GJ2
4,000 4/7 GJ2
800 4/9 GJ2
594 4/12 GJ2
700 4/28 GJ2
Prepaid Insurance 116
Dr.
Cr.
4/2 GJ2 900
Accounts Payable 211
Dr.
Cr.
4/7 GJ2 4,000
4/9 GJ2 200
4/12 GJ2 600
4,800
5,050 4/3 GJ2
4,000 4/4 GJ2
800 4/6 GJ2
980 4/7 GJ2
600 4/12 GJ2
500 4/25 GJ2
11,930
7,130 Bal.
Purchases 511
Dr.
Cr.
4/3 GJ2 5,000
4/6 GJ2 800
4/7 GJ2 980
4/9 GJ2 800
4/12 GJ2 600
Purchases Returns and Allowances 513
Dr.
Cr.
200 4/9 GJ2
Purchases Discount 512
Dr.
Cr.
6 4/12 GJ2
Salaries Expense 611
Dr.
Cr.
4/28 GJ2 700

ART'S WHOLESALE CLOTHING COMPANY
SCHEDULE OF ACCOUNTS PAYABLE
APRIL 30, 200X

Abby Blake Co.	$5 650 00
John Sullivan Co.	1 480 00
Total Accounts Payable	$7 130 00

FIGURE 10.15 Schedule of Accounts Payable

Partial General Ledger

Account No.	Balance
Cash 110	$700
Accounts Payable 210	500
Purchases Discount 511	—
Advertising Expense 610	—

200X

June 1 Issued check no. 15 to Al Jeep in payment of its May 25 invoice no. 410, less purchases discount of 2%.

8 Issued check no. 16 to Moss Advertising Co. to pay advertising bill due, $75, no discount.

9 Issued check no. 17 to Bob Finkelstein in payment of its May 28 invoice no. 488, less purchases discount of 2%.

Solution to Self-Review Quiz 10-3

MELISSA COMPANY
GENERAL JOURNAL
Page 2

Date		Account Titles and Description	PR	Dr.	Cr.
200X					
June	1	Accounts Payable, Al Jeep	210/✓	200 00	
		Purchases Discount	511		4 00
		Cash	110		196 00
		Paid invoice no. 410			
	8	Advertising Expense	610	75 00	
		Cash	110		75 00
		Paid Advertising Bill			
	9	Accounts Payable, Bob Finkelstein	210/✓	300 00	
		Purchases Discount	511		6 00
		Cash	110		294 00
		Paid invoice no. 488			

ACCOUNTS PAYABLE SUBSIDIARY LEDGER

Bob Finkelstein

Dr.	Cr.
6/9 GJ2 300	300 Bal.

Al Jeep

Dr.	Cr.
6/1 GJ2 200	200 Bal.

PARTIAL GENERAL LEDGER

Cash 110

Dr.	Cr.
Bal. 700	196 6/1 GJ2
	75 6/8 GJ2
	294 6/9 GJ2

Purchases Discount 511

Dr.	Cr.
	4 6/1 GJ2
	6 6/9 GJ2

Accounts Payable 210

Dr.	Cr.
6/1 GJ2 200	500 Bal.
6/9 GJ2 300	

Advertising Expense 610

Dr.	Cr.
6/8 GJ2 75	

Learning Unit 10-4 Introduction to a Merchandise Company Using a Perpetual Inventory System

LO6

Introduction to the Merchandise Cycle

In this learning unit we will focus on recording transactions using a **perpetual inventory system.** This means an inventory system that continually monitors its levels of inventory. The previous units were based on a **periodic inventory system.** This means that at the end of each accounting period the cost of unsold goods is calculated. There is no continual tracking of inventory.

Let's use Wal-Mart as an example as both the buyer and seller. We know that Wal-Mart must buy inventory from suppliers to sell to you, the customer. This inventory is called **merchandise inventory.** It is an asset sold to you for cash or accounts receivable and represents *sales revenue* or sales for Wal-Mart.

What did it cost Wal-Mart to bring the inventory into the store? The **cost of goods sold** is the total cost of merchandise inventory brought into the store and sold. These costs do not include any operating expenses such as heat, advertising, and salaries. To find Wal-Mart's profit before operating expenses, we take the sales revenue less cost of goods sold. Figure 10.16 is called *gross profit on sales.*

Wal-Mart Sales Revenue − Cost of Goods Sold = Gross Profit on Sales

FIGURE 10.16 Calculating Gross Profit on Sales

For example, if Wal-Mart sells a TV for $500 that cost $300 to bring into the store, its gross profit is $200. To find its net income or net loss, Wal-Mart would subtract its operating expenses. Figure 10.17 shows how a merchandiser calculates its net income or net loss. *Note:* In step 1 the sales provide an inflow of cash or accounts receivable. Step 2 shows that when the inventory is sold, it is recognized as a cost (cost of goods sold). By subtracting sales less cost of goods sold, we arrive at the gross profit in step 3. Step 4 shows that operating expenses subtracted from gross profit result in a net income or net loss in step 5.

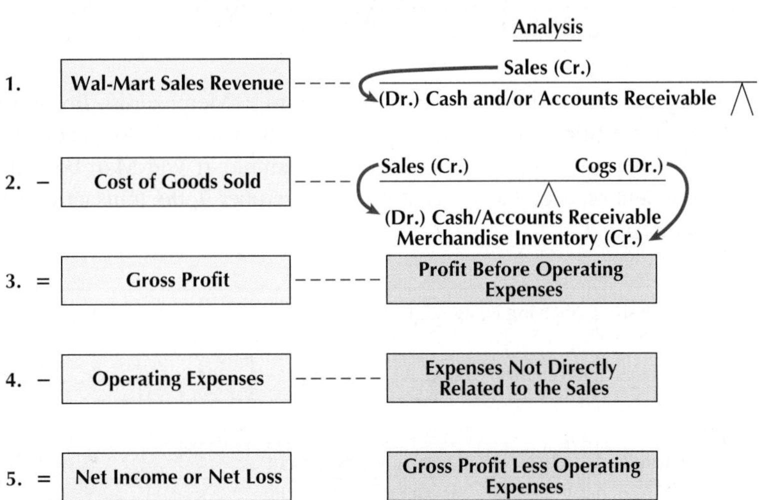

FIGURE 10.17 Introduction to Perpetual Inventory for a Merchandise Company

What Inventory System Wal-Mart Uses

When you pay at Wal-Mart you see the use of bar codes and optical scanners. Wal-Mart keeps detailed records of the inventory it brings into the store and what inventory is sold. With this method, Wal-Mart keeps track of what it costs to make the sale (cost of goods sold) by matching revenues and costs (see Fig. 10.18 on the following page).

FIGURE 10.18 Matching Revenues and Costs

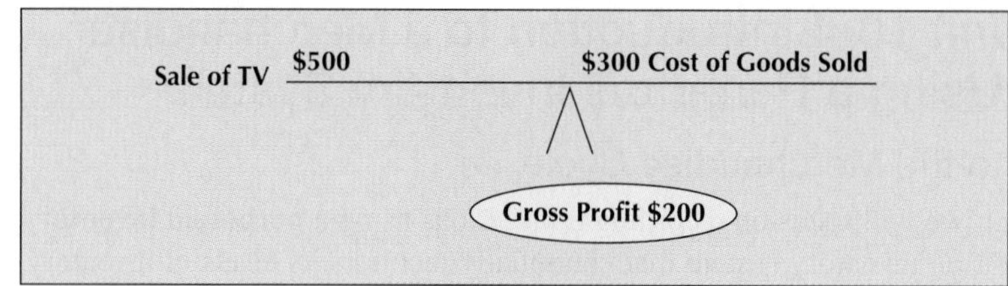

More and more companies, large or small, are using the perpetual inventory system due to increasing computerization. Wal-Mart knows that using the perpetual inventory system will help control stocks of inventory as well as lost or stolen goods.

Recording Merchandise Transactions

Now let's look at Wal-Mart as both a buyer and seller. Let's first focus on Wal-Mart the buyer.

Wal-Mart: The Buyer When Wal-Mart brings merchandise inventory into the stores from suppliers it is recorded in the *Merchandise Inventory account.* Think of this account as purchases of merchandise—for cash or on account—that is for resale to customers. Each order is documented by an invoice for Wal-Mart. Keep in mind that Merchandise Inventory is the cost of bringing the merchandise into the store, not the price at which the merchandise will be sold to customers. Let's assume on July 9 that Wal-Mart bought flat-screen TVs from Sony Corp. for $7,000 with terms 2/10, n/30. Wal-Mart would record the purchase as shown in Figure 10.19.

FIGURE 10.19 Purchase Inventory on Account

Analysis:

Account	Category	↑ ↓	Dr./Cr.	Amount
Merchandise Inventory	A	↑	Dr.	$7,000
Accounts Payable	L	↑	Cr.	$7,000

Journal Entry:

Date		Account	Dr.	Cr.
July	9	Merchandise Inventory	7 0 0 0 00	
		Accounts Payable		7 0 0 0 00
		Purchased inventory on account		
		from Sony 2/10, n/30		

Keep in mind that not all purchases will go to Merchandise Inventory. Wal-Mart will buy supplies, equipment, and so forth that are not for resale to customers. These amounts will be debited to the specific account. For example, if Wal-Mart bought $5,000 of shelving equipment on account for its store on November 9, the transaction would be recorded as in Figure 10.20.

FIGURE 10.20 Purchasing of Equipment on Account

Analysis:

Account	Category	↑ ↓	Dr./Cr.	Amount
Shelving Equipment	A	↑	Dr.	$5,000
Accounts Payable	L	↑	Cr.	$5,000

Journal Entry:

Date		Account	Dr.	Cr.
Nov.	9	Shelving Equipment	5 0 0 0 00	
		Accounts Payable		5 0 0 0 00
		Purchased equipment on account		

What happens if Wal-Mart finds a defective TV among its purchase from Sony?

Recording Purchases Returns and Allowances Because Wal-Mart noticed a damaged TV in the shipment on July 14, it issues a debit memorandum. This document notifies Sony, the supplier, that Wal-Mart is reducing what is owed Sony by $600, the cost of the

TV (to bring it into the store) and that the TV is being returned. On Wal-Mart's books the analysis and journal entry in Figure 10.21 resulted.

FIGURE 10.21 Recording a Debit Memorandum

Analysis:

Account				
Accounts Payable	L	↓	Dr.	$600
Merchandise Inventory	A	↓	Cr.	$600

Journal Entry:

July	14	Accounts Payable	600 00	
		Merchandise Inventory		600 00
		To record debit memo no. 10		

Note that the cost of merchandise inventory has been reduced by $600 due to the return. In the perpetual inventory system there is no purchases, returns, and allowances title. The reduction in cost from the return is recorded *directly* into the Merchandise Inventory account. Let's now look at how Wal-Mart would record any cash discounts it would receive due to payment of the Sony bill within the discount period.

Recording Purchase Discounts Let's assume Wal-Mart pays Sony within the first 10 days. Keep in mind that we take no discounts on returned goods (the $600 return). The amount of purchase discount will be recorded as a reduction to the cost of merchandise inventory. Figure 10.22 shows the analysis and journal entry on July 16. A discount lowers the cost of inventory.

FIGURE 10.22 Recording a Purchase Discount

Analysis:

Account				
Accounts Payable	L	↓	Dr.	$6,400
Cash	A	↓	Cr.	$6,272
Merchandise Inventory	A	↓	Cr.	$ 128

($7,000 – $600 Return)

Journal Entry:

July	14	Accounts Payable	6400 00	
		Cash		6272 00
		Merchandise Inventory		128 00

2% × $6,400

Keep in mind that had Wal-Mart missed the discount period it would have debited $6,400 to Accounts Payable and credited Cash for $6,400. Merchandise Inventory would not be reduced.

Recording Cost of Freight The cost of freight ($300) is to be paid by Wal-Mart. When the purchaser is responsible for cost of freight, it is added to the cost of merchandise inventory. If the cost of freight is paid by the seller, it could be recorded in an operating expense account called Freight-Out. Figure 10.23 is the analysis and journal entry for freight on July 10.

FIGURE 10.23 Recording Cost of Freight

Analysis:

Merchandise Inventory	A	↑	Dr.	$300
Cash	A	↓	Cr.	$300

Freight Cost added to Merchandise Inventory

Journal Entry:

July	10	Merchandise Inventory	300 00	
		Cash		300 00
		Payment of freight		

Wal-Mart: The Seller Now let's look at Wal-Mart as the *seller* of merchandise.

Recording Sales at Wal-Mart Sales revenues are earned at Wal-Mart when the goods are transferred to the buyer. The earned revenue can be for cash and/or credit. Let's look at the following example of the sale of a TV at Wal-Mart for $950 on credit on August 10, which cost Wal-Mart $600. Keep in mind when using the perpetual inventory system that at the time of the earned sale Wal-Mart will

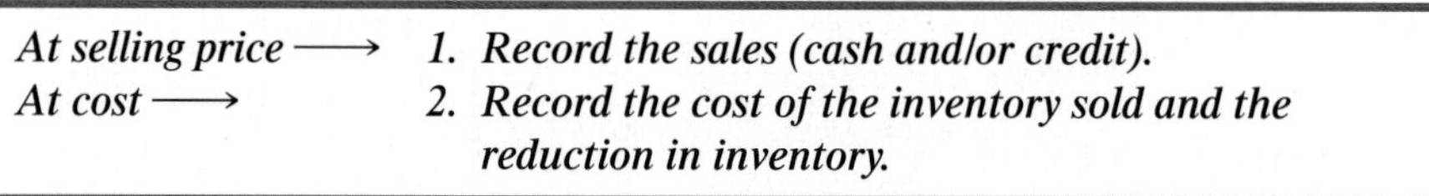

At selling price ⟶ 1. *Record the sales (cash and/or credit).*
At cost ⟶ 2. *Record the cost of the inventory sold and the reduction in inventory.*

First, let's analyze the transaction in Figure 10.24. Note that we will have two entries, one to record the sale and one to show a new cost and less inventory on hand.

FIGURE 10.24 Recording Sales and Cost of Goods Sold

	Account	Category	↑ ↓	Dr./Cr.	Amount
Selling < Price	Accounts Receivable	Asset	↑	Dr.	$950
	Sales	Revenue	↑	Cr.	$950
Cost to < Make sale	Cost of Goods Sold	Cost	↑	Dr.	$600
	Merchandise Inventory	Asset	↓	Cr.	$600

Journal Entries:

Date		Account	Dr.	Cr.
Aug.	10	Accounts Receivable	950 00	
		Sales		950 00
		Charge sales		
	10	Cost of Goods Sold	600 00	
		Merchandise Inventory		600 00
		To record cost of merchandise sold on account		

Be sure to go back to steps 1 and 2 of Figure 10.17. These two steps reinforce the preceding journal entries. Remember that if the sale were a cash sale, we would have debited Cash instead of Accounts Receivable. Note also that the Sales account only records sales of goods held for resale.

How Wal-Mart Records Sales Returns Allowances and Sales Discounts Keep in mind that we are now looking at how the *seller* of merchandise records a transaction giving the customer a credit due to an allowance or a return of goods from a previous sale. Usually, the seller will issue a *credit memorandum*, a document informing the customer of the adjustment due to the return or allowance. For example, on August 15, let's look at a customer who returned a $950 TV that had been purchased at Wal-Mart. On Wal-Mart's books, the analysis and journal entry in Figure 10.25 resulted.

The first entry records the return at the original selling price using the contra-revenue account Sales Returns and Allowances. The second entry records putting the inventory back in Wal-Mart's books at cost and reducing its Cost of Goods Sold because the inventory was not sold. Remember that we only record the Cost of Goods Sold when the sale has been earned. Keep in mind that if the customer kept the TV but at a reduced price, no entry affecting Merchandise Inventory and Cost of Goods Sold would be needed.

FIGURE 10.25 Return of Goods

The Analysis: at Selling Price	Sales Returns and Allowances	Contra-Revenue	↑	Dr.	$950
	Accounts Receivable	Asset	↓	Cr.	$950
At Cost	Merchandise Inventory	Asset	↑	Dr.	$600
	Costs of Goods Sold	Cost	↓	Cr.	$600

Journal Entries:

Date		Account	Dr.	Cr.
Aug.	15	Sales Returns and Allowances	950 00	
		Accounts Receivable*		950 00
		Returned goods		
	15	Merchandise Inventory	600 00	
		Cost of Goods Sold		600 00

*If it were a *cash* customer cash would be credited.

Let's assume a customer on August 25 gets a 2% discount for paying for a $950 TV early. The analysis and entry in Figure 10.26 would result on the seller's book:

FIGURE 10.26 Recording Sales Discount

The Analysis:				
Cash	Asset	↑	Dr.	$931
Sales Discount	Contra-Revenue	↑	Dr.	$ 19
Accounts Receivable	Asset	↓	Cr.	$950

Journal Entry:

Date		Account	Dr.	Cr.
Aug.	25	Cash	931 00	
		Sales Discount	19 00	
		Accounts Receivable		950 00

Now let's summarize (Figure 10.27) all the entries for both the buyer and the seller (in this case, Wal-Mart).

FIGURE 10.27

Wal-Mart the Buyer		Wal-Mart the Seller	
Bought Inventory for Resale on Account	Merchandise Inventory → At Cost Accounts Payable	Sold Inventory on Account	Accounts Receivable → At Selling Price Sales Cost of Goods Sold → At Cost Merchandise Inventory
Issued a Debit Memo for Merchandise Returned	Accounts Payable → At Cost Merchandise Inventory	Issued a Credit Memo for Returned Merchandise	Sales Returns and Allowances → At Selling Price Accounts Receivable Merchandise Inventory → At Cost Cost of Goods Sold
Recorded a Purchase Discount	Accounts Payable Cash Merchandise Inventory (← Amount of discount)	Recorded a Sales Discount	Cash Sales Discount Accounts Receivable

Amount of discount

Figure 10.28 shows a comparison of Perpetual and Periodic Systems.

FIGURE 10.28 Comparison of Perpetual and Periodic Systems

Transaction	Perpetual System			Periodic System		
(A) Sold merchandise that cost $8,000 on account for $20,000.	Accts. Receivable	20000 00		Accts. Receivable	20000 00	
	Sales		20000 00	Sales		20000 00
	Cost of Goods Sold	8000 00				
	Merch. Inventory		8000 00			
(B) Purchased $900 of merchandise on account.	Merch. Inventory	900 00		Purchases	900 00	
	Accts. Payable		900 00	Accts. Payable		900 00
(C) Paid $50 freight charges.	Merch. Inventory	50 00		Freight-In	50 00	
	Cash		50 00	Cash		50 00
(D) Cash customer returned $200 of merchandise. Cost of merchandise was $100.	Sales Ret. & Allow.	200 00		Sales Ret. & Allow.	200 00	
	Cash*		200 00	Cash*		200 00
	Merch. Inventory	100 00				
	Cost of Goods Sold		100 00			
(E) Returned $400 of merchandise previously bought on account due to defects.	Accts. Payable	400 00		Accts. Payable	400 00	
	Merch. Inventory		400 00	Pur. Ret. & Allow.		400 00

* or accounts receivable if made to charge customers

LEARNING UNIT 10-4 REVIEW

AT THIS POINT you should be able to

- Define the terms *merchandise inventory*, *sales*, and *cost of goods sold.*
- Explain how discounts are recorded in a perpetual inventory system.
- Journalize transactions for a merchandise company using a perpetual system.

Self-Review Quiz 10-4

Pete's Clock Shops completed the following merchandise transactions in the month of June:

200X		
June	1	Purchased merchandise on account from Clock Suppliers, $4,000; terms 2/10, n/30.
	3	Sold merchandise on account, $2,000; terms 2/10, n/30. The cost of the merchandise sold was $1,200.
	4	Received credit from Clock Suppliers for merchandise returned, $400.
	10	Received collections in full, less discounts, from June 3 sales.
	11	Paid Clock Suppliers in full, less discount.
	14	Purchased office equipment for cash, $500.
	15	Purchased $2,800 of merchandise from Abe's Distribution for cash.
	16	Received a refund due to defective merchandise from supplier on cash purchase of $400.
	17	Purchased merchandise from Rose Corp., $6,000, free on board shipping point (buyer pays freight); terms 2/10, n/30. Freight to be paid on June 20.
	18	Sold merchandise for $3,000 cash; the cost of the merchandise sold was $1,600.
	20	Paid freight on June 17 purchase, $180.
	25	Purchased merchandise from Lee Co., $1,400, free on board destination (seller pays freight); terms 2/10, n/30.
	26	Paid Rose Corp. in full, less discount.
	27	Made refunds to cash customers for returned clocks, $300. The cost of the defective clocks was $120.

Pete's Clock Shop accounts included the following:

Cash, 101; Accounts Receivable, 112; Merchandise Inventory, 120; Office Equipment, 124; Accounts Payable, 201; P. Rings, Capital, 301; Sales, 401; Sales Discount, 412; Cost of Goods Sold, 501.

Journalize the transactions using a perpetual inventory system.

Solution to Self-Review Quiz 10-4

GENERAL JOURNAL					Page 2
Date		Account Titles and Description	PR	Dr.	Cr.
200X					
June	1	Merchandise Inventory		4 0 0 0 00	
		Accounts Payable			4 0 0 0 00
	3	Accounts Receivable		2 0 0 0 00	
		Sales			2 0 0 0 00
		Cost of Goods Sold		1 2 0 0 00	
		Merchandise Inventory			1 2 0 0 00
	4	Accounts Payable		4 0 0 00	
		Merchandise Inventory			4 0 0 00
	10	Cash		1 9 6 0 00	
		Sales Discount		4 0 00	
		Accounts Receivable			2 0 0 0 00
	11	Accounts Payable		3 6 0 0 00	
		Cash			3 5 2 8 00
		Merchandise Inventory			7 2 00
	14	Office Equipment		5 0 0 00	
		Cash			5 0 0 00
	15	Merchandise Inventory		2 8 0 0 00	
		Cash			2 8 0 0 00
	16	Cash		4 0 0 00	
		Merchandise Inventory			4 0 0 00
	17	Merchandise Inventory		6 0 0 0 00	
		Accounts Payable			6 0 0 0 00
	18	Cash		3 0 0 0 00	
		Sales			3 0 0 0 00
		Cost of Goods Sold		1 6 0 0 00	
		Merchandise Inventory			1 6 0 0 00
	20	Merchandise Inventory		1 8 0 00	
		Cash			1 8 0 00
	25	Merchandise Inventory		1 4 0 0 00	
		Accounts Payable			1 4 0 0 00
	26	Accounts Payable		6 0 0 0 00	
		Cash			5 8 8 0 00
		Merchandise Inventory			1 2 0 00
	27	Sales Returns and Allowances		3 0 0 00	
		Cash*			3 0 0 00
		Merchandise Inventory		1 2 0 00	
		Cost of Goods Sold			1 2 0 00

* If this were a charge customer it would have been Accounts Receivable.

CHAPTER ASSIGNMENTS

SUMMARY OF KEY POINTS

LEARNING UNIT 10-1

1. Purchases are merchandise for resale. It is a cost.
2. Purchases Returns and Allowances and Purchases Discount are contra-costs.
3. *F.O.B. shipping point* means that the purchaser of the goods is responsible for covering the shipping costs. If the terms were *F.O.B. destination,* the seller would be responsible for covering the shipping costs until the goods reached the purchaser's destination.
4. Purchases discounts are not taken on freight.

LEARNING UNIT 10-2

1. The steps for buying merchandise from a company may include the following:
   - **a.** The requesting department prepares a purchase requisition.
   - **b.** The purchasing department prepares a purchase order.
   - **c.** Seller receives the order and prepares a sales invoice (a purchase invoice from the buyer).
   - **d.** Buyer receives the goods and prepares a receiving report.
   - **e.** Accounting department verifies and approves the invoice for payment.
2. The general journal records the buying of merchandise or other items on account.
3. The accounts payable subsidiary ledger, organized in alphabetical order, is not in the same book as Accounts Payable, the controlling account in the general ledger.
4. At the end of the month the total of all creditors' ending balances in the accounts payable subsidiary ledger should equal the ending balance in Accounts Payable, the controlling account in the general ledger.
5. A debit memorandum (issued by the buyer) indicates that the amount owed from a previous purchase is being reduced because some goods were defective or not up to a specific standard and thus were returned or an allowance requested. On receiving the debit memorandum, the seller will issue a credit memorandum.

LEARNING UNIT 10-3

1. All payments of cash (check) are recorded in the general journal.
2. At the end of the month, the schedule of accounts payable, a list of ending amounts owed individual creditors, should equal the ending balance in Accounts Payable, the controlling account in the general ledger.

LEARNING UNIT 10-4

1. In a perpetual inventory system, when a sale is recognized the cost of goods sold and merchandise inventory must be updated.
2. Purchases discounts on returns are reflected in the Merchandise Inventory account for a perpetual inventory system.

KEY TERMS

Accounts payable subsidiary ledger A book or file that contains, in alphabetical order, the name of the creditor and amount owed from purchases on account.

Controlling account The account in the general ledger that summarizes or controls a subsidiary ledger. Example: The Accounts Payable account in the general ledger is the controlling account for the accounts payable subsidiary ledger. After postings are complete, it shows the total amount owed from purchases made on account.

Cost of goods sold In a perpetual inventory system, an account that records the cost of merchandise inventory used to make the sale.

Debit memorandum A memo issued by a purchaser to a seller, indicating that some Purchases Returns and Allowances have occurred and therefore the purchaser now owes less money on account.

F.O.B. Free on board, which means without shipping charge either to the buyer or seller up to or from a specified location. In the view of one or the other, the shipment is *free* on board the carrier.

F.O.B. destination *Seller* pays or is responsible for the cost of freight to purchaser's location or destination.

F.O.B. shipping point *Purchaser* pays or is responsible for the shipping costs from seller's shipping point to purchaser's location.

Invoice approval form Used by the accounting department in checking the invoice and finally approving it for recording and payment.

Merchandise Inventory A perpetual inventory system account that records purchases of merchandise. Discounts and returns are recorded in this account for the buyer.

Periodic inventory system An inventory system that, at the *end* of each accounting period, calculates the cost of the unsold goods on hand by taking the cost of each unit times the number of units of each product on hand.

Perpetual inventory system An inventory system that keeps *continual track* of each type of inventory by recording units on hand at beginning, units sold, and the current balance after each sale or purchase.

Purchase invoice The seller's sales invoice, which is sent to the purchaser.

Purchase order A form used in business to place an order for the buying of goods from a seller.

Purchase requisition A form used within a business by the requesting department asking the purchasing department of the business to buy specific goods.

Purchases Merchandise for resale. It is a cost.

Purchases Discount A contra-cost account in the general ledger that records discounts offered by suppliers of merchandise for prompt payment of purchases by buyers.

Purchases Returns and Allowances A contra-cost account in the ledger that records the amount of defective or unacceptable merchandise returned to suppliers and/or price reductions given for defective items.

Receiving report A business form used to notify the appropriate people of the ordered goods received along with the quantities and specific condition of the goods.

BLUEPRINT

Periodic		Perpetual
Purchases	→	Merchandise Inventory
Purchase Discounts	→	Merchandise Inventory
Sales/Accounts Receivable	→	Sales/Accounts Receivable Cost of Goods Sold/Merchandise Inventory
Freight-In	→	Merchandise Inventory
Sales Discounts	→	Sales Discounts
Sales Returns and Allowances	→	Sales Returns and Allowances

QUESTIONS, CLASSROOM DEMONSTRATION EXERCISES, EXERCISES, AND PROBLEMS

Discussion Questions and Critical Thinking/Ethical Case

1. Explain how net purchases is calculated.
2. What is the normal balance of Purchases Discount?
3. What is a contra-cost?
4. Explain the difference between F.O.B. shipping point and F.O.B. destination.
5. F.O.B. destination means that title to the goods will switch to the buyer when goods are shipped. Agree or disagree? Why?
6. What is the normal balance of each creditor in the accounts payable subsidiary ledger?
7. Why could the balance of the controlling account, Accounts Payable, equal the sum of the accounts payable subsidiary ledger during the month?
8. What is the relationship between a purchase requisition and a purchase order?
9. What purpose could a typical invoice approval form serve?
10. Explain the difference between merchandise and equipment.
11. Why would the purchaser issue a debit memorandum?
12. Explain why a trade discount is not a cash discount.
13. What new account is used in a perpetual system compared to the periodic system?
14. What is the normal balance of cost of goods sold?
15. How are discounts recorded in a perpetual system?
16. Spring Co. bought merchandise from All Co. with terms 2/10, n/30. Joanne Ring, the bookkeeper, forgot to pay the bill within the first 10 days. She went to Mel Ryan, the head accountant, who told her to backdate the check so that it looked like the bill was paid within the discount period. Joanne told Mel that she thought they could get away with it. Should Joanne and Mel backdate the check to take advantage of the discount? You make the call. Write down your specific recommendations to Joanne.

Classroom Demonstration Exercises

SET A

Questions 1–6 are based on a periodic inventory system.

Questions 7–10 are based on a perpetual inventory system.

Accounts for Purchase Activities *LO1, 2, 3 (10 min)*

1. Complete the following table:

To the Seller		To the Buyer
Sales	⟷	a. ____________
Sales returns and allowances	⟷	b. ____________
Sales discount	⟷	c. ____________
Credit memorandum	⟷	d. ____________
Schedule of accounts receivable	⟷	e. ____________
Accounts receivable subsidiary ledger	⟷	f. ____________

LO1 (5 min) **Accounts**

2. Complete the following table:

Account	Category	↑	↓	Temporary or Permanent
Purchases				
Purchases Returns and Allowances				
Purchases Discount				

LO1 (5 min) **Calculating Net Purchases**

3. Calculate Net Purchases from the following: Purchases, $12; Purchases Returns and Allowances, $4; Purchases Discounts, $2.

LO1, 2, 3 (10 min) **Purchases Journal, General Journal, Recording, and Posting**

4. Match the following to the three business transactions (more than one number can be used).
   1. Recorded to the accounts payable subsidiary ledger.
   2. Recorded to the general journal.
   3. Posted to the general ledger.
   _____ **a.** Bought merchandise on account from Long.com, invoice no. 12, $60.
   _____ **b.** Bought equipment on account from Lee Co., invoice no. 13, $90.
   _____ **c.** Issued debit memo no. 1 to Long.com for merchandise returned, $10, from invoice no. 12.

LO1, 5 (15 min) **Journalizing Transactions**

5. Journalize the following transactions:
   a. Issued credit memo no. 2, $40, to Small Co.
   b. Cash sales, $180.
   c. Received check from Blue Co., $50, less 3% discount.
   d. Bought merchandise on account from Mel Co., $35, invoice no. 20; terms 1/10, n/30.
   e. Cash purchase, $15.
   f. Issued debit memo to Mel Co., $15, for merchandise returned from invoice no. 20.

LO5 (10 min) 6. From the following prepare a schedule of Accounts Payable for Web.Com for May 31, 200X:

Accounts Payable Subsidiary Ledger

Rowe Co.

	Dr.	Cr.	
		60	5/7 GJ1

Bloss Co

	Dr.	Cr.	
5/25 GJ1	10	50	5/20 GJ1

General Ledger

Accounts Payable

	Dr.	Cr.	
5/31	GJ1 10	110	5/31 GJ1

LO6 (15 min) 7. Draw a seesaw similar to the one shown in Figure 10.18 and show a sale of $900 that cost the store $400. Be sure to label all the accounts.

8. Bob C. paid $200 to Pete Co. and received a $20 purchases discount. Journalize the entry. *LO6 (10 min)*
9. Pete Morse returned $300 of merchandise to Logan Co. What would be the journal entry on the books of both the buyer and seller? *LO6 (10 min)*
10. Jeans Co. paid the cost of freight, $100. Journalize the transaction. *LO6 (10 min)*

SET B

Questions 1–6 are based on a periodic inventory system.

Questions 7–10 are based on a perpetual inventory system.

Accounts for Purchase Activities

LO1, 2, 3 (10 min)

1. Complete the following table:

		Account
A cost	a.	___________
A contra-cost	b.	___________
A contra-cost discount	c.	___________
Opposite of accounts receivable ledger	d.	___________
Cost of freight to seller	e.	___________

Accounts

LO1 (5 min)

2. Complete the following table:

Account	Category	↑	↓	Temporary or Permanent
Sales				
Sales Returns and Allowances				
Sales Discount				

Calculating Net Purchases

LO1 (5 min)

3. Calculate Net Purchases from the following: Purchases, $15; Purchases Returns and Allowances, $4; Purchases Discounts, $3.

Business Transaction, General Journal, Recording, and Posting

LO1, 2, 3 (10 min)

4. Match the following activities to the three business transactions (more than one number can be used).
   1. Recorded to the accounts payable subsidiary ledger.
   2. Recorded in the general journal.
   3. Posted to the general ledger.
      a. Bought merchandise on account from Ace.com, invoice no. 12, $70.
      b. Bought equipment on account from Mabel Co., invoice no. 13, $120.
      c. Issued debit memo no. 1 to Ace.com for merchandise returned, $7, from invoice no. 12.

Journalizing Transaction

LO1, 5 (15 min)

5. Journalize the following transactions.
   a. Issued credit memo no. 2 to Rose, $50.
   b. Cash sales, $210.
   c. Received check from Lew Co., $90, less 3% discount.

d. Bought merchandise on account from Mel Co., $50, invoice no. 20; terms 1/10, n/30.
e. Cash purchase, $25.
f. Issued debit memo to Ling Co., $15, for merchandise returned from invoice no. 20.

LO5 (10 min) **6.** From the following, prepare a schedule of accounts payable for Web.Com for May 31, 200X:

Accounts Payable Subsidiary Ledger

Jones Co.

	Dr.	Cr.	
		70	5/7 GJ1

Ring Co.

	Dr.	Cr.	
5/25 GJ1	20	60	5/20 GJ1

General Ledger

Accounts Payable

	Dr.	Cr.	
5/31 GJ1	10	120	5/31 GJ1

LO6 (15 min) **7.** Calculate the gross profit: sales, $50,000; cost of goods sold, $18,000; sales discount, $6,000.

LO6 (10 min) **8.** Long paid $500 to James Co. and received a $40 purchases discount. Journalize to entry.

LO6 (10 min) **9.** Lois Long received $400 of merchandise from Blue Co. What would be the journal entry on the books of both the buyer and seller?

LO6 (10 min) **10.** Jeff Co., the buyer, paid the cost of freight, $60. Journalize the transaction.

Exercises

Exercises 1–6 are based on a periodic inventory system.

Exercises 7–10 are based on a perpetual inventory system.

LO1 (15 min) **10-1.** From the general journal in Figure 10.29, record to the accounts payable subsidiary ledger and post to general ledger accounts as appropriate.

FIGURE 10.29

GENERAL JOURNAL — Page 2

Date			PR	Dr.	Cr.
200X					
June	3	Purchases		900 00	
		Accounts Payable, Leese.com			900 00
		Purchased merchandise on account			
	4	Purchases		600 00	
		Accounts Payable, Lane.com			600 00
		Purchased merchandise on account			
	8	Equipment		200 00	
		Accounts Payable, Sail.com			200 00
		Bought equipment on account			

Partial Accounts Payable Subsidiary Ledger

Lee's.com

Dr.	Cr.

Lane.com

Dr.	Cr.

Sail.com

Dr.	Cr.

Partial General Ledger

Equipment 120

Dr.	Cr.

Accounts Payable 210

Dr.	Cr.

Purchases 510

Dr.	Cr.

10-2. On July 10, 200X, Aster Co. issued debit memorandum no. 1 for $400 to Reel Co. for merchandise returned from invoice no. 312. Your task is to journalize, record, and post this transaction as appropriate. *LO3 (15 min)*

10-3. Journalize, record, and post when appropriate the following transactions into the general journal (p. 2) for Morgan's Clothing. All purchases discounts are 2/10, n/30. *LO4, 5 (20 min)*

Accounts Payable Subsidiary Ledger

Name	Balance	Invoice No.
A. James	$1,000	522
B. Foss	400	488
J. Ranch	900	562
B. Swanson	100	821

Partial General Ledger

Account	Balance
Cash 110	$3,000
Accounts Payable 210	2,400
Purchases Discount 511	
Advertising Expense 610	

200X		
Apr.	1	Issued check no. 20 to A. James Company in payment of its March 28 invoice no. 522.
	8	Issued check no. 21 to Flott Advertising in payment of its advertising bill, $100, no discount.
	15	Issued check no. 22 to B. Foss in payment of its March 25 invoice no. 488.

10-4. From Exercise 10-3, prepare a schedule of accounts payable and verify that the total of the schedule equals the amount in the controlling account. *LO5 (10 min)*

10-5. Record the following transaction in a transaction analysis chart for the buyer: Bought merchandise for $9,000 on account. Shipping terms were F.O.B. destination. The cost of shipping was $500. *LO1 (10 min)*

10-6. Angie Rase bought merchandise with a list price of $4,000. Angie was entitled to a 30% trade discount as well as a 3% cash discount. What was Angie's actual cost of buying this merchandise after the cash discount? *LO1 (10 min)*

LO6 (15 min) **10-7.** Journalize the following transactions:

200X		
April	8	Purchased merchandise on account from Jones Suppliers, $14,000; terms 2/10, n/30.
	15	Sold merchandise on account, $6,000; terms 2/10, n/30. The cost of merchandise was $4,500.
	20	Received credit from Jones Suppliers for merchandise returned, $150.

LO6 (15 min) **10-8.** Journalize the following transactions:

200X		
May	4	Sold merchandise for $500 cash. The cost of merchandise was $300.
	9	Purchased merchandise from Ree Co., $3,000, free on board shipping (buyer pays freight); terms 2/10, n/30. Freight to be paid on May 20.
	20	Paid freight on May 9 purchase, $100.

LO6 (15 min) **10-9.** Journalize the following transactions:

200X		
April	5	Sold merchandise for $1,200 cash. The cost of the merchandise was $900.
	16	Made refunds to cash customers for defective merchandise, $60. The cost of defective merchandise was $20.

LO6 (15 min) **10-10.** Journalize the following transactions:

200X		
July	8	Sold merchandise on account, $600, Ring; terms 2/10, n/30. Cost of merchandise was $400.
	12	Purchased office equipment on account from Rej Co., $1,000.
	13	Made refunds to cash customers, $200, for defective merchandise. The cost of defective merchandise was $50.

Group A Problems

LO1, 2 (30 min) **10A-1.** Ron Klay recently opened Ron's Skate Shop. As the bookkeeper of the company, please journalize, record, and post when appropriate the following transactions (account numbers are Store Supplies, 115; Store Equipment, 121; Accounts Payable, 210; Purchases, 510):

Check Figure: Accounts payable ending Bal. $8,700

200X		
June	4	Bought $900 of merchandise on account from Mail.Com, invoice no. 442, dated June 5; terms 2/10, n/30.
	5	Bought $5,000 of store equipment from Norton Co., invoice no. 502, dated June 6.
	8	Bought $1,600 of merchandise on account from Rolo Co., invoice no. 401, dated June 9; terms 2/10, n/30.
	14	Bought $1,200 of store supplies on account from Mail.Com, invoice no. 419, dated June 14.

LO1, 2, 5 (45 min) **10A-2.** The following transactions occurred for Mabel's Natural Food.

200X		
May	8	Purchased $600 of merchandise on account from Aton Co., invoice no. 400, dated May 9; terms 2/10, n/60.
	10	Purchased $1,200 of merchandise on account from Broward Co., invoice no. 420, dated May 11; terms 2/10, n/60.

12 Purchased $500 of store supplies on account from Midden Co., invoice no. 510, dated May 13.

14 Issued debit memo no. 8 to Aton Co. for merchandise returned, $400, from invoice no. 400.

17 Purchased $560 of office equipment on account from Relar Co., invoice no. 810, dated May 18.

24 Purchased $650 of additional store supplies on account from Midden Co., invoice no. 516, dated May 25; terms 2/10, n/30.

Check Figure: Total schedule of accounts payable $5,810

Your tasks are to

1. Journalize the transactions.

2. Post and record as appropriate.

3. Prepare a schedule of accounts payable.

Accounts Payable Subsidiary Ledger

Name	Balance
Aton Co.	$ 400
Broward Co.	600
Midden Co.	1,200
Relar Co.	500

Partial General Ledger

Account	Number	Balance
Store Supplies	110	$ —
Office Equipment	120	—
Accounts Payable	210	2,700
Purchases	510	16,000
Purchases Returns and Allowances	512	—

Check Figure: Total of schedule of accounts payable $1,900

10A-3. Wendy Jones operates a wholesale computer center. The account balances as of May 1, 200X, are as follows:

LO1, 2, 3, 4, 5 (45 min)

Accounts Payable Subsidiary Ledger

Name	Balance
Alvin Co.	$1,200
Henry Co.	600
Soy Co.	800
Xon Co.	1,400

Partial General Ledger

Account	Number	Balance
Cash	110	$17,000
Delivery Truck	150	—
Accounts Payable	210	4,000
Computer Purchases	510	—
Computer Purchases Discount	511	—
Rent Expense	610	—
Utilities Expense	620	—

Your tasks are to

1. Journalize the following transactions.
2. Record to the accounts payable subsidiary ledger and post to the general ledger as appropriate.
3. Prepare a schedule of accounts payable.

200X		
May	1	Paid half the amount owed Henry Co. from previous purchases of appliances on account, less a 2% purchases discount, check no. 21.
	3	Bought a delivery truck for $8,000 cash, check no. 22, payable to Bill Ring Co.
	6	Bought computer merchandise from Lectro Co., check no. 23, $2,900.
	18	Bought additional computer merchandise from Pulse Co., check no. 24, $800.
	24	Paid Xon Co. the amount owed, less a 2% purchases discount, check no. 25.
	28	Paid rent expense to King's Realty Trust, check no. 26, $2,000.
	29	Paid utilities expense to Stone Utility Co., check no. 27, $300.
	30	Paid half the amount owed Soy Co., no discount, check no. 28.

LO1, 2, 3, 4, 5 (130 min)

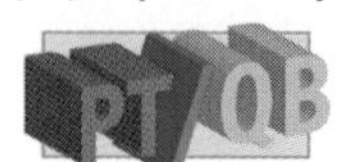

10A-4. Abby Ellen opened Abby's Toy House. As her newly hired accountant, your tasks are to

1. Journalize the transactions for the month of March.
2. Record to subsidiary ledgers and post to the general ledger as appropriate.
3. Prepare a schedule of accounts receivable and a schedule of accounts payable.

The following is the partial chart of accounts for Abby's Toy House:

Check Figures: Total of schedule of accounts receivable $7,600. Total of schedule of accounts payable $9,000

Abby's Toy House Chart of Accounts

Assets		**Revenue**	
110	Cash	410	Toy Sales
112	Accounts Receivable	412	Sales Returns and Allowances
114	Prepaid Rent	414	Sales Discounts
121	Delivery Truck	**Cost of Goods**	
Liabilities		510	Toy Purchases
210	Accounts Payable	512	Purchases Returns and Allowances
Owner's Equity		514	Purchases Discount
310	A. Ellen, Capital	**Expenses**	
		610	Salaries Expense
		612	Cleaning Expense

200X		
Mar.	1	Abby Ellen invested $8,000 in the toy store.
	1	Paid three months' rent in advance, check no. 1, $3,000.
	1	Purchased merchandise from Earl Miller Company on account, $4,000, invoice no. 410, dated March 2; terms 2/10, n/30.
	3	Sold merchandise to Bill Burton on account, $1,000, invoice no. 1; terms 2/10, n/30.
	6	Sold merchandise to Jim Rex on account, $700, invoice no. 2; terms 2/10, n/30.
	8	Purchased merchandise from Earl Miller Co. on account, $1,200, invoice no. 415, dated March 9; terms 2/10, n/30.
	9	Sold merchandise to Bill Burton on account, $600, invoice no. 3; terms 2/10, n/30.
	9	Paid cleaning service, check no. 2, $300.

10	Jim Rex returned merchandise that cost $300 to Abby's Toy House. Abby issued credit memorandum no. 1 to Jim Rex for $300.
10	Purchased merchandise from Minnie Katz on account, $4,000, invoice no. 311, dated March 11; terms 1/15, n/60.
12	Paid Earl Miller Co. invoice no. 410, dated March 2, check no. 3.
13	Sold $1,300 of toy merchandise for cash.
13	Paid salaries, $600, check no. 4.
14	Returned merchandise to Minnie Katz in the amount of $1,000. Abby's Toy House issued debit memorandum no. 1 to Minnie Katz.
15	Sold merchandise for $4,000 cash.
16	Received payment from Jim Rex, invoice no. 2 (less returned merchandise) less discount.
16	Bill Burton paid invoice no. 1.
16	Sold toy merchandise to Amy Rose on account, $4,000, invoice no. 4; terms 2/10, n/30.
20	Purchased delivery truck on account from Sam Katz Garage, $3,000, invoice no. 111, dated March 21 (no discount).
22	Sold to Bill Burton merchandise on account, $900, invoice no. 5; terms 2/10, n/30.
23	Paid Minnie Katz balance owed, check no. 5.
24	Sold toy merchandise on account to Amy Rose, $1,100, invoice no. 6; terms 2/10, n/30.
25	Purchased toy merchandise, $600, check no. 6.
26	Purchased toy merchandise from Woody Smith on account, $4,800, invoice no. 211, dated March 27; terms 2/10, n/30.
28	Bill Burton paid invoice no. 5, dated March 22.
28	Amy Rose paid invoice no. 6, dated March 24.
28	Abby invested an additional $5,000 in the business.
28	Purchased merchandise from Earl Miller Co., $1,400, invoice no. 436, dated March 29; terms 2/10, n/30.
30	Paid Earl Miller Co. invoice no. 436, check no. 7.
30	Sold merchandise to Bonnie Flow Company on account, $3,000, invoice no. 7; terms 2/10, n/30.

10A-5. Jan's Toy Shop completed the following merchandise transactions in the month of April:

LO6 (40 min)

200X		
April	2	Purchased merchandise on account to Fred Mills from Lowe Suppliers, $3,000; terms 2/10, n/30.
	4	Sold merchandise on account, $500; terms 2/10, n/30. The cost of the merchandise sold was $300.
	4	Received credit from Lowe Suppliers for merchandise returned, $200.
	10	Received collections in full, less discounts, from April 4 sales.
	11	Paid Lowe Suppliers in full, less discount.
	14	Purchased store equipment for cash, $300.
	15	Purchased $1,000 of merchandise from Leesy Distribution for cash.
	16	Received a refund due to defective merchandise from supplier on cash purchase of $100.
	17	Purchased merchandise from Logan Corp., $4,000, free on board shipping point (buyer pays freight); terms 2/10, n/30. Freight to be paid on April 21.
	18	Sold merchandise for $3,000 cash; the cost of merchandise sold was $1,600.
	21	Paid freight on April 17 purchase, $120.

Check Figure:
Dr. Merchandise inventory 120
Cr. Cash 120

(*continued on next page*)

25	Purchased merchandise from Aster Co., $1,200, free on board destination (seller pays freight); terms 2/10, n/30.
26	Paid Logan Corp. in full, less discount.
27	Made refunds to cash customers for defective toys, $200. The cost of the defective toys was $140.

Jan's Toy Shop accounts included the following: Cash, 101; Accounts Receivable, 112; Merchandise Inventory, 120; Store Equipment; 124; Accounts Payable, 201; J. Jan, Capital, 301; Sales, 401; Sales Discounts, 412; Sales Returns and Allowances, 414; Cost of Goods Sold, 501.

Assignment

Journalize the transactions using a perpetual inventory system.

Group B Problems

LO1, 2 (30 min)

10B-1. From the following transactions of Ron's Skate Shop, journalize, record, and post as appropriate:

Check Figure: Accounts payable ending balance $9,400

200X		
June	4	Bought merchandise on account from Rolo Co., invoice no. 400, dated June 5, $1,800; terms 2/10, n/30.
	5	Bought store equipment from Norton Co., invoice no. 518, dated June 6, $6,000.
	8	Bought merchandise on account from Mail.Com, invoice no. 411, dated June 5, $400; terms 2/10, n/30.
	14	Bought store supplies on account from Mail.Com, invoice no. 415, dated June 13, $1,200.

LO1, 2, 5 (45 min)

10B-2. As the accountant of Mabel's Natural Food Store (1) journalize the following transactions into the general journal (p. 2), (2) record and post as appropriate, and (3) prepare a schedule of accounts payable. Beginning balances are in the *Study Guide and Working Papers.*

Check Figure: Total of schedule of accounts payable $6,000

200X		
May	8	Purchased merchandise on account from Broward Co., invoice no. 420, dated May 9, $500; terms 2/10, n/60.
	10	Purchased merchandise on account from Aton Co., invoice no. 400, dated May 11, $900; terms 2/10, n/60.
	12	Purchased store supplies on account from Midden Co., invoice no. 510, dated May 13, $700.
	14	Issued debit memo no. 7 to Aton Co. for merchandise returned, $400, from invoice no. 400.
	17	Purchased office equipment on account from Relar Co., invoice no. 810, dated May 18, $750.
	24	Purchased additional store supplies on account from Midden Co., invoice no. 516, dated May 25, $850.

LO1, 2, 3, 4, 5 (45 min)

10B-3. Wendy Jones has hired you as her bookkeeper to record the following transactions. She would like you to record and post as appropriate and supply her with a schedule of accounts payable. (Beginning balances are in your workbook or Problem 10A-3 in the text.)

200X		
May	1	Bought a delivery truck for $8,000 cash, check no. 21, payable to Randy Rosse Co.
	3	Paid half the amount owed Henry Co. from previous purchases of computer merchandise on account, less a 5% purchases discount, check no. 22.
	6	Bought computer merchandise from Jane Co. for $900 cash, check no. 23.
	18	Bought additional computer merchandise from Jane Co., check no. 24, $1,000.
	24	Paid Xon Co. the amount owed, less a 5% purchases discount, check no. 25.
	28	Paid rent expense to Regan Realty Trust, check no. 26, $3,000.
	29	Paid half the amount owed Soy Co., no discount, check no. 27.
	30	Paid utilities expense to French Utility, check no. 28, $425.

Check Figure: Total of schedule of accounts payable $1,900

10B-4. As the new accountant for Abby's Toy House, your tasks are to

1. Journalize the transactions for the month of March.
2. Record to subsidiary ledgers and post to the general ledger as appropriate.
3. Prepare a schedule of accounts receivable and a schedule of accounts payable.

(Use the same chart of accounts as in Problem 10A-4. Your *Study Guide and Working Papers* has all the forms you need to complete this problem.)

LO1, 2, 3, 4, 5 (130 min)

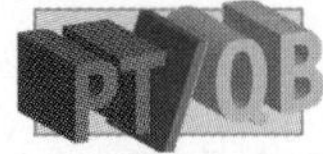

Check Figure: Total of schedule of accounts receivable $9,900. Total of schedule of accounts payable $9,200

200X		
Mar.	1	Abby invested $4,000 in the new toy store.
	1	Paid two months' rent in advance, check no. 1, $1,000.
	1	Purchased merchandise from Earl Miller Company, invoice no. 410, dated March 2, $6,000; terms 2/10, n/30.
	3	Sold merchandise to Bill Burton on account, $1,600, invoice no. 1; terms 2/10, n/30.
	6	Sold merchandise to Jim Rex on account, $800, invoice no. 2; terms 2/10, n/30.
	8	Purchased merchandise from Earl Miller Company, $800, invoice no. 415, dated March 9; terms 2/10, n/30.
	9	Sold merchandise to Bill Burton on account, $700, invoice no. 3; terms 2/10, n/30.
	9	Paid cleaning service, $400, check no. 2.
	10	Jim Rex returned merchandise that cost $200 to Abby. Abby issued credit memorandum no. 1 to Jim Rex for $200.
	10	Purchased merchandise from Minnie Katz, $7,000, invoice no. 311, dated March 11; terms 1/15, n/60.
	12	Paid Earl Miller Co. invoice no. 410, dated March 2, check no. 3.
	13	Sold $1,500 of toy merchandise for cash.
	13	Paid salaries, $700, check no. 4.
	14	Returned merchandise to Minnie Katz in the amount of $500. Abby issued debit memorandum no. 1 to Minnie Katz.
	15	Sold merchandise for cash, $4,800.
	16	Received payment from Jim Rex for invoice no. 2 (less returned merchandise), less discount.
	16	Bill Burton paid invoice no. 1.
	16	Sold toy merchandise to Amy Rose on account, $6,000, invoice no. 4; terms 2/10, n/30.
	20	Purchased delivery truck on account from Sam Katz Garage, $2,500, invoice no. 111, dated March 21 (no discount).
	22	Sold to Bill Burton merchandise on account, $2,000, invoice no. 5; terms 2/10, n/30.

(continued on next page)

	23	Paid Minnie Katz balance owed, check no. 5.
	24	Sold toy merchandise on account to Amy Rose, $2,000, invoice no. 6; terms 2/10, n/30.
	25	Purchased toy merchandise, $800, check no. 6.
	26	Purchased toy merchandise from Woody Smith on account, $5,900, invoice no. 211, dated March 27; terms 2/10, n/30.
	28	Bill Burton paid invoice no. 5, dated March 22.
	28	Amy Rose paid invoice no. 6, dated March 24.
	28	Abby invested an additional $3,000 in the business.
	28	Purchased merchandise from Earl Miller Co., $4,200, invoice no. 436, dated March 29; terms 2/10, n/30.
	30	Paid Earl Miller Co. invoice no. 436, check no. 7.
	30	Sold merchandise to Bonnie Flow Company on account, $3,200, invoice no. 7; terms 2/10, n/30.

LO1, 2, 3, 4, 5 (40 min) **10B-5.** Bob's Sporting Goods Shop completed the following merchandise transactions in the month of August:

200X		
Aug.	1	Purchased merchandise on account from Bob's Suppliers, $6,000; terms 2/10, n/30.
	2	Sold merchandise on account $1,500; terms 2/10, n/30. The cost of the merchandise sold was $800.
	4	Received credit from Bob's Suppliers for merchandise returned, $300.
	10	Received collections in full, less discounts, from August 2 sales.
	11	Paid Bob's Suppliers in full, less discount.
	14	Purchased office equipment for cash, $700.
	15	Purchased $3,000 of merchandise from Abe's Distribution for cash.
	16	Received a refund due for defective merchandise from supplier on cash purchase of $300.
	17	Purchased merchandise from Lee Corp., $5,000, free on board shipping point (buyer pays freight); terms 2/10, n/3. Freight to be paid on August 23.
	18	Sold merchandise for $4,000 cash; the cost of the merchandise sold was $2,700.
	23	Paid freight on August 17 purchase, $180.
	25	Purchased merchandise from Ron Co., $1,300, free on board destination (seller pays freight); terms 2/10, n/30.
	26	Paid Lee Corp., in full, less discount.
	27	Made refunds to cash customers for defective goods, $500. The cost of the defective goods were $350.

Check Figure:
Dr. Merchandise Inventory $180
Cr. Case $180

Bob's Sporting Goods accounts included the following: Cash, 101; Accounts Receivable, 112; Merchandise Inventory, 120; Office Equipment, 124; Accounts Payable, 201; B. Bob, Capital, 301; Sales, 401; Sales Discounts, 412; Sales Returns and Allowances, 414; Cost of Goods Sold, 501.

Assignment

Journalize the transactions using the perpetual inventory system.

ON-THE-JOB TRAINING

T-1. Angie Co. bought merchandise for $1,000 with credit terms of 2/10, n/30. Owing to the bookkeeper's incompetence, the 2% cash discount was missed. The bookkeeper told Pete Angie, the owner, not to get excited. After all, it was a $20 discount that was missed, not hundreds of dollars. Could you please act as Mr. Angie's assistant and show the bookkeeper that his $20 represents a sizable equivalent interest cost? In your calculation assume a 360-day year. Make some written recommendations so that this situation will not happen again. ***LO1 (20 min)***

FINANCIAL REPORT PROBLEM

Reading the Kellogg's Annual Report

LO1 (15 min)

Go to Appendix A and locate the balance sheet. How much has merchandise inventory increased from 2005 to 2006?

INTERNET PROJECT

Del Monte

Go to the Web and search: Annual Report Del Monte 2008.
Click on Investors Relations.
List out the latest news Del Monte is providing to its investors.
Order a free annual report.

CONTINUING PROBLEM

Sanchez Computer Center

LO1, 2, 3, 4, 5 (60 min)

The following is an updated schedule of accounts payable as of January 31, 200X.

Schedule of Accounts Payable

Office Depot	$ 50
System Design Furniture	1,400
Pac Bell	150
Multi Systems, Inc.	450
Total Accounts Payable	$ 2,050

Assignment

1. Journalize the transactions.
2. Record in the accounts payable subsidiary ledger and post to the general ledger as appropriate. A partial general ledger is included in the *Study Guide and Working Papers*.
3. Prepare a schedule of accounts payable as of February 28, 200X.

The transactions for the month of February are as follows:

200X		
Feb.	1	Prepaid the rent for the months of February, March, and April, $1,200, check no. 2585.
	4	Bought merchandise on account from Multi Systems, Inc., purchase order no. 4010, $450; terms 3/10, n/30.

(continued on next page)

8 Bought office supplies on account from Office Depot, purchase order no. 4011, $250; terms n/30.

9 Purchased merchandise on account from Computer Connection, purchase order no. 4012, $500; terms 1/30, n/60.

15 Paid purchase order no. 4010 in full to Multi Systems, Inc., check no. 2586.

21 Issued debit memorandum no. 10 to Computer Connection for merchandise returned from purchase order no. 4012, $100.

27 Paid for office supplies, $50, check no. 2587.

PEACHTREE COMPUTER WORKSHOP

COMPUTERIZED ACCOUNTING APPLICATION FOR CHAPTER 10

Refresher on using Peachtree Complete Accounting

Before starting this assignment, you may want to refresh your memory by reading the following PDF documents in the multimedia library of the MyAccountingLab Web site. Remember to choose the PDF document for your version of Peachtree.

1. An Introduction to Peachtree Complete Accounting
2. Correcting Peachtree Transactions
3. How to Repeat or Restart a Peachtree Assignment
4. Backing Up and Restoring Your Work in Peachtree

You also should have completed the following workshops:

1. Workshop 1 Atlas Company from Chapter 3
2. Workshop 2 Zell Company from Chapter 4
3. Workshop 3 Sullivan Realty from Chapter 5
4. Workshop 4 Pete's Market from Chapter 8

Workshop 5:

PART A: Recording Transactions in the Sales, Receipts, Purchases, and Payments Journals

PART B: Accounting Cycle Mini Practice Set with Sales and Purchasing

Part A:

In this part of the workshop you will learn to record customer sales on account, customer credit memos, customer cash receipts, purchases from vendors on account, and payments to vendors for Mars Company using Peachtree. You will also print the aged receivables and aged payables reports and the sales journal, cash receipts journal, purchasing journal, and cash disbursement journals.

Instructions and the data file for completing Part A of the assignment are in the multimedia library of the MyAccountingLab Web site. Open the ***Workshop 5 Part A Mars Company*** PDF document for your version of Peachtree and download the ***Mars Company*** data file for your version of Peachtree.

Part B:

In this part of the workshop you will complete a mini practice set of March accounting transactions for Abby's Toy House using Peachtree. Transactions include customer sales on account, customer credit memos, customer cash receipts, purchases from vendors on account, payments to vendors, and general journal entries in Peachtree. You will also print the aged receivables and aged payables reports and the general journal and general ledger reports.

Instructions and the data file for completing Part B of the assignment are in the multimedia library of the MyAccountingLab Web site. Open the ***Workshop 5 Part B Abby's Toy House*** PDF document for your version of Peachtree and download the ***Abby's Toy House*** data file for your version of Peachtree.

QUICKBOOKS COMPUTER WORKSHOP

COMPUTERIZED ACCOUNTING APPLICATION FOR CHAPTER 10

Refresher on Using QuickBooks Pro

Before starting this assignment, you may want to refresh your memory by reading the following PDF documents in the multimedia library of the MyAccountingLab Web site. Remember to choose the PDF document for your version of QuickBooks.

1. An Introduction to QuickBooks Pro
2. Correcting QuickBooks Transactions
3. How to Repeat or Restart a QuickBooks Assignment
4. Backing Up and Restoring Your Work in QuickBooks

You also should have completed the following workshops:

1. Workshop 1 Atlas Company from Chapter 3
2. Workshop 2 Zell Company from Chapter 4
3. Workshop 3 Sullivan Realty from Chapter 5
4. Workshop 4 Pete's Market from Chapter 8

Workshop 5:

PART A: Recording Transactions in the Sales, Receipts, Purchases, and Payments Journals

PART B: Accounting Cycle Mini Practice Set with Sales and Purchasing

Part A:

In this part of the workshop you will learn to record customer sales on account, customer credit memos, customer cash receipts, purchases from vendors on account, and payments to vendors for Mars Company using QuickBooks. You will also print the aged receivables and aged payables reports and the sales journal, cash receipts journal, purchasing journal, and cash disbursement journals.

Instructions and the data file for completing Part A of the assignment are in the multimedia library of the MyAccountingLab Web site. Open the ***Workshop 5 Part A Mars Company*** PDF document for your version of QuickBooks and download the ***Mars Company*** data file for your version of QuickBooks.

Part B:

In this part of the workshop, you will complete a mini practice set of March accounting transactions for Abby's Toy House using QuickBooks. Transactions include customer sales on account, customer credit memos, customer cash receipts, purchases from vendors on account, payments to vendors, and general journal entries in Peachtree. You will also print the aged receivables and aged payables reports and the general journal and general ledger reports.

Instructions and the data file for completing Part B of the assignment are in the multimedia library of the MyAccountingLab Web site. ***Open the Workshop 5 Part B Abby's Toy House*** PDF document for your version of QuickBooks and download the ***Abby's Toy House*** data file for your version of QuickBooks.

APPENDIX A

SPECIAL JOURNALS WITH PROBLEM MATERIAL

Classroom Demonstration Problem: Periodic Method

All credit sales are 2/10, n/30. All merchandise purchased on account has 3/10, n/30 credit terms. Record the following transactions into special or general journals. Record and post as appropriate.

Solution Tips to Journalizing

200X			
Mar.	1	J. Ling invested $2,000 into the business.	CRJ
	1	Sold merchandise on account to Balder Co., $500, invoice no. 1.	SJ
	2	Purchased merchandise on account from Case Co., $500.	PJ
	4	Sold $2,000 of merchandise for cash.	CRJ
	6	Paid Case Co. from previous purchases on account, check no. 1.	CPJ
	8	Sold merchandise on account to Lewis Co., $1,000, invoice no. 2.	SJ
	10	Received payment from Balder for invoice no. 1.	CRJ
	12	Issued a credit memorandum to Lewis Co. for $200 for faulty merchandise.	GJ
	14	Received payment from Lewis Co.	CRJ
	16	Purchased merchandise on account from Noone Co., $1,000.	PJ
	17	Purchased equipment on account from Case Co., $300.	PJ
	18	Issued a debit memorandum to Noone Co. for $500 for defective merchandise.	GJ
	20	Paid salaries, $300, check no. 2.	CPJ
	24	Paid Noone balance owed, check no. 3.	CPJ

FIGURE A.1 Sales Journal

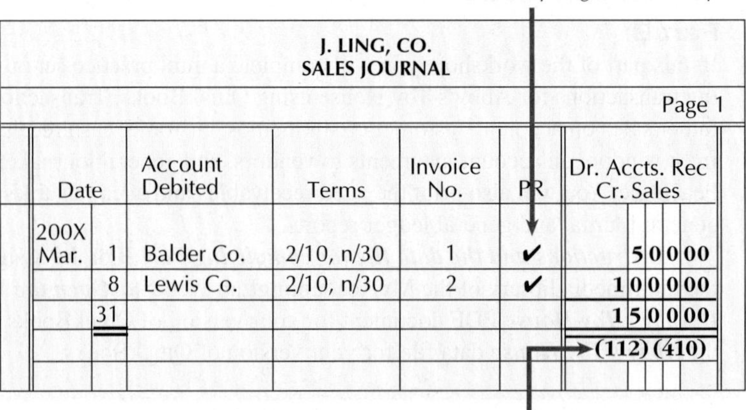
Record accounts receivable subsidiary ledger immediately.
Total posted at end of month to these accounts.

J. LING, CO.
SALES JOURNAL

Page 1

Date		Account Debited	Terms	Invoice No.	PR	Dr. Accts. Rec Cr. Sales
200X Mar.	1	Balder Co.	2/10, n/30	1	✔	500 00
	8	Lewis Co.	2/10, n/30	2	✔	1000 00
	31					1500 00
						(112) (410)

FIGURE A.2 Purchases Journal

J. LING, CO.
PURCHASES JOURNAL

Page 1

Date		Account Credited	Terms	PR	Accounts Payable Cr.	Purchases Dr.	Sundry–Dr. Acct.	Sundry–Dr. PR	Sundry–Dr. Amount
200X Mar.	2	Case Co.	3/10, n/30	✔	500 00	500 00			
	16	Noone Co.	3/10, n/30	✔	1000 00	1000 00			
	17	Case Co.	3/10, n/30	✔	300 00		Equip.	116	300 00
	31				1800 00	1500 00			300 00
					(210)	(510)			(X)

Record to accounts payable subsidiary ledger immediately.

Post totals at end of month to general ledger.

Post immediately to Equipment in general ledger.

Do not post total.

FIGURE A.3 Cash Receipts Journal

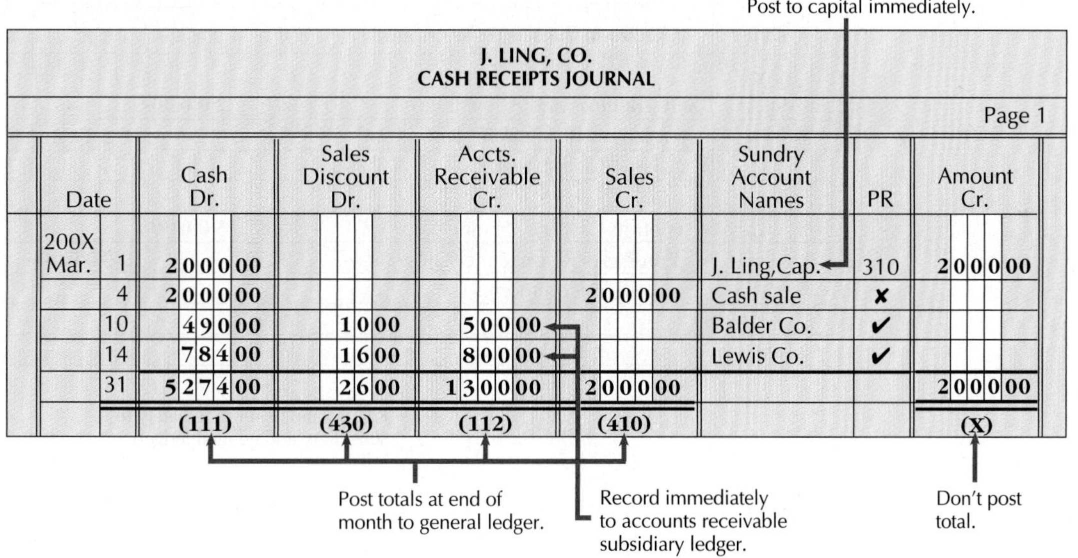

J. LING, CO.
CASH RECEIPTS JOURNAL

Page 1

Date		Cash Dr.	Sales Discount Dr.	Accts. Receivable Cr.	Sales Cr.	Sundry Account Names	PR	Amount Cr.
200X Mar.	1	2000 00				J. Ling,Cap.	310	2000 00
	4	2000 00			2000 00	Cash sale	✘	
	10	490 00	10 00	500 00		Balder Co.	✔	
	14	784 00	16 00	800 00		Lewis Co.	✔	
	31	5274 00	26 00	1300 00	2000 00			2000 00
		(111)	(430)	(112)	(410)			(X)

FIGURE A.4 Cash Payments Journal

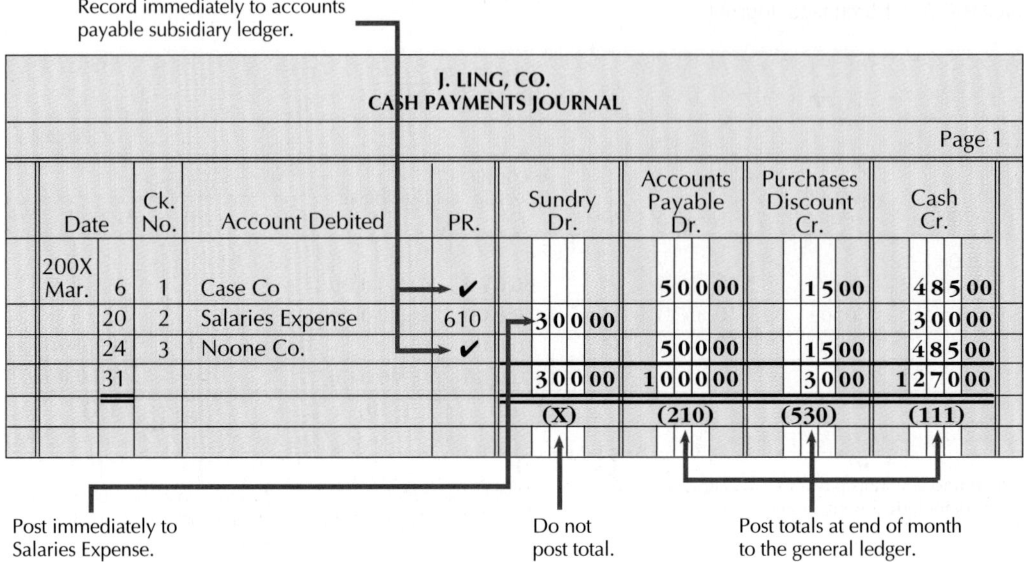
Record immediately to accounts payable subsidiary ledger.
Post immediately to Salaries Expense.
Do not post total.
Post totals at end of month to the general ledger.

J. LING, CO.
CASH PAYMENTS JOURNAL

Page 1

Date		Ck. No.	Account Debited	PR.	Sundry Dr.	Accounts Payable Dr.	Purchases Discount Cr.	Cash Cr.
200X Mar.	6	1	Case Co	✔		500 00	15 00	485 00
	20	2	Salaries Expense	610	300 00			300 00
	24	3	Noone Co.	✔		500 00	15 00	485 00
	31				300 00	1000 00	30 00	1270 00
					(X)	(210)	(530)	(111)

FIGURE A.5 General Journal

GENERAL JOURNAL — Page 1

Date		Account Titles and Description	PR	Dr.	Cr.
200X Mar.	12	Sales Returns and Allowances	420	200 00	
		Accounts Receivable, Lewis Co.	112/✔		200 00
		Issued credit memo			
	18	Accounts Payable, Noone Co.	210/✔	500 00	
		Purchases Returns and Allowances	520		500 00
		Issued debit memo			

Record and post immediately to subsidiary and general ledgers.

FIGURE A.6 Subsidiary and General Ledgers

ACCOUNTS RECEIVABLE SUBSIDIARY LEDGER

Balder Company

Date	PR	Dr.	Cr.	Dr. Bal.
200X 3/1	SJ1	500		500
3/10	CRJ1		500	—

Lewis Company

Date	PR	Dr.	Cr.	Dr. Bal.
200X 3/8	SJ1	1,000		1,000
3/12	GJ1		200	800
3/14	CPJ1		800	—

ACCOUNTS PAYABLE SUBSIDIARY LEDGER

Case Company

Date	PR	Dr.	Cr.	Cr. Bal.
200X 3/2	PJ1		500	500
3/6	CPJ1	500		—
3/17	PJ1		300	300

Noone Company

Date	PR	Dr.	Cr.	Cr. Bal.
200X 3/16	PJ1		1,000	1,000
3/18	GJ1	500		500
3/24	CPJ1	500		—

GENERAL LEDGER

Cash 111

Dr.	Cr.
3/31 CRJ1 5,274	1,270 3/31 CPJ1
Bal. 4,004	

Accounts Receivable 112

Dr.	Cr.
3/31 SJ1 1,500	200 3/12 GJ1
Bal. 0	1,300 3/31 CRJ1

Equipment 116

Dr.	Cr.
3/17 PJ1 300	

Accounts Payable 210

Dr.	Cr.
3/18 GJ1 500	1,800 3/31 PJ1
3/31 CPJ1 1,000	300 *Bal.*

J. Ling, Capital 310

Dr.	Cr.
	2,000 3/1 CRJ1

Sales 410

Dr.	Cr.
	1,500 3/31 SJ1
	2,000 3/31 CRJ1
	3,500 *Bal.*

Sales Returns and Allowances 420

Dr.	Cr.
3/12 GJ1 200	

Sales Discount 430

Dr.	Cr.
3/31 CRJ1 26	

Purchases 510

Dr.	Cr.
3/31 PJ1 1,500	

Purchase Returns and Allowances 520

Dr.	Cr.
	500 3/18 GJ1

Purchase Discount 530

Dr.	Cr.
	30 3/31 CPJ1

Salaries Expense 610

Dr.	Cr.
3/20 CPJ1 300	

Summary of Solution Tips

Seller	Buyer
Sales journal	Purchases journal
Cash receipts journal	Cash payments journal
Accounts receivable subsidiary ledger	Accounts payable subsidiary ledger
Sales (Cr.)	Purchases (Dr.)
Sales Returns and Allowances (Dr.)	Purchase Returns and Allowances (Cr.)
Sales Discounts (Dr.)	Purchase Discounts (Cr.)
Accounts Receivable (Dr.)	Accounts Payable (Cr.)
Issue a credit memo	Receive a credit memo
or	or
Receive a debit memo	Issue a debit memo
Schedule of accounts receivable	Schedule of accounts payable

A Step-by-Step Walk-Through of This Classroom Demonstration Problem

Transaction		What to Do Step-by-Step
200X		
Mar.	1	*Money Received:* Record in cash receipts journal. Post immediately to J. Ling, Capital, because it is in sundry.
	1	*Sale on Account:* Record in sales journal. Record immediately to Balder Co. in accounts receivable subsidiary ledger. Place a ✓ in Post. Ref. column of sales journal when subsidiary is updated.
	2	*Buy Merchandise on Account:* Record in purchases journal. Record to Case Co. immediately in the accounts payable subsidiary ledger.
	4	*Money In:* Record in cash receipts journal. No posting needed (put an × in Post. Ref. column).
	6	*Money Out:* Record in cash payments journal. Save \$15, which is a Purchases Discount. Record immediately to Case Co. in accounts payable subsidiary ledger (the full amount of \$500).
	8	*Sales on Account:* Record in sales journal. Update immediately to Lewis in accounts receivable subsidiary ledger.
	10	*Money In:* Record in cash receipts journal. Because Balder pays within 10 days, it gets a \$10 discount. Record the full amount immediately to Balder in the accounts receivable subsidiary ledger.
	12	*Returns:* Record in general journal. Seller issues credit memo resulting in higher sales returns and customers owing less. All postings and recordings are done immediately.
	14	*Money In:* Record in cash receipts journal: $\$1{,}000 - \$200 \text{ returns} = \$800$; $\times .02$; $\$\ 16$ discount. Record immediately the \$800 to Lewis in the accounts receivable subsidiary ledger.
	16	*Buy Now, Pay Later:* Record in purchases journal. Record immediately to Noone Co. in the accounts payable subsidiary ledger.
	17	*Buy Now, Pay Later:* Record in purchases journal in Sundry. This item is not merchandise for resale. Record and post immediately.

18	*Returns:* Record in general ledger. Buyer issues a debit memo reducing the Accounts Payable due to purchases return and allowances. Post and record immediately.
20	*Salaries:* Record in cash payments journal, sundry column. Post immediately to Salaries Expense.
24	*Money Out:* Record in cash payments journal. Save 3% ($15), a purchases discount. Record immediately to accounts payable subsidiary ledger that you reduce Noone by $500.

End of Month Post totals (except sundry) of special journal to the general ledger.

Note: In this problem at the end of the month, (1) Accounts Receivable in the general ledger, the controlling account, has a zero balance, as does each title in the accounts receivable subsidiary ledger; and (2) the balance in Accounts Payable (the controlling account) is $300. In the accounts payable subsidiary ledger, we owe Case $300. The sum of the accounts payable subsidiary ledger does equal the balance in the controlling account at the end of the month.

Appendix A Problems

A-1. Jill Blue opened Food.com, a wholesale grocery and pizza company. The following transactions occurred in June:

200X		
June	1	Sold grocery merchandise to Duncan Co. on account, $500, invoice no. 1.
	4	Sold pizza merchandise to Sue Moore Co. on account, $600, invoice no. 2.
	8	Sold grocery merchandise to Long Co. on account, $700, invoice no. 3.
	10	Issued credit memorandum no. 1 to Duncan Co. for $150 of grocery merchandise returned due to spoilage.
	15	Sold pizza merchandise to Sue Moore Co. on account, $160, invoice no. 4.
	19	Sold grocery merchandise to Long Co. on account, $300, invoice no. 5.
	25	Sold pizza merchandise to Duncan Co. on account, $1,200, invoice no. 6.

Required

1. Journalize the transactions in the appropriate journals.
2. Record to the accounts receivable subsidiary ledger and post to the general ledger as appropriate.
3. Prepare a schedule of accounts receivable.

Check Figure: Schedule of accounts receivable $3,310

A-2. The following transactions of Ted's Auto Supply occurred in November (your working papers have balances as of November 1 for certain general ledger and accounts receivable ledger accounts):

200X		
Nov.	1	Sold auto parts merchandise to R. Volan on account, $1,000, invoice no. 60, plus 5% sales tax.
	5	Sold auto parts merchandise to J. Seth on account, $800, invoice no. 61, plus 5% sales tax.
	8	Sold auto parts merchandise to Lance Corner on account, $9,000, invoice no. 62, plus 5% sales tax.
	10	Issued credit memorandum no. 12 to R. Volan for $500 for defective auto parts merchandise returned from Nov. 1 transaction. (Be careful to record the reduction in Sales Tax Payable as well.)
	12	Sold auto parts merchandise to J. Seth on account, $600, invoice no. 63, plus 5% sales tax.

Required

1. Journalize the transactions in the appropriate journals.
2. Record to the accounts receivable subsidiary ledger and post to the general ledger as appropriate.
3. Prepare a schedule of accounts receivable.

Check Figure: Schedule of accounts receivable $13,045

A-3. Abby Kim recently opened Skates.com. As the bookkeeper of her company, please journalize, record, and post when appropriate the following transactions (account numbers are Store Supplies, 115; Store Equipment, 121; Accounts Payable, 210; Purchases, 510):

Check Figure: Total of purchases column $2,100

200X		
June	4	Bought $700 of merchandise on account from Mail.com, invoice no. 442, dated June 5; terms 2/10, n/30.
	5	Bought $4,000 of store equipment from Norton Co., invoice no. 502, dated June 6.
	8	Bought $1,400 of merchandise on account from Rolo Co., invoice no. 401, dated June 9; terms 2/10, n/30.
	14	Bought $900 of store supplies on account from Mail.com, invoice no. 419, dated June 14.

A-4. Mabel's Natural Food Store uses a purchases journal and a general journal to record the following transactions (continued from April):

Check Figure: Total schedule of accounts payable $5,810

200X		
May	8	Purchased $600 of merchandise on account from Aton Co., invoice no. 400, dated May 9; terms 2/10, n/60.
	10	Purchased $1,200 of merchandise on account from Broward Co., invoice no. 420, dated May 11; terms 2/10, n/60.
	12	Purchased $500 of store supplies on account from Midden Co., invoice no. 510, dated May 13.
	14	Issued debit memo no. 8 to Aton Co., for merchandise returned, $400, from invoice no. 400.
	17	Purchased $560 of office equipment on account from Relar Co., invoice no. 810, dated May 18.
	24	Purchased $650 of additional store supplies on account from Midden Co., invoice no. 516, dated May 25; terms 2/10, n/30.

The food store decided to keep a separate column for the purchases of supplies in the purchases journal. Your tasks are to

1. Journalize the transactions.
2. Post and record as appropriate.
3. Prepare a schedule of accounts payable.

A-5. Abby Ellen opened Abby's Toy House. As her newly hired accountant, your tasks are to

1. Journalize the transactions for the month of March.
2. Record to subsidiary ledgers and post to the general ledger as appropriate.
3. Total and rule the journals.
4. Prepare a schedule of accounts receivable and a schedule of accounts payable.

The following is the partial chart of accounts for Abby's Toy House:

Abby's Toy House Chart of Accounts

Assets		**Revenue**	
110	Cash	410	Toy Sales
112	Accounts Receivable	412	Sales Returns and Allowances
114	Prepaid Rent	414	Sales Discounts
121	Delivery Truck	**Cost of Goods**	
Liabilities		510	Toy Purchases
210	Accounts Payable	512	Purchases Returns and Allowances
Owner's Equity		514	Purchases Discount
310	A. Ellen, Capital	**Expenses**	
		610	Salaries Expense
		612	Cleaning Expense

Check Figures: Total of schedule of accounts receivable $7,600
Total of schedule of accounts payable $9,000

200X		
Mar.	1	Abby Ellen invested $8,000 in the toy store.
	1	Paid three months' rent in advance, check no. 1, $3,000.
	1	Purchased merchandise from Earl Miller Company on account, $4,000, invoice no. 410, dated March 2; terms 2/10, n/30.
	3	Sold merchandise to Bill Burton on account, $1,000, invoice no. 1; terms 2/10, n/30.
	6	Sold merchandise to Jim Rex on account, $700, invoice no. 2; terms 2/10, n/30.
	8	Purchased merchandise from Earl Miller Co. on account, $1,200, invoice no. 415, dated March 9; terms 2/10, n/30.
	9	Sold merchandise to Bill Burton on account, $600, invoice no. 3; terms 2/10, n/30.
	9	Paid cleaning service, check no. 2, $300.
	10	Jim Rex returned merchandise that cost $300 to Abby's Toy House. Abby issued credit memorandum no. 1 to Jim Rex for $300.
	10	Purchased merchandise from Minnie Katz on account, $4,000, invoice no. 311, dated March 11; terms 1/15, n/60.
	12	Paid Earl Miller Co. invoice no. 410, dated March 2, check no. 3.
	13	Sold $1,300 of toy merchandise for cash.
	13	Paid salaries, $600, check no. 4.
	14	Returned merchandise to Minnie Katz in the amount of $1,000. Abby's Toy House issued debit memorandum no. 1 to Minnie Katz.
	15	Sold merchandise for $4,000 cash.
	16	Received payment from Jim Rex, invoice no. 2 (less returned merchandise) less discount.
	16	Bill Burton paid invoice no. 1.
	16	Sold toy merchandise to Amy Rose on account, $4,000, invoice no. 4; terms 2/10, n/30.
	20	Purchased delivery truck on account from Sam Katz Garage, $3,000, invoice no. 111, dated March 21 (no discount).
	22	Sold to Bill Burton merchandise on account, $900, invoice no. 5; terms 2/10, n/30.
	23	Paid Minnie Katz balance owed, check no. 5.
	24	Sold toy merchandise on account to Amy Rose, $1,100, invoice no. 6; terms 2/10, n/30.

(continued on next page)

25 Purchased toy merchandise, $600, check no. 6.

26 Purchased toy merchandise from Woody Smith on account, $4,800, invoice no. 211, dated March 27; terms 2/10, n/30.

28 Bill Burton paid invoice no. 5, dated March 22.

28 Amy Rose paid invoice no. 6, dated March 24.

28 Abby invested an additional $5,000 in the business.

28 Purchased merchandise from Earl Miller Co., $1,400, invoice no. 436, dated March 29; terms 2/10, n/30.

30 Paid Earl Miller Co. invoice no. 436, check no. 7.

30 Sold merchandise to Bonnie Flow Company on account, $3,000, invoice no. 7; terms 2/10, n/30.

Sales and Cash Receipts Journal in a Perpetual Accounting System for Art's Wholesale Clothing

FIGURE A.7 A Sales Journal Under a Perpetual System

ART'S WHOLESALE CLOTHING COMPANY
SALES JOURNAL

Page 1

Date		Account Debited	Terms	Invoice No.	Post. Ref.	Dr. Acc. Rec Cr. Sales	Cost of Goods Sold Dr. Merchandise Inventory Cr.
200X Apr.	3	Hal's Clothing	2/10, n/30	1	✔	800 00	560 00
	6	Bevans Company	2/10, n/30	2	✔	1600 00	1120 00
	18	Roe Company	2/10, n/30	3	✔	2000 00	1400 00
	24	Roe Company	2/10, n/30	4	✔	500 00	350 00
	28	Mel's Dept. Store	2/10, n/30	5	✔	900 00	630 00
	29	Mel's Dept. Store	2/10, n/30	6	✔	700 00	490 00
	30						
						6500 00	4550 00
						(113) (411)	(510) (114)

What's new:

In the journal: New columns for Cost of Goods Sold (Dr.) and Inventory (Cr.). Each time a charge sale is earned, the Cost of Goods Sold increases and the amount of Inventory at cost is reduced.

In the general ledger: New ledger accounts for Inventory and Cost of Goods Sold.

Example: On April 3, Art's Wholesale sold Hal's Clothing $800 of merchandise on account. This sale cost Art's $560 to bring this merchandise into the store.

FIGURE A.8 A Cash Receipts Journal Under a Perpetual System

ART'S WHOLESALE CLOTHING COMPANY
CASH RECEIPTS JOURNAL
Page 1

Date		Cash Dr.	Sales Discount Dr.	Accounts Receivable Cr.	Sales Cr.	Sundry Account Name	Sundry Post. Ref.	Sundry Amount Cr.	Costs of Goods Sold Dr. Merchandise Inventory Cr.
200X Apr.	1	8 0 0 0 00				Art Newner, Capital	311	8 0 0 0 00	
	4	7 8 4 00	1 6 00	8 0 0 00		Hal's Clothing	✔		
	15	9 0 0 00			9 0 0 00	Cash Sales	x		6 3 0 00
	16	9 8 0 00	2 0 00	1 0 0 0 00		Bevans Company	✔		
	22	1 9 6 0 00	4 0 00	2 0 0 0 00		Roe Company	✔		
	27	5 0 0 00				Store Equipment	121	5 0 0 00	
	30	1 2 0 0 00			1 2 0 0 00	Cash Sales	x		8 4 0 00
		14 3 2 4 00	7 6 00	3 8 0 0 00	2 1 0 0 00			8 5 0 0 00	1 4 7 0 00
		(111)	(413)	(113)	(411)			(X)	(510) (114)

What's new:

In the journal: New columns for Cost of Goods Sold (Dr.) and Inventory (Cr.). Each time a cash sale is earned, the Cost of Goods Sold increases and the amount of Inventory at cost is reduced.

11

Preparing a Worksheet for a Merchandise Company

DID YOU KNOW? If you received a gift card from Build-A-Bear, do you know how the company would treat it in its accounting records? Unredeemed gift cards are recorded as current liabilities on the balance sheet. Visit *www.buildabear.com* to find more information about Build-A-Bear.

LEARNING OBJECTIVES

1. Figuring adjustments for merchandise inventory, unearned rent, supplies used, insurance expired, depreciation expense, and salaries accrued.
2. Preparing a worksheet for a merchandise company.

When you build a bear at Build-A-Bear Workshop, do you ever wonder how the workshop controls its inventory? In Chapters 9 and 10 we discussed the subsidiary ledgers as well as entries for a merchandise company. Additional material provided an introduction to perpetual inventory. Now we shift our attention to recording adjustments and completing a worksheet for a merchandise company. Note that the appendix at the end of the chapter shows worksheets for a perpetual system.

LO1

Learning Unit 11-1 Adjustments for Merchandise Inventory and Unearned Rent

The Merchandise Inventory account shows the goods that a merchandise company has available to sell to customers. Companies have several ways to keep track of the **cost of goods sold** (the total cost of the goods sold to customers) and the quantity of inventory on hand. In this chapter we discuss the **periodic inventory system,** in which the balance in inventory is updated only at the end of the accounting period.* This system is used by companies, such as Art's Wholesale Clothing Company, that sell a variety of merchandise with low unit prices.

Net sales
− Cost of goods sold
= Gross profit
− Operating expenses
= Net income

Assume Art's Wholesale Clothing Company started the year with $19,000 worth of merchandise. This merchandise is called **beginning merchandise inventory** or simply **beginning inventory.** The balance of beginning inventory never changes during the accounting period. Instead, all purchases of merchandise are recorded in the Purchases account. During the accounting period $52,000 worth of such purchases were made and recorded in the Purchases account.

At the end of the period, the company takes a physical count of the merchandise in stock; this amount is called **ending merchandise inventory** or simply **ending inventory.** It is calculated on an inventory sheet as shown in Figure 11.1. This $4,000, which is the ending inventory for this period, will be the beginning inventory for the next period.

When the income statement is prepared, the cost of goods sold section requires two distinct numbers for inventory. The beginning inventory adds to the cost of goods sold, and the ending inventory is subtracted from the cost of goods sold (see margin aids at left). Remember that the two figures for beginning and ending inventory were calculated months apart. Thus, combining these amounts to come up with one inventory figure would not be accurate.

Cost of goods sold
Beginning inventory
+ Net purchases
+ Freight-in
− Ending inventory
= Cost of goods sold

Note that in the calculation (in the margin) of cost of goods sold a title called **Freight-In** is shown. Freight-In is a cost of goods sold account that records the shipping cost to the buyer. Note that net sales (gross sales less sales returns and allowances and sales discounts) less cost of goods sold equals **gross profit.** Subtracting operating expenses from gross profits equals net income.

FIGURE 11.1 Ending Inventory Sheet

ART'S WHOLESALE CLOTHING COMPANY
ENDING INVENTORY SHEET
AS OF DECEMBER 31, 20X2

Amount	Explanation	Unit Cost	Total
20	Ladies' Jackets code 14-0	$50	$1,000
10	Men's Hats code 327	10	100
90	Men's Shirts code 423	10	900
100	Ladies' Blouses code 481	20	2,000
			$4,000

Counted by ______ Checked and priced by ______

*For a discussion of the **perpetual inventory system,** see Learning Unit 10-4.

Adjustment for Merchandise Inventory

Adjusting the Merchandise Inventory account is a two-step process because we must record the beginning inventory and ending inventory amounts separately. The first step deals with beginning merchandise inventory.

Given: Beginning Inventory, $19,000 Our first adjustment removes beginning inventory from the asset account (Merchandise Inventory) and transfers it to Income Summary. We do so by crediting Merchandise Inventory for $19,000 and debiting Income Summary for the same amount. This adjustment is shown in the following T account form and on a transaction analysis chart.

Note that Income Summary has no normal balance of debit or credit.

Merchandise Inventory 114					Income Summary 313			
Bal.	**19,000**	**Adj.**	**19,000**		**Adj.**	**19,000**		

(A)

Accounts Affected	Category	↑ ↓	Rules
Income Summary	—	—	Dr.
Merchandise Inventory	Asset	↓	Cr.

(The adjusting entries would be recorded first on the worksheet and then in the general journal.)

The second step is entering the amount of ending inventory ($4,000) in the Merchandise Inventory account. This step is done to record the amount of goods on hand at the end of the period as an asset and to subtract this amount from the cost of goods sold (because we have not sold this inventory yet). To do so, we debit Merchandise Inventory for $4,000 and credit Income Summary for the same amount. This adjustment is shown in the following T account form.

Second adjustment updates inventory account with a figure for ending inventory.

Merchandise Inventory 114					Income Summary 313			
Bal.	**19,000**	**Adj.**	**19,000**		**Adj.**	**19,000**	**Adj.**	**4,000**
Adj.	**4,000**							

(B)

Beginning inventory	$19,000
+ Net cost of purchases*	50,910
= Cost of goods available for sale	$69,910
− Ending inventory	4,000
= Cost of goods sold	$65,910

*$52,000 Purchases − $860 PD − $680 PRA + $450 Freight-In

Let's look at how this process or method of recording merchandise inventory is reflected in the balance sheet and income statement (see Figure 11.2 on following page). Note that the $19,000 of beginning inventory is assumed sold and is shown on the income statement as part of the cost of goods sold. The ending inventory of $4,000 is assumed not to be sold and is subtracted from the cost of goods sold on the income statement. The ending inventory becomes next month's beginning inventory on the balance sheet. When the income statement is prepared, we will need a figure for beginning inventory as well as a figure for ending inventory. The goal of this adjustment is to wipe out the old inventory (a cost) and show the new inventory (not yet a cost).

Adjustment for Unearned Rent

A second new account we have not seen before is a liability called Unearned Rent or Rent Received in Advance. This account records the amount collected for rent before the service (renting the space) has been provided.

Suppose Art's Wholesale Clothing Company is subletting a portion of its space to Jesse Company for $200 per month. Jesse Company sends Art's cash for $600 for three months' rent paid in advance. This unearned rent ($600) is a liability on the balance sheet because Art's Wholesale owes Jesse Company three months' worth of occupancy.

FIGURE 11.2 Recording Inventory on a Partial Balance Sheet and Income Statement

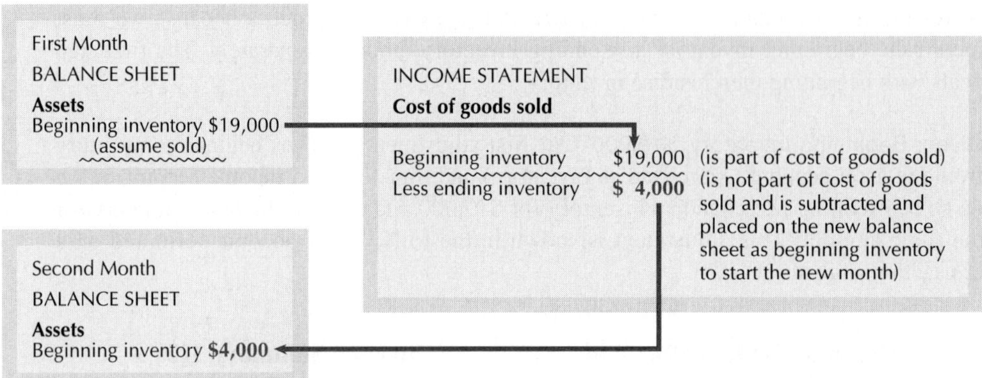

Received cash for renting space in future:

Cash	Asset	↑	Dr.
Unearned Rent	Liab.	↑	Cr.

When Art's Wholesale fulfills a portion of the rental agreement—when Jesse Company has been in the space for a period of time—this liability account will be reduced and the Rental Income account will be increased. Rental Income is another type of revenue for Art's Wholesale.

The adjustment when rental income is earned:

Unearned Rent	Liab.	↓	Dr.
Rental Income	Rev.	↑	Cr.

Remember that under accrual accounting, revenue is recognized when it is earned, whether payment is received then or not. Here, Art's Wholesale collected cash in advance for a service that it has not performed as yet. A liability called Unearned Rent is the result. Art's Wholesale may have the cash, but the Rental Income is not recorded until it is earned. Examples of other types of unearned revenue besides unearned rent include subscriptions for magazines, legal fees collected before the work is performed, and insurance.

LEARNING UNIT 11-1 REVIEW

AT THIS POINT you should be able to

- Define the periodic method of inventory accounting.
- Explain why beginning and ending inventory are two separate figures in the cost of goods sold section on the income statement.
- Calculate net sales, cost of goods sold, gross profit, and net income.
- Show how to calculate a figure for ending inventory.
- Explain why Unearned Rent is a *liability* account.

Self-Review Quiz 11-1

Given the following, prepare the two *adjusting* entries for Merchandise Inventory on 12/31/0X.

Merchandise Inventory, 1/1/0X	$ 8,000
Purchases	9,000
Purchases Returns and Allowances	3,000
Merchandise Inventory, 12/31/0X	4,000
Cost of Goods Sold	10,000
Unearned Magazine Subscriptions	8,000

Solution to Self-Review Quiz 11-1

Dec.	31	Income Summary	800000	
		Merchandise Inventory		800000
	31	Merchandise Inventory	400000	
		Income Summary		400000

FIGURE 11.3 Merchandise Inventory Adjustments

Note that Unearned Magazine Subscriptions is a liability and is not involved in the adjustment for Merchandise Inventory.

Learning Unit 11-2 Completing the Worksheet

LO 2

In this unit we prepare a worksheet for Art's Wholesale Clothing Company. For convenience, we reproduce the company's chart of accounts in Figure 11.4.

Figure 11.5 on the following page shows the trial balance that was prepared on December 31, 200X, from Art's Wholesale ledger. (Note that it is placed directly in the first two columns of the worksheet.)

In looking at the trial balance, we see many new titles that appeared after we completed a trial balance for a service company in Chapter 5. Let's look specifically at these new titles shown in Table 11.1.

Note the following:

- **Mortgage Payable** is a liability account that records the increases and decreases in the amount of debt owed on a mortgage. We discuss this account more in the next chapter, when financial reports are prepared.

CHART OF ACCOUNTS

Assets 100–199
111 Cash
112 Petty Cash
113 Accounts Receivable
114 Merchandise Inventory
115 Supplies
116 Prepaid Insurance
121 Store Equipment
122 Accum. Depreciation, Store Equipment

Liabilities 200–299
211 Accounts Payable
212 Salaries Payable
213 Federal Income Tax Payable
214 FICA—Social Security Payable
215 FICA—Medicare Payable
216 State Income Tax Payable
217 SUTA Tax Payable
218 FUTA Tax Payable
219 Unearned Rent*
220 Mortgage Payable

Owner's Equity 300–399
311 Art Newner, Capital
312 Art Newner, Withdrawals
313 Income Summary

Revenue 400–499
411 Sales
412 Sales Returns and Allowances
413 Sales Discount
414 Rental Income

Cost of Goods Sold 500–599
511 Purchases
512 Purchases Discount
513 Purchases Returns and Allowances
514 Freight-In

Expenses 600–699
611 Salaries Expense
612 Payroll Tax Expense
613 Depreciation Expense, Store Equipment
614 Supplies Expense
615 Insurance Expense
616 Postage Expense
617 Miscellaneous Expense
618 Interest Expense
619 Cleaning Expense
620 Delivery Expense

*Although Unearned Rent is the only term under Liabilities not using payable, it is a liability.

FIGURE 11.4 Art's Wholesale Clothing Company Chart of Accounts

FIGURE 11.5 Trial Balance Section of the Worksheet

	Trial Balance Dr.	Trial Balance Cr.
Cash	12 9 2 0 00	
Petty Cash	1 0 0 00	
Accounts Receivable	14 5 0 0 00	
Merchandise Inventory	19 0 0 0 00	
Supplies	8 0 0 00	
Prepaid Insurance	9 0 0 00	
Store Equipment	4 0 0 0 00	
Acc. Dep., Store Equipment		4 0 0 00
Accounts Payable		17 9 0 0 00
Federal Income Tax Payable		8 0 0 00
FICA—Soc. Sec. Payable		4 5 4 00
FICA—Medicare Payable		1 0 6 00
State Income Tax Payable		2 0 0 00
SUTA Tax Payable		1 0 8 00
FUTA Tax Payable		3 2 00
Unearned Rent		6 0 0 00
Mortgage Payable		2 3 2 0 00
Art Newner, Capital		7 9 0 5 00
Art Newner, Withdrawals	8 6 0 0 00	
Income Summary		
Sales		95 0 0 0 00
Sales Returns and Allowances	9 5 0 00	
Sales Discount	6 7 0 00	
Purchases	52 0 0 0 00	
Purchases Discount		8 6 0 00
Purchases Returns and Allowances		6 8 0 00
Freight-In	4 5 0 00	
Salaries Expense	11 7 0 0 00	
Payroll Tax Expense	4 2 0 00	
Postage Expense	2 5 00	
Miscellaneous Expense	3 0 00	
Interest Expense	3 0 0 00	
	127 3 6 5 00	127 3 6 5 00

- **Interest Expense** represents a nonoperating expense for Art's Wholesale and thus is categorized as Other Expense. We look at this expense in the next chapter.
- **Unearned Revenue** is a liability account that records receipt of payment for goods and services in advance of delivery. Unearned Rent is a particular example of this general type of account.

We already discussed the adjustments that make up the two-step process involved in adjusting Merchandise Inventory at the end of the accounting period. Now we show T accounts and transaction analysis charts for other adjustments that need to be made at this point for a merchandise firm, just as they must for a service company.

Adjustment C: Rental Income Earned by Art's Wholesale, $200 A month ago, Cash was increased by $600, as was a liability, Unearned Rent. Art's Wholesale received payment in advance but had not earned the rental income. Now, because $200 has been

TABLE 11.1 Summary of New Account Titles

Title	Category	Report(s) Found on	Normal Balance	Temporary or Permanent
Petty Cash	Asset	Balance Sheet	Dr.	Permanent
Merchandise Inventory* (Beginning)	Asset	Balance Sheet from prior period	Dr.	Permanent
	Cost of Goods Sold	Income Statement of current period		
Federal Income Tax Payable	Liability	Balance Sheet	Cr.	Permanent
FICA—Social Security Payable	Liability	Balance Sheet	Cr.	Permanent
FICA—Medicare Payable	Liability	Balance Sheet	Cr.	Permanent
State Income Tax Payable	Liability	Balance Sheet	Cr.	Permanent
SUTA Tax Payable	Liability	Balance Sheet	Cr.	Permanent
FUTA Tax Payable	Liability	Balance Sheet	Cr.	Permanent
Unearned Rent†	Liability	Balance Sheet	Cr.	Permanent
Mortgage Payable	Liability	Balance Sheet	Cr.	Permanent
Sales	Revenue	Income Statement	Cr.	Temporary
Sales Returns and Allowances	Contra-Revenue	Income Statement	Dr.	Temporary
Sales Discount	Contra-Revenue	Income Statement	Dr.	Temporary
Purchases§	Cost of Goods Sold	Income Statement	Dr.	Temporary
Purchases Discount	Contra-Cost of Goods Sold	Income Statement	Cr.	Temporary
Purchases Returns and Allowances	Contra-Cost of Goods Sold	Income Statement	Cr.	Temporary
Freight-In	Cost of Goods Sold	Income Statement	Dr.	Temporary
Payroll Tax Expense	Expense	Income Statement	Dr.	Temporary
Postage Expense	Expense	Income Statement	Dr.	Temporary
Interest Expense	Other Expense	Income Statement	Dr.	Temporary

*The ending inventory of current period is a contra-cost of goods sold on the income statement and will be an asset on the balance sheet for the next period.
†Referred to as Unearned Revenue.
§Note that the categories for Purchases and Freight-In are Cost of Goods Sold, whereas Purchases Discounts and Purchases Returns and Allowances are Contra-Cost of Goods Sold.

earned, the liability is reduced and Rental Income can be recorded for the $200. This step is shown as follows:

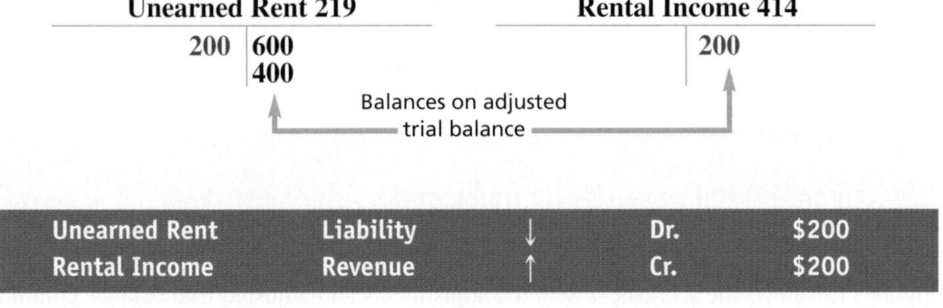

Adjustment D: Supplies on Hand, $300 Because $500 worth of supplies were used up, Supplies Expense is increased, and the asset Supplies is decreased.

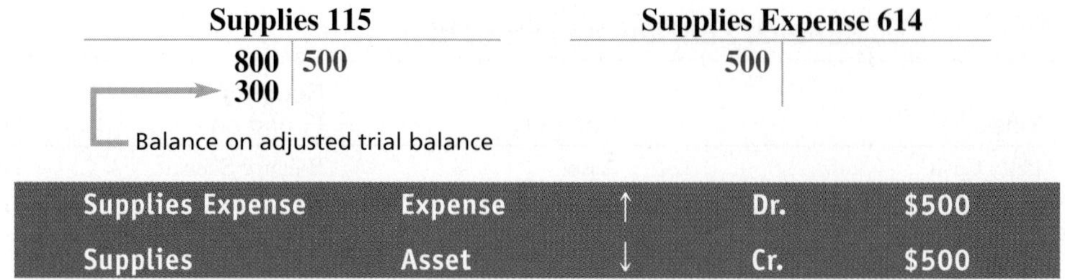

Supplies Expense	Expense	↑	Dr.	$500
Supplies	Asset	↓	Cr.	$500

Adjustment E: Insurance Expired, $300 Because insurance has expired by $300, Insurance Expense is increased by $300 and the asset Prepaid Insurance is decreased by $300.

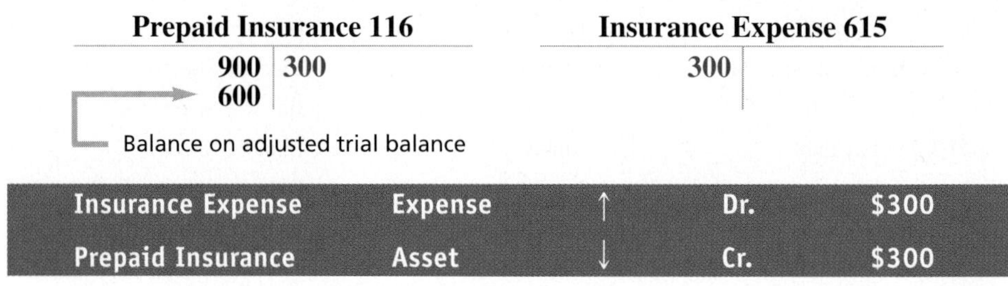

Insurance Expense	Expense	↑	Dr.	$300
Prepaid Insurance	Asset	↓	Cr.	$300

Adjustment F: Depreciation Expense, $50 When depreciation is taken, Depreciation Expense and Accumulated Depreciation are both increased by $50. Note that the cost of the store equipment remains the same.

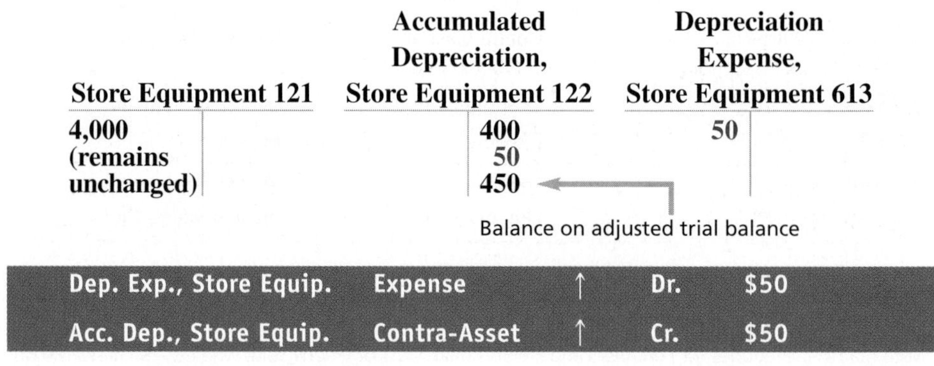

Dep. Exp., Store Equip.	Expense	↑	Dr.	$50
Acc. Dep., Store Equip.	Contra-Asset	↑	Cr.	$50

Adjustment G: Salaries Accrued, $600 The $600 in accrued salaries causes an increase in Salaries Expense and Salaries Payable.

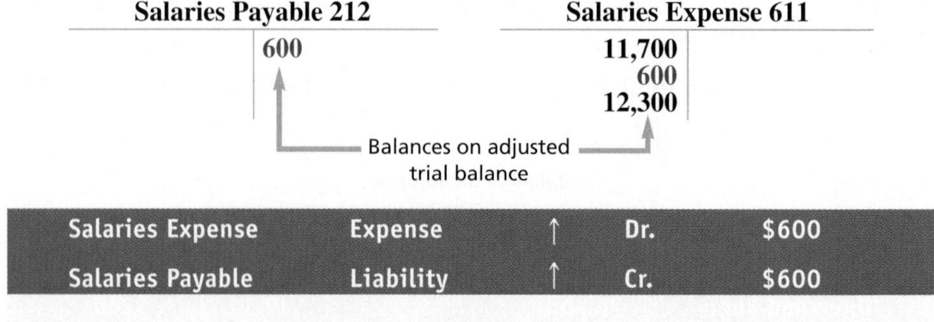

Salaries Expense	Expense	↑	Dr.	$600
Salaries Payable	Liability	↑	Cr.	$600

Figure 11.6 shows the worksheet with the adjustments and adjusted trial balance columns filled out. Note that the adjustment numbers in the Income Summary from beginning and ending inventory are also carried over to the adjusted trial balance and are not combined.

The next step in completing the worksheet is to fill out the income statement columns from the adjusted trial balance, as shown in Figure 11.7.

FIGURE 11.6 Worksheet with Three Columns Filled Out

	Trial Balance		Adjustments		Adjusted Trial Balance	
	Dr.	Cr.	Dr.	Cr.	Dr.	Cr.
Cash	12920 00				12920 00	
Petty Cash	100 00				100 00	
Accounts Receivable	14500 00				14500 00	
Merchandise Inventory	19000 00		(B) 4000 00	(A) 19000 00	4000 00	
Supplies	800 00			(D) 500 00	300 00	
Prepaid Insurance	900 00			(E) 300 00	600 00	
Store Equipment	4000 00				4000 00	
Acc. Dep., Store Equipment		400 00		(F) 50 00		450 00
Accounts Payable		17900 00				17900 00
Federal Income Tax Payable		800 00				800 00
FICA—Soc. Sec. Payable		454 00				454 00
FICA—Medicare Payable		106 00				106 00
State Income Tax Payable		200 00				200 00
SUTA Tax Payable		108 00				108 00
FUTA Tax Payable		32 00				32 00
Unearned Rent		600 00	(C) 200 00			400 00
Mortgage Payable		2320 00				2320 00
Art Newner, Capital		7905 00				7905 00
Art Newner, Withdrawals	8600 00				8600 00	
Income Summary			(A) 19000 00	(B) 4000 00	19000 00	4000 00
Sales		95000 00				95000 00
Sales Returns and Allowances	950 00				950 00	
Sales Discount	670 00				670 00	
Purchases	52000 00				52000 00	
Purchases Discount		860 00				860 00
Purchases Returns and Allowances		680 00				680 00
Freight-In	450 00				450 00	
Salaries Expense	11700 00		(G) 600 00		12300 00	
Payroll Tax Expense	420 00				420 00	
Postage Expense	25 00				25 00	
Miscellaneous Expense	30 00				30 00	
Interest Expense	300 00				300 00	
	127365 00	127365 00				
Rental Income				(C) 200 00		200 00
Supplies Expense			(D) 500 00		500 00	
Insurance Expense			(E) 300 00		300 00	
Depreciation Expense, Store Equip.			(F) 50 00		50 00	
Salaries Payable				(G) 600 00		600 00
			24650 00	24650 00	132015 00	132015 00

The next step in completing the worksheet is to fill out the balance sheet columns (Fig. 11.8). Note how ending inventory is carried over to the balance sheet from the adjusted trial balance column. Take time also to look at the placement of the payroll tax liabilities as well as Unearned Rent on the worksheet.

Figure 11.9 is the completed worksheet.

Remember: We do not combine the $19,000 and $4,000 in Income Summary. When we prepare the cost of goods sold section for the formal income statement, we will need both a beginning and an ending figure for inventory.

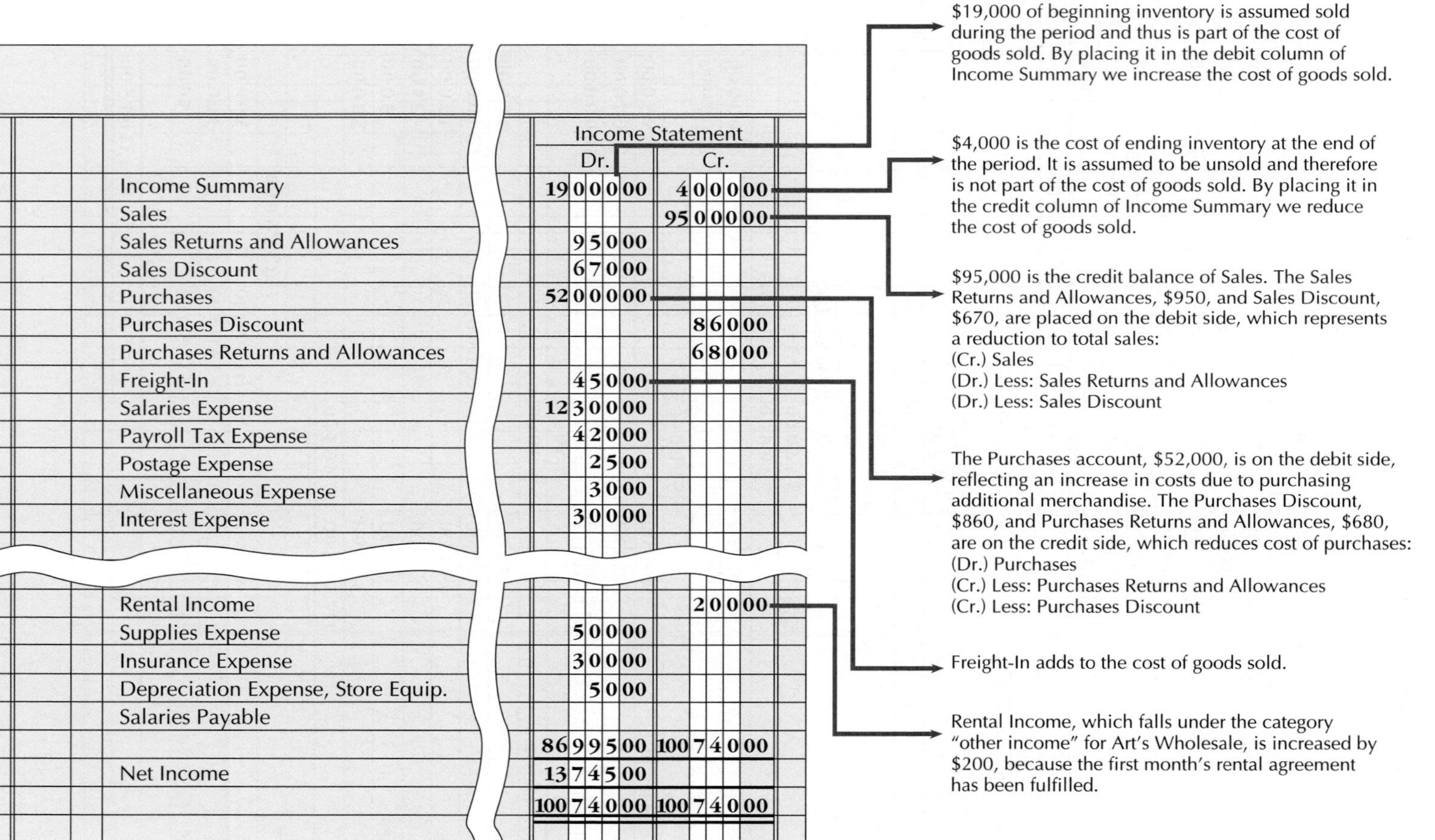

	Income Statement	
	Dr.	Cr.
Income Summary	19000 00	4000 00
Sales		95000 00
Sales Returns and Allowances	950 00	
Sales Discount	670 00	
Purchases	52000 00	
Purchases Discount		860 00
Purchases Returns and Allowances		680 00
Freight-In	450 00	
Salaries Expense	12300 00	
Payroll Tax Expense	420 00	
Postage Expense	25 00	
Miscellaneous Expense	30 00	
Interest Expense	300 00	
Rental Income		200 00
Supplies Expense	500 00	
Insurance Expense	300 00	
Depreciation Expense, Store Equip.	50 00	
Salaries Payable		
	86995 00	100740 00
Net Income	13745 00	
	100740 00	100740 00

$19,000 of beginning inventory is assumed sold during the period and thus is part of the cost of goods sold. By placing it in the debit column of Income Summary we increase the cost of goods sold.
$4,000 is the cost of ending inventory at the end of the period. It is assumed to be unsold and therefore is not part of the cost of goods sold. By placing it in the credit column of Income Summary we reduce the cost of goods sold.
$95,000 is the credit balance of Sales. The Sales Returns and Allowances, $950, and Sales Discount, $670, are placed on the debit side, which represents a reduction to total sales:
(Cr.) Sales
(Dr.) Less: Sales Returns and Allowances
(Dr.) Less: Sales Discount
The Purchases account, $52,000, is on the debit side, reflecting an increase in costs due to purchasing additional merchandise. The Purchases Discount, $860, and Purchases Returns and Allowances, $680, are on the credit side, which reduces cost of purchases:
(Dr.) Purchases
(Cr.) Less: Purchases Returns and Allowances
(Cr.) Less: Purchases Discount
Freight-In adds to the cost of goods sold.
Rental Income, which falls under the category "other income" for Art's Wholesale, is increased by $200, because the first month's rental agreement has been fulfilled.

FIGURE 11.7 Income Statement Section of the Worksheet

FIGURE 11.8 Balance Sheet Section of the Worksheet

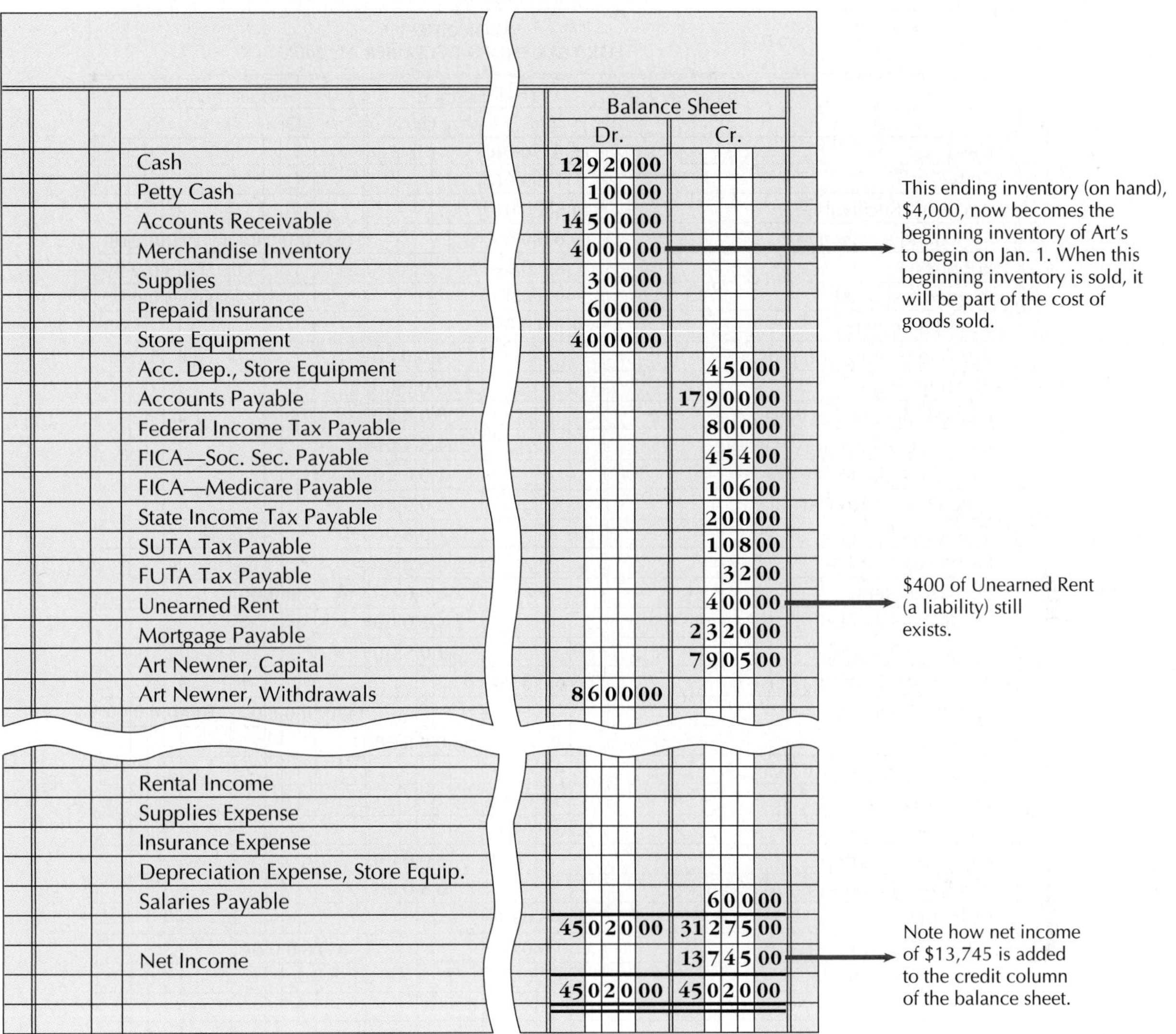

	Balance Sheet	
	Dr.	Cr.
Cash	12,920.00	
Petty Cash	100.00	
Accounts Receivable	14,500.00	
Merchandise Inventory	4,000.00	
Supplies	300.00	
Prepaid Insurance	600.00	
Store Equipment	4,000.00	
Acc. Dep., Store Equipment		450.00
Accounts Payable		17,900.00
Federal Income Tax Payable		800.00
FICA—Soc. Sec. Payable		454.00
FICA—Medicare Payable		106.00
State Income Tax Payable		200.00
SUTA Tax Payable		108.00
FUTA Tax Payable		32.00
Unearned Rent		400.00
Mortgage Payable		2,320.00
Art Newner, Capital		7,905.00
Art Newner, Withdrawals	8,600.00	
Rental Income		
Supplies Expense		
Insurance Expense		
Depreciation Expense, Store Equip.		
Salaries Payable		600.00
	45,020.00	31,275.00
Net Income		13,745.00
	45,020.00	45,020.00

This ending inventory (on hand), $4,000, now becomes the beginning inventory of Art's to begin on Jan. 1. When this beginning inventory is sold, it will be part of the cost of goods sold.
$400 of Unearned Rent (a liability) still exists.
Note how net income of $13,745 is added to the credit column of the balance sheet.

FIGURE 11.9 Completed Worksheet

WORKSHEET
FOR YEAR ENDED DECEMBER 31, 200X

	Trial Balance		Adjustments	
	Dr.	Cr.	Dr.	Cr.
Cash	12920 00			
Petty Cash	100 00			
Accounts Receivable	14500 00			
Merchandise Inventory	19000 00		(B) 4000 00	(A) 19000 00
Supplies	800 00			(D) 500 00
Prepaid Insurance	900 00			(E) 300 00
Store Equipment	4000 00			
Acc. Dep., Store Equipment		400 00		(F) 50 00
Accounts Payable		17900 00		
Federal Income Tax Payable		800 00		
FICA—Social Security Payable		454 00		
FICA—Medicare Payable		106 00		
State Income Tax Payable		200 00		
SUTA Tax Payable		108 00		
FUTA Tax Payable		32 00		
Unearned Rent		600 00	(C) 200 00	
Mortgage Payable		2320 00		
Art Newner, Capital		7905 00		
Art Newner, Withdrawals	8600 00			
Income Summary			(A) 19000 00	(B) 4000 00
Sales		95000 00		
Sales Returns and Allowances	950 00			
Sales Discount	670 00			
Purchases	52000 00			
Purchases Discount		860 00		
Purchases Returns and Allowances		680 00		
Freight-In	450 00			
Salaries Expense	11700 00		(G) 600 00	
Payroll Tax Expense	420 00			
Postage Expense	25 00			
Miscellaneous Expense	30 00			
Interest Expense	300 00			
	127365 00	127365 00		
Rental Income				(C) 200 00
Supplies Expense			(D) 500 00	
Insurance Expense			(E) 300 00	
Depreciation Expense, Store Equip.			(F) 50 00	
Salaries Payable				(G) 600 00
			24650 00	24650 00
Net Income				

FIGURE 11.9 *(continued)*

Adjusted Trial Bal.		Income Statement		Balance Sheet	
Dr.	Cr.	Dr.	Cr.	Dr.	Cr.
12920 00				12920 00	
100 00				100 00	
14500 00				14500 00	
4000 00				4000 00	
300 00				300 00	
600 00				600 00	
4000 00				4000 00	
	450 00				450 00
	17900 00				17900 00
	800 00				800 00
	454 00				454 00
	106 00				106 00
	200 00				200 00
	108 00				108 00
	32 00				32 00
	400 00				400 00
	2320 00				2320 00
	7905 00				7905 00
8600 00				8600 00	
19000 00	4000 00	19000 00	4000 00		
	95000 00		95000 00		
950 00		950 00			
670 00		670 00			
52000 00		52000 00			
	860 00		860 00		
	680 00		680 00		
450 00		450 00			
12300 00		12300 00			
420 00		420 00			
25 00		25 00			
30 00		30 00			
300 00		300 00			
	200 00		200 00		
500 00		500 00			
300 00		300 00			
50 00		50 00			
	600 00				600 00
132015 00	132015 00	86995 00	100740 00	45020 00	31275 00
		13745 00			13745 00
		100740 00	100740 00	45020 00	45020 00

LEARNING UNIT 11-2 REVIEW

AT THIS POINT you should be able to

- Complete adjustments for a merchandise company.
- Complete a worksheet.

Self-Review Quiz 11-2

From the trial balance shown in Figure 11.10, complete a worksheet for Ray Company. Additional data include the following: (A and B) On December 31, 200X, ending inventory was calculated as \$200; (C) Storage Fees Earned, \$516; (D) Rent Expired, \$100; (E) Depreciation Expense, Office Equipment, \$60; (F) Salaries Accrued, \$200.

FIGURE 11.10 Trial Balance of Ray Company

Account Title	Trial Balance Dr.	Trial Balance Cr.
Cash	2486 00	
Merchandise Inventory	824 00	
Prepaid Rent	1152 00	
Prepaid Insurance	60 00	
Office Equipment	2160 00	
Accumulated Depreciation, Office Equipment		560 00
Unearned Storage Fees		2516 00
Accounts Payable		100 00
B. Ray, Capital		1932 00
Income Summary	—	—
Sales		11040 00
Sales Returns and Allowances	546 00	
Sales Discount	216 00	
Purchases	5256 00	
Purchases Returns and Allowances		168 00
Purchases Discount		102 00
Salaries Expense	2016 00	
Insurance Expense	1392 00	
Utilities Expense	96 00	
Plumbing Expense	214 00	
	16418 00	16418 00

The ending inventory of \$200 becomes next month's beginning inventory.

Solution to Self-Review Quiz 11-2

The solution is shown in Figure 11.11.

RAY COMPANY WORKSHEET FOR YEAR ENDED DECEMBER 31, 200X	Trial Balance		Adjustments		Adjusted Trial Balance		Income Statement		Balance Sheet	
	Dr.	Cr.	Dr.	Cr.	Dr.	Cr.	Dr.	Cr.	Dr.	Cr.
Cash	2486 00				2486 00				2486 00	
Merchandise Inventory	824 00		(B) 200 00	(A) 824 00	200 00				200 00	
Prepaid Rent	1152 00			(D) 100 00	1052 00				1052 00	
Prepaid Insurance	60 00				60 00				60 00	
Office Equipment	2160 00				2160 00				2160 00	
Acc. Dep., Office Equipment		560 00		(E) 60 00		620 00				620 00
Unearned Storage Fees		2516 00	(C) 516 00			2000 00				2000 00
Accounts Payable		100 00				100 00				100 00
B. Ray, Capital		1932 00				1932 00				1932 00
Income Summary			(A) 824 00	(B) 200 00	824 00	200 00	824 00	200 00		
Sales		11040 00				11040 00		11040 00		
Sales Returns and Allowances	546 00				546 00		546 00			
Sales Discount	216 00				216 00		216 00			
Purchases	5256 00				5256 00		5256 00			
Purchases Returns and Allowances		168 00				168 00		168 00		
Purchases Discount		102 00				102 00		102 00		
Salaries Expense	2016 00		(F) 200 00		2216 00		2216 00			
Insurance Expense	1392 00				1392 00		1392 00			
Utilities Expense	96 00				96 00		96 00			
Plumbing Expense	214 00				214 00		214 00			
	16418 00	16418 00								
Storage Fees Earned				(C) 516 00		516 00		516 00		
Rent Expense			(D) 100 00		100 00		100 00			
Depreciation Expense, Equipment			(E) 60 00		60 00		60 00			
Salaries Payable				(F) 200 00		200 00				200 00
			1900 00	1900 00	16878 00	16878 00	10920 00	12026 00	5958 00	4852 00
Net Income							1106 00			1106 00
							12026 00	12026 00	5958 00	5958 00

FIGURE 11.11 Worksheet for Ray Company

CHAPTER ASSIGNMENTS

SUMMARY OF KEY POINTS

LEARNING UNIT 11-1

1. The periodic inventory system updates the record of goods on hand only at the *end* of the accounting period. This system is used for companies with a variety of merchandise with low unit prices. With computers today, many companies switch to a perpetual inventory system.
2. In the periodic inventory system, additional purchases of merchandise during the accounting period will be recorded in the Purchases account. The amount in beginning inventory will remain unchanged during the accounting period. At the end of the period, a new figure for ending inventory will be calculated.
3. Beginning inventory at the end of the accounting period is part of the cost of goods sold, whereas ending inventory is a reduction to cost of goods sold.
4. The perpetual inventory system keeps a continuous record of inventory. It is used by companies with high amounts of inventory.
5. Net sales less cost of goods sold equals gross profit. Gross profit less operating expenses equals net income.
6. Unearned Revenue is a liability account that accumulates revenue that has *not* been earned yet, although the cash has been received. It represents a liability to the seller until the service or product is performed or delivered.

LEARNING UNIT 11-2

1. Two important adjustments in the accounting for a merchandise company deal with the Merchandise Inventory account and with the Unearned Revenue account (unearned rent).
2. When a company delivers goods or services for which it has been paid in advance, an adjustment is made to reduce the liability account Unearned Revenue and to increase an earned revenue account.

KEY TERMS

Beginning merchandise inventory (beginning inventory) The cost of goods on hand in a company to *begin* an accounting period.

Cost of goods sold Total cost of goods sold to customers.

Ending merchandise inventory (ending inventory) The cost of goods that remain unsold at the *end* of the accounting period. It is an asset on the new balance sheet.

Freight-In A cost of goods sold account that records the shipping cost to the buyer.

Gross profit Net sales less cost of goods sold.

Interest Expense The cost of borrowing money.

Mortgage Payable A liability account showing amount owed on a mortgage.

Periodic inventory system An inventory system that, at the *end* of each accounting period, calculates the cost of the unsold goods on hand by taking the cost of each unit times the number of units of each product on hand.

Perpetual inventory system An inventory system that keeps *continual track* of each type of inventory by recording units on hand at the beginning, units sold, and the current balance after each sale or purchase.

Unearned Revenue A liability account that records amount owed for goods or services in advance of delivery. The Cash account would record the receipt of cash.

BLUEPRINT: A WORKSHEET FOR A MERCHANDISE COMPANY

Account Titles	Adjustments		Adjusted Trial Balance		Income Statement		Balance Sheet	
	Dr.	Cr.	Dr.	Cr.	Dr.	Cr.	Dr.	Cr.
Cash			X				X	
Petty Cash			X				X	
Accounts Receivable			X				X	
Merchandise Inventory	X-E	X-B	X-E				X-E	
Supplies			X				X	
Equipment			X				X	
Acc. Dep., Store Equipment				X				X
Accounts Payable				X				X
Federal Income Tax Payable				X				X
FICA—Social Security Payable				X				X
FICA—Medicare Payable				X				X
State Income Tax Payable				X				X
SUTA Tax Payable				X				X
FUTA Tax Payable				X				X
Unearned Sales				X				X
Mortgage Payable				X				X
A. Flynn, Capital				X				X
A. Flynn, Withdrawals			X				X	
Income Summary*	X-B	X-E	X-B	X-E	X-B	X-E		
Sales				X		X		
Sales Returns and Allow.			X		X			
Sales Discount			X		X			
Purchases			X		X			
Purchases Ret. and Allow.				X		X		
Purchases Discount				X		X		
Freight-In			X		X			
Salaries Expense			X		X			
Payroll Tax Expense			X		X			
Insurance Expense			X		X			
Depreciation Expense			X		X			
Salaries Payable				X				X
Rental Income				X		X		

* Note that the figures for beginning (X-B) and ending inventory (X-E) are never combined on the Income Summary line of the worksheet. When the formal income statement is prepared, two distinct figures for inventory will be used to explain and calculate cost of goods sold. Beginning inventory adds to cost of goods sold; ending inventory reduces cost of goods sold.

QUESTIONS, CLASSROOM DEMONSTRATION EXERCISES, EXERCISES, AND PROBLEMS

Discussion and Critical Thinking Questions/Ethical Case

1. What is the function of the Purchases account?
2. Explain why Unearned Revenue is a liability account.
3. In a periodic system of inventory, the balance of beginning inventory will remain unchanged during the period. True or false?
4. What is the purpose of an inventory sheet?

5. Why do many Unearned Revenue accounts have to be adjusted?

6. Explain why figures for beginning and ending inventory are not combined on the Income Summary line of the worksheet.

7. Jim Heary is the custodian of petty cash. Jim, who is short of personal cash, decided to pay his home electrical and phone bill from petty cash. He plans to pay it back next month. Do you feel Jim should do so? You make the call. Write down your specific recommendations to Jim.

Classroom Demonstration Exercises

SET A

LO1 (10 min) **Adjustment for Merchandise Inventory**

1. Given the following, journalize the adjusting entries for Merchandise Inventory. Note that ending inventory has a balance of $18,000.

Merchandise Inventory 114	
60,000	

Income Summary 313	

LO1 (15 min) **Adjustment for Unearned Fees**

2. a. Given the following, journalize the adjusting entry. By December 31, $210 of the unearned dog walking fees were earned.

Unearned Dog Walking Fees 225	
	900 12/1/XX

Earned Dog Walking Fees 441	
	5,000 12/1/XX

b. What is the category of unearned dog walking fees?

LO2 (10 min) **Worksheet**

3. Match the following:

1. Located on the Income Statement debit column of the worksheet.
2. Located on the Income Statement credit column of the worksheet.
3. Located on the Balance Sheet debit column of the worksheet.
4. Located on the Balance Sheet credit column of the worksheet.

_____ **a.** Beginning Merchandise Inventory
_____ **b.** Sales Returns and Allowance
_____ **c.** Salaries Payable
_____ **d.** Sales
_____ **e.** Ending Merchandise Inventory
_____ **f.** Accounts Receivable

LO1 (10 min) **Merchandise Inventory Adjustment**

4. Given beginning merchandise inventory of $2,000 and ending merchandise inventory of $50, what would be the adjusting entries?

LO2 (10 min) **Income Summary on the Worksheet**

5.

	Adj.		ATB		Income Statement	
	Dr.	Cr.	Dr.	Cr.	Dr.	Cr.
Income Summary	A	B	C	D	E	F

Given a figure of beginning inventory of $400 and a $900 figure for ending inventory, place these numbers on the Income Summary line of this partial worksheet.

SET B

Adjustment for Merchandise Inventory

LO1 (10 min)

1. Given the following, journalize the adjusting entries for Merchandise Inventory. Note that ending inventory has a balance of $17,000.

Merchandise Inventory 114	
60,000	

Income Summary 313	

Adjustment for Unearned Fees

LO1 (15 min)

2. a. Given the following, journalize the adjusting entry. By December 31, $300 of the unearned dog walking fees were earned.

Unearned Dog Walking Fees 225	
	650 12/1/XX

Earned Dog Walking Fees 441	
	4,000 12/1/XX

b. What is the category of unearned dog walking fees?

Worksheet

LO2 (10 min)

3. Match the following:
   1. Located on the Income Statement debit column of the worksheet.
   2. Located on the Income Statement credit column of the worksheet.
   3. Located on the Balance Sheet debit column of the worksheet.
   4. Located on the Balance Sheet credit column of the worksheet.

   _____ a. Ending Merchandise Inventory
   _____ b. Unearned Rent
   _____ c. Sales Discount
   _____ d. Purchases
   _____ e. Rental Income
   _____ f. Petty Cash

Merchandise Inventory Adjustment on Worksheet

LO1 (10 min)

4. Adjustment column of a worksheet:

Merchandise Inventory	(A)	(B)
Income Summary	(B)	(A)

Explain what the letters A and B represent. Why are they never combined?

Income Summary on the Worksheet

LO2 (10 min)

5.

	Adj.		ATB		Income Statement	
	Dr.	Cr.	Dr.	Cr.	Dr.	Cr.
Income Summary	A	B	C	D	E	F

Given a figure of beginning inventory of $500 and a $700 figure for ending inventory, place these numbers on the Income Summary line of this partial worksheet.

Exercises

LO1 (10 min) **11-1.** Indicate the normal balance and category of each of the following accounts:

a. Unearned Revenue
b. Merchandise Inventory (beginning of period)
c. Freight-In
d. Payroll Tax Expense
e. Purchases Discount
f. Sales Discount
g. FICA—Social Security Payable
h. Purchases Returns and Allowances

LO1 (15 min) **11-2.** From the following, calculate (a) net sales, (b) cost of goods sold, (c) gross profit, and (d) net income: Sales, $22,000; Sales Discount, $500; Sales Returns and Allowances, $250; Beginning Inventory, $650; Net Purchases, $13,200; Ending Inventory, $510; Operating Expenses, $3,600.

LO1 (10 min) **11-3.** Allan Co. had the following balances on December 31, 200X:

Cash	
2,100	

Unearned Janitorial Service	
	600

Janitorial Service	
	7,200

The accountant for Allan has asked you to make an adjustment because $400 of janitorial services has just been performed for customers who had paid for two months. Construct a transaction analysis chart.

LO1, 2 (15 min) **11-4.** Lesan Co. purchased merchandise costing $400,000. Calculate the cost of goods sold under the following different situations:

a. Beginning inventory $40,000 and no ending inventory
b. Beginning inventory $50,000 and a $60,000 ending inventory
c. No beginning inventory and a $30,000 ending inventory

LO2 (20 min) **11-5.** Prepare a worksheet for Moore Co. from the following information using Figure 11.12:

a/b. Merchandise Inventory, ending	13
c. Store Supplies on hand	4
d. Depreciation on Store Equipment	4
e. Accrued Salaries	2

Group A Problems

You can also use the foldout worksheets at the end of the *Study Guide and Working Papers.*

LO1 (30 min) **11A-1.** Based on the following accounts, calculate

Check Figure:
Net income $2,125

a. Net sales.
b. Cost of goods sold.
c. Gross profit.
d. Net income.

Accounts Payable	$ 6,000
Operating Expenses	2,000
Bing.com, Capital	19,400
Purchases	1,500
Freight-In	90
Ending Merchandise Inventory, Dec. 31, 200X	65
Sales	6,000

MOORE CO. TRIAL BALANCE DECEMBER 31, 200X	Dr.	Cr.
Cash	800	
Accounts Receivable	500	
Merchandise Inventory	1100	
Store Supplies	1000	
Store Equipment	2000	
Accumulated Depreciation, Store Equipment		600
Accounts Payable		500
J. Moore, Capital		3400
Income Summary	—	—
Sales		6400
Sales Returns and Allowances	900	
Purchases	2300	
Purchases Discount		300
Freight-In	300	
Salaries Expense	1000	
Advertising Expense	1300	
Totals	11200	11200

FIGURE 11.12 Trial Balance for Moore Co.

Accounts Receivable	500
Cash	800
Purchases Discount	50
Sales Returns and Allowances	300
Beg. Merchandise Inventory, Jan. 1, 200X	80
Purchases Returns and Allowances	70
Sales Discount	90

11A-2. From the trial balance in Figure 11.13 on the following page, complete a worksheet for Jim's Hardware. Assume the following:

a/b. Ending inventory on December 31 is calculated at $310.
c. Insurance expired, $150.
d. Depreciation on store equipment, $60.
e. Accrued wages, $90.

LO2 (60 min)

Check Figure:
Net income $1,984

11A-3. The owner of Waltz Company asked you to prepare a worksheet from the trial balance in Figure 11.14 on the following page.

LO2 (60 min)

Check Figure:
Net income $5,300

Additional Data

a/b. Ending merchandise inventory on December 31, $1,805.
c. Office supplies used up, $210.
d. Rent expired, $195.
e. Depreciation expense on office equipment, $550.
f. Office salaries earned but not paid, $310.

11A-4. From the trial balance in Figure 11.15 and additional data, complete the worksheet for Ron's Wholesale Clothing Company.

LO1, 2 (60 min)

Check Figure:
Net loss $824

Additional Data

a/b. Ending merchandise inventory on December 31, $6,000.
c. Supplies on hand, $400.
d. Insurance expired, $600.
e. Depreciation on store equipment, $400.
f. Storage fees earned, $176.

FIGURE 11.13 Trial Balance for Jim's Hardware

JIM'S HARDWARE
TRIAL BALANCE
DECEMBER 31, 200X

	Dr.	Cr.
Cash	786.00	
Accounts Receivable	1152.00	
Merchandise Inventory	600.00	
Prepaid Insurance	684.00	
Store Equipment	2160.00	
Accumulated Depreciation, Store Equipment		660.00
Accounts Payable		516.00
Jim Spool, Capital		1632.00
Income Summary	—	—
Hardware Sales		11040.00
Hardware Sales Returns and Allowances	546.00	
Hardware Sales Discount	216.00	
Purchases	5256.00	
Purchases Discount		168.00
Purchases Returns and Allowances		102.00
Wages Expense	1716.00	
Rent Expense	792.00	
Telephone Expense	114.00	
Miscellaneous Expense	96.00	
	14118.00	14118.00

FIGURE 11.14 Trial Balance for Waltz Company

WALTZ COMPANY
TRIAL BALANCE
DECEMBER 31, 200X

	Dr.	Cr.
Cash	5408.00	
Petty Cash	240.00	
Accounts Receivable	2512.00	
Beginning Merchandise Inventory, Jan. 1	5092.00	
Prepaid Rent	616.00	
Office Supplies	944.00	
Office Equipment	9280.00	
Accumulated Depreciation, Office Equipment		7600.00
Accounts Payable		5964.00
K. Waltz, Capital		5476.00
K. Waltz, Withdrawals	4800.00	
Income Summary	—	—
Sales		52484.00
Sales Returns and Allowances	96.00	
Sales Discount	2400.00	
Purchases	29316.00	
Purchases Discount		16.00
Purchases Returns and Allowances		348.00
Office Salaries Expense	7408.00	
Insurance Expense	2400.00	
Advertising Expense	800.00	
Utilities Expense	576.00	
	71888.00	71888.00

RON'S WHOLESALE CLOTHING COMPANY TRIAL BALANCE DECEMBER 31, 200X		
	Dr.	Cr.
Cash	4 460 00	
Petty Cash	300 00	
Accounts Receivable	7 500 00	
Merchandise Inventory	9 000 00	
Supplies	1 000 00	
Prepaid Insurance	850 00	
Store Equipment	2 500 00	
Acc. Dep., Store Equipment		1 500 00
Accounts Payable		10 635 00
Federal Income Tax Payable		500 00
FICA—Social Security Payable		454 00
FICA—Medicare Payable		106 00
State Income Tax Payable		150 00
SUTA Tax Payable		108 00
FUTA Tax Payable		32 00
Unearned Storage Fees		325 00
Ron Win, Capital		12 500 00
Ron Win, Withdrawals	4 300 00	
Income Summary	—	—
Sales		45 000 00
Sales Returns and Allowances	1 475 00	
Sales Discount	1 335 00	
Purchases	26 000 00	
Purchases Discount		550 00
Purchases Returns and Allowances		400 00
Freight-In	225 00	
Salaries Expense	12 000 00	
Payroll Tax Expense	420 00	
Interest Expense	895 00	
	72 260 00	72 260 00

FIGURE 11.15 Trial Balance for Ron's Wholesale Clothing Company

Group B Problems

11B-1. From the following accounts, calculate (a) net sales, (b) cost of goods sold, (c) gross profit, and (d) net income.

LO1 (30 min)

Sales Discount	$ 500
Purchases Returns and Allowances	64
Beginning Merchandise Inventory, Jan 1, 200X	79
Sales Returns and Allowances	191
Purchases Discounts	42
Cash	3,895
Accounts Receivable	441
Sales	3,950
Ending Merchandise Inventory, Dec. 31, 200X	75
Freight-In	41

Check Figure:
Net income $1,273

(continued on next page)

Purchases	1,152
R. Roland, Capital	1,950
Operating Expenses	895
Accounts Payable	129

LO1, 2 (60 min)

Check Figure:
Net income $1,336

11B-2. As the accountant for Jim's Hardware, you have been asked to complete a worksheet from the trial balance in Figure 11.16 as well as additional data.

Additional Data

a/b. Cost of ending inventory on December 31, $480.
c. Insurance expired, $112.
d. Depreciation on store equipment, $90.
e. Accrued wages, $150.

LO1, 2 (60 min)

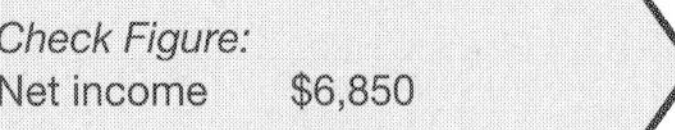

Check Figure:
Net income $6,850

11B-3. From Figure 11.17, complete a worksheet for Waltz Company.

Additional Data

a/b. Ending merchandise inventory on December 31, $1,600.
c. Office supplies on hand, $90.
d. Rent expired, $110.
e. Depreciation expense on office equipment, $250.
f. Salaries accrued, $180.

LO1, 2 (60 min)

Check Figure:
Net income $8,686

11B-4. From the trial balance in Figure 11.18, and additional data, complete the worksheet for Ron's Wholesale Clothing Company.

Additional Data

a/b. Ending merchandise inventory on December 31, $9,000.
c. Supplies on hand, $50.
d. Insurance expired, $55.
e. Depreciation on store equipment, $100.
f. Storage fees earned, $115.

FIGURE 11.16 Trial Balance for Jim's Hardware

JIM'S HARDWARE
TRIAL BALANCE
DECEMBER 31, 200X

	Dr.	Cr.
Cash	960 00	
Accounts Receivable	1600 00	
Merchandise Inventory	736 00	
Prepaid Insurance	1112 00	
Store Equipment	3200 00	
Accumulated Depreciation, Store Equipment		1680 00
Accounts Payable		1408 00
J. Spool, Capital		2576 00
Income Summary	—	—
Hardware Sales		14800 00
Hardware Sales Returns and Allowances	728 00	
Hardware Sales Discount	688 00	
Purchases	7088 00	
Purchases Discounts		240 00
Purchases Returns and Allowances		248 00
Wages Expense	2304 00	
Rent Expense	1840 00	
Telephone Expense	552 00	
Miscellaneous Expense	144 00	
	20952 00	20952 00

WALTZ COMPANY
TRIAL BALANCE
DECEMBER 31, 200X

	Dr.	Cr.
Cash	3800 00	
Petty Cash	100 00	
Accounts Receivable	3400 00	
Merchandise Inventory	5204 00	
Prepaid Rent	1200 00	
Office Supplies	1360 00	
Office Equipment	9680 00	
Accumulated Depreciation, Office Equipment		4040 00
Accounts Payable		7964 00
K. Waltz, Capital		5476 00
K. Waltz, Withdrawals	5000 00	
Income Summary	—	—
Sales		52462 00
Sales Returns and Allowances	116 00	
Sales Discount	2200 00	
Purchases	29296 00	
Purchases Discounts		1208 00
Purchases Returns and Allowances		1350 00
Office Salaries Expense	7408 00	
Insurance Expense	2200 00	
Advertising Expense	800 00	
Utilities Expense	736 00	
	72500 00	72500 00

FIGURE 11.17 Trial Balance for Waltz Company

ON-THE-JOB TRAINING

T-1. Kim Andrews prepared the income statement in Figure 11.19 on a cash basis for Ed Sloan, M.D. ***LO1 (20 min)***

Dr. Sloan has requested written information from Kim as to what his professional fees earned would be under the accrual-basis system of accounting. Kim has asked you to provide Dr. Sloan with this information, based on the following facts that Kim ignored in the original preparation of the financial report:

	20X1	20X2
Accrued Professional Fees	$4,200	$5,300
Unearned Professional Fees	6,200	4,250

Make a written recommendation about the advantages of an accrual system to Dr. Sloan.

T-2. Abby Jay is having a difficult time understanding the relationship of sales, cost of goods sold, gross profit, and net income for a merchandise company. As the accounting lab tutor, you have been asked to sit down with Abby and explain how to calculate the missing amounts in each situation listed here. Keep in mind that each situation is a distinct and separate business problem. ***LO1 (20 min)***

FIGURE 11.18 Trial Balance for Ron's Wholesale Clothing Company

RON'S WHOLESALE CLOTHING COMPANY
TRIAL BALANCE
DECEMBER 31, 200X

	Dr.	Cr.
Cash	260000	
Petty Cash	3000	
Accounts Receivable	300000	
Merchandise Inventory	360000	
Supplies	27000	
Prepaid Insurance	18000	
Store Equipment	100000	
Accumulated Depreciation, Store Equipment		49600
Accounts Payable		459000
FIT Payable		35000
FICA—Social Security Payable		19400
FICA—Medicare Payable		4600
SIT Payable		10000
SUTA Tax Payable		6000
FUTA Tax Payable		1400
Unearned Storage Fees		35000
Ron Win, Capital		273400
Ron Win, Withdrawals	180000	
Income Summary	—	—
Sales		1940000
Sales Returns and Allowances	56000	
Sales Discount	48000	
Purchases	860000	
Purchases Discount		24000
Purchases Returns and Allowances		16000
Freight-In	10000	
Salaries Expense	600000	
Payroll Tax Expense	19400	
Interest Expense	32000	
	2873400	2873400

	Sales	Beg. Inv.	Purchases	End Inv.	Cost of Goods Sold	Gross Profit	Expense	Net Income or Loss
Sit. 1	320,000	200,000	160,000	?	260,000	?	80,000	?
Sit. 2	380,000	140,000	?	180,000	200,000	?	100,000	80,000
Sit. 3	480,000	200,000	?	160,000	?	220,000	140,000	80,000
Sit. 4	?	160,000	280,000	140,000	?	160,000	140,000	?
Sit. 5	440,000	160,000	260,000	?	240,000	?	100,000	?
Sit. 6	280,000	120,000	?	140,000	160,000	?	?	40,000
Sit. 7	?	160,000	200,000	120,000	?	160,000	?	−20,000
Sit. 8	320,000	?	200,000	140,000	?	120,000	?	40,000

Explain in writing why gross profit does not always mean cash.

ED SLOAN, M.D. INCOME STATEMENT FOR YEAR ENDED DECEMBER 31, 20X2	
Professional Fees Earned	5000000
Expenses	1800000
Net Income	3200000

FIGURE 11.19 Income Statement for Ed Sloan, M.D.

FINANCIAL REPORT PROBLEM

Reading the Kellogg's Annual Report

LO1 (10 min)

Go to Appendix A and find the Consolidated Statement of Earnings. What is the cost of goods sold in 2006?

INTERNET PROJECT

Build-A-Bear

Go to the Web and search: Annual Report Build-A-Bear 2008.
Click on Investors Relations.
List out the latest news Build-A-Bear is providing to its investors.
Order a free annual report.

CONTINUING PROBLEM

Sanchez Computer Center

LO1, 2 (60 min)

The first six months of the year have concluded for Sanchez Computer Center, and Tony wants to make the necessary adjustments to his accounts to prepare accurate financial statements.

Assignment

To prepare these adjustments, use the trial balance in Figure 11.20 and the following inventory that Tony took at the end of March:

10 dozen ¼″ screws at a cost of $10 a dozen

5 dozen ½″ screws at a cost of $7 a dozen

2 feet of coaxial cable at a cost of $5 per foot

Merchandise left in stock was valued at $300.

Depreciation of Computer Equipment:

Computer depreciates at $33 a month; purchased July 5.

Computer workstations depreciate at $20 per month; purchased September 17.

Shop benches depreciate at $25 per month; purchased November 5.

Depreciation of Office Equipment:

Office equipment depreciates at $10 per month; purchased July 17.

Fax machine depreciates at $10 per month; purchased November 20.

Six months' worth of rent at a rental rate of $400 per month has expired.

Remember: If any long-term asset is purchased in the first 15 days of the month, Tony will charge depreciation for the full month. If an asset is purchased later than the 15th, he will not charge depreciation in the month it was purchased.

Complete the 10-column worksheet for the six months ended March 31, 200X.

FIGURE 11.20 Trial Balance for Sanchez Computer March 31, 200X

Account Titles	Trial Balance Dr.	Trial Balance Cr.
Cash	1251665	
Petty Cash	10000	
Accounts Receivable	1190000	
Prepaid Rent	280000	
Supplies	43200	
Merchandise Inventory		
Computer Shop Equipment	380000	
Accumulated Dep., C.S. Equip.		9900
Office Equipment	105000	
Accum. Dep., Office Equip.		2000
Accounts Payable		284000
T. Freedman, Capital		740600
T. Freedman, Withdrawals	201500	
Income Summary		
Service Revenue		1980000
Sales		970000
Sales Return and Allowances	40000	
Sales Discounts	22000	
Advertising Expense	80000	
Rent Expense		
Utilities Expense	29000	
Phone Expense	15000	
Supplies Expense		
Insurance Expense	10000	
Postage Expense	17500	
Depreciation Exp., C.S. Equip.		
Depreciation Exp., Office Equip.		
Miscellaneous Expense	1000	
Wage Expense	203000	
Payroll Tax Expense	22635	
Purchases	95000	
Purchase Ret. & Allow.		10000
Totals	3996500	3996500

APPENDIX

A WORKSHEET FOR ART'S WHOLESALE CLOTHING CO. USING A PERPETUAL INVENTORY SYSTEM

What's New: The Merchandise Inventory account (in Figure A.1 on the following page) does not need to be adjusted. The $4,000 figure for merchandise is the up-to-date balance in the account. The difference between beginning inventory and ending inventory will be part of a new account called *Cost of Goods Sold* on the worksheet.

How the $65,910 of Cost of Goods Sold was calculated from a periodic setup:

Purchases	$52,000	← **Assumed sold; part of cost**
+ Merchandise Inventory	$15,000	← **Beg. Inv. − Ending Inv.** **$19,000 − $4,000**
− Purchases Discount	860	→ **Reduces costs**
− Purchases Returns and Allowances	680	↗
+ Freight-In	450	→ **Adds to cost**
	$65,910	**Cost of Goods Sold**

What's Deleted from the Periodic Worksheet: Account titles for Purchases, Purchases Discounts, Purchases Returns and Allowances, and Freight-In.

Note: Net income is the same on the periodic and the perpetual worksheets.

Problem for Appendix

Using the solution to Self-Review Quiz 11-2 about Ray Company, convert this worksheet to a perpetual inventory system worksheet.

ART'S WHOLESALE CLOTHING CO.
WORKSHEET
FOR YEAR ENDED DECEMBER 31, 200X

Account Titles	Trial Balance Dr.	Trial Balance Cr.	Adjustments Dr.	Adjustments Cr.	Adjusted Trial Balance Dr.	Adjusted Trial Balance Cr.	Income Statement Dr.	Income Statement Cr.	Balance Sheet Dr.	Balance Sheet Cr.
Cash	12,920.00				12,920.00				12,920.00	
Petty Cash	100.00				100.00				100.00	
Accounts Receivable	14,500.00				14,500.00				14,500.00	
Merchandise Inventory	4,000.00				4,000.00				4,000.00	
Supplies	800.00			(B) 500.00	300.00				300.00	
Prepaid Insurance	900.00			(C) 300.00	600.00				600.00	
Store Equipment	4,000.00				4,000.00				4,000.00	
Acc. Dep., Store Equip.		400.00		(D) 50.00		450.00				450.00
Accounts Payable		1,790.00				1,790.00				1,790.00
Federal Income Tax		800.00				800.00				800.00
FICA—Social Security		454.00				454.00				454.00
FICA—Medicare		106.00				106.00				106.00
State Income Tax		200.00				200.00				200.00
SUTA Tax		108.00				108.00				108.00
FUTA Tax Payable		32.00				32.00				32.00
Unearned Rent		600.00	(A) 200.00			400.00				400.00
Mortgage Payable		2,320.00				2,320.00				2,320.00
Art Newner, Capital		7,905.00				7,905.00				7,905.00
Art Newner, Withdrawal	8,600.00				8,600.00				8,600.00	
Sales		95,000.00				95,000.00		95,000.00		
Sales Returns and Allow.	950.00				950.00		950.00			
Sales Discount	670.00				670.00		670.00			
Cost of Goods Sold	65,910.00				65,910.00		65,910.00			
Salaries Expense	11,700.00		(E) 600.00		12,300.00		12,300.00			
Payroll Tax Expense	420.00				420.00		420.00			
Postage Expense	25.00				25.00		25.00			
Miscellaneous Expense	30.00				30.00		30.00			
Interest Expense	300.00				300.00		300.00			
	125,825.00	125,825.00								
Rental Income				(A) 200.00		200.00		200.00		
Supplies Expense			(B) 500.00		500.00		500.00			
Insurance Expense			(C) 300.00		300.00		300.00			
Dep. Exp., Store Equip.			(D) 50.00		50.00		50.00			
Salaries Payable				(E) 600.00		600.00				600.00
			1,650.00	1,650.00	126,475.00	126,475.00	81,455.00	95,200.00	45,020.00	31,275.00
Net Income							13,745.00			13,745.00
							95,200.00	95,200.00	45,020.00	45,020.00

FIGURE A.1 Worksheet for Art's Wholesale Clothing Co. Using a Perpetual Inventory System

RAY COMPANY
WORKSHEET
FOR YEAR ENDED DECEMBER 31, 200X

Account Titles	Trial Balance Dr.	Trial Balance Cr.	Adjustments Dr.	Adjustments Cr.	Adjusted Trial Balance Dr.	Adjusted Trial Balance Cr.	Income Statement Dr.	Income Statement Cr.	Balance Sheet Dr.	Balance Sheet Cr.
Cash	2486 00				2486 00				2486 00	
Merchandise Inventory	200 00				200 00				200 00	
Prepaid Rent	1152 00			(B) 100 00	1052 00				1052 00	
Prepaid Insurance	60 00				60 00				60 00	
Office Equipment	2160 00				2160 00				2160 00	
Accumulated Dep., Off. Equip.		560 00		(C) 60 00		620 00				620 00
Unearned Storage Fees		2516 00	(A) 516 00			2000 00				2000 00
Accounts Payable		100 00				100 00				100 00
B. Ray, Capital		1932 00				1932 00				1932 00
Sales		11040 00				11040 00		11040 00		
Sales Returns and Allowances	546 00				546 00		546 00			
Sales Discounts	216 00				216 00		216 00			
COGS*	5610 00				5610 00		5610 00			
Salaries Expense	2016 00		(D) 200 00		2216 00		2216 00			
Insurance Expense	1392 00				1392 00		1392 00			
Utilities Expense	96 00				96 00		96 00			
Plumbing Expense	214 00				214 00		214 00			
	16148 00	16148 00								
Storage Fees Earned				(A) 516 00		516 00		516 00		
Rent Expense			(B) 100 00		100 00		100 00			
Dep. Expense, Equip.			(C) 60 00		60 00		60 00			
Salaries Payable				(D) 200 00		200 00				200 00
			876 00	876 00	16408 00	16408 00	10450 00	11556 00	5958 00	4852 00
							1106 00			1106 00
Net Income							11556 00	11556 00	5958 00	5958 00

*$624 ($824 − $200) + $5,256 − $168 − $102.

FIGURE A.2 Worksheet for Ray Company Using a Perpetual Inventory System

12

Completion of the Accounting Cycle for a Merchandise Company

DID YOU KNOW? Chiquita now packages single bananas to go that can stay ripe for seven days or more. Any shipping or handling fees are included in net sales as part of cost of sales. Visit *www.chiquita.com* to find more information about Chiquita.

LEARNING OBJECTIVES

1. Preparing financial statements for a merchandise company.
2. Recording adjusting and closing entries.
3. Preparing post-closing trial balance.
4. Completing reversing entries.

When you eat that Chiquita banana just keep in mind all the steps Chiquita must take to complete its accounting cycle. In this chapter we discuss the steps involved in completing the accounting cycle for a merchandise company. These steps include preparing financial reports, journalizing and posting adjusting and closing entries, preparing a post-closing trial balance, and reversing entries.

When setting up a new entity in QuickBooks or Peachtree, be careful to select the correct type of entity and to select the correct type of Chart of Accounts. Careful selection will ensure that your financial statements will include all of the necessary sections.

Learning Unit 12-1 Preparing Financial Statements

As we discussed in Chapter 5, when we were dealing with a service company rather than a merchandise company, the three financial statements can be prepared from the worksheet. Let's begin by looking at how Art's Wholesale Clothing Company prepares the income statement.

LO1

The Income Statement

Art is interested in knowing how well his shop performed for the year ended December 31, 200X. What were its net sales? What was the level of returns of goods from dissatisfied customers? What was the cost of the goods brought into the store versus the selling price received? How many goods were returned to suppliers? What is the cost of the goods that have not been sold? What was the cost of the Freight-In account? The income statement in Figure 12.1 is prepared from the income statement columns of the worksheet. Note that no debit or credit columns appear on the formal income statement; the inside columns in financial reports are used for subtotaling, not for debit and credit.

The income statement is broken down into several sections. Remembering the sections can help you set it up correctly on your own. The income statement shows the following:

Net Sales
− Cost of Goods Sold
= Gross Profit
− Operating Expenses
= Net Income from Operations
+ Other Income
− Other Expenses
= Net Income

Let's take these sections one at a time and see where the figures come from on the worksheet.

Sales
− Sales Ret. & Allow.
− Sales Discount
= Net Sales

Revenue Section

Net Sales The first major category of the income statement shows net sales. The figure here—$93,380—is not on the worksheet. Instead, the accountant must combine the amounts for gross sales, sales returns and allowances, and sales discount found on the worksheet to arrive at a figure for net sales. Thus these individual amounts are not summarized in a single figure for net sales until the formal income statement is prepared.

Beg. Inventory
+ Net Cost of Purchases
− Ending Inventory
= Cost of Goods Sold

Remember: In the periodic inventory system, goods brought in during the accounting period are added to the Purchases account, not to the Merchandise Inventory account.

Cost of Goods Sold Section The figures for Merchandise Inventory are shown separately on the worksheet. The $19,000 represents the beginning inventory of the period, and the $4,000, calculated from an inventory sheet is the ending inventory. Note on the financial report that the cost of goods sold section uses two separate figures for inventory.

Note that the following numbers are not found on the worksheet but are shown on the formal income statement (they are combined by the accountant in preparing the income statement):

- Net Purchases: $50,460 (Purchases − Purchases Discount − Purchases Returns and Allowances)
- Net Cost of Purchases: $50,910 (Net Purchases + Freight-In)
- Cost of Goods Available for Sale: $69,910 (Beginning Inventory + Net Cost of Purchases)
- Cost of Goods Sold: $65,910 (Cost of Goods Available for Sale − Ending Inventory)

ART'S WHOLESALE CLOTHING COMPANY
PARTIAL WORKSHEET
FOR YEAR ENDED DECEMBER 31, 200X

	Income Statement	
	Dr.	Cr.
Income Summary	1900000	400000
Sales		9500000
Sales Returns and Allowances	95000	
Sales Discount	67000	
Purchases	5200000	
Purchases Discount		86000
Purchases Returns and Allowances		68000
Freight-In	45000	
Salaries Expense	1230000	
Payroll Tax Expense	42000	
Postage Expense	2500	
Miscellaneous Expense	3000	
Interest Expense	30000	
Rental Income		20000
Supplies Expense	50000	
Insurance Expense	30000	
Depreciation Expense, Store Equip.	5000	
Salaries Payable		
	8699500	10074000
Net Income	1374500	
	10074000	10074000

ART'S WHOLESALE CLOTHING COMPANY
INCOME STATEMENT
FOR YEAR ENDED DECEMBER 31, 200X

Revenue:				
Gross Sales				$9500000
Less: Sales Ret. and Allow.			$ 95000	
Sales Discount			67000	162000
Net Sales				$9338000
Cost of Goods Sold:				
Merchandise Inventory, 1/1/0X			$1900000	
Purchases		$5200000		
Less: Purch. Discount	$ 86000			
Purch. Ret. and Allow.	68000	154000		
Net Purchases		$5046000		
Add: Freight-In		45000		
Net Cost of Purchases			5091000	
Cost of Goods Available for Sale			$6991000	
Less: Merch. Inv., 12/31/0X			400000	
Cost of Goods Sold				6591000
Gross Profit				$2747000
Operating Expenses:				
Salaries Expense			$1230000	
Payroll Tax Expense			42000	
Dep. Exp., Store Equip.			5000	
Supplies Expense			50000	
Insurance Expense			30000	
Postage Expense			2500	
Miscellaneous Expense			3000	
Total Operating Expenses				1362500
Net Income from Operations				$1384500
Other Income:				
Rental Income			$ 20000	
Other Expenses:				
Interest Expense			30000	10000
Net Income				$1374500

FIGURE 12.1 Partial Worksheet and Income Statement

Gross Profit Gross profit ($27,470) is calculated by subtracting the cost of goods sold from net sales ($93,380 − $65,910). The amount is not found on the worksheet.

Operating Expenses Section Like the other figures we have discussed, the business's operating expenses do not appear on the worksheet. To get this figure ($13,625), the accountant adds up all the expenses on the worksheet.

Many operating companies break expenses down into those directly related to the selling activity of the company (**selling expenses**) and those related to administrative or office activity (**administrative expenses** or **general expenses**). Here's a sample list broken down into these two categories:

OPERATING EXPENSES

- Selling Expenses:

  Sales Salaries Expense
  Delivery Expense
  Advertising Expense
  Depreciation Expense, Store Equipment
  Insurance Expense
  Total Selling Expenses

- Administrative Expenses:

  Rent Expense
  Office Salaries Expense
  Utilities Expense
  Supplies Expense
  Depreciation Expense, Office Equipment
  Total Administrative Expenses
  Total Operating Expenses

Other Income (or Other Revenue) Section The **other income,** or other revenue, section is used to record any revenue other than revenue from sales. For example, Art's Wholesale makes a profit from subletting a portion of a building. The $200 of rental income the company earns from this is recorded in the other income section.

Other Expenses Section The **other expenses** section is used to record nonoperating expenses, that is, expenses that are not related to the main operating activities of the business. For example, Art's Wholesale owes $300 interest on money it has borrowed. That expense is shown in the other expenses section.

Statement of Owner's Equity

The statement of owner's equity is the same for a merchandise business as for a service firm.

The information used to prepare the statement of owner's equity comes from the balance sheet columns of the worksheet. Keep in mind that the capital account in the ledger should be checked to see whether any additional investments occurred during the period. Figure 12.2 shows how the worksheet aids in this step. The ending figure of $13,050 for Art Newner, Capital, is carried over to the balance sheet, which is the final report we look at in this chapter.

The Balance Sheet

Figure 12.3 (on the next page spread) shows how a worksheet is used to aid in the preparation of a **classified balance sheet.** A classified balance sheet breaks down the assets and liabilities into more detail. Classified balance sheets provide management, owners, creditors, and

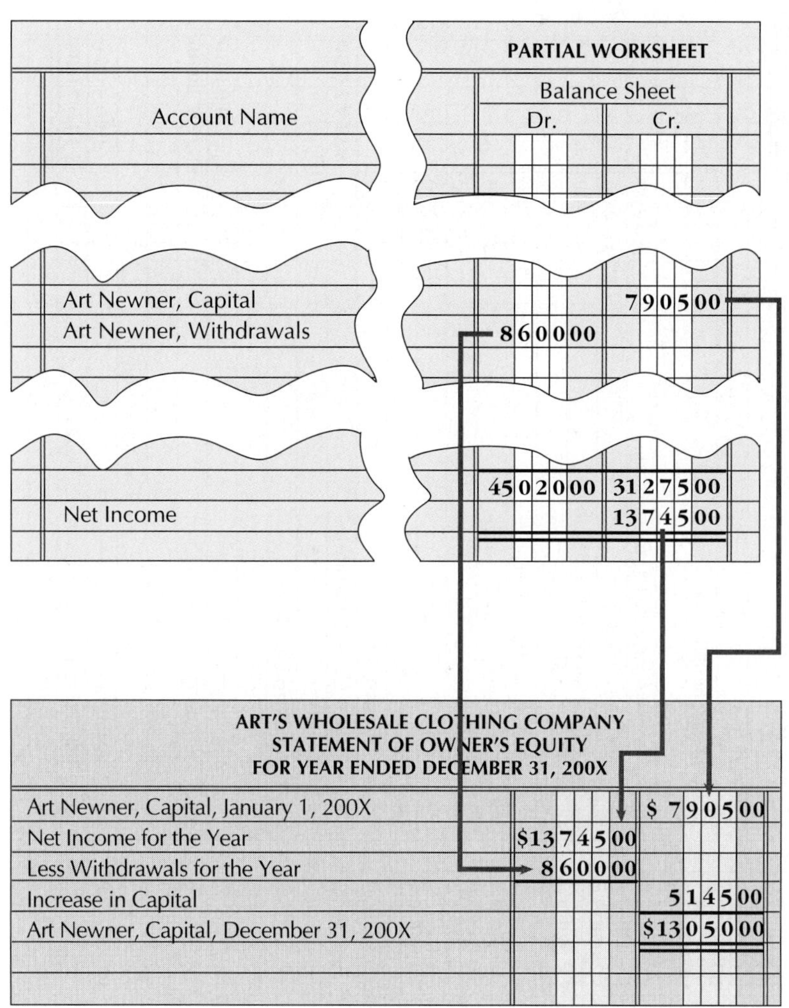

PARTIAL WORKSHEET
Account Name
Balance Sheet
Dr.
Cr.
Art Newner, Capital
7 9 0 5 00
Art Newner, Withdrawals
8 6 0 0 00
45 0 2 0 00
31 2 7 5 00
Net Income
13 7 4 5 00

ART'S WHOLESALE CLOTHING COMPANY
STATEMENT OF OWNER'S EQUITY
FOR YEAR ENDED DECEMBER 31, 200X

Art Newner, Capital, January 1, 200X		$ 7 9 0 5 00
Net Income for the Year	$13 7 4 5 00	
Less Withdrawals for the Year	8 6 0 0 00	
Increase in Capital		5 1 4 5 00
Art Newner, Capital, December 31, 200X		$13 0 5 0 00

FIGURE 12.2 Preparing Statement of Owner's Equity from the Worksheet

Any additional investment by the owner would be added to his or her beginning capital amount.

suppliers with more information about the company's ability to pay current and long-term debts. They also provide a more complete financial picture of the firm.

The categories on the classified balance sheet are as follows:

- **Current assets** are defined as cash and assets that will be converted into cash or used up during the normal operating cycle of the company or one year, whichever is longer. (Think of the **operating cycle** as the time period it takes a company to buy and sell merchandise and then collect accounts receivable.)

  Accountants list current assets in order of how easily they can be converted into cash (called *liquidity*). In most cases, Accounts Receivable can be turned into cash more quickly than Merchandise Inventory. For example, it can be quite difficult to sell an outdated computer in a computer store or to sell last year's model car this year.
- **Plant and equipment** are long-lived assets that are used in the production or sale of goods or services. Art's Wholesale has only one plant asset, store equipment; other plant assets could include buildings and land. The assets are usually listed in order according to how long they will last; the shortest-lived assets are listed first. Land would always be the last asset listed (and land is never depreciated). Note that we still show the cost of the asset less its accumulated depreciation.

ART'S WHOLESALE CLOTHING COMPANY
WORKSHEET
FOR YEAR ENDED DECEMBER 31, 200X

	Balance Sheet Dr.	Balance Sheet Cr.
Cash	12920 00	
Petty Cash	100 00	
Accounts Receivable	14500 00	
Merchandise Inventory	4000 00	
Supplies	300 00	
Prepaid Insurance	600 00	
Store Equipment	4000 00	
Acc. Dep., Store Equipment		450 00
Accounts Payable		17900 00
Federal Income Tax Payable		800 00
FICA—Social Security Payable		454 00
FICA—Medicare Payable		106 00
State Income Tax Payable		200 00
SUTA Tax Payable		108 00
FUTA Tax Payable		32 00
Unearned Rent		400 00
Mortgage Payable		2320 00
Art Newner, Capital		7905 00
…		
Salaries Payable		600 00
	45020 00	31275 00
Net Income		13745 00
	45020 00	45020 00

ART'S WHOLESALE CLOTHING COMPANY
CLASSIFIED BALANCE SHEET
FOR YEAR ENDED DECEMBER 31, 200X

Assets		
Current Assets:		
Cash	$12920 00	
Petty Cash	100 00	
Accounts Receivable	14500 00	
Merchandise Inventory	4000 00	
Supplies	300 00	
Prepaid Insurance	600 00	
Total Current Assets		$32420 00
Plant and Equipment:		
Store Equipment	$4000 00	
Less: Accum. Depreciation	450 00	3550 00
Total Assets		$35970 00
Liabilities		
Current Liabilities:		
Mortgage Payable (current portion)	$ 320 00	
Accounts Payable	17900 00	
Federal Income Tax Payable	800 00	
FICA—Social Security Payable	454 00	
FICA—Medicare Payable	106 00	
State Income Tax Payable	200 00	
SUTA Tax Payable	108 00	
FUTA Tax Payable	32 00	
Salaries Payable	600 00	
Unearned Rent	400 00	
Total Current Liabilities		$20920 00
Long-Term Liabilities		
Mortgage Payable		2000 00
Total Liabilities		$22920 00
Owner's Equity		
Art Newner, Capital, December 31, 200X		13050 00
Total Liabilities and Owner's Equity		$35970 00

FIGURE 12.3 Partial Worksheet and Classified Balance Sheet

- **Current liabilities** are the debts or obligations of Art's Wholesale that must be paid within one year or one operating cycle. The order of listing accounts in this section is not always the same; many times companies will list their liabilities in the order they expect to pay them off. Note that the current portion of the mortgage, $320 (that portion due within one year), is listed before Accounts Payable.
- **Long-term liabilities** are debts or obligations that are not due and payable for a comparatively long period, usually for more than one year. For Art's Wholesale the only long-term liability is Mortgage Payable. The long-term portion of the mortgage is listed here; the current portion, due within one year, is listed under current liabilities.

Mortgage Payable:
$2,320
− 320 current portion
$2,000 long-term liability

LEARNING UNIT 12-1 REVIEW

AT THIS POINT you should be able to

- Prepare a detailed income statement from the worksheet.
- Explain the difference between selling and administrative expenses.
- Explain which columns of the worksheet are used in preparing a statement of owner's equity.
- Explain as well as compare current assets with plant and equipment.
- Using Mortgage Payable as an example, explain the difference between current and long-term liabilities.
- Prepare a classified balance sheet from a worksheet.

Self-Review Quiz 12-1

Using the worksheet from Self-Review Quiz 11-2 in Chapter 11, prepare in proper form (1) an income statement, (2) a statement of owner's equity, (3) a classified balance sheet for Ray Company.

Solutions to Self-Review Quiz 12-1

1.

FIGURE 12.4 Income Statement for Ray Company

RAY COMPANY
INCOME STATEMENT
FOR YEAR ENDED DECEMBER 31, 200X

Revenue:				
Sales				$11,040.00
Less: Sales Ret. and Allow.			$546.00	
Sales Discount			216.00	762.00
Net Sales				$10,278.00
Cost of Goods Sold:				
Merchandise Inventory, 1/1/0X			$824.00	
Purchases		$5,256.00		
Less: Pur. Ret. and Allow.	$168.00			
Purchases Discount	102.00	270.00		
Net Purchases			4,986.00	
Cost of Goods Available for Sale			$5,810.00	
Less: Merchandise Inv., 12/31/0X			200.00	
Cost of Goods Sold				5,610.00
Gross Profit				$4,668.00
Operating Expenses:				
Salaries Expense		$2,216.00		
Insurance Expense		1,392.00		
Utilities Expense		96.00		
Plumbing Expense		214.00		
Rent Expense		100.00		
Depreciation Exp., Equip.		60.00		
Total Operating Expenses				4,078.00
Net Income from Operations				$590.00
Other Income:				
Storage Fees				516.00
Net Income				$1,106.00

2.

FIGURE 12.5 Statement of Owner's Equity for Ray Company

RAY COMPANY
STATEMENT OF OWNER'S EQUITY
FOR YEAR ENDED DECEMBER 31, 200X

B. Ray, Capital, 1/1/0X	$1,932.00
Net Income for the Year	1,106.00
B. Ray, Capital, 12/31/0X	$3,038.00

3.

RAY COMPANY BALANCE SHEET DECEMBER 31, 200X		
Assets		
Current Assets:		
Cash	$2486 00	
Merchandise Inventory	200 00	
Prepaid Rent	1052 00	
Prepaid Insurance	60 00	
Total Current Assets		$3798 00
Plant and Equipment:		
Office Equipment	$2160 00	
Less: Accumulated Depreciation	620 00	1540 00
Total Assets		$5338 00
Liabilities		
Current Liabilities		
Accounts Payable	$ 100 00	
Salaries Payable	200 00	
Unearned Storage Fees	2000 00	
Total Liabilities		$2300 00
Owner's Equity		
B. Ray, Capital, December 31, 200X		3038 00
Total Liabilities and Owner's Equity		$5338 00

FIGURE 12.6 Balance Sheet for Ray Company

Learning Unit 12-2 Journalizing and Posting Adjusting and Closing Entries; Preparing the Post-Closing Trial Balance

LO2

QuickBooks and Peachtree programs do not use worksheets. Adjustments are made from preparing the trial balance and are recorded in the general journal. Entries are both journalized and posted at the same time when the user selects Save in the General Journal screen.

Journalizing and Posting Adjusting Entries

From the worksheet of Art's Wholesale (repeated in Fig. 12.7 on the following page for your convenience), the adjusting entries can be journalized from the adjustments column and posted to the ledger. Keep in mind that the adjustments have been placed only on the worksheet, not in the journal or in the ledger. At this point, the journal does not reflect adjustments and the ledger still contains only unadjusted amounts.

Partial Ledger

Merchandise Inventory 114

Dr.	Cr.
19,000	19,000
4,000	

Income Summary 313

Dr.	Cr.
19,000	4,000

FIGURE 12.7 Completed Worksheet

ART'S WHOLESALE CLOTHING CO.
WORKSHEET
FOR YEAR ENDED DECEMBER 31, 200X

	Trial Balance		Adjustments	
	Dr.	Cr.	Dr.	Cr.
Cash	12920 00			
Petty Cash	100 00			
Accounts Receivable	14500 00			
Merchandise Inventory	19000 00		(B)4000 00	(A)19000 00
Supplies	800 00			(D)500 00
Prepaid Insurance	900 00			(E)300 00
Store Equipment	4000 00			
Acc. Dep., Store Equipment		400 00		(F) 50 00
Accounts Payable		17900 00		
Federal Income Tax Payable		800 00		
FICA—Social Security Payable		454 00		
FICA—Medicare Payable		106 00		
State Income Tax Payable		200 00		
SUTA Tax Payable		108 00		
FUTA Tax Payable		32 00		
Unearned Rent		600 00	(C)200 00	
Mortgage Payable		2320 00		
Art Newner, Capital		7905 00		
Art Newner, Withdrawals	8600 00			
Income Summary			(A)19000 00	(B)4000 00
Sales		95000 00		
Sales Returns and Allowances	950 00			
Sales Discount	670 00			
Purchases	52000 00			
Purchases Discount		860 00		
Purchases Returns and Allowances		680 00		
Freight-In	450 00			
Salaries Expense	11700 00		(G)600 00	
Payroll Tax Expense	420 00			
Postage Expense	25 00			
Miscellaneous Expense	30 00			
Interest Expense	300 00			
	127365 00	127365 00		
Rental Income				(C)200 00
Supplies Expense			(D)500 00	
Insurance Expense			(E)300 00	
Depreciation Expense, Store Equip.			(F) 50 00	
Salaries Payable				(G)600 00
			24650 00	24650 00
Net Income				

FIGURE 12.7 *(continued)*

Adjusted Trial Bal.		Income Statement		Balance Sheet	
Dr.	Cr.	Dr.	Cr.	Dr.	Cr.
12920 00				12920 00	
100 00				100 00	
14500 00				14500 00	
4000 00				4000 00	
300 00				300 00	
600 00				600 00	
4000 00				4000 00	
	450 00				450 00
	17900 00				17900 00
	800 00				800 00
	454 00				454 00
	106 00				106 00
	200 00				200 00
	108 00				108 00
	32 00				32 00
	400 00				400 00
	2320 00				2320 00
	7905 00				7905 00
8600 00				8600 00	
19000 00	4000 00	19000 00	4000 00		
	95000 00		95000 00		
950 00		950 00			
670 00		670 00			
52000 00		52000 00			
	860 00		860 00		
	680 00		680 00		
450 00		450 00			
12300 00		12300 00			
420 00		420 00			
25 00		25 00			
30 00		30 00			
300 00		300 00			
	200 00		200 00		
500 00		500 00			
300 00		300 00			
50 00		50 00			
	600 00				600 00
132015 00	132015 00	86995 00	100740 00	45020 00	31275 00
		13745 00			13745 00
		100740 00	100740 00	45020 00	45020 00

Supplies 115

Dr.	Cr.
800	500

Supplies Expense 614

Dr.	Cr.
500	

Prepaid Insurance 116

Dr.	Cr.
900	300

Insurance Expense 615

Dr.	Cr.
300	

Accum. Dep., Store Equipment 122

Dr.	Cr.
	400
	50

Dep. Expense, Store Equip. 613

Dr.	Cr.
50	

Salaries Payable 212

Dr.	Cr.
	600

Salaries Exp. 611

Dr.	Cr.
11,700	
600	

Unearned Rent 219

Dr.	Cr.
200	600

Rental Income 414

Dr.	Cr.
	200

The journalized and posted adjusting entries are shown in Figure 12.8. Note that the liability Unearned Rent is reduced by $200 and Rental Income has increased by $200.

> Closing is not a necessary step when using Peachtree or QuickBooks. Net income is calculated after each transaction, and financial statements are current.

Journalizing and Posting Closing Entries

In Chapter 5, we discussed the closing process for a service company. The goals of closing are the same for a merchandise company. These goals are (1) to clear all temporary accounts in the ledger to zero and (2) to update capital in the ledger to its latest balance. The company must use the worksheet and the steps listed here to complete the closing process.

Step 1 Close all balances on the income statement credit column of the worksheet, except Income Summary, by debits.
Then credit the total to the Income Summary account.

Step 2 Close all balances on the income statement debit column of the worksheet, except Income Summary, by credits.
Then debit the total to the Income Summary account.

Step 3 Transfer the balance of the Income Summary account to the Capital account.

Step 4 Transfer the balance of the owner's Withdrawals account to the Capital account.

Let's look now at the journalized closing entries in Figure 12.9. When these entries are posted, all the temporary accounts will have zero balances in the ledger, and the Capital account will be updated with a new balance.

Let's take a moment to look at the Income Summary account in T account form:

Income Summary 313

	Dr.	Cr.	
Adj.	19,000	4,000	Adj.
Clos.	67,995	96,740	Clos.
	86,995	100,740	
Net Income → Clos.	13,745		

FIGURE 12.8 Journalized and Posted Adjusting Entries

ART'S WHOLESALE CLOTHING CO. GENERAL JOURNAL				
				Page 2
Date	Account Titles and Description	PR	Dr.	Cr.
	Adjusting Entries			
31	Income Summary	313	19 0 0 0 00	
	Merchandise Inventory	114		19 0 0 0 00
	Transferred beginning inventory			
	to Income Summary			
31	Merchandise Inventory	114	4 0 0 0 00	
	Income Summary	313		4 0 0 0 00
	Records cost of ending inventory			
31	Unearned Rent	219	2 0 0 00	
	Rental Income	414		2 0 0 00
	Rental income earned			
31	Supplies Expense	614	5 0 0 00	
	Supplies	115		5 0 0 00
	Supplies consumed			
31	Insurance Expense	615	3 0 0 00	
	Prepaid Insurance	116		3 0 0 00
	Insurance expired			
31	Dep. Exp., Store Equipment	613	5 0 00	
	Acc. Dep., Store Equipment	122		5 0 00
	Depreciation on equipment			
31	Salaries Expense	611	6 0 0 00	
	Salaries Payable	212		6 0 0 00
	Accrued salaries			

Note that Income Summary before the closing process contains the adjustments for Merchandise Inventory. The end result is that the net income of $13,745 is closed to the Capital account.

The Post-Closing Trial Balance

LO3

The post-closing trial balance shown in Figure 12.10 (on the following page spread) is prepared from the general ledger. Note first that all temporary accounts have been closed and thus are not shown on this post-closing trial balance. Note also that the ending inventory figure of the last accounting period, $4,000, becomes the beginning inventory figure on January 1, 20X3.

FIGURE 12.9 General Journal Closing Entries

ART'S WHOLESALE CLOTHING CO.
GENERAL JOURNAL

Page 2

Date		Account Titles and Description	PR	Dr.	Cr.
		Closing Entries			
	31	Sales	411	95 000 00	
		Rental Income	414	200 00	
		Purchases Discount	512	860 00	
		Purchases Ret. and Allow.	513	680 00	
		Income Summary	313		96 740 00
		Transfers credit account balances			
		on income statement column of			
		worksheet to Income Summary			
	31	Income Summary	313	67 995 00	
		Sales Returns and Allowances	412		950 00
		Sales Discount	413		670 00
		Purchases	511		52 000 00
		Freight-In	514		450 00
		Salaries Expense	611		12 300 00
		Payroll Tax Expense	612		420 00
		Postage Expense	616		25 00
		Miscellaneous Expense	617		30 00
		Interest Expense	618		300 00
		Supplies Expense	614		500 00
		Insurance Expense	615		300 00
		Depreciation Expense, Store Equip.	613		50 00
		Transfers all expenses, and			
		deductions to Sales are			
		closed to Income Summary			
	31	Income Summary	313	13 745 00	
		A. Newner, Capital	311		13 745 00
		Transfer of net income to			
		Capital from Income Summary			
	31	A. Newner, Capital	311	8 600 00	
		A. Newner, Withdrawals	312		8 600 00
		Closes withdrawals to			
		Capital Account			

LEARNING UNIT 12-2 REVIEW

AT THIS POINT you should be able to

- Journalize and post adjusting entries for a merchandise company.
- Explain the relationship of the worksheet to the adjusting and closing process.
- Complete the closing process for a merchandise company.
- Prepare a post-closing trial balance and explain why ending Merchandise Inventory is not a temporary account.

Self-Review Quiz 12-2

Using the worksheet from Self-Review Quiz 11-2 in Chapter 11, journalize the closing entries.

ART'S WHOLESALE CLOTHING COMPANY POSTCLOSING TRIAL BALANCE DECEMBER 31, 200X		
	Dr.	Cr.
Cash	12920 00	
Petty Cash	100 00	
Accounts Receivable	14500 00	
Merchandise Inventory	4000 00	
Supplies	300 00	
Prepaid Insurance	600 00	
Store Equipment	4000 00	
Accum. Depreciation, Store Equipment		450 00
Accounts Payable		17900 00
Federal Income Tax Payable		800 00
FICA—Social Security Payable		454 00
FICA—Medicare Payable		106 00
State Income Tax Payable		200 00
SUTA Tax Payable		108 00
FUTA Tax Payable		32 00
Salary Payable		600 00
Unearned Rent		400 00
Mortgage Payable		2320 00
Art Newner, Capital		13050 00
	36420 00	36420 00

FIGURE 12.10 Post-Closing Trial Balance for Art's Wholesale Clothing Company

Solution to Self-Review Quiz 12-2

				Page 2
Date	Account Titles and Description	PR	Dr.	Cr.
	Closing Entries			
Dec. 31	Sales		11040 00	
	Storage Fees Earned		516 00	
	Purchases Returns and Allowances		168 00	
	Purchases Discount		102 00	
	Income Summary			11826 00
31	Income Summary		10096 00	
	Sales Returns and Allowances			546 00
	Sales Discount			216 00
	Purchases			5256 00
	Salaries Expense			2216 00
	Insurance Expense			1392 00
	Utilities Expense			96 00
	Plumbing Expense			214 00
	Rent Expense			100 00
	Depreciation Exp., Equipment			60 00
31	Income Summary		1106 00	
	B. Ray, Capital			1106 00

FIGURE 12.11 Closing Entries Journalized

LO4 Learning Unit 12-3 Reversing Entries (Optional Section)

The accounting cycle for Art's Wholesale Clothing Company is completed. Now let's look at **reversing entries,** an optional way of handling some adjusting entries. Reversing entries are general journal entries that are the opposite of adjusting entries. Reversing entries help reduce potential errors and simplify the recordkeeping process. If Art's accountant does reversing entries, routine transactions can be done in the usual steps.

Reversing entries are an option; they are not mandatory.

To help explain the concept of reversing entries, let's look at these two adjustments that could be reversed:

1. When an increase occurs in an asset account (no previous balance).
   Example: Interest Receivable
   Interest Income
   (Interest earned but not collected is covered in later chapters.)
2. When an increase occurs in a liability account (no previous balance).
   Example: Wages Expense
   Wages Payable

With the exception of businesses in their first year of operation, accounts such as Accumulated Depreciation or Inventory cannot be reduced because they have previous balances.

Art's bookkeeper handles an entry without reversing for salaries at the end of the year (see Fig. 12.12). Note that the permanent account, Salaries Payable, carries over to the new accounting period a $600 balance. Remember that the $600 was an expense of the prior year.

FIGURE 12.12 Reversing Entries Not Used

❶ On December 31, an adjusting entry was journalized and posted for $600 of salaries incurred but not paid.

ADJUSTING JOURNAL ENTRY

Account	Dr.	Cr.
Salaries Expense	600 00	
Salaries Payable		600 00

T ACCOUNT UPDATE

Salaries Exp. (Dr.)	Salaries Exp. (Cr.)	Salaries Pay. (Dr.)	Salaries Pay. (Cr.)
11,700			600
600			

❷ On January 8 after closing entries have been journalized and posted, Salaries Expense has a zero balance.

Account	Dr.	Cr.
Income Summary	XXX	
Salaries Expense		12 300 00

Salaries Exp. (Dr.)	Salaries Exp. (Cr.)	Salaries Pay. (Dr.)	Salaries Pay. (Cr.)
11,700	12,300		600
600			

On January 8 of the new year, the payroll to be paid is $2,000. If the optional reversing entry is *not* used, the bookkeeper must make the journal entry in Figure 12.13.

To do so, the bookkeeper has to refer back to the adjustment on December 31 to determine how much of the salary of $2,000 is indeed a new salary expense and what portion was shown in the old year although not paid. It is easy to see how potential errors can result if the bookkeeper pays the payroll but forgets about the adjustment in the previous year. In this way, reversing entries can help avoid potential errors.

Figure 12.14 shows the four steps the bookkeeper would take if reversing entries were used. Note that steps 1 and 2 are the same whether the accountant uses reversing entries or not.

Note that the balance of Salaries Expense is indeed only $1,400, the *true* expense in the new year. Reversing results in switching the adjustment the first day of the new period. Also note that each of the accounts ends up with the same balance no matter which method is chosen. Using a reversing entry for salaries, however, allows the accountant to make the normal entry when it is time to pay salaries.

FIGURE 12.13 Entry When Optional Reversing Entry Is Not Used

			Dr.	Cr.
		Salaries Payable	600 00	
		Salaries Expense	1 400 00	
		Cash		2 000 00

Salaries Exp.		Salaries Pay.		Cash	
1,400		600	600		2,000

FIGURE 12.14 Reversing Entries Used

❶ On December 31, an adjustment for salary was recorded.

Salaries Exp.		Salaries Pay.	
11,700			600
600			

❷ Closing entry on December 31.

Salaries Exp.		Salaries Pay.	
11,700	12,300		600
600			

❸ On January 1 (first day of the following fiscal period), a reverse adjusting entry was made for salary on December 31 (a "flipping" adjustment).

			Dr.	Cr.
Jan.	1	Salaries Payable	600 00	
		Salaries Expense		600 00

Salaries Exp.		Salaries Pay.	
	600	600	600

This way, the liability is reduced to 0. We know it will be paid in this new period, but the Salaries Expense has a credit balance of $600 until the payroll is paid. When the payroll of $2,000 is paid, the following results:

❹ Paid Payroll $2,000.

			Dr.	Cr.
Jan.	1	Salaries Expense	2 000 00	
		Cash		2 000 00

Salaries Exp.		Cash	
2,000	600		2,000

LEARNING UNIT 12-3 REVIEW

AT THIS POINT you should be able to

- Explain the purpose of reversing entries.
- Complete a reversing entry.
- Explain when reversing entries can be used.

Self-Review Quiz 12-3

Explain which of the following situations could be reversed:

1.

Supplies Exp.		Supplies	
	200	800	200

2.

Wages Exp.		Wages Payable	
3,200			200
200			

3.

Sales		Unearned Sales	
	4,000	50	200
	50		

Solutions to Self-Review Quiz 12-3

1. Not reversed: asset Supplies is decreasing, not increasing.
2. Reversed: liability is increasing and no previous balance exists.
3. Not reversed: liability is decreasing and a previous balance exists.

CHAPTER ASSIGNMENTS

SUMMARY OF KEY POINTS

LEARNING UNIT 12-1

1. The formal income statement can be prepared from the income statement columns of the worksheet.
2. No debit or credit columns are used on the formal income statement.
3. The cost of goods sold section has a figure for beginning inventory and a separate figure for ending inventory.
4. Operating expenses could be broken down into selling and administrative expenses.
5. The ending figure for Capital is not found on the worksheet. It comes from the statement of owner's equity.
6. A classified balance sheet breaks assets into current and plant and equipment. Liabilities are broken down into current and long-term.

LEARNING UNIT 12-2

1. The information for journalizing, adjusting, and closing entries can be obtained from the worksheet.
2. In the closing process all temporary accounts will be zero and the Capital account is brought up to its new balance.
3. Inventory is not a temporary account. The ending inventory, along with other permanent accounts, will be listed in the post-closing trial balance.

LEARNING UNIT 12-3

1. Reversing entries are optional. They can aid in reducing potential errors and simplify the recordkeeping process.
2. The reversing entry "flips" the adjustment on the first day of a new fiscal period. Thus, the bookkeeper need *not* look back at what happened in the old year when recording the current year's transactions.
3. Reversing entries are only used if (a) assets are increasing and have no previous balance or (b) liabilities are increasing and have no previous balance.

KEY TERMS

Administrative expenses (general expenses) Expenses such as general office expenses that are incurred indirectly in the selling of goods.

Classified balance sheet A balance sheet that categorizes assets as current or plant and equipment and groups liabilities as current or long-term.

Current assets Assets that can be converted into cash or used within one year or the normal operating cycle of the business, whichever is longer.

Current liabilities Obligations that will come due within one year or within the operating cycle, whichever is longer.

Long-term liabilities Obligations that are not due or payable for a long time, usually for more than a year.

Operating cycle Average time it takes to buy and sell merchandise and then collect accounts receivable.

Other expenses Nonoperating expenses that do not relate to the main operating activities of the business; they appear in a separate section on the income statement. One example given in the text is Interest Expense, interest owed on money borrowed by the company.

Other income Any revenue other than revenue from sales. It appears in a separate section on the income statement. Examples: Rental Income and Storage Fees.

Plant and equipment Long-lived assets such as buildings or land that are used in the production or sale of goods or services.

Reversing entries Optional bookkeeping technique in which certain adjusting entries are reversed or switched on the first day of the new accounting period so that transactions in the new period can be recorded without referring back to prior adjusting entries.

Selling expenses Expenses directly related to the sale of goods.

QUESTIONS, CLASSROOM DEMONSTRATION EXERCISES, EXERCISES, AND PROBLEMS

Discussion and Critical Thinking Questions/Ethical Case

1. Which columns of the worksheet aid in the preparation of the income statement?
2. Explain the components of cost of goods sold.
3. Explain how operating expenses can be broken down into different categories.
4. What is the difference between current assets and plant and equipment?
5. What is an operating cycle?
6. Why journalize adjusting entries *after* the formal reports in a manual system have been prepared?
7. Explain the steps of closing for a merchandise company.
8. Temporary accounts could appear on a post-closing trial balance. Agree or disagree?
9. What is the purpose of using reversing entries? Are they mandatory? When should they be used?
10. Janet Flynn, owner of Reel Company, plans to apply for a bank loan at Petro National Bank. Because the company has a lot of debt on its balance sheet, Janet does not plan to show the loan officer the balance sheet. She plans only to bring the income statement. Do you feel that this move is a sound financial move by Janet? You make the call. Write down your specific recommendations to Janet.

Classroom Demonstration Exercises

SET A

Calculate Net Sales

LO1 (5 min)

1. From the following, calculate net sales:

Purchases	$100	Sales Discount	$20
Gross Sales	180	Operating Expenses	50
Sales Returns and Allowances	15		

Calculate Cost of Goods Sold

LO1 (5 min)

2. Calculate Cost of Goods Sold:

Freight-In	$ 6	Ending Inventory	$ 4
Beginning Inventory	12	Net Purchases	66

Calculate Gross Profit and Net Income

LO1 (10 min)

3. Using Exercises 1 and 2, calculate the following:
   a. Gross profit
   b. Net income or net loss

LO1, 2 (15 min) **Classification of Accounts**

4. Match the following categories to each account listed.

1. Current Asset
2. Plant and Equipment
3. Current Liabilities
4. Long-Term Liabilities

_____	**a.** Petty Cash	_____	**f.** Mortgage Payable (Current)
_____	**b.** Accounts Receivable	_____	**g.** SUTA Payable
_____	**c.** Prepaid Rent	_____	**h.** Accumulated Depreciation
_____	**d.** FICA Payable	_____	**i.** Computer Equipment
_____	**e.** Store Supplies	_____	**j.** Unearned Rent

LO4 (10 min) **Reversing Entries**

5. a. On January 1, prepare a reversing entry. On January 8, journalize the entry to record the paying of salary expense, $800.

b. What will be the balance in Salaries Expense on January 8 (after posting)?

December 31:

Salaries Expense		Salaries Payable	
Dr.	**Cr.**	**Dr.**	**Cr.**
800	**1,200 closing**		**400 Adj.**
Adj. 400			

SET B

LO1 (5 min) **Calculate Net Sales**

1. From the following, calculate net sales:

Purchases	$ 90	Sales Discount	$ 10
Gross Sales	280	Operating Expenses	100
Sales Returns and Allowances	50		

LO1 (5 min) **Calculate Cost of Goods Sold**

2. Calculate Cost of Goods Sold:

Freight-In	$ 5	Ending Inventory	$15
Beginning Inventory	20	Net Purchases	50

LO1 (10 min) **Calculate Gross Profit and Net Income**

3. Using Exercises 1 and 2, calculate the following:

a. Gross profit
b. Net income or net loss

BLUEPRINT: FINANCIAL STATEMENTS

(1) INCOME STATEMENT

Revenue:				
Sales				$ XXX
Less: Sales Ret. and Allow.			$ XXX	
Sales Discount			XXX	XXX
Net Sales				$ XXXX
Cost of Goods Sold:				
Merchandise Inventory, 1/1/0X			$ XXX	
Purchases		$XXX		
Less: Purchases Discount	$XXX			
Purch. Ret. and Allow.	XXX	XXX		
Net Purchases		XXX		
Add: Freight-In		XXX		
Net Cost of Purchases			XXX	
Cost of Goods Avail. for Sale			$XXXX	
Less: Merch. Inv., 12/31/0X			XXX	
Cost of Goods Sold				XXXX
Gross Profit				$XXXX
Operating Expenses:				
~~			$XXX	
~~			XXX	
~~			XXX	
Total Operating Expenses				XXX
Net Income from Operations				$ XXX
Other Income:				
Rental Income			$ XXX	
Storage Fees Income			XXX	
Total Other Income			$ XXX	
Other Expenses:				
Interest Expenses			XXX	XXX
Net Income:				$ XXX

(2) STATEMENT OF OWNER'S EQUITY

Beginning Capital		$XXX
Additional Investments		XXX
Total Investment		$XXX
Net Income	$XXX	
Less: Withdrawals	XXX	
Increase in Capital		XXX
Ending Capital		$XXX

(3) BALANCE SHEET			
Assets			
Current Assets:			
Cash		$ XXXX	
Acccounts Receivable		XXXX	
Merchandise Inventory		XXXX	
Prepaid Insurance		XXX	
Total Current Assets			$ XXXX
Plant and Equipment:			
Store Equipment	$XXXX		
Less Accumulated Depreciation	XXXX	$XXXX	
Office Equipment	$XXXX		
Less Accumulated Depreciation	XXX	XXX	
Total Plant and Equipment			XXXX
Total Assets			$XXXX
Liabilities			
Current Liabilities:			
Unearned Revenue		$XXX	
Mortgage Payable (current portion)		XXX	
Accounts Payable		XXX	
Salaries Payable		XX	
FICA—Social Security Payable		XX	
FICA—Medicare Payable		XX	
Income Taxes Payable		XX	
Total Current Liabilities			$XXX
Long-Term Liabilities			
Mortgage Payable			$XXX
Total Liabilities			$XXXX
Owner's Equity			
Capital*			XXXX
Total Liabilities and Owner's Equity			$XXXX

* From statement of owner's equity

Classification of Accounts

LO4 (15 min)

4. Match the following categories to each account listed:

1. Current Asset
2. Plant and Equipment
3. Current Liabilities
4. Long-Term Liabilities

_____	**a.** Merchandise Inventory	_____	**f.** Mortgage Payable (Not Current)
_____	**b.** Unearned Rent	_____	**g.** FUTA Payable
_____	**c.** Prepaid Insurance	_____	**h.** Accumulated Depreciation
_____	**d.** SUTA Payable	_____	**i.** FICA—Social Security Payable
_____	**e.** Store Equipment	_____	**j.** Petty Cash

Reversing Entries

LO4 (10 min)

5. a. On January 1, prepare a reversing entry. On January 8, journalize the entry to record the paying of salary expense, $900.

b. What will be the balance in Salaries Expense on January 8 (after posting)?

December 31:

Salaries Expense		Salaries Payable	
Dr.	**Cr.**	**Dr.**	**Cr.**
900	**1,200 closing**		**300 Adj.**
Adj. 300			

Exercises

12-1. From the following accounts, prepare a cost of goods sold section in proper form: Merchandise Inventory, 12/31/X1, $9,000; Purchases Discount, $900; Merchandise Inventory, 12/1/X1, $4,000; Purchases, $58,000; Purchases Returns and Allowances, $1,000; Freight-In, $300. *LO1 (15 min)*

12-2. Give the category, the classification, and the report(s) on which each of the following appears (for example: Cash—asset, current asset, balance sheet): *LO1 (10 min)*

a. Salaries Payable
b. Accounts Payable
c. Mortgage Payable
d. Unearned Legal Fees
e. SIT Payable
f. Office Equipment
g. Land

12-3. From the partial worksheet in Fig. 12.15 on the following page, journalize the closing entries of December 31 for A. Slow Co. *LO2 (10 min)*

12-4. From the worksheet in Exercise 12-3, prepare the assets section of a classified balance sheet. *LO1 (15 min)*

12-5. On December 31, 20X1, $300 of salaries has been accrued. (Salaries before the accrued amount totaled $26,000.) The next payroll to be paid will be on February 3, 20X2, for $6,000. Please do the following: *LO2, 4 (30 min)*

a. Journalize and post the adjusting entry (use T accounts).
b. Journalize and post the reversing entry on January 1.
c. Journalize and post the payment of the payroll. Cash has a balance of $15,000 before the payment of payroll on February 3.

FIGURE 12.15
Worksheet for A. Slow Co.

A. SLOW CO.
WORKSHEET
FOR YEAR ENDED DECEMBER 31, 200X

Account Titles	Income Statement		Balance Sheet	
	Dr.	Cr.	Dr.	Cr.
Cash			193 00	
Merchandise Inventory			450 00	
Prepaid Advertising			561 00	
Prepaid Insurance			30 00	
Office Equipment			1080 00	
Accum. Dep., Office Equip.				210 00
Accounts Payable				258 00
A. Slow, Capital				966 00
Income Summary	362 00	450 00		
Sales		5520 00		
Sales Returns and Allowances	223 00			
Sales Discount	108 00			
Purchases	2628 00			
Purchases Returns and Allow.		34 00		
Purchases Discount		51 00		
Salaries Expense	1083 00			
Insurance Expense	696 00			
Utilities Expense	48 00			
Plumbing Expense	57 00			
Advertising Expense	15 00			
Dep. Expenses, Office Equip.	30 00			
Salaries Payable				75 00
	5250 00	6055 00	2314 00	1509 00
Net Income	805 00			805 00
	6055 00	6055 00	2314 00	2314 00

Group A Problems

LO1 (30 min)

Check Figure:
Net Income from operations $761

12A-1. Prepare a formal income statement from the partial worksheet for Ring.com in Figure 12.16.

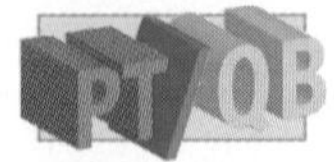

LO1 (40 min)

Check Figure:
Total Assets $33,340

12A-2. Prepare a statement of owner's equity and a classified balance sheet from the worksheet for James Company in Figure 12.17. (*Note:* Of the Mortgage Payable, $200 is due within one year.)

LO1, 2 (90 min)

Check Figure:
Net Income $4,340

12A-3. **a.** Complete the worksheet for Jay's Supplies in Figure 12.18.
b. Prepare an income statement, a statement of owner's equity, and a classified balance sheet. (*Note:* The amount of the mortgage due the first year is $800.)
c. Journalize the adjusting and closing entries.

LO1, 2, 3, 4 (150 min)

Check Figure:
Net Income $4,336

12A-4. Using the ledger balances and additional data shown on the following pages, do the following for Callahan Lumber for the year ended December 31, 200X:
1. Prepare the worksheet.
2. Prepare the income statement, statement of owner's equity, and balance sheet.

FIGURE 12.16 Partial Worksheet for Ring.Com

RING.COM
PARTIAL WORKSHEET
FOR YEAR ENDED DECEMBER 31, 200X

Account Titles	Income Statement Dr.	Income Statement Cr.
Income Summary	370 00	260 00
Sales		2800 00
Sales Returns and Allowances	119 00	
Sales Discount	64 00	
Purchases	870 00	
Purchases Returns and Allow.		167 00
Purchases Discount		129 00
Freight-In	102 00	
Salaries Expense	300 00	
Insurance Expense	200 00	
Advertising Expense	155 00	
Rental Income		200 00
Rent Expense	215 00	
Dep. Exp., Store Equip.	200 00	
Salaries Payable		
	2595 00	3556 00
Net Income	961 00	
	3556 00	3556 00

3. Journalize and post adjusting and closing entries. (Be sure to put beginning balances in the ledger first.)
4. Prepare a post-closing trial balance.
5. Journalize the reversing entry for wages accrued.

Account Balances for Callahan Lumber

Acct. No.		
110	Cash	$ 1,340
111	Accounts Receivable	1,300
112	Merchandise Inventory	4,550
113	Lumber Supplies	269
114	Prepaid Insurance	218
121	Lumber Equipment	3,000
122	Accum. Dep., Lumber Equipment	490
220	Accounts Payable	1,160
221	Wages Payable	—
330	J. Callahan, Capital	7,352
331	J. Callahan, Withdrawals	3,000
332	Income Summary	—
440	Sales	22,800
441	Sales Returns and Allowances	200
550	Purchases	14,800
551	Purchases Discount	285
552	Purchases Returns and Allowances	300

(continued on next page)

FIGURE 12.17 Partial Worksheet for James Company

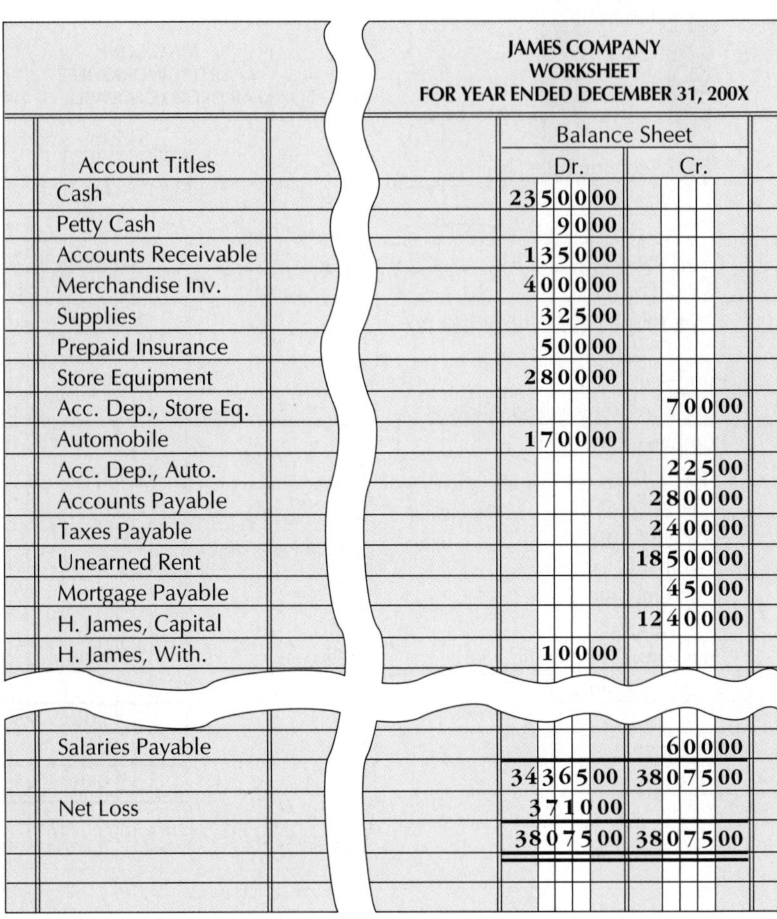

JAMES COMPANY
WORKSHEET
FOR YEAR ENDED DECEMBER 31, 200X

Account Titles	Balance Sheet Dr.	Balance Sheet Cr.
Cash	23500 00	
Petty Cash	90 00	
Accounts Receivable	1350 00	
Merchandise Inv.	4000 00	
Supplies	325 00	
Prepaid Insurance	500 00	
Store Equipment	2800 00	
Acc. Dep., Store Eq.		700 00
Automobile	1700 00	
Acc. Dep., Auto.		225 00
Accounts Payable		2800 00
Taxes Payable		2400 00
Unearned Rent		18500 00
Mortgage Payable		450 00
H. James, Capital		12400 00
H. James, With.	100 00	
Salaries Payable		600 00
	34365 00	38075 00
Net Loss	3710 00	
	38075 00	38075 00

Account Balances for Callahan Lumber (continued)

660	Wages Expense	2,480
661	Advertising Expense	400
662	Rent Expense	830
663	Dep. Expense, Lumber Equipment	—
664	Lumber Supplies Expense	—
665	Insurance Expense	—

Additional Data

a./b. Merchandise inventory, December 31	$ 4,900
c. Lumber supplies on hand, December 31	75
d. Insurance expired	150
e. Depreciation for the year	250
f. Accrued wages on December 31	95

Group B Problems

PT/QB *LO1 (70 min)*

Check Figure:
Net income from operations $845

12B-1. From the partial worksheet shown in Figure 12.19, prepare a formal income statement.

FIGURE 12.18
Worksheet for Jay's Supplies

JAY'S SUPPLIES
WORKSHEET
FOR YEAR ENDED DECEMBER 31, 200X

	Trial Balance		Adjustments	
Account Titles	Dr.	Cr.	Dr.	Cr.
Cash	2000 00			
Accounts Receivable	3000 00			
Merch. Inventory, 1/1/XX	11000 00		(B) 10400 00	11000 00 (A)
Prepaid Insurance	1880 00			500 00 (E)
Equipment	3400 00			
Accum. Dep., Equipment		1080 00		400 00 (D)
Accounts Payable		5080 00		
Unearned Training Fees		2120 00	(C) 320 00	
Mortgage Payable		1200 00		
P. Jay, Capital		10560 00		
P. Jay, Withdrawals	4280 00			
Income Summary			(A) 11000 00	10400 00 (B)
Sales		95800 00		
Sales Returns and Allowances	3200 00			
Sales Discount	2600 00			
Purchases	63600 00			
Purchases Returns and Allow.		13600 00		
Purchases Discount		3200 00		
Freight-In	2680 00			
Advertising Expense	11400 00			
Rent Expense	10000 00			
Salaries Expense	13600 00			
	132640 00	132640 00		
Training Fees Earned				320 00 (C)
Dep. Exp., Equipment			(D) 400 00	
Insurance Expense			(E) 500 00	
			22620 00	22620 00

12B-2. From the worksheet shown in Figure 12.20, complete the following:

a. Statement of owner's equity

b. Classified balance sheet

(*Note:* Of the Mortgage Payable, $3,000 is due within one year.)

LO1 (40 min)

Check Figure:
Total Assets $28,294

12B-3. From the partial worksheet for Jay's Supplies in Figure 12.21, do the following:

1. Complete the worksheet.
2. Prepare the income statement, statement of owner's equity, and classified balance sheet. (The amount of the mortgage due the first year is $800.)
3. Journalize the adjusting and closing entries.

LO1, 2 (90 min)

Check Figure:
Net Loss $12,050

12B-4. From the following ledger balances and additional data shown on the following pages, do the following for Callahan Lumber for the year ended December 31, 200X.

1. Prepare the worksheet.
2. Prepare the income statement, statement of owner's equity, and balance sheet.
3. Journalize and post adjusting and closing entries. (Be sure to put beginning balances in the ledger first.)
4. Prepare a post-closing trial balance.
5. Journalize the reversing entry for wages accrued.

LO1, 2, 3, 4 (150 min)

Check Figure:
Net Income $2,730

FIGURE 12.19 Partial Worksheet of Ring.Com

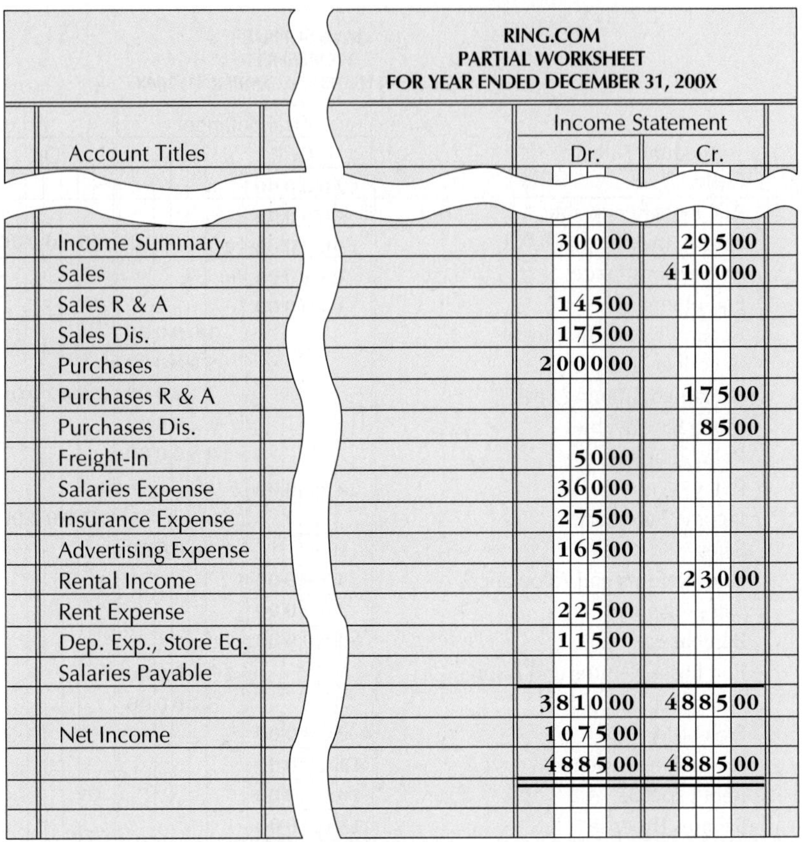

RING.COM
PARTIAL WORKSHEET
FOR YEAR ENDED DECEMBER 31, 200X

Account Titles	Income Statement Dr.	Income Statement Cr.
Income Summary	300 00	295 00
Sales		4100 00
Sales R & A	145 00	
Sales Dis.	175 00	
Purchases	2000 00	
Purchases R & A		175 00
Purchases Dis.		85 00
Freight-In	50 00	
Salaries Expense	360 00	
Insurance Expense	275 00	
Advertising Expense	165 00	
Rental Income		230 00
Rent Expense	225 00	
Dep. Exp., Store Eq.	115 00	
Salaries Payable		
	3810 00	4885 00
Net Income	1075 00	
	4885 00	4885 00

Account Balances of Callahan Lumber

Acct. No.		
110	Cash	$ 940
111	Accounts Receivable	1,470
112	Merchandise Inventory	5,600
113	Lumber Supplies	260
114	Prepaid Insurance	117
121	Lumber Equipment	2,600
122	Acc. Dep., Lumber Equipment	340
220	Accounts Payable	1,330
221	Wages Payable	
330	J. Callahan, Capital	7,562
331	J. Callahan, Withdrawals	3,500
332	Income Summary	—
440	Sales	23,000
441	Sales Returns and Allowances	400
550	Purchases	14,700
551	Purchases Discount	440
552	Purchases Returns and Allowances	545
660	Wages Expense	2,390
661	Advertising Expense	400
662	Rent Expense	840
663	Dep. Exp., Lumber Equipment	—
664	Lumber Supplies Expense	—
665	Insurance Expense	—

FIGURE 12.20 Worksheet for James Company

JAMES COMPANY
WORKSHEET
FOR YEAR ENDED DECEMBER 31, 200X

Account Titles	Balance Sheet Dr.	Balance Sheet Cr.
Cash	2500 00	
Petty Cash	50 00	
Accts. Receivable	1300 00	
Merch. Inventory	4250 00	
Supplies	344 00	
Prepaid Ins.	600 00	
Store Equip.	18000 00	
Acc. Dep., Store Eq.		750 00
Automobile	2500 00	
Acc. Dep., Auto.		500 00
Accts. Payable		3450 00
Taxes Payable		2100 00
Unearned Rent		1100 00
Mortgage Payable		8000 00
H. James, Capital		10500 00
H. James, Withd.	4000 00	
Salaries Payable		100 00
	33544 00	36400 00
Net Loss	2856 00	
	36400 00	36400 00

Additional Data

a./b. Merchandise inventory, December 31	$ 3,900
c. Lumber supplies on hand, December 31	60
d. Insurance expired	50
e. Depreciation for the year	400
f. Accrued wages on December 31	175

ON-THE-JOB TRAINING

T-1. Chan Company recently had most of its records destroyed in a fire. The information for 20X1 (Fig. 12.22) was discovered by the bookkeeper. Please assist the bookkeeper in reconstructing an income statement for 20X1. *LO1, 2 (60 min)*

T-2. Hope Lang, a junior accountant, has the December 31, 200X, trial balance of Gregot Company sitting on her desk. Attached is a memo from her supervisor requesting that a classified balance sheet be prepared. Hope gathers the following data: *LO1, 2 (60 min)*

1. A physical inventory of merchandise at December 31 showed $80,000 on hand.
2. Office supplies on hand totaled $600.
3. Insurance unexpired was $750.
4. Depreciation (straight-line) is based on a 25-year life.

Using the trial balance of Gregot Co. in Figure 12.23, please assist Hope with this project. *Hint:* Ending figure for capital is $115,850.

FIGURE 12.21
Worksheet for Jay's Supplies

JAY'S SUPPLIES WORKSHEET FOR YEAR ENDED DECEMBER 31, 200X				
	Trial Balance		Adjustments	
Account Titles	Dr.	Cr.	Dr.	Cr.
Cash	3000 00			
Accounts Receivable	3000 00			
Merch. Inventory, 1/1/XX	11700 00		(B) 8000 00	11700 00 (A)
Prepaid Insurance	1000 00			350 00 (E)
Equipment	5000 00			
Accum. Dep., Equipment		1900 00		500 00 (D)
Accounts Payable		2100 00		
Unearned Training Fees		1450 00	(C) 400 00	
Mortgage Payable		2400 00		
P. Jay, Capital		27750 00		
P. Jay, Withdrawals	4000 00			
Income Summary			(A) 11700 00	8000 00 (B)
Sales		100800 00		
Sales Returns and Allowances	4100 00			
Sales Discount	2800 00			
Purchases	70000 00			
Purchases Returns and Allow.		2000 00		
Purchases Discounts		1400 00		
Freight-In	2700 00			
Advertising Expense	8000 00			
Rent Expense	8500 00			
Salaries Expense	16000 00			
	139800 00	139800 00		
Training Fees Earned				400 00 (C)
Dep. Exp., Equipment			(D) 500 00	
Insurance Expense			(E) 350 00	
			20950 00	20950 00

FINANCIAL REPORT PROBLEM

LO2, 3 (5 min)

Reading the Kellogg's Annual Report

Go to Appendix A and locate the consolidated statement of earnings. How much has Selling and general administrative expense increased from 2005 to 2006?

INTERNET PROJECT

Chiquita

Go to the Web and search: Annual Report Chiquita 2008.
Click on Investors Relations.
List out the latest news Chiquita is providing to its investors.
Order a free annual report.

FIGURE 12.22 General Journal for Chan Company

Beg. Inv. $1,400
End. Inv. 3,000

CHAN COMPANY GENERAL JOURNAL					
					Page 2
20X1 Date		Description	PR	Dr.	Cr.
Dec.	31	Income Summary	312	3630 00	
		Sales Returns and Allowances	420		140 00
		Sales Discount	430		30 00
		Purchases	500		2400 00
		Delivery Expense	600		90 00
		Salaries Expense	610		840 00
		Rent Expense	620		30 00
		Office Supplies Expense	630		50 00
		Advertising Expense	640		10 00
		Dep. Exp., Store Equipment	650		40 00
	31	Sales	410	5542 00	
		Purchases Discount	510	120 00	
		Purchases Returns and Allowances	520	100 00	
		Income Summary	312		5762 00
	31	Income Summary	312	3732 00	
		J. Chan, Capital	310		3732 00

GREGOT COMPANY TRIAL BALANCE DECEMBER 31, 200X		
	Dr.	Cr.
Cash	11000 00	
Accounts Receivable	38000 00	
Merchandise Inventory, Jan. 1	80000 00	
Prepaid Insurance	2000 00	
Office Supplies	1000 00	
Land	17500 00	
Building	50000 00	
Accumulated Depreciation, Building		10000 00
Notes Payable		40000 00
Accounts Payable		30000 00
G. Gregot, Capital		98400 00
G. Gregot, Withdrawals	13000 00	
Income Summary	—	—
Retail Sales		329000 00
Sales Returns and Allowances	21000 00	
Sales Discount	8000 00	
Purchases	215500 00	
Purchases Returns and Allowances		11600 00
Purchases Discount		4000 00
Freight-In	5000 00	
Advertising Expense	2500 00	
Wage Expense	55000 00	
Utilities Expense	3500 00	
	523000 00	523000 00

FIGURE 12.23 Trial Balance for Gregot Company

CONTINUING PROBLEM

LO1, 2 (60 min)

Sanchez Computer Center

Using the worksheet in Chapter 11 for Sanchez Computer Center, journalize and post the adjusting entries and prepare the financial statements.

MINI PRACTICE SET

THE CORNER DRESS SHOP

Reviewing the Accounting Cycle for a Merchandise Company

This practice set will help you review all the key concepts of a merchandise company, along with the integration of payroll, including the preparation of Form 941.

Because you are the bookkeeper of the Corner Dress Shop, we have gathered the following information for you. It will be your task to complete the accounting cycle for March.

Betty Loeb's dress shop is located at 1 Milgate Rd., Marblehead, MA 01945. Its identification number is 33-4158215.

THE CORNER DRESS SHOP
POST-CLOSING TRIAL BALANCE
FEBRUARY 28, 200X

	1	2
Cash	2231 90	
Accounts Receivable	2200 00	
Petty Cash	35 00	
Merchandise Inventory	5600 00	
Prepaid Rent	1800 00	
Delivery Truck	6000 00	
Accumulated Depreciation, Truck		1500 00
Accounts Payable		1900 00
FIT Payable		1013 00
FICA—OASDI Payable		1339 20
FICA—Medicare Payable		313 20
SIT Payable		756 00
SUTA Payable		979 20
FUTA Payable		163 20
Unearned Rent		800 00
B. Loeb, Capital		9103 10
Total	17866 90	17866 90

Balances in subsidiary ledgers as of March 1 are as follows:

Accounts Receivable		Accounts Payable	
Bing Co.	$ 2,200	Blew Co.	$ 1,900
Blew Co.	—	Jones Co.	—
Ronald Co.	—	Moe's Garage	—
		Morris Co.	—

Payroll is paid monthly:

FICA rate	OASDI 6.2% on $102,000
	Medicare 1.45% on all earnings
SUTA rate	4.8% on $7,000
FUTA rate	.8% on $7,000
SIT rate	7%
FIT	Use the table provided at the end of this practice set.

The payroll register for January and February is provided. In March, salaries are as follows:

Mel Case	$3,325
Jane Holl	4,120
Jackie Moore	4,760

Your tasks are to do the following:

1. Set up a general ledger, accounts receivable subsidiary ledger and accounts payable subsidiary ledger, auxiliary petty cash record, and payroll register. (Be sure to update ledger accounts based on information given in the post-closing trial balance for February 28 before beginning.)
2. Journalize the transactions, and prepare the payroll register.
3. Update the accounts payable and accounts receivable subsidiary ledgers.
4. Post to the general ledger.
5. Prepare a trial balance on a worksheet and complete the worksheet.
6. Prepare an income statement, statement of owner's equity, and classified balance sheet.
7. Journalize the adjusting and closing entries.
8. Post the adjusting and closing entries to the ledger.
9. Prepare a post-closing trial balance.
10. Complete Form 941 and sign it as of the last day in April.

Chart of Accounts
for the Corner Dress Shop

Assets	**Revenue**
110 Cash	410 Sales
111 Accounts Receivable	412 Sales Returns and Allowances
112 Petty Cash	414 Sales Discount
114 Merchandise Inventory	416 Rental Income
116 Prepaid Rent	
120 Delivery Truck	**Cost of Goods Sold**
121 Accumulated Depreciation, Truck	510 Purchases
	512 Purchases Returns and Allowances
Liabilities	514 Purchases Discount
210 Accounts Payable	
212 Salaries Payable	**Expenses**
214 Federal Income Tax Payable	610 Sales Salaries Expense
216 FICA—OASDI Payable	611 Office Salaries Expense
218 FICA—Medicare Payable	612 Payroll Tax Expense

(continued on next page)

220 State Income Tax Payable
222 SUTA Tax Payable
224 FUTA Tax Payable
226 Unearned Rent

Owner's Equity
310 B. Loeb, Capital
320 B. Loeb, Withdrawals
330 Income Summary

614 Cleaning Expense
616 Depreciation Expense, Truck
618 Rent Expense
620 Postage Expense
622 Delivery Expense
624 Miscellaneous Expense

THE CORNER DRESS SHOP
PAYROLL REGISTER
JANUARY AND FEBRUARY 200X

Employees	Allow. and Marital Status	Cum. Earnings	Salary	Earnings Reg.	O/T	Gross	Cum. Earnings
Mel Case	M – 2	—	3300 00	3300 00		3300 00	3300 00
Jane Holl	M – 1	—	3400 00	3400 00		3400 00	3400 00
Jackie Moore	M – 0	—	4100 00	4100 00		4100 00	4100 00
Totals for Jan.			10800 00	10800 00		10800 00	10800 00
Mel Case	M – 2	3300 00	3300 00	3300 00		3300 00	6600 00
Jane Holl	M – 1	3400 00	3400 00	3400 00		3400 00	6800 00
Jackie Moore	M – 0	4100 00	4100 00	4100 00		4100 00	8200 00
Totals for Feb.		10800 00	10800 00	10800 00		10800 00	21600 00

PAYROLL REGISTER

Taxable Earnings			Deductions						Distribution	
	FICA		FICA							
Unemp.	Soc. Sec.	Medicare	OASDI	Medicare	FIT	SIT	Net Pay	Ck. No.	Office Salary Expense	Sales Salary Expense
3300 00	3300 00	3300 00	204 60	47 85	250 00	231 00	2566 55		3300 00	
3400 00	3400 00	3400 00	210 80	49 30	310 00	238 00	2591 90			3400 00
4100 00	4100 00	4100 00	254 20	59 45	453 00	287 00	3046 35			4100 00
10800 00	10800 00	10800 00	669 60	156 60	1013 00	756 00	8204 80		3300 00	7500 00
3300 00	3300 00	3300 00	204 60	47 85	250 00	231 00	2566 55		3300 00	
3400 00	3400 00	3400 00	210 80	49 30	310 00	238 00	2591 90			3400 00
2900 00	4100 00	4100 00	254 20	59 45	453 00	287 00	3046 35			4100 00
9600 00	10800 00	10800 00	669 60	156 60	1013 00	756 00	8204 80		3300 00	7500 00

200X		
Mar.	1	Bing paid balance owed, no discount.
	2	Purchased merchandise from Morris Company on account, $10,000; terms 2/10, n/30.
	2	Paid $6 from the petty cash fund for cleaning package, voucher no. 18 (consider it a cleaning expense).
	3	Sold merchandise to Ronald Company on account, $7,000, invoice no. 51; terms 2/10, n/30.
	5	Paid $3 from the petty cash fund for postage, voucher no. 19.
	6	Sold merchandise to Ronald Company on account, $5,000, invoice no. 52; terms 2/10, n/30.
	8	Paid $10 from the petty cash fund for first aid emergency, voucher no. 20.
	9	Purchased merchandise from Morris Company on account, $5,000; terms 2/10, n/30.
	9	Paid $5 for delivery expense from petty cash fund, voucher no. 21.
	9	Sold more merchandise to Ronald Company on account, $3,000, invoice no. 53; terms 2/10, n/30.
	9	Paid cleaning service, $300, check no. 110.
	10	Ronald Company returned merchandise costing $1,000 from invoice no. 52; the Corner Dress shop issued credit memo no. 10 to Ronald Company for $1,000.
	11	Purchased merchandise from Jones Company on account, $10,000; terms 1/15, n/60.
	12	Paid Morris Company invoice dated March 2, check no. 111.
	13	Sold $7,000 of merchandise for cash.
	14	Returned merchandise to Jones Company in amount of $2,000; the Corner Dress Shop issued debit memo no. 4 to Jones Company.
	14	Paid $5 from the petty cash fund for delivery expense, voucher no. 22.
	15	Paid taxes due for FICA (OASDI and Medicare) and FIT for February payroll, check no. 112.
	15	Sold Merchandise for $29,000 cash.
	15	Betty withdrew $100 for her own personal expenses, check no. 113.
	15	Paid state income tax for February payroll, check no. 114.
	16	Received payment from Ronald Company for invoice no. 52, less discount.
	16	Ronald Company paid invoice no. 51, $7,000.
	16	Sold merchandise to Bing Company on account, $3,200, invoice no. 54; terms 2/10, n/30.
	21	Purchased delivery truck on account from Moe's Garage, $17,200.
	22	Sold merchandise to Ronald Company on account, $4,000, invoice no. 55; terms 2/10, n/30.
	23	Paid Jones Company the balance owed, check no. 115.
	24	Sold merchandise to Bing Company on account, $2,000, invoice no. 56; terms 2/10, n/30.
	25	Purchased merchandise for $1,000 check no. 116.
	27	Purchased merchandise from Blew Company on account, $6,000; terms 2/10, n/30.
	27	Paid $2 postage from the petty cash fund, voucher no. 23.
	28	Ronald Company paid invoice no. 55 dated March 22, less discount.

(continued on next page)

28	Bing Company paid invoice no. 54 dated March 16.
29	Purchased merchandise from Morris Company on account, $9,000; terms 2/10, n/30.
30	Sold merchandise to Blew Company on account, $10,000, invoice no. 57; terms 2/10, n/30.
30	Issued check no. 117 to replenish to the same level the petty cash fund.
30	Recorded payroll in payroll register.
30	Journalized payroll entry (to be paid on 31st).
30	Journalized employer's payroll tax expense.
31	Paid payroll checks no. 118, no. 119, and no. 120.

Additional Data

a./b. Ending merchandise inventory, $13,515.

c. During March, rent expired, $600.

d. Truck depreciated, $150.

e. Rental income earned, $200 (one month's rent from subletting).

MARRIED Persons—**MONTHLY** Payroll Period

(For Wages Paid in 2008)

If the wages are–		And the number of withholding allowances claimed is—										
At least	But less than	0	1	2	3	4	5	6	7	8	9	10
		The amount of income tax to be withheld is—										
$3,240	$3,280	$324	$280	$237	$193	$149	$114	$84	$55	$26	$0	$0
3,280	3,320	330	286	243	199	155	118	88	59	30	1	0
3,320	3,360	336	292	249	205	161	122	92	63	34	5	0
3,360	3,400	342	298	255	211	167	126	96	67	38	9	0
3,400	3,440	348	304	261	217	173	130	100	71	42	13	0
3,440	3,480	354	310	267	223	179	135	104	75	46	17	0
3,480	3,520	360	316	273	229	185	141	108	79	50	21	0
3,520	3,560	366	322	279	235	191	147	112	83	54	25	0
3,560	3,600	372	328	285	241	197	153	116	87	58	29	0
3,600	3,640	378	334	291	247	203	159	120	91	62	33	4
3,640	3,680	384	340	297	253	209	165	124	95	66	37	8
3,680	3,720	390	346	303	259	215	171	128	99	70	41	12
3,720	3,760	396	352	309	265	221	177	134	103	74	45	16
3,760	3,800	402	358	315	271	227	183	140	107	78	49	20
3,800	3,840	408	364	321	277	233	189	146	111	82	53	24
3,840	3,880	414	370	327	283	239	195	152	115	86	57	28
3,880	3,920	420	376	333	289	245	201	158	119	90	61	32
3,920	3,960	426	382	339	295	251	207	164	123	94	65	36
3,960	4,000	432	388	345	301	257	213	170	127	98	69	40
4,000	4,040	438	394	351	307	263	219	176	132	102	73	44
4,040	4,080	444	400	357	313	269	225	182	138	106	77	48
4,080	4,120	450	406	363	319	275	231	188	144	110	81	52
4,120	4,160	456	412	369	325	281	237	194	150	114	85	56
4,160	4,200	462	418	375	331	287	243	200	156	118	89	60
4,200	4,240	468	424	381	337	293	249	206	162	122	93	64
4,240	4,280	474	430	387	343	299	255	212	168	126	97	68
4,280	4,320	480	436	393	349	305	261	218	174	130	101	72
4,320	4,360	486	442	399	355	311	267	224	180	136	105	76
4,360	4,400	492	448	405	361	317	273	230	186	142	109	80
4,400	4,440	498	454	411	367	323	279	236	192	148	113	84
4,440	4,480	504	460	417	373	329	285	242	198	154	117	88
4,480	4,520	510	466	423	379	335	291	248	204	160	121	92
4,520	4,560	516	472	429	385	341	297	254	210	166	125	96
4,560	4,600	522	478	435	391	347	303	260	216	172	129	100
4,600	4,640	528	484	441	397	353	309	266	222	178	134	104
4,640	4,680	534	490	447	403	359	315	272	228	184	140	108
4,680	4,720	540	496	453	409	365	321	278	234	190	146	112
4,720	4,760	546	502	459	415	371	327	284	240	196	152	116
4,760	4,800	552	508	465	421	377	333	290	246	202	158	120
4,800	4,840	558	514	471	427	383	339	296	252	208	164	124
4,840	4,880	564	520	477	433	389	345	302	258	214	170	128
4,880	4,920	570	526	483	439	395	351	308	264	220	176	133
4,920	4,960	576	532	489	445	401	357	314	270	226	182	139
4,960	5,000	582	538	495	451	407	363	320	276	232	188	145
5,000	5,040	588	544	501	457	413	369	326	282	238	194	151
5,040	5,080	594	550	507	463	419	375	332	288	244	200	157
5,080	5,120	600	556	513	469	425	381	338	294	250	206	163
5,120	5,160	606	562	519	475	431	387	344	300	256	212	169
5,160	5,200	612	568	525	481	437	393	350	306	262	218	175
5,200	5,240	618	574	531	487	443	399	356	312	268	224	181
5,240	5,280	624	580	537	493	449	405	362	318	274	230	187
5,280	5,320	630	586	543	499	455	411	368	324	280	236	193
5,320	5,360	636	592	549	505	461	417	374	330	286	242	199
5,360	5,400	642	598	555	511	467	423	380	336	292	248	205
5,400	5,440	648	604	561	517	473	429	386	342	298	254	211
5,440	5,480	654	610	567	523	479	435	392	348	304	260	217
5,480	5,520	660	616	573	529	485	441	398	354	310	266	223
5,520	5,560	666	622	579	535	491	447	404	360	316	272	229
5,560	5,600	672	628	585	541	497	453	410	366	322	278	235
5,600	5,640	678	634	591	547	503	459	416	372	328	284	241
5,640	5,680	684	640	597	553	509	465	422	378	334	290	247
5,680	5,720	690	646	603	559	515	471	428	384	340	296	253
5,720	5,760	696	652	609	565	521	477	434	390	346	302	259
5,760	5,800	702	658	615	571	527	483	440	396	352	308	265
5,800	5,840	708	664	621	577	533	489	446	402	358	314	271
5,840	5,880	714	670	627	583	539	495	452	408	364	320	277

$5,880 and over Use Table 4(b) for a **MARRIED person** on page 38. Also see the instructions on page 36.

PEACHTREE COMPUTER WORKSHOP

COMPUTERIZED ACCOUNTING APPLICATION FOR CHAPTER 12

Refresher on using Peachtree Complete Accounting

Before starting this assignment, you may want to refresh your memory by reading the following PDF documents in the multimedia library of the MyAccountingLab Web site. Remember to choose the PDF document for your version of Peachtree.

1. An Introduction to Peachtree Complete Accounting
2. Correcting Peachtree Transactions
3. How to Repeat or Restart a Peachtree Assignment
4. Backing Up and Restoring Your Work in Peachtree

You also should have completed the following workshops:

1. Workshop 1 Atlas Company from Chapter 3
2. Workshop 2 Zell Company from Chapter 4
3. Workshop 3 Sullivan Realty from Chapter 5
4. Workshop 4 Pete's Market from Chapter 8
5. Workshop 5 Part A Mars Company from Chapter 10
6. Workshop 5 Part B Abby's Toy House from Chapter 10

Workshop 6:

Accounting Cycle for a Merchandising Company

In this workshop you complete an accounting cycle for a merchandising business owned by the Corner Dress Shop using Peachtree. Tasks include maintaining inventory, recording sales on account, merchandise returns, merchandise purchases, vendor payments, and payroll. You will also prepare inventory reports, aged receivables and aged payable reports, general journal and general ledger reports, a trial balance, and financial statements. Finally, you will close the accounting period.

Instructions and the data file for completing this assignment are in the multimedia library of the MyAccountingLab Web site. Open the ***Workshop 6 The Corner Dress Shop*** PDF document for your version of Peachtree and download ***The Corner Dress Shop*** data file for your version of Peachtree.

QUICKBOOKS COMPUTER WORKSHOP

COMPUTERIZED ACCOUNTING APPLICATION FOR CHAPTER 12

Refresher on using QuickBooks Pro

Before starting this assignment, you may want to refresh your memory by reading the following PDF documents in the multimedia library of the MyAccountingLab Web site. Remember to choose the PDF document for your version of QuickBooks.

1. An Introduction to QuickBooks Pro
2. Correcting QuickBooks Transactions
3. How to Repeat or Restart a QuickBooks Assignment
4. Backing Up and Restoring Your Work in QuickBooks

You also should have completed the following workshops:

1. Workshop 1 Atlas Company from Chapter 3
2. Workshop 2 Zell Company from Chapter 4
3. Workshop 3 Sullivan Realty from Chapter 5
4. Workshop 4 Pete's Market from Chapter 8
5. Workshop 5 Part A Mars Company from Chapter 10
6. Workshop 5 Part B Abby's Toy House from Chapter 10

Workshop 6:

Accounting Cycle for a Merchandising Company

In this workshop you complete an accounting cycle for a merchandising business owned by the Corner Dress Shop using QuickBooks. Tasks include maintaining inventory, recording sales on account, merchandise returns, merchandise purchases, vendor payments, and payroll. You will also prepare inventory reports, aged receivables and aged payable reports, general journal and general ledger reports, a trial balance, and financial statements. Finally, you will close the accounting period.

Instructions and the data file for completing this assignment are in the multimedia library of the MyAccountingLab Web site. Open the ***Workshop 6 The Corner Dress Shop*** PDF document for your version of Quickbooks and download the ***The Corner Dress Shop*** data file for your version of Quickbooks.

Appendix A
Kellogg Financial Report

Appendix A Kellogg Financial Report

Kellogg Company and Subsidiaries

Consolidated Statement of Earnings

(millions, except per share data)	**2006**	2005	2004
Net sales	**$10,906.7**	$10,177.2	$9,613.9
Cost of goods sold	**6,081.5**	5,611.6	5,298.7
Selling, general, and administrative expense	**3,059.4**	2,815.3	2,634.1
Operating profit	**$ 1,765.8**	$ 1,750.3	$1,681.1
Interest expense	**307.4**	300.3	308.6
Other income (expense), net	**13.2**	(24.9)	(6.6)
Earnings before income taxes	**$ 1,471.6**	$ 1,425.1	$1,365.9
Income taxes	**466.5**	444.7	475.3
Earnings (loss) from joint venture	**(1.0)**	—	—
Net earnings	**$ 1,004.1**	$ 980.4	$ 890.6
Per share amounts:			
Basic	**$ 2.53**	$ 2.38	$ 2.16
Diluted	**2.51**	2.36	2.14

Refer to Notes to Consolidated Financial Statements.

Consolidated Statement of Shareholders' Equity

(millions)	Common Stock Shares	Common Stock Amount	Capital in Excess of Par Value	Retained Earnings	Treasury Stock Shares	Treasury Stock Amount	Accumulated Other Comprehensive Income	Total Shareholders' Equity	Total Comprehensive Income
Balance, December 27, 2003	415.5	$103.8	$ 24.5	$2,247.7	5.8	$(203.6)	$ (729.2)	$1,443.2	$ 911.3
Common stock repurchases					7.3	(297.5)		(297.5)	
Net earnings				890.6				890.6	890.6
Dividends				(417.6)				(417.6)	
Other comprehensive income							289.3	289.3	289.3
Stock options exercised and other			(24.5)	(19.4)	(10.7)	393.1		349.2	
Balance, January 1, 2005	415.5	$103.8	$ —	$2,701.3	2.4	$(108.0)	$ (439.9)	$2,257.2	$1,179.9
Common stock repurchases					15.4	(664.2)		(664.2)	
Net earnings				980.4				980.4	980.4
Dividends				(435.2)				(435.2)	
Other comprehensive income							(136.2)	(136.2)	(136.2)
Stock options exercised and other	3.0	.8	58.9	19.6	(4.7)	202.4		281.7	
Balance, December 31, 2005	418.5	$104.6	$ 58.9	$3,266.1	13.1	$(569.8)	$ (576.1)	$2,283.7	$ 844.2
Revision (a)			101.4	(101.4)				—	
Common stock repurchases					14.9	(649.8)		(649.8)	
Net earnings				1,004.1				1,004.1	1,004.1
Dividends				(449.9)				(449.9)	
Other comprehensive income							121.8	121.8	121.8
Stock compensation			85.7					85.7	
Stock options exercised and other			46.3	(88.5)	(7.2)	307.5		265.3	
Impact of adoption of SFAS No. 158 (a)							(591.9)	(591.9)	
Balance, December 30, 2006	**418.5**	**$104.6**	**$292.3**	**$3,630.4**	**20.8**	**$(912.1)**	**$(1,046.2)**	**$2,069.0**	**$1,125.9**

Refer to Notes to Consolidated Financial Statements.
(a) Refer to Note 5 for further information on these items.

Kellogg Company and Subsidiaries

Consolidated Balance Sheet

(millions, except share data)	**2006**	2005
Current assets		
Cash and cash equivalents	**$ 410.6**	$ 219.1
Accounts receivable, net	**944.8**	879.1
Inventories	**823.9**	717.0
Other current assets	**247.7**	381.3
Total current assets	**$ 2,427.0**	$ 2,196.5
Property, net	**2,815.6**	2,648.4
Other assets	**5,471.4**	5,729.6
Total assets	**$10,714.0**	$10,574.5
Current liabilities		
Current maturities of long-term debt	**$ 723.3**	$ 83.6
Notes payable	**1,268.0**	1,111.1
Accounts payable	**910.4**	883.3
Other current liabilities	**1,118.5**	1,084.8
Total current liabilities	**$ 4,020.2**	$ 3,162.8
Long-term debt	**3,053.0**	3,702.6
Other liabilities	**1,571.8**	1,425.4
Shareholders' equity		
Common stock, $.25 per value, 1,000,000,000 shares authorized		
Issued: 418,515,339 shares in 2006 and 418,451,198 shares in 2005	**104.6**	104.6
Capital in excess of par value	**292.3**	58.9
Retained earnings	**3,630.4**	3,266.1
Treasury stock at cost:		
20,817,930 shares in 2006 and 13,121,446 shares in 2005	**(912.1)**	(569.8)
Accumulated other comprehensive income (loss)	**(1,046.2)**	(576.1)
Total shareholders' equity	**$ 2,069.0**	$ 2,283.7
Total liabilities and shareholders' equity	**$10,714.0**	$10,574.5

Refer to Notes to Consolidated Financial Statements. In particular, refer to Note 15 for supplemental information on various balance sheet captions and Note 1 for details on the impact of adopting SFAS No. 158 "Employers' Accounting for Defined Benefit Pension and Other Postretirement Plans."

Kellogg Company and Subsidiaries

Consolidated Statement of Cash Flows

(millions)	**2006**	2005	2004
Operating activities			
Net earnings	**$1,004.1**	$ 980.4	$ 890.6
Adjustments to reconcile net earnings to operating cash flows:			
Depreciation and amortization	**352.7**	391.8	410.0
Deferred income taxes	**(43.7)**	(59.2)	57.7
Other (a)	**235.2**	199.3	104.5
Pension and other postretirement benefit plan contributions	**(99.3)**	(397.3)	(204.0)
Changes in operating assets and liabilities	**(38.5)**	28.3	(29.8)
Net cash provided by operating activities	**$1,410.5**	$1,143.3	$1,229.0
Investing activities			
Additions to properties	**$ (453.1)**	$ (374.2)	$ (278.6)
Acquisitions of businesses	—	(50.4)	—
Property disposals	**9.4**	9.8	7.9
Investment in joint venture and other	**(1.7)**	(.2)	.3
Net cash used in investing activities	**$ (445.4)**	$ (415.0)	$ (270.4)
Financing activities			
Net increase (reduction) of notes payable, with maturities less than or equal to 90 days	**$ (344.2)**	$ 360.2	$ 388.3
Issuances of notes payable, with maturities greater than 90 days	**1,065.4**	42.6	142.3
Reductions of notes payable, with maturities greater than 90 days	**(565.2)**	(42.3)	(141.7)
Issuances of long-term debt	—	647.3	7.0
Reductions of long-term debt	**(84.7)**	(1,041.3)	(682.2)
Issuances of common stock	**217.5**	221.7	291.8
Common stock repurchases	**(649.8)**	(664.2)	(297.5)
Cash dividends	**(449.9)**	(435.2)	(417.6)
Other	**21.9**	5.9	(6.7)
Net cash used in financing activities	**$ (789.0)**	$ (905.3)	$ (716.3)
Effect of exchange rate changes on cash	**15.4**	(21.3)	33.9
Increase (decrease) in cash and cash equivalents	**$ 191.5**	$ (198.3)	$ 276.2
Cash and cash equivalents at beginning of year	**219.1**	417.4	141.2
Cash and cash equivalents at end of year	**$ 410.6**	$ 219.1	$ 417.4

Refer to Notes to Consolidated Financial Statements.

(a) Consists principally of non-cash expense accruals for employee compensation and benefit obligations.

Note 1 Accounting Policies

Basis of Presentation

The consolidated financial statements include the accounts of Kellogg Company and its majority-owned subsidiaries. Intercompany balances and transactions are eliminated.

The Company's fiscal year normally ends on the Saturday closest to December 31 and as a result, a 53rd week is added approximately every sixth year. The Company's 2006 and 2005 fiscal years ended on December 30 and December 31, respectively. The Company's 2004 fiscal year ended on January 1, 2005, and included a 53rd week.

Cash and cash equivalents

Highly liquid temporary investments with original maturities of less than three months are considered to be cash equivalents. The carrying amount approximates fair value.

Accounts receivable

Accounts receivable consist principally of trade receivables, which are recorded at the invoiced amount, net of allowances for doubtful accounts and prompt payment discounts. Trade receivables generally do not bear interest. Terms and collection patterns vary around the world and by channel. In the United States, the Company generally has required payment for goods sold eleven or sixteen days subsequent to the date of invoice as 2% 10/net 11 or 1% 15/net 16, and days sales outstanding (DSO) has averaged approximately 19 days during the periods presented. The allowance for doubtful accounts represents management's estimate of the amount of probable credit losses in existing accounts receivable, as determined from a review of past due balances and other specific account data. Account balances are written off against the allowance when management determines the receivable is uncollectible. The Company does not have any off-balance sheet credit exposure related to its customers. Refer to Note 15 for an analysis of the Company's accounts receivable and allowance for doubtful account balances during the periods presented.

Inventories

Inventories are valued at the lower of cost (principally average) or market.

In November 2004, the Financial Accounting Standards Board (FASB) issued Statement of Financial Accounting Standard (SFAS) No. 151 "Inventory Costs" to converge U.S. GAAP principles with International Accounting Standards on inventory valuation. SFAS No. 151 clarifies that abnormal amounts of idle facility expense, freight, handling costs, and spoilage should be recognized as period charges, rather than as inventory value. This standard also provides that fixed production overheads should be allocated to units of production based on the normal capacity of production facilities, with excess overheads being recognized as period charges. The provisions of this standard are effective for inventory costs incurred during fiscal years beginning after June 15, 2005, with earlier application permitted. The Company adopted this standard at the beginning of its 2006 fiscal year. The Company's pre-existing accounting policy for inventory valuation was generally consistent with this guidance. Accordingly, the adoption of SFAS No. 151 did not have a significant impact on the Company's 2006 financial results.

Property

The Company's property consists mainly of plant and equipment used for manufacturing activities. These assets are recorded at cost and depreciated over estimated useful lives using straight-line methods for financial reporting and accelerated methods, where permitted, for tax reporting. Major property categories are depreciated over various periods as follows (in years): manufacturing machinery and equipment 5-20; computer and other office equipment 3-5; building components 15-30; building structures 50. Cost includes an amount of interest associated with significant capital projects. Plant and equipment are reviewed for impairment when conditions indicate that the carrying value may not be recoverable. Such conditions include an extended period of idleness or a plan of disposal. Assets to be abandoned at a future date are depreciated over the remaining period of use. Assets to be sold are written down to realizable value at the time the assets are being actively marketed for sale and the disposal is expected to occur within one year. As of year-end 2005 and 2006, the carrying value of assets held for sale was insignificant.

Goodwill and other intangible assets

The Company's intangible assets consist primarily of goodwill and major trademarks arising from the 2001 acquisition of Keebler Foods Company ("Keebler"). Management expects the Keebler trademarks, collectively, to contribute indefinitely to the cash flows of the Company. Accordingly, this asset has been classified as an "indefinite-lived" intangible pursuant to SFAS No. 142 "Goodwill and Other Intangible Assets." Under this standard, goodwill and indefinite-lived intangibles are not amortized, but are tested at least annually for impairment. Goodwill impairment testing first requires a comparison between the carrying value and fair value of a "reporting unit," which for the Company is generally equivalent to a North American product group or International country market. If carrying value exceeds fair value, goodwill is considered impaired and is reduced to the implied fair value. Impairment testing for non-amortized intangibles requires a comparison between the fair value and carrying value of the intangible asset. If carrying value exceeds fair value, the intangible is considered impaired and is reduced to fair value. The Company uses various market valuation techniques to determine the fair value of intangible assets and periodically engages third-party valuation consultants for this purpose. Refer to Note 2 for further information on goodwill and other intangible assets.

Revenue recognition and measurement

The Company recognizes sales upon delivery of its products to customers net of applicable provisions for discounts, returns, allowances, and various government withholding taxes. Methodologies for determining these provisions are dependent on local customer pricing and promotional practices, which range from contractually fixed percentage price reductions to reimbursement based on actual occurrence or performance. Where applicable, future reimbursements are estimated based on a combination of historical patterns and future expectations regarding specific in-market product performance. The Company classifies promotional payments to its customers, the cost of consumer coupons, and other cash redemption offers in net sales. The cost of promotional package inserts are recorded in cost of goods sold. Other types of consumer promotional expenditures are normally recorded in selling, general, and administrative (SGA) expense.

Advertising

The costs of advertising are generally expensed as incurred and are classified within SGA expense.

Research and development

The costs of research and development (R&D) are generally expensed as incurred and are classified within SGA expense. R&D includes expenditures for new product and process innovation, as well as significant technological improvements to existing products and processes. Total annual expenditures for R&D are disclosed in Note 15 and are principally comprised of internal salaries, wages, consulting, and supplies attributable to time spent on R&D activities. Other costs include depreciation and maintenance of research facilities and equipment, including assets at manufacturing locations that are temporarily engaged in pilot plant activities.

Stock compensation

The Company uses various equity-based compensation programs to provide long-term performance incentives for its global workforce. Refer to Note 8 for further information on these programs and the amount of compensation expense recognized during the periods presented.

In December 2004, the FASB issued SFAS No. 123(R) "Share-Based Payment," which generally requires public companies to measure the cost of employee services received in exchange for an award of equity instruments based on the grant-date fair value and to recognize this cost over the requisite service period. The Company adopted SFAS No. 123(R) as of the beginning of its 2006 fiscal year, using the modified prospective method. Accordingly, prior years were not restated, but 2006 results include compensation expense associated with unvested equitybased awards, which were granted prior to 2006.

Prior to adoption of SFAS No. 123(R), the Company used the intrinsic value method prescribed by Accounting Principles Board Opinion (APB) No. 25 "Accounting for Stock Issued to Employees" to account for its employee stock options and other stock-based compensation. Under this method, because the exercise price of stock options granted to employees and directors equaled the market price of the underlying stock on the date of the grant, no compensation expense was recognized. Expense attributable to other types of stock-based awards was generally recognized in the Company's reported results under APB No. 25.

Certain of the Company's equity-based compensation plans contain provisions that accelerate vesting of awards upon retirement, disability, or death of eligible employees and directors. Prior to adoption of SFAS No. 123(R), the Company generally recognized stock compensation expense over the stated vesting period of the award, with any unamortized expense recognized immediately if an acceleration event occurred. SFAS No. 123(R) specifies that a stock-based award is considered vested for expense attribution purposes when the employee's retention of the award is no longer contingent on providing subsequent service. Accordingly, beginning in 2006, the Company has prospectively revised its expense attribution method so that the related compensation cost is recognized immediately for awards granted to retirement-eligible individuals or over the period from the grant date to the date retirement eligibility is achieved, if less than the stated vesting period.

The Company classifies pre-tax stock compensation expense principally in SGA expense within its corporate operations. Expense attributable to awards of equity instruments is accrued in capital in excess of par value within the Consolidated Balance Sheet.

SFAS No. 123(R) also provides that any corporate income tax benefit realized upon exercise or vesting of an award in excess of that previously recognized in earnings (referred to as a "windfall tax benefit") will be presented in the Consolidated Statement of Cash Flows as a financing (rather than an operating) cash flow. Realized windfall tax benefits are credited to capital in excess of par value in the Consolidated Balance Sheet. Realized shortfall tax benefits (amounts which are less than that previously recognized in earnings) are first offset against the cumulative balance of windfall tax benefits, if any, and then charged directly to income tax expense. Under the transition rules for adopting SFAS No. 123(R) using the modified prospective method, the Company was permitted to calculate a cumulative memo balance of windfall tax benefits from post-1995 years for the purpose of accounting for future shortfall tax benefits. The Company completed such study prior to the first period of adoption and currently has sufficient cumulative memo windfall tax benefits to absorb arising shortfalls, such that earnings were not affected in 2006. Correspondingly, the Company includes the impact of pro forma deferred tax assets (i.e., the "as if" windfall or shortfall) for purposes of determining assumed proceeds in the treasury stock calculation of diluted earnings per share under SFAS No. 128 "Earnings Per Share."

Employee postretirement and postemployment benefits

The Company sponsors a number of U.S. and foreign plans to provide pension, health care, and other welfare benefits to retired employees, as well as salary continuance, severance, and long-term disability to former or inactive employees. Refer to Notes 9 and 10 for further information on these benefits and the amount of expense recognized during the periods presented.

In order to improve the reporting of pension and other postretirement benefit plans in the financial statements, in September 2006, the FASB issued SFAS No. 158 "Employers' Accounting for Defined Benefit Pension and Other Postretirement Plans," which is effective at the end of fiscal years ending after December 15, 2006. Prior periods are not restated. The standard generally requires company plan sponsors to measure the net over- or under-funded position of a defined postretirement benefit plan as of the sponsor's fiscal year end and to display that position as an asset or liability on the balance sheet. Any unrecognized prior service cost, experience gains/losses, or transition obligation are reported as a component of other comprehensive income, net of tax, in shareholders' equity. In contrast, under preexisting guidance, these unrecognized amounts were generally disclosed only in financial statement footnotes, often resulting in a disparity between plan balance sheet positions and the funded status. Furthermore, plan measurement dates could occur up to three months prior to year end.

The Company adopted SFAS No. 158 as of the end of its 2006 fiscal year. The Company had previously applied postretirement accounting concepts for purposes of recognizing its postemployment benefit obligations; accordingly, the adoption of SFAS No. 158 as of December 30, 2006, affected the balance sheet display of both the Company's postretirement and postemployment benefit obligations, as follows:

(millions)	Before application of SFAS No. 158 (a)	Adjustments	After application of SFAS No. 158
Other assets:			
Other intangibles — pension	$ 9.5	$ (9.5)	$ —
Pension	855.5	(502.9)	352.6
	$865.0	**$(512.4)**	**$ 352.6**
Total assets	**$865.0**	**$(512.4)**	**$ 352.6**
Other current liabilities:			
Pension, postretirement, and postemployment benefits	53.0	(34.2)	18.8
	$ 53.0	**$ (34.2)**	**$ 18.8**
Other liabilities:			
Pension, postretirement, and postemployment benefits (a)	287.2	412.6	699.8
Deferred income taxes (b)	(6.8)	(298.9)	(305.7)
	$280.4	**$ 113.7**	**$ 394.1**
Total liabilities	**$333.4**	**$ 79.5**	**$ 412.9**
Accumulated other comprehensive income (loss) (a)	**$ (12.2)**	**$(591.9)**	**$(604.1)**

(a) Includes additional minimum pension liability adjustment under pre-existing guidance of $28.5, which reduced accumulated other comprehensive income by $12.2 on an after-tax basis.

(b) Represents an asset component of deferred tax liabilities, which are presented on a net basis at the jurisdiction level.

The Company's net earnings, cash flow, liquidity, debt covenants, and plan funding requirements were not affected by this change in accounting principle. The Company has historically used its fiscal year end as the measurement date for its company-sponsored defined benefit plans.

Recently issued pronouncements

Uncertain tax positions

In July 2006, the FASB issued Interpretation No. 48 "Accounting for Uncertainty in Income Taxes" (FIN No. 48) to clarify what criteria must be met prior to recognition of the financial statement benefit, in accordance with FASB Statement No. 109, "Accounting for Income Taxes," of a position taken in a tax return. The provisions of the final interpretation apply broadly to all tax positions taken by an enterprise, including the decision not to report income in a tax return or the decision to classify a transaction as tax exempt. The prescribed approach is based on a two-step benefit recognition model. The first step is to evaluate the tax position for recognition by determining if the weight of available evidence indicates it is more likely than not, based on the technical merits and without consideration of detection risk, that the position will be sustained on audit, including resolution of related appeals or litigation processes, if any. The second step is to measure the appropriate amount of the benefit to recognize. The amount of benefit to recognize is measured as the largest amount of tax benefit that is greater than 50 percent likely of being ultimately realized upon settlement. The tax position must be derecognized when it is no longer more likely than not of being sustained. The interpretation also provides guidance on recognition and classification of related penalties and interest, classification of liabilities, and disclosures of unrecognized tax benefits. The change in net assets, if any, as a result of applying the provisions of this interpretation is considered a change in accounting principle with the cumulative effect of the change treated as an offsetting adjustment to the opening balance of retained earnings in the period of transition. The final interpretation is effective for the first annual period beginning after December 15, 2006, with earlier application encouraged.

The Company adopted FIN No. 48 as of the beginning of its 2007 fiscal year. Prior to adoption, the Company's preexisting policy was to establish reserves for uncertain tax positions that reflected the probable outcome of known tax contingencies. As compared to the Company's historical approach, the application of FIN No. 48 resulted in a net decrease to accrued income tax and related interest liabilities of approximately $2 million, with an offsetting increase to retained earnings.

Interest recognized in accordance with FIN No. 48 may be classified in the financial statements as either income taxes or interest expense, based on the accounting policy election of the enterprise. Similarly, penalties may be classified as income taxes or another expense. The Company has historically classified income tax-related interest and penalties as interest expense and SGA expense, respectively, and will continue to do so under FIN No. 48.

Fair value

In September 2006, the FASB issued SFAS No. 157 "Fair Value Measurements" to provide enhanced guidance for using fair value to measure assets and liabilities. The standard also expands disclosure requirements for assets and liabilities measured at fair value, how fair value is determined, and the effect of fair value measurements on earnings. The standard applies whenever other authoritative literature requires (or permits) certain assets or liabilities to be measured at fair value, but does not expand the use of fair value. SFAS No. 157 is effective for financial statements issued for fiscal years beginning after November 15, 2007, and interim periods within those years. Early adoption is permitted. The Company plans to adopt SFAS No. 157 in the first quarter of its 2008 fiscal year. For the Company, balance sheet items carried at fair value consist primarily of derivatives and other financial instruments, assets held for sale, exit liabilities, and the trust asset component of net benefit plan obligations. Additionally, the Company uses fair value concepts to test various long-lived assets for impairment and to initially measure assets and liabilities acquired in a business combination. Management is currently evaluating the impact of adoption on how these assets and liabilities are currently measured.

Use of estimates

The preparation of financial statements in conformity with generally accepted accounting principles requires management to make estimates and assumptions that affect the reported amounts of assets and liabilities and disclosure of contingent assets and liabilities at the date of the financial statements and the reported amounts of revenues and expenses during the reporting period. Actual results could differ from those estimates.

Note 2 Acquisitions, Other Investments, and Intangibles

Acquisitions

In order to support the continued growth of its North American fruit snacks business, the Company completed two separate business acquisitions during 2005 for a total of approximately $50 million in cash, including related transaction costs. In June 2005, the Company acquired a fruit snacks manufacturing facility and related assets from Kraft Foods Inc. The facility is located in Chicago, Illinois and employs approximately 400 active hourly and salaried employees. In November 2005, the Company acquired substantially all of the assets and certain liabilities of a Washington State-based manufacturer of natural and organic fruit snacks. Assets, liabilities, and results of the acquired businesses have been included in the Company's consolidated financial statements since the respective dates of acquisition. The combined purchase price for both transactions was allocated to property ($22 million); goodwill and other indefinite-lived intangibles ($16 million); and inventory and other working capital ($12 million).

Joint venture arrangement

In early 2006, a subsidiary of the Company formed a joint venture with a third-party company domiciled in Turkey, for the purpose of selling co-branded products in the surrounding region. As of December 30, 2006, the Company had contributed approximately $3.5 million in cash for a 50% equity interest in this arrangement. The Turkish joint venture is reflected in the consolidated financial statements on the equity basis of accounting. Accordingly, the Company records its share of the earnings or loss from this arrangement as well as other direct transactions with or on behalf of the joint venture entity such as product sales and certain administrative expenses. Summary financial information for one hundred percent of the joint venture is as follows:

(millions)	2006
Net sales	$ 6.0
Gross profit	1.9
Net earnings (loss)	(1.9)
Current assets	5.9
Noncurrent assets	—
Current liabilities	1.3
Noncurrent liabilities	—

Goodwill and other intangible assets

For 2004, the Company recorded in selling, general, and administrative expense impairment losses of $10.4 million to write off the remaining carrying value of a $7.9 million contract-based intangible asset in North America and $2.5 million of goodwill in Latin America.

For the periods presented, the Company's intangible assets consisted of the following:

Intangible assets subject to amortization				
(millions)	Gross carrying amount		Accumulated amortization	
	2006	2005	**2006**	2005
Trademarks	**$29.5**	$29.5	**$21.6**	$20.5
Other	**29.1**	29.1	**27.5**	27.1
Total	**$58.6**	$58.6	**$49.1**	$47.6

	2006	2005
Amortization expense (a)	**$1.5**	$1.5

(a) The currently estimated aggregate amortization expense for each of the four succeeding fiscal years is approximately $1.5 per year and $1.1 for the fifth succeeding fiscal year.

Intangible assets not subject to amortization

(millions)	Total carrying amount	
	2006	2005
Trademarks	**$1,410.2**	$1,410.2
Pension (a)	—	17.0
Total	**$1,410.2**	$1,427.2

(a) The Company adopted SFAS No. 158 "Employers' Accounting for Defined Benefit Pension and Other Postretirement Plans" as of the end of its 2006 fiscal year. The standard generally requires company plan sponsors to reflect the net over- or under-funded position of a defined postretirement benefit plan as an asset or liability on the balance sheet. Accordingly, the pension-related intangible included in the preceding table for 2005 was eliminated by the adoption of this standard. Refer to Note 1 for further information.

Changes in the carrying amount of goodwill

(millions)	United States	Europe	Latin America	Asia Pacific (a)	Consolidated
January 1, 2005	$3,443.3	—	—	$2.2	$3,445.5
Acquisitions	10.2	—	—	—	10.2
Other	(.3)	—	—	(.1)	(.4)
December 31, 2005	$3,453.2	—	—	$2.1	$3,455.3
Purchase accounting adjustments (b)	**(7.0)**	—	—	—	**(7.0)**
Other	**(.1)**	—	—	**.1**	—
December 30, 2006	**$3,446.1**	—	—	**$2.2**	**$3,448.3**

(a) Includes Australia and Asia.

(b) Relates principally to the recognition of an acquired tax benefit arising from the purchase of Keebler Foods Company in 2001.

Note 3 Cost-Reduction Initiatives

The Company views its continued spending on cost-reduction initiatives as part of its ongoing operating principles to reinvest earnings so as to provide greater reliability in meeting long-term growth targets. Initiatives undertaken must meet certain pay-back and internal rate of return (IRR) targets. Each cost-reduction initiative is normally one to three years in duration. Upon completion (or as each major stage is completed in the case of multi-year programs), the project begins to deliver cash savings and/or reduced depreciation, which is then used to fund new initiatives. To implement these programs, the Company has incurred various up-front costs, including asset write-offs, exit charges, and other project expenditures.

Cost summary

For 2006, the Company recorded total program-related charges of approximately $82 million, comprised of $20 million of asset write-offs, $30 million for severance and other exit costs, $9 million for other cash expenditures, $4 million for a multiemployer pension plan withdrawal liability, and $19 million for pension and other postretirement plan curtailment losses and special termination benefits. Approximately $74 million of the total 2006 charges were recorded in cost of goods sold within operating segment results, with approximately $8 million recorded in selling, general, and administrative (SGA) expense within corporate results. The Company's operating segments were impacted as follows (in millions): North America–$46; Europe–$28.

For 2005, the Company recorded total program-related charges of approximately $90 million, comprised of $16 million for a multiemployer pension plan withdrawal liability, $44 million of asset write-offs, $21 million for severance and other exit costs, and $9 million for other cash expenditures. All of the 2005 charges were recorded in cost of goods sold within the Company's North America operating segment.

For 2004, the Company recorded total program-related charges of approximately $109 million, comprised of $41 million in asset write-offs, $1 million for special pension termination benefits, $15 million in severance and other exit costs, and $52 million in other cash expenditures such as relocation and consulting. Approximately $46 million of the total 2004 charges were recorded in cost of goods sold, with approximately $63 million recorded in SGA expense. The 2004 charges impacted the Company's operating segments as follows (in millions): North America–$44; Europe–$65. Exit cost reserves were approximately $14 million at December 30, 2006, consisting principally of severance obligations associated with projects commenced in 2006, which are expected to be paid out in 2007. At December 31, 2005, exit cost reserves were approximately $13 million, primarily representing severance costs that were substantially paid out in 2006.

Specific initiatives

In September 2006, the Company approved a multi-year European manufacturing optimization plan to improve utilization of its facility in Manchester, England and to better align production in Europe. Based on forecasted foreign exchange rates, the Company currently expects to incur approximately $60 million in total up-front costs (including those already incurred in 2006), comprised of approximately 80% cash and 20% non-cash asset writeoffs, to complete this initiative. The cash portion of the total up-front costs results principally from management's plan to eliminate approximately 220 hourly and salaried positions from the Manchester facility by the end of 2008 through voluntary early retirement and severance programs. The pension trust funding requirements of these early retirements are expected to exceed the recognized benefit expense impact by approximately $10 million; most of this incremental funding occurred in 2006. During this period, certain manufacturing equipment will also be removed from service. For 2006, the Company incurred approximately $28 million of total up-front costs, including $9 million of pension plan curtailment losses and special termination benefits.

During 2006, the Company commenced several initiatives to enhance the productivity and efficiency of its U.S. cereal manufacturing network, primarily through technological and sourcing improvements in warehousing and packaging operations. In conjunction with these initiatives, the Company offered voluntary separation incentives, which resulted in the retirement of approximately 80 hourly employees by early 2007. During the fourth quarter of 2006, the Company incurred approximately $15 million of total up-front costs, comprised of approximately 20% asset write-offs and 80% cash costs, including $10 million of pension and other postretirement plan curtailment losses.

Also during 2006, the Company undertook an initiative to improve customer focus and selling efficiency within a particular Latin American market, leading to a shift from a third-party distributor to a direct sales force model. As a result of this initiative, the Company paid $8 million in cash during the fourth quarter of 2006 to exit the existing distribution arrangement.

To improve operational efficiency and better position its North American snacks business for future growth, during 2005, the Company undertook an initiative to consolidate U.S. bakery capacity, which was completed by the end of 2006. The project resulted in the closure and sale of the Company's Des Plaines, Illinois facility in late 2005 and closure of its Macon, Georgia facility in April 2006, with sale occurring in September 2006. These closures resulted in the elimination of over 700 hourly and salaried employee positions, through the combination of involuntary severance and attrition. Related to this initiative, the Company incurred up-front costs of approximately $80 million in 2005, comprised of approximately one-half asset write-offs and one-half cash costs, including $16 million for the present value of a projected multiemployer pension plan withdrawal liability associated with closure of the Macon facility. The Company incurred approximately $31 million in up-front costs for 2006, comprised of approximately one-third asset write-offs and two-thirds cash costs, including a $4 million increase in the Company's estimated pension plan withdrawal liability to $20 million. This increase was principally attributable to investment loss experienced during 2005 in conjunction with increased benefit levels for all participating employers. The final calculation of this liability is pending full-year 2007 employee hours attributable to the Company's remaining participation in this plan, and is therefore subject to adjustment in early 2008. The associated cash obligation is payable to the pension fund over a 20-year maximum period; management has not currently determined the actual period over which the payments will be made. Except for this pension plan withdrawal liability, the Company's cash obligations attributable to this initiative were substantially paid out by year end 2006.

During 2004, the Company commenced an operational improvement initiative which resulted in the consolidation of veggie foods manufacturing at its Zanesville, Ohio facility and the closure and sale of its Worthington, Ohio facility by mid 2005. As a result of this closing, approximately 280 employee positions were eliminated through separation and attrition. Related to this initiative, the Company recognized approximately $20 million of up-front costs in 2004 and $10 million in 2005. For both years, the total amounts were comprised of approximately two-thirds asset writeoffs and one-third cash costs such as severance and removal, which were entirely paid out by the end of 2005.

During 2004, the Company's global rollout of its SAP information technology system resulted in accelerated depreciation of legacy software assets to be abandoned in 2005, as well as related consulting and other implementation expenses. Total incremental costs for 2004 were approximately $30 million. In close association with this SAP rollout, management undertook a major initiative to improve the organizational design and effectiveness of pan-European operations. Specific benefits of this initiative were expected to include improved marketing and promotional coordination across Europe, supply chain network savings, overhead cost reductions, and tax savings. To achieve these benefits, management implemented, at the beginning of 2005, a new European legal and operating structure headquartered in Ireland, with strengthened pan-European management authority and coordination. During 2004, the Company incurred various up-front costs, including relocation, severance, and consulting, of approximately $30 million. Additional relocation and other costs to complete this business transformation after 2004 have been insignificant.

In order to integrate it with the rest of our U.S. operations, during 2004, the Company completed the relocation of its U.S. snacks business unit from Elmhurst, Illinois (the former headquarters of Keebler Foods Company) to Battle Creek, Michigan. About one-third of the approximately 300 employees affected by this initiative accepted relocation or reassignment offers. The recruiting effort to fill the remaining open positions was substantially completed by year-end 2004. Attributable to this initiative, the Company incurred approximately $15 million in relocation, recruiting, and severance costs during 2004. Subject to achieving certain employment levels and other regulatory requirements, management expects to defray a significant portion of these up-front costs through various multi-year tax incentives, which began in 2005. The Elmhurst office building was sold in late 2004, and the net sales proceeds approximated carrying value.

Note 4 Other Income (Expense), Net

Other income (expense), net includes non-operating items such as interest income, charitable donations, and foreign exchange gains and losses. Net foreign exchange transaction losses for the periods presented were approximately (in millions): 2006–$2; 2005–$2; 2004–$15.

Other expense includes charges for contributions to the Kellogg's Corporate Citizenship Fund, a private trust established for charitable giving, as follows (in millions): 2006–$3; 2005–$16; 2004–$9. Other expense for 2005 also includes a charge of approximately $7 million to reduce the carrying value of a corporate commercial facility to estimated selling value. This facility was sold in August 2006.

Note 5 Equity

During the year ended December 30, 2006, the Company revised the classification of $101.4 million of prior net losses realized upon reissuance of treasury shares from capital in excess of par value to retained earnings on the Consolidated Balance Sheet. Such reissuances occurred in connection with employee and director stock option exercises and other share-based settlements. The revision did not have an effect on the Company's results of operations, total shareholders' equity, or cash flows.

Earnings per share

Basic net earnings per share is determined by dividing net earnings by the weighted-average number of common shares outstanding during the period. Diluted net earnings per share is similarly determined, except that the denominator is increased to include the number of additional common shares that would have been outstanding if all dilutive potential common shares had been issued. Dilutive potential common shares are comprised principally of employee stock options issued by the Company. Basic net earnings per share is reconciled to diluted net earnings per share in the following table. The total number of anti-dilutive potential common shares excluded from the reconciliation for each period was (in millions): 2006–.7; 2005–1.5; 2004–4.3.

(millions, except per share data)	Earnings	Average shares outstanding	Per share
2006			
Basic	**$1,004.1**	**397.0**	**$2.53**
Dilutive potential common shares	**—**	**3.4**	**(.02)**
Diluted	**$1,004.1**	**400.4**	**$2.51**
2005			
Basic	$ 980.4	412.0	$2.38
Dilutive potential common shares	—	3.6	(.02)
Diluted	$ 980.4	415.6	$2.36
2004			
Basic	$890.6	412.0	$2.16
Dilutive potential common shares	—	4.4	(.02)
Diluted	$890.6	416.4	$2.14

Stock transactions

The Company issues shares to employees and directors under various equity-based compensation and stock purchase programs, as further discussed in Note 8. The number of shares issued during the periods presented was (in millions): 2006–7.2; 2005–7.7; 2004–10.7. Additionally, during 2006, the Company established *Kellogg Direct*™, a direct stock purchase and dividend reinvestment plan for U.S. shareholders and issued less than .1 million shares for that purpose in 2006.

To offset these issuances and for general corporate purposes, the Company's Board of Directors has authorized management to repurchase specified amounts of the Company's common stock in each of the periods presented. In 2006, the Company spent $650 million to repurchase approximately 14.9 million shares. This activity consisted principally of a February 2006 private transaction with the W.K. Kellogg Foundation Trust to repurchase approximately 12.8 million shares for $550 million. In 2005, the Company spent $664 million to repurchase approximately 15.4 million shares. This activity consisted principally of a November 2005 private transaction with the W.K. Kellogg Foundation Trust to repurchase approximately 9.4 million shares for $400 million. In 2004, the Company spent $298 million to repurchase approximately 7.3 million shares.

On December 8, 2006, the Company's Board of Directors authorized a stock repurchase program of up to $650 million for 2007.

Comprehensive Income

Comprehensive income includes net earnings and all other changes in equity during a period except those resulting from investments by or distributions to shareholders. Other comprehensive income for the periods presented consists of foreign currency translation adjustments pursuant to SFAS No. 52 "Foreign Currency Translation," unrealized gains and losses on cash flow hedges pursuant to SFAS No. 133 "Accounting for Derivative Instruments and Hedging Activities," and minimum pension liability adjustments pursuant to SFAS No. 87 "Employers' Accounting for Pensions." Additionally, accumulated other comprehensive income at December 30, 2006, reflects the adoption of SFAS No. 158 "Employers' Accounting for Defined Benefit Pension and Other Postretirement Plans" as of the Company's 2006 fiscal year end. Refer to Note 1 for further information.

(millions)	Pretax amount	Tax (expense) benefit	After-tax amount
2006			
Net earnings			**$1,004.1**
Other comprehensive income:			
Foreign currency translation adjustments	**$ 10.0**	**$ —**	**10.0**
Cash flow hedges:			
Unrealized loss on cash flow hedges	**(12.6)**	**4.6**	**(8.0)**
Reclassification to net earnings	**11.9**	**(4.3)**	**7.6**
Minimum pension liability adjustments	**172.3**	**(60.1)**	**112.2**
	$ 181.6	**$(59.8)**	**121.8**
Total comprehensive income			**$1,125.9**
2005			
Net earnings			$ 980.4
Other comprehensive income:			
Foreign currency translation adjustments	$ (85.2)	$ —	(85.2)
Cash flow hedges:			
Unrealized loss on cash flow hedges	(3.7)	1.6	(2.1)
Reclassification to net earnings	26.4	(9.9)	16.5
Minimum pension liability adjustments	(102.7)	37.3	(65.4)
	$(165.2)	$ 29.0	(136.2)
Total comprehensive income			$ 844.2
2004			
Net earnings			$ 890.6
Other comprehensive income:			
Foreign currency translation adjustments	$ 71.7	$ —	71.7
Cash flow hedges:			
Unrealized loss on cash flow hedges	(10.2)	3.1	(7.1)
Reclassification to net earnings	19.3	(6.9)	12.4
Minimum pension liability adjustments	308.9	(96.6)	212.3
	$389.7	$(100.4)	289.3
Total comprehensive income			$1,179.9

Accumulated other comprehensive income (loss) at year end consisted of the following:

(millions)	2006	2005
Foreign currency translation adjustments	**$ (409.5)**	$(419.5)
Cash flow hedges — unrealized net loss	**(32.6)**	(32.2)
Minimum pension liability adjustments	**—**	(124.4)
Postretirement and postemployment benefits:		
Net experience loss	**(540.5)**	—
Prior service cost	**(63.6)**	—
Total accumulated other comprehensive income (loss)	**$(1,046.2)**	$(576.1)

Note 6 Leases and Other Commitments

The Company's leases are generally for equipment and warehouse space. Rent expense on all operating leases was (in millions): 2006–$122.8; 2005–$115.1; 2004–$107.4. Additionally, the Company is subject to a residual value guarantee on one operating lease of approximately $13 million which expires in July 2007. At December 30, 2006, the Company had not recorded any liability related to this residual value guarantee. During 2006 and 2005, the Company entered into approximately $2 million and $3 million, respectively, in capital lease agreements to finance the purchase of equipment. Similar transactions in 2004 were insignificant.

At December 30, 2006, future minimum annual lease commitments under noncancelable operating and capital leases were as follows:

(millions)	Operating leases	Capital leases
2007	$119.7	$ 2.1
2008	103.4	1.4
2009	85.9	1.3
2010	67.7	1.0
2011	49.8	.6
2012 and beyond	148.6	3.0
Total minimum payments	$575.1	$ 9.4
Amount representing interest		(1.6)
Obligations under capital leases		7.8
Obligations due within one year		(2.1)
Long-term obligations under capital leases		$ 5.7

One of the Company's subsidiaries is guarantor on loans to independent contractors for the purchase of DSD route franchises. At year-end 2006, there were total loans outstanding of $16.0 million to 517 franchisees. All loans are variable rate with a term of 10 years. Related to this arrangement, the Company has established with a financial institution a one-year renewable loan facility up to $17.0 million with a five-year term-out and servicing arrangement. The Company has the right to revoke and resell the route franchises in the event of default or any other breach of contract by franchisees. Revocations are infrequent. The Company's maximum potential future payments under these guarantees are limited to the outstanding loan principal balance plus unpaid interest. The estimated fair value of these guarantees is recorded in the Consolidated Balance Sheet and was insignificant for the periods presented.

The Company has provided various standard indemnifications in agreements to sell business assets and lease facilities over the past several years, related primarily to pre-existing tax, environmental, and employee benefit obligations. Certain of these indemnifications are limited by agreement in either amount and/or term and others are unlimited. The Company has also provided various "hold harmless" provisions within certain service type agreements. Because the Company is not currently aware of any actual exposures associated with these indemnifications, management is unable to estimate the maximum potential future payments to be made. At December 30, 2006, the Company had not recorded any liability related to these indemnifications.

Note 7 Debt

Notes payable at year-end consisted of commercial paper borrowings in the United States and to a lesser extent, bank loans and commercial paper of foreign subsidiaries at competitive market rates, as follows:

(dollars in millions)	**2006**		2005	
	Principal amount	Effective interest rate	Principal amount	Effective interest rate
U.S. commercial paper	**$1,140.7**	**5.3%**	$ 797.3	4.4%
Canadian commercial paper	**87.5**	**4.4%**	260.4	3.4%
Other	**39.8**		53.4	
	$1,268.0		$1,111.1	

Long-term debt at year end consisted primarily of issuances of fixed rate U.S. Dollar and floating rate Euro Notes, as follows:

(millions)	**2006**	2005
(a) 6.6% U.S. Dollar Notes due 2011	**$1,496.2**	$1,495.4
(a) 7.45% U.S. Dollar Debentures due 2031	**1,087.8**	1,087.3
(b) 4.49% U.S. Dollar Notes due 2006	—	75.0
(c) 2.875% U.S. Dollar Notes due 2008	**464.6**	464.6
(d) Guaranteed Floating Rate Euro Notes due 2007	**722.1**	650.6
Other	**5.6**	13.3
	3,776.3	3,786.2
Less current maturities	**(723.3)**	(83.6)
Balance at year-end	**$3,053.0**	$3,702.6

(a) In March 2001, the Company issued $4.6 billion of long-term debt instruments, primarily to finance the acquisition of Keebler Foods Company. The preceding table reflects the remaining principal amounts outstanding as of year-end 2006 and 2005. The effective interest rates on these Notes, reflecting issuance discount and swap settlement, were as follows: due 2011 – 7.08%; due 2031 – 7.62%. Initially, these instruments were privately placed, or sold outside the United States, in reliance on exemptions from registration under the Securities Act of 1933, as amended (the "1933 Act"). The Company then exchanged new debt securities for these initial debt instruments, with the new debt securities being substantially identical in all respects to the initial debt instruments, except for being registered under the 1933 Act. These debt securities contain standard events of default and covenants. The Notes due 2011 and the Debentures due 2031 may be redeemed in whole or in part by the Company at any time at prices determined under a formula (but not less than 100% of the principal amount plus unpaid interest to the redemption date).

(b) In November 2001, a subsidiary of the Company issued $375 million of five-year 4.49% fixed rate U.S. Dollar Notes to replace other maturing debt. These Notes were guaranteed by the Company and matured $75 million per year over the five-year term, with the final principal payment made in November 2006. These Notes, which were privately placed, contained standard warranties, events of default, and covenants. They also required the maintenance of a specified consolidated interest expense coverage ratio, and limited capital lease obligations and subsidiary debt. In conjunction with this issuance, the subsidiary of the Company entered into a $375 million notional US$/Pound Sterling currency swap, which effectively converted this debt into a 5.302% fixed rate Pound Sterling obligation for the duration of the five-year term.

(c) In June 2003, the Company issued $500 million of five-year 2.875% fixed rate U.S. Dollar Notes, using the proceeds from these Notes to replace maturing long-term debt. These Notes were issued under an existing shelf registration statement. The effective interest rate on these Notes, reflecting issuance discount and swap settlement, is 3.35%. The Notes contain customary covenants that limit the ability of the Company and its restricted subsidiaries (as defined) to incur certain liens or enter into certain sale and lease-back transactions. In December 2005, the Company redeemed $35.4 million of these Notes.

(d) In November 2005, a subsidiary of the Company (the "Borrower") issued Euro 550 million of Guaranteed Floating Rate Notes (the "Euro Notes") due May 2007. The Euro Notes were issued and sold in transactions outside the United States in reliance on exemptions from registration under the 1933 Act. The Euro Notes are guaranteed by the Company and bear interest at a rate of 0.12% per annum above three-month EURIBOR for each quarterly interest period. The Euro Notes contain customary covenants that limit the ability of the Company and its restricted subsidiaries (as defined) to incur certain liens or enter into certain sale and lease-back transactions. The Euro Notes were redeemable in whole or in part at par on interest payment dates or upon the occurrence of certain events in 2006 and 2007. In accordance with these terms, on January 31, 2007, the Borrower announced that it had exercised its right to call for early redemption all of the outstanding Euro Notes effective February 28, 2007, at a redemption price equal to the principal amount, plus accrued and unpaid interest through the redemption date.

At December 30, 2006, the Company had $2.2 billion of shortterm lines of credit, virtually all of which were unused and available for borrowing on an unsecured basis. These lines were comprised principally of an unsecured Five-Year Credit Agreement, which the Company entered into during November 2006 to replace an existing facility, which would have expired in 2009. The agreement allows the Company to borrow, on a revolving credit basis, up to $2.0 billion, to obtain letters of credit in an aggregate amount up to $75 million, and to provide a procedure for lenders to bid on short-term debt of the Company. The agreement contains customary covenants and warranties, including specified restrictions on indebtedness, liens, sale and leaseback transactions, and a specified interest coverage ratio. If an event of default occurs, then, to the extent permitted, the administrative agent may terminate the commitments under the credit facility, accelerate any outstanding loans, and demand the deposit of cash collateral equal to the lender's letter of credit exposure plus interest. The facility is available for general corporate purposes, including commercial paper back-up, although the Company does not currently anticipate any usage under the facility.

Scheduled principal repayments on long-term debt are (in millions): 2007–$723.3; 2008–$466.1; 2009–$1.2; 2010 –$1.1; 2011–$1,500.5; 2012 and beyond–$1,100.2.

Interest paid was (in millions): 2006–$299; 2005–$295; 2004–$333. Interest expense capitalized as part of the construction cost of fixed assets was (in millions): 2006–$2.7; 2005–$1.2; 2004–$.9.

Subsequent events

As discussed in preceding subnote (d), on January 31, 2007, a subsidiary of the Company announced an early redemption, effective February 28, 2007, of Euro 550 million of Guaranteed Floating Rate Notes otherwise due May 2007. To partially refinance this redemption, the Company and two of its subsidiaries (the "Issuers") established a program under which the Issuers may issue euro-commercial paper notes up to a maximum aggregate amount outstanding at any time of $750 million or its equivalent in alternative currencies. The notes may have maturities ranging up to 364 days and will be senior unsecured obligations of the applicable Issuer. Notes issued by subsidiary Issuers will be guaranteed by the Company. The notes may be issued at a discount or may bear fixed or floating rate interest or a coupon calculated by reference to an index or formula.

In connection with these financing activities, the Company increased its short-term lines of credit from $2.2 billion at December 30, 2006 to approximately $2.6 billion, via a $400 million unsecured 364-Day Credit Agreement effective January 31, 2007. The 364-Day Agreement contains customary covenants, warranties, and restrictions similar to those described herein for the Five-Year Credit Agreement. The facility is available for general corporate purposes, including commercial paper back-up, although the Company does not currently anticipate any usage under the facility.

Note 8 Stock Compensation

The Company uses various equity-based compensation programs to provide long-term performance incentives for its global workforce. Currently, these incentives consist principally of stock options, and to a lesser extent, executive performance shares and restricted stock grants. The Company also sponsors a discounted stock purchase plan in the United States and matching-grant programs in several international locations. Additionally, the Company awards stock options and restricted stock to its outside directors. These awards are administered through several plans, as described within this Note.

The 2003 Long-Term Incentive Plan ("2003 Plan"), approved by shareholders in 2003, permits benefits to be awarded to employees and officers in the form of incentive and nonqualified stock options, performance units, restricted stock or restricted stock units, and stock appreciation rights. The 2003 Plan authorizes the issuance of a total of (a) 25 million shares plus (b) shares not issued under the 2001 Long-Term Incentive Plan, with no more than 5 million shares to be issued in satisfaction of performance units, performance based restricted shares and other awards (excluding stock options and stock appreciation rights), and with additional annual limitations on awards or payments to individual participants. At December 30, 2006, there were 15.0 million remaining authorized, but unissued, shares under the 2003 Plan. During the periods presented, specific awards and terms of those awards granted under the 2003 Plan are described in the following sections of this Note.

The Non-Employee Director Stock Plan ("Director Plan") was approved by shareholders in 2000 and allows each eligible non-employee director to receive 1,700 shares of the Company's common stock annually and annual grants of options to purchase 5,000 shares of the Company's common stock. At December 30, 2006, there were .4 million remaining authorized, but unissued, shares under this plan. Shares other than options are placed in the Kellogg Company Grantor Trust for Non-Employee Directors (the "Grantor Trust"). Under the terms of the Grantor Trust, shares are available to a director only upon termination of service on the Board. Under this plan, awards were as follows: 2006–50,000 options and 17,000 shares; 2005–55,000 options and 17,000 shares; 2004–55,000 options and 18,700 shares. Options granted to directors under this plan are included in the option activity tables within this Note.

The 2002 Employee Stock Purchase Plan was approved by shareholders in 2002 and permits eligible employees to purchase Company stock at a discounted price. This plan allows for a maximum of 2.5 million shares of Company stock to be issued at a purchase price equal to the lesser of 85% of the fair market value of the stock on the first or last day of the quarterly purchase period. Total purchases through this plan for any employee are limited to a fair market value of $25,000 during any calendar year. At December 30, 2006, there were 1.5 million remaining authorized, but unissued, shares under this plan. Shares were purchased by employees under this plan as follows (approximate number of shares): 2006–237,000; 2005–218,000; 2004–214,000. Options granted to employees to repurchase discounted stock under this plan are included in the option activity tables within this Note.

Additionally, during 2002, a foreign subsidiary of the Company established a stock purchase plan for its employees. Subject to limitations, employee contributions to this plan are matched 1:1 by the Company. Under this plan, shares were granted by the Company to match an approximately equal number of shares purchased by employees as follows (approximate number of shares): 2006–80,000; 2005–80,000; 2004–82,000.

The Executive Stock Purchase Plan was established in 2002 to encourage and enable certain eligible employees of the Company to acquire Company stock, and to align more closely the interests of those individuals and the Company's shareholders. This plan allows for a maximum of 500,000 shares of Company stock to be issued. At December 30, 2006, there were .5 million remaining authorized, but unissued, shares under this plan. Under this plan, shares were granted by the Company to executives in lieu of cash bonuses as follows (approximate number of shares): 2006–4,000; 2005–2,000; 2004–8,000.

For 2006, the Company used the fair value method prescribed by SFAS No. 123(R) "Share-Based Payment" to account for its equity-based compensation programs. Prior to 2006, the Company used the intrinsic value method prescribed by Accounting Principles Board Opinion (APB) No. 25 "Accounting for Stock Issued to Employees." Refer to Note 1 for further information on the Company's accounting policy for stock compensation.

For the year ended December 30, 2006, compensation expense for all types of equity-based programs and the related income tax benefit recognized was $95.7 million and $34.0 million, respectively. As a result of adopting SFAS No. 123(R) in 2006, the Company's reported pre-tax stock-based compensation expense for the year was $65.4 million higher (with net earnings and net earnings per share (basic and diluted) correspondingly lower by $42.4 million and $.11, respectively) than if it had continued to account for its equity-based programs under APB No. 25. Amounts for the prior years are presented in the following table in accordance with SFAS No. 123 "Accounting for Stock-Based Compensation" and related interpretations. Reported amounts consist principally of expense recognized for executive performance share and restricted stock awards; pro forma amounts are attributable primarily to stock option grants.

(millions, except per share data)	2005	2004
Stock-based compensation expense, pre-tax:		
As reported	$ 18.5	$ 17.5
Pro forma	$ 76.4	$ 64.1
Associated income tax benefit recognized:		
As reported	$ 6.7	$ 6.1
Pro forma	$ 27.7	$ 22.3
Stock-based compensation expense, net of tax:		
As reported	$ 11.8	$ 11.4
Pro forma	$ 48.7	$ 41.8
Net earnings:		
As reported	$980.4	$890.6
Pro forma	$943.5	$860.2
Basic net earnings per share:		
As reported	$ 2.38	$ 2.16
Pro forma	$ 2.29	$ 2.09
Diluted net earnings per share:		
As reported	$ 2.36	$ 2.14
Pro forma	$ 2.27	$ 2.07

As of December 30, 2006, total stock-based compensation cost related to nonvested awards not yet recognized was approximately $36 million and the weighted-average period over which this amount is expected to be recognized was approximately 1.4 years.

Cash flows realized upon exercise or vesting of stock-based awards in the periods presented are included in the following table. Within this table, the 2006 windfall tax benefit (amount realized in excess of that previously recognized in earnings) of $21.5 million represents the operating cash flow reduction (and financing cash flow increase) related to the Company's adoption of SFAS No. 123(R) in 2006. (Refer to Note 1 for further information on the Company's accounting policies regarding tax benefit windfalls and shortfalls.) Cash used by the Company to settle equity instruments granted under stock-based awards was insignificant.

(millions)	**2006**	2005	2004
Total cash received from option exercises and similar instruments	**$217.5**	$221.7	$291.8
Tax benefits realized upon exercise or vesting of stock-based awards:			
Windfall benefits classified as financing cash flow	**$ 21.5**	n/a	n/a
Other amounts classified as operating cash flow	**23.4**	40.3	38.6
Total	**$ 44.9**	$ 40.3	$ 38.6

Shares used to satisfy stock-based awards are normally issued out of treasury stock, although management is authorized to issue new shares to the extent permitted by respective plan provisions. Refer to Note 5 for information on shares issued during the periods presented to employees and directors under various long-term incentive plans and share repurchases under the Company's stock repurchase authorizations. The Company does not currently have a policy of repurchasing a specified number of shares issued under employee benefit programs during any particular time period.

Stock Options

During the periods presented, non-qualified stock options were granted to eligible employees under the 2003 Plan with exercise prices equal to the fair market value of the Company's stock on the grant date, a contractual term of ten years, and a two-year graded vesting period. Grants to outside directors under the Non-Employee Director Stock Plan included similar terms, but vested immediately. Additionally, "reload" options were awarded to eligible employees and directors to replace previously-owned Company stock used by those individuals to pay the exercise price, including related employment taxes, of vested pre-2004 option awards containing this accelerated ownership feature. These reload options are immediately vested, with an expiration date which is the same as the original option grant.

Management estimates the fair value of each annual stock option award on the date of grant using a lattice-based option valuation model. Due to the already-vested status and short expected term of reload options, management uses a Black-Scholes model to value such awards. Composite assumptions, which are not materially different for each of the two models, are presented in the following table. Weighted-average values are disclosed for certain inputs which incorporate a range of assumptions. Expected volatilities are based principally on historical volatility of the Company's stock, and to a lesser extent, on implied volatilities from traded options on the Company's stock. For the lattice-based model, historical volatility corresponds to the contractual term of the options granted; whereas, for the Black-Scholes model, historical volatility corresponds to the expected term. The Company generally uses historical data to estimate option exercise and employee termination within the valuation models; separate groups of employees that have similar historical exercise behavior are considered separately for valuation purposes. The expected term of options granted (which is an input to the Black-Scholes model and an output from the lattice-based model) represents the period of time that options granted are expected to be outstanding; the weighted-average expected term for all employee groups is presented in the following table. The risk-free rate for periods within the contractual life of the options is based on the U.S. Treasury yield curve in effect at the time of grant.

Stock option valuation model assumptions for grants within the year ended:	**2006**	**2005**	**2004**
Weighted-average expected volatility	**17.94%**	22.00%	23.00%
Weighted-average expected term (years)	**3.21**	3.42	3.69
Weighted-average risk-free interest rate	**4.65%**	3.81%	2.73%
Dividend yield	**2.40%**	2.40%	2.60%
Weighed-average fair value of options granted	**$ 6.67**	$ 7.35	$ 6.39

A summary of option activity for the year ended December 30, 2006, is presented in the following table:

Employee and director stock options	Shares (millions)	Weighted-average exercise price	Weighted-average remaining contractual term (yrs.)	Aggregate intrinsic value (millions)
Outstanding, beginning of year	28.8	$38		
Granted	9.6	46		
Exercised	(10.9)	37		
Forfeitures	(.3)	43		
Expirations	(.2)	43		
Outstanding, end of year	27.0	$41	6.1	$243.0
Exercisable, end of year	19.9	$40	5.1	$199.0

Additionally, option activity for comparable prior-year periods is presented in the following table:

(millions, except per share data)	2005	2004
Outstanding, beginning of year	32.5	37.0
Granted	8.3	9.7
Exercised	(10.9)	(12.9)
Forfeitures and expirations	(1.1)	(1.3)
Outstanding, end of year	28.8	32.5
Exercisable, end of year	21.3	22.8
Weighted-average exercise price:		
Outstanding, beginning of year	$ 35	$ 33
Granted	44	40
Exercised	34	32
Forfeitures and expirations	41	41
Outstanding, end of year	$ 38	$ 35
Exercisable, end of year	$ 37	$ 35

The total intrinsic value of options exercised during the periods presented was (in millions): 2006–$114; 2005–$116; 2004–$119.

Other stock-based awards During the periods presented, other stock-based awards consisted principally of executive performance shares and restricted stock granted under the 2003 Plan.

In 2005 and 2006, the Company granted performance shares to a limited number of senior executive-level employees, which entitled these employees to receive a specified number of shares of the Company's common stock on the vesting date, provided cumulative three-year net sales growth targets were achieved. Subsequent to the adoption of SFAS No. 123(R), management has estimated the fair value of performance share awards based on the market price of the underlying stock on the date of grant, reduced by the present value of estimated dividends foregone during the performance period. The 2005 and 2006 target grants (as revised for non-vested forfeitures and other adjustments) currently correspond to approximately 275,000 and 260,000 shares, respectively; each with a grant-date fair value of approximately $41 per share. The actual number of shares issued on the vesting date could range from zero to 200% of target, depending on actual performance achieved. Based on the market price of the Company's common stock at year-end 2006, the maximum future value that could be awarded on the vesting date is (in millions): 2005 award–$27.5; 2006 award–$25.8. In addition to these performance share plans, a 2003 performance unit plan (payable in stock or cash under certain conditions) was settled at 74% of target in February 2006 for a total dollar equivalent of $2.9 million. The Company also periodically grants restricted stock and restricted stock units to eligible employees under the 2003 Plan. Restrictions with respect to sale or transferability generally lapse after three years and the grantee is normally entitled to receive shareholder dividends during the vesting period. Management estimates the fair value of restricted stock grants based on the market price of the underlying stock on the date of grant. A summary of restricted stock activity for the year ended December 30, 2006, is presented in the following table:

Employee restricted stock and restricted stock units	Shares (thousands)	Weighted-average grant-date fair value
Non-vested, beginning of year	447	$39
Granted	190	47
Vested	(176)	34
Forfeited	(27)	43
Non-vested, end of year	434	$45

Grants of restricted stock and restricted stock units for comparable prior-year periods were: 2005–141,000; 2004–140,000.

The total fair value of restricted stock and restricted stock units vesting in the periods presented was (in millions): 2006–$8; 2005–$4; 2004–$4.

Note 9 Pension Benefits

The Company sponsors a number of U.S. and foreign pension plans to provide retirement benefits for its employees. The majority of these plans are funded or unfunded defined benefit plans, although the Company does participate in a few multiemployer or other defined contribution plans for certain employee groups. Defined benefits for salaried employees are generally based on salary and years of service, while union employee benefits are generally a negotiated amount for each year of service. The Company uses its fiscal year end as the measurement date for its defined benefit plans.

Obligations and funded status

The aggregate change in projected benefit obligation, plan assets, and funded status is presented in the following tables. The Company adopted SFAS No. 158 "Employers'

Accounting for Defined Benefit Pension and Other Postretirement Plans" as of the end of its 2006 fiscal year. The impact of the adoption is discussed in Note 1. The standard generally requires company plan sponsors to reflect the net over- or under-funded position of a defined postretirement benefit plan as an asset or liability on the balance sheet.

(millions)	2006	2005
Change in projected benefit obligation		
Beginning of year	**$3,145.1**	$2,972.9
Service cost	**94.2**	80.2
Interest cost	**172.0**	160.1
Plan participants' contributions	**1.7**	2.5
Amendments	**24.2**	42.2
Actuarial loss (gain)	**(96.7)**	114.3
Benefits paid	**(160.4)**	(144.0)
Curtailment and special termination benefits	**15.3**	1.3
Foreign currency adjustments and other	**113.9**	(84.4)
End of year	**$3,309.3**	$3,145.1
Change in plan assets		
Fair value beginning of year	**$2,922.6**	$2,685.9
Actual return on plan assets	**448.4**	277.9
Employer contributions	**85.7**	156.4
Plan participants' contributions	**1.7**	2.5
Benefits paid	**(149.6)**	(132.3)
Foreign currency adjustments and other	**117.7**	(67.8)
Fair value end of year	**$3,426.5**	$2,922.6
Funded status at year end	**$ 117.2**	$ (222.5)
Unrecognized net loss	—	826.3
Unrecognized transition amount	—	1.9
Unrecognized prior service cost	—	100.1
Net balance sheet position	**$ 117.2**	$ 705.8
Amounts recognized in the Consolidated Balance Sheet consist of		
Prepaid benefit cost		$ 683.3
Accrued benefit liability		(185.8)
Intangible asset		17.0
Other comprehensive income — minimum pension liability		191.3
Noncurrent assets	**$ 352.6**	
Current liabilities	**(9.6)**	
Noncurrent liabilities	**(225.8)**	
Net amount recognized	**$ 117.2**	$ 705.8
Amounts recognized in accumulated other comprehensive income consist of		
Net experience loss	**$ 502.7**	
Prior service cost	**115.5**	
Net amount recognized	**$ 618.2**	$191.3

The accumulated benefit obligation for all defined benefit pension plans was $2.99 billion and $2.87 billion at December 30, 2006 and December 31, 2005, respectively. Information for pension plans with accumulated benefit obligations in excess of plan assets were:

(millions)	2006	2005
Projected benefit obligation	**$253.4**	$1,621.4
Accumulated benefit obligation	**202.5**	1,473.7
Fair value of plan assets	**55.5**	1,289.1

The significant decrease in accumulated benefit obligations in excess of plan assets for 2006 is due primarily to favorable asset returns in a major U.S. pension plan.

Expense

The components of pension expense are presented in the following table. Pension expense for defined contribution plans relates principally to multiemployer plans in which the Company participates on behalf of certain unionized workforces in the United States. The amounts for 2006 and 2005 include charges of approximately $4 million and $16 million, respectively, for the Company's current estimate of a multiemployer plan withdrawal liability, which is further described in Note 3.

(millions)	2006	2005	2004
Service cost	**$ 94.2**	$ 80.2	$ 76.0
Interest cost	**172.0**	160.1	157.3
Expected return on plan assets	**(256.7)**	(229.0)	(238.1)
Amortization of unrecognized transition obligation	—	.3	.2
Amortization of unrecognized prior service cost	**12.4**	10.0	8.2
Recognized net loss	**79.8**	64.5	54.1
Curtailment and special termination benefits — net loss	**16.7**	1.6	12.2

Pension expense:			
Defined benefit plans	**118.4**	87.7	69.9
Defined contribution plans	**18.7**	31.9	14.4
Total	**$137.1**	$119.6	$84.3

Any arising obligation-related experience gain or loss is amortized using a straight-line method over the average remaining service period of active plan participants. Any asset-related experience gain or loss is recognized as described on page 46. The estimated net experience loss and prior service cost for defined benefit pension plans that will be amortized from accumulated other comprehensive income into pension expense over the next fiscal year are approximately $61 million and $13 million, respectively.

Net losses from curtailment and special termination benefits recognized in 2006 are related primarily to plant workforce reductions in the United States and England, as further described in Note 3. Net losses from curtailment and special termination benefits recognized in 2004 are related primarily to special termination benefits granted to the Company's former CEO and other former executive officers pursuant to separation agreements, and to a lesser extent, liquidation of the Company's pension fund in South Africa and plant workforce reductions in Great Britain.

Certain of the Company's subsidiaries sponsor 401(k) or similar savings plans for active employees. Expense relatedto these plans was (in millions): 2006–$33; 2005–$30; 2004–$26. Company contributions to these savings plans approximate annual expense. Company contributions to multiemployer and other defined contribution pension plans approximate the amount of annual expense presented in the preceding table.

Assumptions

The worldwide weighted-average actuarial assumptions used to determine benefit obligations were:

	2006	2005	2004
Discount rate	**5.7%**	5.4%	5.7%
Long-term rate of compensation increase	**4.4%**	4.4%	4.3%

The worldwide weighted-average actuarial assumptions used to determine annual net periodic benefit cost were:

	2006	2005	2004
Discount rate	**5.4%**	5.7%	5.9%
Long-term rate of compensation increase	**4.4%**	4.3%	4.3%
Long-term rate of return on plan assets	**8.9%**	8.9%	9.3%

To determine the overall expected long-term rate of return on plan assets, the Company works with third party financial consultants to model expected returns over a 20-year investment horizon with respect to the specific investment mix of its major plans. The return assumptions used reflect a combination of rigorous historical performance analysis and forward-looking views of the financial markets including consideration of current yields on long-term bonds, priceearnings ratios of the major stock market indices, and long-term inflation. The U.S. model, which corresponds to approximately 70% of consolidated pension and other postretirement benefit plan assets, incorporates a longterm inflation assumption of 2.8% and an active management premium of 1% (net of fees) validated by historical analysis. Similar methods are used for various foreign plans with invested assets, reflecting local economic conditions. Although management reviews the Company's expected long-term rates of return annually, the benefit trust investment performance for one particular year does not, by itself, significantly influence this evaluation. The expected rates of return are generally not revised, provided these rates continue to fall within a "more likely than not" corridor of between the 25th and 75th percentile of expected long-term returns, as determined by the Company's modeling process. The expected rate of return for 2006 of 8.9% equated to approximately the 50th percentile expectation. Any future variance between the expected and actual rates of return on plan assets is recognized in the calculated value of plan assets over a five-year period and once recognized, experience gains and losses are amortized using a declining-balance method over the average remaining service period of active plan participants.

Plan assets

The Company's year-end pension plan weighted-average asset allocations by asset category were:

	2006	2005
Equity securities	**76%**	73%
Debt securities	**21%**	24%
Other	**3%**	3%
Total	**100%**	100%

The Company's investment strategy for its major defined benefit plans is to maintain a diversified portfolio of asset classes with the primary goal of meeting long-term cash requirements as they become due. Assets are invested in a prudent manner to maintain the security of funds while maximizing returns within the Company's guidelines. The current weighted-average target asset allocation reflected by this strategy is: equity securities–74%; debt securities–24%; other–2%. Investment in Company common stock represented 1.5% of consolidated plan assets at December 30, 2006 and December 31, 2005. Plan funding strategies are influenced by tax regulations. The Company currently expects to contribute approximately $39 million to its defined benefit pension plans during 2007.

Benefit payments

The following benefit payments, which reflect expected future service, as appropriate, are expected to be paid (in millions): 2007–$169; 2008–$174; 2009–$184; 2010–$189; 2011–$191; 2012 to 2016–$1,075.

Note 10 Nonpension Postretirement and Postemployment Benefits

Postretirement

The Company sponsors a number of plans to provide health care and other welfare benefits to retired employees in the United States and Canada, who have met certain age and service requirements. The majority of these plans are funded or unfunded defined benefit plans, although the Company does participate in a few multiemployer or other defined contribution plans for certain employee groups. The Company contributes to voluntary employee benefit association (VEBA) trusts to fund certain U.S. retiree health and welfare benefit obligations. The Company uses its fiscal year end as the measurement date for these plans.

Obligations and funded status

The aggregate change in accumulated postretirement benefit obligation, plan assets, and funded status is presented in the following tables. The Company adopted SFAS No. 158 "Employers' Accounting for Defined Benefit Pension and Other Postretirement Plans" as of the end of its 2006 fiscal year. The impact of the adoption is discussed in Note 1. The standard generally requires company plan sponsors to reflect the net over- or under-funded position of a defined postretirement benefit plan as an asset or liability on the balance sheet.

(millions)	**2006**	**2005**
Change in accumulated benefit obligation		
Beginning of year	**$1,224.9**	$1,046.7
Service cost	**17.4**	14.5
Interest cost	**65.8**	58.3
Actuarial loss (gain)	**(54.4)**	164.6
Amendments	**3.6**	—
Benefits paid	**(56.0)**	(60.4)
Curtailment and special termination benefits	**6.2**	—
Foreign currency adjustments	**.1**	1.2
End of year	**$1,207.6**	$1,224.9
Change in plan assets		
Fair value beginning of year	**$ 682.7**	$ 468.4
Actual return on plan assets	**123.6**	32.5
Employer contributions	**13.6**	240.9
Benefits paid	**(56.0)**	(59.1)
Fair value end of year	**$ 763.9**	$ 682.7
Funded status	**$(443.7)**	$(542.2)
Unrecognized net loss	—	446.0
Unrecognized prior service cost	—	(26.3)
Accrued postretirement benefit cost	**$(443.7)**	$(122.5)
Amounts recognized in the Consolidated Balance Sheet consist of		
Current liabilities	**$ (1.4)**	
Noncurrent liabilities	**(442.3)**	
Total liabilities	**$(443.7)**	$(122.5)
Amounts recognized in accumulated other comprehensive income consist of		
Net experience loss	**$ 294.8**	$ —
Prior service credit	**(19.2)**	—
Net amount recognized	**$ 275.6**	$ —

Expense

Components of postretirement benefit expense were:

(millions)	**2006**	**2005**	**2004**
Service cost	**$ 17.4**	$ 14.5	$ 12.1
Interest cost	**65.8**	58.3	55.6
Expected return on plan assets	**(58.2)**	(42.1)	(39.8)
Amortization of unrecognized prior service credit	**(2.6)**	(2.9)	(2.9)
Recognized net loss	**30.6**	19.8	14.8
Curtailment and special termination benefits — net loss	**6.2**	—	—
Postretirement benefit expense:			
Defined benefit plans	**59.2**	47.6	39.8
Defined contribution plans	**1.9**	1.3	1.8
Total	**$ 61.1**	$ 48.9	$ 41.6

Any arising health care claims cost-related experience gain or loss is recognized in the calculated amount of claims experience over a four-year period and once recognized, is amortized using a straight-line method over 15 years, resulting in at least the minimum amortization prescribed by SFAS No. 106. Any asset-related experience gain or loss is recognized as described for pension plans on page 46. The estimated net experience loss for defined benefit plans that will be amortized from accumulated other comprehensive income into nonpension postretirement benefit expense over the next fiscal year is approximately $24 million, partially offset by amortization of prior service credit of $3 million.

Net losses from curtailment and special termination benefits recognized in 2006 are related primarily to plant workforce reductions in the United States as further described in Note 3.

Assumptions

The weighted-average actuarial assumptions used to determine benefit obligations were:

	2006	2005	2004
Discount rate	**5.9%**	5.5%	5.8%

The weighted-average actuarial assumptions used to determine annual net periodic benefit cost were:

	2006	2005	2004
Discount rate	**5.5%**	5.8%	6.0%
Long-term rate of return on plan assets	**8.9%**	8.9%	9.3%

The Company determines the overall expected long-term rate of return on VEBA trust assets in the same manner as that described for pension trusts in Note 9.

The assumed health care cost trend rate is 9.5% for 2007, decreasing gradually to 4.75% by the year 2012 and remaining at that level thereafter. These trend rates reflect the Company's recent historical experience and management's expectations regarding future trends. A one percentage point change in assumed health care cost trend rates would have the following effects:

(millions)	One percentage point increase	One percentage point decrease
Effect on total of service and interest cost components	$ 9.2	$ (10.5)
Effect on postretirement benefit obligation	$127.8	$(125.4)

Plan assets

The Company's year-end VEBA trust weighted-average asset allocations by asset category were:

	2006	2005
Equity securities	**77%**	78%
Debt securities	**22%**	22%
Other	**1%**	—
Total	**100%**	100%

The Company's asset investment strategy for its VEBA trusts is consistent with that described for its pension trusts in Note 9. The current target asset allocation is 75% equity securities and 25% debt securities. The Company currently expects to contribute approximately $15 million to its VEBA trusts during 2007.

Postemployment

Under certain conditions, the Company provides benefits to former or inactive employees in the United States and several foreign locations, including salary continuance, severance, and long-term disability. The Company recognizes an obligation for any of these benefits that vest or accumulate with service. Postemployment benefits that do not vest or accumulate with service (such as severance based solely on annual pay rather than years of service) or costs arising from actions that offer benefits to employees in excess of those specified in the respective plans are charged to expense when incurred. The Company's postemployment benefit plans are unfunded. Actuarial assumptions used are generally consistent with those presented for pension benefits on page 46. The Company previously applied postretirement accounting concepts for purposes of recognizing its postemployment benefit obligations. Accordingly, the Company's adoption of SFAS No. 158 "Employers' Accounting for Defined Benefit Pension and Other Postretirement Plans" as of the end of its 2006 fiscal year impacted its presentation of postemployment benefits as discussed in Note 1. The aggregate change in accumulated postemployment benefit obligation and the net amount recognized were:

(millions)	2006	2005
Change in accumulated benefit obligation		
Beginning of year	**$42.2**	$37.9
Service cost	**4.3**	4.5
Interest cost	**2.0**	2.0
Actuarial loss (gain)	**(.8)**	7.4
Benefits paid	**(8.6)**	(9.0)
Foreign currency adjustments	**.4**	(.6)
End of year	**$39.5**	$42.2

Funded status	**$(39.5)**	$(42.2)
Unrecognized net loss	**—**	19.1
Accrued postemployment benefit cost	**$(39.5)**	$(23.1)
Amounts recognized in the Consolidated Balance Sheet consist of		
Current liabilities	**$ (7.8)**	
Noncurrent liabilities	**(31.7)**	
Total liabilities	**$(39.5)**	$(23.1)
Amounts recognized in accumulated other comprehensive income consist of		
Net experience loss	**$ 16.0**	$ —
Net amount recognized	**$ 16.0**	$ —

Components of postemployment benefit expense were:

(millions)	**2006**	2005	2004
Service cost	**$4.3**	$ 4.5	$3.5
Interest cost	**2.0**	2.0	1.9
Recognized net loss	**2.4**	3.5	4.5
Postemployment benefit expense	**$8.7**	$10.0	$9.9

All gains and losses are recognized over the average remaining service period of active plan participants. The estimated net experience loss that will be amortized from accumulated other comprehensive income into postemployment benefit expense over the next fiscal year is approximately $2 million.

Benefit payments

The following benefit payments, which reflect expected future service, as appropriate, are expected to be paid:

(millions)	Postretirement	Postemployment
2007	$ 64.0	$ 8.0
2008	67.7	7.3
2009	71.2	7.0
2010	73.9	7.3
2011	76.5	7.7
2012–2016	397.5	44.4

Note 11 Income Taxes

Earnings before income taxes and the provision for U.S. federal, state, and foreign taxes on these earnings were:

(millions)	**2006**	2005	2004
Earnings before income taxes			
United States	**$1,048.3**	$ 971.4	$ 952.0
Foreign	**423.3**	453.7	413.9
	$1,471.6	$1,425.1	$1,365.9
Income taxes			
Currently payable			
Federal	**$ 342.0**	$ 376.8	$ 249.8
State	**34.1**	26.4	30.0
Foreign	**134.1**	100.7	137.8
	510.2	503.9	417.6
Deferred			
Federal	**(9.6)**	(69.6)	51.5
State	**(4.4)**	.6	5.3
Foreign	**(29.7)**	9.8	.9
	(43.7)	(59.2)	57.7
Total income taxes	**$ 466.5**	$ 444.7	$ 475.3

The difference between the U.S. federal statutory tax rate and the Company's effective income tax rate was:

	2006	2005	2004
U.S. statutory income tax rate	**35.0%**	35.0%	35.0%
Foreign rates varying from 35%	**−3.5**	−3.8	−.5
State income taxes, net of federal benefit	**1.3**	1.2	1.7
Foreign earnings repatriation	**1.2**	—	2.1
Tax audit settlements	**−1.7**	—	—
Net change in valuation allowances	**.5**	−.2	−1.5
Statutory rate changes, deferred tax impact	**—**	—	.1
Other	**−1.1**	−1.0	−2.1
Effective income tax rate	**31.7%**	31.2%	34.8%

As presented in the preceding table, the Company's 2006 consolidated provision for income taxes included two significant, but partially-offsetting, discrete adjustments. First, during the second quarter, the Company revised its repatriation plan for certain foreign earnings, giving rise to an incremental net tax cost of $18 million. Also in the second quarter, the Company reduced its reserves for uncertain tax positions by $25 million, related principally to closure of several domestic tax audits.

The consolidated effective income tax rate for 2004 of nearly 35% was higher than the rates for 2006 and 2005 primarily because this period preceded the final reorganization of the Company's European operations which favorably affected the country-weighting impact on the rate. (Refer to Note 3 for further information on this initiative.) Additionally, the 2004 consolidated effective income tax rate included a provision of approximately $40 million, partially offset by related foreign tax credits of approximately $12 million, for approximately $1.1 billion of dividends from foreign subsidiaries which the Company elected to repatriate in 2005 under the American Jobs Creation Act. Finally, 2005 was the first year in which the Company was permitted to claim a phased-in deduction from U.S. taxable income equal to a stipulated percentage of qualified production income ("QPI").

Generally, the changes in valuation allowances on deferred tax assets and corresponding impacts on the effective income tax rate result from management's assessment of the Company's ability to utilize certain operating loss and tax credit carryforwards prior to expiration. For 2004, the 1.5 percent rate reduction presented in the preceding table primarily reflects reversal of a valuation allowance against U.S. foreign tax credits, which were utilized in conjunction with the aforementioned 2005 foreign earnings repatriation. Total tax benefits of carryforwards at year-end 2006 and 2005 were approximately $29 million and $23 million, respectively. Of the total carryforwards at year-end 2006, less than $2 million expire in 2007 with the remainder principally expiring after five years. After valuation allowance, the carrying value of carryforward tax benefits at year-end 2006 was only $1 million.

The deferred tax assets and liabilities included in the balance sheet at year end are presented in a table on page 50. The Company adopted SFAS No. 158 "Employers' Accounting for Defined Benefit Pension and Other Postretirement Plans" as of the end of its 2006 fiscal year. The standard generally requires company plan sponsors to reflect the net over- or under-funded position of a defined postretirement benefit plan as an asset or liability on the balance sheet. Any unrecognized prior service cost, experience gains/losses, or transition obligation are reported as a component of other comprehensive income, net of tax, in shareholders' equity. As a result of adopting this standard, the employee benefits component of the Company's deferred tax assets increased (or liabilities decreased) by a total of $298.9 million at December 30, 2006. Refer to Note 1 for further information.

	Deferred tax assets		Deferred tax liabilities	
(millions)	**2006**	2005	**2006**	2005
Current:				
U.S. state income taxes	**$ 7.6**	$ 12.1	**$ —**	$ —
Advertising and promotion-related	**19.7**	19.4	**11.0**	8.8
Wages and payroll taxes	**26.3**	28.8	**—**	—
Inventory valuation	**22.5**	25.5	**4.6**	6.3
Employee benefits	**18.0**	32.0	**—**	—
Operating loss and credit carryforwards	**13.9**	7.0	**—**	—
Hedging transactions	**19.2**	17.5	**.8**	.1
Depreciation and asset disposals	**.1**	.1	**—**	—
Deferred intercompany revenue	**6.1**	76.3	**—**	—
Other	**26.4**	22.6	**15.2**	22.8
	159.8	241.3	**31.6**	38.0
Less valuation allowance	**(15.2)**	(3.2)	**—**	—
	$144.6	$238.1	**$31.6**	$38.0
Noncurrent:				
U.S. state income taxes	**$ —**	$ —	**$ 47.0**	$ 54.4
Employee benefits	**217.4**	20.4	**53.2**	129.7
Operating loss and credit carryforwards	**15.2**	15.5	**—**	—
Hedging transactions	**2.0**	1.7	**—**	—
Depreciation and asset disposals	**15.1**	12.7	**306.5**	340.8
Capitalized interest	**5.3**	5.1	**11.9**	12.7
Trademarks and other intangibles	**.1**	.1	**473.9**	472.4
Deferred compensation	**40.6**	34.9	**—**	—
Stock options	**22.4**	—	**—**	—
Other	**12.0**	15.3	**6.3**	2.1
	330.1	105.7	**898.8**	1,012.1
Less valuation allowance	**(13.0)**	(16.2)	**—**	—
	317.1	89.5	**898.8**	1,012.1
Total deferred taxes	**$461.7**	$327.6	**$930.4**	$1,050.1

The change in valuation allowance against deferred tax assets was:

(millions)	**2006**	2005	2004
Balance at beginning of year	**$19.4**	$22.3	$ 36.8
Additions charged to income tax expense	**11.4**	.2	13.3
Reductions credited to income tax expense	**(3.6)**	(3.2)	(28.9)
Currency translation adjustments	**1.0**	.1	1.1
Balance at end of year	**$28.2**	$19.4	$ 22.3

At December 30, 2006, accumulated foreign subsidiary earnings of approximately $1.1 billion were considered permanently invested in those businesses. Accordingly, U.S. income taxes have not been provided on these earnings.

Cash paid for income taxes was (in millions): 2006–$428; 2005–$425; 2004–$421. Income tax benefits realized from stock option exercises and deductibility of other equity-based awards are presented in Note 8.

Note 12 Financial Instruments and Credit Risk Concentration

The fair values of the Company's financial instruments are based on carrying value in the case of short-term items, quoted market prices for derivatives and investments, and in the case of long-term debt, incremental borrowing rates currently available on loans with similar terms and maturities. The carrying amounts of the Company's cash, cash equivalents, receivables, and notes payable approximate fair value. The fair value of the Company's long-term debt at December 30, 2006, exceeded its carrying value by approximately $275 million.

The Company is exposed to certain market risks which exist as a part of its ongoing business operations. Management uses derivative financial and commodity instruments, where appropriate, to manage these risks. In general, instruments used as hedges must be effective at reducing the risk associated with the exposure being hedged and must be designated as a hedge at the inception of the contract. In accordance with SFAS No. 133, the Company designates derivatives as either cash flow hedges, fair value hedges, net investment hedges, or other contracts used to reduce volatility in the translation of foreign currency earnings to U.S. Dollars. The fair values of all hedges are recorded in accounts receivable or other current liabilities. Gains and losses representing either hedge ineffectiveness, hedge components excluded from the assessment of effectiveness, or hedges of translational exposure are recorded in other income (expense), net. Within the Consolidated Statement of Cash Flows, settlements of cash flow and fair value hedges are classified as an operating activity; settlements of all other derivatives are classified as a financing activity.

Cash flow hedges

Qualifying derivatives are accounted for as cash flow hedges when the hedged item is a forecasted transaction. Gains and losses on these instruments are recorded in other comprehensive income until the underlying transaction is recorded in earnings. When the hedged item is realized, gains or losses are reclassified from accumulated other comprehensive income to the Consolidated Statement of Earnings on the same line item as the underlying transaction. For all cash flow hedges, gains and losses representing either hedge ineffectiveness or hedge components excluded from the assessment of effectiveness were insignificant during the periods presented.

The total net loss attributable to cash flow hedges recorded in accumulated other comprehensive income at December 30, 2006, was $32.6 million, related primarily to forward interest rate contracts settled during 2001 and 2003 in conjunction with fixed rate long-term debt issuances and to a lesser extent, to 10-year natural gas price swaps entered into in 2006. The interest rate contract losses will be reclassified into interest expense over the next 25 years. The natural gas swap losses will be reclassified to cost of goods sold over 10 years. Other insignificant amounts related to foreign currency and commodity price cash flow hedges will be reclassified into earnings during the next 18 months.

Fair value hedges

Qualifying derivatives are accounted for as fair value hedges when the hedged item is a recognized asset, liability, or firm commitment. Gains and losses on these instruments are recorded in earnings, offsetting gains and losses on the hedged item. For all fair value hedges, gains and losses representing either hedge ineffectiveness or hedge components excluded from the assessment of effectiveness were insignificant during the periods presented.

Net investment hedges

Qualifying derivative and nonderivative financial instruments are accounted for as net investment hedges when the hedged item is a nonfunctional currency investment in a subsidiary. Gains and losses on these instruments are recorded as a foreign currency translation adjustment in other comprehensive income.

Other contracts

The Company also periodically enters into foreign currency forward contracts and options to reduce volatility in the translation of foreign currency earnings to U.S. Dollars.

Gains and losses on these instruments are recorded in other income (expense), net, generally reducing the exposure to translation volatility during a full-year period.

Foreign exchange risk

The Company is exposed to fluctuations in foreign currency cash flows related primarily to third-party purchases, intercompany transactions, and nonfunctional currency denominated third-party debt. The Company is also exposed to fluctuations in the value of foreign currency investments in subsidiaries and cash flows related to repatriation of these investments. Additionally, the Company is exposed to volatility in the translation of foreign currency earnings to U.S. Dollars. Management assesses foreign currency risk based on transactional cash flows and translational volatility and enters into forward contracts, options, and currency swaps to reduce fluctuations in net long or short currency positions. Forward contracts and options are generally less than 18 months duration. Currency swap agreements are established in conjunction with the term of underlying debt issues.

For foreign currency cash flow and fair value hedges, the assessment of effectiveness is generally based on changes in spot rates. Changes in time value are reported in other income (expense), net.

Interest rate risk

The Company is exposed to interest rate volatility with regard to future issuances of fixed rate debt and existing issuances of variable rate debt. The Company periodically uses interest rate swaps, including forward-starting swaps, to reduce interest rate volatility and funding costs associated with certain debt issues, and to achieve a desired proportion of variable versus fixed rate debt, based on current and projected market conditions.

Variable-to-fixed interest rate swaps are accounted for as cash flow hedges and the assessment of effectiveness is based on changes in the present value of interest payments on the underlying debt. Fixed-to-variable interest rate swaps are accounted for as fair value hedges and the assessment of effectiveness is based on changes in the fair value of the underlying debt, using incremental borrowing rates currently available on loans with similar terms and maturities.

Price risk

The Company is exposed to price fluctuations primarily as a result of anticipated purchases of raw and packaging materials, fuel, and energy. The Company has historically used the combination of long-term contracts with suppliers, and exchange-traded futures and option contracts to reduce price fluctuations in a desired percentage of forecasted raw material purchases over a duration of generally less than 18 months. During 2006, the Company entered into two separate 10-year over-the-counter commodity swap transactions to reduce fluctuations in the price of natural gas used principally in its manufacturing processes.

Commodity contracts are accounted for as cash flow hedges. The assessment of effectiveness for exchange-traded instruments is based on changes in futures prices. The assessment of effectiveness for over-the-counter transactions is based on changes in designated indexes.

Credit risk concentration

The Company is exposed to credit loss in the event of nonperformance by counterparties on derivative financial and commodity contracts. This credit loss is limited to the cost of replacing these contracts at current market rates. Management believes the probability of such loss is remote.

Financial instruments, which potentially subject the Company to concentrations of credit risk are primarily cash, cash equivalents, and accounts receivable. The Company places its investments in highly rated financial institutions and investment-grade short-term debt instruments, and limits the amount of credit exposure to any one entity. Management believes concentrations of credit risk with respect to accounts receivable is limited due to the generally high credit quality of the Company's major customers, as well as the large number and geographic dispersion of smaller customers. However, the Company conducts a disproportionate amount of business with a small number of large multinational grocery retailers, with the five largest accounts comprising approximately 27% of consolidated accounts receivable at December 30, 2006.

Note 13 Quarterly Financial Data (Unaudited)

	Net sales		*Gross profit*	
(millions, except per share data)	**2006**	2005	**2006**	2005
First	**$ 2,726.5**	$ 2,572.3	**$1,196.7**	$1,135.9
Second	**2,773.9**	2,587.2	**1,235.5**	1,198.6
Third	**2,822.4**	2,623.4	**1,273.3**	1,186.0
Fourth	**2,583.9**	2,394.3	**1,119.7**	1,045.1
	$10,906.7	$10,177.2	**$4,825.2**	$4,565.6

	Net earnings		*Net earnings per share*			
	2006	2005	**2006**		2005	
			Basic	Diluted	Basic	Diluted
First	**$ 274.1**	$254.7	**$.69**	**$.68**	$.62	$.61
Second	**266.5**	259.0	**.68**	**.67**	.63	.62
Third	**281.1**	274.3	**.71**	**.70**	.66	.66
Fourth	**182.4**	192.4	**.46**	**.45**	.47	.47
	$1,004.1	$980.4				

The principal market for trading Kellogg shares is the New York Stock Exchange (NYSE). The shares are also traded on the Boston, Chicago, Cincinnati, Pacific, and Philadelphia Stock Exchanges. At year-end 2006, the closing price (on the NYSE) was $50.06 and there were 41,450 shareholders of record.

Dividends paid per share and the quarterly price ranges on the NYSE during the last two years were:

	Dividend per share	*Stock Price* High	Low
2006–Quarter			
First	**$ .2775**	**$45.78**	**$42.41**
Second	**.2775**	**48.50**	**43.06**
Third	**.2910**	**50.87**	**47.31**
Fourth	**.2910**	**50.95**	**47.71**
	$1.1370		
2005–Quarter			
First	$ .2525	$45.59	$42.41
Second	.2525	46.89	42.35
Third	.2775	46.99	43.42
Fourth	.2775	46.70	43.22
	$1.0600		

Note 14 Operating Segments

Kellogg Company is the world's leading producer of cereal and a leading producer of convenience foods, including cookies, crackers, toaster pastries, cereal bars, fruit snacks, frozen waffles, and veggie foods. Kellogg products are manufactured and marketed globally. Principal markets for these products include the United States and United Kingdom. The Company currently manages its operations in four geographic operating segments, comprised of North America and the three International operating segments of Europe, Latin America, and Asia Pacific. For the periods presented, the Asia Pacific operating segment included Australia and Asian markets. Beginning in 2007, this segment will also include South Africa, which was formerly a part of Europe.

The measurement of operating segment results is generally consistent with the presentation of the Consolidated Statement of Earnings and Balance Sheet. Intercompany transactions between operating segments were insignificant in all periods presented.

(millions)	2006	2005	2004
Net sales			
North America	**$ 7,348.8**	$ 6,807.8	$ 6,369.3
Europe	**2,143.8**	2,013.6	2,007.3
Latin America	**890.8**	822.2	718.0
Asia Pacific (a)	**523.3**	533.6	519.3
Consolidated	**$ 10,906.7**	$10,177.2	$ 9,613.9
Segment operating profit			
North America	**$ 1,340.5**	$ 1,251.5	$ 1,240.4
Europe	**334.1**	330.7	292.3
Latin America	**220.1**	202.8	185.4
Asia Pacific (a)	**76.9**	86.0	79.5
Corporate	**(205.8)**	(120.7)	(116.5)
Consolidated	**$ 1,765.8**	$ 1,750.3	$ 1,681.1

(a) Includes Australia and Asia.

	2006	2005	2004
Depreciation and amortization			
North America	**$ 241.8**	272.3	$ 261.4
Europe	**66.4**	61.2	95.7
Latin America	**21.9**	20.0	15.4
Asia Pacific (a)	**17.2**	20.9	20.9
Corporate	**5.4**	17.4	16.6
Consolidated	**$ 352.7**	391.8	$ 410.0
Interest expense			
North America	**$ 8.7**	$ 1.4	$ 1.7
Europe	**27.0**	12.4	15.6
Latin America	**.1**	.2	.2
Asia Pacific (a)	**.4**	.3	.2
Corporate	**271.2**	286.0	290.9
Consolidated	**$ 307.4**	$ 300.3	$ 308.6
Income taxes			
North America	**$ 396.2**	$ 372.7	$ 371.5
Europe	**9.8**	30.2	64.5
Latin America	**31.8**	21.5	39.8
Asia Pacific (a)	**14.4**	12.4	(.8)
Corporate	**14.3**	7.9	.3
Consolidated	**$ 466.5**	$ 444.7	$ 475.3
Total assets (b)			
North America	**$ 7,996.2**	$ 7,944.6	$ 7,641.5
Europe	**2,380.7**	2,356.7	2,324.2
Latin America	**661.4**	450.6	411.1
Asia Pacific (a)	**328.8**	294.7	347.4
Corporate	**4,934.0**	5,336.4	5,619.0
Elimination entries	**(5,587.1)**	(5,808.5)	(5,781.3)
Consolidated	**$ 10,714.0**	$10,574.5	$10,561.9

(millions)	2006	2005	2004
Additions to long-lived assets (c)			
North America	**$316.0**	$317.0	$167.4
Europe	**62.6**	42.3	59.7
Latin America	**52.8**	38.1	37.2
Asia Pacific (a)	**18.9**	14.4	9.9
Corporate	**2.8**	.4	4.4
Consolidated	**$453.1**	$412.2	$278.6

(a) Includes Australia and Asia.

(b) The Company adopted SFAS No. 158 "Employers' Accounting for Defined Benefit Pension and Other Postretirement Plans" as of the end of its 2006 fiscal year. The standard generally requires company plan sponsors to reflect the net over- or under-funded position of a defined postretirement benefit plan as an asset or liability on the balance sheet. Accordingly, the Company's consolidated and corporate total assets for 2006 were reduced by $512.4 and $152.4 respectively. Operating segment total assets were reduced as follows: North America–$71.8; Europe–$284.3; Latin America–$2.9; Asia Pacific–$1.0. Refer to Note 1 for further information.

(c) Includes plant, property, equipment, and purchased intangibles.

The Company's largest customer, Wal-Mart Stores, Inc. and its affiliates, accounted for approximately 18% of consolidated net sales during 2006, 17% in 2005, and 14% in 2004, comprised principally of sales within the United States.

Supplemental geographic information is provided below for net sales to external customers and long-lived assets:

(millions)	2006	2005	2004
Net sales			
United States	**$ 6,842.8**	$ 6,351.6	$5,968.0
United Kingdom	**893.9**	836.9	859.6
Other foreign countries	**3,170.0**	2,988.7	2,786.3
Consolidated	**$10,906.7**	$10,177.2	$9,613.9
Long-lived assets (a)			
United States	**$ 6,629.5**	$ 6,576.8	$6,539.2
United Kingdom	**369.2**	323.8	432.5
Other foreign countries	**684.9**	641.3	631.1
Consolidated	**$ 7,683.6**	$ 7,541.9	$7,602.8

(a) Includes plant, property, equipment, and purchased intangibles.

Supplemental product information is provided below for net sales to external customers:

(millions)	2006	2005	2004
North America			
Retail channel cereal	**$ 2,667.0**	$ 2,587.7	$2,404.5
Retail channel snacks	**3,318.4**	2,976.6	2,801.4
Frozen and speciality channels	**1,363.4**	1,243.5	1,163.4
International			
Cereal	**3,010.3**	2,932.8	2,829.2
Convenience foods	**547.6**	436.6	415.4
Consolidated	**$10,906.7**	$10,177.2	$9,613.9

Note 15 Supplemental Financial Statement Data

(millions)

Consolidated Statement of Earnings	2006	2005	2004
Research and development expense	**$190.6**	$181.0	$148.9
Advertising expense	**$915.9**	$857.7	$806.2

Consolidated Statement of Cash Flows	2006	2005	2004
Trade receivables	**$ (57.7)**	$(86.2)	$ 13.8
Other receivables	**(21.0)**	(25.4)	(39.5)
Inventories	**(107.0)**	(24.8)	(31.2)
Other current assets	**(10.8)**	(15.3)	(17.8)
Accounts payable	**27.5**	156.4	63.4
Accrued income taxes	**65.6**	74.7	(13.5)
Accrued interest expense	**4.3**	(6.3)	(38.4)
Other current liabilities	**60.6**	(44.8)	33.4
Changes in operating assets and liabilities	**$ (38.5)**	$ 28.3	$(29.8)

(millions)

Consolidated Balance Sheet	2006	2005
Trade receivables	**$839.4**	$782.7
Allowance for doubtful accounts	**(5.9)**	(6.9)
Other receivables	**111.3**	103.3
Accounts receivable, net	**$944.8**	$879.1
Raw materials and supplies	**$200.7**	$188.6
Finished goods and materials in process	**623.2**	528.4
Inventories	**$823.9**	$717.0
Deferred income taxes	**$115.9**	$207.6
Other prepaid assets	**131.8**	173.7

(millions)

Consolidated Balance Sheet	2006	2005
Other current assets	**$ 247.7**	$ 381.3
Land	**$ 77.5**	$ 75.5
Buildings	**1,521.3**	1,458.8
Machinery and equipment (a)	**4,992.0**	4,692.4
Construction in progress	**326.8**	237.3
Accumulated depreciation	**(4,102.0)**	(3,815.6)
Property, net	**$2,815.6**	$2,648.4
Goodwill	**$3,448.3**	$3,455.3
Other intangibles (b)	**1,468.8**	1,485.8
–Accumulated amortization	**(49.1)**	(47.6)
Pension (b)	**352.6**	629.8
Other	**250.8**	206.3
Other assets	**$5,471.4**	$5,729.6
Accrued income taxes	**$ 151.7**	$ 148.3
Accrued salaries and wages	**311.1**	276.5
Accrued advertising and promotion	**338.0**	320.9
Other (b)	**317.7**	339.1
Other current liabilities	**$1,118.5**	$1,084.8
Nonpension postretirement benefits (b)	**$ 442.3**	$ 74.5
Deferred income taxes (b)	**619.3**	945.8
Other (b)	**510.2**	405.1
Other liabilities	**$1,571.8**	$1,425.4

(a) Includes an insignificant amount of capitalized internal-use software.

(b) The Company adopted SFAS No. 158 "Employers' Accounting for Defined Benefit Pension and Other Postretirement Plans" as of the end of its 2006 fiscal year. The standard generally requires company plan sponsors to reflect the net over- or under-funded position of a defined postretirement benefit plan as an asset or liability on the balance sheet. Accordingly, the 2006 balances associated with the identified captions within the preceding table were materially affected by the adoption of this standard. Refer to Note 1 for further information.

(millions)

Allowance for doubtful accounts	2006	2005	2004
Balance at beginning of year	**$ 6.9**	$13.0	$15.1
Additions charged to expense	**1.6**	—	2.1
Doubtful accounts charged to reserve	**(2.8)**	(7.4)	(4.3)
Currency translation adjustments	**.2**	1.3	.1
Balance at end of year	**$ 5.9**	$ 6.9	$13.0

Management's Responsibility for Financial Statements

Management is responsible for the preparation of the Company's consolidated financial statements and related notes. We believe that the consolidated financial statements present the Company's financial position and results of operations in conformity with accounting principles that are generally accepted in the United States, using our best estimates and judgments as required.

The independent registered public accounting firm audits the Company's consolidated financial statements in accordance with the standards of the Public Company Accounting Oversight Board and provides an objective, independent review of the fairness of reported operating results and financial position.

The Board of Directors of the Company has an Audit Committee composed of three non-management Directors. The Committee meets regularly with management, internal auditors, and the independent registered public accounting firm to review accounting, internal control, auditing and financial reporting matters.

Formal policies and procedures, including an active Ethics and Business Conduct program, support the internal controls and are designed to ensure employees adhere to the highest standards of personal and professional integrity. We have a vigorous internal audit program that independently evaluates the adequacy and effectiveness of these internal controls.

Management's Report on Internal Control over Financial Reporting

Our management is responsible for establishing and maintaining adequate internal control over financial reporting, as such term is defined in Exchange Act Rules 13a-15(f). Under the supervision and with the participation of management, we conducted an evaluation of the effectiveness of our internal control over financial reporting based on the framework in *Internal Control—Integrated Framework* issued by the Committee of Sponsoring Organizations of the Treadway Commission.

Because of its inherent limitations, internal control over financial reporting may not prevent or detect misstatements. Also, projections of any evaluation of effectiveness to future periods are subject to risk that controls may become inadequate because of changes in conditions, or that the degree of compliance with the policies or procedures may deteriorate.

Based on our evaluation under the framework in *Internal Control—Integrated Framework,* management concluded that our internal control over financial reporting was effective as of December 30, 2006. Our management's assessment of the effectiveness of our internal control over financial reporting as of December 30, 2006 has been audited by PricewaterhouseCoopers LLP, an independent registered public accounting firm, as stated in their report which follows on page 56.

A.D. David Mackay
President and Chief Executive Officer

John A. Bryant
Executive Vice President,
Chief Financial Officer, Kellogg Company
and President, Kellogg International

Report of Independent Registered Public Accounting Firm

To the Shareholders and Board of Directors of Kellogg Company:

We have completed integrated audits of Kellogg Company's consolidated financial statements and of its internal control over financial reporting as of December 30, 2006, in accordance with the standards of the Public Company Accounting Oversight Board (United States). Our opinions, based on our audits, are presented below.

Consolidated financial statements

In our opinion, the consolidated financial statements listed in the index appearing under Item 15(a)1 present fairly, in all material respects, the financial position of Kellogg Company and its subsidiaries at December 30, 2006 and December 31, 2005, and the results of their operations and their cash flows for each of the three years in the period ended December 30, 2006 in conformity with accounting principles generally accepted in the United States of America. These financial statements are the responsibility of the Company's management. Our responsibility is to express an opinion on these financial statements based on our audits. We conducted our audits of these statements in accordance with the standards of the Public Company Accounting Oversight Board (United States). Those standards require that we plan and perform the audit to obtain reasonable assurance about whether the financial statements are free of material misstatement. An audit of financial statements includes examining, on a test basis, evidence supporting the amounts and disclosures in the financial statements, assessing the accounting principles used and significant estimates made by management, and evaluating the overall financial statement presentation. We believe that our audits provide a reasonable basis for our opinion.

As discussed in Note 1 to the consolidated financial statements, the Company changed the manner in which it accounted for share-based compensation and defined benefit pension, other postretirement, and postemployment plans in 2006.

Internal control over financial reporting

Also, in our opinion, management's assessment, included in Management's Report on Internal Control over Financial Reporting, appearing under Item 8, that the Company maintained effective internal control over financial reporting as of December 30, 2006 based on criteria established in *Internal Control—Integrated Framework* issued by the Committee of Sponsoring Organizations of the Treadway Commission (COSO), is fairly stated, in all material respects, based on those criteria. Furthermore, in our opinion, the Company maintained, in all material respects, effective internal control over financial reporting as of December 30, 2006, based on criteria established in *Internal Control—Integrated Framework* issued by the COSO. The Company's management is responsible for maintaining effective internal control over financial reporting and for its assessment of the effectiveness of internal control over financial reporting. Our responsibility is to express opinions on management's assessment and on the effectiveness of the Company's internal control over financial reporting based on our audit. We conducted our audit of internal control over financial reporting in accordance with the standards of the Public Company Accounting Oversight Board (United States). Those standards require that we plan and perform the audit to obtain reasonable assurance about whether effective internal control over financial reporting was maintained in all material respects. An audit of internal control over financial reporting includes obtaining an understanding of internal control over financial reporting, evaluating management's assessment, testing and evaluating the design and operating effectiveness of internal control, and performing such other procedures as we consider necessary in the circumstances. We believe that our audit provides a reasonable basis for our opinions.

A company's internal control over financial reporting is a process designed to provide reasonable assurance regarding the reliability of financial reporting and the preparation of financial statements for external purposes in accordance with generally accepted accounting principles. A company's internal control over financial reporting includes those policies and procedures that (i) pertain to the maintenance of records that, in reasonable detail, accurately and fairly reflect the transactions and dispositions of the assets of the company; (ii) provide reasonable assurance that transactions are recorded as necessary to permit preparation of financial statements in accordance with generally accepted accounting principles, and that receipts and expenditures of the company are being made only in accordance with authorizations of management and directors of the company; and (iii) provide reasonable assurance regarding prevention or timely detection of unauthorized acquisition, use, or disposition of the company's assets that could have a material effect on the financial statements.

Because of its inherent limitations, internal control over financial reporting may not prevent or detect misstatements. Also, projections of any evaluation of effectiveness to future periods are subject to the risk that controls may become inadequate because of changes in conditions, or that the degree of compliance with the policies or procedures may deteriorate.

PricewaterhouseCoopers LLP

Battle Creek, Michigan
February 23, 2007

Index

A

B

C

F

J

L

M

N

O

P

T

Photo Credits

Chapter 1, page 1, Adrian Sanchez-Gonzalez\Landov Media

Chapter 2, page 39, Neal Hamburg/Bloomberg News./Landov

Chapter 3, page 77, © George Hall/CORBIS All Rights Reserved

Chapter 4, page 121, Adam Rountree\Landov Media

Chapter 5, page 163, Ken James\Landov Media

Chapter 6, page 221, Bankrate, Inc.

Chapter 7, page 255, Rob Kim\Landov Media

Chapter 8, page 283, Getty Images

Chapter 9, page 327, Ty Wright\Landov Media

Chapter 10, page 357, Lisa Poole\AP Wide World Photos

Chapter 11, page 409, Alamy Images

Chapter 12, page 441, Esteban Felix\AP Wide World Photos

STUDY GUIDE AND WORKING PAPERS CHAPTERS 1–12

COLLEGE ACCOUNTING

Eleventh Edition

Jeffrey Slater

North Shore Community College
Danvers, Massacusetts

Prentice Hall

Boston Columbus Indianapolis New York San Francisco Upper Saddle River
Amsterdam Cape Town Dubai London Madrid Milan Munich Paris
Montreal Toronto Delhi Mexico City Sao Paulo Sydney Hong Kong Seoul
Singapore Taipei Tokyo

VP/Editorial Director: Natalie Anderson
AVP/Executive Editor: Jodi McPherson
Development Editor: Karen Misler
Assistant Editor: Melissa Arlio
Editorial Assistant: Christina Rumbaugh
AVP/Director of Marketing: Kate Valentine
Senior Marketing Manager: Maggie Moylan Leen
Marketing Assistant: Justin Jacob
Senior Managing Editor: Cynthia Zonneveld
Project Manager: Rhonda Aversa
Senior Operations Specialist: Nick Sklitsis
Senior Art Director: Jonathan Boylan
AVP/Director of Product Development: Lisa Strite
Media Editors: Ashley Lulling/Allison Longley
Media Project Manager, Production: John Cassar
Full-Service Project Management: GEX Publishing Services
Composition: GEX Publishing Services
Printer/Binder: Courier/Kendallville
Cover Printer: Lehigh-Phoenix Color/Hagerstown
Text Font: Times Roman 10/12

Pearson Education LTD.
Pearson Education Singapore, Pte. Ltd
Pearson Education, Canada, Ltd
Pearson Education–Japan
Pearson Education Australia PTY, Limited
Pearson Education North Asia Ltd
Pearson Educación de Mexico, S.A. de C.V.
Pearson Education Malaysia, Pte. Ltd

Prentice Hall
is an imprint of

www.pearsonhighered.com

10 9 8 7 6 5
ISBN 10: 0-13-606572-4
ISBN 13: 978-0-13-606572-2

Contents

STUDY GUIDE AND WORKING PAPERS CHAPTERS 1–12

1 INTRODUCTION TO ACCOUNTING CONCEPTS AND PROCEDURES

SELF-REVIEW QUIZ 1-1

GRACIE RYAN REAL ESTATE

	ASSETS			=	LIABILITIES	+	OWNER'S EQUITY
	Cash	+	Computer Equipment	=	Accounts Payable	+	Gracie Ryan, Capital
TRANSACTION 1							
NEW BALANCE				=			
TRANSACTION 2							
NEW BALANCE				=			
TRANSACTION 3							
ENDING BALANCE		+		=		+	
				=			

Name ______________________ Class ______________ Date ______________

SELF-REVIEW QUIZ 1-4

(1)

(2)

Name ______________________ Class ______________ Date ______________

(3)

____

____

____

ASSETS			LIABILITIES AND OWNER'S EQUITY		

Name ______________________ Class ______________ Date ______________

FORMS FOR DEMONSTRATION PROBLEM

(A)

MICHAEL BROWN, ATTORNEY AT LAW

ASSETS = LIABILITIES + OWNER'S EQUITY

	Cash	+	Accounts Receivable	+	Office Equipment	=	Accounts Payable	+	M. Brown, Capital	−	M. Brown Withd.	+	Legal fees	−	Expenses
1.															
Balance															
2.															
Balance															
3.															
Balance															
4.															
Balance															
5.															
Balance															
6.															
Balance															
7.															
Balance															
8.															
Balance															
9.															
Ending Balance		+		+		=		+		−		+		−	

_______ = _______

Name ______________________ Class ______________ Date ______________

DEMONSTRATION PROBLEM (CONTINUED)

B-1

MICHAEL BROWN, ATTORNEY AT LAW
INCOME STATEMENT
FOR MONTH ENDED JUNE 30, 200X

B-2

MICHAEL BROWN, ATTORNEY AT LAW
STATEMENT OF OWNER'S EQUITY
FOR MONTH ENDED JUNE 30, 200X

B-3

MICHAEL BROWN, ATTORNEY AT LAW
BALANCE SHEET
JUNE 30, 200X

ASSETS		LIABILITIES AND OWNER'S EQUITY	

Name ______________________ Class ______________ Date ______________

CHAPTER 1
FORMS FOR CLASSROOM DEMONSTRATION EXERCISES SET A OR SET B

1. A. ______________
B. ______________
C. ______________
D. ______________
E. ______________
F. ______________

2. A. ______________
B. ______________
C. ______________

3. A. ______________
B. ______________

4. ______________
____
____

5. ______________
____
____
____
____

6. ______________
____
____
____

7. A. ______________
B. ______________
C. ______________
D. ______________

8. A. ______________
B. ______________
C. ______________
D. ______________
E. ______________
F. ______________
G. ______________
H. ______________

9. A. ______________
B. ______________
C. ______________
D. ______________

Name ______________________ Class ______________ Date ______________

FORMS FOR EXERCISES

1-1.

A. ______________________

B. ______________________

C. ______________________

1-2.

ASSETS	=	LIABILITIES	+	OWNER'S EQUITY
A.				
B.				
C.				

1-3.

RANGE CO.
BALANCE SHEET
NOVEMBER 30, 200X

ASSETS			LIABILITIES AND OWNER'S EQUITY	

Name ____________ Class ____________ Date ____________

EXERCISES (CONTINUED)

1-4.

	ASSETS			= LIABILITIES +	OWNER'S EQUITY			
	Cash	+ Accounts Receivable	+ Computer Equipment	= Accounts Payable	+ B. Bell Capital	− B. Bell Withd.	+ Revenue	− Expenses
A.								
B								
C.								
D								
E.								
F								
G.								
Ending Balance								
			=					

Name ____________________ Class ____________ Date ____________

EXERCISES (CONCLUDED)

1-5.

(A)

FRENCH REALTY
INCOME STATEMENT
FOR MONTH ENDED JUNE 30, 200X

(B)

FRENCH REALTY
STATEMENT OF OWNER'S EQUITY
FOR MONTH ENDED JUNE 30, 200X

(C)

FRENCH REALTY
BALANCE SHEET
JUNE 30, 200X

ASSETS			LIABILITIES AND OWNER'S EQUITY		

Name ____________________ Class ____________________ Date ____________________

END OF CHAPTER PROBLEMS

PROBLEM 1A-1 OR PROBLEM 1B-1

MIA'S NAIL SPA

	ASSETS			=	LIABILITIES	+	OWNER'S EQUITY
	Cash	+	Store Equipment	=	Accounts Payable	+	Mia Annabelle, Capital
TRANSACTION A							
NEW BALANCE							
TRANSACTION B							
NEW BALANCE							
TRANSACTION C							
NEW BALANCE							
TRANSACTION D							
ENDING BALANCE							

PROBLEM 1A-2 OR PROBLEM 1B-2

SEE'S INTERNET SERVICE
BALANCE SHEET
SEPTEMBER 30, 200X

ASSETS			LIABILITIES AND OWNER'S EQUITY		

Name ____________________ Class ____________ Date ____________

PROBLEM 1A-3 OR PROBLEM 1B-3

RICK FOX
TYPING SERVICE

	ASSETS					= LIABILITIES +		OWNER'S EQUITY						
	Cash	+	Accounts Receivable	+	Office Equipment	=	Accounts Payable	+	R. Fox, Capital	–	R. Fox, Withd.	+	Typing Revenue	–	Expenses
A.															
BALANCE															
B.															
BALANCE															
C.															
BALANCE															
D.															
BALANCE															
E.															
BALANCE															
F.															
BALANCE															
G.															
BALANCE															
H.															
ENDING BALANCE															

Name ______________________ Class ______________ Date ______________

PROBLEM 1A-4 OR PROBLEM 1B-4

(A)

WEST STENCILING SERVICE
INCOME STATEMENT
FOR MONTH ENDED JUNE 30, 200X

(B)

WEST STENCILING SERVICE
STATEMENT OF OWNER'S EQUITY
FOR MONTH ENDED JUNE 30, 200X

Name ______________________ Class ______________ Date ______________

PROBLEM 1A-4 OR PROBLEM 1B-4 (CONCLUDED)

(C)

WEST STENCILING SERVICE
BALANCE SHEET
JUNE 30, 200X

ASSETS			LIABILITIES AND OWNER'S EQUITY		

Name ______________________ Class ______________ Date ______________

PROBLEM 1A-5 OR PROBLEM 1B-5

(A)

TOBEY'S CATERING SERVICE

	ASSETS			= LIABILITIES +	OWNER'S EQUITY			
	Cash	+ Accounts Receivable	+ Equipment	= Accounts Payable	+ J. Tobey, Capital	− J. Tobey, Withd.	+ Catering Revenue	− Expenses
10/25								
BALANCE								
10/27								
BALANCE								
10/28								
BALANCE								
10/29								
BALANCE								
11/1								
BALANCE								
11/5								
BALANCE								
11/8								
BALANCE								
11/10								
BALANCE								
11/15								
BALANCE								
11/17								
BALANCE								
11/20								
BALANCE								
11/25								
BALANCE								
11/28								
BALANCE								
11/30								
END. BAL.								

=

Name ____________ Class ____________ Date ____________

PROBLEM 1A-5 OR PROBLEM 1B-5 (CONTINUED)

(B)

TOBEY'S CATERING SERVICE
BALANCE SHEET
OCTOBER 31, 200X

ASSETS		LIABILITIES AND OWNER'S EQUITY	

(C)

TOBEY'S CATERING SERVICE
INCOME STATEMENT
FOR MONTH ENDED NOVEMBER 30, 200X

Name ______________________ Class ______________ Date ______________

PROBLEM 1A-5 OR PROBLEM 1B-5 (CONCLUDED)

(D)

TOBEY'S CATERING SERVICE
STATEMENT OF OWNER'S EQUITY
FOR MONTH ENDED NOVEMBER 30, 200X

(E)

TOBEY'S CATERING SERVICE
BALANCE SHEET
NOVEMBER 30, 200X

ASSETS | LIABILITIES AND OWNER'S EQUITY

Name ______________________ Class ______________ Date ______________

CHAPTER 1
SUMMARY PRACTICE TEST:
INTRODUCTION TO ACCOUNTING CONCEPTS AND PROCEDURES

Part I Instructions

Fill in the blank(s) to complete the statement.

1. ______________ was passed to prevent corporate fraud.
2. ______________ – Liabilities = Owner's Equity
3. The owner's current investment or equity in the assets of a business is called ______________.
4. A list of assets, liabilities, and owner's equity as of a particular date is reported on a(n) ______________ ______________.
5. ______________ create an outward or potential outward flow of assets.
6. Revenue earned not on account creates an asset entitled ______________.
7. ______________ record personal expenses that are not related to the business. They are a subdivision of owner's equity.
8. The ______________ ______________ reports how well a business performs for a period of time.
9. The ______________ ______________ ______________ ______________ is a report that shows changes in capital.
10. The ending figure for capital from the statement of owner's equity is placed on the ______________ ______________.

Part II Instructions

Answer true or false to the following statements.

1. Accounts Receivable is a liability.
2. Liabilities produce revenue.
3. Revenue is an asset.
4. Capital means cash.
5. Bookkeeping is 50% of accounting.
6. The balance sheet lists assets, revenue, and owner's equity.
7. The balance sheet shows where we are now for a specific period of time.
8. Revenue creates an outward flow of assets.
9. Expenses are a subdivision of owner's equity.
10. Withdrawals are the only subdivision of owner's equity.
11. Withdrawals are listed on the income statement.
12. Revenue is a subdivision of owner's equity.
13. Revenues and withdrawals are listed on the income statement.
14. The income statement helps update the statement of owner's equity, and the statement of owner's equity helps update the balance sheet.
15. Withdrawals are listed on the statement of owner's equity.

Name ____________________ Class ____________ Date ____________

Part III Instructions

In column B, record the appropriate code(s) that result from recording the transaction in column A.

1. Increase in assets
2. Decrease in assets
3. Increase in liabilities
4. Decrease in liabilities
5. Increase in capital
6. Increase in revenues
7. Increase in expenses
8. Increase in withdrawals

	Column A	Column B
1.	EXAMPLE: Pete Smith invested $5,000 in his business.	1,5
2.	Bought computer equipment on account for $600.	
3.	Paid salaries of $70.	
4.	Bought additional computer equipment for $750 cash.	
5.	Paid rent expense of $90.	
6.	Received $5,000 in cash from revenue earned.	
7.	Paid heat expense of $15.	
8.	Earned revenue of $500 that will not be received until next month.	
9.	Paid amount owed on equipment previously purchased on account.	
10.	Paid for cleaning supplies expense, $15.	
11.	Customers paid $10 of amount previously owed.	
12.	Bought additional equipment of $1,000, half paid in cash and half charged.	
13.	Charged customer $100 for services performed.	
14.	Pete paid home phone bill from the company's cash.	
15.	Advertising expense incurred but not to be paid until next month.	

CHAPTER 1 SOLUTIONS TO SUMMARY PRACTICE TEST

Part I

1. The Sarbanes-Oxley Act
2. Assets
3. capital
4. balance sheet
5. Expenses
6. Cash
7. Withdrawals
8. income statement
9. statement of owner's equity
10. balance sheet

Name ______________________ Class ______________ Date ______________

Part II

1. false
2. false
3. false
4. false
5. false
6. false
7. false
8. false
9. true
10. false
11. false
12. true
13. false
14. true
15. true

Part III

1. 1,5
2. 1,3
3. 7,2
4. 1,2
5. 7,2
6. 1,6
7. 7,2
8. 1,6
9. 4,2
10. 7,2
11. 1,2
12. 1,2,3
13. 1,6
14. 8,2
15. 7,3

Name ______________________ Class ______________ Date ______________

CONTINUING PROBLEM FOR CHAPTER 1

SANCHEZ COMPUTER CENTER

ASSETS = LIABILITIES + OWNER'S EQUITY

	Cash	+	Supplies	+	Computer Shop Equipment	+	Office Equipment	=	Accounts Payable	+	Freedman Capital	–	Freedman, Withdrawals	+	Revenue	–	Expenses
a																	
BALANCE																	
b																	
BALANCE																	
c																	
BALANCE																	
d																	
BALANCE																	
e																	
BALANCE																	
f																	
BALANCE																	
g																	
BALANCE																	
h																	
BALANCE																	
i																	
BALANCE																	
j																	
END BAL.		+		+		+		=		+		–		+		–	

______ = ______

Name ______________________ Class ______________ Date ______________

SANCHEZ COMPUTER CENTER
INCOME STATEMENT
FOR THE MONTH ENDED JULY 31, 200X

SANCHEZ COMPUTER CENTER
STATEMENT OF OWNER'S EQUITY
FOR MONTH ENDED JULY 31, 200X

SANCHEZ COMPUTER CENTER
BALANCE SHEET
JULY 31, 200X

ASSETS			LIABILITIES AND OWNER'S EQUITY		

2 DEBITS AND CREDITS: ANALYZING AND RECORDING BUSINESS TRANSACTIONS

SELF-REVIEW QUIZ 2-1

1. ____________ 4. ____________
2. ____________ 5. ____________
3. ____________

SELF-REVIEW QUIZ 2-2

A. 1.	2.	3.	4.	5.
Accounts Affected	Category	↑↓	Rules	T Account Update

B. 1.	2.	3.	4.	5.
Accounts Affected	Category	↑↓	Rules	T Account Update

Name ______________________ Class ______________ Date ______________

C. 1.	2.	3.	4.	5.
Accounts Affected	Category	↑↓	Rules	T Account Update

D. 1.	2.	3.	4.	5.
Accounts Affected	Category	↑↓	Rules	T Account Update

E. 1.	2.	3.	4.	5.
Accounts Affected	Category	↑↓	Rules	T Account Update

Name ______________________ Class ______________ Date ______________

SELF-REVIEW QUIZ 2-3

Cash 111

Dr.	Cr.
4,500	300
2,000	100
1,000	1,200
300	1,300
	2,600

Accounts Payable 211

Dr.	Cr.
300	700

Salon Fees 411

Dr.	Cr.
	3,500
	1,000

Accounts Receivable 121

Dr.	Cr.
1,000	300

Pam Jay, Capital 311

Dr.	Cr.
	4,000

Rent Expense 511

Dr.	Cr.
1,200	

Salon Equipment 131

Dr.	Cr.
700	

Pam Jay, Withdrawals 321

Dr.	Cr.
100	

Salon Supplies Exp. 521

Dr.	Cr.
1,300	

Salaries Expense 531

Dr.	Cr.
2,600	

Name ______________________ Class ______________ Date ______________

(1)

(2)

Name ____________________ Class ______________ Date ______________

(3)

(4)

Name ______________ Class ______________ Date ______________

FORMS FOR DEMONSTRATION PROBLEM

(1,2,3)

Advertising Expense 511

Gas Expense 512

Salaries Expense 513

Telephone Expense 514

Accounts Payable 211

Mel Free, Capital 311

Mel Free, Withdrawals 312

Delivery Fees Earned 411

Cash 111

Accounts Receivable 112

Office Equipment 121

Delivery Trucks 122

Name ______________________ Class ______________ Date ______________

FORMS FOR DEMONSTRATION PROBLEM (CONTINUED)

(4)

MEL'S DELIVERY SERVICE
TRIAL BALANCE
JULY 31, 200X

	Dr.	Cr.

(5A)

MEL'S DELIVERY SERVICE
INCOME STATEMENT
FOR MONTH ENDED JULY 31, 200X

Name ______________________ Class ______________ Date ______________

FORMS FOR DEMONSTRATION PROBLEM (CONCLUDED)

(5B)

MEL'S DELIVERY SERVICE
STATEMENT OF OWNER'S EQUITY
FOR MONTH ENDED JULY 31, 200X

(5C)

MEL'S DELIVERY SERVICE
BALANCE SHEET
JULY 31, 200X

ASSETS			LIABILITIES AND OWNER'S EQUITY	

Name ______________________ Class ______________ Date ______________

CHAPTER 2
FORMS FOR CLASSROOM DEMONSTRATION EXERCISES SET A OR SET B

1.

2. A.
B.
C.
D.
E.
F.
G.

3.

4.

5. A.
B.
C.
D.
E.
F.
G.
H.
I.
J.
K.

Name ______________________ Class ______________ Date ______________

FORMS FOR EXERCISES

2-1.

2-2.

1. Accounts Affected	2. Category	3. ↑ ↓	4. Rules	5. T Account Update

2-3.

Account	Category	↑↓	Financial Statement

Name ______________________ Class ______________ Date ______________

EXERCISES (CONTINUED)

2-4.

	Dr.	Cr.
A.	8	1
B.		
C.		
D.		
E.		
F.		
G.		
H.		
I.		

2-5.

(1)

HALL'S CLEANERS
INCOME STATEMENT
FOR MONTH ENDED JULY 31, 200X

(2)

HALL'S CLEANERS
STATEMENT OF OWNER'S EQUITY
FOR MONTH ENDED JULY 31, 200X

Name ______________ Class ______________ Date ______________

EXERCISES (CONCLUDED)

(3)

HALL'S CLEANERS
BALANCE SHEET
JULY 31, 200X

ASSETS			LIABILITIES AND OWNER'S EQUITY		

Name ______________________ Class ______________ Date ______________

END OF CHAPTER PROBLEMS

PROBLEM 2A-1 OR PROBLEM 2B-1

Accounts Affected	Category	↑ Inc. ↓ Dec.	Rules	T Account Update
A.				
B.				
C.				
D.				
E.				
F.				

Name ______________________ Class ______________ Date ______________

PROBLEM 2A-2 OR PROBLEM 2B-2

Cash	111

Office Equipment	121

Accounts Payable	211

Bernie Pillows, Capital	311

Bernie Pillows, Withdrawals	312

Consulting Fees Earned	411

Advertising Expense	511

Rent Expense	512

Name ______________________ Class ______________ Date ______________

PROBLEM 2A-3 OR PROBLEM 2B-3

(A)

Cash	111

Accounts Payable	211

Fees Earned	411

Accounts Receivable	112

Barry Joy, Capital	311

Rent Expense	511

Office Equipment	121

Barry Joy, Withdrawals	312

Utilities Expense	512

(B)

BARRY'S CLEANING SERVICE
TRIAL BALANCE
MAY 31, 200X

	Dr.	Cr.

Name ____________________ Class ____________ Date ____________

PROBLEM 2A-4 OR PROBLEM 2B-4

(A)

GRACIE LANTZ, ATTORNEY AT LAW
INCOME STATEMENT
FOR MONTH ENDED MAY 31, 200X

(B)

GRACIE LANTZ, ATTORNEY AT LAW
STATEMENT OF OWNER'S EQUITY
FOR MONTH ENDED MAY 31, 200X

Name ________________________ Class ________________ Date ________________

PROBLEM 2A-4 OR PROBLEM 2B-4 (CONCLUDED)

(C)

GRACIE LANTZ, ATTORNEY AT LAW
BALANCE SHEET
MAY 31, 200X

ASSETS

LIABILITIES AND OWNER'S EQUITY

Name ______________________ Class ______________ Date ______________

PROBLEM 2A-5 OR PROBLEM 2B-5

(1,2,3)

Cash 111

Accounts Receivable 112

Office Equipment 121

Delivery Trucks 122

Accounts Payable 211

A. Angel, Capital 311

A. Angel, Withdrawals 312

Delivery Fees Earned 411

Advertising Expense 511

Gas Expense 512

Salaries Expense 513

Telephone Expense 514

Name ______________________ Class ______________ Date ______________

PROBLEM 2A-5 OR PROBLEM 2-B5 (CONTINUED)

(4)

ANGEL'S DELIVERY SERVICE
TRIAL BALANCE
MARCH 31, 200X

	Dr.	Cr.

(5A)

ANGEL'S DELIVERY SERVICE
INCOME STATEMENT
FOR MONTH ENDED MARCH 31, 200X

Name ____________________ Class ____________ Date ____________

PROBLEM 2A-5 OR PROBLEM 2B-5 (CONCLUDED)

(5B)

ANGEL'S DELIVERY SERVICE
STATEMENT OF OWNER'S EQUITY
FOR MONTH ENDED MARCH 31, 200X

(5C)

ANGEL'S DELIVERY SERVICE
BALANCE SHEET
MARCH 31, 200X

ASSETS		LIABILITIES AND OWNER'S EQUITY	

Name ______________________ Class ______________ Date ______________

CHAPTER 2
SUMMARY PRACTICE TEST:
DEBITS AND CREDITS: ANALYZING AND RECORDING BUSINESS TRANSACTIONS

Part I Instructions

Fill in the blank(s) to complete the statement.

1. Financial reports do not contain ______________ or ______________.
2. The right side of any T account is called the ______________ ______________.
3. Assets are increased by ______________.
4. The process of balancing an account involves ______________.
5. Transaction analysis charts are an aid in recording ______________ ______________.
6. The ______________ ______________ ______________ indicates the names and numbering system of accounts.
7. A(n) ______________ is a group of accounts.
8. A(n) ______________ ______________ is an informal report that lists accounts and their balances.
9. Withdrawals are increased by ______________.
10. The income statement, statement of owner's equity, and balance sheet may be prepared from a(n) ______________ ______________.
11. Cash, Accounts Receivable, and Equipment are examples of ______________.
12. Increasing expenses ultimately cause owner's equity to ______________.
13. An increase in rent expense is a(n) ______________ by the rules of debits and credits.
14. A debit to one asset and a credit to another asset for the same transaction reflect a(n) ______________ in assets.
15. The category of accounts receivable is a(n) ______________.

Part II Instructions

Bea Paul opened a shuttle service company. From the following chart of accounts, indicate in column B (by account number) which account (s) will be debited or credited as related to the transaction in column A.

Name ______________________ Class ______________________ Date ______________________

Chart of Accounts

ASSETS	LIABILITIES	EXPENSES
10 Cash	50 Accounts Payable	80 Advertising
20 Accounts Receivable		90 Gas
30 Equipment	OWNER'S EQUITY	100 Salaries
40 Shuttle Bus	60 B. Paul, Capital	110 Telephone
	62 B. Paul, Withdrawals	
	REVENUE	
	70 Taxi Fees Earned	

	COLUMN A	COLUMN B DEBIT(S)	CREDIT(S)
1.	EXAMPLE: Bea Paul invested $40,000 in the shuttle service.	10	60
2.	Purchased a shuttle bus on account for $25,000.	______	______
3.	Bought equipment on account for $3,000.	______	______
4.	Advertising bill received, but not paid until next month, $60.	______	______
5.	Bea paid home telephone bill from company checkbook, $20.	______	______
6.	Collected $100 in cash from daily shuttle fees earned.	______	______
7.	Customer charged a shuttle ride of $20.	______	______
8.	Received partial payment for Transaction #7 of $10.	______	______
9.	Paid business telephone bill, $32.	______	______
10.	Purchased additional equipment for cash, $550.	______	______
11.	Paid shuttle driver salaries of $150.	______	______
12.	Drove customer on account to local train station for $6.	______	______
13.	Received $5 from customer who hired a shuttle for ride across town.	______	______
14.	Collected from past charged revenue, $15.	______	______
15.	Bought office equipment on account for $110.	______	______

Part III Instructions

Answer true or false to the following statements.

1. There are no debit and credit columns found on the three financial statements.
2. A trial balance could balance but be wrong.
3. Withdrawals are listed on the credit column of the trial balance.
4. Double entry bookkeeping results in a system where the sum of all the debits is equal to the sum of all the credits.
5. The ledger is numbered like a textbook.

6. Withdrawals are always increased by credits.
7. An expense could create a liability.
8. A shift in assets means the total of assets must change.
9. The rules of debit and credit are constantly changing.
10. The transaction analysis chart is a teaching device.
11. The chart of accounts makes locating and identifying accounts easier.
12. The left side of any account is a credit.
13. A debit means all accounts are decreasing.
14. Financial statements are prepared from a trial balance.
15. The statement of owner's equity is prepared before the income statement.
16. Liabilities increase by credits.
17. Footings aid in balancing accounts.
18. Withdrawals are listed on the income statement.
19. The balance sheet contains the old figure for capital.
20. Think of a credit as always meaning something good.

CHAPTER 2
SOLUTIONS TO SUMMARY PRACTICE TEST

Part I

1. debits/credits
2. credit side
3. debits
4. footings
5. business transactions
6. chart of accounts
7. ledger (general)
8. trial balance
9. debits
10. trial balance
11. assets
12. decrease
13. debit
14. shift
15. asset

Part II

	Debit	Credit
1.	10	60
2.	40	50
3.	30	50
4.	80	50
5.	62	10
6.	10	70
7.	20	70
8.	10	20
9.	110	10
10.	30	10
11.	100	10
12.	20	70
13.	10	70
14.	10	20
15.	30	50

Part III

1. true
2. true
3. false
4. true
5. false
6. false
7. true
8. false
9. false
10. true
11. true
12. false
13. false
14. true
15. false
16. true
17. true
18. false
19. false
20. false

Name ______________________ Class ______________ Date ______________

CONTINUING PROBLEM FOR CHAPTER 2

Cash 1000	
Bal. 3,850	

Accounts Receivable 1020	

Supplies 1030	
Bal. 250	

Computer Shop Equipment 1080	
Bal. 1,200	

Office Equipment 1090	
Bal. 600	

Accounts Payable 2000	
	335 Bal.

Freedman, Capital 3000	
	4,500 Bal.

Freedman, Withdrawals 3010	
Bal. 100	

Service Revenue 4000	
	1,650 Bal.

Advertising Expense 5010	

Rent Expense 5020	
Bal. 400	

Utilities Expense 5030	
Bal. 85	

Phone Expense 5040	

Supplies Expense 5050	

Insurance Expense 5060	

Postage Expense 5070	

Name ______________________ Class ______________ Date ______________

SANCHEZ COMPUTER CENTER
TRIAL BALANCE
AUGUST 31, 200X

	Dr.	Cr.

SANCHEZ COMPUTER CENTER
INCOME STATEMENT
FOR THE TWO MONTHS ENDED AUGUST 31, 200X

Name ______________________ Class ______________________ Date ______________________

SANCHEZ COMPUTER CENTER
STATEMENT OF OWNER'S EQUITY
FOR THE TWO MONTHS ENDED AUGUST 31, 200X

SANCHEZ COMPUTER CENTER
BALANCE SHEET
AUGUST 31, 200X

ASSETS			LIABILITIES AND OWNER'S EQUITY		

3

Beginning the Accounting Cycle: Journalizing, Posting, and the Trial Balance

SELF-REVIEW QUIZ 3-1

LOWE'S REPAIR SERVICE
GENERAL JOURNAL

PAGE 1

Date		Account Titles and Description	PR	Dr.	Cr.

Name ______________________ Class ______________ Date ______________

LOWE'S REPAIR SERVICE
GENERAL JOURNAL

PAGE 1 (Cont.)

Date		Account Titles and Description	PR	Dr.	Cr.

Name ______________________ Class ______________ Date ______________

SELF-REVIEW QUIZ 3-2

CLARK'S WORD PROCESSING SERVICES
GENERAL JOURNAL

PAGE 1

Date 200X		Account Titles and Description	PR	Dr.	Cr.
May	1	Cash		10 000 00	
		Brenda Clark, Capital			10 000 00
		Initial investment of cash by owner			
	1	Word Processing Equipment		6 000 00	
		Cash			1 000 00
		Accounts Payable			5 000 00
		Purchase of equip. from Ben Co.			
	1	Prepaid Rent		1 200 00	
		Cash			1 200 00
		Rent paid in advance (3 months)			
	3	Office Supplies		600 00	
		Accounts Payable			600 00
		Purchase of supplies on acct. from Norris			
	7	Cash		3 000 00	
		Word Processing Fees			3 000 00
		Cash received for services rendered			
	13	Office Salaries Expense		650 00	
		Cash			650 00
		Payment of office salaries			
	18	Advertising Expense		250 00	
		Accounts Payable			250 00
		Bill received but not paid from Al's News			
	20	Brenda Clark, Withdrawals		625 00	
		Cash			625 00
		Personal withdrawal of cash			
	22	Accounts Receivable		5 000 00	
		Word Processing Fees			5 000 00
		Billed Morris Co. for fees earned			

Name ____________________ Class ____________ Date ____________

CLARK'S WORD PROCESSING SERVICES
GENERAL JOURNAL

PAGE 2

Date 200X		Account Titles and Description	PR	Dr.	Cr.
May	27	Office Salaries Expense		650 00	
		Cash			650 00
		Payment of office salaries			
	28	Accounts Payable		2 500 00	
		Cash			2 500 00
		Paid half the amount owed Ben Co.			
	29	Telephone Expense		220 00	
		Cash			220 00
		Paid telephone bill			

Name ______________________ Class ______________ Date ______________

PARTIAL LEDGER OF CLARK'S WORD PROCESSING SERVICE

CASH **ACCOUNT NO. 111**

Date		Explanation	Post Ref.	Debit	Credit	Balance Debit	Balance Credit

ACCOUNTS RECEIVABLE **ACCOUNT NO. 112**

Date		Explanation	Post Ref.	Debit	Credit	Balance Debit	Balance Credit

Name ______________ Class ______________ Date ______________

OFFICE SUPPLIES **ACCOUNT NO. 114**

Date	Explanation	Post Ref.	Debit	Credit	Balance	
					Debit	Credit

PREPAID RENT **ACCOUNT NO. 115**

Date	Explanation	Post Ref.	Debit	Credit	Balance	
					Debit	Credit

WORD PROCESSING EQUIPMENT **ACCOUNT NO. 121**

Date	Explanation	Post Ref.	Debit	Credit	Balance	
					Debit	Credit

ACCOUNTS PAYABLE **ACCOUNT NO. 211**

Date	Explanation	Post Ref.	Debit	Credit	Balance	
					Debit	Credit

Name ______________________ Class ______________ Date ______________

BRENDA CLARK, CAPITAL **ACCOUNT NO. 311**

Date		Explanation	Post Ref.	Debit	Credit	Balance	
						Debit	Credit

BRENDA CLARK, WITHDRAWALS **ACCOUNT NO. 312**

Date		Explanation	Post Ref.	Debit	Credit	Balance	
						Debit	Credit

WORD PROCESSING FEES **ACCOUNT NO. 411**

Date		Explanation	Post Ref.	Debit	Credit	Balance	
						Debit	Credit

OFFICE SALARIES EXPENSE **ACCOUNT NO. 511**

Date		Explanation	Post Ref.	Debit	Credit	Balance	
						Debit	Credit

Name ______________________ Class ______________ Date ______________

ADVERTISING EXPENSE **ACCOUNT NO. 512**

Date		Explanation	Post Ref.	Debit	Credit	Balance	
						Debit	Credit

TELEPHONE EXPENSE **ACCOUNT NO. 513**

Date		Explanation	Post Ref.	Debit	Credit	Balance	
						Debit	Credit

Name ______________________ Class ______________ Date ______________

SELF-REVIEW QUIZ 3-3

1. ____

GENERAL JOURNAL

2. PAGE 4

Date		Account Titles and Description	PR	Dr.	Cr.

Name ______________________ Class ______________ Date ______________

FORMS FOR DEMONSTRATION PROBLEM

(A, B)

ABBY'S EMPLOYMENT AGENCY
GENERAL JOURNAL

PAGE 1

Date		Account Titles and Description	PR	Dr.	Cr.

Name ______________________ Class ______________ Date ______________

FORMS FOR DEMONSTRATION PROBLEM (CONTINUED)

GENERAL LEDGER OF ABBY'S EMPLOYMENT AGENCY

CASH — **ACCOUNT NO. 111**

Date	Explanation	Post Ref.	Debit	Credit	Balance Debit	Balance Credit

ACCOUNTS RECEIVABLE — **ACCOUNT NO. 112**

Date	Explanation	Post Ref.	Debit	Credit	Balance Debit	Balance Credit

SUPPLIES — **ACCOUNT NO. 131**

Date	Explanation	Post Ref.	Debit	Credit	Balance Debit	Balance Credit

EQUIPMENT — **ACCOUNT NO. 141**

Date	Explanation	Post Ref.	Debit	Credit	Balance Debit	Balance Credit

Name ______________________ Class ______________ Date ______________

FORMS FOR DEMONSTRATION PROBLEM (CONTINUED)

ACCOUNTS PAYABLE — ACCOUNT NO. 211

Date		Explanation	Post Ref.	Debit	Credit	Balance	
						Debit	Credit

A. TODD, CAPITAL — ACCOUNT NO. 311

Date		Explanation	Post Ref.	Debit	Credit	Balance	
						Debit	Credit

A. TODD, WITHDRAWALS — ACCOUNT NO. 321

Date		Explanation	Post Ref.	Debit	Credit	Balance	
						Debit	Credit

EMPLOYMENT FEES EARNED — ACCOUNT NO. 411

Date		Explanation	Post Ref.	Debit	Credit	Balance	
						Debit	Credit

Name ______________________ Class ______________ Date ______________

FORMS FOR DEMONSTRATION PROBLEM (CONTINUED)

WAGE EXPENSE **ACCOUNT NO. 511**

Date	Explanation	Post Ref.	Debit	Credit	Balance	
					Debit	Credit

TELEPHONE EXPENSE **ACCOUNT NO. 521**

Date	Explanation	Post Ref.	Debit	Credit	Balance	
					Debit	Credit

ADVERTISING EXPENSE **ACCOUNT NO. 531**

Date	Explanation	Post Ref.	Debit	Credit	Balance	
					Debit	Credit

Name ______________________ Class ______________ Date ______________

FORMS FOR DEMONSTRATION PROBLEM (CONCLUDED)

ABBY'S EMPLOYMENT AGENCY
TRIAL BALANCE
MARCH 31, 200X

	Dr.	Cr.

Name ____________________ Class ____________________ Date ____________________

CHAPTER 3
FORMS FOR CLASSROOM DEMONSTRATION EXERCISES SET A OR SET B

1. A. ____________________ E. ____________________
B. ____________________ F. ____________________
C. ____________________ G. ____________________
D. ____________________ H. ____________________
I. ____________________

2. A. ____________________
B. ____________________
C. ____________________

3.

CASH **ACCOUNT NO. 111**

Date		Explanation	Post Ref.	Debit	Credit	Balance Debit	Balance Credit

____
____

4.

LEE CO.
TRIAL BALANCE
OCTOBER 31, 200X

	Dr.	Cr.

Name ______________________ Class ______________ Date ______________

FORMS FOR CLASSROOM DEMONSTRATION EXERCISES SET A OR SET B (CONCLUDED)

5.

Date		Account Titles and Description	PR	Dr.	Cr.

FORMS FOR EXERCISES

3-1.

Date		Account Titles and Description	PR	Dr.	Cr.

Name ____________________ Class ____________________ Date ____________________

EXERCISES (CONTINUED)

3-2.

Date	Account Titles and Description	PR	Dr.	Cr.

Name ____________ Class ____________ Date ____________

EXERCISES (CONTINUED)

3-3.

Date		Account Titles and Description	PR	Dr.	Cr.
200X					
April	6	Cash		15 000 —	
		A. King, Capital			15 000 —
		Cash investment			
	14	Equipment		9 000 —	
		Cash			4 000 —
		Accounts Payable			5 000 —
		Purchase of Equipment			

CASH **ACCOUNT NO. 111**

Date		Explanation	Post Ref.	Debit	Credit	Balance	
						Debit	Credit

EQUIPMENT **ACCOUNT NO. 121**

Date		Explanation	Post Ref.	Debit	Credit	Balance	
						Debit	Credit

ACCOUNTS PAYABLE **ACCOUNT NO. 211**

Date		Explanation	Post Ref.	Debit	Credit	Balance	
						Debit	Credit

A. KING, CAPITAL **ACCOUNT NO. 311**

Date		Explanation	Post Ref.	Debit	Credit	Balance	
						Debit	Credit

Name ______________ Class ______________ Date ______________

EXERCISES (CONTINUED)

3-4.

(A)

PAGE 1

Date		Account Titles and Description	PR	Dr.	Cr.

(B)

CASH **ACCOUNT NO. 111**

Date		Explanation	Post Ref.	Debit	Credit	Balance Debit	Balance Credit

ACCOUNTS RECEIVABLE **ACCOUNT NO. 112**

Date		Explanation	Post Ref.	Debit	Credit	Balance Debit	Balance Credit

Name ______________________ Class ______________ Date ______________

EXERCISES (CONTINUED)

EQUIPMENT — **ACCOUNT NO. 121**

Date	Explanation	Post Ref.	Debit	Credit	Balance Debit	Balance Credit

ACCOUNTS PAYABLE — **ACCOUNT NO. 211**

Date	Explanation	Post Ref.	Debit	Credit	Balance Debit	Balance Credit

J. LOWE, CAPITAL — **ACCOUNT NO. 311**

Date	Explanation	Post Ref.	Debit	Credit	Balance Debit	Balance Credit

J. LOWE, WITHDRAWALS — **ACCOUNT NO. 312**

Date	Explanation	Post Ref.	Debit	Credit	Balance Debit	Balance Credit

FEES EARNED — **ACCOUNT NO. 411**

Date	Explanation	Post Ref.	Debit	Credit	Balance Debit	Balance Credit

SALARIES EXPENSE — **ACCOUNT NO. 511**

Date	Explanation	Post Ref.	Debit	Credit	Balance Debit	Balance Credit

Name ______________________ Class ______________ Date ______________

EXERCISES (CONCLUDED)

(C)

LOWE COMPANY
TRIAL BALANCE
JULY 31, 200X

	Dr.	Cr.

3-5.

SUNG CO.
TRIAL BALANCE
MARCH 31, 200X

	Dr.	Cr.

3-6.

	Dr.	Cr.

Name ______________________ Class ______________ Date ______________

END OF CHAPTER PROBLEMS

PROBLEM 3A-1 OR PROBLEM 3B-1

JACK'S CLEANING SERVICE
GENERAL JOURNAL

PAGE 1

Date		Account Titles and Description	PR	Dr.	Cr.

Name ______________________ Class ______________ Date ______________

PROBLEM 3A-1 OR PROBLEM 3B-1 (CONCLUDED)

JACK'S CLEANING SERVICE
GENERAL JOURNAL

PAGE 2

Date		Account Titles and Description	PR	Dr.	Cr.

Name ____________________ Class ____________ Date ____________

PROBLEM 3A-2 OR PROBLEM 3B-2

(A, B)

BETTY'S ART STUDIO
GENERAL JOURNAL

PAGE 1

Date		Account Titles and Description	PR	Dr.	Cr.

Name ______________________ Class ______________ Date ______________

PROBLEM 3A-2 OR PROBLEM 3B-2 (CONTINUED)

GENERAL LEDGER OF BETTY'S ART STUDIO

CASH ACCOUNT NO. 111

Date	Explanation	Post Ref.	Debit	Credit	Balance Debit	Balance Credit

ACCOUNTS RECEIVABLE ACCOUNT NO. 112

Date	Explanation	Post Ref.	Debit	Credit	Balance Debit	Balance Credit

PREPAID RENT ACCOUNT NO. 114

Date	Explanation	Post Ref.	Debit	Credit	Balance Debit	Balance Credit

ART SUPPLIES ACCOUNT NO. 121

Date	Explanation	Post Ref.	Debit	Credit	Balance Debit	Balance Credit

Name ______________________ Class ______________ Date ______________

PROBLEM 3A-2 OR PROBLEM 3B-2 (CONTINUED)

EQUIPMENT **ACCOUNT NO. 131**

Date	Explanation	Post Ref.	Debit	Credit	Balance	
					Debit	Credit

ACCOUNTS PAYABLE **ACCOUNT NO. 211**

Date	Explanation	Post Ref.	Debit	Credit	Balance	
					Debit	Credit

BETTY RICE, CAPITAL **ACCOUNT NO. 311**

Date	Explanation	Post Ref.	Debit	Credit	Balance	
					Debit	Credit

BETTY RICE, WITHDRAWALS **ACCOUNT NO. 312**

Date	Explanation	Post Ref.	Debit	Credit	Balance	
					Debit	Credit

Name ____________________ Class ____________________ Date ____________________

PROBLEM 3A-2 OR PROBLEM 3B-2 (CONTINUED)

ART FEES EARNED **ACCOUNT NO. 411**

Date	Explanation	Post Ref.	Debit	Credit	Balance Debit	Balance Credit

ELECTRICAL EXPENSE **ACCOUNT NO. 511**

Date	Explanation	Post Ref.	Debit	Credit	Balance Debit	Balance Credit

SALARIES EXPENSE **ACCOUNT NO. 521**

Date	Explanation	Post Ref.	Debit	Credit	Balance Debit	Balance Credit

TELEPHONE EXPENSE **ACCOUNT NO. 531**

Date	Explanation	Post Ref.	Debit	Credit	Balance Debit	Balance Credit

Name ______________ Class ______________ Date ______________

PROBLEM 3A-2 OR PROBLEM 3B-2 (CONCLUDED)

(C)

BETTY'S ART STUDIO
TRIAL BALANCE
JUNE 30, 200X

	Dr.	Cr.

Name ______________________ Class ______________ Date ______________

PROBLEM 3A-3 OR PROBLEM 3B-3
(A, B)

A. FRENCH'S PLACEMENT AGENCY
GENERAL JOURNAL

PAGE 1

Date		Account Titles and Description	PR	Dr.	Cr.

Name ______________________ Class ______________ Date ______________

PROBLEM 3A-3 OR PROBLEM 3B-3 (CONTINUED)

GENERAL LEDGER OF A. FRENCH'S PLACEMENT AGENCY

CASH — ACCOUNT NO. 111

Date	Explanation	Post Ref.	Debit	Credit	Balance	
					Debit	Credit

ACCOUNTS RECEIVABLE — ACCOUNT NO. 112

Date	Explanation	Post Ref.	Debit	Credit	Balance	
					Debit	Credit

SUPPLIES — ACCOUNT NO. 131

Date	Explanation	Post Ref.	Debit	Credit	Balance	
					Debit	Credit

EQUIPMENT — ACCOUNT NO. 141

Date	Explanation	Post Ref.	Debit	Credit	Balance	
					Debit	Credit

Name ______________________ Class ______________ Date ______________

PROBLEM 3A-3 OR PROBLEM 3B-3 (CONTINUED)

ACCOUNTS PAYABLE **ACCOUNT NO. 211**

Date		Explanation	Post Ref.	Debit	Credit	Balance	
						Debit	Credit

A. FRENCH, CAPITAL **ACCOUNT NO. 311**

Date		Explanation	Post Ref.	Debit	Credit	Balance	
						Debit	Credit

A. FRENCH,WITHDRAWALS **ACCOUNT NO. 312**

Date		Explanation	Post Ref.	Debit	Credit	Balance	
						Debit	Credit

PLACEMENT FEES EARNED **ACCOUNT NO. 411**

Date		Explanation	Post Ref.	Debit	Credit	Balance	
						Debit	Credit

Name ____________________ Class ____________ Date ____________

PROBLEM 3A-3 OR PROBLEM 3B-3 (CONTINUED)

WAGE EXPENSE — **ACCOUNT NO. 511**

Date		Explanation	Post Ref.	Debit	Credit	Balance	
						Debit	Credit

TELEPHONE EXPENSE — **ACCOUNT NO. 521**

Date		Explanation	Post Ref.	Debit	Credit	Balance	
						Debit	Credit

ADVERTISING EXPENSE — **ACCOUNT NO. 531**

Date		Explanation	Post Ref.	Debit	Credit	Balance	
						Debit	Credit

Name ______________________ Class ______________ Date ______________

PROBLEM 3A-3 OR PROBLEM 3B-3 (CONCLUDED)

(C)

A. FRENCH'S PLACEMENT AGENCY
TRIAL BALANCE
JUNE 30, 200X

	Dr.	Cr.

Name ______________________ Class ______________ Date ______________

CHAPTER 3
SUMMARY PRACTICE TEST: BEGINNING THE ACCOUNTING CYCLE: JOURNALIZING, POSTING, AND THE TRIAL BALANCE

Part I Instructions

Fill in the blank(s) to complete the statement.

1. A fiscal year runs for ______________ months.
2. ______________ ______________ are prepared for parts of a fiscal year (monthly, quarterly, etc.).
3. The ______________ ______________ ______________ eliminates the need for footings.
4. The positive balance of each account is referred to as its ______________ ______________.
5. The process of recording transactions in a journal is called ______________.
6. Entries are journalized in ______________ ______________.
7. A ledger is often called a(n) ______________ ______________ ______________ ______________.
8. The ______________ portion of a journal entry is indented and placed below the ______________ portion.
9. A journal entry requiring three or more accounts is called a(n) ______________ ______________ ______________.
10. Accounts receivable is a(n) ______________ on the balance sheet.
11. When supplies are used up or consumed they become a(n) ______________.
12. The book of original entry usually refers to a(n) ______________.
13. The process of transferring information from a journal to a ledger is called ______________.
14. ______________ ______________ deals with the process of updating the PR of the journal from the account number of the ledger to indicate to which account in the ledger information has been posted.
15. Recording $995.00 as $99.50 is an example of a(n) ______________.

Name ______________________ Class ______________ Date ______________

Part II Instructions

Match the term in column A to the definition, example, or phrase in column B. Be sure to use a letter only once.

COLUMN A

__g__ **1.** EXAMPLE: Book of original entry

_____ **2.** Non-Business Expense

_____ **3.** Slide

_____ **4.** Transposition

_____ **5.** Posting

_____ **6.** General Journal

_____ **7.** Cross-reference

_____ **8.** Journalizing

_____ **9.** Balance Sheet prepared monthly

_____ **10.** A fiscal year

COLUMN B

a. 243 — 2430

b. Transferring information from a general journal to a ledger

c. Chronological order

d. Increased by a credit

e. Withdrawal

f. Compound journal entry

g. General journal

h. Rearrangement of digits of a number by accident

i. Updating PR column of journal from ledger account

j. Trial balance

k. Place to record transactions

l. Accounting cycle

m. Accounting period

n. Interim statements

Part III Instructions

Answer true or false to the following statements.

1. A slide cannot affect position of numbers.

2. The totals of a trial balance may possibly not balance due to transpositions.

3. Withdrawals has a normal balance of a credit.

4. The running balance of an account can be kept in a four-column account.

5. The journal links debits and credits in alphabetical order.

6. The ledger accumulates information from the journal.

7. The post reference column of a ledger records the account number of that account.

8. An accounting cycle must be from January 1 to December 31.

9. The ledger is the book of original entry.

10. The income statement is prepared for a specific accounting period.

11. Interim statements are prepared for an entire fiscal year.

12. A calendar year could be a fiscal year.

13. 390 written by mistake as 3,900 is an example of a slide.

14. If the totals of a trial balance balance, the individual balance of items must be correct.
15. The equality of debits and credits on a trial balance does not guarantee that transactions have been properly recorded.
16. The trial balance is prepared from the journal.
17. Cross-referencing means never updating the post reference column of the journal.
18. Journals and ledgers are always in the same book.
19. The normal balance of each account is located on the same side that increases the acccount.
20. Ruling of four-column accounts is eliminated.

CHAPTER 3
SOLUTIONS TO SUMMARY PRACTICE TEST

Part I

1. 12
2. Interim statements
3. four-column ledger
4. normal balance
5. journalizing
6. chronological order
7. book of final entry
8. credit, debit
9. compound journal entry
10. asset
11. expense
12. journal
13. posting
14. Cross-reference
15. slide

Part II

1. g
2. e
3. a
4. h
5. b
6. k
7. i
8. c
9. n
10. m

Part III

1. false
2. true
3. false
4. true
5. false
6. true
7. false
8. false
9. false
10. true
11. false
12. true
13. true
14. false
15. true
16. false
17. false
18. false
19. true
20. true

Name ______________________ Class ______________ Date ______________

CONTINUING PROBLEM FOR CHAPTER 3

SANCHEZ COMPUTER CENTER
GENERAL JOURNAL

PAGE 1

Date		Account Titles and Description	PR	Dr.	Cr.

Name ______________________ Class ______________ Date ______________

SANCHEZ COMPUTER CENTER
GENERAL JOURNAL

PAGE 1 (Cont.)

Date		Account Titles and Description	PR	Dr.	Cr.

Name ______________________ Class ______________ Date ______________

CASH **ACCOUNT NO. 1000**

Date		Explanation	Post Ref.	Debit	Credit	Balance Debit	Balance Credit
9/1	0X	Balance forward	✓			2 8 6 5 00	

Name ____________________ Class ______________ Date ______________

ACCOUNTS RECEIVABLE **ACCOUNT NO. 1020**

Date		Explanation	Post Ref.	Debit	Credit	Balance Debit	Balance Credit
9/1	0X	Balance forward	✓			850 00	

PREPAID RENT **ACCOUNT NO. 1025**

Date		Explanation	Post Ref.	Debit	Credit	Balance Debit	Balance Credit

SUPPLIES **ACCOUNT NO. 1030**

Date		Explanation	Post Ref.	Debit	Credit	Balance Debit	Balance Credit
9/1	0X	Balance forward	✓			450 00	

COMPUTER SHOP EQUIPMENT **ACCOUNT NO. 1080**

Date		Explanation	Post Ref.	Debit	Credit	Balance Debit	Balance Credit
9/1	0X		✓			1 200 00	

Name ____________________ Class ____________ Date ____________

OFFICE EQUIPMENT **ACCOUNT NO. 1090**

Date		Explanation	Post Ref.	Debit	Credit	Balance Debit	Balance Credit
9/1	0X	Balance forward	✓			600 00	

ACCOUNTS PAYABLE **ACCOUNT NO. 2000**

Date		Explanation	Post Ref.	Debit	Credit	Balance Debit	Balance Credit
9/1	0X	Balance forward	✓				405 00

FREEDMAN, CAPITAL **ACCOUNT NO. 3000**

Date		Explanation	Post Ref.	Debit	Credit	Balance Debit	Balance Credit
9/1	0X	Balance forward	✓				4 500 00

FREEDMAN, WITHDRAWALS **ACCOUNT NO. 3010**

Date		Explanation	Post Ref.	Debit	Credit	Balance Debit	Balance Credit
9/1	0X	Balance forward	✓			100 00	

Name ______________________ Class ______________ Date ______________

SERVICE REVENUE **ACCOUNT NO. 4000**

Date		Explanation	Post Ref.	Debit	Credit	Balance Debit	Balance Credit
9/1	0X	Balance forward	✓				3 4 0 0 00

ADVERTISING EXPENSE **ACCOUNT NO. 5010**

Date		Explanation	Post Ref.	Debit	Credit	Balance Debit	Balance Credit
9/1	0X	Balance forward	✓			1 4 0 0 00	

RENT EXPENSE **ACCOUNT NO. 5020**

Date		Explanation	Post Ref.	Debit	Credit	Balance Debit	Balance Credit
9/1	0X	Balance forward	✓			4 0 0 00	

Name ______________________ Class ______________ Date ______________

UTILITIES EXPENSE **ACCOUNT NO. 5030**

Date		Explanation	Post Ref.	Debit	Credit	Balance Debit	Balance Credit
9/1	0X	Balance forward	✓			85 00	

PHONE EXPENSE **ACCOUNT NO. 5040**

Date		Explanation	Post Ref.	Debit	Credit	Balance Debit	Balance Credit
9/1	0X	Balance forward	✓			155 00	

SUPPLIES EXPENSE **ACCOUNT NO. 5050**

Date		Explanation	Post Ref.	Debit	Credit	Balance Debit	Balance Credit

Name ______________________ Class ______________ Date ______________

INSURANCE EXPENSE **ACCOUNT NO. 5060**

Date		Explanation	Post Ref.	Debit	Credit	Balance Debit	Balance Credit
9/1	0X	Balance forward	✓			150 00	

POSTAGE EXPENSE **ACCOUNT NO. 5070**

Date		Explanation	Post Ref.	Debit	Credit	Balance Debit	Balance Credit
9/1	0X	Balance forward	✓			50 00	

Name ______________________ Class ______________ Date ______________

SANCHEZ COMPUTER CENTER
TRIAL BALANCE
SEPTEMBER 30, 200X

	Dr.	Cr.

Name ______________________ Class ______________ Date ______________

SANCHEZ COMPUTER CENTER
INCOME STATEMENT
FOR THE QUARTER ENDED 9/30/0X

SANCHEZ COMPUTER CENTER
STATEMENT OF OWNER'S EQUITY
FOR THE QUARTER ENDED 9/30/0X

SANCHEZ COMPUTER CENTER
BALANCE SHEET
9/30/0X

ASSETS				LIABILITIES AND OWNER'S EQUITY			

4 THE ACCOUNTING CYCLE CONTINUED: PREPARING WORKSHEETS AND FINANCIAL STATEMENTS

SELF-REVIEW QUIZ 4-1

Use one of the blank fold-out worksheets that accompanied your textbook.

Name ______________________ Class ______________ Date ______________

SELF-REVIEW QUIZ 4-2

(1)

(2)

Name ______________________ Class ______________ Date ______________

(3)

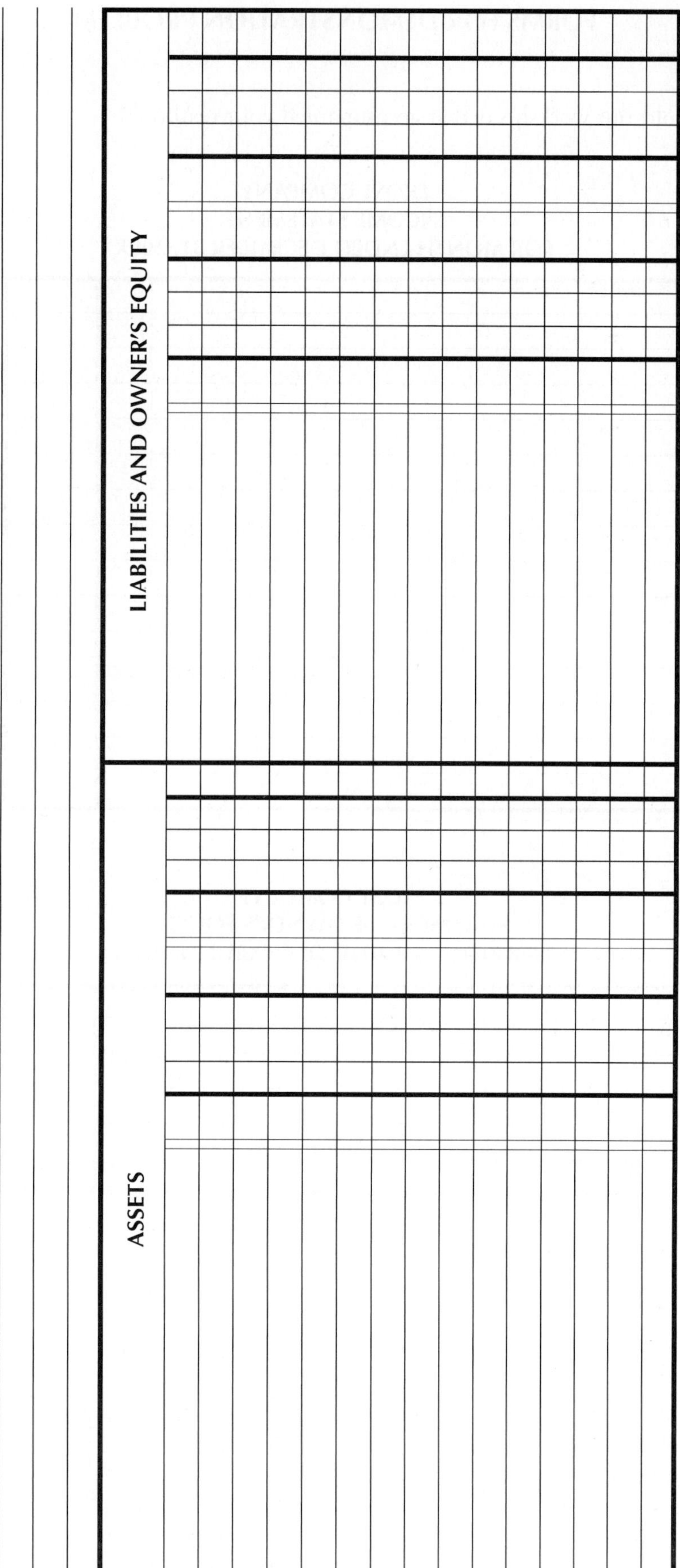

ASSETS

LIABILITIES AND OWNER'S EQUITY

Name ______________________ Class ______________ Date ______________

FORMS FOR DEMONSTRATION PROBLEM

(1)

Use one of the blank fold-out worksheets that accompanied your textbook.

(2)

FROST COMPANY
INCOME STATEMENT
FOR MONTH ENDED DECEMBER 31, 200X

(2)

FROST COMPANY
STATEMENT OF OWNER'S EQUITY
FOR MONTH ENDED DECEMBER 31, 200X

Name ______________________ Class ______________ Date ______________

DEMONSTRATION PROBLEM (CONCLUDED)

(2)

FROST COMPANY
BALANCE SHEET
DECEMBER 31, 200X

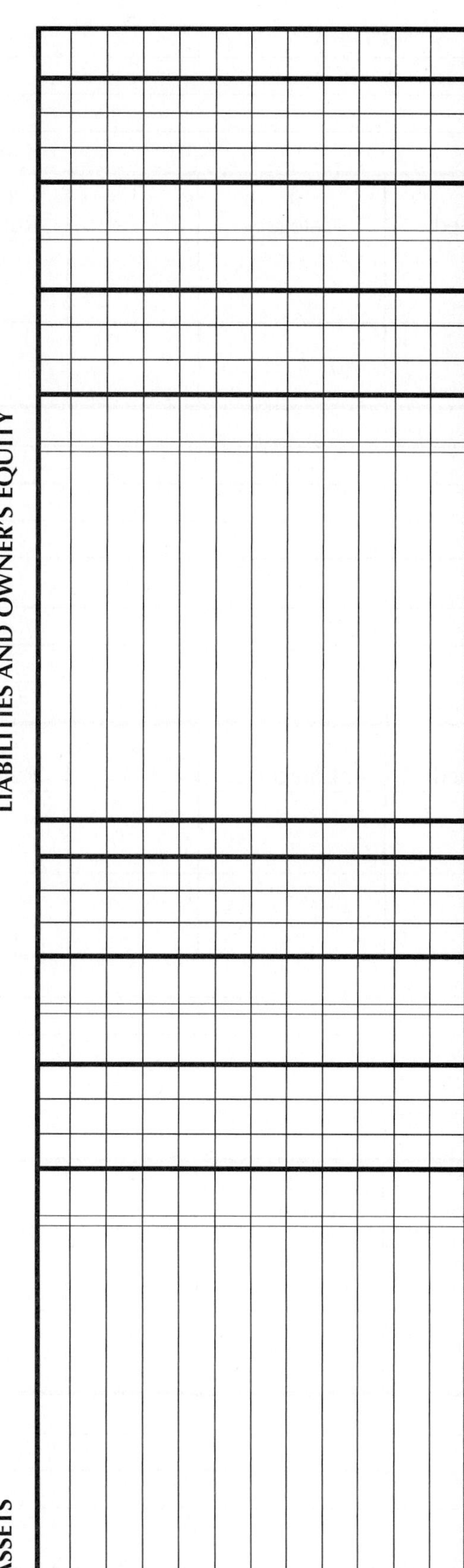

Name ____________________ Class ____________ Date ____________

CHAPTER 4
FORMS FOR CLASSROOM DEMONSTRATION EXERCISES SET A OR SET B

1. A.

B.

1. Accounts Affected	2. Category	3. ↑ ↓	4. Rules	5. T Account

C.

2. A.

B.

1. Accounts Affected	2. Category	3. ↑ ↓	4. Rules	5. T Account

C.

3. A.

B.

C.

1. Accounts Affected	2. Category	3. ↑ ↓	4. Rules	5. T Account

D.

Name ______________ Class ______________ Date ______________

4. A.

1. Accounts Affected	2. Category	3. ↑ ↓	4. Rules	5. T Account

B. ______________

5.

A. ______________ H. ______________
B. ______________ I. ______________
C. ______________ J. ______________
D. ______________ K. ______________
E. ______________ L. ______________
F. ______________ M. ______________
G. ______________ N. ______________

6.

A. ______________

B. ______________

Name ______________________ Class ______________ Date ______________

FORMS FOR EXERCISES

4-1.

Account	Category	Normal Balance	Financial Statement(s) Found on

4-2.

Accounts Affected	Category	↑ ↓	Rules	Amount
A.				
B.				

4-3.

A. ______________________________

____

B. ______________________________

____

____

4-4.

Use one of the blank fold-out worksheets that accompanied your textbook.

Name ______________________ Class ______________ Date ______________

EXERCISES (CONTINUED)

4-5.
(A)

J. TRENT
INCOME STATEMENT
FOR MONTH ENDED DECEMBER 31, 200X

(B)

J. TRENT
STATEMENT OF OWNER'S EQUITY
FOR MONTH ENDED DECEMBER 31, 200X

Name ____________________ Class ____________ Date ____________

EXERCISES (CONCLUDED)
(C)

J. TRENT
BALANCE SHEET
DECEMBER 31, 200X

ASSETS		LIABILITIES AND OWNER'S EQUITY	

Name ______________________ Class ______________ Date ______________

END OF CHAPTER PROBLEMS

PROBLEM 4A-1 OR PROBLEM 4B-1

Use one of the blank fold-out worksheets that accompanied your textbook.

PROBLEM 4A-2 OR PROBLEM 4B-2

Use one of the blank fold-out worksheets that accompanied your textbook.

PROBLEM 4A-3 OR PROBLEM 4B-3

Use one of the blank fold-out worksheets that accompanied your textbook.

(2)

KEVIN'S MOVING CO.
INCOME STATEMENT
FOR MONTH ENDED OCTOBER 31, 200X

KEVIN'S MOVING CO.
STATEMENT OF OWNER'S EQUITY
FOR MONTH ENDED OCTOBER 31, 200X

(2)

Name ______________________ Class ______________ Date ______________

PROBLEM 4A-3 OR PROBLEM 4B-3 (CONCLUDED)

(2)

KEVIN'S MOVING CO.
BALANCE SHEET
OCTOBER 31, 200X

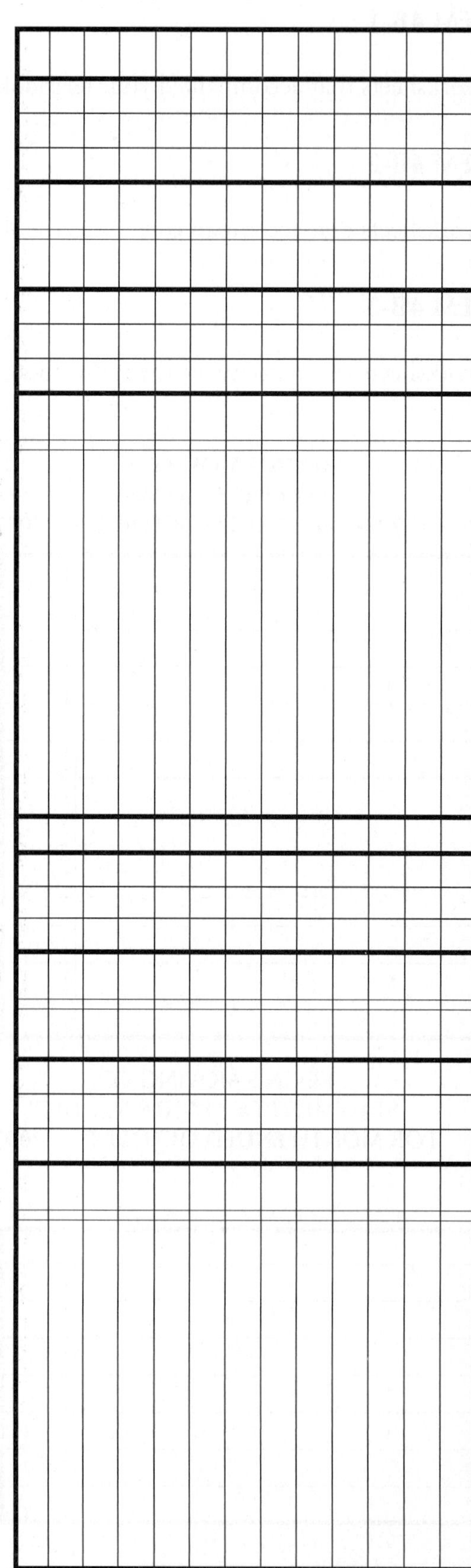

ASSETS

LIABILITIES AND OWNER'S EQUITY

Name ______________________ Class ______________ Date ______________

PROBLEM 4A-4 OR PROBLEM 4B-4

Use one of the blank fold-out worksheets that accompanied your textbook.

(2)

DICK'S REPAIR SERVICE
INCOME STATEMENT
FOR MONTH ENDED NOVEMBER 30, 200X

(2)

DICK'S REPAIR SERVICE
STATEMENT OF OWNER'S EQUITY
FOR MONTH ENDED NOVEMBER 30, 200X

Name ______________ Class ______________ Date ______________

PROBLEM 4A-4 OR PROBLEM 4B-4 (CONCLUDED)

(2)

DICK'S REPAIR SERVICE
BALANCE SHEET
NOVEMBER 30, 200X

ASSETS

LIABILITIES AND OWNER'S EQUITY

Name ______________________ Class ______________ Date ______________

CHAPTER 4
SUMMARY PRACTICE TEST: THE ACCOUNTING CYCLE CONTINUED: PREPARING WORKSHEETS AND FINANCIAL STATEMENTS

Part I Instructions

Fill in the blank(s) to complete the statement.

1. ______________ is an estimate.
2. A(n) ______________ will decrease accumulated depreciation.
3. ______________ affect both the income statement and balance sheet.
4. The adjustment for supplies reflects the amount of supplies ______________ ______________.
5. Supplies Expense is found on the income statement. Supplies are found on the ______________ ______________.
6. ______________ ______________ reflects the cost of equipment at time of purchase.
7. Depreciation Expense is found on the ______________ ______________.
8. ______________ ______________ is a contra asset that has a credit balance.
9. Accumulated Depreciation, a contra asset, is found on the ______________ ______________.
10. Historical or original cost of an auto less ______________ ______________ reflects the unused amount of the auto on the accounting books.
11. Withdrawals are found in the ______________ column of the balance sheet section of the worksheet.
12. Salaries Payable is a liability that will appear in the ______________ ______________ ______________ ______________ of the worksheet.
13. The figure for net income on the worksheet is carried over to the ______________ column of the balance sheet.
14. A worksheet is a(n) ______________ report.
15. ______________ ______________ are prepared after the completion of the worksheet.

Part II Instructions

Complete the following statements by circling the letter of the appropriate answer.

Name ______________________ Class ______________ Date ______________

1. The adjustment for depreciation results in Accumulated Depreciation
   a. decreasing.
   b. staying the same.
   c. increasing.
2. The historical or original cost of an asset on the worksheet
   a. never changes.
   b. sometimes changes.
   c. continually changes.
3. Net income on the worksheet is carried over to the
   a. trial balance.
   b. adjusted trial balance.
   c. balance sheet column.
4. Accumulated Depreciation is found on
   a. a worksheet.
   b. an income statement.
   c. both a worksheet and an income statement.
5. Accumulated Depreciation, a contra asset, is increased by a
   a. debit.
   b. credit.
   c. both a and b.
6. A worksheet is usually completed
   a. one column at a time.
   b. two columns at a time.
   c. three columns at a time.
7. Withdrawals on the worksheet are found in the
   a. debit column of the income statement.
   b. debit column of the balance sheet.
   c. both a and b.
8. The worksheet specifically shows the
   a. beginning figure for owner capital.
   b. ending figure for owner capital.
   c. average figure for owner capital.
9. The total of the assets on a formal balance sheet will __________ equal the total of the debit column of the balance sheet on the worksheet.
   a. always
   b. sometimes
   c. never
10. The adjustment for depreciation affects
   a. the income statement.
   b. the balance sheet.
   c. both a and b.
11. The adjustment for supplies requires one to know
   a. beginning supplies plus supplies purchased.
   b. supplies on hand.
   c. both a and b.

12. The purpose of adjustments is to
    a. bring general journals up to date.
    b. bring ledger accounts up to proper balances in the journal.
    c. bring ledger accounts to proper balance.
13. Book values equals cost less
    a. expenses.
    b. accumulated depreciation.
    c. neither a nor b.
14. The __________ is an informal report.
    a. income statement
    b. balance sheet
    c. worksheet

Part III Instructions

Answer true or false to the following statements.

1. The normal balance of accumulated depreciation is a credit.
2. Liabilities are only income statement accounts.
3. The total of the adjustments column may balance but be incorrect.
4. Prepaid rent is found on the income statement.
5. Rent expense is found on the income statement.
6. Debits and credits are found on financial statements.
7. Historical cost relates only to automobiles.
8. Accumulated Depreciation is found on the income statement.
9. As Accumulated Depreciation increases, the historical cost changes.
10. The adjustment for depreciation directly affects cash.
11. An expense is only recorded when it is paid.
12. The ending figure for owner capital does not have to be calculated from the worksheet.
13. Withdrawals have the same balance as Accumulated Depreciation.
14. Salaries Payable is an asset on the income statement.
15. Net loss would never be shown on a worksheet.
16. The net income on the worksheet is the same amount on the income statement.
17. Worksheets must use dollar signs.
18. The worksheet eliminates the need to prepare financial statements.
19. Cost less accumulated depreciation equals book value.
20. Accrued Salaries are expenses that have already been paid for.

Name ______________________ Class ______________ Date ______________

CHAPTER 4
SOLUTIONS TO SUMMARY PRACTICE TEST

Part I

1. Depreciation
2. debit
3. Adjustments
4. used up
5. balance sheet
6. Historical (original) cost
7. income statement
8. Accumulated Depreciation
9. balance sheet
10. accumulated depreciation
11. debit
12. balance sheet credit column
13. credit
14. informal
15. Financial statements

Part II

1. c
2. a
3. c
4. a
5. b
6. b
7. b
8. a
9. c
10. c
11. c
12. c
13. b
14. c

Part III

1. true
2. false
3. true
4. false
5. true
6. false
7. false
8. false
9. false
10. false
11. false
12. true
13. false
14. false
15. false
16. true
17. false
18. false
19. true
20. false

Name ____________________ Class ____________________ Date ____________________

CONTINUING PROBLEM FOR CHAPTER 4*

SANCHEZ COMPUTER CENTER
INCOME STATEMENT
FOR THE THREE MONTHS ENDED SEPTEMBER 30, 200X

SANCHEZ COMPUTER CENTER
STATEMENT OF OWNER'S EQUITY
FOR THE THREE MONTHS ENDED SEPTEMBER 30, 200X

*Use one of the blank fold-out worksheets that accompanied your textbook.

Name ____________________ Class ____________ Date ____________

SANCHEZ COMPUTER CENTER
BALANCE SHEET
SEPTEMBER 30, 200X

ASSETS

LIABILITIES AND OWNER'S EQUITY

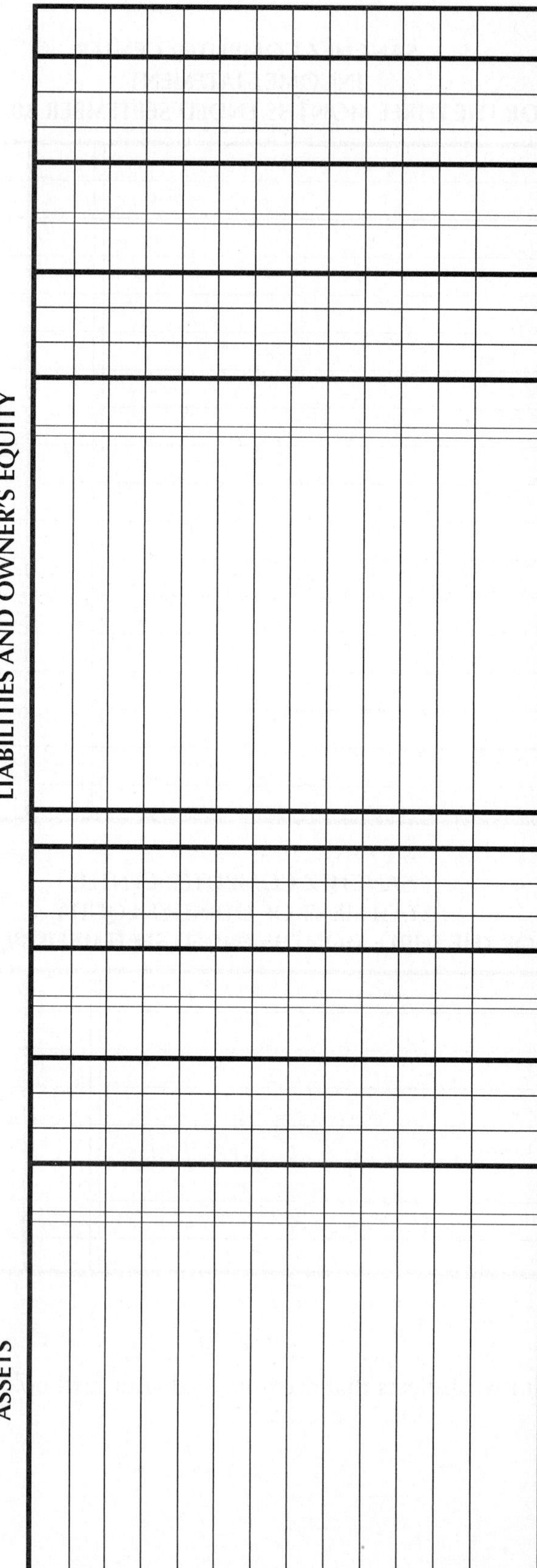

5

The Accounting Cycle Completed: Adjusting, Closing, and the Post-Closing Trial Balance

SELF-REVIEW QUIZ 5-1

(1)

PAGE 2

Date		Account Titles and Description	PR	Dr.	Cr.

Name ______________________ Class ______________ Date ______________

(2) Partial Ledger

Depreciation Expense, Store Equipment 511	

Accumulated Depreciation, Store Equipment 122	
	4

Prepaid Insurance 116	
3	

Insurance Expense 516	

Store Supplies 114	
5	

Supplies Expense 514	

Salaries Expense 512	
8	

Salaries Payable 212	

Name ______________________ Class ______________ Date ______________

SELF-REVIEW QUIZ 5-2

(1)

P. Logan, Capital 310

Dr.	Cr.
	14

Revenue from Clients 410

Dr.	Cr.
	25

Supplies Expense 514

Dr.	Cr.
4	

P. Logan, Withdrawals 311

Dr.	Cr.
3	

Depreciation Expense, Store Equipment 510

Dr.	Cr.
1	

Insurance Expense 516

Dr.	Cr.
2	

Income Summary 312

Dr.	Cr.

Salaries Expense 512

Dr.	Cr.
11	

Rent Expense 518

Dr.	Cr.
2	

Name ______________________ Class ______________ Date ______________

(2)

SELF-REVIEW QUIZ 5-3

Name ____________________ Class ____________ Date ____________

FORMS FOR DEMONSTRATION PROBLEM

Use one of the blank fold-out worksheets that accompanied your textbook.

ROLO COMPANY
GENERAL JOURNAL

PAGE 1

Date		Account Titles and Description	PR	Dr.	Cr.

Name ______________________ Class ______________ Date ______________

FORMS FOR DEMONSTRATION PROBLEM (CONTINUED)

ROLO COMPANY
GENERAL JOURNAL

PAGE 2

Date		Account Titles and Description	PR	Dr.	Cr.

Name ______________________ Class ______________ Date ______________

FORMS FOR DEMONSTRATION PROBLEM (CONTINUED)

CASH **ACCOUNT NO. 111**

Date		Explanation	Post Ref.	Debit	Credit	Balance	
						Debit	Credit

ACCOUNTS RECEIVABLE **ACCOUNT NO. 112**

Date		Explanation	Post Ref.	Debit	Credit	Balance	
						Debit	Credit

PREPAID RENT **ACCOUNT NO. 114**

Date		Explanation	Post Ref.	Debit	Credit	Balance	
						Debit	Credit

OFFICE SUPPLIES **ACCOUNT NO. 115**

Date		Explanation	Post Ref.	Debit	Credit	Balance	
						Debit	Credit

Name ______________________ Class ______________ Date ______________

FORMS FOR DEMONSTRATION PROBLEM (CONTINUED)

OFFICE EQUIPMENT **ACCOUNT NO. 121**

Date	Explanation	Post Ref.	Debit	Credit	Balance Debit	Balance Credit

ACCUMULATED DEPRECIATION, OFFICE EQUIPMENT **ACCOUNT NO. 122**

Date	Explanation	Post Ref.	Debit	Credit	Balance Debit	Balance Credit

ACCOUNTS PAYABLE **ACCOUNT NO. 211**

Date	Explanation	Post Ref.	Debit	Credit	Balance Debit	Balance Credit

Name ____________________ Class ____________ Date ____________

FORMS FOR DEMONSTRATION PROBLEM (CONTINUED)

SALARIES PAYABLE **ACCOUNT NO. 212**

Date	Explanation	Post Ref.	Debit	Credit	Balance	
					Debit	Credit

ROLO KERN, CAPITAL **ACCOUNT NO. 311**

Date	Explanation	Post Ref.	Debit	Credit	Balance	
					Debit	Credit

ROLO KERN, WITHDRAWALS **ACCOUNT NO. 312**

Date	Explanation	Post Ref.	Debit	Credit	Balance	
					Debit	Credit

INCOME SUMMARY **ACCOUNT NO. 313**

Date	Explanation	Post Ref.	Debit	Credit	Balance	
					Debit	Credit

FEES EARNED **ACCOUNT NO. 411**

Date	Explanation	Post Ref.	Debit	Credit	Balance	
					Debit	Credit

Name ______________________ Class ______________ Date ______________

FORMS FOR DEMONSTRATION PROBLEM (CONTINUED)

SALARIES EXPENSE **ACCOUNT NO. 511**

Date		Explanation	Post Ref.	Debit	Credit	Balance	
						Debit	Credit

ADVERTISING EXPENSE **ACCOUNT NO. 512**

Date		Explanation	Post Ref.	Debit	Credit	Balance	
						Debit	Credit

RENT EXPENSE **ACCOUNT NO. 513**

Date		Explanation	Post Ref.	Debit	Credit	Balance	
						Debit	Credit

OFFICE SUPPLIES EXPENSE **ACCOUNT NO. 514**

Date		Explanation	Post Ref.	Debit	Credit	Balance	
						Debit	Credit

DEPRECIATION EXPENSE, OFFICE EQUIPMENT **ACCOUNT NO. 515**

Date		Explanation	Post Ref.	Debit	Credit	Balance	
						Debit	Credit

Name ______________________ Class ______________ Date ______________

FORMS FOR DEMONSTRATION PROBLEM (CONTINUED)

ROLO COMPANY
INCOME STATEMENT
FOR MONTH ENDED JANUARY 31, 200X

ROLO COMPANY
STATEMENT OF OWNER'S EQUITY
FOR MONTH ENDED JANUARY 31, 200X

Name ____________ Class ____________ Date ____________

FORMS FOR DEMONSTRATION PROBLEM (CONTINUED)

ROLO COMPANY
BALANCE SHEET
JANUARY 31, 200X

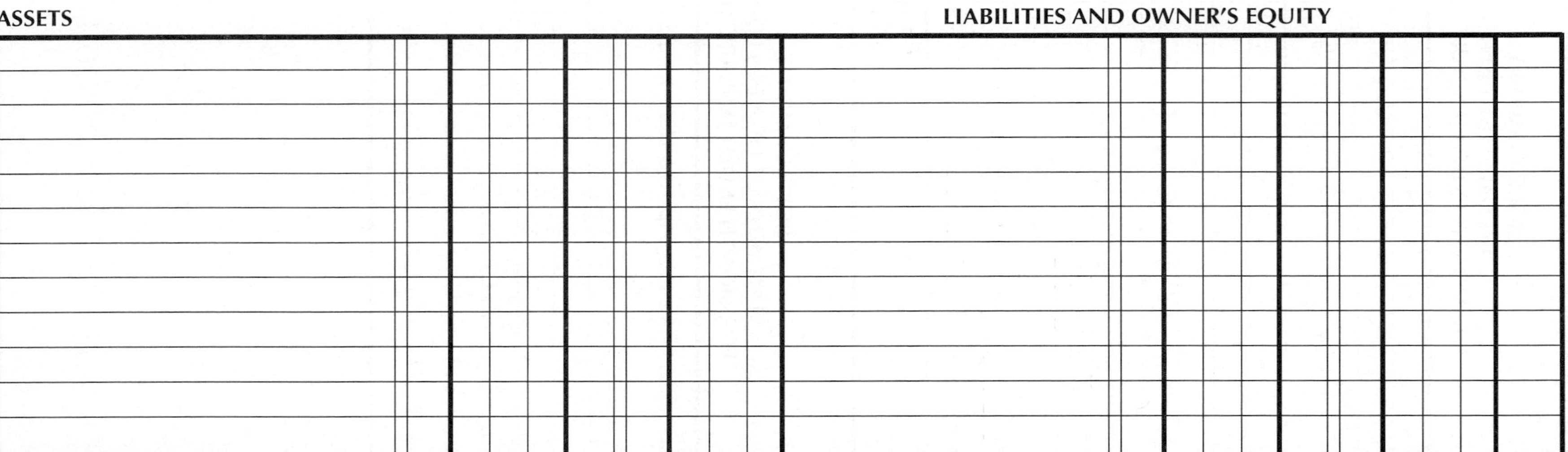

Name ______________________ Class ______________ Date ______________

FORMS FOR DEMONSTRATION PROBLEM (CONCLUDED)

ROLO COMPANY
POST-CLOSING TRIAL BALANCE
JANUARY 31, 200X

	Dr.	Cr.

Name ______________________ Class ______________ Date ______________

CHAPTER 5
FORMS FOR CLASSROOM DEMONSTRATION EXERCISES SET A OR SET B

GENERAL JOURNAL

1.

PAGE 3

Date		Account Titles and Description	PR	Dr.	Cr.

Prepaid Insurance 115

Insurance Expense 510

Store Supplies 116

Depreciation Expense, Store Equipment 512

Accumulated Depreciation Store Equipment 119

Supplies Expense 514

Salaries Payable 210

Salaries Expense 516

2. ____

Name ______________ Class ______________ Date ______________

GENERAL JOURNAL

3.

PAGE 4

Date		Account Titles and Description	PR	Dr.	Cr.

4.

Income Summary 314

5.

Mel Blanc, Capital 310

Name ______________________________ Class ____________________ Date ____________________

FORMS FOR EXERCISES

5-1.

Date		Account Titles and Description	PR	Dr.	Cr.

5-2.

	TEMPORARY	PERMANENT	WILL BE CLOSED
1. Income Summary			
2. Jen Rich, Capital			
3. Salary Expense			
4. Jen Rich, Withdrawals			
5. Fees Earned			
6. Accounts Payable			
7. Cash			

Name ______________ Class ______________ Date ______________

EXERCISES (CONTINUED)

5-3.

Date		Account Titles and Description	PR	Dr.	Cr.

Name ______________________ Class ______________ Date ______________

EXERCISES (CONCLUDED)

5-4.

Date		Account Titles and Description	PR	Dr.	Cr.

5-5.

WEY CO.
POST-CLOSING TRIAL BALANCE
DECEMBER 31, 200X

	Dr.	Cr.

Name ______________________ Class ______________ Date ______________

END OF CHAPTER PROBLEMS

PROBLEM 5A-1 OR PROBLEM 5B-1

Use one of the blank fold-out worksheets that accompanied your textbook.

(2)

DEBBIE'S DANCE STUDIO
GENERAL JOURNAL

PAGE 3

Date		Account Titles and Description	PR	Dr.	Cr.

Name ______________________ Class ______________ Date ______________

PROBLEM 5A-2 OR PROBLEM 5B-2

(1)

POTTER CLEANING SERVICE
GENERAL JOURNAL

PAGE 2

Date		Account Titles and Description	PR	Dr.	Cr.

Name ____________________ Class ____________________ Date ____________________

PROBLEM 5A-2 OR PROBLEM 5B-2 (CONTINUED)

CASH **ACCOUNT NO. 112**

Date		Explanation	Post Ref.	Debit	Credit	Balance	
						Debit	Credit

PREPAID INSURANCE **ACCOUNT NO. 114**

Date		Explanation	Post Ref.	Debit	Credit	Balance	
						Debit	Credit

CLEANING SUPPLIES **ACCOUNT NO. 115**

Date		Explanation	Post Ref.	Debit	Credit	Balance	
						Debit	Credit

AUTO **ACCOUNT NO. 121**

Date		Explanation	Post Ref.	Debit	Credit	Balance	
						Debit	Credit

ACCUMULATED DEPRECIATION, AUTO **ACCOUNT NO. 122**

Date		Explanation	Post Ref.	Debit	Credit	Balance	
						Debit	Credit

Name ______________________ Class ______________ Date ______________

PROBLEM 5A-2 OR PROBLEM 5B-2 (CONTINUED)

ACCOUNTS PAYABLE **ACCOUNT NO. 212**

Date		Explanation	Post Ref.	Debit	Credit	Balance	
						Debit	Credit

SALARIES PAYABLE **ACCOUNT NO. 213**

Date		Explanation	Post Ref.	Debit	Credit	Balance	
						Debit	Credit

B. POTTER, CAPITAL **ACCOUNT NO. 312**

Date		Explanation	Post Ref.	Debit	Credit	Balance	
						Debit	Credit

B. POTTER, WITHDRAWALS **ACCOUNT NO. 313**

Date		Explanation	Post Ref.	Debit	Credit	Balance	
						Debit	Credit

INCOME SUMMARY **ACCOUNT NO. 314**

Date		Explanation	Post Ref.	Debit	Credit	Balance	
						Debit	Credit

Name ______________________ Class ______________ Date ______________

PROBLEM 5A-2 OR PROBLEM 5B-2 (CONTINUED)

CLEANING FEES **ACCOUNT NO. 412**

Date		Explanation	Post Ref.	Debit	Credit	Balance Debit	Balance Credit

SALARIES EXPENSE **ACCOUNT NO. 513**

Date		Explanation	Post Ref.	Debit	Credit	Balance Debit	Balance Credit

TELEPHONE EXPENSE **ACCOUNT NO. 514**

Date		Explanation	Post Ref.	Debit	Credit	Balance Debit	Balance Credit

ADVERTISING EXPENSE **ACCOUNT NO. 515**

Date		Explanation	Post Ref.	Debit	Credit	Balance Debit	Balance Credit

GAS EXPENSE **ACCOUNT NO. 516**

Date		Explanation	Post Ref.	Debit	Credit	Balance Debit	Balance Credit

Name ______________________ Class ______________ Date ______________

PROBLEM 5A-2 OR PROBLEM 5B-2 (CONTINUED)

INSURANCE EXPENSE **ACCOUNT NO. 517**

Date		Explanation	Post Ref.	Debit	Credit	Balance	
						Debit	Credit

CLEANING SUPPLIES EXPENSE **ACCOUNT NO. 518**

Date		Explanation	Post Ref.	Debit	Credit	Balance	
						Debit	Credit

DEPRECIATION EXPENSE, AUTO **ACCOUNT NO. 519**

Date		Explanation	Post Ref.	Debit	Credit	Balance	
						Debit	Credit

Name ______________________ Class ______________ Date ______________

PROBLEM 5A-2 OR PROBLEM 5B-2 (CONCLUDED)

(2)

POTTER CLEANING SERVICE
POST-CLOSING TRIAL BALANCE
MARCH 31, 200X

	Dr.	Cr.

PROBLEM 5A-3 OR PROBLEM 5B-3

Use one of the blank fold-out worksheets that accompanied your textbook.

Name ______________________ Class ______________ Date ______________

PROBLEM 5A-3 OR PROBLEM 5B-3 (CONTINUED)

PETE'S PLOWING
GENERAL JOURNAL

PAGE 1

Date		Account Titles and Description	PR	Dr.	Cr.

Name ______________________ Class ______________ Date ______________

PROBLEM 5A-3 OR PROBLEM 5B-3 (CONTINUED)

PETE'S PLOWING
GENERAL JOURNAL

PAGE 2

Date		Account Titles and Description	PR	Dr.	Cr.

Name ____________________ Class ____________ Date ____________

PROBLEM 5A-3 OR PROBLEM 5B-3 (CONTINUED)

PETE'S PLOWING
GENERAL JOURNAL

PAGE 3

Date		Account Titles and Description	PR	Dr.	Cr.

Name ________________ Class ________________ Date ________________

PROBLEM 5A-3 OR PROBLEM 5B-3 (CONTINUED)

CASH **ACCOUNT NO. 111**

Date		Explanation	Post Ref.	Debit	Credit	Balance Debit	Balance Credit

ACCOUNTS RECEIVABLE **ACCOUNT NO. 112**

Date		Explanation	Post Ref.	Debit	Credit	Balance Debit	Balance Credit

PREPAID RENT **ACCOUNT NO. 114**

Date		Explanation	Post Ref.	Debit	Credit	Balance Debit	Balance Credit

SNOW SUPPLIES **ACCOUNT NO. 115**

Date		Explanation	Post Ref.	Debit	Credit	Balance Debit	Balance Credit

Name ____________ Class ____________ Date ____________

PROBLEM 5A-3 OR PROBLEM 5B-3 (CONTINUED)

OFFICE EQUIPMENT **ACCOUNT NO. 121**

Date		Explanation	Post Ref.	Debit	Credit	Balance Debit	Balance Credit

ACCUMULATED DEPRECIATION, OFFICE EQUIPMENT **ACCOUNT NO. 122**

Date		Explanation	Post Ref.	Debit	Credit	Balance Debit	Balance Credit

SNOW EQUIPMENT **ACCOUNT NO. 123**

Date		Explanation	Post Ref.	Debit	Credit	Balance Debit	Balance Credit

ACCUMULATED DEPRECIATION, SNOW EQUIPMENT **ACCOUNT NO. 124**

Date		Explanation	Post Ref.	Debit	Credit	Balance Debit	Balance Credit

ACCOUNTS PAYABLE **ACCOUNT NO. 211**

Date		Explanation	Post Ref.	Debit	Credit	Balance Debit	Balance Credit

Name ______________________ Class ______________ Date ______________

PROBLEM 5A-3 OR PROBLEM 5B-3 (CONTINUED)

SALARIES PAYABLE **ACCOUNT NO. 212**

Date		Explanation	Post Ref.	Debit	Credit	Balance	
						Debit	Credit

PETE MACK, CAPITAL **ACCOUNT NO. 311**

Date		Explanation	Post Ref.	Debit	Credit	Balance	
						Debit	Credit

PETE MACK, WITHDRAWALS **ACCOUNT NO. 312**

Date		Explanation	Post Ref.	Debit	Credit	Balance	
						Debit	Credit

INCOME SUMMARY **ACCOUNT NO. 313**

Date		Explanation	Post Ref.	Debit	Credit	Balance	
						Debit	Credit

PLOWING FEES **ACCOUNT NO. 411**

Date		Explanation	Post Ref.	Debit	Credit	Balance	
						Debit	Credit

Name ______________________ Class ______________ Date ______________

PROBLEM 5A-3 OR PROBLEM 5B-3 (CONTINUED)

SALARIES EXPENSE **ACCOUNT NO. 511**

Date		Explanation	Post Ref.	Debit	Credit	Balance Debit	Balance Credit

ADVERTISING EXPENSE **ACCOUNT NO. 512**

Date		Explanation	Post Ref.	Debit	Credit	Balance Debit	Balance Credit

TELEPHONE EXPENSE **ACCOUNT NO. 513**

Date		Explanation	Post Ref.	Debit	Credit	Balance Debit	Balance Credit

RENT EXPENSE **ACCOUNT NO. 514**

Date		Explanation	Post Ref.	Debit	Credit	Balance Debit	Balance Credit

SNOW SUPPLIES EXPENSE **ACCOUNT NO. 515**

Date		Explanation	Post Ref.	Debit	Credit	Balance Debit	Balance Credit

PROBLEM 5A-3 OR PROBLEM 5B-3 (CONTINUED)

DEPRECIATION EXPENSE, OFFICE EQUIPMENT **ACCOUNT NO. 516**

Date		Explanation	Post Ref.	Debit	Credit	Balance	
						Debit	Credit

DEPRECIATION EXPENSE, SNOW EQUIPMENT **ACCOUNT NO. 517**

Date		Explanation	Post Ref.	Debit	Credit	Balance	
						Debit	Credit

Name ____________________ Class ____________ Date ____________

PROBLEM 5A-3 OR PROBLEM 5B-3 (CONTINUED)

PETE'S PLOWING
INCOME STATEMENT
FOR MONTH ENDED JANUARY 31, 200X

PETE'S PLOWING
STATEMENT OF OWNER'S EQUITY
FOR MONTH ENDED JANUARY 31, 200X

Name ______________________ Class ______________ Date ______________

PROBLEM 5A-3 OR PROBLEM 5B-3 (CONTINUED)

PETE'S PLOWING
BALANCE SHEET
JANUARY 31, 200X

ASSETS

LIABILITIES AND OWNER'S EQUITY

Name ______________________ Class ______________ Date ______________

PROBLEM 5A-3 OR PROBLEM 5B-3 (CONCLUDED)

PETE'S PLOWING
POST-CLOSING TRIAL BALANCE
JANUARY 31, 200X

	Dr.	Cr.

Name ______________________ Class ______________ Date ______________

CHAPTER 5
SUMMARY PRACTICE TEST: THE ACCOUNTING CYCLE COMPLETED: ADJUSTING, CLOSING, AND THE POST-CLOSING TRIAL BALANCE

Part I Instructions

Fill in the blank(s) to complete the statement.

1. After the closing process only ______________ accounts remain with balances.
2. Revenue, Expenses, and Withdrawals are examples of ______________ ______________.
3. ______________ in temporary accounts will not be carried over to the next accounting period.
4. After closing entries are posted, owner's Capital in the ledger will contain the ______________ ______________.
5. Revenue is closed to Income Summary by a(n) ______________ to each revenue account and a(n) ______________ to Income Summary.
6. Expenses are closed to Income Summary by ______________ the individual expenses and ______________ Income Summary.
7. If the balance of Income Summary is a credit, it will be closed by ______________ Income Summary and ______________ owner's Capital.
8. The balance of Withdrawals is closed by a(n) ______________ and the amount transferred to owner's Capital by a(n) ______________.
9. At the end of the closing process, all temporary accounts in the ledger will have a(n) ______________ balance.
10. The ______________ ______________ ______________ ______________ contains a list of permanent accounts after the adjusting and closing entries have been posted to the ledger from a journal.
11. Closing entries can be prepared from a(n) ______________.
12. After closing entries are posted, Income Summary will have a(n) ______________ balance.
13. Journalizing adjustments can be done from the ______________.
14. Cash, Equipment, and Supplies are not part of the ______________ process.
15. Income Summary is a(n) ______________ account.

Part II Instructions

The following is a chart of accounts for Al's Auto Shop. From the chart, indicate in Column B (by account number) which accounts will be debited or credited as related to the transactions in Column A.

Name ____________________ Class ____________ Date ____________

CHART OF ACCOUNTS

ASSETS	OWNER'S EQUITY
112 Cash	340 A. Jones, Capital
114 Accounts Receivable	341 A. Jones, Withdrawals
116 Prepaid Rent	342 Income Summary
118 Auto Supplies	
120 Delivery Truck	REVENUE
121 Accumulated Depreciation, Delivery Truck	450 Fees Earned
LIABILITIES	EXPENSES
230 Accounts Payable	560 Salaries
232 Salaries Payable	562 Advertising
	564 Rent
	566 Auto Supplies
	568 Depreciation Expense, Delivery Truck

COLUMN A	COLUMN B Debit(s)	Credit(s)
1. Closed balance in revenue account to Income Summary.	________	________
2. Closed balance in individual expenses to Income Summary.	________	________
3. Closed balance in Income Summary to owner's Capital. (Assume that it is a net income.)	________	________
4. Closed Withdrawals to owner's Capital.	________	________
5. Recorded auto supplies used up.	________	________
6. Recorded depreciation on delivery truck.	________	________
7. Brought Salaries Expense up to date (an adjustment).	________	________

Part III Instructions

Answer true or false to the following statements.

1. Closing entries are done every other month.
2. Adjustments are journalized before preparing the worksheet.
3. Closing entries can only clear permanent accounts.
4. Income summary is a temporary account.
5. Interim statements can be prepared from worksheets.
6. To clear expenses in the closing process, a compound entry is appropriate.
7. Withdrawals is a temporary account on the income statement.
8. Income Summary helps update withdrawals.

9. Accumulated Depreciation is a permanent account on the income statement.
10. Cash, Rent Expense, and Accounts Receivable need to be closed at the end of the period.
11. Closing entries do not relate to the worksheet.
12. Revenue is closed by a credit.
13. Expenses are placed on the debit side of the Income Summary account.
14. A post-closing trial balance closely resembles the ending balance sheet.
15. Accumulated Depreciation never has to be adjusted.
16. Interim statements are always prepared monthly.
17. A post-closing trial balance is prepared before adjustments are journalized.
18. Income Summary is shown on the balance sheet.
19. The process of closing entries will help update owner's Capital.
20. The normal balance of the Income Summary is a debit.
21. The normal balance of the Income Summary is a credit.
22. The income statement is listed in terms of debits and credits.
23. Closing updates only permanent accounts.
24. The completion of financial statements means that the Capital account in the ledger has been updated.
25. Withdrawals is closed to Income Summary.

SOLUTIONS TO SUMMARY PRACTICE TEST

Part I

1. permanent
2. temporary accounts
3. Balances
4. ending figure (balance)
5. debit, credit
6. crediting, debiting
7. debiting, crediting
8. credit, debit
9. zero
10. post-closing trial balance
11. worksheet
12. zero
13. worksheet
14. closing
15. temporary

Part II

	Debit	Credit
1.	450	342
2.	342	560, 562, 564, 566, 568
3.	342	340
4.	340	341
5.	566	118
6.	568	121
7.	560	232

Name ______________________ Class ______________ Date ______________

Part III

1. false
2. false
3. false
4. true
5. true
6. true
7. false
8. false
9. false
10. false
11. false
12. false
13. true
14. true
15. false
16. false
17. false
18. false
19. true
20. false
21. false
22. false
23. false
24. false
25. false

Name ______________________ Class ______________ Date ______________

CONTINUING PROBLEM FOR CHAPTER 5

SANCHEZ COMPUTER CENTER
GENERAL JOURNAL

PAGE 2

Date		Account Titles and Description	PR	Dr.	Cr.

Name ______________________ Class ______________ Date ______________

CASH ACCOUNT NO. 1000

Date		Explanation	Post Ref.	Debit	Credit	Balance Debit	Balance Credit
9/30	0X	Balance forward	✓			1 645 00	

ACCOUNTS RECEIVABLE ACCOUNT NO. 1020

Date		Explanation	Post Ref.	Debit	Credit	Balance Debit	Balance Credit
9/30	0X	Balance forward	✓			2 600 00	

PREPAID RENT ACCOUNT NO. 1025

Date		Explanation	Post Ref.	Debit	Credit	Balance Debit	Balance Credit
9/30	0X	Balance forward	✓			1 200 00	

SUPPLIES ACCOUNT NO. 1030

Date		Explanation	Post Ref.	Debit	Credit	Balance Debit	Balance Credit
9/30	0X	Balance forward	✓			450 00	

Name ______________________ Class ______________ Date ______________

COMPUTER SHOP EQUIPMENT — ACCOUNT NO. 1080

Date		Explanation	Post Ref.	Debit	Credit	Balance Debit	Balance Credit
9/30	0X	Balance forward	✓			2 4 0 0 00	

ACCUMULATED DEPRECIATION, COMPUTER SHOP EQUIPMENT — ACCOUNT NO. 1081

Date		Explanation	Post Ref.	Debit	Credit	Balance Debit	Balance Credit

OFFICE EQUIPMENT — ACCOUNT NO. 1090

Date		Explanation	Post Ref.	Debit	Credit	Balance Debit	Balance Credit
9/30	0X	Balance forward	✓			6 0 0 00	

ACCUMULATED DEPRECIATION, OFFICE EQUIPMENT — ACCOUNT NO. 1091

Date		Explanation	Post Ref.	Debit	Credit	Balance Debit	Balance Credit

Name ______________________ Class ______________ Date ______________

ACCOUNTS PAYABLE **ACCOUNT NO. 2000**

Date		Explanation	Post Ref.	Debit	Credit	Balance Debit	Balance Credit
9/30	0X	Balance forward	✓				210 00

T. FREEDMAN, CAPITAL **ACCOUNT NO. 3000**

Date		Explanation	Post Ref.	Debit	Credit	Balance Debit	Balance Credit
9/30	0X	Balance forward	✓				4 500 00

T. FREEDMAN, WITHDRAWALS **ACCOUNT NO. 3010**

Date		Explanation	Post Ref.	Debit	Credit	Balance Debit	Balance Credit
9/30	0X	Balance forward	✓			100 00	

Name ______________________ Class ______________ Date ______________

INCOME SUMMARY **ACCOUNT NO. 3020**

Date		Explanation	Post Ref.	Debit	Credit	Balance Debit	Balance Credit

SERVICE REVENUE **ACCOUNT NO. 4000**

Date		Explanation	Post Ref.	Debit	Credit	Balance Debit	Balance Credit
9/30	0X	Balance forward	✓				6685 00

ADVERTISING EXPENSE **ACCOUNT NO. 5010**

Date		Explanation	Post Ref.	Debit	Credit	Balance Debit	Balance Credit
9/30	0X	Balance forward	✓			1400 00	

RENT EXPENSE **ACCOUNT NO. 5020**

Date		Explanation	Post Ref.	Debit	Credit	Balance Debit	Balance Credit
9/30	0X	Balance forward	✓			400 00	

Name ______________________ Class ______________ Date ______________

UTILITIES EXPENSE **ACCOUNT NO. 5030**

Date		Explanation	Post Ref.	Debit	Credit	Balance Debit	Balance Credit
9/30	0X	Balance forward	✓			180 00	

PHONE EXPENSE **ACCOUNT NO. 5040**

Date		Explanation	Post Ref.	Debit	Credit	Balance Debit	Balance Credit
9/30	0X	Balance forward	✓			220 00	

SUPPLIES EXPENSE **ACCOUNT NO. 5050**

Date		Explanation	Post Ref.	Debit	Credit	Balance Debit	Balance Credit

INSURANCE EXPENSE **ACCOUNT NO. 5060**

Date		Explanation	Post Ref.	Debit	Credit	Balance Debit	Balance Credit
9/30	0X	Balance forward	✓			150 00	

Name ______________ Class ______________ Date ______________

POSTAGE EXPENSE **ACCOUNT NO. 5070**

Date		Explanation	Post Ref.	Debit	Credit	Balance Debit	Balance Credit
9/30	0X	Balance forward	✓			50 00	

DEPRECIATION EXPENSE C.S. EQUIPMENT **ACCOUNT NO. 5080**

Date		Explanation	Post Ref.	Debit	Credit	Balance Debit	Balance Credit

DEPRECIATION EXPENSE OFFICE EQUIPMENT **ACCOUNT NO. 5090**

Date		Explanation	Post Ref.	Debit	Credit	Balance Debit	Balance Credit

Name ______________________ Class ______________ Date ______________

SANCHEZ COMPUTER CENTER
POST-CLOSING TRIAL BALANCE
SEPTEMBER 30, 200X

	Dr.	Cr.

Name ______________________ Class ______________ Date ______________

MINI PRACTICE SET
SULLIVAN REALTY

SULLIVAN REALTY
GENERAL JOURNAL

PAGE 1

Date		Account Titles and Description	PR	Dr.	Cr.

Name ______________________ Class ______________ Date ______________

MINI PRACTICE SET
SULLIVAN REALTY

SULLIVAN REALTY
GENERAL JOURNAL

PAGE 2

Date		Account Titles and Description	PR	Dr.	Cr.

Name ______________________ Class ______________ Date ______________

MINI PRACTICE SET
SULLIVAN REALTY

SULLIVAN REALTY
GENERAL JOURNAL

PAGE 3

Date		Account Titles and Description	PR	Dr.	Cr.

Name ______________________ Class ______________ Date ______________

MINI PRACTICE SET
SULLIVAN REALTY

SULLIVAN REALTY
GENERAL JOURNAL

PAGE 4

Date		Account Titles and Description	PR	Dr.	Cr.

Name ______________________ Class ______________ Date ______________

MINI PRACTICE SET
SULLIVAN REALTY

SULLIVAN REALTY
GENERAL JOURNAL

PAGE 5

Date		Account Titles and Description	PR	Dr.	Cr.

Name ______________________ Class ______________ Date ______________

MINI PRACTICE SET
SULLIVAN REALTY

SULLIVAN REALTY
GENERAL JOURNAL

PAGE 6

Date		Account Titles and Description	PR	Dr.	Cr.

Name ______________________ Class ______________ Date ______________

MINI PRACTICE SET
SULLIVAN REALTY

CASH **ACCOUNT NO. 111**

Date	Explanation	Post Ref.	Debit	Credit	Balance	
					Debit	Credit

Name ______________________ Class ______________ Date ______________

MINI PRACTICE SET
SULLIVAN REALTY

ACCOUNTS RECEIVABLE **ACCOUNT NO. 112**

Date	Explanation	Post Ref.	Debit	Credit	Balance Debit	Balance Credit

PREPAID RENT **ACCOUNT NO. 114**

Date	Explanation	Post Ref.	Debit	Credit	Balance Debit	Balance Credit

OFFICE SUPPLIES **ACCOUNT NO. 115**

Date	Explanation	Post Ref.	Debit	Credit	Balance Debit	Balance Credit

OFFICE EQUIPMENT **ACCOUNT NO. 121**

Date	Explanation	Post Ref.	Debit	Credit	Balance Debit	Balance Credit

Name ______________________ Class ______________ Date ______________

MINI PRACTICE SET: SULLIVAN REALTY

ACCUMULATED DEPRECIATION, OFFICE EQUIPMENT ACCOUNT NO. 122

Date	Explanation	Post Ref.	Debit	Credit	Balance Debit	Balance Credit

AUTOMOBILE ACCOUNT NO. 123

Date	Explanation	Post Ref.	Debit	Credit	Balance Debit	Balance Credit

ACCUMULATED DEPRECIATION, AUTOMOBILE ACCOUNT NO. 124

Date	Explanation	Post Ref.	Debit	Credit	Balance Debit	Balance Credit

ACCOUNTS PAYABLE ACCOUNT NO. 211

Date	Explanation	Post Ref.	Debit	Credit	Balance Debit	Balance Credit

SALARIES PAYABLE ACCOUNT NO. 212

Date	Explanation	Post Ref.	Debit	Credit	Balance Debit	Balance Credit

Name ______________________ Class ______________ Date ______________

MINI PRACTICE SET
SULLIVAN REALTY

JOHN SULLIVAN, CAPITAL **ACCOUNT NO. 311**

Date		Explanation	Post Ref.	Debit	Credit	Balance	
						Debit	Credit

JOHN SULLIVAN, WITHDRAWALS **ACCOUNT NO. 312**

Date		Explanation	Post Ref.	Debit	Credit	Balance	
						Debit	Credit

INCOME SUMMARY **ACCOUNT NO. 313**

Date		Explanation	Post Ref.	Debit	Credit	Balance	
						Debit	Credit

Name ______________________ Class ______________ Date ______________

MINI PRACTICE SET
SULLIVAN REALTY

COMMISSIONS EARNED **ACCOUNT NO. 411**

Date		Explanation	Post Ref.	Debit	Credit	Balance	
						Debit	Credit

RENT EXPENSE **ACCOUNT NO. 511**

Date		Explanation	Post Ref.	Debit	Credit	Balance	
						Debit	Credit

SALARIES EXPENSE **ACCOUNT NO. 512**

Date		Explanation	Post Ref.	Debit	Credit	Balance	
						Debit	Credit

Name ______________________ Class ______________ Date ______________

MINI PRACTICE SET
SULLIVAN REALTY

GAS EXPENSE **ACCOUNT NO. 513**

Date		Explanation	Post Ref.	Debit	Credit	Balance	
						Debit	Credit

REPAIRS EXPENSE **ACCOUNT NO. 514**

Date		Explanation	Post Ref.	Debit	Credit	Balance	
						Debit	Credit

TELEPHONE EXPENSE **ACCOUNT NO. 515**

Date		Explanation	Post Ref.	Debit	Credit	Balance	
						Debit	Credit

ADVERTISING EXPENSE **ACCOUNT NO. 516**

Date		Explanation	Post Ref.	Debit	Credit	Balance	
						Debit	Credit

Name ____________ Class ____________ Date ____________

MINI PRACTICE SET
SULLIVAN REALTY

OFFICE SUPPLIES EXPENSE **ACCOUNT NO. 517**

Date	Explanation	Post Ref.	Debit	Credit	Balance Debit	Balance Credit

DEPRECIATION EXPENSE, OFFICE EQUIPMENT **ACCOUNT NO. 518**

Date	Explanation	Post Ref.	Debit	Credit	Balance Debit	Balance Credit

DEPRECIATION EXPENSE, AUTOMOBILE **ACCOUNT NO. 519**

Date	Explanation	Post Ref.	Debit	Credit	Balance Debit	Balance Credit

MISCELLANEOUS EXPENSE **ACCOUNT NO. 524**

Date	Explanation	Post Ref.	Debit	Credit	Balance Debit	Balance Credit

Name ____________ Class ____________ Date ____________

MINI PRACTICE SET
SULLIVAN REALTY

Use the blank fold-out worksheets that accompanied your textbook.

SULLIVAN REALTY
INCOME STATEMENT
FOR MONTH ENDED JUNE 30, 200X

Name ______________________ Class ______________ Date ______________

MINI PRACTICE SET
SULLIVAN REALTY

SULLIVAN REALTY
STATEMENT OF OWNER'S EQUITY
FOR MONTH ENDED JUNE 30, 200X

Name ____________________ Class ____________ Date ____________

MINI PRACTICE SET
SULLIVAN REALTY

SULLIVAN REALTY
BALANCE SHEET
JUNE 30, 200X

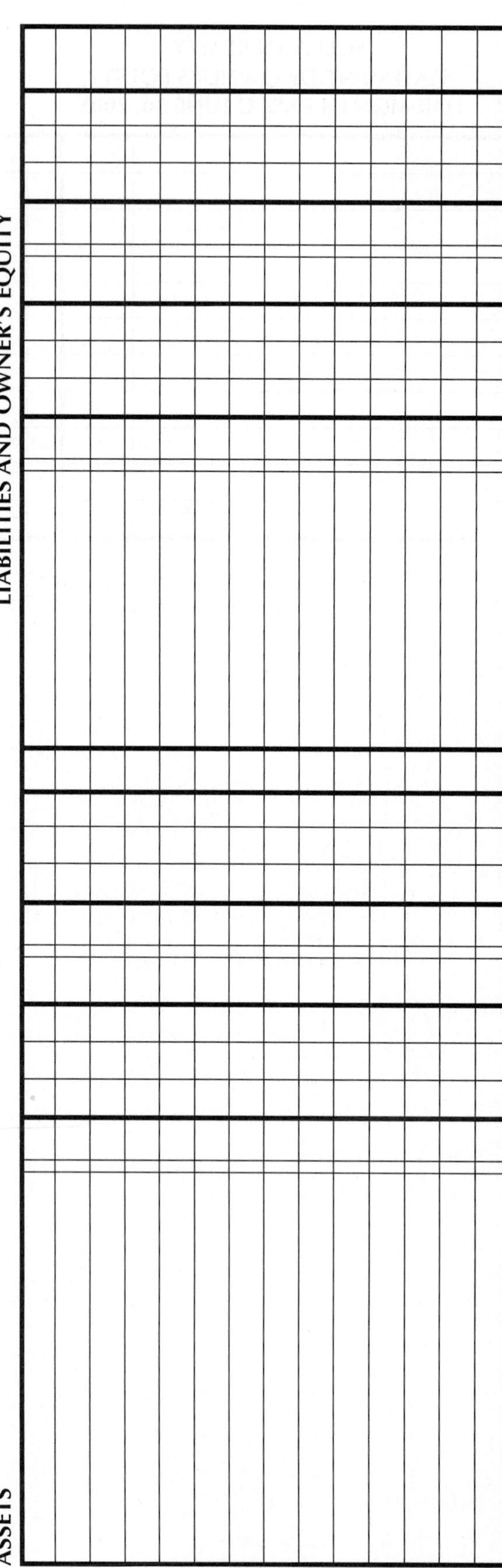

Name ____________________ Class ____________ Date ____________

MINI PRACTICE SET
SULLIVAN REALTY

SULLIVAN REALTY
POST-CLOSING TRIAL BALANCE
JUNE 30, 200X

	Dr.	Cr.

You can find the worksheet for July with the blank fold-out worksheets that accompanied your textbook.

Name ______________________ Class ______________ Date ______________

MINI PRACTICE SET
SULLIVAN REALTY

SULLIVAN REALTY
INCOME STATEMENT
FOR MONTH ENDED JULY 31, 200X

Name ______________________ Class ______________ Date ______________

MINI PRACTICE SET
SULLIVAN REALTY

SULLIVAN REALTY
STATEMENT OF OWNER'S EQUITY
FOR MONTH ENDED JULY 31, 200X

Name ______________________ Class ______________ Date ______________

MINI PRACTICE SET
SULLIVAN REALTY

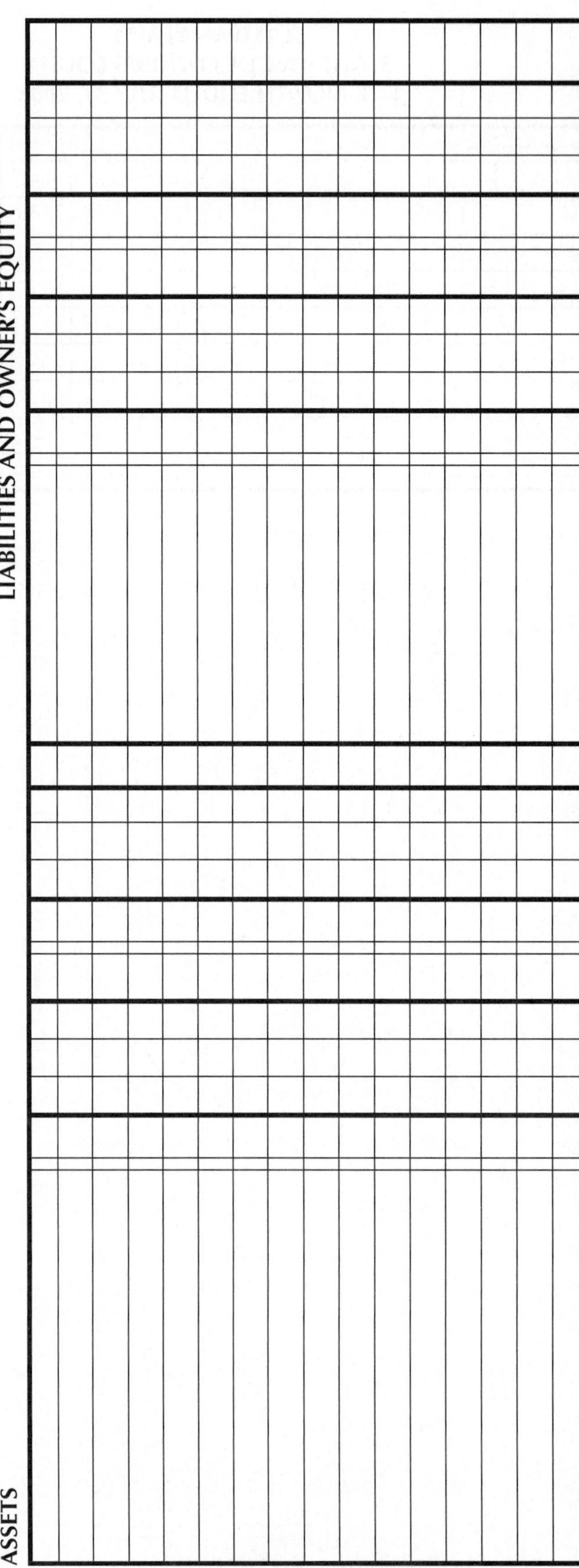

Name ____________________ Class ____________ Date ____________

MINI PRACTICE SET
SULLIVAN REALTY

SULLIVAN REALTY
POST-CLOSING TRIAL BALANCE
JULY 31, 200X

	Dr.	Cr.

6 BANKING PROCEDURES AND CONTROL OF CASH

SELF-REVIEW QUIZ 6-1

Situation	Add to Bank Balance	Deduct from Bank Balance	Add to Checkbook Balance	Deduct from Checkbook Balance
1				
2				
3				
4				
5				
6				
7				
8				

SELF-REVIEW QUIZ 6-2

PAGE 6

Date		Account Titles and Description	PR	Dr.	Cr.

Name ____________ Class ____________ Date ____________

AUXILIARY PETTY CASH RECORD

Date	Voucher No.	Description	Receipts	Payment	Category of Payment			
					Delivery Expense	General Expense	Sundry	
							Account	Amount

Name ______________________ Class ______________ Date ______________

CHAPTER 6

SET A FORMS FOR CLASSROOM DEMONSTRATION EXERCISES

1.

A. ______________ E. ______________

B. ______________ F. ______________

C. ______________

D. ______________

2. ________ ________ ________ ________

3.

ACE CO.
BANK RECONCILIATION
JUNE 30, 200X

Checkbook	Bank

4.

A. ______ ______ ______ E. ______ ______ ______

B. ______ ______ ______ F. ______ ______ ______

C. ______ ______ ______

D. ______ ______ ______

5.

6.

Name ______________________ Class ______________ Date ______________

CHAPTER 6

SET B FORMS FOR CLASSROOM DEMONSTRATION EXERCISES

1.

A. ______________ E. ______________

B. ______________ F. ______________

C. ______________

D. ______________

2. ________ ________ ________ ________

3.

ACE CO.
BANK RECONCILIATION
JUNE 30, 200X

Checkbook	Bank

4.

A. ______ ______ ______ E. ______ ______ ______

B. ______ ______ ______ F. ______ ______ ______

C. ______ ______ ______

D. ______ ______ ______

5.

6.

Name ______________________ Class ______________ Date ______________

FORMS FOR EXERCISES

6-1.

BING CO.
BANK RECONCILIATION AS OF JULY 31, 200X

CHECKBOOK BALANCE		**BALANCE PER BANK**	
Ending Checkbook Balance	________	Ending Bank Statement Balance	________
Deduct:	________	Add:	________
Bank Service Charge	________	Deposit in Transit	________
	________		________
	________	Deduct:	________
	________	Outstanding Checks	________
	________		________
Reconciled Balance	________	Reconciled Balance	________

6-2.

6-3.

Name ____________________ Class ____________ Date ____________

EXERCISES (CONCLUDED)

6-4.

6-5.

Beg. Change Fund
+Cash Register Total
=Cash should have on hand
–Counted Cash
= Cash Shortage

Name ______________________ Class ______________ Date ______________

END OF CHAPTER PROBLEMS

PROBLEM 6A-1 OR PROBLEM 6B-1

LEE.COM
BANK RECONCILIATION AS OF JULY 31, 200X

BALANCE PER BANK			**CHECKBOOK BALANCE**	
Bank Statement Balance			Checkbook Balance	
Add:		______	Add:	
				______
Deduct:	______		Deduct:	
		______		
				______
Reconciled Balance		______	Reconciled Balance	______

Name ______________________ Class ______________ Date ______________

PROBLEM 6A-1 OR PROBLEM 6B-1 (CONCLUDED)

Date		Account Titles and Description	PR	Dr.	Cr.

Name ____________________ Class ______________ Date ______________

PROBLEM 6A-2 OR PROBLEM 6B-2

LOWELL NATIONAL BANK
RIO MEAN BRAND
BUGNA, TEXAS TELEPHONE 555-8311

This form is provided to help you balance your bank statement. If no errors are reported to auditors in ten days, the account will be considered correct.

Please notify us of any change in address.

Checks outstanding
(not charged to account)

Check No.	Amount
Total	

Sort the checks numerically or by date issued.
Check off on the stubs of your checkbook each check paid by bank.
List the numbers and amounts of checks still outstanding in the space provided at the left.
Verify the deposits in your checkbook with deposits credited on this statement. Bank balance show on this statement $__________
Plus: Deposits not credited on this statement $__________
Subtotal $__________
Less: Checks outstanding $__________
Balance $__________

If your checkbook does not agree, enter any necessary adjustments:

Correct checkbook balance $__________

Name ____________________ Class ____________ Date ____________

PROBLEM 6A-2 OR PROBLEM 6B-2 (CONCLUDED)

GENERAL JOURNAL

Date		Account Titles and Description	PR	Dr.	Cr.

Name ______________________ Class ______________ Date ______________

PROBLEM 6A-3 OR PROBLEM 6B-3

MERRY CO.
GENERAL JOURNAL

Date		Account Titles and Description	PR	Dr.	Cr.

Name ________________ Class ________________ Date ________________

PROBLEM 6A-3 OR PROBLEM 6B-3 (CONCLUDED)

MERRY CO.
AUXILIARY PETTY CASH RECORD

Date	Voucher No.	Description	Receipts	Payment	Category of Payment			
					Postage Expense	Office Supplies Expense	Sundry	
							Account	Amount

Name ______________________ Class ______________ Date ______________

PROBLEM 6A-4 OR PROBLEM 6B-4

LOGAN CO.
GENERAL JOURNAL

PAGE 2

Date		Account Titles and Description	PR	Dr.	Cr.

Name ____________________ Class ____________ Date ____________

PROBLEM 6A-4 OR PROBLEM 6B-4 (CONCLUDED)

LOGAN CO.
AUXILIARY PETTY CASH RECORD

Date	Voucher No.	Description	Receipts	Payment	Category of Payment			
					Postage Expense	Delivery Expense	Sundry	
							Account	Amount

Name ______________________ Class ______________ Date ______________

CHAPTER 6
SUMMARY PRACTICE TEST
BANKING PROCEDURES AND CONTROL OF CASH

Part I Instructions

Fill in the blank(s) to complete the statement.

1. Online banking is ______________ due to the internet.
2. Today, use of the ______________ ______________ has greatly increased.
3. All adjustments to the checkbook balance in the reconciliation process will require ______________ ______________.
4. Petty cash is a(n) ______________ found on the balance sheet.
5. The auxiliary petty cash record is not a(n) ______________.
6. A(n) ______________ ______________ is an asset used to make change for customer.
7. A cash overage will be ______________ ______________ on the income statement.
8. ______________ ______________ represents checks not processed by the bank at the time the bank statement was prepared.
9. When a bank credits your account, your balance will ______________.
10. ______________ is a procedure whereby the bank does not return the processed checks.

Part II Instructions

Indicate which of the following procedures are involved in each of the transactions below.

a. Recorded in General Journal
b. Recorded in both general journal and auxiliary petty cash record
c. Recorded only in auxiliary petty cash record
d. New check is written
e. Account petty cash is increased

1. EXAMPLE: Check issued to establish petty cash b,d,e
2. Paid donation from petty cash __________
3. Paid postage from petty cash __________
4. Paid past purchases previously charged __________
5. Paid for business luncheon with petty cash __________
6. Issued check to pay for office supplies __________
7. Replenished petty cash __________
8. Paid local donation from petty cash __________
9. Paid for past purchases bought on account __________
10. Replenished petty cash __________

Name ______________________ Class ______________ Date ______________

Part III Instructions

Answer true or false to the following statements.

1. Online banking is decreasing today.
2. Petty cash is a liability found on the balance sheet.
3. Checks returned from the bank are placed in alphabetical order.
4. ATMs are being used less today than in the past.
5. Bank service charges represent an expense to the business.
6. The bank statement is the same as the bank reconciliation.
7. The balance in the company cash account will always equal the bank balance before the bank statement is received.
8. Deposit slips are needed in writing checks.
9. The signature must be presented when cashing a check.
10. The auxiliary petty cash record is posted monthly.
11. The petty cash account has a debit balance.
12. Replenishment of petty cash requires a new check.
13. The expenses paid from petty cash are journalized at time of replenishment.
14. Internal control only affects large companies.
15. A petty cash voucher records the expense into the ledger.
16. The petty cash fund must be replenished monthly.
17. The petty cash voucher identifies the account that will be charged.
18. The establishment of petty cash may require some judgment as to the amount of petty cash needed.
19. EFT is the same as safekeeping.
20. The drawer is the person who receives the check.
21. A debit memo will increase the depositor's balance.
22. A change fund uses only one denomination.
23. The payer is the person or company the check is payable to.

Part IV Instructions

Based on the following situation, prepare a bank reconciliation.

The checkbook balance of Logan Company is $5,263.08. The bank statement shows a bank balance of $7,980. The bank statement shows interest earned of $42 and a service charge of $29.76. There is a deposit in transit of $2,558.22. Outstanding checks total $3,762.90. The bank collected a note for Moore for $4,200. Moore Company forgot to deduct a check for $2,700 during the month.

Name ______________________ Class ______________ Date ______________

SOLUTIONS TO SUMMARY PRACTICE TEST

Part I

1. increasing
2. debit card
3. journal entries
4. asset
5. journal
6. change fund
7. miscellaneous income
8. Checks outstanding
9. increase
10. Safekeeping

Part II

1. b, d, e
2. c
3. c
4. a, d
5. c
6. a, d
7. b, d
8. c
9. a, d
10. b, d

Part III

1. false
2. false
3. false
4. false
5. true
6. false
7. false
8. false
9. true
10. false
11. true
12. true
13. true
14. false
15. false
16. false
17. true
18. true
19. false
20. false
21. false
22. false
23. false

Part IV

LOGAN CO.				BANK BALANCE	
Checkbook Balance		$5,263.08		Bank Balance	$7,980.00
ADD:				ADD:	
				Deposit	
Interest	$ 42			in Transit	2,558.22
Collection of note	4,200	4,242.00			$9,038.22
		8,005.08			
DEDUCT:				DEDUCT:	
Service Chg.	$ 29.76			Check outstanding	$3,762.90
Error	2,700.00	2,729.76			
Reconciled Balance		$6,775.32		Reconciled Balance	$6,775.32

Name ______________________ Class ______________ Date ______________

CONTINUING PROBLEM FOR CHAPTER 6

SANCHEZ COMPUTER CENTER
GENERAL JOURNAL

PAGE 3

Date		Account Titles and Description	PR	Dr.	Cr.

Name ______________________ Class ______________ Date ______________

CASH **ACCOUNT NO. 1000**

Date		Explanation	Post Ref.	Debit	Credit	Balance Debit	Balance Credit
9/30	0X	Balance forward	✓			1 645 00	

PETTY CASH **ACCOUNT NO. 1010**

Date		Explanation	Post Ref.	Debit	Credit	Balance Debit	Balance Credit

Name ______________________ Class ______________ Date ______________

ACCOUNTS RECEIVABLE ACCOUNT NO. 1020

Date		Explanation	Post Ref.	Debit	Credit	Balance Debit	Balance Credit
9/30	0X	Balance forward	✓			2 6 0 0 00	

PREPAID RENT ACCOUNT NO. 1025

Date		Explanation	Post Ref.	Debit	Credit	Balance Debit	Balance Credit
9/30	0X	Balance forward	✓			4 0 0 00	

SUPPLIES ACCOUNT NO. 1030

Date		Explanation	Post Ref.	Debit	Credit	Balance Debit	Balance Credit
9/30	0X	Balance forward	✓			9 0 00	

COMPUTER SHOP EQUIPMENT ACCOUNT NO. 1080

Date		Explanation	Post Ref.	Debit	Credit	Balance Debit	Balance Credit
9/30	0X	Balance forward	✓			2 4 0 0 00	

Name ______________________ Class ______________ Date ______________

ACCUMULATED DEPRECIATION, COMPUTER SHOP EQUIPMENT **ACCOUNT NO. 1081**

Date		Explanation	Post Ref.	Debit	Credit	Balance Debit	Balance Credit
9/30	0X	Balance forward	✓				9 9 00

OFFICE EQUIPMENT **ACCOUNT NO. 1090**

Date		Explanation	Post Ref.	Debit	Credit	Balance Debit	Balance Credit
9/30	0X	Balance forward	✓			6 0 0 00	

ACCUMULATED DEPRECIATION, OFFICE EQUIPMENT **ACCOUNT NO. 1091**

Date		Explanation	Post Ref.	Debit	Credit	Balance Debit	Balance Credit
9/30	0X	Balance forward	✓				2 0 00

ACCOUNTS PAYABLE **ACCOUNT NO. 2000**

Date		Explanation	Post Ref.	Debit	Credit	Balance Debit	Balance Credit
9/30	0X	Balance forward	✓				2 1 0 00

Name ______________________ Class ______________ Date ______________

T. FREEDMAN, CAPITAL **ACCOUNT NO. 3000**

Date		Explanation	Post Ref.	Debit	Credit	Balance Debit	Balance Credit
9/30	0X	Balance forward	✓				7 406 00

T. FREEDMAN, WITHDRAWALS **ACCOUNT NO. 3010**

Date		Explanation	Post Ref.	Debit	Credit	Balance Debit	Balance Credit

INCOME SUMMARY **ACCOUNT NO. 3020**

Date		Explanation	Post Ref.	Debit	Credit	Balance Debit	Balance Credit

Name ______________________ Class ______________ Date ______________

SERVICE REVENUE — ACCOUNT NO. 4000

Date		Explanation	Post Ref.	Debit	Credit	Balance	
						Debit	Credit

ADVERTISING EXPENSE — ACCOUNT NO. 5010

Date		Explanation	Post Ref.	Debit	Credit	Balance	
						Debit	Credit

RENT EXPENSE — ACCOUNT NO. 5020

Date		Explanation	Post Ref.	Debit	Credit	Balance	
						Debit	Credit

Name ______________________ Class ______________ Date ______________

UTILITIES EXPENSE **ACCOUNT NO. 5030**

Date		Explanation	Post Ref.	Debit	Credit	Balance Debit	Balance Credit

PHONE EXPENSE **ACCOUNT NO. 5040**

Date		Explanation	Post Ref.	Debit	Credit	Balance Debit	Balance Credit

SUPPLIES EXPENSE **ACCOUNT NO. 5050**

Date		Explanation	Post Ref.	Debit	Credit	Balance Debit	Balance Credit

INSURANCE EXPENSE **ACCOUNT NO. 5060**

Date		Explanation	Post Ref.	Debit	Credit	Balance Debit	Balance Credit

Name ________________ Class ________________ Date ________________

POSTAGE EXPENSE **ACCOUNT NO. 5070**

Date		Explanation	Post Ref.	Debit	Credit	Balance Debit	Balance Credit

DEPRECIATION EXPENSE, COMPUTER SHOP EQUIPMENT **ACCOUNT NO. 5080**

Date		Explanation	Post Ref.	Debit	Credit	Balance Debit	Balance Credit

DEPRECIATION EXPENSE, OFFICE EQUIPMENT **ACCOUNT NO. 5090**

Date		Explanation	Post Ref.	Debit	Credit	Balance Debit	Balance Credit

MISCELLANEOUS EXPENSE **ACCOUNT NO. 5100**

Date		Explanation	Post Ref.	Debit	Credit	Balance Debit	Balance Credit

Name ______________________ Class ______________ Date ______________

SANCHEZ COMPUTER CENTER
TRIAL BALANCE
OCTOBER 31, 200X

Name ______________ Class ______________ Date ______________

AUXILIARY PETTY CASH RECORD

Date	Voucher No.	Description	Receipts	Payment	Category of Payment			
					Postage Expense	Supplies Expense	Sundry	
							Account	Amount

Name ______________________ Class ______________ Date ______________

SANCHEZ COMPUTER CENTER
BANK RECONCILIATION AS OF SEPTEMBER 30, 200X

BALANCE PER BANK			**CHECKBOOK BALANCE**	
Bank Statement Balance			Checkbook Balance	
Add:		________	Add:	
				________
Deduct:	________		Deduct:	
		________		
				________
Reconciled Balance		________	Reconciled Balance	________

7

Payroll Concepts and Procedures—Employee Taxes

SELF-REVIEW QUIZ 7-1

REGULAR EARNINGS

OVERTIME

GROSS EARNINGS

SELF-REVIEW QUIZ 7-2

FIT

SIT

FICA - OASDI

FICA - Medicare

NET PAY

Name ______________________ Class ______________ Date ______________

SELF-REVIEW QUIZ 7-3

FICA - OASDI ______________________

FICA - Medicare ______________________

FUTA ______________________

SUTA ______________________

Name ______________________ Class ______________ Date ______________

CHAPTER 7

SET A FORMS FOR CLASSROOM DEMONSTRATION EXERCISES

1. A. ______________________________

____

____

B. ______________________________

____

____

2. ______________________________

____

____

____

____

3. ______________________________

____

____

____

____

____

____

4. A. ______________ D. ______________

B. ______________ E. ______________

C. ______________ F. ______________

5.

A. __________

B. __________

C. __________

D. __________

Name ______________________ Class ______________ Date ______________

CHAPTER 7

SET B FORMS FOR CLASSROOM DEMONSTRATION EXERCISES

1. A. ______________________________

____

____

B. ______________________________

____

____

2. ______________________________

____

____

____

____

3. ______________________________

____

____

____

____

____

____

4.

A.	D.
B.	E.
C.	F.

5.

A. __________

B. __________

C. __________

D. __________

Name ______________ Class ______________ Date ______________

FORMS FOR EXERCISES

7-1.

Carmen ______________

Jill ______________

____

Fred ______________

____

7-2.

Alvin	Angelina

7-3. ______________

7-4. ______________

Name ______________ Class ______________ Date ______________

EXERCISES (CONCLUDED)

7-5. ______________________________

____

____

____

____

7-6. ______________________________

____

____

____

____

7-7.

Employee	Weekly Pay	Weeks	Total	Taxable	Tax Rate	Tax

7-8. ______________________________

____

____

Name ____________________ Class ____________ Date ____________

END OF CHAPTER PROBLEMS

PROBLEM 7A-1 OR PROBLEM 7B-1

Employee	Hourly Rate	# of Hours Worked	Gross Earnings
A.			
B.			
C.			
D.			

A. B.

C. D.

PROBLEM 7A-2 OR PROBLEM 7B-2

Use the fold-out payroll register that accompanied your textbook.

PROBLEM 7A-3 OR PROBLEM 7B-3

Use the fold-out payroll register that accompanied your textbook.

PROBLEM 7A-4 OR PROBLEM 7B-4

Use the fold-out payroll register that accompanied your textbook.

Name ______________________ Class ______________ Date ______________

CHAPTER 7
SUMMARY PRACTICE TEST:
PAYROLL CONCEPTS AND PROCEDURES—EMPLOYEE TAXES

PART I INSTRUCTIONS

Fill in the blank(s) to complete the statement.

1. ______________ ______________ is gross pay less deductions.
2. Form ______________ aids the employer in knowing how much to deduct for federal income tax.
3. The base for OASDI-Medicare will ______________ ______________ from year to year.
4. ______________ ______________ of the employer's tax guide has tables available for deductions for FIT and FICA (OASDI and Medicare).
5. ______________ ______________ ______________ protects employees against losses due to injury or death incurred while on the job.
6. The two primary records used to keep track of payroll information are the ______________ ______________ and ______________ ______________ ______________.
7. The employer is responsible for paying for______________.
8. ______________ ______________ is paid every two weeks.
9. A(n) ______________ employee will only be paid for the hours actually worked.
10. An employer must pay FUTA on wages earned by each employee up to a maximum of $______________.

Part II Instructions

Answer true or false to the following.

1. OASDI is the tax form for SUTA.
2. Employers only pay FUTA and SUTA.
3. Employers pay a higher FICA-OASDI tax rate than employees do.
4. Gross pay plus deductions equals net pay.
5. Form W-4 aids in calculating FICA-OASDI.
6. The employer will match the employee's contribution for FICA (OASDI and Medicare).
7. The maximum tax credit for state unemployment tax is .8%.
8. A company may have different types of employees.
9. The Wage-Bracket Table makes it more difficult to calculate the amount of deductions for FIT.
10. A calendar year has no effect on taxes for FICA-Social Security.

Name ______________________ Class ______________ Date ______________

Part III Instructions

Complete the chart below (use table in text as needed). Use the following information: Before this payroll Pete Bloom had earned $101,000. This week Pete earned $2,000 for the past two weeks. Assume an OASDI rate of Social Security of 6.2% up to $102,000. Medicare, 1.45%. FIT is $238.50. The state income tax is 7 percent.

GROSS PAY	TAXABLE FICA	DEDUCTIONS FICA OASDI	DEDUCTIONS FICA Med.	FIT	SIT	NET PAY

CHAPTER 7
SOLUTIONS TO SUMMARY PRACTICE TEST

Part I

1. Net Pay
2. W-4
3. not change
4. Circular E
5. Workers' Compensation Insurance
6. payroll register, employee earnings record
7. FUTA (SUTA)
8. Biweekly payroll
9. hourly
10. 7,000

Part II

1. false
2. false
3. false
4. false
5. false
6. true
7. false
8. true
9. false
10. false

Part III

OASDI	$1,000 x.062 =	$ 62.00	
Medicare	2,000 x.0145 =	29.00	
FIT		238.50	$2,000.00
SIT	2,000 x.07	140.00	– 469.50
Total deductions		$469.50	$1,530.50

Name ______________________ Class ______________ Date ______________

CONTINUING PROBLEM FOR CHAPTER 7

(1)

SANCHEZ COMPUTER CENTER
GENERAL JOURNAL

PAGE 4

Date		Account Titles and Description	PR	Dr.	Cr.

Name ______________________ Class ______________ Date ______________

SANCHEZ COMPUTER CENTER
GENERAL JOURNAL

PAGE 5

Date		Account Titles and Description	PR	Dr.	Cr.

Name ______________________ Class ______________ Date ______________

CASH **ACCOUNT NO. 1000**

Date		Explanation	Post Ref.	Debit	Credit	Balance Debit	Balance Credit
10/31	0X	Balance forward	✓			4293 00	

PETTY CASH **ACCOUNT NO. 1010**

Date		Explanation	Post Ref.	Debit	Credit	Balance Debit	Balance Credit
10/31	0X	Balance forward	✓			100 00	

ACCOUNTS RECEIVABLE **ACCOUNT NO. 1020**

Date		Explanation	Post Ref.	Debit	Credit	Balance Debit	Balance Credit
10/31	0X	Balance forward	✓			4200 00	

Name ______________________ Class ______________ Date ______________

PREPAID RENT **ACCOUNT NO. 1025**

Date		Explanation	Post Ref.	Debit	Credit	Balance Debit	Balance Credit
10/31	0X	Balance forward	✓			1 600 00	

SUPPLIES **ACCOUNT NO. 1030**

Date		Explanation	Post Ref.	Debit	Credit	Balance Debit	Balance Credit
10/31	0X	Balance forward	✓			90 00	

COMPUTER SHOP EQUIPMENT **ACCOUNT NO. 1080**

Date		Explanation	Post Ref.	Debit	Credit	Balance Debit	Balance Credit
10/31	0X	Balance forward	✓			2 400 00	

ACCUMULATED DEPRECIATION, COMPUTER SHOP EQUIPMENT **ACCOUNT NO. 1081**

Date		Explanation	Post Ref.	Debit	Credit	Balance Debit	Balance Credit
10/31	0X	Balance forward	✓				99 00

Name ______________________ Class ______________ Date ______________

OFFICE EQUIPMENT **ACCOUNT NO. 1090**

Date		Explanation	Post Ref.	Debit	Credit	Balance Debit	Balance Credit
10/31	0X	Balance forward	✓			600 00	

ACCUMULATED DEPRECIATION, OFFICE EQUIPMENT **ACCOUNT NO. 1091**

Date		Explanation	Post Ref.	Debit	Credit	Balance Debit	Balance Credit
10/31	0X	Balance forward	✓				20 00

ACCOUNTS PAYABLE **ACCOUNT NO. 2000**

Date		Explanation	Post Ref.	Debit	Credit	Balance Debit	Balance Credit
10/31	0X	Balance forward	✓				50 00

WAGES PAYABLE **ACCOUNT NO. 2010**

Date		Explanation	Post Ref.	Debit	Credit	Balance Debit	Balance Credit

Name ______________________ Class ______________ Date ______________

FICA—OASDI PAYABLE **ACCOUNT NO. 2020**

Date		Explanation	Post Ref.	Debit	Credit	Balance	
						Debit	Credit

FICA—MEDICARE PAYABLE **ACCOUNT NO. 2030**

Date		Explanation	Post Ref.	Debit	Credit	Balance	
						Debit	Credit

FIT PAYABLE **ACCOUNT NO. 2040**

Date		Explanation	Post Ref.	Debit	Credit	Balance	
						Debit	Credit

SIT PAYABLE **ACCOUNT NO. 2050**

Date		Explanation	Post Ref.	Debit	Credit	Balance	
						Debit	Credit

Name ______________________ Class ______________ Date ______________

T. FREEDMAN CAPITAL | **ACCOUNT NO. 3000**

Date		Explanation	Post Ref.	Debit	Credit	Balance Debit	Balance Credit
10/31	0X	Balance forward	✓				7 406 00

T. FREEDMAN WITHDRAWALS | **ACCOUNT NO. 3010**

Date		Explanation	Post Ref.	Debit	Credit	Balance Debit	Balance Credit
10/31	0X	Balance forward	✓			2 015 00	

SERVICE REVENUE | **ACCOUNT NO. 4000**

Date		Explanation	Post Ref.	Debit	Credit	Balance Debit	Balance Credit
10/31	0X	Balance forward	✓				7 800 00

ADVERTISING EXPENSE | **ACCOUNT NO. 5010**

Date		Explanation	Post Ref.	Debit	Credit	Balance Debit	Balance Credit

RENT EXPENSE | **ACCOUNT NO. 5020**

Date		Explanation	Post Ref.	Debit	Credit	Balance Debit	Balance Credit

Name ______________________ Class ______________ Date ______________

UTILITIES EXPENSE **ACCOUNT NO. 5030**

Date		Explanation	Post Ref.	Debit	Credit	Balance Debit	Balance Credit

PHONE EXPENSE **ACCOUNT NO. 5040**

Date		Explanation	Post Ref.	Debit	Credit	Balance Debit	Balance Credit

SUPPLIES EXPENSE **ACCOUNT NO. 5050**

Date		Explanation	Post Ref.	Debit	Credit	Balance Debit	Balance Credit
10/31	0X		✓			42 00	

INSURANCE EXPENSE **ACCOUNT NO. 5060**

Date		Explanation	Post Ref.	Debit	Credit	Balance Debit	Balance Credit

POSTAGE EXPENSE **ACCOUNT NO. 5070**

Date		Explanation	Post Ref.	Debit	Credit	Balance Debit	Balance Credit
10/31	0X	Balance forward	✓			25 00	

Name ______________ Class ______________ Date ______________

DEPRECIATION EXPENSE C. S. EQUIPMENT **ACCOUNT NO. 5080**

Date		Explanation	Post Ref.	Debit	Credit	Balance	
						Debit	Credit

DEPRECIATION EXPENSE OFFICE EQUIPMENT **ACCOUNT NO. 5090**

Date		Explanation	Post Ref.	Debit	Credit	Balance	
						Debit	Credit

MISCELLANEOUS EXPENSE **ACCOUNT NO. 5100**

Date		Explanation	Post Ref.	Debit	Credit	Balance	
						Debit	Credit
10/31	0X	Balance forward	✓			10 00	

WAGES EXPENSE **ACCOUNT NO. 5110**

Date		Explanation	Post Ref.	Debit	Credit	Balance	
						Debit	Credit

(2) Use the fold-out payroll register that accompanied your textbook.

Name ______________________ Class ______________ Date ______________

(3)

SANCHEZ COMPUTER CENTER
TRIAL BALANCE
NOVEMBER 30, 200X

	Dr.	Cr.

8

THE EMPLOYER'S TAX RESPONSIBILITIES: PRINCIPLES AND PROCEDURES

SELF-REVIEW QUIZ 8-1

GENERAL JOURNAL

PAGE 1

Date		Account Titles and Description	PR	Dr.	Cr.

Name ______________________ Class ______________ Date ______________

SELF-REVIEW QUIZ 8-2

1.

2.

SELF-REVIEW QUIZ 8-3

1. ________ 2. ________ 3. ________ 4. ________ 5. ________ 6. ________

Name ______________________ Class ______________ Date ______________

CHAPTER 8

SET A FORMS FOR CLASSROOM DEMONSTRATION EXERCISES

1.

A. B. C. D. E.			

2.

A. ______________________

B. ______________________

C. ______________________

D. ______________________

3.

____

____

____

____

4.

A. ______________________

B. ______________________

C. ______________________

D. ______________________

E. ______________________

F. ______________________

G. ______________________

5.

A. ____________

B. ____________

C. ____________

D. ____________

E. ____________

Name ____________________ Class ____________ Date ____________

CHAPTER 8

SET B FORMS FOR CLASSROOM DEMONSTRATION EXERCISES

1.

A. B. C. D. E.			

2.

A. ____________________

B. ____________________

C. ____________________

D. ____________________

3.

____

____

____

____

4.

A. ____________________

B. ____________________

C. ____________________

D. ____________________

E. ____________________

F. ____________________

G. ____________________

5.

A. __________

B. __________

C. __________

D. __________

E. __________

Name ______________________ Class ______________ Date ______________

FORMS FOR EXERCISES

8-1.

ACCOUNT	CATEGORY	DR/CR	STATEMENT FOUND ON

8-2.

8-3.

Name ______________________ Class ______________ Date ______________

EXERCISES (CONCLUDED)

8-4.

8-5.

8-6.

8-7.

8-8.

Name ____________ Class ____________ Date ____________

END OF CHAPTER PROBLEMS

PROBLEM 8A-1 OR PROBLEM 8B-1

Employee	Allowance & Marital Status	Gross	FICA OASDI	FICA Medicare	Federal Income Tax

(2)

Name ____________________ Class ____________ Date ____________

PROBLEM 8A-2 OR PROBLEM 8B-2

Date		Account Titles and Description	PR	Dr.	Cr.

Name ______________________ Class ______________ Date ______________

PROBLEM 8A-2 OR PROBLEM 8B-2 (CONCLUDED)

Date		Account Titles and Description	PR	Dr.	Cr.

Name ______________________ Class ______________ Date ______________

PROBLEM 8A-3 OR PROBLEM 8B-3

Form **941 for 200X: Employer's QUARTERLY Federal Tax Return** 990106

(Rev. January 2006) Department of the Treasury — Internal Revenue Service OMB No. 1545-0029

(EIN)
Employer identification number ☐☐ – ☐☐☐☐☐☐☐

Name *(not your trade name)* ______________________

Trade name *(if any)* ______________________

Address ______________________
Number Street Suite or room number
____
City State ZIP code

Report for this Quarter ...
(Check one.)

☐ **1:** January, February, March
☐ **2:** April, May, June
☐ **3:** July, August, September
☐ **4:** October, November, December

Read the separate instructions before you fill out this form. Please type or print within the boxes.

Part 1: Answer these questions for this quarter.

1 **Number of employees who received wages, tips, or other compensation for the pay period including:** ***Mar. 12*** **(Quarter 1),** ***June 12*** **(Quarter 2),** ***Sept. 12*** **(Quarter 3),** ***Dec. 12*** **(Quarter 4)** . . . 1 ______

2 **Wages, tips, and other compensation** . . . 2 ______ .

3 **Total income tax withheld from wages, tips, and other compensation** . . . 3 ______ .

4 **If no wages, tips, and other compensation are subject to social security or Medicare tax** . . ☐ Check and go to line 6.

5 **Taxable social security and Medicare wages and tips:**

	Column 1		*Column 2*
5a **Taxable social security wages**	.	× .124 =	.
5b **Taxable social security tips**	.	× .124 =	.
5c **Taxable Medicare wages & tips**	.	× .029 =	.

5d **Total social security and Medicare taxes** (*Column 2,* lines 5a + 5b + 5c = line 5d) . . 5d ______ .

6 **Total taxes before adjustments** (lines 3 + 5d = line 6) . . . 6 ______ .

7 **TAX ADJUSTMENTS** (Read the instructions for line 7 before completing lines 7a through 7h.):

7a **Current quarter's fractions of cents** . . . ______ .

7b **Current quarter's sick pay** . . . ______ .

7c **Current quarter's adjustments for tips and group-term life insurance** ______ .

7d **Current year's income tax withholding** (attach Form 941c) . . . ______ .

7e **Prior quarters' social security and Medicare taxes** (attach Form 941c) ______ .

7f **Special additions to federal income tax** (attach Form 941c) . . . ______ .

7g **Special additions to social security and Medicare** (attach Form 941c) ______ .

7h **TOTAL ADJUSTMENTS** (Combine all amounts: lines 7a through 7g.) . . . 7h ______ .

8 **Total taxes after adjustments** (Combine lines 6 and 7h.) . . . 8 ______ .

9 **Advance earned income credit (EIC) payments made to employees** . . . 9 ______ .

10 **Total taxes after adjustment for advance EIC** (line 8 – line 9 = line 10) . . . 10 ______ .

11 **Total deposits for this quarter, including overpayment applied from a prior quarter** . . . 11 ______ .

12 **Balance due** (If line 10 is more than line 11, write the difference here.) . . . 12 ______ .
Make checks payable to *United States Treasury.*

13 **Overpayment** (If line 11 is more than line 10, write the difference here.) ______ . Check one ☐ Apply to next return. ☐ Send a refund.

▶ You **MUST** fill out both pages of this form and **SIGN** it.

Next ➡

For Privacy Act and Paperwork Reduction Act Notice, see the back of the Payment Voucher. Cat. No. 17001Z Form **941** (Rev. 1-2006)

Name ______________________ Class ______________ Date ______________

PROBLEM 8A-3 OR PROBLEM 8B-3 (CONCLUDED)

990206

Name *(not your trade name)* | **Employer identification number (EIN)**

Part 2: Tell us about your deposit schedule and tax liability for this quarter.

If you are unsure about whether you are a monthly schedule depositor or a semiweekly schedule depositor, see *Pub. 15 (Circular E)*, section 11.

14 ☐☐ **Write the state abbreviation for the state where you made your deposits** OR **write "MU" if you made your deposits in *multiple* states.**

15 **Check one:** ☐ **Line 10 is less than $2,500.** Go to Part 3.

☐ **You were a monthly schedule depositor for the entire quarter. Fill out your tax liability for each month.** Then go to Part 3.

Tax liability: Month 1 ________ .

Month 2 ________ .

Month 3 ________ .

Total liability for quarter ________ . **Total must equal line 10.**

☐ **You were a semiweekly schedule depositor for any part of this quarter.** Fill out *Schedule B (Form 941): Report of Tax Liability for Semiweekly Schedule Depositors,* and attach it to this form.

Part 3: Tell us about your business. If a question does NOT apply to your business, leave it blank.

16 **If your business has closed or you stopped paying wages** . . . . ☐ Check here, and

enter the final date you paid wages ___ / ___ / ___ .

17 **If you are a seasonal employer and you do not have to file a return for every quarter of the year** . . ☐ Check here.

Part 4: May we speak with your third-party designee?

Do you want to allow an employee, a paid tax preparer, or another person to discuss this return with the IRS? See the instructions for details.

☐ Yes. Designee's name ________________

Phone ( ) – Personal Identification Number (PIN) ☐☐☐☐☐

☐ No.

Part 5: Sign here. You MUST fill out both sides of this form and **SIGN it.**

Under penalties of perjury, I declare that I have examined this return, including accompanying schedules and statements, and to the best of my knowledge and belief, it is true, correct, and complete.

X Sign your name here ________________

Print name and title ________________

Date ___ / ___ / ___ Phone ( ) –

Part 6: For PAID preparers only *(optional)*

Paid Preparer's Signature ________________

Firm's name ________________

Address ________________ EIN ________

________________ ZIP code ________

Date ___ / ___ / ___ Phone ( ) – SSN/PTIN ________

☐ Check if you are self-employed.

Name ______________________ Class ______________ Date ______________

PROBLEM 8A-4 OR PROBLEM 8B-4

Name ______________________ Class ______________ Date ______________

PROBLEM 8A-4 OR PROBLEM 8B-4 (CONTINUED)

Form **941 for 200X: Employer's QUARTERLY Federal Tax Return** 990106

(Rev. January 2006) Department of the Treasury — Internal Revenue Service OMB No. 1545-0029

(EIN)
Employer identification number ☐☐ – ☐☐☐☐☐☐☐

Name *(not your trade name)* ______________________

Trade name *(if any)* ______________________

Address ______________________
Number Street Suite or room number
____
City State ZIP code

Report for this Quarter ...
(Check one.)

☐ **1:** January, February, March
☐ **2:** April, May, June
☐ **3:** July, August, September
☐ **4:** October, November, December

Read the separate instructions before you fill out this form. Please type or print within the boxes.

Part 1: Answer these questions for this quarter.

1 **Number of employees who received wages, tips, or other compensation for the pay period including:** ***Mar. 12*** **(Quarter 1),** ***June 12*** **(Quarter 2),** ***Sept. 12*** **(Quarter 3),** ***Dec. 12*** **(Quarter 4)** . . . 1 ______

2 **Wages, tips, and other compensation** . . . . 2 ______

3 **Total income tax withheld from wages, tips, and other compensation** . . . . 3 ______

4 **If no wages, tips, and other compensation are subject to social security or Medicare tax** . . ☐ Check and go to line 6.

5 **Taxable social security and Medicare wages and tips:**

	Column 1		*Column 2*
5a **Taxable social security wages**	.	× .124 =	.
5b **Taxable social security tips**	.	× .124 =	.
5c **Taxable Medicare wages & tips**	.	× .029 =	.

5d **Total social security and Medicare taxes** (*Column 2,* lines 5a + 5b + 5c = line 5d) . . 5d ______

6 **Total taxes before adjustments** (lines 3 + 5d = line 6) . . . . 6 ______

7 **TAX ADJUSTMENTS** (Read the instructions for line 7 before completing lines 7a through 7h.):

7a **Current quarter's fractions of cents** . . . . ______

7b **Current quarter's sick pay** . . . . ______

7c **Current quarter's adjustments for tips and group-term life insurance** ______

7d **Current year's income tax withholding** (attach Form 941c) . . . ______

7e **Prior quarters' social security and Medicare taxes** (attach Form 941c) ______

7f **Special additions to federal income tax** (attach Form 941c) . . . ______

7g **Special additions to social security and Medicare** (attach Form 941c) ______

7h **TOTAL ADJUSTMENTS** (Combine all amounts: lines 7a through 7g.) . . . . 7h ______

8 **Total taxes after adjustments** (Combine lines 6 and 7h.) . . . . 8 ______

9 **Advance earned income credit (EIC) payments made to employees** . . . . 9 ______

10 **Total taxes after adjustment for advance EIC** (line 8 – line 9 = line 10) . . . . 10 ______

11 **Total deposits for this quarter, including overpayment applied from a prior quarter** . . . 11 ______

12 **Balance due** (If line 10 is more than line 11, write the difference here.) . . . . 12 ______
Make checks payable to *United States Treasury.*

13 **Overpayment** (If line 11 is more than line 10, write the difference here.) ______ Check one ☐ Apply to next return. ☐ Send a refund.

▶ You **MUST** fill out both pages of this form and **SIGN** it.

Next ➔

For Privacy Act and Paperwork Reduction Act Notice, see the back of the Payment Voucher. Cat. No. 17001Z Form **941** (Rev. 1-2006)

Name ______________________ Class ______________ Date ______________

PROBLEM 8A-4 OR PROBLEM 8B-4 (CONCLUDED)

990206

Name *(not your trade name)*	**Employer identification number (EIN)**

Part 2: Tell us about your deposit schedule and tax liability for this quarter.

If you are unsure about whether you are a monthly schedule depositor or a semiweekly schedule depositor, see *Pub. 15 (Circular E),* section 11.

14 ☐☐ **Write the state abbreviation for the state where you made your deposits** OR **write "MU" if you made your deposits in *multiple* states.**

15 Check one: ☐ **Line 10 is less than $2,500.** Go to Part 3.

☐ **You were a monthly schedule depositor for the entire quarter. Fill out your tax liability for each month.** Then go to Part 3.

Tax liability: Month 1 ________ .

Month 2 ________ .

Month 3 ________ .

Total liability for quarter ________ . **Total must equal line 10.**

☐ **You were a semiweekly schedule depositor for any part of this quarter.** Fill out *Schedule B (Form 941): Report of Tax Liability for Semiweekly Schedule Depositors,* and attach it to this form.

Part 3: Tell us about your business. If a question does NOT apply to your business, leave it blank.

16 If your business has closed or you stopped paying wages . . . . ☐ Check here, and

enter the final date you paid wages ___ / ___ / ___ .

17 If you are a seasonal employer and you do not have to file a return for every quarter of the year . . ☐ Check here.

Part 4: May we speak with your third-party designee?

Do you want to allow an employee, a paid tax preparer, or another person to discuss this return with the IRS? See the instructions for details.

☐ Yes. Designee's name ______________________

Phone ( ) – Personal Identification Number (PIN) ☐☐☐☐☐

☐ No.

Part 5: Sign here. You MUST fill out both sides of this form and **SIGN it.**

Under penalties of perjury, I declare that I have examined this return, including accompanying schedules and statements, and to the best of my knowledge and belief, it is true, correct, and complete.

✗ Sign your name here ______________________

Print name and title ______________________

Date ___ / ___ / ___ Phone ( ) –

Part 6: For PAID preparers only *(optional)*

Paid Preparer's Signature ______________________

Firm's name ______________________

Address ______________________ EIN ______________

______________________ ZIP code ______________

Date ___ / ___ / ___ Phone ( ) – SSN/PTIN ______________

☐ Check if you are self-employed.

 Form **941** (Rev. 1-2006)

Name ______________________ Class ______________ Date ______________

PROBLEM 8A-5 OR PROBLEM 8B-5

Form **940 for 200X: Employer's Annual Federal Unemployment (FUTA) Tax Return** 850108

Department of the Treasury — Internal Revenue Service

OMB No. 1545-0028

(EIN)
Employer identification number ☐☐ – ☐☐☐☐☐☐☐

Name *(not your trade name)* ____________

Trade name *(if any)* ____________

Address ____________
Number Street Suite or room number
____
City State ZIP code

Type of Return
(Check all that apply.)

☐ **a.** Amended
☐ **b.** Successor employer
☐ **c.** No payments to employees in 2008
☐ **d.** Final: Business closed or stopped paying wages

Read the separate instructions before you fill out this form. Please type or print within the boxes.

Part 1: Tell us about your return. If any line does NOT apply, leave it blank.

1 **If you were required to pay your state unemployment tax in ...**

1a **One state only,** write the state abbreviation . . . . . 1a ☐☐

- OR -

1b **More than one state** (You are a multi-state employer) . . . . 1b ☐ Check here. Fill out Schedule A.

Skip line 2 for 2008 and go to line 3.

2 **If you paid wages in a state that is subject to CREDIT REDUCTION** . . . . 2 ☐ Check here. Fill out Schedule A (Form 940), Part 2.

Part 2: Determine your FUTA tax before adjustments for 2008. If any line does NOT apply, leave it blank.

3 **Total payments to all employees** . . . . 3 ______ .

4 **Payments exempt from FUTA tax** . . . . 4 ______ .

Check all that apply: 4a ☐ Fringe benefits 4c ☐ Retirement/Pension 4e ☐ Other
4b ☐ Group-term life insurance 4d ☐ Dependent care

5 **Total of payments made to each employee in excess of $7,000** . . . . 5 ______ .

6 **Subtotal** (line 4 + line 5 = line 6) . . . . 6 ______ .

7 **Total taxable FUTA wages** (line 3 – line 6 = line 7) . . . . 7 ______ .

8 **FUTA tax before adjustments** (line 7 × .008 = line 8) . . . . 8 ______ .

Part 3: Determine your adjustments. If any line does NOT apply, leave it blank.

9 **If ALL of the taxable FUTA wages you paid were excluded from state unemployment tax, multiply line 7 by .054** (line 7 × .054 = line 9). Then go to line 12 . . . . 9 ______ .

10 **If SOME of the taxable FUTA wages you paid were excluded from state unemployment tax, OR you paid ANY state unemployment tax late** (after the due date for filing Form 940), fill out the worksheet in the instructions. Enter the amount from line 7 of the worksheet onto line 10 . . 10 ______ .

Skip line 11 for 2008 and go to line 12.

11 **If credit reduction applies,** enter the amount from line 3 of Schedule A (Form 940) . . . . . . 11 ______ .

Part 4: Determine your FUTA tax and balance due or overpayment for 2008. If any line does NOT apply, leave it blank.

12 **Total FUTA tax after adjustments** (lines 8 + 9 + 10 + 11 = line 12) . . . . 12 ______ .

13 **FUTA tax deposited for the year, including any payment applied from a prior year** . . . . 13 ______ .

14 **Balance due** (If line 12 is more than line 13, enter the difference on line 14.)
- If line 14 is more than $500, you must deposit your tax.
- If line 14 is $500 or less, you may pay with this return. For more information on how to pay, see the separate instructions . . . . 14 ______ .

15 **Overpayment** (If line 13 is more than line 12, enter the difference on line 15 and check a box below.) . . . . 15 ______ .

Check one: ☐ Apply to next return. ☐ Send a refund.

▶ You **MUST** fill out both pages of this form and **SIGN** it.

Next ➡

For Privacy Act and Paperwork Reduction Act Notice, see the back of Form 940-V, Payment Voucher. Cat. No. 11234O Form **940** (2008)

PROBLEM 8A-5 OR PROBLEM 8B-5 (CONCLUDED)

Name *(not your trade name)*	**Employer identification number (EIN)**

Part 5: Report your FUTA tax liability by quarter only if line 12 is more than $500. If not, go to Part 6.

16 **Report the amount of your FUTA tax liability for each quarter; do NOT enter the amount you deposited. If you had no liability for a quarter, leave the line blank.**

16a **1st quarter** (January 1 – March 31) . . . . **16a** ______ .

16b **2nd quarter** (April 1 – June 30) . . . . **16b** ______ .

16c **3rd quarter** (July 1 – September 30) . . . . **16c** ______ .

16d **4th quarter** (October 1 – December 31) . . . . **16d** ______ .

17 **Total tax liability for the year** (lines 16a + 16b + 16c + 16d = line 17) **17** ______ . **Total must equal line 12.**

Part 6: May we speak with your third-party designee?

Do you want to allow an employee, a paid tax preparer, or another person to discuss this return with the IRS? See the instructions for details.

☐ **Yes.** Designee's name and phone number ______ (   )   –

Select a 5-digit Personal Identification Number (PIN) to use when talking to IRS ☐☐☐☐☐

☐ **No.**

Part 7: Sign here. You MUST fill out both pages of this form and SIGN it.

Under penalties of perjury, I declare that I have examined this return, including accompanying schedules and statements, and to the best of my knowledge and belief, it is true, correct, and complete, and that no part of any payment made to a state unemployment fund claimed as a credit was, or is to be, deducted from the payments made to employees. Declaration of preparer (other than taxpayer) is based on all information of which preparer has any knowledge.

✗ **Sign your name here** ______

Print your name here ______

Print your title here ______

Date   /   /

Best daytime phone (   )   –

Paid preparer's use only

Check if you are self-employed . . . ☐

Preparer's name ______ Preparer's SSN/PTIN ______

Preparer's signature ______ Date   /   /

Firm's name (or yours if self-employed) ______ EIN ______

Address ______ Phone (   )   –

City ______ State ______ ZIP code ______

Page **2** Form **940** (2008)

Name ______________________ Class ______________ Date ______________

CHAPTER 8
SUMMARY PRACTICE TEST: THE EMPLOYER'S TAX RESPONSIBILITIES: PRINCIPLES AND PROCEDURES

Part I Instructions

Fill in the blank(s) to complete the statement.

1. Form 941 is completed ______________.
2. The payroll tax expense for the employer is made up of ______________, ______________, and FUTA.
3. Data from the ______________ ______________ will provide the needed information to record the payroll in the general journal.
4. SUTA is usually paid ______________.
5. FUTA Payable is a ______________ found on the ______________ ______________.
6. Form 941 summarizes the taxes owed for ______________ and ______________.
7. ______________ ______________ ______________ will tell if a deposit is to be made monthly or semiweekly for FIT and Social Security.
8. Form ______________ is prepared quarterly to summarize tax liabilities for FICA (Social Security and Medicare) and FIT.
9. The ______________ ______________ ______________ ______________ is required to be given to employees by January 31 following the year employed.
10. ______________ does not have a merit rating like SUTA.

Part II Instructions

Answer true or false to the following.

1. Prepaid Workers' Compensation Insurance is a liability.
2. Payroll taxes are recorded as assets for a business.
3. Payroll Tax Expense is made up of FICA, SUTA, and FIT.
4. Frequency of deposits relating to Form 941 is based on amount of tax liability in look-back periods.
5. The normal balance of FIT payable is a debit.
6. The individual earnings record provides the data to prepare W-2s.
7. A tax calendar provides little help to the employer involving the payment of tax liabilities.
8. Form 941 is completed twice a year.
9. A year-end adjusting entry is needed for workers' compensation.
10. Form 8109 relates only to Form 940.

Name ______________________ Class ______________ Date ______________

Part III Instructions

Complete the following table:

ACCOUNT	CATEGORY	FOUND ON WHICH REPORT
1. Salaries Payable		
2. FUTA Payable		
3. SUTA Payable		
4. OASDI Tax Payable—Medicare		
5. FIT Payable		
6. Office Salaries Expense		

Part IV Instructions

Complete the following table:

	4 QUARTERS LOOK-BACK PERIOD LIABILITY	PAYROLL PAID WEEKLY	TAX PAID BY:
Sit. A	$40,000	October	?
Sit. B	75,000		
		on Wed.	?
		on Thurs.	?
		on Fri	?
		on Sat.	?
		on Sun.	?
		on Mon.	?
		on Tues.	?

Why is the depositor in situation A classified as a monthly depositor while in situation B the depositor is classified as semiweekly?

SOLUTIONS TO SUMMARY PRACTICE TEST

Part I

1. quarterly
2. FICA (OASDI and Medicare), SUTA
3. payroll register
4. quarterly
5. liability, balance sheet
6. FICA (OASDI and Medicare), FIT
7. Look-back periods
8. 941
9. Wage and Tax Statement
10. FUTA

Name ____________________ Class ____________ Date ____________

Part II

1.	false	**6.**	true
2.	false	**7.**	false
3.	false	**8.**	false
4.	true	**9.**	true
5.	false	**10.**	false

Part III

1. Liability; Balance Sheet
2. Liability; Balance Sheet
3. Liability; Balance Sheet
4. Liability; Balance Sheet
5. Liability; Balance Sheet
6. Expense; Income Statement

Part IV

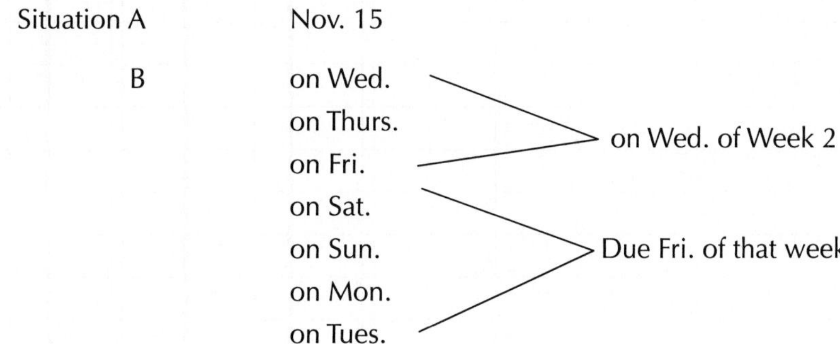

The depositor in situation A is classified as a monthly depositor because its tax liability of $40,000 during the look-back period was less than the $50,000 limit.

On the other hand, the depositor in situation B owed $75,000 during the look-back period. Since this is greater than the $50,000 limit, it was classified as a semiweekly depositor.

Name ______________________ Class ______________ Date ______________

CONTINUING PROBLEM FOR CHAPTER 8
SANCHEZ COMPUTER CENTER

SANCHEZ COMPUTER CENTER
GENERAL JOURNAL

PAGE 5

Date		Account Titles and Description	PR	Dr.	Cr.

Name ______________________ Class ______________ Date ______________

CONTINUING PROBLEM FOR CHAPTER 8
SANCHEZ COMPUTER CENTER

SANCHEZ COMPUTER CENTER
GENERAL JOURNAL

PAGE 6

Date		Account Titles and Description	PR	Dr.	Cr.

Name ______________________ Class ______________ Date ______________

CONTINUING PROBLEM FOR CHAPTER 8
SANCHEZ COMPUTER CENTER

Form **941 for 200X: Employer's QUARTERLY Federal Tax Return** 990106

(Rev. January 2006) Department of the Treasury — Internal Revenue Service OMB No. 1545-0029

(EIN)
Employer identification number ☐☐ – ☐☐☐☐☐☐☐

Name *(not your trade name)*

Trade name *(if any)*

Address
Number Street Suite or room number
City State ZIP code

Report for this Quarter ...
(Check one.)

☐ **1:** January, February, March
☐ **2:** April, May, June
☐ **3:** July, August, September
☐ **4:** October, November, December

Read the separate instructions before you fill out this form. Please type or print within the boxes.

Part 1: Answer these questions for this quarter.

1 **Number of employees who received wages, tips, or other compensation for the pay period including:** ***Mar. 12*** **(Quarter 1),** ***June 12*** **(Quarter 2),** ***Sept. 12*** **(Quarter 3),** ***Dec. 12*** **(Quarter 4)** . . . 1

2 **Wages, tips, and other compensation** . . . 2

3 **Total income tax withheld from wages, tips, and other compensation** . . . 3

4 **If no wages, tips, and other compensation are subject to social security or Medicare tax** . . ☐ Check and go to line 6.

5 **Taxable social security and Medicare wages and tips:**

	Column 1		*Column 2*
5a Taxable social security wages	.	× .124 =	.
5b Taxable social security tips	.	× .124 =	.
5c Taxable Medicare wages & tips	.	× .029 =	.

5d Total social security and Medicare taxes (*Column 2,* lines 5a + 5b + 5c = line 5d) . . 5d

6 **Total taxes before adjustments** (lines 3 + 5d = line 6) . . . 6

7 **TAX ADJUSTMENTS** (Read the instructions for line 7 before completing lines 7a through 7h.):

7a Current quarter's fractions of cents . . .

7b Current quarter's sick pay . . .

7c Current quarter's adjustments for tips and group-term life insurance

7d Current year's income tax withholding (attach Form 941c) . . .

7e Prior quarters' social security and Medicare taxes (attach Form 941c)

7f Special additions to federal income tax (attach Form 941c) . . .

7g Special additions to social security and Medicare (attach Form 941c)

7h TOTAL ADJUSTMENTS (Combine all amounts: lines 7a through 7g.) . . . 7h

8 **Total taxes after adjustments** (Combine lines 6 and 7h.) . . . 8

9 **Advance earned income credit (EIC) payments made to employees** . . . 9

10 **Total taxes after adjustment for advance EIC** (line 8 – line 9 = line 10) . . . 10

11 **Total deposits for this quarter, including overpayment applied from a prior quarter** . . . 11

12 **Balance due** (If line 10 is more than line 11, write the difference here.) . . . 12
Make checks payable to *United States Treasury.*

13 **Overpayment** (If line 11 is more than line 10, write the difference here.) Check one ☐ Apply to next return. ☐ Send a refund.

▶ You **MUST** fill out both pages of this form and **SIGN** it.

Next ➔

For Privacy Act and Paperwork Reduction Act Notice, see the back of the Payment Voucher. Cat. No. 17001Z Form **941** (Rev. 1-2006)

Name ______________________ Class ______________ Date ______________

CONTINUING PROBLEM FOR CHAPTER 8
SANCHEZ COMPUTER CENTER

990206

Name *(not your trade name)*	**Employer identification number (EIN)**

Part 2: Tell us about your deposit schedule and tax liability for this quarter.

If you are unsure about whether you are a monthly schedule depositor or a semiweekly schedule depositor, see ***Pub. 15 (Circular E),*** **section 11.**

14 ☐☐ **Write the state abbreviation for the state where you made your deposits** OR **write "MU" if you made your deposits in** ***multiple*** **states.**

15 **Check one:** ☐ **Line 10 is less than $2,500.** Go to Part 3.

☐ **You were a monthly schedule depositor for the entire quarter. Fill out your tax liability for each month.** Then go to Part 3.

Tax liability: Month 1	.	
Month 2	.	
Month 3	.	
Total liability for quarter	.	**Total must equal line 10.**

☐ **You were a semiweekly schedule depositor for any part of this quarter.** Fill out *Schedule B (Form 941): Report of Tax Liability for Semiweekly Schedule Depositors,* and attach it to this form.

Part 3: Tell us about your business. If a question does NOT apply to your business, leave it blank.

16 **If your business has closed or you stopped paying wages** . . . . ☐ Check here, and

enter the final date you paid wages / / .

17 **If you are a seasonal employer and you do not have to file a return for every quarter of the year** . . ☐ Check here.

Part 4: May we speak with your third-party designee?

Do you want to allow an employee, a paid tax preparer, or another person to discuss this return with the IRS? See the instructions for details.

☐ Yes. Designee's name

Phone ( ) – Personal Identification Number (PIN) ☐☐☐☐☐

☐ No.

Part 5: Sign here. You MUST fill out both sides of this form and **SIGN it.**

Under penalties of perjury, I declare that I have examined this return, including accompanying schedules and statements, and to the best of my knowledge and belief, it is true, correct, and complete.

X Sign your name here

Print name and title

Date / / Phone ( ) –

Part 6: For PAID preparers only ***(optional)***

Paid Preparer's Signature

Firm's name

Address | EIN

ZIP code

Date / / Phone ( ) – SSN/PTIN

☐ Check if you are self-employed.

Page **2** Form **941** (Rev. 1-2006)

Name ______________________ Class ______________ Date ______________

Form **940 for 200X:** **Employer's Annual Federal Unemployment (FUTA) Tax Return** 850108

Department of the Treasury — Internal Revenue Service

OMB No. 1545-0028

(EIN)
Employer identification number ☐☐ – ☐☐☐☐☐☐☐

Name *(not your trade name)* ______________________

Trade name *(if any)* ______________________

Address ______________________
Number Street Suite or room number
____
City State ZIP code

Type of Return
(Check all that apply.)

☐ **a.** Amended

☐ **b.** Successor employer

☐ **c.** No payments to employees in 2008

☐ **d.** Final: Business closed or stopped paying wages

Read the separate instructions before you fill out this form. Please type or print within the boxes.

Part 1: Tell us about your return. If any line does NOT apply, leave it blank.

1 **If you were required to pay your state unemployment tax in ...**

1a **One state only,** write the state abbreviation . . . . . 1a ☐☐

- OR -

1b **More than one state** (You are a multi-state employer) . . . . 1b ☐ Check here. Fill out Schedule A.

Skip line 2 for 2008 and go to line 3.

2 If you paid wages in a state that is subject to CREDIT REDUCTION . . . . 2 ☐ Check here. Fill out Schedule A (Form 940), Part 2.

Part 2: Determine your FUTA tax before adjustments for 2008. If any line does NOT apply, leave it blank.

3 **Total payments to all employees** . . . . 3 ________ .

4 **Payments exempt from FUTA tax** . . . . 4 ________ .

Check all that apply: 4a ☐ Fringe benefits 4c ☐ Retirement/Pension 4e ☐ Other
4b ☐ Group-term life insurance 4d ☐ Dependent care

5 **Total of payments made to each employee in excess of $7,000** . . . . 5 ________ .

6 **Subtotal** (line 4 + line 5 = line 6) . . . . 6 ________ .

7 **Total taxable FUTA wages** (line 3 – line 6 = line 7) . . . . 7 ________ .

8 **FUTA tax before adjustments** (line 7 × .008 = line 8) . . . . 8 ________ .

Part 3: Determine your adjustments. If any line does NOT apply, leave it blank.

9 **If ALL of the taxable FUTA wages you paid were excluded from state unemployment tax, multiply line 7 by .054** (line 7 × .054 = line 9). Then go to line 12 . . . . 9 ________ .

10 **If SOME of the taxable FUTA wages you paid were excluded from state unemployment tax, OR you paid ANY state unemployment tax late** (after the due date for filing Form 940), fill out the worksheet in the instructions. Enter the amount from line 7 of the worksheet onto line 10 . . 10 ________ .

Skip line 11 for 2008 and go to line 12.

11 **If credit reduction applies,** enter the amount from line 3 of Schedule A (Form 940) . . . . . 11 ________ .

Part 4: Determine your FUTA tax and balance due or overpayment for 2008. If any line does NOT apply, leave it blank.

12 **Total FUTA tax after adjustments** (lines 8 + 9 + 10 + 11 = line 12) . . . . 12 ________ .

13 **FUTA tax deposited for the year, including any payment applied from a prior year** . . . . 13 ________ .

14 **Balance due** (If line 12 is more than line 13, enter the difference on line 14.)
- If line 14 is more than $500, you must deposit your tax.
- If line 14 is $500 or less, you may pay with this return. For more information on how to pay, see the separate instructions . . . . 14 ________ .

15 **Overpayment** (If line 13 is more than line 12, enter the difference on line 15 and check a box below.) . . . . 15 ________ .

Check one: ☐ Apply to next return. ☐ Send a refund.

▶ You **MUST** fill out both pages of this form and **SIGN** it.

Next ➡

For Privacy Act and Paperwork Reduction Act Notice, see the back of Form 940-V, Payment Voucher. Cat. No. 11234O Form **940** (2008)

Name ______________________ Class ______________ Date ______________

Name *(not your trade name)*	Employer identification number (EIN)

Part 5: Report your FUTA tax liability by quarter only if line 12 is more than $500. If not, go to Part 6.

16 **Report the amount of your FUTA tax liability for each quarter; do NOT enter the amount you deposited. If you had no liability for a quarter, leave the line blank.**

16a **1st quarter** (January 1 – March 31) . . . . **16a** ________ .

16b **2nd quarter** (April 1 – June 30) . . . . **16b** ________ .

16c **3rd quarter** (July 1 – September 30) . . . . **16c** ________ .

16d **4th quarter** (October 1 – December 31) . . . . **16d** ________ .

17 **Total tax liability for the year** (lines 16a + 16b + 16c + 16d = line 17) **17** ________ . **Total must equal line 12.**

Part 6: May we speak with your third-party designee?

Do you want to allow an employee, a paid tax preparer, or another person to discuss this return with the IRS? See the instructions for details.

☐ **Yes.** Designee's name and phone number ________ ( ) –

Select a 5-digit Personal Identification Number (PIN) to use when talking to IRS ☐☐☐☐☐

☐ **No.**

Part 7: Sign here. You MUST fill out both pages of this form and SIGN it.

Under penalties of perjury, I declare that I have examined this return, including accompanying schedules and statements, and to the best of my knowledge and belief, it is true, correct, and complete, and that no part of any payment made to a state unemployment fund claimed as a credit was, or is to be, deducted from the payments made to employees. Declaration of preparer (other than taxpayer) is based on all information of which preparer has any knowledge.

✗ **Sign your name here** ________

Print your name here ________

Print your title here ________

Date / /

Best daytime phone ( ) –

Paid preparer's use only

Check if you are self-employed . . . ☐

Preparer's name		Preparer's SSN/PTIN	
Preparer's signature		Date	/ /
Firm's name (or yours if self-employed)		EIN	
Address		Phone	( ) –
City	State	ZIP code	

9

Sales and Cash Receipts

SELF-REVIEW QUIZ 9-1

1. ____________ 2. ____________ 3. ____________ 4. ____________ 5. ____________

Name ______________________ Class ______________ Date ______________

SELF-REVIEW QUIZ 9-2

BERNIE COMPANY
GENERAL JOURNAL

PAGE 1

Date		Account Titles and Description	PR	Dr.	Cr.

ACCOUNTS RECEIVABLE SUBSIDIARY LEDGER

NAME LEE CORP.

ADDRESS 118 MORRIS RD., BOSTON, MA 01935

Date		Explanation	Post Ref.	Debit	Credit	Dr. Balance

NAME RING COMPANY

ADDRESS 31 NORRIS ROAD, BOSTON, MA 01935

Date		Explanation	Post Ref.	Debit	Credit	Dr. Balance

Name ______________________ Class ______________ Date ______________

PARTIAL GENERAL LEDGER

ACCOUNT RECEIVABLE — ACCOUNT NO. 141

Date	Explanation	Post Ref.	Debit	Credit	Balance	
					Debit	Credit

SALES — ACCOUNT NO. 310

Date	Explanation	Post Ref.	Debit	Credit	Balance	
					Debit	Credit

SALES RETURNS AND ALLOWANCES — ACCOUNT NO. 312

Date	Explanation	Post Ref.	Debit	Credit	Balance	
					Debit	Credit

Name ______________________ Class ______________ Date ______________

SELF-REVIEW QUIZ 9-3

MABEL CORPORATION
GENERAL JOURNAL

PAGE 3

Date		Account Titles and Description	PR	Dr.	Cr.

Name ________________ Class ________________ Date ________________

PARTIAL GENERAL LEDGER

CASH — ACCOUNT NO. 110

Date 200X		Explanation	Post Ref.	Debit	Credit	Balance Debit	Balance Credit
May	1	Balance	✓			600 00	

ACCOUNTS RECEIVABLE — ACCOUNT NO. 120

Date 200X		Explanation	Post Ref.	Debit	Credit	Balance Debit	Balance Credit
May	1	Balance	✓			700 00	

STORE EQUIPMENT — ACCOUNT NO. 130

Date 200X		Explanation	Post Ref.	Debit	Credit	Balance Debit	Balance Credit
May	1	Balance	✓			600 00	

SALES — ACCOUNT NO. 410

Date 200X		Explanation	Post Ref.	Debit	Credit	Balance Debit	Balance Credit
May	1	Balance	✓				700 00

Name ______________________ Class ______________ Date ______________

SALES DISCOUNT **ACCOUNT NO. 420**

Date 200X		Explanation	Post Ref.	Debit	Credit	Balance Debit	Balance Credit

NAME **JANIS FROSS**

ADDRESS **81 FOSTER RD., BEVERLY, MA 09125**

Date 200X		Explanation	Post Ref.	Debit	Credit	Dr. Balance
May	1	Balance	✓			200 00

ACCOUNTS RECEIVABLE SUBSIDIARY LEDGER

NAME **IRENE WELCH**

ADDRESS **10 RONG RD., BEVERLY, MA 01215**

Date 200X		Explanation	Post Ref.	Debit	Credit	Dr. Balance
May	1	Balance	✓			500 00

Name ______________________ Class ______________ Date ______________

CHAPTER 9
FORMS FOR CLASSROOM DEMONSTRATION EXERCISES SET A OR SET B

1.

2.

3.

A. ________ ________ ________

B. ________ ________ ________

C. ________ ________ ________

4.

Name ______________________ Class ______________ Date ______________

5.

PAGE 6

Date		Account Titles and Description	PR	Dr.	Cr.

6.

BLUE CO.
SCHEDULE OF ACCOUNTS RECEIVABLE
MAY 31, 200X

Name ________________ Class ________________ Date ________________

FORMS FOR EXERCISES

9-1.

Amazon.com	

Accounts Receivable 112	

Bill Valley Co.	

Sales 412	

9-2.

GENERAL JOURNAL

PAGE 1

Date		Account Titles and Description	PR	Dr.	Cr.

Bass Co.	

Sales 411	

Ronald Co.	

Accounts Receivable 112	

Sales Returns & Allowances 412	

Name ______________________ Class ______________ Date ______________

EXERCISES (CONTINUED)

9-3.

9-4.

EDNA CO.
GENERAL JOURNAL

PAGE 1

Date		Account Titles and Description	PR	Dr.	Cr.

Name ______________________ Class ______________ Date ______________

EXERCISES (CONCLUDED)

GENERAL JOURNAL (CONTINUED) PAGE 1

Date		Account Titles and Description	PR	Dr.	Cr.

ACCOUNTS RECEIVABLE SUBSIDIARY LEDGER

Boston Co.

Gary Co.

PARTIAL GENERAL LEDGER

Cash 111

Accounts Receivable 113

Edna Cares, Capital 311

Sales 411

Sales Returns & Allowances 412

Sales Discount 413

EDNA CO.
SCHEDULE OF ACCOUNTS RECEIVABLE
JUNE 30, 200X

9-5.

Name ______________________ Class ______________ Date ______________

END OF CHAPTER PROBLEMS

PROBLEM 9A-1 OR PROBLEM 9B-1

PIZZA AND MORE
GENERAL JOURNAL

PAGE 1

Date		Account Titles and Description	PR	Dr.	Cr.

Name ______________________ Class ______________________ Date ______________________

PROBLEM 9A-1 OR PROBLEM 9B-1 (CONTINUED)

ACCOUNTS RECEIVABLE SUBSIDIARY LEDGER

NAME CINDY CO.

ADDRESS 942 MOSE ST., REVERE, MA 01938

Date		Explanation	Post Ref.	Debit	Credit	Dr. Balance

NAME FRENCH CO.

ADDRESS 8 JOSS AVE., LYNN, MA 01947

Date		Explanation	Post Ref.	Debit	Credit	Dr. Balance

NAME GROOM CO.

ADDRESS 10 LOST RD., TOPSFIELD, MA 01998

Date		Explanation	Post Ref.	Debit	Credit	Dr. Balance

Name ______________________ Class ______________ Date ______________

PROBLEM 9A-1 OR PROBLEM 9B-1 (CONTINUED)

PIZZA AND MORE
GENERAL LEDGER

ACCOUNTS RECEIVABLE — **ACCOUNT NO. 112**

Date	Explanation	Post Ref.	Debit	Credit	Balance	
					Debit	Credit

PIZZA SALES — **ACCOUNT NO. 410**

Date	Explanation	Post Ref.	Debit	Credit	Balance	
					Debit	Credit

GROCERY SALES — **ACCOUNT NO. 411**

Date	Explanation	Post Ref.	Debit	Credit	Balance	
					Debit	Credit

SALES RETURNS AND ALLOWANCES — **ACCOUNT NO. 412**

Date	Explanation	Post Ref.	Debit	Credit	Balance	
					Debit	Credit

Name ______________________ Class ______________ Date ______________

PROBLEM 9A-1 OR PROBLEM 9B-1 (CONCLUDED)

PIZZA AND MORE
SCHEDULE OF ACCOUNTS RECEIVABLE
JUNE 30, 200X

PROBLEM 9A-2 OR PROBLEM 9B-2

TED'S AUTO SUPPLY
GENERAL JOURNAL

PAGE 2

Date		Account Titles and Description	PR	Dr.	Cr.

Name ______________________ Class ______________ Date ______________

PROBLEM 9A-2 OR PROBLEM 9B-2 (CONTINUED)

ACCOUNTS RECEIVABLE SUBSIDIARY LEDGER

NAME LANCE CORNER

ADDRESS 9 ROE ST., BARTLETT, NH 01382

Date 200X		Explanation	Post Ref.	Debit	Credit	Dr. Balance
Nov	1	Balance	✓			400 00

NAME J. SETH

ADDRESS 22 REESE ST., LACONIA, NH 04321

Date 200X		Explanation	Post Ref.	Debit	Credit	Dr. Balance
Nov	1	Balance	✓			200 00

NAME R. VOLAN

ADDRESS 12 ASTER RD., MERRIMACK, NH 02134

Date 200X		Explanation	Post Ref.	Debit	Credit	Dr. Balance
Nov	1	Balance	✓			1 000 00

Name ______________________ Class ______________ Date ______________

PROBLEM 9A-2 OR PROBLEM 9B-2 (CONTINUED)

TED'S AUTO SUPPLY
PARTIAL GENERAL LEDGER

ACCOUNTS RECEIVABLE **ACCOUNT NO. 110**

Date 200X		Explanation	Post Ref.	Debit	Credit	Balance Debit	Balance Credit
Nov	1	Balance	✓			1 6 0 0 00	

SALES TAX PAYABLE **ACCOUNT NO. 210**

Date 200X		Explanation	Post Ref.	Debit	Credit	Balance Debit	Balance Credit
Nov	1	Balance	✓				1 6 0 0 00

AUTO PARTS SALES **ACCOUNT NO. 410**

Date		Explanation	Post Ref.	Debit	Credit	Balance Debit	Balance Credit

SALES RETURNS AND ALLOWANCES **ACCOUNT NO. 420**

Date		Explanation	Post Ref.	Debit	Credit	Balance Debit	Balance Credit

Name ______________________ Class ______________ Date ______________

PROBLEM 9A-2 OR PROBLEM 9B-2 (CONCLUDED)

(3)

TED'S AUTO SUPPLY
SCHEDULE OF ACCOUNTS RECEIVABLE
NOVEMBER 30, 200X

Name ______________________ Class ______________ Date ______________

PROBLEM 9A-3 OR PROBLEM 9B-3

(1,2)

PEAKER'S SNEAKER SHOP
GENERAL JOURNAL

PAGE 2

Date		Account Titles and Description	PR	Dr.	Cr.

Name ______________________ Class ______________ Date ______________

PROBLEM 9A-3 OR PROBLEM 9B-3 (CONTINUED)

(1,2)

PEAKER'S SNEAKER SHOP
GENERAL JOURNAL

PAGE 3

Date		Account Titles and Description	PR	Dr.	Cr.

Name ______________________ Class ______________ Date ______________

PROBLEM 9A-3 OR PROBLEM 9B-3 (CONTINUED)

ACCOUNTS RECEIVABLE SUBSIDIARY LEDGER

NAME B. DALE

ADDRESS 1822 RIVER RD., MEMPHIS, TN 09111

Date 200X		Explanation	Post Ref.	Debit	Credit	Dr. Balance
May	1	Balance	✓			400 00

NAME RON LESTER

ADDRESS 18 MASS. AVE., SAN DIEGO, CA 01999

Date		Explanation	Post Ref.	Debit	Credit	Dr. Balance
May	1	Balance	✓			800 00

ACCOUNTS RECEIVABLE SUBSIDIARY LEDGER

NAME PAM PRY

ADDRESS 918 MOORE DR., HOMEWOOD, IL 60430

Date 200X		Explanation	Post Ref.	Debit	Credit	Dr. Balance
May	1	Balance	✓			600 00

Name ______________ Class ______________ Date ______________

PROBLEM 9A-3 OR PROBLEM 9B-3 (CONTINUED)

NAME JIM ZON

ADDRESS 2 CHESTNUT ST., SWAMPSCOTT, MA 01970

Date 200X		Explanation	Post Ref.	Debit	Credit	Dr. Balance
May	1	Balance	✓			400 00

PEAKER'S SNEAKER SHOP
PARTIAL GENERAL LEDGER

CASH **ACCOUNT NO. 10**

Date 200X		Explanation	Post Ref.	Debit	Credit	Balance Debit	Balance Credit
May	1	Balance	✓			15 500 00	

PROBLEM 9A-3 OR PROBLEM 9B-3 (CONTINUED)

ACCOUNTS RECEIVABLE **ACCOUNT NO. 12**

Date 200X		Explanation	Post Ref.	Debit	Credit	Balance Debit	Balance Credit
May	1	Balance	✓			2 2 0 0 00	

SNEAKER RACK EQUIPMENT **ACCOUNT NO. 14**

Date 200X		Explanation	Post Ref.	Debit	Credit	Balance Debit	Balance Credit
May	1	Balance	✓			1 0 0 0 00	

MARK PEAKER, CAPITAL **ACCOUNT NO. 30**

Date 200X		Explanation	Post Ref.	Debit	Credit	Balance Debit	Balance Credit
May	1	Balance	✓				40 0 0 0 00

Name ____________ Class ____________ Date ____________

PROBLEM 9A-3 OR PROBLEM 9B-3 (CONTINUED)

SALES **ACCOUNT NO. 40**

Date 200X	Explanation	Post Ref.	Debit	Credit	Balance Debit	Balance Credit
May 1	Balance	✓				2 2 0 0 00

SALES DISCOUNT **ACCOUNT NO. 42**

Date 200X	Explanation	Post Ref.	Debit	Credit	Balance Debit	Balance Credit

SALES RETURNS & ALLOWANCES **ACCOUNT NO. 44**

Date 200X	Explanation	Post Ref.	Debit	Credit	Balance Debit	Balance Credit

Name ______________________ Class ______________ Date ______________

PROBLEM 9A-3 OR PROBLEM 9B-3 (CONCLUDED)

(3)

PEAKER'S SNEAKER SHOP
SCHEDULE OF ACCOUNTS RECEIVABLE
MAY 31, 200X

Name ______________________ Class ______________ Date ______________

PROBLEM 9A-4 OR PROBLEM 9B-4

BILL'S COSMETIC MARKET
GENERAL JOURNAL

PAGE 1

Date		Account Titles and Description	PR	Dr.	Cr.

Name ______________________ Class ______________ Date ______________

PROBLEM 9A-4 OR PROBLEM 9B-4 (CONTINUED)

BILL'S COSMETIC MARKET
GENERAL JOURNAL

PAGE 2

Date		Account Titles and Description	PR	Dr.	Cr.

Name ______________________ Class ______________ Date ______________

PROBLEM 9A-4 OR PROBLEM 9B-4 (CONTINUED)

ACCOUNTS RECEIVABLE SUBSIDIARY LEDGER

NAME ALICE KOY CO.

ADDRESS 2 RYAN RD., BUFFALO, NY 09113

Date		Explanation	Post Ref.	Debit	Credit	Debit Balance

Name ______________________ Class ______________ Date ______________

PROBLEM 9A-4 OR PROBLEM 9B-4 (CONTINUED)

ACCOUNTS RECEIVABLE SUBSIDIARY LEDGER

NAME RUSTY NEAL CO.

ADDRESS 4 REEL RD., LANCASTER, PA 04332

Date		Explanation	Post Ref.	Debit	Credit	Debit Balance

NAME MARIKA SANCHEZ CO.

ADDRESS 14 BONE DR., ENGLEWOOD CLIFFS, NJ 07632

Date		Explanation	Post Ref.	Debit	Credit	Debit Balance

NAME JEFF TONG CO.

ADDRESS 2 MARION RD., BOSTON, MA 01981

Date		Explanation	Post Ref.	Debit	Credit	Debit Balance

Name ____________________ Class ____________ Date ____________

PROBLEM 9A-4 OR PROBLEM 9B-4 (CONTINUED)

BILL'S COSMETIC MARKET
GENERAL LEDGER

CASH **ACCOUNT NO. 10**

Date	Explanation	Post Ref.	Debit	Credit	Balance Debit	Balance Credit

ACCOUNTS RECEIVABLE **ACCOUNT NO. 12**

Date	Explanation	Post Ref.	Debit	Credit	Balance Debit	Balance Credit

Name ______________________ Class ______________ Date ______________

PROBLEM 9A-4 OR PROBLEM 9B-4 (CONTINUED)

SALES TAX PAYABLE **ACCOUNT NO. 20**

Date		Explanation	Post Ref.	Debit	Credit	Balance	
						Debit	Credit

BILL MURRAY, CAPITAL **ACCOUNT NO. 30**

Date		Explanation	Post Ref.	Debit	Credit	Balance	
						Debit	Credit

LIPSTICK SALES **ACCOUNT NO. 40**

Date		Explanation	Post Ref.	Debit	Credit	Balance	
						Debit	Credit

Name ______________________ Class ______________ Date ______________

PROBLEM 9A-4 OR PROBLEM 9B-4 (CONCLUDED)

SALES RETURNS & ALLOWANCES, LIPSTICK **ACCOUNT NO. 42**

Date		Explanation	Post Ref.	Debit	Credit	Balance Debit	Balance Credit

EYE SHADOW SALES **ACCOUNT NO. 44**

Date		Explanation	Post Ref.	Debit	Credit	Balance Debit	Balance Credit

(3)

BILL'S COSMETIC MARKET
SCHEDULE OF ACCOUNTS RECEIVABLE
APRIL 30, 200X

Name ________________________ Class ______________ Date ______________

CHAPTER 9
SUMMARY PRACTICE TEST
SALES AND CASH RECEIPTS

Part I Instructions

Fill in the blank(s) to complete the statement.

1. The normal balance of sales returns and allowances is ____________.
2. ____________ ____________ and ____________ is a contra-revenue account.
3. Sales is a(n) ____________ account.
4. A discount period is less time than the ____________ ____________.
5. A debit to accounts receivable and a credit to sales records the sale of merchandise ____________ ____________.
6. The ____________ ____________ ____________ ____________ lists in alphabetical order an account for each customer.
7. ____________ ____________ in the general ledger is called the controlling account.
8. The (✓) in the PR column of the general journal indicates that the accounts receivable ledger has been updated ____________ ____________ ____________.
9. Issuing ____________ ____________ results in a debit to sales returns and allowancs and a credit to accounts receivable.
10. In a wholesale company there is no ____________ tax.
11. Sales Tax Payable is a(n) ____________ in the general ledger.
12. Cash sales result in a(n) ____________ to cash and a ____________ to sales.
13. Sales Returns and Allowances is a(n) ____________ ____________ account.
14. The ____________ ____________ has to be posted to the general as well as the sales ledger.
15. No ____________ ____________ are taken on sales tax.
16. A(n) ____________ ____________ ____________ ____________ lists the ending balances from the accounts receivable ledger.

Part II

Complete the following chart:

	Transaction	Dr.	Cr.
1.	Sale for cash	____________	____________
2.	Issued credit memo	____________	____________
3.	Sale on account	____________	____________
4.	Received cash payment less discount	____________	____________

Partial Chart of Accounts

10 Cash
20 Accounts Receivable

40 Sales
42 Sales Discount
44 Sales Returns and Allowances

Name ______________________ Class ______________ Date ______________

Part III Instructions

Answer true or false to the following statements.

1. A schedule of accounts receivable shows what customers do not owe.
2. A perpetual system would keep continual track of inventory.
3. Sales Discount policies can never change.
4. Sales Tax Payable is an asset.
5. Sales Discount is a contra asset.
6. Issuing a credit memorandum results in Sales, Returns and Allowances decreasing with Accounts Receivable increasing.
7. The sum of the accounts receivable subsidiary ledger is equal to the balance in the controlling account at the end of the month.
8. The buyer issues the credit memo.
9. The accounts receivable subsidiary ledger is listed in numerical order.
10. Sales Discount is a contra-revenue account.
11. Net sales = gross sales – SRA-SD.
12. The normal balance of an Accounts Receivable ledger is a debit.
13. Discounts are taken on sales tax.
14. 2/10, N/30 means a cash discount is good for 30 days.
15. The accounts receivable subsidiary ledger is always located in the general ledger.
16. Gross profit plus operating expenses equals net income.
17. A credit period is longer than the discount period.
18. In the accounts receivable subsidiary ledger each account is debited to record amounts customers owe.
19. Sales Tax Payable is an asset.

CHAPTER 9
SOLUTIONS TO SUMMARY PRACTICE TEST

Part I

1. debit
2. Sales Returns, Allowances
3. revenue
4. credit period
5. on account
6. accounts receivable subsidiary ledger
7. Accounts Receivable
8. during the month
9. credit memorandum
10. sales
11. liability
12. debit, credit
13. contra-revenue
14. journalized transaction
15. cash discounts
16. schedule of accounts receivable

Name ______________________ Class ______________ Date ______________

Part II

	Dr.	Cr.
1.	10	40
2.	44	20
3.	20	40
4.	10	20
	42	

Part III

1. false
2. true
3. false
4. false
5. false
6. false
7. true
8. false
9. false
10. true
11. true
12. true
13. false
14. false
15. false
16. false
17. true
18. true
19. false

Name ______________________ Class ______________ Date ______________

CONTINUING PROBLEM FOR CHAPTER 9

SANCHEZ COMPUTER CENTER
GENERAL JOURNAL

PAGE 4

Date		Account Titles and Description	PR	Dr.	Cr.

Name ______________________ Class ______________ Date ______________

SANCHEZ COMPUTER CENTER
SCHEDULE OF ACCOUNTS RECEIVABLE
1/31/0X

____

____

____

____

CASH **ACCOUNT NO. 1000**

Date		Explanation	Post Ref.	Debit	Credit	Balance Debit	Balance Credit
1/1	0X	Balance Forward	✓			3 336 65	

Name ______________ Class ______________ Date ______________

SANCHEZ COMPUTER CENTER
PARTIAL GENERAL LEDGER

ACCOUNTS RECEIVABLE **ACCOUNT NO. 1020**

Date		Explanation	Post Ref.	Debit	Credit	Balance Debit	Balance Credit
1/1	0X	Balance Forward	✓			13 600 00	

SALES **ACCOUNT NO. 4010**

Date		Explanation	Post Ref.	Debit	Credit	Balance Debit	Balance Credit

SALES RETURNS & ALLOWANCES **ACCOUNT NO. 4020**

Date		Explanation	Post Ref.	Debit	Credit	Balance Debit	Balance Credit

Name ______________________ Class ______________ Date ______________

SALES DISCOUNTS **ACCOUNT NO. 4030**

Date		Explanation	Post Ref.	Debit	Credit	Balance Debit	Balance Credit

ACCOUNTS RECEIVABLE
SUBSIDIARY LEDGER

NAME **TAYLOR GOLF** **ACCOUNT NO. 100**

ADDRESS **1010 MOCKINGBIRD LANE, CARLSBAD, CA 92008**

Date		Explanation	Post Ref.	Debit	Credit	Dr. Balance
1/1	0X	Balance forward	✓			2 9 0 0 00

NAME **VITA NEEDLE** **ACCOUNT NO. 101**

ADDRESS **144 CANTATA, IRVINE, CA 92606**

Date		Explanation	Post Ref.	Debit	Credit	Dr. Balance
1/1	0X	Balance	✓			6 8 0 0 00

Name ______________________ Class ______________ Date ______________

ACCOUNTS RECEIVABLE SUBSIDIARY LEDGER

NAME ACCU PAC **ACCOUNT NO.** 103

ADDRESS 1717 JORDAN ST., SAN CLEMENTE, CA 91607

Date		Explanation	Post Ref.	Debit	Credit	Dr. Balance
1/1	0X	Balance	✓			3 9 0 0 00

NAME ANTHONY J. PITALE **ACCOUNT NO.** 104

ADDRESS 600 NEWPORT BEACH, NEWPORT, CA 91600

Date		Explanation	Post Ref.	Debit	Credit	Dr. Balance

10

PURCHASES AND CASH PAYMENTS

SELF-REVIEW QUIZ 10-1

1. ________ 2. ________ 3. ________ 4. ________ 5. ________

Name ______________________ Class ______________ Date ______________

SELF-REVIEW QUIZ 10-2

MUNROE CO.
GENERAL JOURNAL

PAGE 1

Date		Account Titles and Description	PR	Dr.	Cr.

Name ______________________ Class ______________ Date ______________

ACCOUNTS PAYABLE SUBSIDIARY LEDGER

NAME JOHN BUTLER COMPANY

ADDRESS 18 REED RD., HOMEWOOD, IL 60430

Date		Explanation	Post Ref.	Debit	Credit	Cr. Balance

NAME FLYNN COMPANY

ADDRESS 15 FOSS AVE., ENGLEWOOD CLIFFS, NJ 07632

Date		Explanation	Post Ref.	Debit	Credit	Cr. Balance

PARTIAL GENERAL LEDGER

EQUIPMENT **ACCOUNT NO. 121**

Date		Explanation	Post Ref.	Debit	Credit	Balance	
						Debit	Credit

Name ______________________ Class ______________ Date ______________

ACCOUNTS PAYABLE ACCOUNT NO. 212

Date		Explanation	Post Ref.	Debit	Credit	Balance Debit	Balance Credit

PURCHASES ACCOUNT NO. 512

Date		Explanation	Post Ref.	Debit	Credit	Balance Debit	Balance Credit

PURCHASES RETURNS AND ALLOWANCES ACCOUNT NO. 513

Date		Explanation	Post Ref.	Debit	Credit	Balance Debit	Balance Credit

Name ______________________ Class ______________ Date ______________

SELF-REVIEW QUIZ 10-3

MELISSA COMPANY
GENERAL JOURNAL

PAGE 2

Date		Account Titles and Description	PR	Dr.	Cr.

ACCOUNTS PAYABLE SUBSIDIARY LEDGER

NAME **BOB FINKELSTEIN**

ADDRESS **112 FLYING HIGHWAY, TRENTON, NJ 00861**

Date 200X		Explanation	Post Ref.	Debit	Credit	Cr. Balance
June	1	Balance	✓			300 00

NAME **AL JEEP**

ADDRESS **118 WANG RD., SAUGUS, MA 01432**

Date 200X		Explanation	Post Ref.	Debit	Credit	Cr. Balance
June	1	Balance	✓			200 00

Name ______________________ Class ______________ Date ______________

PARTIAL GENERAL LEDGER

CASH — ACCOUNT NO. 110

Date 200X		Explanation	Post Ref.	Debit	Credit	Balance Debit	Balance Credit
June	1	Balance	✓			700 00	

ACCOUNTS PAYABLE — ACCOUNT NO. 210

Date 200X		Explanation	Post Ref.	Debit	Credit	Balance Debit	Balance Credit
June	1	Balance	✓				500 00

PURCHASES DISCOUNT — ACCOUNT NO. 511

Date		Explanation	Post Ref.	Debit	Credit	Balance Debit	Balance Credit

ADVERTISING EXPENSE — ACCOUNT NO. 610

Date		Explanation	Post Ref.	Debit	Credit	Balance Debit	Balance Credit

Name ______________ Class ______________ Date ______________

SELF-REVIEW QUIZ 10-4

PETE'S CLOCK SHOP
GENERAL JOURNAL

PAGE 2

Date		Account Titles and Description	PR	Dr.	Cr.

Name ______________________ Class ______________ Date ______________

PETE'S CLOCK SHOP
GENERAL JOURNAL

PAGE 3

Date		Account Titles and Description	PR	Dr.	Cr.

Name ______________________ Class ______________ Date ______________

CHAPTER 10
FORMS FOR CLASSROOM DEMONSTRATION EXERCISES SET A OR SET B

1. A. ______________ D. ______________

B. ______________ E. ______________

C. ______________ F. ______________

2.

3. ____

4. A. ______________

B. ______________

C. ______________

5.

Name ______________________ Class ______________ Date ______________

6.

WEB.COM
SCHEDULE OF ACCOUNTS PAYABLE
MAY 31, 200X

7.

FORM FOR CLASSROOM DEMONSTRATION EXERCISES 8, 9, 10

Date		Account Titles and Description	PR	Dr.	Cr.

Name ______________________ Class ______________ Date ______________

FORMS FOR EXERCISES

10-1.

Lee's.com		Equipment 120	

Lane.com		Accounts Payable 210	

Sail.com		Purchases 510	

10-2.

PAGE 1

Reel Co.		Accounts Payable 211		Purchases Returns and Allowances 513	

Name ______________________ Class ______________ Date ______________

EXERCISES (CONTINUED)

10-3.

PAGE 2

Date		Account Titles and Description	PR	Dr.	Cr.

ACCOUNTS PAYABLE SUBSIDIARY LEDGER

A. James	
	1,000

B. Foss	
	400

J. Ranch	
	900

B. Swanson	
	100

PARTIAL GENERAL LEDGER

Cash 110	
3,000	

Accounts Payable 210	
	2,400

Purchases Discount 511	

Advertising Expense 610	

Name ______________________ Class ______________ Date ______________

EXERCISES (CONTINUED)

10-4.

MORGAN'S CLOTHING
SCHEDULE OF ACCOUNTS PAYABLE
APRIL 30, 200X

Accounts Payable 210

10-5.

Accounts Affected	Category	↑ ↓	Rules

10-6.

Name ______________________ Class ______________ Date ______________

FORM FOR EXERCISES 10-7, 10-8, 10-9, 10-10

Date	Account Titles and Description	PR	Dr.	Cr.

Name ______________________ Class ______________ Date ______________

FORM FOR EXERCISES 10-7, 10-8, 10-9, 10-10 (CONTINUED)

Date		Account Titles and Description	PR	Dr.	Cr.

CALCULATIONS PAGE FOR 10-7 TO 10-10

Name ____________________ Class ____________ Date ____________

END OF CHAPTER PROBLEMS

PROBLEM 10A-1 OR PROBLEM 10B-1

RON'S SKATE SHOP
GENERAL JOURNAL

PAGE 2

Date		Account Titles and Description	PR	Dr.	Cr.

Name ______________________ Class ______________ Date ______________

PROBLEM 10A-1 OR PROBLEM 10B-1 (CONTINUED)

ACCOUNTS PAYABLE SUBSIDIARY LEDGER

NAME MAIL.COM

ADDRESS 12 SMITH ST., DEARBORN, MI 09113

Date		Explanation	Post Ref.	Debit	Credit	Cr. Balance

NAME NORTON CO.

ADDRESS 1 RANTOUL RD., CHARLOTTE, NC 01114

Date		Explanation	Post Ref.	Debit	Credit	Cr. Balance

NAME ROLO CO.

ADDRESS 2 WEST RD., LYNN, MA 01471

Date		Explanation	Post Ref.	Debit	Credit	Cr. Balance

PARTIAL GENERAL LEDGER

STORE SUPPLIES **ACCOUNT NO. 115**

Date		Explanation	Post Ref.	Debit	Credit	Balance	
						Debit	Credit

Name ______________________ Class ______________ Date ______________

PROBLEM 10A-1 OR PROBLEM 10B-1 (CONCLUDED)

STORE EQUIPMENT **ACCOUNT NO. 121**

Date		Explanation	Post Ref.	Debit	Credit	Balance Debit	Balance Credit

ACCOUNTS PAYABLE **ACCOUNT NO. 210**

Date		Explanation	Post Ref.	Debit	Credit	Balance Debit	Balance Credit

PURCHASES **ACCOUNT NO. 510**

Date		Explanation	Post Ref.	Debit	Credit	Balance Debit	Balance Credit

Name ______________________ Class ______________ Date ______________

PROBLEM 10A-2 OR PROBLEM 10B-2

MABEL'S NATURAL FOOD

PAGE 2

Date		Account Titles and Description	PR	Dr.	Cr.

Name ____________ Class ____________ Date ____________

PROBLEM 10A-2 OR PROBLEM 10B-2 (CONTINUED)

ACCOUNTS PAYABLE SUBSIDIARY LEDGER

NAME ATON CO.

ADDRESS 11 LYNNWAY AVE., NEWPORT, RI 03112

Date 200X		Explanation	Post Ref.	Debit	Credit	Cr. Balance
May	1	Balance	✓			400 00

NAME BROWARD CO.

ADDRESS 21 RIVER ST., ANAHEIM, CA 43110

Date 200X		Explanation	Post Ref.	Debit	Credit	Cr. Balance
May	1	Balance	✓			600 00

NAME MIDDEN CO.

ADDRESS 10 ASTER RD., DUBUQUE, IA 80021

Date 200X		Explanation	Post Ref.	Debit	Credit	Cr. Balance
May	1	Balance	✓			1 200 00

NAME RELAR CO.

ADDRESS 22 GERALD RD., SMITH, CO 43138

Date 200X		Explanation	Post Ref.	Debit	Credit	Cr. Balance
May	1	Balance	✓			500 00

Name ______________________ Class ______________ Date ______________

PROBLEM 10A-2 OR PROBLEM 10B-2 (CONTINUED)

PARTIAL GENERAL LEDGER

STORE SUPPLIES — **ACCOUNT NO. 110**

Date		Explanation	Post Ref.	Debit	Credit	Balance Debit	Balance Credit

OFFICE EQUIPMENT — **ACCOUNT NO. 120**

Date		Explanation	Post Ref.	Debit	Credit	Balance Debit	Balance Credit

ACCOUNTS PAYABLE — **ACCOUNT NO. 210**

Date 200X		Explanation	Post Ref.	Debit	Credit	Balance Debit	Balance Credit
May	1	Balance	✓				2 700 00

PURCHASES — **ACCOUNT NO. 510**

Date 200X		Explanation	Post Ref.	Debit	Credit	Balance Debit	Balance Credit
May	1	Balance	✓			16 000 00	

Name ______________________ Class ______________ Date ______________

PROBLEM 10A-2 OR PROBLEM 10B-2 (CONCLUDED)

PURCHASES RETURNS AND ALLOWANCES **ACCOUNT NO. 512**

Date		Explanation	Post Ref.	Debit	Credit	Balance	
						Debit	Credit

MABEL'S NATURAL FOOD

SCHEDULE OF ACCOUNTS PAYABLE

MAY 31, 200X

Name ______________________ Class ______________ Date ______________

PROBLEM 10A-3 OR PROBLEM 10B-3

PAGE 5

Date		Account Titles and Description	PR	Dr.	Cr.

Name ______________________ Class ______________ Date ______________

PROBLEM 10A-3 OR PROBLEM 10B-3 (CONTINUED)

ACCOUNTS PAYABLE SUBSIDIARY LEDGER

NAME ALVIN CO.

ADDRESS 1 REACH RD., IPSWICH, MA 01932

Date 200X		Explanation	Post Ref.	Debit	Credit	Cr. Balance
May	1	Balance	✓			1 2 0 0 00

NAME HENRY CO.

ADDRESS 1 RALPH RD., REVERE, MA 01321

Date 200X		Explanation	Post Ref.	Debit	Credit	Cr. Balance
May	1	Balance	✓			6 0 0 00

NAME SOY CO.

ADDRESS 7 PLYMOUTH AVE., GLENN, NH 01218

Date 200X		Explanation	Post Ref.	Debit	Credit	Cr. Balance
May	1	Balance	✓			8 0 0 00

NAME XON CO.

ADDRESS 22 REY RD., BOCA RATON, FL 99132

Date 200X		Explanation	Post Ref.	Debit	Credit	Cr. Balance
May	1	Balance	✓			1 4 0 0 00

Name ______________ Class ______________ Date ______________

PROBLEM 10A-3 OR PROBLEM 10B-3 (CONTINUED)

PARTIAL GENERAL LEDGER

CASH — **ACCOUNT NO. 110**

Date 200X		Explanation	Post Ref.	Debit	Credit	Balance Debit	Balance Credit
May	1	Balance	✓			17 0 0 0 00	

DELIVERY TRUCK — **ACCOUNT NO. 150**

Date 200X		Explanation	Post Ref.	Debit	Credit	Balance Debit	Balance Credit

ACCOUNTS PAYABLE — **ACCOUNT NO. 210**

Date 200X		Explanation	Post Ref.	Debit	Credit	Balance Debit	Balance Credit
May	1	Balance	✓				4 0 0 0 00

COMPUTER PURCHASES — **ACCOUNT NO. 510**

Date 200X		Explanation	Post Ref.	Debit	Credit	Balance Debit	Balance Credit

Name ______ Class ______ Date ______

PROBLEM 10A-3 OR PROBLEM 10B-3 (CONCLUDED)

COMPUTER PURCHASES DISCOUNT **ACCOUNT NO. 511**

Date		Explanation	Post Ref.	Debit	Credit	Balance	
						Debit	Credit

RENT EXPENSE **ACCOUNT NO. 610**

Date		Explanation	Post Ref.	Debit	Credit	Balance	
						Debit	Credit

UTILITIES EXPENSE **ACCOUNT NO. 620**

Date		Explanation	Post Ref.	Debit	Credit	Balance	
						Debit	Credit

JONES COMPUTER CENTER
SCHEDULE OF ACCOUNTS PAYABLE
MAY 31, 200X

Name ______________________ Class ______________ Date ______________

PROBLEM 10A-4 OR PROBLEM 10B-4

(1)

ABBY'S TOY HOUSE
GENERAL JOURNAL

PAGE 1

Date	Account Titles and Description	PR	Dr.	Cr.

Name ______________________ Class ______________ Date ______________

PROBLEM 10A-4 OR PROBLEM 10B-4 (CONTINUED)

PAGE 2

Date		Account Titles and Description	PR	Dr.	Cr.

Name ______________________ Class ______________ Date ______________

PROBLEM 10A-4 OR PROBLEM 10B-4 (CONTINUED)

PAGE 3

Date		Account Titles and Description	PR	Dr.	Cr.

Name ______________________ Class ______________ Date ______________

PROBLEM 10A-4 OR PROBLEM 10B-4 (CONTINUED)

PAGE 4

Date		Account Titles and Description	PR	Dr.	Cr.

Name ______________________ Class ______________ Date ______________

PROBLEM 10A-4 OR PROBLEM 10B-4 (CONTINUED)

PAGE 5

Date	Account Titles and Description	PR	Dr.	Cr.

Name ______________ Class ______________ Date ______________

PROBLEM 10A-4 OR PROBLEM 10B-4 (CONTINUED)

(2) ACCOUNTS PAYABLE SUBSIDIARY LEDGER

NAME MINNIE KATZ

ADDRESS 87 GARFIELD AVE., REVERE, MA 01245

Date	Explanation	Post Ref.	Debit	Credit	Cr. Balance

NAME SAM KATZ GARAGE

ADDRESS 22 REGIS RD., BOSTON, MA 01950

Date	Explanation	Post Ref.	Debit	Credit	Cr. Balance

NAME EARL MILLER CO.

ADDRESS 22 RETTER ST., SAN DIEGO, CA 01211

Date	Explanation	Post Ref.	Debit	Credit	Cr. Balance

NAME WOODY SMITH

ADDRESS 2 SPRING ST., WEERS, ND 02118

Date	Explanation	Post Ref.	Debit	Credit	Cr. Balance

Name ______________________ Class ______________ Date ______________

PROBLEM 10A-4 OR PROBLEM 10B-4 (CONTINUED)

ACCOUNTS RECEIVABLE SUBSIDIARY LEDGER

NAME BILL BURTON

ADDRESS 24 RYAN RD., BUIKE, OH 02183

Date		Explanation	Post Ref.	Debit	Credit	Dr. Balance

NAME BONNIE FLOW CO.

ADDRESS 2 SMITH RD., DALLAS, TX 22210

Date		Explanation	Post Ref.	Debit	Credit	Dr. Balance

NAME JIM REX

ADDRESS 1 SCHOOL ST., CLEVELAND, OH 22441

Date		Explanation	Post Ref.	Debit	Credit	Dr. Balance

Name ____________ Class ____________ Date ____________

PROBLEM 10A-4 OR PROBLEM 10B-4 (CONTINUED)

NAME AMY ROSE

ADDRESS 18 VEEK RD., CHESTER, CT 80111

Date		Explanation	Post Ref.	Debit	Credit	Dr. Balance

GENERAL LEDGER

CASH **ACCOUNT NO. 110**

Date		Explanation	Post Ref.	Debit	Credit	Balance	
						Debit	Credit

Name ______________________ Class ______________ Date ______________

PROBLEM 10A-4 OR PROBLEM 10B-4 (CONTINUED)

ACCOUNTS RECEIVABLE **ACCOUNT NO. 112**

Date		Explanation	Post Ref.	Debit	Credit	Balance Debit	Balance Credit

PREPAID RENT **ACCOUNT NO. 114**

Date		Explanation	Post Ref.	Debit	Credit	Balance Debit	Balance Credit

DELIVERY TRUCK **ACCOUNT NO. 121**

Date		Explanation	Post Ref.	Debit	Credit	Balance Debit	Balance Credit

Name ______________________ Class ______________ Date ______________

PROBLEM 10A-4 OR PROBLEM 10B-4 (CONTINUED)

ACCOUNTS PAYABLE **ACCOUNT NO. 210**

Date		Explanation	Post Ref.	Debit	Credit	Balance Debit	Balance Credit

A. ELLEN, CAPITAL **ACCOUNT NO. 310**

Date		Explanation	Post Ref.	Debit	Credit	Balance Debit	Balance Credit

TOY SALES **ACCOUNT NO. 410**

Date		Explanation	Post Ref.	Debit	Credit	Balance Debit	Balance Credit

Name ______________________ Class ______________ Date ______________

PROBLEM 10A-4 OR PROBLEM 10B-4 (CONTINUED)

SALES RETURNS AND ALLOWANCES **ACCOUNT NO. 412**

Date		Explanation	Post Ref.	Debit	Credit	Balance	
						Debit	Credit

SALES DISCOUNTS **ACCOUNT NO. 414**

Date		Explanation	Post Ref.	Debit	Credit	Balance	
						Debit	Credit

TOY PURCHASES **ACCOUNT NO. 510**

Date		Explanation	Post Ref.	Debit	Credit	Balance	
						Debit	Credit

PURCHASES RETURNS AND ALLOWANCES **ACCOUNT NO. 512**

Date		Explanation	Post Ref.	Debit	Credit	Balance	
						Debit	Credit

Name ______________________ Class ______________ Date ______________

PROBLEM 10A-4 OR PROBLEM 10B-4 (CONTINUED)

PURCHASES DISCOUNT **ACCOUNT NO. 514**

Date		Explanation	Post Ref.	Debit	Credit	Balance Debit	Balance Credit

SALARIES EXPENSE **ACCOUNT NO. 610**

Date		Explanation	Post Ref.	Debit	Credit	Balance Debit	Balance Credit

CLEANING EXPENSE **ACCOUNT NO. 612**

Date		Explanation	Post Ref.	Debit	Credit	Balance Debit	Balance Credit

Name ______________________ Class ______________ Date ______________

PROBLEM 10A-4 OR PROBLEM 10B-4 (CONCLUDED)

(3)

ABBY'S TOY HOUSE
SCHEDULE OF ACCOUNTS RECEIVABLE
MARCH 31, 200X

(3)

ABBY'S TOY HOUSE
SCHEDULE OF ACCOUNTS PAYABLE
MARCH 31, 200X

Name ____________________ Class ______________ Date ______________

PROBLEM 10A-5 OR PROBLEM 10B-5

PAGE 3

Date		Account Titles and Description	PR	Dr.	Cr.

Name ____________ Class ____________ Date ____________

PROBLEM 10A-5 OR PROBLEM 10B-5 (CONCLUDED)

PAGE 4

Date		Account Titles and Description	PR	Dr.	Cr.

Name ______________________ Class ______________ Date ______________

CHAPTER 10
SUMMARY PRACTICE TEST
PURCHASES AND CASH PAYMENTS

Part I Instructions

Fill in the blank(s) to complete the statement.

1. The trend in accounting is more to ______________ inventory rather than ______________ inventory.
2. Purchase discounts are categorized as a(n) ______________ ______________ account.
3. The Purchases account has a ______________ balance.
4. Purchases are defined as merchandise for ______________ to customers.
5. The accounts payable subsidiary ledger represents a potential ______________ of cash.
6. The controlling account in the general ledger for the accounts payable subsidiary ledger is called ______________ ______________.
7. The accounts payable subsidiary ledger would be recorded ______________.
8. The balance in the Accounts Payable controlling account should be equal to the sum of the accounts payable subsidiary ledger accounts ______________ ______________ ______________ ______________.
9. In perpetual inventory, purchases are recorded as ______________ ______________.
10. The ✓ in the reference column indicates that the ______________ ______________ ______________ ______________ has been updated.
11. A(n) ______________ ______________ that is issued means the buyer owes less money, as merchandise is being returned or an allowance received.
12. A debit memorandum issued or a credit memorandum received results in a(n) ______________ to Accounts Payable and a credit to Purchases, Returns and Allowances.
13. List price − net price = ______________ ______________ amount.
14. The accounts payable subsidiary ledger is listed in ______________ ______________.
15. Purchases Returns and Allowances is increased by a(n) ______________.
16. Cost of goods sold is classified as a(n) ______________.
17. In a perpetual inventory system, freight is recorded in the ______________ ______________ account.
18. Purchases Discounts is increased by ______________.
19. A(n) ______________ ______________ provides the purchasing department the information to then prepare a purchase order.
20. A(n) ______________ ______________ is made out after a company inspects received shipments.

Name ______________________ Class ______________ Date ______________

Part II

Complete the following table:

	Account Title	CAT	↑ ↓	Financial Statement
1.	Purchases			
2.	Purchase Discount			
3.	Accounts Receivable			
4.	Cost of Goods Sold			
5.	Salary Expenses			
6.	Accounts Payable			
7.	Purchase Returns and Allowances			
8.	Cash			
9.	Supplies			
10.	Sale Discount			

Name ______________________ Class ______________ Date ______________

Part III Instructions

Answer true or false to the following statements.

1. F.O.B. shipping point means the seller is responsible to cover shipping costs.
2. The Purchases account is a contra-cost of goods sold account.
3. Purchases discounts are the result of paying for equipment within the discount period.
4. F.O.B. Destination means the seller is responsible to cover shipping costs.
5. Purchases discounts are taken on freight.
6. Merchandise inventory is an asset.
7. Cost of goods sold is a cost.
8. The balance in Accounts Payable, the controlling account, will be equal to the sum of the accounts receivable subsidiary ledger at the end of the month.
9. A purchase order is completed after the purchase requisition.
10. On receiving a purchase order, the seller may issue a sales invoice.
11. The normal balance of Purchases Discount is a debit balance.
12. The seller will often issue a debit memorandum to the buyer.
13. Cost of goods sold is used in a periodic inventory system.
14. Returned equipment by a buyer results in a change in Purchases Returns and Allowances.
15. Trade discounts do not occur because of early payments of one's bills.
16. A seller's sales discount on purchases is the buyer's purchases discount.
17. Buying of equipment on account is only recorded in the general ledger.
18. On receiving a debit memorandum, the seller will issue a credit memorandum.
19. Returns in a perpetual accounting system are recorded in the merchandise inventory account.
20. Purchases are contra costs.

CHAPTER 10
SOLUTIONS TO SUMMARY PRACTICE TEST

Part I

1. perpetual, periodic
2. contra-cost
3. debit
4. resale
5. outflow
6. accounts payable
7. daily
8. at end of month
9. merchandise inventory
10. accounts payable subsidiary ledger
11. debit memorandum
12. debit
13. trade discount
14. alphabetical order
15. credit
16. cost
17. merchandise inventory
18. credits
19. purchase requisition
20. receiving report

Name ______________________ Class ______________ Date ______________

Part II

1.	cost	Dr	Cr	Income Statement
2.	contra-cost	Cr	Dr	Income Statement
3.	asset	Dr	Cr	Balance Sheet
4.	cost	Dr	Cr	Income Statement
5.	expense	Dr	Cr	Income Statement
6.	liability	Cr	Dr	Balance Sheet
7.	contra-cost	Cr	Dr	Income Statement
8.	asset	Dr	Cr	Balance Sheet
9.	asset	Dr	Cr	Balance Sheet
10.	contra-revenue	Dr	Cr	Income Statement

Part III

1. false
2. false
3. true
4. true
5. false
6. true
7. true
8. false
9. true
10. true
11. false
12. false
13. false
14. true
15. true
16. true
17. false
18. true
19. true
20. false

Name ____________________ Class ______________ Date ______________

CONTINUING PROBLEM FOR CHAPTER 10

SANCHEZ COMPUTER CENTER
GENERAL JOURNAL

PAGE 5

Date		Account Titles and Description	PR	Dr.	Cr.

Name ______________________ Class ______________ Date ______________

PARTIAL GENERAL LEDGER

CASH — **ACCOUNT NO. 1000**

Date		Explanation	Post Ref.	Debit	Credit	Balance Debit	Balance Credit
2/1	0X	Balance forward	✓			15 1 1 6 65	

SUPPLIES — **ACCOUNT NO. 1030**

Date		Explanation	Post Ref.	Debit	Credit	Balance Debit	Balance Credit
2/1	0X	Balance forward	✓			1 3 2 00	

MERCHANDISE INVENTORY — **ACCOUNT NO. 1040**

Date		Explanation	Post Ref.	Debit	Credit	Balance Debit	Balance Credit

Name ____________________ Class ____________________ Date ____________________

PREPAID RENT **ACCOUNT NO. 1025**

Date		Explanation	Post Ref.	Debit	Credit	Balance Debit	Balance Credit
2/1	0X	Balance forward	✓			1 6 0 0 00	

ACCOUNTS PAYABLE **ACCOUNT NO. 2000**

Date		Explanation	Post Ref.	Debit	Credit	Balance Debit	Balance Credit
2/1	0X	Balance forward	✓				2 0 5 0 00

PURCHASES **ACCOUNT NO. 6000**

Date		Explanation	Post Ref.	Debit	Credit	Balance Debit	Balance Credit

PURCHASE RETURNS AND ALLOWANCES **ACCOUNT NO. 6010**

Date		Explanation	Post Ref.	Debit	Credit	Balance Debit	Balance Credit

PURCHASE DISCOUNTS **ACCOUNT NO. 6020**

Date		Explanation	Post Ref.	Debit	Credit	Balance Debit	Balance Credit

Name ____________ Class ____________ Date ____________

SANCHEZ COMPUTER CENTER
SCHEDULE OF ACCOUNTS PAYABLE
2/28/0X

ACCOUNTS PAYABLE SUBSIDIARY LEDGER

NAME **MULTI SYSTEMS, INC.** **# 6A3**

ADDRESS **1919 MORAN ST., ANAHEIM, CA 92606**

Date		Explanation	Post Ref.	Debit	Credit	Cr. Balance
2/1	0X	Balance forward	✓			450 00

NAME **OFFICE DEPOT** **# 6A4**

ADDRESS **460 ESCONDIDO BLVD., ESCONDIDO, CA 92025**

Date		Explanation	Post Ref.	Debit	Credit	Cr. Balance
2/1	0X	Balance forward	✓			50 00

Name ______________________ Class ______________ Date ______________

NAME SAN DIEGO ELECTRIC # 6A5

ADDRESS 606 INDUSTRIAL ST., SAN DIEGO, CA 92121

Date		Explanation	Post Ref.	Debit	Credit	Cr. Balance

NAME PAC BELL # 6A6

ADDRESS 101 BELL AVE., SAN DIEGO, CA 92101

Date		Explanation	Post Ref.	Debit	Credit	Cr. Balance
2/1	0X	Balance forward	✓			150 00

NAME COMPUTER CONNECTION # 6A7

ADDRESS 1020 WIL LANE, LOS ANGELES, CA 92405

Date		Explanation	Post Ref.	Debit	Credit	Cr. Balance

Name ______________________ Class ______________ Date ______________

NAME **SYSTEM DESIGN FURNITURE** **# 6A8**

ADDRESS **2070 FIRST ST., SAN DIEGO, CA 92101**

Date		Explanation	Post Ref.	Debit	Credit	Cr. Balance
2/1	0X	Balance forward	✓			1 400 00

Name ______________________ Class ______________ Date ______________

APPENDIX 10A
FORMS FOR CLASSROOM DEMONSTRATION PROBLEM — SPECIAL JOURNALS

J. LING CO.
SALES JOURNAL

PAGE 1

Date	Account Debited	Terms	Invoice No.	Post Ref.	**Dr. Acc. Receivable** Cr. Sales

CASH RECEIPTS JOURNAL

PAGE 1

Date	Cash Dr.	Sales Discounts Dr.	Accounts Receivable Cr.	Sales Cr.	Sundry		
					Account Name	PR	Amount Cr.

PURCHASES JOURNAL

PAGE 1

Date	Account Credited	Terms	PR	Accounts Payable Cr.	Purchases Dr.	Sundry Dr.		
						Account	PR	Amount

CASH PAYMENTS JOURNAL

PAGE 1

Date	Check No.	Accounts Debited	PR	Sundry Account Dr.	Accounts Payable Dr.	Purchases Discounts Cr.	Cash Cr.

Name ______________________ Class ______________ Date ______________

DEMONSTRATION PROBLEM (CONTINUED)

GENERAL JOURNAL

PAGE 1

Date		Account Titles and Description	PR	Dr.	Cr.

ACCOUNTS RECEIVABLE SUBSIDIARY LEDGER

NAME **BALDER CO.**

ADDRESS **1 ROCK RD., DENVER, CO 66083**

Date		Explanation	Post Ref.	Debit	Credit	Dr. Balance

NAME **LEWIS CO.**

ADDRESS **15 SMITH AVE., REVERE, MA 01545**

Date		Explanation	Post Ref.	Debit	Credit	Dr. Balance

Name ______________________ Class ______________ Date ______________

DEMONSTRATION PROBLEM (CONCLUDED)

ACCOUNTS PAYABLE SUBSIDIARY LEDGER

NAME CASE CO.

ADDRESS 1 LONG RD., MARLBOROUGH, MA 01545

Date	Explanation	Post Ref.	Debit	Credit	Cr. Balance

NAME NOONE CO.

ADDRESS 11 MILL RD., MALDEN, OK 01143

Date	Explanation	Post Ref.	Debit	Credit	Cr. Balance

PARTIAL GENERAL LEDGER

Cash 111

Sales 410

Purchases Discounts 530

Accounts Receivable 112

Sales Returns & Allowances 420

Salaries Expense 610

Equipment 116

Sales Discount 430

Accounts Payable 210

Purchases 510

J. Ling, Capital 310

Purchases Returns & Allowances 520

Name ______________________ Class ______________ Date ______________

CHAPTER 10A APPENDIX FORMS

PROBLEM A-1

(1,2)

FOOD.COM
SALES JOURNAL

PAGE 1

Date	Account Debited	Invoice No.	PR	Accounts Receivable Dr.	Pizza Sales Cr.	Grocery Sales Cr.

(1,2)

FOOD.COM
GENERAL JOURNAL

PAGE 1

Date	Account Titles and Description	PR	Dr.	Cr.

Name ________________ Class ________________ Date ________________

PROBLEM A-1 (CONTINUED)

ACCOUNTS RECEIVABLE SUBSIDIARY LEDGER

NAME **DUNCAN CO.**

ADDRESS **942 MOSE ST., REVERE, MA 01938**

Date		Explanation	Post Ref.	Debit	Credit	Dr. Balance

NAME **LONG CO.**

ADDRESS **8 JOSS AVE., LYNN, MA 01947**

Date		Explanation	Post Ref.	Debit	Credit	Dr. Balance

NAME **SUE MOORE CO.**

ADDRESS **10 LOST RD., TOPSFIELD, MA 01998**

Date		Explanation	Post Ref.	Debit	Credit	Dr. Balance

Name ______________________ Class ______________ Date ______________

PROBLEM A-1 (CONTINUED)

FOOD.COM
GENERAL LEDGER

ACCOUNTS RECEIVABLE **ACCOUNT NO. 112**

Date	Explanation	Post Ref.	Debit	Credit	Balance	
					Debit	Credit

PIZZA SALES **ACCOUNT NO. 410**

Date	Explanation	Post Ref.	Debit	Credit	Balance	
					Debit	Credit

GROCERY SALES **ACCOUNT NO. 411**

Date	Explanation	Post Ref.	Debit	Credit	Balance	
					Debit	Credit

SALES RETURNS AND ALLOWANCES **ACCOUNT NO. 412**

Date	Explanation	Post Ref.	Debit	Credit	Balance	
					Debit	Credit

Name ____________ Class ____________ Date ____________

PROBLEM A-1 (CONCLUDED)

FOOD.COM
SCHEDULE OF ACCOUNTS RECEIVABLE
JUNE 30, 200X

PROBLEM A-2

(1,2)

TED'S AUTO SUPPLY
SALES JOURNAL

PAGE 4

Date		Customer's Name Account Receivable	Invoice No.	PR	Accounts Receivable Dr.	Sales Tax Payable Cr.	Auto Parts Sales Cr.

Name ______________________ Class ______________ Date ______________

PROBLEM A-2 (CONTINUED)

(1,2)

TED'S AUTO SUPPLY
GENERAL JOURNAL

PAGE 2

Date		Account Titles and Description	PR	Dr.	Cr.

Name ____________________ Class ____________ Date ____________

PROBLEM A-2 (CONTINUED)

ACCOUNTS RECEIVABLE SUBSIDIARY LEDGER

NAME **LANCE CORNER**

ADDRESS **9 ROE ST., BARTLETT, NH 01382**

Date 200X		Explanation	Post Ref.	Debit	Credit	Dr. Balance
Nov	1	Balance	✓			400 00

NAME **J. SETH**

ADDRESS **22 REESE ST., LACONIA, NH 04321**

Date 200X		Explanation	Post Ref.	Debit	Credit	Dr. Balance
Nov	1	Balance	✓			200 00

NAME **R. VOLAN**

ADDRESS **12 ASTER RD., MERRIMACK, NH 02134**

Date 200X		Explanation	Post Ref.	Debit	Credit	Dr. Balance
Nov	1	Balance	✓			1000 00

Name ____________________ Class ____________ Date ____________

PROBLEM A-2 (CONTINUED)

TED'S AUTO SUPPLY
GENERAL JOURNAL

ACCOUNTS RECEIVABLE — **ACCOUNT NO. 110**

Date 200X		Explanation	Post Ref.	Debit	Credit	Balance Debit	Balance Credit
Nov	1	Balance	✓			1 6 0 0 00	

SALES TAX PAYABLE — **ACCOUNT NO. 210**

Date 200X		Explanation	Post Ref.	Debit	Credit	Balance Debit	Balance Credit
Nov	1	Balance	✓				1 6 0 0 00

AUTO PARTS SALES — **ACCOUNT NO. 410**

Date		Explanation	Post Ref.	Debit	Credit	Balance Debit	Balance Credit

SALES RETURNS AND ALLOWANCES — **ACCOUNT NO. 420**

Date		Explanation	Post Ref.	Debit	Credit	Balance Debit	Balance Credit

Name ______________________ Class ______________ Date ______________

PROBLEM A-2 (CONCLUDED)

(3)

TED'S AUTO SUPPLY
SCHEDULE OF ACCOUNTS RECEIVABLE
NOVEMBER 30, 200X

Name ______________________ Class ______________ Date ______________

PROBLEM A-3

SKATES.COM
PURCHASES JOURNAL

PAGE 3

Date	Account Credited	Date of Invoice	Inv. No.	Terms	PR	Accounts Payable Cr.	Purchases Dr.	Sundry Dr.		
								Account	PR	Amount

Name ______________________ Class ______________ Date ______________

PROBLEM A-3 (CONTINUED)

ACCOUNTS PAYABLE SUBSIDIARY LEDGER

NAME MAIL.COM

ADDRESS 12 SMITH ST., DEARBORN, MI 09113

Date		Explanation	Post Ref.	Debit	Credit	Cr. Balance

NAME NORTON CO.

ADDRESS 1 RANTOUL RD., CHARLOTTE, NC 01114

Date		Explanation	Post Ref.	Debit	Credit	Cr. Balance

NAME ROLO CO.

ADDRESS 2 WEST RD., LYNN, MA 01471

Date		Explanation	Post Ref.	Debit	Credit	Cr. Balance

PARTIAL GENERAL LEDGER

STORE SUPPLIES **ACCOUNT NO. 115**

Date		Explanation	Post Ref.	Debit	Credit	Balance	
						Debit	Credit

Name ______________ Class ______________ Date ______________

PROBLEM A-3 (CONCLUDED)

STORE EQUIPMENT **ACCOUNT NO. 121**

Date		Explanation	Post Ref.	Debit	Credit	Balance	
						Debit	Credit

ACCOUNTS PAYABLE **ACCOUNT NO. 210**

Date		Explanation	Post Ref.	Debit	Credit	Balance	
						Debit	Credit

PURCHASES **ACCOUNT NO. 510**

Date		Explanation	Post Ref.	Debit	Credit	Balance	
						Debit	Credit

Name ______________________ Class ______________ Date ______________

PROBLEM A-4

MABEL'S NATURAL FOOD STORE
PURCHASES JOURNAL

PAGE 10

Date	Account Credited	Date of Invoice	Inv. No.	Terms	PR	Accounts Payable Cr.	Purchases Dr.	Store Supplies Dr.	Sundry Dr.		
									Account	PR	Amount

Name ______________________ Class ______________ Date ______________

PROBLEM A-4 (CONTINUED)

ACCOUNTS PAYABLE SUBSIDIARY LEDGER

NAME ATON CO.

ADDRESS 11 LYNNWAY AVE., NEWPORT, RI 03112

Date 200X		Explanation	Post Ref.	Debit	Credit	Cr. Balance
May	1	Balance	✓			400 00

NAME BROWARD CO.

ADDRESS 21 RIVER ST., ANAHEIM, CA 43110

Date 200X		Explanation	Post Ref.	Debit	Credit	Cr. Balance
May	1	Balance	✓			600 00

NAME MIDDEN CO.

ADDRESS 10 ASTER RD., DUBUQUE, IA 80021

Date 200X		Explanation	Post Ref.	Debit	Credit	Cr. Balance
May	1	Balance	✓			1 200 00

NAME RELAR CO.

ADDRESS 22 GERALD RD., SMITH, CO 43138

Date 200X		Explanation	Post Ref.	Debit	Credit	Cr. Balance
May	1	Balance	✓			500 00

Name ______________________ Class ______________ Date ______________

PROBLEM A-4 (CONTINUED)

PARTIAL GENERAL LEDGER

STORE SUPPLIES — **ACCOUNT NO. 110**

Date		Explanation	Post Ref.	Debit	Credit	Balance Debit	Balance Credit

OFFICE EQUIPMENT — **ACCOUNT NO. 120**

Date		Explanation	Post Ref.	Debit	Credit	Balance Debit	Balance Credit

ACCOUNTS PAYABLE — **ACCOUNT NO. 210**

Date 200X		Explanation	Post Ref.	Debit	Credit	Balance Debit	Balance Credit
May	1	Balance	✓				2 700 00

PURCHASES — **ACCOUNT NO. 510**

Date 200X		Explanation	Post Ref.	Debit	Credit	Balance Debit	Balance Credit
May	1	Balance	✓			16 700 00	

Name ______________________ Class ______________ Date ______________

PROBLEM A-4 (CONCLUDED)

PURCHASES RETURNS AND ALLOWANCES **ACCOUNT NO. 512**

Date		Explanation	Post Ref.	Debit	Credit	Balance	
						Debit	Credit

GENERAL JOURNAL PAGE 2

Date		Account Titles and Description	PR	Dr.	Cr.

MABEL'S NATURAL FOOD STORE
SCHEDULE OF ACCOUNTS PAYABLE
MAY 31, 200X

Name ______________________ Class ______________ Date ______________

PROBLEM A-5

(1,3)

ABBY'S TOY HOUSE
PURCHASES JOURNAL

PAGE 1

Date	Account Credited	Date of Inv.	Inv. No.	Terms	PR	Accounts Payable Cr.	Toy Purchases Dr.	Sundry Dr.		
								Accounts	PR	Amount

Name ______________________ Class ______________ Date ______________

PROBLEM A-5 (CONTINUED)

ABBY'S TOY HOUSE
CASH RECEIPTS JOURNAL

PAGE 1

Date	Cash Dr.	Sales Discounts Dr.	Accounts Receivable Cr.	Toy Sales Cr.	Sundry		
					Account	PR	Amount Cr.

Name ____________________ Class ____________ Date ____________

PROBLEM A-5 (CONTINUED)

ABBY'S TOY HOUSE
CASH PAYMENTS JOURNAL

PAGE 1

Date	Check No.	Account Debited	PR	Sundry Dr.	Accounts Payable Dr.	Purchases Discount Cr.	Cash Cr.

Name ______________________ Class ______________ Date ______________

PROBLEM A-5 (CONTINUED)

ABBY'S TOY HOUSE
SALES JOURNAL
MARCH 31, 200X

PAGE 1

Date	Account Debited	Invoice No.	Terms	PR	Accounts Rec. – Dr. Toy Sales – Cr.

ABBY'S TOY HOUSE
GENERAL JOURNAL
MARCH 31, 200X

PAGE 1

Date	Account Titles and Description	PR	Dr.	Cr.

Name ____________ Class ____________ Date ____________

PROBLEM A-5 (CONTINUED)

(2) ACCOUNTS PAYABLE SUBSIDIARY LEDGER

NAME MINNIE KATZ

ADDRESS 87 GARFIELD AVE., REVERE, MA 01245

Date		Explanation	Post Ref.	Debit	Credit	Cr. Balance

NAME SAM KATZ GARAGE

ADDRESS 22 REGIS RD., BOSTON, MA 01950

Date		Explanation	Post Ref.	Debit	Credit	Cr. Balance

NAME EARL MILLER CO.

ADDRESS 22 RETTER ST., SAN DIEGO, CA 01211

Date		Explanation	Post Ref.	Debit	Credit	Cr. Balance

NAME WOODY SMITH

ADDRESS 2 SPRING ST., WEERS, ND 02118

Date		Explanation	Post Ref.	Debit	Credit	Cr. Balance

Name ______________________ Class ______________ Date ______________

PROBLEM A-5 (CONTINUED)

ACCOUNTS RECEIVABLE SUBSIDIARY LEDGER

NAME **BILL BURTON**

ADDRESS **24 RYAN RD., BUIKE, OH 02183**

Date		Explanation	Post Ref.	Debit	Credit	Dr. Balance

NAME **BONNIE FLOW CO.**

ADDRESS **2 SMITH RD., DALLAS, TX 22210**

Date		Explanation	Post Ref.	Debit	Credit	Dr. Balance

NAME **JIM REX**

ADDRESS **1 SCHOOL ST., CLEVELAND, OH 22441**

Date		Explanation	Post Ref.	Debit	Credit	Dr. Balance

Name ______________ Class ______________ Date ______________

PROBLEM A-5 (CONTINUED)

NAME AMY ROSE

ADDRESS 18 VEEK RD., CHESTER, CT 80111

Date		Explanation	Post Ref.	Debit	Credit	Dr. Balance

GENERAL LEDGER

CASH ACCOUNT NO. 110

Date		Explanation	Post Ref.	Debit	Credit	Balance	
						Debit	Credit

ACCOUNTS RECEIVABLE ACCOUNT NO. 112

Date		Explanation	Post Ref.	Debit	Credit	Balance	
						Debit	Credit

PREPAID RENT ACCOUNT NO. 114

Date		Explanation	Post Ref.	Debit	Credit	Balance	
						Debit	Credit

Name ______________________ Class ______________ Date ______________

PROBLEM A-5 (CONTINUED)

DELIVERY TRUCK **ACCOUNT NO. 121**

Date	Explanation	Post Ref.	Debit	Credit	Balance Debit	Balance Credit

ACCOUNTS PAYABLE **ACCOUNT NO. 210**

Date	Explanation	Post Ref.	Debit	Credit	Balance Debit	Balance Credit

A. ELLEN, CAPITAL **ACCOUNT NO. 310**

Date	Explanation	Post Ref.	Debit	Credit	Balance Debit	Balance Credit

TOY SALES **ACCOUNT NO. 410**

Date	Explanation	Post Ref.	Debit	Credit	Balance Debit	Balance Credit

Name ______________________ Class ______________ Date ______________

PROBLEM A-5 (CONTINUED)

SALES RETURNS AND ALLOWANCES **ACCOUNT NO. 412**

Date		Explanation	Post Ref.	Debit	Credit	Balance Debit	Balance Credit

SALES DISCOUNTS **ACCOUNT NO. 414**

Date		Explanation	Post Ref.	Debit	Credit	Balance Debit	Balance Credit

TOY PURCHASES **ACCOUNT NO. 510**

Date		Explanation	Post Ref.	Debit	Credit	Balance Debit	Balance Credit

PURCHASES RETURNS AND ALLOWANCES **ACCOUNT NO. 512**

Date		Explanation	Post Ref.	Debit	Credit	Balance Debit	Balance Credit

Name ______________________ Class ______________ Date ______________

PROBLEM A-5 (CONTINUED)

PURCHASES DISCOUNT **ACCOUNT NO. 514**

Date		Explanation	Post Ref.	Debit	Credit	Balance	
						Debit	Credit

SALARIES EXPENSE **ACCOUNT NO. 610**

Date		Explanation	Post Ref.	Debit	Credit	Balance	
						Debit	Credit

CLEANING EXPENSE **ACCOUNT NO. 612**

Date		Explanation	Post Ref.	Debit	Credit	Balance	
						Debit	Credit

Name ______________________ Class ______________ Date ______________

PROBLEM A-5 (CONCLUDED)

(4)

ABBY'S TOY HOUSE
SCHEDULE OF ACCOUNTS RECEIVABLE
MARCH 31, 200X

(4)

ABBY'S TOY HOUSE
SCHEDULE OF ACCOUNTS PAYABLE
MARCH 31, 200X

Preparing a Worksheet for a Merchandise Company

11

SELF-REVIEW QUIZ 11-1

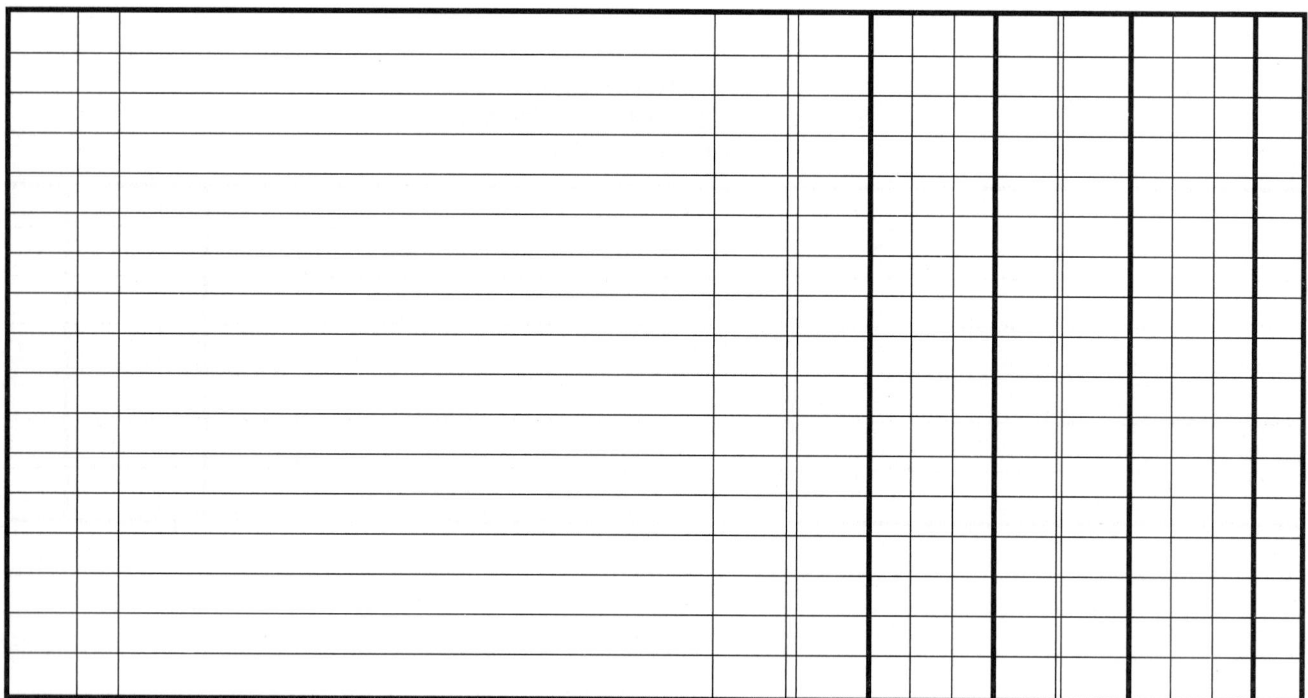

SELF-REVIEW QUIZ 11-2

Use one of the blank fold-out worksheets that accompanied your textbook.

CHAPTER 11
FORMS FOR CLASSROOM DEMONSTRATION EXERCISES SET A OR SET B

1.													
2.													

3. A. ____________ E. ____________
B. ____________ F. ____________
C. ____________
D. ____________

4. ____

____

____

____

____

____

____

5.

A. ________ B. ________ C. ________ D. ________ E. ________ F. ________

Name ______________________ Class ______________ Date ______________

FORMS FOR EXERCISES

11-1.

A. ______________________
B. ______________________
C. ______________________
D. ______________________
E. ______________________
F. ______________________
G. ______________________
H. ______________________

11-2.

A. ______________________

B. ______________________

C. ______________________

D. ______________________

11-3.

Accounts Affected	Category	↑↓	Rules

11-4.

A. ______________________
B. ______________________
C. ______________________

11-5.

Use one of the blank fold-out worksheets that accompanied your textbook.

Name ______________________ Class ______________ Date ______________

END OF CHAPTER PROBLEMS

PROBLEM 11A-1 OR PROBLEM 11B-1

A.	
B.	
C.	
D.	

PROBLEM 11A-2 OR PROBLEM 11B-2;
PROBLEM 11A-3 OR PROBLEM 11B-3;
PROBLEM 11A-4 OR PROBLEM 11B-4

Use blank fold-out worksheets that accompanied your textbook.

Name ______________________ Class ______________ Date ______________

CHAPTER 11
SUMMARY PRACTICE TEST: PREPARING A WORKSHEET FOR A MERCHANDISE COMPANY

Part I Instructions

Fill in the blank(s) to complete the statement.

1. The ______________ ______________ system keeps a continual track of the quantity and cost of the inventory on hand.
2. In the periodic inventory system, new inventories bought is recorded in the ______________ account.
3. A continuous record of inventory is kept in a(n) ______________ ______________ system.
4. When using the periodic system, ______________ ______________ will remain unchanged.
5. ______________ ______________ represents a liability on the balance sheet and records money received for a sale or service not yet performed.
6. Freight-in is ______________ to the cost of goods sold.
7. Net Sales less Cost of Goods Sold equals ______________ ______________.
8. ______________ ______________ equals Gross Sales less Sales Discounts and Sales Returns and Allowances.
9. Net Purchases equals Purchases less ______________ ______________ and ______________ ______________ ______________ ______________.
10. A(n) ______________ ______________ helps calculate ending inventory.
11. Ending inventory is ______________ from the cost of goods available for sale.
12. Net purchases are ______________ to Beginning Inventory to get the cost of goods available for sale.
13. Gross Profit less ______________ equals Net Income.
14. Purchase discounts ______________ the total cost of merchandise sold.
15. Beginning inventory at the end of the period is assumed to be ______________, and thus a ______________.
16. The ending inventory of one period becomes the ______________ ______________ next period.
17. Ending inventory represents goods not ______________.
18. The inventory account is ______________ at the end of the period.
19. Purchases are increased by a(n) ______________.
20. Sales returns and allowances are used in calculating ______________ ______________.
21. Beginning Inventory plus Net Purchases equals ______________ ______________ ______________ ______________ ______________ ______________.
22. Beginning Inventory and Ending Inventory are never ______________ on the worksheet.

Name ______________________ Class ______________ Date ______________

Part II Instructions

Answer true or false to the following statements.

1. Unearned Revenue is a liability.
2. Perpetual inventory keeps a continuous record of inventory.
3. Purchases increase cost of goods sold.
4. Freight-in is added to cost of goods sold.
5. Figures for Beginning and Ending Inventory are combined on the worksheet.
6. A periodic system is used by companies with low volume and high unit prices.
7. Merchandise Inventory is an asset.
8. Unearned Revenue is a liability on the income statement.
9. Inventory is always taken 10 times per year.
10. Purchases replace ending inventory in a periodic system.
11. A trial balance may be placed directly on a worksheet.
12. The adjustment process updates the inventory account.
13. A post-closing trial balance has no temporary accounts.
14. Sales Discounts is a permanent account.
15. Gross sales are located on the balance sheet.
16. The Sales Returns and Allowances account has a normal balance of a credit.
17. Ending inventory of one period is the beginning inventory of the following period.
18. Net income always means cash.
19. Ending inventory increases cost of goods sold.
20. Net purchases is always the same as total purchases.
21. Gross profit plus expenses equals net income.
22. Unearned Storage Fees is a liability.
23. Merchandise inventory that is sold is assumed to be a cost.
24. Accumulated Depreciation is increased by a debit.
25. Merchandise Inventory can never be listed on a trial balance.
26. Ending Merchandise Inventory can only be found on a balance sheet.
27. The amount of rent expired is used in the adjustment process.
28. Adjustments help update individual ledger accounts.
29. Purchases Returns and Allowances is found on a balance sheet.
30. Beginning Merchandise Inventory found on the balance sheet from the prior period will also be placed in the cost of goods sold section of the balance sheet.
31. Sales always means cash received.
32. Ending Merchandise Inventory of the current period is found only on the balance sheet.
33. Purchases adds to the cost of goods sold.
34. Purchases discounts reduce the cost of purchases on the balance sheet.
35. Beginning inventory can never be assumed sold by the end of a period.

Name ______________________ Class ______________ Date ______________

36. Ending inventory in one period becomes beginning inventory for the next two periods.

37. The ending inventory may be calculated from an inventory sheet.

38. Income Summary is used in the adjustment of merchandise inventory.

39. Ending inventory not sold is only placed in the credit column of the balance sheet section on the worksheet.

40. Purchases Discount is recorded in the credit column of the income statement section on the worksheet.

41. Gross profit and net income mean the same.

42. All companies must give sales discounts.

43. A merchandise company does not need a cost of goods sold section on the income statement.

44. Cost of goods available to sell less ending inventory equals cost of goods not sold.

SOLUTIONS TO SUMMARY PRACTICE TEST

Part I

1. perpetual inventory
2. Purchases
3. perpetual inventory
4. beginning inventory
5. Unearned Revenue
6. added
7. Gross Profit
8. Net sales
9. Purchases Discounts, Purchases Returns and Allowances
10. Inventory sheet (record)
11. subtracted
12. added
13. Expenses
14. reduce
15. sold, cost
16. begining inventory
17. sold
18. adjusted
19. debit
20. net sales
21. Cost of Goods Available for Sale
22. combined

Name ______________________ Class ______________ Date ______________

Part II

1. true
2. true
3. true
4. true
5. false
6. false
7. true
8. false
9. false
10. false
11. true
12. true
13. true
14. false
15. false
16. false
17. true
18. false
19. false
20. false
21. false
22. true
23. true
24. false
25. false
26. false
27. true
28. true
29. false
30. false
31. false
32. false
33. true
34. false
35. false
36. false
37. true
38. true
39. false
40. true
41. false
42. false
43. false
44. false

CONTINUING PROBLEM FOR CHAPTER 11

Use the blank fold-out worksheet that accompanied your textbook.

12

Completion of the Accounting Cycle for a Merchandise Company

Name ______________________ Class ______________ Date ______________

SELF-REVIEW QUIZ 12-1

(1)

Name ______________________ Class ______________ Date ______________

(2)

Name ______________________ Class ______________ Date ______________

(3)

Name ______________________ Class ______________ Date ______________

SELF-REVIEW QUIZ 12-2

GENERAL JOURNAL PAGE 2

Date		Account Titles and Description	PR	Dr.	Cr.

Name ______________________ Class ______________ Date ______________

SELF-REVIEW QUIZ 12-3

Situation 1

Situation 2

Situation 3

Name ______________________ Class ______________ Date ______________

CHAPTER 12
FORMS FOR CLASSROOM DEMONSTRATION EXERCISES SET A OR SET B

1.

2.

3.

4. A. ______ F. ______
B. ______ G. ______
C. ______ H. ______
D. ______ I. ______
E. ______ J. ______

5.

Name ______________________ Class ______________ Date ______________

FORMS FOR EXERCISES

12-1.

COST OF GOODS SOLD

Merchandise Inv. 12/01/X1	
Purchases	
Less: Purchases Disc.	
Purch. R. & A.	
Net Purchases	
Add: Freight-in	
Net Cost of Purchases	
Cost of Goods Available for Sale	
Less: Merchandise Inv. 12/31/X1	
Cost of Goods Sold	

12-2.

A. ______________________

B. ______________________

C. ______________________

D. ______________________

E. ______________________

F. ______________________

G. ______________________

12-3.

Name ______________________ Class ______________ Date ______________

EXERCISES (CONCLUDED)

12-4.

A. SLOW COMPANY
BALANCE SHEET
DECEMBER 31, 200X

12-5.

(A)

Salaries Expense

Salaries Payable

(B)

Salaries Expense

Salaries Expense

(C)

Salaries Expense

Cash

Name ______________________ Class ______________ Date ______________

END OF CHAPTER PROBLEMS

PROBLEM 12A-1 OR PROBLEM 12B-1

RING.COM
INCOME STATEMENT
FOR YEAR ENDED DECEMBER 31, 200X

Name ______________________ Class ______________ Date ______________

PROBLEM 12A-2 OR PROBLEM 12B-2

JAMES CO.
STATEMENT OF OWNER'S EQUITY
FOR MONTH ENDED DECEMBER 31, 200X

Name ____________________ Class ____________ Date ____________

PROBLEM 12A-2 OR PROBLEM 12B-2 (CONCLUDED)

JAMES CO.
BALANCE SHEET
DECEMBER 31, 200X

Name ______________________ Class ______________ Date ______________

PROBLEM 12A-3 OR PROBLEM 12B-3

Use one of the blank fold-out worksheets that accompanied your textbook.

JAY'S SUPPLIES
INCOME STATEMENT
FOR YEAR ENDED DECEMBER 31, 200X

Name ____________ Class ____________ Date ____________

PROBLEM 12A-3 OR PROBLEM 12B-3 (CONTINUED)

JAY'S SUPPLIES
STATEMENT OF OWNER'S EQUITY
FOR YEAR ENDED DECEMBER 31, 200X

Name ______________________ Class ______________ Date ______________

PROBLEM 12A-3 OR PROBLEM 12B-3 (CONTINUED)

JAY'S SUPPLIES
BALANCE SHEET
DECEMBER 31, 200X

Name ________________ Class ________________ Date ________________

PROBLEM 12A-3 OR PROBLEM 12B-3 (CONTINUED)

GENERAL JOURNAL

PAGE 2

Date		Account Titles and Description	PR	Dr.	Cr.

Name ____________________ Class ____________ Date ____________

PROBLEM 12A-3 OR PROBLEM 12B-3 (CONCLUDED)

GENERAL JOURNAL

PAGE 3

Date		Account Titles and Description	PR	Dr.	Cr.

Name ______________________ Class ______________ Date ______________

PROBLEM 12A-4 OR PROBLEM 12B-4

Use one of the blank fold-out worksheets that accompanied your textbook.

CALLAHAN LUMBER
INCOME STATEMENT
FOR YEAR ENDED DECEMBER 31, 200X

Name ______________________ Class ______________ Date ______________

PROBLEM 12A-4 OR PROBLEM 12B-4 (CONTINUED)

Use one of the blank fold-out worksheets that accompanied your textbook.

CALLAHAN LUMBER
STATEMENT OF OWNER'S EQUITY
FOR YEAR ENDED DECEMBER 31, 200X

Name ______________________ Class ______________ Date ______________

PROBLEM 12A-4 OR PROBLEM 12B-4 (CONTINUED)

CALLAHAN LUMBER
BALANCE SHEET
DECEMBER 31, 200X

Name ______________________ Class ______________ Date ______________

PROBLEM 12A-4 OR PROBLEM 12B-4 (CONTINUED)

GENERAL JOURNAL

PAGE 2

Date		Account Titles and Description	PR	Dr.	Cr.

Name ______________________ Class ______________ Date ______________

PROBLEM 12A-4 OR PROBLEM 12B-4 (CONTINUED)

CALLAHAN LUMBER
GENERAL LEDGER

CASH — **ACCOUNT NO. 110**

Date		Explanation	Post Ref.	Debit	Credit	Balance Debit	Balance Credit

ACCOUNTS RECEIVABLE — **ACCOUNT NO. 111**

Date		Explanation	Post Ref.	Debit	Credit	Balance Debit	Balance Credit

MERCHANDISE INVENTORY — **ACCOUNT NO. 112**

Date		Explanation	Post Ref.	Debit	Credit	Balance Debit	Balance Credit

LUMBER SUPPLIES — **ACCOUNT NO. 113**

Date		Explanation	Post Ref.	Debit	Credit	Balance Debit	Balance Credit

Name ______________ Class ______________ Date ______________

PROBLEM 12A-4 OR PROBLEM 12B-4 (CONTINUED)

PREPAID INSURANCE **ACCOUNT NO. 114**

Date	Explanation	Post Ref.	Debit	Credit	Balance Debit	Balance Credit

LUMBER EQUIPMENT **ACCOUNT NO. 121**

Date	Explanation	Post Ref.	Debit	Credit	Balance Debit	Balance Credit

ACCUMULATED DEPRECIATION, LUMBER EQUIPMENT **ACCOUNT NO. 122**

Date	Explanation	Post Ref.	Debit	Credit	Balance Debit	Balance Credit

ACCOUNTS PAYABLE **ACCOUNT NO. 220**

Date	Explanation	Post Ref.	Debit	Credit	Balance Debit	Balance Credit

WAGES PAYABLE **ACCOUNT NO. 221**

Date	Explanation	Post Ref.	Debit	Credit	Balance Debit	Balance Credit

PROBLEM 12A-4 OR PROBLEM 12B-4 (CONTINUED)

J. CALLAHAN, CAPITAL — **ACCOUNT NO. 330**

Date	Explanation	Post Ref.	Debit	Credit	Balance Debit	Balance Credit

J. CALLAHAN, WITHDRAWALS — **ACCOUNT NO. 331**

Date	Explanation	Post Ref.	Debit	Credit	Balance Debit	Balance Credit

INCOME SUMMARY — **ACCOUNT NO. 332**

Date	Explanation	Post Ref.	Debit	Credit	Balance Debit	Balance Credit

SALES — **ACCOUNT NO. 440**

Date	Explanation	Post Ref.	Debit	Credit	Balance Debit	Balance Credit

SALES RETURNS AND ALLOWANCES — **ACCOUNT NO. 441**

Date	Explanation	Post Ref.	Debit	Credit	Balance Debit	Balance Credit

Name ______________________ Class ______________ Date ______________

PROBLEM 12A-4 OR PROBLEM 12B-4 (CONTINUED)

PURCHASES **ACCOUNT NO. 550**

Date		Explanation	Post Ref.	Debit	Credit	Balance	
						Debit	Credit

PURCHASES DISCOUNT **ACCOUNT NO. 551**

Date		Explanation	Post Ref.	Debit	Credit	Balance	
						Debit	Credit

PURCHASES RETURNS AND ALLOWANCES **ACCOUNT NO. 552**

Date		Explanation	Post Ref.	Debit	Credit	Balance	
						Debit	Credit

WAGES EXPENSE **ACCOUNT NO. 660**

Date		Explanation	Post Ref.	Debit	Credit	Balance	
						Debit	Credit

ADVERTISING EXPENSE **ACCOUNT NO. 661**

Date		Explanation	Post Ref.	Debit	Credit	Balance	
						Debit	Credit

Name ______________________ Class ______________ Date ______________

PROBLEM 12A-4 OR PROBLEM 12B-4 (CONTINUED)

RENT EXPENSE **ACCOUNT NO. 662**

Date		Explanation	Post Ref.	Debit	Credit	Balance	
						Debit	Credit

DEPRECIATION EXPENSE, LUMBER EQUIPMENT **ACCOUNT NO. 663**

Date		Explanation	Post Ref.	Debit	Credit	Balance	
						Debit	Credit

LUMBER SUPPLIES EXPENSE **ACCOUNT NO. 664**

Date		Explanation	Post Ref.	Debit	Credit	Balance	
						Debit	Credit

INSURANCE EXPENSE **ACCOUNT NO. 665**

Date		Explanation	Post Ref.	Debit	Credit	Balance	
						Debit	Credit

Name ____________________ Class ____________ Date ____________

PROBLEM 12A-4 OR PROBLEM 12B-4 (CONCLUDED)

CALLAHAN LUMBER
POST-CLOSING TRIAL BALANCE
DECEMBER 31, 200X

	Dr.	Cr.

Name ______________________ Class ______________ Date ______________

CHAPTER 12
SUMMARY PRACTICE TEST: COMPLETION OF THE ACCOUNTING CYCLE FOR A MERCHANDISE COMPANY

Part I Instructions

Fill in the blank(s) to complete the statement.

1. There are no debits or credits on ____________ ____________.
2. The fomal income statement uses ____________ ____________ figures for inventory.
3. The gross profit figure ____________ (is/is not) found on the worksheet.
4. ____________ expenses are related to the general activity.
5. ____________ ____________ are related to the administrative function.
6. ____________ ____________ could be broken down into selling and administrative expenses.
7. The ____________ figure for capital is not found on the worksheet.
8. ____________ ____________ are cash or other assets that will be converted into cash during the normal operating cycle of the company or one year, whichever is longer.
9. ____________ and ____________ are long-lived assets used for the production or sale of other assets or services.
10. Debts or obligations that are to be paid with current assets within one year or one operating cycle are called ____________ ____________.
11. Mortgage Payable is an example of a(n) ____________ ____________ ____________.
12. Ending merchandise inventory is a(n) ____________ ____________.
13. By the adjusting process, the beginning inventory of the period is transferred to ____________ ____________.
14. The ____________ ____________ ____________ ____________ contains no temporary accounts.
15. A reversing entry involves certain ____________ entries.
16. Reversing entries are used only if assets are ____________ and have no previous balance and liabilities are ____________ and have no balance.

Name ______________________ Class ______________ Date ______________

Part II Instructions

Match the term in the last column to the definition, example, or phrase in the right column. Be sure to use a letter only once.

d	**1.** EXAMPLE: Computer Equipment	a.	Subtotaling
______	**2.** Net Sales-Cost of Goods Sold	b.	Unearned Revenue
______	**3.** Operating Cycle	c.	Current asset
______	**4.** Inside Columns of Financial Reports	d.	Plant and Equipment
______	**5.** Gross Profit-Operating Expenses	e.	Reversing Entry
______	**6.** Operating Expenses	f.	Time Period
______	**7.** Temporary Account	g.	Net Income
______	**8.** OASDI	h.	Current Liability
______	**9.** Result of an adjusting entry	i.	When earned reduced by a debit
______	**10.** Petty Cash	j.	Gross Profit
______	**11.** An asset that is adjsuted	k.	Merchandise Inventory
______	**12.** Ending Capital	l.	Debit Balance
______	**13.** A Liability showing revenue no earned	m.	Not found on worksheet
______	**14.** Unearned training fees	n.	Income Summary
		o.	Selling and Administrative

Part III Instructions

Answer true or false to the following statements.

1. A balance sheet records all revenue.
2. Cost of goods sold contains only ending inventory.
3. Net sales less cost of goods sold equals gross profit.
4. Operating expenses can only be administrative.
5. Supplies is part of Plant and Equipment.
6. Unearned Rent is an asset.
7. An operating cycle of a business must be one year.
8. Accumulated Depreciation is a current asset.
9. Long-term liabilities are due within one year.
10. Merchandise Inventory is a temporary account.
11. The normal balance of merchandise inventory is a debit.
12. The post-closing trial balance will not contain any unearned revenue accounts.
13. Ending inventory is closed directly to Capital.
14. Reversing entries cannot be applied to all adjustments.
15. Reversing entries are optional at the end of each month before the close of the year.
16. Reversing entries switch closing entries on the first day of the new period.
17. An adjusting entry with an asset decreasing with no prevoius balance cannot be reversed.
18. Closing entries will update the merchandise inventory account.
19. Beginning merchandise inventory of a period is assumed sold by the end of the period.
20. An adjusting entry for Accrued Wages can be reversed.

Name ____________ Class ____________ Date ____________

CHAPTER 12
SOLUTIONS TO SUMMARY PRACTICE TEST

Part I

1. financial reports
2. two separate
3. is not
4. General
5. Administrative expenses
6. Operating expenses
7. ending
8. Current assets
9. Plant, Equipment
10. current liabilities
11. long-term liability
12. permanent account
13. Income Summary
14. post-closing trial balance
15. adjusting
16. increasing, increasing

Part II

1. d
2. j
3. f
4. a
5. g
6. o
7. n
8. h
9. e
10. l
11. k
12. m
13. b
14. i

Part III

1. false
2. false
3. true
4. false
5. false
6. false
7. false
8. false
9. false
10. false
11. true
12. false
13. false
14. true
15. false
16. false
17. true
18. false
19. true
20. true

Name ______________________ Class ______________ Date ______________

CONTINUING PROBLEM FOR CHAPTER 12

SANCHEZ COMPUTER CENTER
GENERAL JOURNAL

PAGE 12

Date		Account Titles and Description	PR	Dr.	Cr.

Name ______________________ Class ______________ Date ______________

SANCHEZ COMPUTER CENTER
GENERAL LEDGER

CASH — **ACCOUNT NO. 1000**

Date		Explanation	Post Ref.	Debit	Credit	Balance Debit	Balance Credit
3/1	0X	Balance forward	✓			12 516 65	

PETTY CASH — **ACCOUNT NO. 1010**

Date		Explanation	Post Ref.	Debit	Credit	Balance Debit	Balance Credit
3/1	0X	Balance forward	✓			100 00	

ACCOUNTS RECEIVABLE — **ACCOUNT NO. 1020**

Date		Explanation	Post Ref.	Debit	Credit	Balance Debit	Balance Credit
3/1	0X	Balance forward	✓			11 900 00	

PREPAID RENT — **ACCOUNT NO. 1025**

Date		Explanation	Post Ref.	Debit	Credit	Balance Debit	Balance Credit
3/1	0X	Balance forward	✓			2 800 00	

Name ______________________ Class ______________ Date ______________

SUPPLIES ACCOUNT NO. 1030

Date		Explanation	Post Ref.	Debit	Credit	Balance Debit	Balance Credit
3/1	0X	Balance forward	✓			432 00	

MERCHANDISE INVENTORY ACCOUNT NO. 1040

Date		Explanation	Post Ref.	Debit	Credit	Balance Debit	Balance Credit

COMPUTER SHOP EQUIPMENT ACCOUNT NO. 1080

Date		Explanation	Post Ref.	Debit	Credit	Balance Debit	Balance Credit
3/1	0X	Balance forward	✓			3 800	

ACCUMULATED DEPRECIATION, C.S. EQUIPMENT ACCOUNT NO. 1081

Date		Explanation	Post Ref.	Debit	Credit	Balance Debit	Balance Credit
3/1	0X	Balance forward	✓				99 00

OFFICE EQUIPMENT ACCOUNT NO. 1090

Date		Explanation	Post Ref.	Debit	Credit	Balance Debit	Balance Credit
3/1	0X	Balance forward	✓			1 050 00	

Name ______________________ Class ______________ Date ______________

ACCUMULATED DEPRECIATION, OFFICE EQUIPMENT — ACCOUNT NO. 1091

Date		Explanation	Post Ref.	Debit	Credit	Balance Debit	Balance Credit
3/1	0X	Balance forward	✓				20 00

ACCOUNTS PAYABLE — ACCOUNT NO. 2000

Date		Explanation	Post Ref.	Debit	Credit	Balance Debit	Balance Credit
3/1	0X	Balance forward	✓				2 840 00

WAGES PAYABLE — ACCOUNT NO. 2010

Date		Explanation	Post Ref.	Debit	Credit	Balance Debit	Balance Credit

FICA OASDI PAYABLE — ACCOUNT NO. 2020

Date		Explanation	Post Ref.	Debit	Credit	Balance Debit	Balance Credit

FICA MEDICARE PAYABLE — ACCOUNT NO. 2030

Date		Explanation	Post Ref.	Debit	Credit	Balance Debit	Balance Credit

Name ______________________ Class ______________ Date ______________

FIT PAYABLE ACCOUNT NO. 2040

Date		Explanation	Post Ref.	Debit	Credit	Balance Debit	Balance Credit

SIT PAYABLE ACCOUNT NO. 2050

Date		Explanation	Post Ref.	Debit	Credit	Balance Debit	Balance Credit

FUTA PAYABLE ACCOUNT NO. 2060

Date		Explanation	Post Ref.	Debit	Credit	Balance Debit	Balance Credit

SUTA PAYABLE ACCOUNT NO. 2070

Date		Explanation	Post Ref.	Debit	Credit	Balance Debit	Balance Credit

T. FREEDMAN, CAPITAL ACCOUNT NO. 3000

Date		Explanation	Post Ref.	Debit	Credit	Balance Debit	Balance Credit
3/1	0X	Balance forward	✓				7 4 0 6 00

Name ______________ Class ______________ Date ______________

T. FREEDMAN WITHDRAWALS ACCOUNT NO. 3010

Date		Explanation	Post Ref.	Debit	Credit	Balance Debit	Balance Credit
3/1	0X	Balance forward	✓			2 0 1 5 00	

INCOME SUMMARY ACCOUNT NO. 3020

Date		Explanation	Post Ref.	Debit	Credit	Balance Debit	Balance Credit

SERVICE REVENUE ACCOUNT NO. 4000

Date		Explanation	Post Ref.	Debit	Credit	Balance Debit	Balance Credit
3/1	0X	Balance forward	✓				19 8 0 0 00

SALES ACCOUNT NO. 4010

Date		Explanation	Post Ref.	Debit	Credit	Balance Debit	Balance Credit
3/1	0X	Balance forward	✓				9 7 0 0 00

Name ____________________ Class ____________ Date ____________

GENERAL LEDGER

SALES RETURNS AND ALLOWANCES — ACCOUNT NO. 4020

Date		Explanation	Post Ref.	Debit	Credit	Balance Debit	Balance Credit
3/1	0X	Balance forward	✓			400 00	

SALES DISCOUNTS — ACCOUNT NO. 4030

Date		Explanation	Post Ref.	Debit	Credit	Balance Debit	Balance Credit
3/1	0X	Balance forward	✓			220 00	

ADVERTISING EXPENSE — ACCOUNT NO. 5010

Date		Explanation	Post Ref.	Debit	Credit	Balance Debit	Balance Credit
3/1	0X	Balance forward	✓			800 00	

RENT EXPENSE — ACCOUNT NO. 5020

Date		Explanation	Post Ref.	Debit	Credit	Balance Debit	Balance Credit

UTILITIES EXPENSE — ACCOUNT NO. 5030

Date		Explanation	Post Ref.	Debit	Credit	Balance Debit	Balance Credit
3/1	0X	Balance forward	✓			290 00	

Name ______________________ Class ______________ Date ______________

PHONE EXPENSE **ACCOUNT NO. 5040**

Date		Explanation	Post Ref.	Debit	Credit	Balance	
						Debit	Credit
3/1	0X	Balance forward	✓			150 00	

SUPPLIES EXPENSE **ACCOUNT NO. 5050**

Date		Explanation	Post Ref.	Debit	Credit	Balance	
						Debit	Credit

INSURANCE EXPENSE **ACCOUNT NO. 5060**

Date		Explanation	Post Ref.	Debit	Credit	Balance	
						Debit	Credit
3/1	0X	Balance forward	✓			100 00	

POSTAGE EXPENSE **ACCOUNT NO. 5070**

Date		Explanation	Post Ref.	Debit	Credit	Balance	
						Debit	Credit
3/1	0X	Balance forward	✓			175 00	

DEPRECIATION EXPENSE C.S. EQUIPMENT **ACCOUNT NO. 5080**

Date		Explanation	Post Ref.	Debit	Credit	Balance	
						Debit	Credit

Name ____________ Class ____________ Date ____________

DEPRECIATION EXPENSE OFFICE EQUIPMENT ACCOUNT NO. 5090

Date		Explanation	Post Ref.	Debit	Credit	Balance Debit	Balance Credit

MISCELLANEOUS EXPENSE ACCOUNT NO. 5100

Date		Explanation	Post Ref.	Debit	Credit	Balance Debit	Balance Credit
3/1	0X	Balance forward	✓			10 00	

WAGE EXPENSE ACCOUNT NO. 5110

Date		Explanation	Post Ref.	Debit	Credit	Balance Debit	Balance Credit
3/1	0X	Balance forward	✓			2 030 00	

PAYROLL TAX EXPENSE ACCOUNT NO. 5120

Date		Explanation	Post Ref.	Debit	Credit	Balance Debit	Balance Credit
3/1	0X	Balance forward	✓			226 35	

INTEREST EXPENSE ACCOUNT NO. 5130

Date		Explanation	Post Ref.	Debit	Credit	Balance Debit	Balance Credit

Name ______________________ Class ______________ Date ______________

BAD DEBT EXPENSE ACCOUNT NO. 5140

Date		Explanation	Post Ref.	Debit	Credit	Balance Debit	Balance Credit

PURCHASES ACCOUNT NO. 6000

Date		Explanation	Post Ref.	Debit	Credit	Balance Debit	Balance Credit
3/1	0X	Balance forward	✓			950 00	

PURCHASE RETURNS AND ALLOWANCES ACCOUNT NO. 6010

Date		Explanation	Post Ref.	Debit	Credit	Balance Debit	Balance Credit
3/1	0X	Balance forward	✓				100 00

PURCHASE DISCOUNTS ACCOUNT NO. 6020

Date		Explanation	Post Ref.	Debit	Credit	Balance Debit	Balance Credit

FREIGHT IN ACCOUNT NO. 6030

Date		Explanation	Post Ref.	Debit	Credit	Balance Debit	Balance Credit

Name ______________________ Class ______________ Date ______________

SANCHEZ COMPUTER CENTER
INCOME STATEMENT
FOR THE SIX MONTHS ENDED MARCH 31, 200X

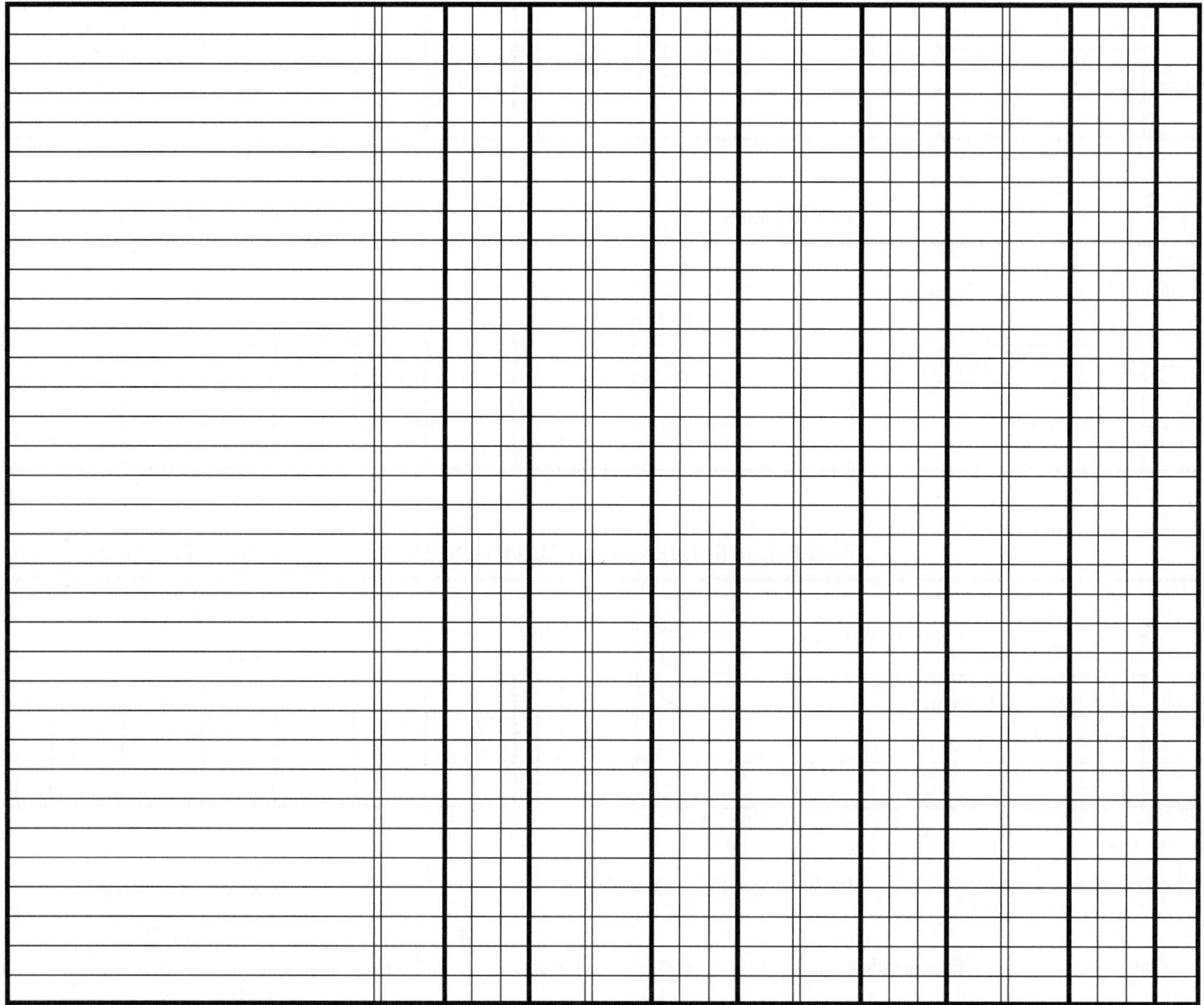

Name ______________________ Class ______________ Date ______________

SANCHEZ COMPUTER CENTER
STATEMENT OF OWNER'S EQUITY
FOR THE SIX MONTHS ENDED MARCH 31, 200X

Name ______________________ Class ______________ Date ______________

SANCHEZ COMPUTER CENTER
BALANCE SHEET
MARCH 31, 200X

Name ______________________ Class ______________ Date ______________

MINI PRACTICE SET

THE CORNER DRESS SHOP
GENERAL JOURNAL

PAGE 4

Date		Account Titles and Description	PR	Dr.	Cr.

THE CORNER DRESS SHOP

Use a blank fold-out worksheet and a blank payroll register that accompanied your textbook.

Name ________________ Class ________________ Date ________________

MINI PRACTICE SET

Use the blank fold-out worksheets that accompanied your textbook.

THE CORNER DRESS SHOP
GENERAL JOURNAL

PAGE 5

Date		Account Titles and Description	PR	Dr.	Cr.

Name ______________________ Class ______________ Date ______________

MINI PRACTICE SET

THE CORNER DRESS SHOP
GENERAL JOURNAL

PAGE 6

Date		Account Titles and Description	PR	Dr.	Cr.

Name ____________________ Class ____________________ Date ____________________

MINI PRACTICE SET

THE CORNER DRESS SHOP
GENERAL JOURNAL

PAGE 7

Date		Account Titles and Description	PR	Dr.	Cr.

Name ______________________ Class ______________ Date ______________

MINI PRACTICE SET

THE CORNER DRESS SHOP
GENERAL JOURNAL

PAGE 8

Date		Account Titles and Description	PR	Dr.	Cr.

Name ______________________ Class ______________ Date ______________

MINI PRACTICE SET

THE CORNER DRESS SHOP
GENERAL JOURNAL

PAGE 9

Date		Account Titles and Description	PR	Dr.	Cr.

Name ______________________________ Class ________________ Date ________________

MINI PRACTICE SET

THE CORNER DRESS SHOP
AUXILIARY PETTY CASH RECORD

Date	Voucher No.	Description	Receipts	Payment	Category of Payment			
					Postage Expense	Delivery Expense	Sundry	
							Account	Amount

Name ______________________ Class ______________ Date ______________

MINI PRACTICE SET

ACCOUNTS PAYABLE SUBSIDIARY LEDGER

NAME **BLEW CO.**

Date 200X		Explanation	Post Ref.	Debit	Credit	Credit Balance
Mar	1	Balance	✓			1 9 0 0 00

NAME **JONES CO.**

Date 200X		Explanation	Post Ref.	Debit	Credit	Credit Balance

NAME **MOE'S GARAGE**

Date 200X		Explanation	Post Ref.	Debit	Credit	Credit Balance

Name ______ Class ______ Date ______

MINI PRACTICE SET

NAME **MORRIS CO.**

Date 200X		Explanation	Post Ref.	Debit	Credit	Credit Balance

ACCOUNTS RECEIVABLE SUBSIDIARY LEDGER

NAME **BING CO.**

Date 200X		Explanation	Post Ref.	Debit	Credit	Debit Balance
Mar	1	Balance	✓			2 2 0 0 00

NAME **BLEW CO.**

Date 200X		Explanation	Post Ref.	Debit	Credit	Debit Balance

Name ______________________ Class ______________ Date ______________

MINI PRACTICE SET

NAME **RONALD CO.**

Date 200X		Explanation	Post Ref.	Debit	Credit	Debit Balance

GENERAL LEDGER

CASH **ACCOUNT NO. 110**

Date 200X		Explanation	Post Ref.	Debit	Credit	Balance Debit	Balance Credit
Mar	1	Balance	✓			2 2 3 1 90	

Name ______________________ Class ______________ Date ______________

MINI PRACTICE SET

ACCOUNTS RECEIVABLE

ACCOUNT NO. 111

Date 200X		Explanation	Post Ref.	Debit	Credit	Balance Debit	Balance Credit
Mar	1	Balance	✓			2 2 0 0 00	

PETTY CASH

ACCOUNT NO. 112

Date 200X		Explanation	Post Ref.	Debit	Credit	Balance Debit	Balance Credit
Mar	1	Balance	✓			3 5 00	

MERCHANDISE INVENTORY

ACCOUNT NO. 114

Date 200X		Explanation	Post Ref.	Debit	Credit	Balance Debit	Balance Credit
Mar	1	Balance	✓			5 6 0 0 00	

Name ____________ Class ____________ Date ____________

MINI PRACTICE SET

PREPAID RENT — ACCOUNT NO. 116

Date 200X		Explanation	Post Ref.	Debit	Credit	Balance Debit	Balance Credit
Mar	1	Balance	✓			1 800 00	

DELIVERY TRUCK — ACCOUNT NO. 120

Date 200X		Explanation	Post Ref.	Debit	Credit	Balance Debit	Balance Credit
Mar	1	Balance	✓			6 000 00	

ACCUMULATED DEPRECIATION, TRUCK — ACCOUNT NO. 121

Date 200X		Explanation	Post Ref.	Debit	Credit	Balance Debit	Balance Credit
Mar	1	Balance	✓				1 500 00

Name ______________ Class ______________ Date ______________

MINI PRACTICE SET

ACCOUNTS PAYABLE — **ACCOUNT NO. 210**

Date 200X		Explanation	Post Ref.	Debit	Credit	Balance Debit	Balance Credit
Mar	1	Balance	✓				1 900 00

SALARIES PAYABLE — **ACCOUNT NO. 212**

Date 200X		Explanation	Post Ref.	Debit	Credit	Balance Debit	Balance Credit

FIT PAYABLE — **ACCOUNT NO. 214**

Date 200X		Explanation	Post Ref.	Debit	Credit	Balance Debit	Balance Credit
Mar	1	Balance	✓				1 013 00

Name ____________________ Class ____________ Date ____________

MINI PRACTICE SET

FICA-OASDI PAYABLE — ACCOUNT NO. 216

Date 200X		Explanation	Post Ref.	Debit	Credit	Balance Debit	Balance Credit
Mar	1	Balance	✓				1 339 20

FICA-MEDICARE PAYABLE — ACCOUNT NO. 218

Date 200X		Explanation	Post Ref.	Debit	Credit	Balance Debit	Balance Credit
Mar	1	Balance	✓				313 20

SIT PAYABLE — ACCOUNT NO. 220

Date 200X		Explanation	Post Ref.	Debit	Credit	Balance Debit	Balance Credit
Mar	1	Balance	✓				756 00

SUTA TAX PAYABLE — ACCOUNT NO. 222

Date 200X		Explanation	Post Ref.	Debit	Credit	Balance Debit	Balance Credit
Mar	1	Balance	✓				979 20

FUTA TAX PAYABLE — ACCOUNT NO. 224

Date 200X		Explanation	Post Ref.	Debit	Credit	Balance Debit	Balance Credit
Mar	1	Balance	✓				163 20

UNEARNED RENT — ACCOUNT NO. 226

Date 200X		Explanation	Post Ref.	Debit	Credit	Balance Debit	Balance Credit
Mar	1	Balance	✓				800 00

Name ______________________ Class ______________ Date ______________

MINI PRACTICE SET

B. LOEB, CAPITAL — ACCOUNT NO. 310

Date 200X		Explanation	Post Ref.	Debit	Credit	Balance Debit	Balance Credit
Mar	1	Balance	✓				9 103 10

B. LOEB, WITHDRAWALS — ACCOUNT NO. 320

Date 200X		Explanation	Post Ref.	Debit	Credit	Balance Debit	Balance Credit

INCOME SUMMARY — ACCOUNT NO. 330

Date 200X		Explanation	Post Ref.	Debit	Credit	Balance Debit	Balance Credit

SALES — ACCOUNT NO. 410

Date 200X		Explanation	Post Ref.	Debit	Credit	Balance Debit	Balance Credit

SALES RETURNS AND ALLOWANCES — ACCOUNT NO. 412

Date 200X		Explanation	Post Ref.	Debit	Credit	Balance Debit	Balance Credit

Name ______________________ Class ______________ Date ______________

MINI PRACTICE SET

SALES DISCOUINT **ACCOUNT NO. 414**

Date 200X		Explanation	Post Ref.	Debit	Credit	Balance Debit	Balance Credit

RENTAL INCOME **ACCOUNT NO. 416**

Date 200X		Explanation	Post Ref.	Debit	Credit	Balance Debit	Balance Credit

PURCHASES **ACCOUNT NO. 510**

Date 200X		Explanation	Post Ref.	Debit	Credit	Balance Debit	Balance Credit

PURCHASES RETURNS AND ALLOWANCES **ACCOUNT NO. 512**

Date 200X		Explanation	Post Ref.	Debit	Credit	Balance Debit	Balance Credit

PURCHASES DISCOUNT **ACCOUNT NO. 514**

Date 200X		Explanation	Post Ref.	Debit	Credit	Balance Debit	Balance Credit

Name ______________ Class ______________ Date ______________

MINI PRACTICE SET

SALES SALARY EXPENSE — **ACCOUNT NO. 610**

Date 200X		Explanation	Post Ref.	Debit	Credit	Balance Debit	Balance Credit

OFFICE SALARY EXPENSE — **ACCOUNT NO. 611**

Date 200X		Explanation	Post Ref.	Debit	Credit	Balance Debit	Balance Credit

PAYROLL TAX EXPENSE — **ACCOUNT NO. 612**

Date 200X		Explanation	Post Ref.	Debit	Credit	Balance Debit	Balance Credit

CLEANING EXPENSE — **ACCOUNT NO. 614**

Date 200X		Explanation	Post Ref.	Debit	Credit	Balance Debit	Balance Credit

DEPRECIATION EXPENSE, TRUCK — **ACCOUNT NO. 616**

Date 200X		Explanation	Post Ref.	Debit	Credit	Balance Debit	Balance Credit

Name ______________________ Class ______________ Date ______________

MINI PRACTICE SET

RENT EXPENSE

ACCOUNT NO. 618

Date 200X		Explanation	Post Ref.	Debit	Credit	Balance	
						Debit	Credit

POSTAGE EXPENSE

ACCOUNT NO. 620

Date 200X		Explanation	Post Ref.	Debit	Credit	Balance	
						Debit	Credit

DELIVERY EXPENSE

ACCOUNT NO. 622

Date 200X		Explanation	Post Ref.	Debit	Credit	Balance	
						Debit	Credit

MISCELLANEOUS EXPENSE

ACCOUNT NO. 624

Date 200X		Explanation	Post Ref.	Debit	Credit	Balance	
						Debit	Credit

Name ______________________ Class ______________ Date ______________

MINI PRACTICE SET

THE CORNER DRESS SHOP
SCHEDULE OF ACCOUNTS RECEIVABLE
MARCH 31, 200X

THE CORNER DRESS SHOP
SCHEDULE OF ACCOUNTS PAYABLE
MARCH 31, 200X

Name ____________________ Class ____________________ Date ____________________

MINI PRACTICE SET

THE CORNER DRESS SHOP
INCOME STATEMENT
FOR MONTH ENDED MARCH 31, 200X

Name ______________________ Class ______________ Date ______________

MINI PRACTICE SET

THE CORNER DRESS SHOP
STATEMENT OF OWNER'S EQUITY
FOR MONTH ENDED MARCH 31, 200X

Name ____________________ Class ____________________ Date ____________________

MINI PRACTICE SET

THE CORNER DRESS SHOP
BALANCE SHEET
MARCH 31, 200X

Name ____________ Class ____________ Date ____________

MINI PRACTICE SET

THE CORNER DRESS SHOP
POST-CLOSING TRIAL BALANCE
MARCH 31, 200X

Name ______________________ Class ______________ Date ______________

MINI PRACTICE SET

Form **941 for 200X: Employer's QUARTERLY Federal Tax Return** 990106

(Rev. January 2006) Department of the Treasury — Internal Revenue Service OMB No. 1545-0029

(EIN)
Employer identification number [ ][ ] – [ ][ ][ ][ ][ ][ ][ ]

Name *(not your trade name)* ______________________

Trade name *(if any)* ______________________

Address ______________________
Number Street Suite or room number
____
City State ZIP code

Report for this Quarter ...
(Check one.)

- [ ] **1:** January, February, March
- [ ] **2:** April, May, June
- [ ] **3:** July, August, September
- [ ] **4:** October, November, December

Read the separate instructions before you fill out this form. Please type or print within the boxes.

Part 1: Answer these questions for this quarter.

1 **Number of employees who received wages, tips, or other compensation for the pay period including:** ***Mar. 12*** **(Quarter 1),** ***June 12*** **(Quarter 2),** ***Sept. 12*** **(Quarter 3),** ***Dec. 12*** **(Quarter 4)** . . . 1 ______

2 **Wages, tips, and other compensation** . . . . 2 ______ .

3 **Total income tax withheld from wages, tips, and other compensation** . . . . 3 ______ .

4 **If no wages, tips, and other compensation are subject to social security or Medicare tax** . . [ ] Check and go to line 6.

5 **Taxable social security and Medicare wages and tips:**

	Column 1		*Column 2*
5a **Taxable social security wages**	.	× .124 =	.
5b **Taxable social security tips**	.	× .124 =	.
5c **Taxable Medicare wages & tips**	.	× .029 =	.

5d **Total social security and Medicare taxes** (*Column 2,* lines 5a + 5b + 5c = line 5d) . . 5d ______ .

6 **Total taxes before adjustments** (lines 3 + 5d = line 6) . . . . 6 ______ .

7 **TAX ADJUSTMENTS** (Read the instructions for line 7 before completing lines 7a through 7h.):

7a **Current quarter's fractions of cents** . . . . ______ .

7b **Current quarter's sick pay** . . . . ______ .

7c **Current quarter's adjustments for tips and group-term life insurance** ______ .

7d **Current year's income tax withholding** (attach Form 941c) . . . ______ .

7e **Prior quarters' social security and Medicare taxes** (attach Form 941c) ______ .

7f **Special additions to federal income tax** (attach Form 941c) . . . ______ .

7g **Special additions to social security and Medicare** (attach Form 941c) ______ .

7h **TOTAL ADJUSTMENTS** (Combine all amounts: lines 7a through 7g.) . . . . 7h ______ .

8 **Total taxes after adjustments** (Combine lines 6 and 7h.) . . . . 8 ______ .

9 **Advance earned income credit (EIC) payments made to employees** . . . . 9 ______ .

10 **Total taxes after adjustment for advance EIC** (line 8 – line 9 = line 10) . . . . 10 ______ .

11 **Total deposits for this quarter, including overpayment applied from a prior quarter** . . . 11 ______ .

12 **Balance due** (If line 10 is more than line 11, write the difference here.) . . . . 12 ______ .
Make checks payable to *United States Treasury.*

13 **Overpayment** (If line 11 is more than line 10, write the difference here.) ______ . Check one [ ] Apply to next return. [ ] Send a refund.

▶ You **MUST** fill out both pages of this form and **SIGN** it.

Next ➡

For Privacy Act and Paperwork Reduction Act Notice, see the back of the Payment Voucher. Cat. No. 17001Z Form **941** (Rev. 1-2006)

Name ______________________ Class ______________ Date ______________

MINI PRACTICE SET

990206

Name *(not your trade name)* | Employer identification number (EIN)

Part 2: Tell us about your deposit schedule and tax liability for this quarter.

If you are unsure about whether you are a monthly schedule depositor or a semiweekly schedule depositor, see *Pub. 15 (Circular E)*, section 11.

14 ☐☐ **Write the state abbreviation for the state where you made your deposits** OR **write "MU" if you made your deposits in *multiple* states.**

15 Check one: ☐ **Line 10 is less than $2,500.** Go to Part 3.

☐ **You were a monthly schedule depositor for the entire quarter. Fill out your tax liability for each month.** Then go to Part 3.

Tax liability: Month 1 ________ .

Month 2 ________ .

Month 3 ________ .

Total liability for quarter ________ . **Total must equal line 10.**

☐ **You were a semiweekly schedule depositor for any part of this quarter.** Fill out *Schedule B (Form 941): Report of Tax Liability for Semiweekly Schedule Depositors,* and attach it to this form.

Part 3: Tell us about your business. If a question does NOT apply to your business, leave it blank.

16 If your business has closed or you stopped paying wages . . . . ☐ Check here, and

enter the final date you paid wages ___ / ___ / ___ .

17 If you are a seasonal employer and you do not have to file a return for every quarter of the year . . ☐ Check here.

Part 4: May we speak with your third-party designee?

Do you want to allow an employee, a paid tax preparer, or another person to discuss this return with the IRS? See the instructions for details.

☐ Yes. Designee's name ________________

Phone ( ) – Personal Identification Number (PIN) ☐☐☐☐☐

☐ No.

Part 5: Sign here. You MUST fill out both sides of this form and **SIGN it.**

Under penalties of perjury, I declare that I have examined this return, including accompanying schedules and statements, and to the best of my knowledge and belief, it is true, correct, and complete.

X Sign your name here ________________

Print name and title ________________

Date ___ / ___ / ___ Phone ( ) –

Part 6: For PAID preparers only *(optional)*

Paid Preparer's Signature ________________

Firm's name ________________

Address ________________ EIN ________

________________ ZIP code ________

Date ___ / ___ / ___ Phone ( ) – SSN/PTIN ________

☐ Check if you are self-employed.

Page **2** Form **94**

41 (Rev. 1-2006)